Laudemus viros gloriosos

Thomistic Studies

Sponsored by the Center for Thomistic Studies
Houston, Texas

Laudemus viros gloriosos

Essays in Honor of

ARMAND MAURER, CSB

edited by

R. E. HOUSER

University of Notre Dame Press

Notre Dame, Indiana

Library of Congress Cataloging-in-Publication Data

Laudemus viros gloriosos : essays in honor of Armand Maurer / edited by R. E. Houser.
    p.   cm. — (Thomistic studies)
    Includes bibliographical references and index.
    ISBN-13: 978-0-268-03103-9 (cloth : alk. paper)
    ISBN-10: 0-268-03103-7 (cloth : alk. paper)
    1. Philosophy, Medieval.   I. Maurer, Armand A. (Armand Augustine), 1915–
II. Houser, R. E.
    B721.L335   2007
    189—dc22   2006039811

Contents

Introduction: Armand Maurer: Disciple, Historian, Philosopher   **1**
R. E. HOUSER

Chapter 1
On the Original Nature of Christian Philosophy   **13**
JOHN M. RIST

Chapter 2
Averroes: God and the Noble Lie   **38**
RICHARD C. TAYLOR

Chapter 3
Undoing the Past: Fishacre and Rufus on the Limits of God's Power   **60**
R. JAMES LONG

Chapter 4
The Real Distinction and the Principles of Metaphysics: Avicenna
and Aquinas   **75**
R. E. HOUSER

Chapter 5
Faith and Reason: The Synthesis of St. Thomas Aquinas   **109**
LEO J. ELDERS, SVD

Chapter 6

St. Thomas and Analogy: The Logician and the Metaphysician   132

LAWRENCE DEWAN, OP

Chapter 7

To Which "God" Must a Proof of God's Existence Conclude for Aquinas?   146

DAVID B. TWETTEN

Chapter 8

Defense and Discovery: Brother Thomas's *Contra impugnantes*   184

MARY C. SOMMERS

Chapter 9

A Note on Love and Governance   209

JAMES P. REILLY, JR.

Chapter 10

Godfrey of Fontaines and the Condemnation of March 7, 1277   213

JOHN F. WIPPEL

Chapter 11

Franciscan Attitudes toward Philosophy: 1274–1300   238

TIMOTHY B. NOONE

Chapter 12

Peter of Candia's Portrait of Late Thirteenth-Century Problems
concerning Faith and Reason in *Book I of the Sentences*   254
STEPHEN F. BROWN

Chapter 13

What Was Contingency?   283

CALVIN G. NORMORE

Chapter 14

Francis Mayronis on Cognition: Abstractive and Intuitive-Abstractive   **297**

GIRARD J. ETZKORN

Chapter 15

Mastrius on *Esse Cognitum*   **327**

NORMAN WELLS

Recollections of Times Past   **362**

ARMAND MAURER

Bibliography of the Writings of Armand A. Maurer, CSB   **373**

JAMES K. FARGE, CSB

Contributors   **379**

Index   **383**

Armand Maurer, CSB

About 1990

Introduction

Armand Maurer: Disciple, Historian, Philosopher

R. E. H O U S E R

Armand Maurer was born 21 January 1915 in Rochester, New York. He received his education at the University of Toronto (BA, MA, PhD) and the Pontifical Institute of Mediaeval Studies, Toronto (MSL), and was ordained in the Congregation of St. Basil on 15 August 1945. A lovely memoir of his training in Toronto as scholar and priest, "Recollections of Times Past," is included here, and I would like to thank Fr. Maurer for it. No one could have told his story, so intimately bound up with that of the Pontifical Institute of Mediaeval Studies, better than Fr. Maurer himself. At the point where his recollections end, his scholarly life was just beginning. My remarks here are designed simply to orient the reader toward his writings, for here too there is no substitute for Maurer himself.

As is often true for outstanding scholars, Maurer's life has not been peripatetic in its externals. Throughout his long career he has remained in one city, teaching for many years at the University of Toronto, in both St. Michael's College and the Graduate Department of Philosophy, and at the Pontifical Institute of Mediaeval Studies, where he is still active as Senior Fellow Emeritus. His journeys have been adventures of ideas, conducted by looking back in history. To meet this extraordinary guide, one would pass through the heavy outer doors of the Pontifical Institute—often escaping the Canadian snow—and trudge up the stone stairs to a second door, the door of an academic office. From behind this door Fr. Maurer peered with his mind's eye out on the historical course of philosophy and charted the excursions set out in his many writings. The articles from friends contained in this volume cover the millenium and a half that ranges from the earliest Christian philosophers to contemporaries of Descartes, a breadth appropriate because Fr. Maurer himself has ranged over that whole period, and beyond.

From his aerie on the grounds of the Pontifical Institute, Armand Maurer became an author and translator of world renown. He has been honored as Guggenheim Fellow, Aquinas Lecturer, Fellow of the Royal Society of Canada, President of the American Catholic Philosophical Association, and recipient of its Aquinas medal. Maurer's writing combines the Cartesian values of clarity and distinctness with the intellectual rigor and precision that come from a lifelong study of the thought of St. Thomas Aquinas. In his writing one gets the truth of the matter, set out briefly, with absolute precision and utter clarity. To my mind, this is why readers around the world have returned again and again to his writings. It also explains how he can have so successfully combined two crafts not often found in the same man: translator and philosopher.

Fr. Maurer's "Recollections" show how he was drawn to the study of medieval philosophy, to which he added the task of preserving the approach to the subject begun by Étienne Gilson. Maurer's first and critical step was to think of himself modestly as a disciple of that great historian. However, for a few in every trade apprenticeship turns into mastery; and Maurer thus became a master historian in his own right, and via this route a philosopher. Maurer's way of philosophizing, then, was "Gilson's way" or "the Institute way." As an introduction to the vast scope of his writings, let us look briefly at three themes they exhibit: Maurer as disciple, historian, and philosopher.

DISCIPLE OF ÉTIENNE GILSON

After the retirement of Étienne Gilson, Fr. Maurer began a series of essays on his beloved teacher, essays that illuminate his reasons for apprenticing himself to Gilson just as much as they explain the French historian's thought.[1] In his 1974 essay "Medieval Philosophy and its Historians," Maurer eschewed the opportunity to engage in Toronto-Louvain polemics, choosing instead to position Gilson (and himself) within a dispassionate and objective review of two centuries of scholarship about medieval philosophy.

As Maurer tells the tale, "the scientific study of the history of medieval philosophy began in the early nineteenth century, when the romantic movement was awakening curiosity in the Gothic culture of the Middle Ages."[2] He begins with two figures: Victor Cousin and Barthélémy Hauréau. Cousin thought the Middle Ages not a distinct epoch in history but "the cradle of modern society, and medieval philosophy the cradle of modern philosophy." Cousin's study of Ablelard and Heloise led him to insist on the name "scholasticism" for medieval philosophy, in order to signify reason's subservience to the Christian religion and "ecclesiastical authority," which assured a uniformity of doctrine but also meant that "scholasticism was not strictly speaking philosophy at all. Its proper name is theology."[3] By contrast, the "rationalist and free-thinker" Hauréau saw "in medieval scholasticism 'the passionate work of minds who, too long enslaved to revealed dogma, were trying to merit and gain their emancipation.'" Scholasticism was truly philosophy, and what gave scholastics their distinctive character was not subservience to religious authority, but the fact that "Aristotle was their master."[4]

The second phase in Maurer's tale can be dated from 1879, when Pope Leo XIII issued the encyclical *Aeterni patris* and brought medieval philosophy to the forefront of Catholic interests. The Chair in Thomistic philosophy at the University of Louvain in Belgium that the pope requested in 1880 was awarded to Désiré (later Cardinal) Mercier, whose job was "to revive scholastic philosophy in the modern world."[5] For historical help he turned to Maurice De Wulf, who held two "important" theses. In one thesis he took sides "with Hauréau against Victor Cousin," affirming "the independence of medieval philosophy from medieval theology." Scholastic reasoning was autonomous philosophical reasoning, even though De Wulf admitted that the scholastics had a passion "for combining (but not confusing) philosophical and theological questions in the same work," as Aquinas did in the *Summa theologiae*.[6]

De Wulf's other thesis concerned the content of scholastic philosophy. The similarities among medieval philosophers were not due to subservience to Church authority, as Cousin had said, nor simply to Aristotelian form, as Hauréau held. There was in medieval philosophy a common *content*, a "common scholastic synthesis," with the consequence that "the scholastics formed a school in the strict sense of the term." De Wulf placed individual medieval philosophers along an historical trend-line that began with "pre-scholastics" in the early middle ages, moved to "pre-Thomists such as Alexander of Hales and Bonaventure" in the early thirteenth century, and culminated in Thomas Aquinas, whose philosophy was "set forth as a grand and enduring system," one worthy of reappropriation by the Church in the early twentieth century.[7] "De Wulf's notion of a common scholastic philosophy came under severe criticism as early as the first decades of the twentieth century" and he "somewhat modifed his views," but De Wulf "never abandoned his thesis of a common body of philosophical ideas shared by the leading scholastics and expressed most systematically by Thomas Aquinas."[8]

The third phase of Maurer's story concerns Étienne Gilson, whose career began in earnest after World War I, when De Wulf was at the height of his fame. Though a Catholic, Gilson was not trained in scholastic philosophy but at the Sorbonne during the high tide of positivism, where he learned the skills of the historian of philosophy. Gilson would do for medieval philosophy what he had seen his teacher Lucien Lévy-Bruhl do for Hume. He concluded that De Wulf's two central theses were both demonstrably wrong. First, there was no "common scholastic synthesis." Gilson's proof can be seen by comparing his *Le thomisme* (1919), a doctrinal study of Aquinas, with his *La philosophie de saint Bonaventure* (1924), whose "most remarkable conclusion" was that "the thought of Bonaventure cannot be described as an inferior form of Thomism, a *thomisme manqué*. Like the philosophy of St. Thomas, that of St. Bonaventure is thoroughly Christian in inspiration and purpose, and yet it is a different philosophy, neither conflicting nor coinciding with Thomism."[9] By interpreting what united medieval philosophers as common *doctrinal* content, De Wulf had distorted the facts, a matter that can be resolved by looking closely at medieval philosophical texts.

But if so, how explain the remarkable similarities among medieval philosophies? And should not Christianity play a role here? Here Gilson saw the shortcomings of De Wulf's other "important thesis," that philosophy in the middle ages was "independent" of theology. None of Gilson's three predecessors had seen the subtlety of the very real connection between philosophy and faith. "Gilson's study of the Middle Ages convinced him that it produced, besides a Christian literature and art, a Christian philosophy," the reality of which "was forced upon Gilson by historical facts." It was because they "were created under the influence of the same Christian revelation" that there was "a kind of unity among the philosophies of the Middle Ages." As a result, "Gilson in effect substituted the notion of Christian philosophy for the outmoded concept of a common scholasticism. But Christian philosophy, in his view, had no doctrinal unity; it embraced a number of diverse and even mutually incompatible philosophical syntheses, the chief of which were Augustinism, Albertism, Bonaventurianism, Thomism, Scotism, and Ockhamism."[10] Gilson's notion of "Christian philosophy" does have one consequence that he was slow to embrace, but eventually accepted: ". . . what he presented as the Christian *philosophy* of St. Thomas is in reality a part of his *theology*—the part, namely, which St. Thomas considered to be demonstrable by reason. In short, what Gilson called medieval philosophies were in fact 'truncated theologies.'"[11]

Fr. Maurer summarizes his results by returning to the nineteenth century:

Thus Gilson proved that Victor Cousin was right: the philosophy of the Middle Ages was in fact theology. But he also proved that Barthélémy Hauréau was right: schoolmen such as St. Thomas developed strictly rational philosophies worthy of the name. This must be qualified, however, by adding that unlike modern philosophies those of the Middle Ages were created within theologies for theological purposes.[12]

Maurer learned the Gilsonian position from the master himself and accepted the truth that there was no scholastic synthesis, but that medievals developed what could be called Christian philosophy. The philosophy of the theologians was the dominant strain of Christian philosophy, but philosophy was also taught and developed by Masters in the Arts faculties. While most Masters of Arts were unwilling to accept a conflict between faith and reason, those called "radical Aristotelians" or "Latin Averroists" like Siger of Brabant are important precisely because they do not fit the model of "Christian philosophy." Maurer notes that "radical Aristotelianism is important in the history of philosophy because it introduced into the medieval world the separation of philosophy from faith and theology that became the ideal of modern thought."[13] Current attempts to find an "enlightenment" philosophy in the thirteenth century, one that is a source of modern philosophy's wall of separation between faith and reason, have focused on the Arts faculty and the radical Aristotelians in particular, a result quite in accord with Maurer's story. Maurer was not content to investigate just one form of medieval philosophy. In the compendium of his articles entitled *Being and Knowing,* he included studies of philosophizing theologians: the Dominicans Thomas Aquinas and Dietrich of Freiberg, the Franciscans William of Ockham and Francis of Meyronnes, and Henry Harclay, a secular master; but he also treats radical Aristotelian Masters of Arts Siger of Brabant and John of Jandun.

HISTORIAN OF PHILOSOPHY

The flavor of Maurer's historical studies is readily perceived in his studies of two Masters, where Maurer's efforts moved scholarship well beyond Gilson. He has devoted a considerable body of work, spanning thirty-seven years, to Siger of Brabant. With his usual precision, he summed up his view of Siger in the introduction to his edition of the *Quaestiones in Metaphysicam* (1983). I translate from Maurer's French:

> In his commentary on the *Metaphysics,* Siger depended upon numerous sources, but in the end the philosophy contained in its lectures is his own philosophy. It cannot be reduced to that of any of his predecessors, even Aristotle. Siger has been called a "heterodox Aristotelian," and rightly so, since Aristotle was his preferred philosopher and, on occasion, he did not hesitate to follow him even when such fidelity put him in contradiction with the Christian faith. He has also been presented as a "Latin Averroist," owing to the influence of Averroes on his thought; but he was too independent to follow Averroes slavishly, and sometimes he left Averroes in favor of Avicenna, Proclus, or Thomas Aquinas for the solution to a philosophical problem. All things considered, the philosophy of Siger is a personal synthesis, nourished no doubt by numerous sources, but incontestably marked by the seal of its author.[14]

It is impossible to read Maurer's phrase "personal synthesis" and not see him following the path pointed out by Gilson; and it is equally impossible to read the Latin text of Siger that Maurer has edited and not see how much farther down that path Maurer has proceeded.

Maurer has spent even more time with the theologian William of Ockham. In his book on Ockham, published in 1999 at the age of 84, Maurer introduces his concluding chapter this way:

> Martin Heidegger once made the perceptive observation: "Every thinker thinks but one single thought." . . . If we were to choose a single thought that plays this role in Ockham's philosophy, what would it be? The divine omnipotence and the razor are likely candidates because of their prominence in shaping his philosophy. But neither was original with him, nor was he the only one who used them; they were common coin for the schoolmen. It is true that he interpreted them in his own way, but always under the influence of his new notion of the individual. The evidence presented here leads to the conclusion that the central theme of Ockham's philosophy is the singular or individual thing (*res singularis*), as common nature (*natura communis*) is the focal point of Scotism and the act of existing (*esse*) is at the heart of Thomism.[15]

In this short passage, Fr. Maurer manages not only to point out the central theme of Ockham's philosophy, but also to offer a memorable comparison with Scotism and Thomism. He can do so because he looks at Ockham's philosophy doctrinally, that is, he concentrates on showing how Ockham's important conclusions flow from his even more important principles. Hence, the full title of the book: *The Philosophy of William of Ockham in the Light of Its Principles*.

In this respect, Maurer's work can be viewed as a reply to Marilyn M. Adams's huge 1989 work, *William Ockham*. Though a treasure trove of detailed arguments, its bulk is so overwhelming that the reader can lose sight of Ockham's overall doctrine. Always a gentleman, Maurer does not explicitly present his own book as a response; but it is. And Maurer's way of presenting Ockham's thought may well last as long as Gilson's book on Bonaventure, still the premier work on the topic three quarters of a century after it was first published.

THOMIST PHILOSOPHER

For Fr. Maurer, the history of philosophy was his own chosen route into philosophy itself. Of all the historical figures he has studied, the most important is Thomas

Aquinas; and when Maurer philosophizes he philosophizes as a Thomist. For this reason, some of his most important philosophical contributions take the form of his own presentations of Thomas Aquinas or of his favorite expositor of St. Thomas, Étienne Gilson. To get a feel for the range and importance of Maurer's own contributions to the long history of Thomism, let us glance at three of his favorite topics: Christian philosophy; the "division and methods of the sciences," to use Maurer's own phrase; and Thomistic existentialism.

Since Maurer adopted the idea of "Christian philosophy" from Gilson, some of his most memorable formulations of this doctrine come in the course of his explanations of Gilson's thought. In the "Translator's Introduction" to his 1993 translation of Gilson's 1960 work, *Christian Philosophy: An Introduction,* Maurer reminds his reader of Gilson's "first description of Christian philosophy" in his Gifford lectures, *The Spirit of Mediaeval Philosophy* (1931–32): "every philosophy which, although keeping the two orders [of philosophy and supernatural revelation] formally distinct, nevertheless considers the Christian revelation as an indispensable auxiliary to reason."[16] Looking back over several decades at this much disputed definition, Maurer then offers his own gloss on Gilson:

> When philosophy is incorporated in theology, as it is in the theology of St. Thomas and other scholastic theologians, it can be viewed from two different angles. As philosophy, it retains its essential rationality, deepened and enlightened by the higher wisdom in which it dwells. Thus Gilson insists that the theology of St. Thomas "includes, not only in fact but necessarily, a strictly rational philosophy." But that same philosophy is theological when it enters into the service of theology, for then it belongs to its household. Formally distinct as philosophy and theology, these two different wisdoms intimately collaborate with each other without any confusion between them. With the help of philosophy, theology achieves the structure and status of a science, and it gains a deeper understanding of the contents of faith. Philosophy in turn benefits from its service to theology; for example, metaphysics makes deeper progress in understanding the primary notion of being.[17]

Here Maurer, the second Master, is clearer than Gilson, the first.

In typical fashion, Maurer then goes on to draw a lesson that covers the history of modern philosophy in a glance:

> The theologians of the Middle Ages produced a variety of metaphysics as their instruments. With Descartes the ties between religion and metaphysics were cut, as metaphysics prided itself in dispensing with the theology from which it came. Metaphysics then lost its sense of identity, and philosophy took up arms against

it with Kant's critique and Comte's positivism. Metaphysics died at their hands, and the condition of its revival is the return to theology.[18]

The ties that should bind faith and reason began to loosen in the lecture halls along the Street of Straw in Paris in the thirteenth century; they were fully "cut" by Descartes, writing in a farmhouse in Holland in the seventeenth century; with the result that metaphysics "died" in the nineteenth century. Not content to explain its demise, Maurer ends on a prophetic note. To rise again metaphysics must be reconnected to religion, a prescription not irrelevant to the practical task of developing in the twenty-first century a philosophical curriculum that fulfills the program of John Paul II's *Ex corde ecclesiae.*

In his attempts to counter the positivistic foreshortening of the "range of reason" and to resurrect metaphysics in his 1932 book *The Degrees of Knowledge,* Jacques Maritain had made use of Aquinas's *Commentary on the De trinitate of Boethius.* Maurer subsequently made this work his own, translating Aquinas's questions 1–4 as *Faith, Reason, and Theology* and questions 5 and 6 as *The Division and Methods of the Sciences.* In his "Introduction" to the latter, Maurer explains Aquinas's rationale for following the Aristotelian division of theoretical knowledge into the physical sciences, the mathematical sciences, and metaphysics. Maurer notes the difference between "empiriological knowledge gained through controlled observation and measurement of the physical world" as found in modern science, and the kind of "philosophical" or "ontological" knowledge "of the very being and essential structure of things."[19] As an historian, he concentrates on the latter. For Aquinas, the scope and differences among sciences are determined by their "subjects," which in turn are understood through the doctrine of abstraction. Three kinds of abstraction locate the three kinds of sciences.

The first is "abstraction of the whole" universal from individuals possessing a common feature. "All the sciences use this type of abstraction, for they all leave aside the individual and accidental features of their object of study and concentrate on those that belong to it necessarily and universally. However, it is especially characteristic of natural philosophy, which studies the natures of material things."[20] Consequently, Aristotle had written different books devoted to different "subjects," such as moveable being, soul, animal, and dreams.

The second is "abstraction of form from sensible matter." This is the abstraction of the quantitative features that are only part of the reality of physical substances, from their substantial natures that characterizes the mathematical sciences. "Quantity is not abstracted from substance, but from the sensible qualities and the activities and passivities of material substance."[21] It cannot be completely abstracted from matter because quantity is an accident of substance, but mathematicians ignore substance in favor of quantity—both medieval mathematicians who knew only arithmetic and geometry, and moderns who have expanded the frontiers, but not the nature, of mathematics.

Maurer is most concerned with the third kind of abstraction, because it authorizes the revival of metaphysics after its apparent death at the hands of Kant and Comte. Here Maurer sets out Aquinas's teaching in a masterful overview of an exceedingly contentious topic:

> The abstraction used by the metaphysician to grasp his subject is properly called separation: *separatio.* This is a radically different mode of abstraction from those we have already discussed, for it is effected through negative judgment, not through simple apprehension. . . . For judgment is primarily pointed to the act of existing of things, whereas simple apprehension has to do rather with their essences or natures. As a result, the subject of metaphysics will have an existential character not found in those of the other two speculative sciences . . . the subject of this science is universal being (*ens commune*), or being as being (*ens inquantum ens*). It also deals with the transcendental properties of being, such as goodness and truth, as well as with God, who is the first cause of universal being. Now none of these depends on matter and motion for its existence, as do the objects of natural philosophy and mathematics. Some of them *can* exist in matter and motion, as for instance being, goodness, act and potency; but these can also be found apart from matter in spiritual being. God, of course, exists absolutely independent of matter and movement. We can conclude, therefore, that the objects with which the metaphysician is concerned either actually exist or can exist without matter. And it is this truth that is grasped by him in a negative judgment in which he denies that being is necessarily bound up with matter and material conditions. Through a judgment of this sort he grasps being in its pure intelligibility, and primarily in its value of existence, and forms the metaphysical conception of being as being.[22]

On the doctrine of essence and existence, Maurer's introduction to his translation of *De ente et essentia* contains an unsurpassed short description:

> The basic metaphysical themes [Aquinas] adopted at the beginning of his career remained the same throughout his life; yet he developed and deepened them as the years went by. Already in *On Being and Essence* he describes being (*esse*) as the actuality of essence, the two forming a composition that results in a being (*ens*). God has no other essence or nature than being; he is being in all its purity (*esse tantum*). Creatures receive being as a participation of the divine being, their essences limiting the degree of this participation.[23]

Ever the historian, Maurer again sets Aquinas's doctrine within a picture of the history of metaphysics his reader can take in at a glance:

> While not neglecting other aspects of being, such as form and essence, St. Thomas offers a radically new interpretation of being by emphasizing its existential side. This was a decisive moment in the history of Western metaphysics, for St. Thomas was transforming previous Greek and mediaeval conceptions of being, which gave primary place to form. Before St. Thomas, important progress had been made in the direction of an existential interpretation of being by the Arabian philosophers Alfarabi and Avicenna, and by the Christian theologian-philosopher William of Auvergne. But St. Thomas was the first to appreciate fully the supremacy of the act of existing over essence.[24]

By helping us understand the past, Maurer illuminates a central metaphysical thesis relevant to this and every age.

The themes I have pointed out here are but a few of the many found in Maurer's writings, but they are important themes, important enough to be reflected in several of the pieces here offered to him by students, colleagues, and friends. Speaking for all the authors here assembled, as well as his many other students, friends, and readers, let me close by noting simply that these offerings are our humble way of saying: "*Laudemus virum gloriosum* (let us praise an illustrious man)," one in particular, Armand Maurer.

———

Thanks are due to many for this book. Let me begin by thanking the authors who contributed to this appreciation. All are scholars well-recognized in their own right, and I want to thank them all for taking time in the midst of their various projects to sing the praises of Fr. Maurer here.

I would also like to thank Barbara Hanrahan, Rebecca DeBoer, Margaret Hyre, and all those at the University of Notre Dame Press. The quality of the end product, it seems to me, speaks for itself.

In addition, let me take this opportunity to express my gratitude to a number of people at the Center for Thomistic Studies in the University of St. Thomas, Houston, who have taken an active role in its publication: Rev. Jack Gallagher, CSB, former Director of the Center and Publications Director, approved the initial plan for this book. Subsequently, several Center officials helped move the project along: Christopher Martin, Daniel McInerny, Mary C. Sommers, and John Deely. Finally, let me thank Kevin White and Thomas Osborne, whose care as readers is greatly appreciated.

The editing process in Houston took a long time, but it would have been longer still without excellent help from David Arias, Mark Barker, and Benjamin Smith. Philip

Edmundson contributed the index. I would also like to mention Jeffrey Zents, whose computer wizardry came to the rescue on more than one occasion. Claudia Sommers Brown took the photographs for the cover, and James K. Farge, CSB, jack of all trades and master of them, too, provided the bibliography of Maurer's writings and expedited communications between Toronto and Houston.

Most of all, however, I would like to thank Armand Maurer himself. He has been for many years the living personification of an historical way of doing philosophy coming out of the Pontifical Institute of Mediaeval Studies in Toronto. His way is not the only way to do philosophy or to study the history of philosophy or even to follow the inspiration of Thomas Aquinas; it is simply the best way.

28 January 2004,
Feast of the Translation of the Relics of St. Thomas Aquinas

Notes

1. In Maurer's bibliography, nos. 21, 48, 61, 67, 71, 74, 77, 83, 89.

2. A. Maurer, "Medieval Philosophy and its Historians," in *Essays on the Reconstruction of Medieval History*, ed. V. Murdoch and G.S. Couse (Montréal / London: McGill–Queens University Press, 1974), 69–84; repr. A. Maurer, *Being and Knowing* (Toronto: Pontifical Institute of Mediaeval Studies, 1990), 461–80. Quoted from the reprint, p. 462.

3. Ibid., 462–63.

4. Ibid., 463–65.

5. Ibid., 471.

6. Ibid., 470–71.

7. Ibid., 468.

8. Ibid., 469–70.

9. Ibid., 474.

10. Ibid., 476–77.

11. Ibid., 477–78. Emphasis added.

12. Ibid., 478.

13. Ibid., 475.

14. Siger of Brabant, *Quaestiones in Metaphysicam*, ed. A.A. Maurer (Louvain: Éditions de l'Institut Supérieur de philosophie, 1983), 19–20.

15. Armand Maurer, *The Philosophy of William of Ockham in the Light of Its Principles*, in Studies and Texts 133 (Toronto: Pontifical Institute of Mediaeval Studies, 1999), 540.

16. Étienne Gilson, *The Spirit of Mediaeval Philosophy* (New York: Scribner, 1936; repr. Notre Dame, Ind.: University of Notre Dame Press, 1991), 37.

17. Étienne Gilson, *Christian Philosophy: An Introduction*, trans. Armand Maurer (Toronto: Pontifical Institute of Mediaeval Studies, 1993), xvi–xvii.

18. Ibid., xviii–xix.

19. Armand Maurer, *St. Thomas Aquinas: The Division and Methods of the Sciences*, 4th ed. (Toronto: Pontifical Institute of Mediaeval Studies, 1986), x.

20. Ibid., xx–xxi.

21. Ibid., xxi–xxii.

22. Ibid., xxii–xxiii.

23. Armand Maurer, CSB, "Introduction," *St. Thomas Aquinas: On Being and Essence,* 2nd ed. (Toronto: Pontifical Institute of Mediaeval Studies, 1968), 9–10.

24. Ibid., 10–11.

| *Chapter 1* |

On the Original Nature
of Christian Philosophy

JOHN M. RIST

By the fourteenth century, of which our knowledge has been so signally increased by Armand Maurer, Christians had been philosophizing for more than a thousand years, and although there still remained a few—their number was later to increase—who objected to the practice, it had long been institutionalized, provided with a curriculum, and widely approved. During the thirteenth century, Western "Aristotelianized" Augustinians[1] had largely overcome the suspicions of their more fundamentalist co-religionists whose counterparts had prevailed in Islam. But in the beginning Christians did not philosophize: neither the Old Testament prophets nor Christ himself was a philosopher, nor were the Apostles and Paul, who inveighed against "vain philosophy" (Col. 2:8; cf. 1 Tim. 6:20).[2] But philosophy did come to attract Christians, and although the history of that attraction is rather bedevilled by large gaps in our sources—which are in any case uneven in time and space—some aspects of it have been subjected to considerable scholarly scrutiny. Given the right approach, however, more precision can be achieved, and if the original nature of Christian philosophizing can be better understood, it may be of use to those wishing to continue in the tradition.

HOW TO TRAVEL FROM JERUSALEM TO ATHENS

A long line of historians and theologians,[3] reaching back through Harnack to Luther—whose hostility to Aristotle ("that fool who misled the Church") and to what he supposed to be scholasticism is palpable—has dreaded the contamination of Christianity by metaphysics and the consequent loss of the prophetic spirit of the Evangelists. In any consideration of the origins of Christian philosophy, it is fitting to touch on the rationale of that fear as well as its ultimate futility. For Luther, the metaphysical rot was largely to be blamed on the scholastics, but in the last two centuries there has been a recurrent belief that as early as the second century Christianity was somehow infected, even replaced, by a metaphysical idol. Harnack saw Hellenic corruptions even in the Gospel of John, but to go as far as that is to test the Christian sources by a standard of "orthodoxy" which cannot itself be tested historically, which may never have existed, and which can only derive from the modern critic's assurance that he can divine a pure Hellene-free Christianity.

Of more interest is to examine the steadily growing Christian literature in post-Biblical times, searching for philosophical items. But what would such items look like? To answer that would require a thesis about the basic nature of philosophy itself. To know what a philosopher says, even to use some of his more famous remarks, is hardly to philosophize, but at least it shows a more or less serious interest in the activities of philosophers. And from being interested in the activities of philosophers, from coming to believe that philosophers may confirm, or make more plausible, some pre-philosophical belief, one may (but need not) move towards doing philosophy. For a religious tradition to become philosophical it may pass through a number of stages — as, I shall argue, was the case with ancient Christianity. First comes a pre-philosophical period in which philosophy is viewed as useless, irrelevant, or hostile. Then some may find philosophical insights concordant with views learned from more specifically religious sources, which opens up the possibility that the writings of the philosophers need not be irrelevant or hostile; they may in certain respects even add to the deposit of truth or give it independent intelligibility, justification, and credibility. In considering this second stage, however, we must avoid the danger just observed[4] of confusing philosophizing with thinking — and specifically arguing — more generally: to think about the import of a prophecy, or to attempt to harmonize a set of prophetic utterances, is normally not philosophy but exegesis, whether performed intelligently or not. Which brings us back to the need for some kind of account, however stipulative, of what it is to philosophize, for without that it will obviously be difficult to ask whether, if, and when the Christians began to do it.

Aristotle's remark (*Met.* A.1) that philosophy begins with wonder is a reasonable place to start. Philosophers are puzzled about why things are as they are, but all investigations are not philosophical investigations. Philosophy seems to have to do with whether proposed explanations, of any sort, make sense: that is why there is a philosophy of physics, a philosophy of mind, and a philosophy of religion. In a sense philosophy is concerned with making sense of *both* phenomena *and* possible explanations of those phenomena: "What exactly does it mean to propose that *p*?" Clearly, when applied to early Christianity this means that thinking about how the Old Testament prophecies have been fulfilled, or what the relationship is between Christianity and Judaism, is not to be counted as philosophizing, but — to select a pair of relevant examples—to ask "What does it mean to say that God is omnipotent?" or "What sense can be attached to the proposition that God created the world *ex nihilo?*" is to raise philosophical questions. What we need to consider, therefore, is which and when such specific questions were first asked by Christians and what intellectual activities, if any, were pursued in earlier years, for some of these activities could hardly fail to raise philosophical questions.

Revelation, tradition, and authority could provide the early Christians with important facts about the world; they could, that is, provide the basis for faith; what they could less easily provide was a basis for understanding. For people in such circumstances, to philosophize would be to enquire why what is true is true and how what is true is intelligible: in other words, in Augustine's later formulation,[5] it would be to try to understand what one believes, to seek to give some kind of rationale (what Plato in the *Republic* had called a *logos*) of that understanding. For it is clearly absurd to say that I understand something without being able to provide any justification other than an appeal to revelation or authority—though the justification may include the claim that it makes sense to defer to some particular kind of authority.

Clearly the early Christians had to learn—at the very least for various proselytizing purposes—why it is important to be able to justify, though not of course always to demonstrate, what they held to be true. When they reached that stage, they had passed the two previous stages: the one, the contempt for philosophy or dismissal of it as wholly unnecessary, the other, a claim that non-Christian philosophers (and others, perhaps poets) have said some Christian-sounding things and thus that Christian claims are not altogether outlandish, as the Areopagites seem to have considered Paul's views of resurrection. Stage three began when Christians themselves attempted to understand not merely historical truth (about the relationship between their Messianic beliefs and the Old Testament prophecies and the Jewish Bible in general) nor about mere exegesis and application (how do we apply Jesus' stricter regulations about divorce to our Mosaic understanding and the present circumstances in our community?), but rather, for example: on the assumption that man is free and God is omnipotent, what does it mean to be free or omnipotent? And not merely to ask that question, but to answer it not by citation of authority but by making sense of the citation of authority and of what authority proposes.

But first, a methodological problem of some difficulty. A distinguished historian of early Christian ideas has remarked that "like Justin, therefore, Clement judges the individual philosophical systems from the point of view of Middle Platonism. His philosophical education has not been effaced by his conversion to Christianity."[6] The second of these sentences is true, the first (and in this the author is not untypical) is more questionable. An alternative (and perhaps more interesting and accurate) way of explaining the same data would be to say that Justin and Clement's philosophical judgment is that the truth is better explicated by Middle Platonists than by other philosophical groups. Put that way it suggests that Justin also judges the quality of Middle Platonism itself. It is not simply that Middle Platonism in and of itself is the standard of truth, but that from the philosophical options of his day, Justin's faith finds its best reflection among the Middle Platonists. If that is right, then a further question will arise not merely as to when Christians began to philosophize, but as to why and when they found Middle (or other forms of) Platonism the most congenial—if still defective—philosophical approach on offer. That in turn will raise for the contemporary reader questions about the content of any possible Christian philosophy which is to be genuinely *Christian*, that is, capable of expressing a philosophical justification of Christian truth. At least we can see that the early Christians rejected certain modes of philosophizing out of hand as wholly incompatible with Christianity while variously modifying others (rightly or wrongly) almost beyond recognition.

A by-product of our *historical* examination of the early Christian thinkers will suggest why they deployed no formal distinction between philosophy and theology. That distinction, as currently adopted, itself depends on a distinction between the "raw material" considered suitable within the two disciplines, but no such distinction existed in patristic times when "philosophy," if Christianized, had to retain its pagan sense of a (proper) way of life, while at the same time referring (as in the time of Socrates) to an "examined" way of life, that is to a way of life which its devotees would wish to *understand* with the aid of whatever data is available. Christian "philosophy" in the ancient world, then, will turn out to be the pursuit and rational justification of a properly Christian way of life. "Philosophy" and "theology" as we know them are subordinated to an all-embracing search not for certainty but for an understanding of an intelligible universe—which would also identify what Plato in the *Meno* (98A3) had called "an account of its cause (αἰτίας λογισμός)."

A Pre-Philosophical Phase

During the period from the Crucifixion and Resurrection to the sack of Jerusalem in A.D.70 and that subsequent Jewish Synod of Jamnia which signalled *inter alia* the failure of the first phase of the Christian mission, or rather of the hope of Christian Jews that Judaism would be transformed as a whole into Christianity, Christians normally expected the imminent end of the world and the ushering in of Christ's kingdom, with or without the thousand-year reign of the saints on a new earth. This expectation, though subject to increasing strain as the years passed ("Too many Gentiles, too few Jews and no End in sight," as one scholar put it[7]) was strengthened by the appearance of the book of Revelation (presumably a fruit of Domitian's persecution) and persisted in mainstream Christianity for many centuries, always encouraging those sections of the movement which saw little point in arguing with non-Christians: sufficient only to warn them of their impending doom if they declined to repent.

Though appealing also to "god-fearers" (Gentiles who had previously converted to some form of Jewish belief, who attended synagogue services, but who were not required to meet the halakhic requirements, especially circumcision) and to Gentiles more widely, the original rhetoric of the *ecclesia* as a Messianic movement within Judaism meant that much of the intellectual effort of the earlier Christians (still visible in Justin's mid-second century *Dialogue with Trypho*) was directed to persuading their fellow Jews that the Messianic prophecies had been fulfilled in Jesus of Nazareth, notwithstanding his shameful death. As yet there was no New Testament, though Christian writings did exist—first, many of the Pauline Epistles, then the "Memoirs of the Apostles," then the rest which were eventually to form the core of the New Testament canon when it became, somehow, more or less fixed throughout the world in the middle to late second century.

Jesus had been executed by the Romans as a political agitator, feared as such by his Jewish enemies, and desideratively considered such by many of his nationalist Jewish friends. And his enemies had indeed legitimate fear of political agitators; they knew well that Rome would not tolerate them, and that, if provoked, the Roman hand would come down hard on the entire Jewish community. ("It is good that one man should die for the people.") Similarly, after Jesus' disappearance—at least in the Jewish communities of the Diaspora such as that of Damascus in which Saul of Tarsus had in his earlier days been some kind of religious official—Jewish concern to keep on the right side of the Roman authorities was of paramount importance, and contributed at least in part to their fear of the growing group of Christians in their midst whose activities might compromise the community as a whole, for the Jewish community depended for its security from pagan mobs on Roman presence and protection.

Just as the Jews feared Christians as a danger to their entire community, and increasingly sought to distance themselves from them, so the Christians too realized that they needed to persuade the Roman authorities that they were no threat to the civic order: no easy task with ill-wishers spreading stories of their atheism, incestuous unions, and Thyestian banquets at their "love-feasts." Moreover, their refusal of the civic religion—a concession allowed to the Jews but not to this increasingly un-Jewish subgroup—made them immediately suspect as a threat to the daily life of the community and a possible cause of an enmity of the gods which might be made manifest in the form of floods, fires, or famines. Not by chance did Christian activities provoke the cry "Christians to the lion," when the notorious religious charlatan Alexander of Abonoteichos was able to have the herald of his new cult (complete with talking snake) proclaim at the dawn of each new day, "Atheists away, Christians and Epicureans away" (*Alex.* 38).

Soon, however, Christians had to face a different kind of reality. While Judaism went its own way, while the Day of Judgment still remained in the indefinite future, there were problems to be faced with the Gentiles quite unconnected with persecution. For increasingly Gentiles were becoming the majority in Christian groups. Perhaps at first most were uneducated, but before long Christian missioners would be confronted by more educated pagans (as Justin by the Cynic Crescens), inevitably including those with some knowledge of the various schools of philosophy. Mere contact with them could only serve to diminish by familiarity the more "fideist" tendencies in the Christian groups, while any attempt to convert them would bring the Christian missioners face to face with the matter of what to do with "philosophical" questions, that is, with those kinds of philosophical questions which were currently in circulation. The long process by which Christianity tried to sort out what kinds of philosophy might be compatible with its beliefs had thus begun. Let us first approach this by the conventional route, by considering the first person often claimed as a Christian philosopher.

JUSTIN MARTYR

Paul's debate on the Areopagus apart, we do not know when Christians first encountered pagan philosophers,[8] let alone pagan philosophical doctrines: urban Christians could take in with the air they breathed philosophical ideas of various sorts without recognizing them as philosophical.[9] Possibly there were Christians who took an interest in philosophy before Justin, but Justin is the earliest example we have. Before converting, he had made the rounds of the philosophical schools, preferring Platonic theorizing to the alternatives on offer—Pythagoreans, Aristotelians, and Stoics (*Dial.* 2)—and reaching a critical awareness of certain philosophical commonplaces at odds with Christianity, such as the notion that man's soul is naturally immortal, "akin to" rather than an image of God (*Dial.* 5). Of course, a man whose turn to philosophy had preceded his conversion to Christianity and who still wore the philosopher's cloak as a Christian would differ substantially from a more "ordinary" Christian (like Irenaeus) who was drawn by the personal circumstances of his own struggle for truth to defend himself by rational argument on what might at times look like philosophical themes. In other words, whereas Justin has a certain first-hand experience of the philosophical world,[10] is proud to be called a philosopher, and indeed hails Christianity itself as the true philosophy (*Dial.* 8), Irenaeus, in arguing for a rational and intelligible Christianity, could have found himself philosophizing without so intending, and with only a minimal knowledge of contemporary philosophical practice. Whereas Justin is willing to apply his knowledge of philosophical traditions, at least to a degree, to the understanding of philosophical difficulties, Irenaeus, rather more Socratically, may perhaps at times reinvent the philosophical wheel.

What we might expect in Justin is some contribution of an argumentative sort on "philosophical questions," plus a limited use of philosophical texts to support his Christian positions. In fact Justin has an important defense mechanism: philosophy is justified *because* the philosophers originally learned their wisdom from the prophets, a significant use of bogus history (*Dial.* 7). Socrates, he tells us (2 *Apol.* 10), had a partial knowledge of Christianity. And again (13.2), the "teachings" of Plato are "not alien to those of Christianity, but not wholly similar." To understand the force of this latter claim we must understand what Justin takes to be the teaching of Plato, and we may approach that topic by noting that Justin and his character Trypho agree that it is the business of philosophy to "enquire about the divine" (*Dial.* 1.3; cf. 2.6 on Plato). Yet for all Justin's knowledge of at least a number of substantial philosophical themes— some of which we shall identify—and for all that he can introduce his dialogue with Trypho with echoes of several Platonic dialogues, including the *Republic* and *Phaedrus*, his main importance lies in his attempt to insert himself into contemporary debate rather than merely reverting to the prophetic or exegetical mode.

What had Athens to do with Jerusalem? If enough Athenian material were to be introduced into the Jerusalem mentality, then that mentality would increasingly allow for the possibility not merely of preaching what is true but of explaining why what is true is true. In the first instance such an explanation will reveal itself as the claim that the Christian faith makes sense. That is not a claim to be philosophizing in some Cartesian manner, engaging, that is, in a pursuit of certainty; it is showing both that Christianity is coherent by current standards and that supposedly intellectual attacks on it are themselves intellectually flawed.

In 1 *Apol.* 20 (cf. *Dial.* 5.4) Justin tells us that when we say that God created and arranged all things we seem to repeat the thinking of Plato's *Timaeus*. But what he repeats of Plato are his dogmas, not his arguments. Insofar as Justin is a Platonist, it is because Platonism is selectively congenial to his Christianity. In a similar vein he observes that various poets and philosophers have indicated postmortem penalties similar to those preached in Christian literature, and when he introduces Plato's account in the *Timaeus* of "shapeless matter" (1 *Apol.* 59; cf. 1 *Apol.* 10) he invokes the claim that Plato plagiarized the idea from Moses.[11]

More philosophically interesting is Justin's use (1 *Apol.* 43–44) of *Republic* 10, 617E4, where Plato exonerates God from responsibility for human wrongdoing. Here Justin offers something like an argument: unless man were responsible, then rewards and punishments are by fate, so choice must be in our power. Man, claims Justin in Plato's steps, is a unique creature in that he has the power of freely choosing, and therefore he is liable for praise and blame.

I have not listed all the philosophical pickings in Justin, but though significant they are still comparatively scanty.

A New Approach: Four Examples

The principal philosophical effect of Justin's work was to familiarize Christians with an appeal (however justified) to Greek philosophy. But to appeal to the authority of philosophers to corroborate ideas derived solely from revelation and Christian tradition is not yet to philosophize. Yet it may lead to philosophizing, because it may (even unintentionally) bring out philosophical confusion, or at least the need for philosophical clarification, either within the pagan philosophical texts or within the Christian tradition, which appeal to those texts is supposed to elucidate. But if we want to study not the developing preconditions for philosophy among the early Christians, but the activity itself, we must look not at whether, say, Justin is a "Christian philosopher," but at what philosophy is being done.

To achieve this we require a less conventional approach. Christian philosophy began in two ways: either because of the need to clarify conceptual ambiguities in the Christian tradition which no mere exegesis could resolve, since the problems now being proposed to the texts were not in the minds of their original authors; or because a willingness to cite Greek philosophers awakens a Christian awareness that *further* progress on certain "philosophical" questions would be helpful for the intelligent pursuit of a Christian life—and that the progress could not be achieved merely by the repetition of traditional or revealed doctrinal statements. Examples of the first sort are difficulties about the nature of God's creatorship—the problem of the developing Christian theme of *creatio ex nihilo*—and attempts to grasp what it could mean to call God "omnipotent." In these cases we recognize the emergence, in a Christian setting, of new problems of metaphysics or the philosophy of religion.

A second group of problems will be represented in the present discussion by two traditional topics of Greek philosophy which find new forms in a Christian context, but which derive their origin in Christian writers less from understanding what a "Christian" notion such as omnipotence[12] or *creatio ex nihilo* means (or to what possible reality such language could refer) than from trying to clarify the general philosophical conditions within which a Christian philosophy of man and of morality could be formulated. The two examples I shall consider under this head will be the problem of "free will" and its relationship to the Christian belief that somehow we shall be held responsible for our actions—this has already been seen in Justin—and the problem of the metaphysical nature of evil which Christian thinkers were inclined to believe had been inadequately treated (even when properly raised) by the pagans.

In selecting these four topics (which will turn out to be interestingly interrelated), I have neglected other possible themes often emphasized in earlier treatments of the origin of Christian philosophy: not least the defence of monotheism itself—or rather the argument from design in some monotheistic version (cf. Tatian, *Orat.* 4; Irenaeus,

Adv. Haer. 2.9.1; 4.6.6). We should note that even Stead,[13] who sees very little significant philosophical interest among Christians prior to the fourth century, allows that "positive arguments for God's unity and transcendence deriving ultimately from Plato and Aristotle . . . are to be found in Justin and Irenaeus and are rather more coherently stated by Clement, though for a more considered approach we have to wait for Augustine."

(a) Creatio ex Nihilo

Biblical support for the idea that God created the world out of nothing[14] is very limited: the most plausible candidate is 2 Macc. 7:28, where it is said that God made things from what is not (ἐξ οὐκ ὄντων ἐποίησεν ὁ Θεος). The interpretation of this is disputed and will probably never be settled: ἐξ οὐκ ὄντων could mean either from what does not exist at all, i.e., from nothing—though ἐξ οὐκ ὄντος might seem more plausible Greek for that—or "from things which do not exist," i.e., from things which are not specific (ὄντα would then, as commonly, suggest ὄντα τινά), from some indefinite material substrate. If the latter is the case, it might be paralleled by Wisdom 11:17 where God is said to have created the world (κτίσασα τὸν κόσμον) from shapeless matter (ἐξ ἀμόρφου ὕλης). Of course, anyone determined to read *creatio ex nihilo* into the Old Testament can always add that at some earlier time God also "created" the shapeless matter. And other texts often later *taken* to refer to *creatio ex nihilo* would include Genesis 1:1: "In the beginning God created the heavens and the earth, the earth was without form and void and darkness covered the abyss."

Fortunately it is not our present concern to determine the "intended" meaning of the Old Testament texts, though it is hard not to conclude that none of their authors had *creatio ex nihilo* in mind; what they were concerned to identify was the absolute dependence of the universe on God. Genesis clearly emphasizes that God's creative activity (signified by the Hebrew *bara*) is thus unique, while the language of 2 Maccabees may suggest that Hellenistic categories (being vs. non-being) are now being introduced. That may be so, but it does not settle the problem of a possible *creatio ex nihilo*.

The possibility of *creatio ex nihilo* is a metaphysical question, and anyone who maintained it in the ancient world would have to deny (at least implicitly) an axiom (obeyed even if not recognized as such) dating back to Parmenides: nothing arises from nothing (*nihil ex nihilo fit*). That axiom justifies the normal view of ancient philosophers that the world has (and could have) no beginning in time. Unless, that is, it began not from nothing but from God, that is, that it is somehow created from God's substance (*de Deo*). But to be so "created," it would have to be "created" somewhere. That is something like the position of Plato's *Timaeus*, at least in what I believe to be the most plausible reading.[15] And Plato's *Timaeus*, however interpreted, underlies almost all non-Stoic and non-Epicurean accounts of the origin of the cosmos available in the second century of our era—available, that is, to pagans and, insofar as they were willing to use it, to Christians. As we have seen, Justin was aware of it—probably directly, and at least indirectly through manuals and philosophical talk (1 *Apol.* 59–60).[16]

But of course we find references to creation before Justin, and by looking at them we can see how something like a philosophical treatment took root. Clement of Rome refers to God as the great Craftsman and in a passage in which Stoic echoes have been noted (1 Clement 20) goes on to speak of providence and the evidence of God's goodness in the universe. More interestingly there appears to be an unambiguous reference to *creatio ex nihilo* in the early second century *Shepherd of Hermas* (*Mandate* 1.1): "God," says Hermas, "created (κτίσας) the universe . . . and made from that which does not exist (ἐκ τοῦ μὴ ὄντος) all that exists." Here Hermas not only uses the "Hellenistic" categories of being and non-being, but in the more interesting singular form—with negative μή—which seems a more likely indication of *creatio ex nihilo* than the passage of 2 Maccabees from which perhaps it draws its inspiration; though it also repeats simpler "Hebrew" notions of the superiority of God: He alone is "uncontained (ἀχώρητος)" and of the dependence of the creation which he himself "contains."

Hermas might seem to confirm Torchia's suggestion that "a faith commitment to the notion of creation from nothing in an absolute sense was present in the Christian tradition from the outset."[17] In view of the possible ambiguity of ὄν, however, we should hesitate; perhaps we are still, despite the being/non-being language, in a world in which the question "What does non-being mean?" has not yet been formulated. It will require, it seems, a thesis *about* non-being—which more deliberate use of traditions influenced by Plato's *Timaeus* will provide—to offer sufficient challenge to the Christian "philosopher" for him to think more precisely about the nature of God's creative activity. But if there is literally nothing "*from* which" the universe could be created, perhaps a Christian might now take up the option that it is from God's own generative being that the world derives,[18] or perhaps this *generative* model was to be put not to philosophical but to purely Trinitarian work.

Recognition that Justin is the earliest Christian known to have significant firsthand knowledge of some of the philosophical schools might lead us to suppose that the problem of how to interpret scriptural notions about God's creativity in terms of Greek concepts of being and non-being would now be brought to the foreground, and this expectation is strengthened when we find him using the term ἀγέννητος (unbegotten, *Dial.* 5) for God alone.[19] That again certainly suggests the *Timaeus* (52A), but our hopes are disappointed. Justin, as we have seen, holds that we learn from Christian tradition that in the beginning God "crafted" (or "created"—δημιουργῆσαι) everything from shapeless matter—as in Wisdom 11:17—for the sake of man (1 *Apol.* 10), and he uses the same phrase "shapeless matter," which God changed (στρέψαντα) a little later (1 *Apol.* 59).[20] Those still wishing to allow that Justin advocated *creatio ex nihilo* have suggested that he could have accepted a two-stage creation, first unformed matter, then a cosmos; others have more plausibly denied this—and indeed there is no evidence for it. For all Justin's use of the *Timaeus* he still accepts the Old Testament attitude to creation (perhaps influenced by Philo[21]). The "Greek" problem of the *relationship* between non-being and chaos is not yet in his sights. And the same is true of Athenagoras (*Leg.* 15.2, 19.4; *De Res.* 3.2).

When, however, we reach Justin's pupil Tatian and Theophilus of Antioch, we find a recognition that the relationship between the scriptural doctrine of "creation" and the tradition of inchoate unformed matter must be thought through; familiarity with Greek ideas has forced Christian authors to raise questions perhaps implicit but certainly unconsidered in their Jewish originals.

Tatian unambiguously offers a two-stage creation of the universe: "In the beginning" the *logos* was begotten (γεννηθείς) and in its turn begat (ἀντιγεννάω seems a new term) our world by "crafting" (δημιουργήσας) matter, but this matter is brought into existence by the sole craftsman of the universe (προβεβλημένη—another neologism, *Orat.* 5): in this sense it is not "without beginning" (ἄναρχον). A little later the process is spelled out clearly: the cosmos is created "from matter" and matter is brought into existence (προβεβλημένην again) by God. On the one hand (*Orat.* 12) before they are marked off (πρὸ τοῦ διάκριοιν λαβεῖν) there are no "beings"—matter is resourceless and formless; on the other, after its "division" (διαιρεῖν) it is ordered and well arranged. In an address "To the Greeks" this can only be a repudiation of any theory (however misunderstood) of an organization of matter by God from a coexistent formless chaos.

It only remained for Theophilus, *Ad Autol.* 1.4 (after 180), again with specific reference (direct or indirect) to the *Timaeus* (cf. 2.4) to insist—with an eye on 2 Maccabees—that God brought all things into being from what does not exist (ἐξ οὐκ ὄντων εἰς τὸ εἶναι, 1.4); Plato and his followers are wrong (2.4) to suppose that "God and matter are both uncreated; if they were, God would not enjoy absolute monarchy." Here then is a philosophical retort—governed by Christian axioms—to a fundamental position of Greek philosophy. And there is at least implicit argumentation. If matter were coeternal, God would not be God in the strict sense. We are beginning, that is, to think about what it is to speak clearly about God's nature: "What is great about God making the cosmos from a material substrate (ἐξ ὑποκειμένης ὕλης)?" It is a specific difference between divine and human nature that God can make things "out of what does not exist, as many as he wishes and how he wishes."

Once stated, the doctrine of *creatio ex nihilo* is free to develop, and there is no space to pursue these developments—not least those implicit in Tatian's "brought into being" (προβεβλημένη) which leaves open the possibility (we noted the concern of

Hermogenes) that *ex nihilo* could be evaded by supposing that matter is created not "from nothing" but "from God" (*ex Deo*). And Theophilus' claim that God can do "as he wills" brings us to the next of our four topics: God's omnipotence. But before leaving *ex nihilo* we should note that, as yet, nothing has been said about the implications of *creatio ex nihilo* for man's moral nature. That is another story, and especially about Augustine.[22]

(b) Omnipotence

"We (in contrast to Moses) do not think in that way; we say that certain things are impossible by nature and these God does not attempt" (Galen, *De usu partium* xi.14.906; cf. Osborn, *Justin* 50–51).

Discussion of *creatio ex nihilo* is a special case of a possible discussion about the nature of God's power. Arguments for *creatio ex nihilo* are arguments that in the world of nature nothing can exist in any way, formed or unformed, without the creative act of God. But it seems that the claim that God—to be God in the strict sense—must have created everything from nothing, did not lead directly to the further more general question of what exactly God can or cannot do, though it certainly preceded it in time in the Christian community.[23]

From earliest times Christians, following Old Testament texts, had called God "almighty (παντοκράτωρ)"—though the word occurs very rarely in the New Testament (cf. 2 Cor. 6:18; Rev. 1:8, etc.[24])—often combining "almighty" with "God" (ὁ παντο-κράτωρ Θεός, *Deus omnipotens*), and it seems that by the late second or early third century belief in "God the Father Almighty" (εἰς Θεὸν πατέρα παντοκράτορα)— the Greek probably precedes the Latin *in Deum patrem omnipotentem*—had been accepted as a standard credal formula in Rome. And the association of "almighty" with "father" suggests that "almighty" refers to the creative powers of God, that is, in philosophical terms, to the role and power of God in the creating and/or ordering of the physical universe.

 But as the case of Philo shows, to call God omnipotent is not necessarily to understand much about the sense in which he is omnipotent, though it seems that originally it referred to God's ability to make and order the natural cosmos. But if God can "make," presumably he can destroy. Or can he? Or rather, perhaps, in what circumstances can he destroy or at least allow to be destroyed? Once these questions are asked and answered by Christians, we can say again that they are doing philosophy: that is, in this case, considering the philosophical problem of omnipotence.

The problem of what a non-omnipotent God can do had been raised as far back as Plato's *Republic*, and indeed in pre-Socratic times. Certainly Justin is aware that in the *Republic* Plato had asserted that God—however he thought of him or however

Justin thought he had thought of him—cannot cause evil: Justin, as we have seen (1 *Apol.* 44), cites the words "God is not responsible," Θεὸς ἀναίτιος, from *Republic* 10, 617E. But it is likely that possible "restrictions" on God's power will become more problematic if God is regularly stated to be "omnipotent."

It seems that it was not until the time of Origen in the third century that the problem of omnipotence was treated more seriously.[25] Origen's comments, however, interesting though they are, leave much more to be said, and Augustine and Boethius still find the territory strange and difficult.[26] It is uncertain whether it was biblical exegesis or the challenge of secular philosophers, in particular Celsus, which compelled Origen to face the issue. Sometimes he seems focused on what are largely exegetical problems: so in his *Commentary on Matthew* (95), in discussing Jesus' prayer, "If it be possible, let this cup be taken from me," he tries to identify the features of God which must be considered when we ask, "Was it *possible* for the cup to be taken away?" These features are God's absolute power—absoluteness, even arbitrariness, is suggested by Rufinus' *potentia* for whatever was Origen's Greek original—and God's justice, "for so far as God's power goes, all things both just and unjust are possible for him." By this Origen clearly means that although in some sense of "possible" it is possible, e.g., for God deliberately and directly to injure an innocent person, if we consider God's justice, such actions are not possible: if you like, Origen has identified a "moral" sense of "impossible," a moral way in which God "cannot" do certain things—though in the *Commentary on Matthew* there is no analysis of "cannot"; rather he speaks of the Father's will (*contra voluntatem paternam,* perhaps for the Greek προαίρεσις), that will being assumed to be just.

Origen's first approaches to omnipotence had been in the *De Principiis* (2.9.1; 4.4.8). Both these texts have comparatively little interest and suggest that he is not yet aware (as he is in the *Commentary on Matthew*) of the seriousness of the problem. In 2.9 he argues against "certain people" who hold that there is an infinite number of creatures, for if so, they cannot be understood or framed, while Scripture says that God created all things "with number and measure." A similar position is taken in 4.4, though perhaps with an allusion to the *Timaeus;* Origen now speaks of God's will and that he is good by nature. Here, however, the exegesis does not lead, as in the *Commentary on Matthew*, to any philosophical account either of God's goodness or of his power, beyond the suggestion that God can grasp all things (*virtute sua omnia comprehendit*).

It is not only in the *Commentary on Matthew* that Origen considers the nature of God's power. The most interesting contexts are not exegetical but philosophical—and in one text (*Contra Celsum*) the direct result of a philosophical challenge: something akin to the philosophical challenge answered by Theophilus about *creatio ex nihilo*. But Origen offers not merely a reply to Celsus; he argues against Celsus' position. Celsus, he claims, is intellectually confused.

In the reply to Celsus we see Origen's striking philosophical talent at work, demolishing the pretensions and arguments of his Platonist opponent in philosophical terms. Celsus's charge is harsh and direct: the Christians outrageously dissolve problems about the resurrected body (5.23) by saying that "anything is possible for God." (Indeed Justin had done so in 1 *Apol.* 18.6.) Celsus, says Origen (3.70), in attributing to us the view that "everything is possible for God," takes us to mean that God will be able to do anything, thus indicating that he fails to understand how we use the term "everything" when we say "God would be able to do everything"; nor does he grasp the relevant sense of "can."

In leaving aside Celsus's closing point in 3.70, Origen makes the "professional" comment that there are in fact arguments, though they are not compelling, in favour of a more sweeping account of omnipotence which Celsus could have made, but did not; perhaps, Origen allows, Celsus was able to see through them himself. But in 5.23 he returns to the terms "all" and "can." To say that God is all-powerful (δυνήσεται πάντα) does not imply that he has power over what does not actually exist (ἀνύπαρκτόν): thus God could not feed a chimera, since there are no chimeras. Nor can he deal in things which are "inconceivable" (ἀδιανοήτων). Nor can he do what is base. In general, then, Origen is recognizing "logical" limits on God's omnipotence.

In both 3.70 and 5.23 Origen also broaches ethical questions similar to those we have found in the *Commentary on Matthew,* but there is also something new. In the *Commentary* he says that we must consider not only God's power but also God's justice. There is a sense in which God cannot do what is unjust—though he would have the raw power to do it. (If I say, "I cannot bring myself to shoot X," it does not mean that I don't have the power to pull the trigger.) But in 3.70, to *potentia* and *iustitia* (profiting from Celsus' comments) Origen adds as clarification (cf. *De Princ.* 4.4) the notion of God's will: God can do nothing wrong, not merely because he does not (arbitrarily) so will, but because such action would contradict his nature. Just as light cannot darken, so God can do nothing wrong. Here the "argument from ethics" is linked to a metaphysical point. A logical account of God in which he would do wrong is inherently contradictory—and in saying this Origen is hearkening back to older Stoic, Platonic, and even pre-Socratic arguments. As for whatever beings have a "natural" tendency to injustice, that is because, unlike God, there is nothing in their nature which rules out such possibilities. Thus, contrary to Celsus, who suggests un-Platonically that God might be able to act unjustly but does not will to do so, Origen insists that such talk is mistaken. God's nature *rules out* any possibility of attributing an unjust will to him; his will is all of a piece.

In 5.23 Origen introduces additional material: in a way Celsus is right to say that "God does not will what is contrary to nature." If by "contrary to nature," Celsus means only "what is wicked or irrational," that is fine, but if he wishes to enclose God in a natural dimension, denying, that is, that God is the master of nature, then his metaphysics is (Stoically and improperly for a Platonist) misconceived. Nature, Origen holds, has a vulgar sense by which we refer only to human nature or the nature of the cosmos, but there is "a superior and more divine nature" available.

Once again, as we saw Theophilus reacting to "Platonic" claims about matter in arguing philosophically to the necessary origin of matter, so Celsus's accusations of uncritical Christian language about God's power bring out the philosophical spirit in Origen and set up a "philosophical" problem for future Christian thinkers. Yet it is probably going too far to say that Origen specifically recognized a "problem about omnipotence" in the way that he would have recognized, from the pagan philosophical tradition, a problem about the freedom of the will.

As I have argued elsewhere,[27] even Augustine, who often discusses God's omnipotence, is unable to bring omnipotence to the surface *as a problem*.[28] Interestingly, however, unlike with Origen, some of Augustine's remarks occur in discussions of the Apostles' Creed (as in *Sermon* 213). Augustine argues first that we need God to be "almighty"; otherwise he could not forgive sins. And he repeats Origen's "ethical" though not his purely "logical" limitations: "God cannot die, he cannot sin, he cannot be deceived. . . . so many things he cannot do; if he could do them he would not be almighty."

In the much earlier *Sermon* 214 (of 391), Augustine's discussion is more elaborate: God cannot do what he does not will—this is now supported by reference to 2 Timothy 2:13: he cannot deny himself. "Justice," continues Augustine, "cannot have the will to do what is unjust, wisdom what is foolish, truth what is false." And in *The Trinity* (13.13.17) we read that *potentia* must serve *iustitia*.[29]

Much more could be said about the development of a conscious awareness of the problem of omnipotence. We should have to investigate the impact in Christian circles (especially in Gregory of Nyssa) of the notion of God as "infinite,"[30] either in himself or in his power, a notion strongly present in Plotinus and reappearing, whether through direct influence or by parallel reflection, in Cappadocia. But again that is another story; for the present we merely record the problem of omnipotence as growing ever more complex as Christians faced various versions of a Greek challenge to the intelligibility of one of their most deep-seated beliefs.

(c) Free Will

To pass from omnipotence to free will is to see how new Christian problems soon became locked into a variety of much older philosophical dilemmas. In classical Christian texts such as Augustine's *De Libero Arbitrio*, the problem of the "free choice of the will" is inextricably tied up with the question of omnipotence, for how the will of an omnipotent God can be frustrated puzzles Augustine. Obviously, as we have already seen, the problem is with the rational, beneficent will of a good God. For if the will (expressing the nature) of a good God is frustrated, this is another (and more worrying) diminution of his omnipotence. Notoriously, Augustine has difficulties with the text of 1 Timothy 2:4, "God wishes all men to be saved," and these difficulties are roughly generated as follows: God wishes to save all; free choice suggests a real possibility of a permanent choice of evil; in those cases God's will to save all is frustrated —unless he overrides the "free" choice. This is not the place to consider Augustine's dilemmas, for Christians recognized almost from the beginning that God's justice seems absurd, to say the least, if we are punished for sins which we have no choice but to commit. And whatever problems there may be about what was later to be called "traducianism," all seemed to agree that at least Adam and Eve chose to sin. And that mere "fact" puts Christians in line to accept some form of the "free will defense," that is, that we, or some of us, are justly held to be responsible for our actions. This then being apparently a philosophical problem which Christians could hardly avoid facing for long, two interesting questions arise: When did they first become aware of it, and, in that awareness, how relevant are the Greek treatments of the same topic? For any providential system, not merely one in which God or the gods are omnipotent, will generate problems about free will, and at the purely philosophical level such problems can also arise (as in the worlds of Aristotle and Epicurus) where there is no providence at all.

Unsurprisingly, Justin's first reference to "free choice" introduces not only men but (fallen) angels (1 *Apol.* 28.1). Christ has foretold that Satan, with his followers human and demonic, will be cast into the fire, but this has not yet happened because God foreknows that some men will repent. When man was created, he was intelligent, able to choose the true and to act well. All men can reason and reflect and thus have no excuse for wrongdoing. This all seems commonsensical, and there is no evident philosophical background: the key term αὐτεξούσιος—in the sense of self-determining, freely choosing—does not occur.

As a philosophical term, αὐτεξούσιος has a strange history. Perhaps deriving originally from Chrysippus (*SVF* 2.975), it is found very occasionally in Epictetus (4.1.62ff.) and Musonius (fr.12 p. 66 Hense), but it is more frequent in Philo. Surprisingly and significantly it becomes important and common in Plotinus (see Sleeman-Pollet's index), but its future lay especially with Christianity; Justin uses it twice, both times in passages where he is contradicting the Stoic doctrine of fate and defending "autonomy" both for men and for angels, so as to defend God's justice.[31]

As Telfer points out, the religious use of the *concept* is not original with Justin; it is "abundantly present in Scripture." But that is to neglect the importance of the actual identification of an idea *as* an idea when it is given a philosophical tag. Here, of course, Justin may have followed Philo (or others). What is certain, however, is that by speaking of both angels and men as "autonomous" (able to act well or ill) (*Dial.* 102.4; cf. 2 *Apol.*7.5), Justin establishes the concept at the heart of Christian accounts of man, and hence puts in place one of the key planks of the later version of the problem of evil: for if man's autonomy is "guarded" by God, as Justin puts it, then God is committed to making man *capable* of doing wrong. In other words Justin's God has preferred to make men capable of sinning (in full knowledge of the possibility that some men *will* sin) rather than making them sinless by nature. Hence two potential problems: (1) *Could* God have made them sinless? (2) Would it not have been better for him to have made them sinless? If the latter question is to be answered in the negative, then God's will to save all is, by his own choice, suspended for the greater good of granting autonomy.[32] Such questions are not yet clear in Justin's mind, but the stage is being set for them. As far as Justin is concerned, his immediate project is to argue against the supposedly Stoic position that "if all things are fated, then nothing is in our power" (1 *Apol.* 43.1ff.)— and hence that we shall not be rewarded and punished for what we cannot help.[33]

Justin never points out that the Stoics themselves tried to avoid such conclusions.[34] He does, however, at least offer something of an argument—and thus may be said not merely to allude to the old philosophical puzzle, but to make some attempt to resolve it. Men are different from trees and quadrupeds precisely in that these cannot choose (προαιρέσει). Plato is right (1 *Apol.* 44.8); God is not responsible (*Rep.* 10, 617E4).

What we miss in this, of course, is any explanation by Justin of why it was better for God to create man autonomous—let alone any theory as to why only by being so created could man learn the "godlikeness" of using his autonomy well. We may note that it is not a Christian thinker, but rather Plotinus, who seems to have been the first to see something of the point at issue when he makes the suggestion that those who return to the One may become "more than autonomous" (*Enn.* 6.8.15.20); it would take further moves in the pagan world to prompt Christian thinkers to scrutinize the problem of "autonomy" further. It must also be admitted that the Christians were not very successful in that scrutiny, precisely because (following Justin!) they did not identify *their* problem as a problem, contenting themselves with the notion that God did as he did "because it was good."

Underlying all such difficulties lurks the last of our immediate problems, that of the origin of evil—and in the Christian schema the emergence of the difficulty that all (good) beings must be created out of "defective" nothingness! Our four problems— *creatio ex nihilo,* omnipotence, free will, and evil—are more closely linked both in fact and in their emergence in Christianity than we have demonstrated so far.

(d) Evil

Vitiating most ancient talk of "freedom" or "autonomy" lurks a lack of analysis of the concept itself. For Seneca, for example, freedom is self-sufficiency, while for St. Paul it is being liberated (or redeemed) from the slavery of sin. Beneath that, we can see that for Seneca to be self-sufficient is to be good, while for St. Paul it is to be cast back on one's own sinful devices. Thus in Seneca we see the pearl-in-the-oyster pattern of much of Stoic and Platonic morality: we are "basically" sound, healthy, spiritually good. The Pauline account implies that we are now in our fallen nature disastrously unsound, unhealthy, and spiritually weak or evil. Thus, as Augustine would put it, for Seneca it is good to be *free*, for Paul it is good to be *freed*.

This situation leaves the Christian with a major philosophical problem to which our earlier treatments of the origin of philosophical debate about *creatio ex nihilo*, omnipotence, and free will must be related. If God is good and omnipotent, and we are free to choose good or evil, what is this evil from which we need to be freed? And to that question, as we have already noticed, a second is to be added: if we are "originally" free to do evil as well as good, why is it best for God to create us? But to approach the latter question we need to know the "nature" of the evil which it is somehow better to be able to choose. And related to that again, what is our basic nature like (compared, that is, with God's) insofar as we must somehow be able to choose that evil: on pain, perhaps, of not existing at all?

The proposition that God is a *creator ex nihilo* and the attempt to formulate his omnipotence entailed at some point that for the Christians the further problem of the nature and "origin" of evil must become pressing. But when Christians turned to look at the available philosophical accounts of evil, they could identify confusion, but form little idea of some of the purely "philosophical" sources of that confusion. Broadly speaking, amid the disagreements of the philosophers (cf. Origen, *Contra Celsum* 4.62–70), they would normally have recognized three possible accounts (or are they reducible to one?) of evil: either evil is somehow identical with matter, or it is caused by the soul "falling into" matter, or it is the product of an evil (perhaps material) soul. It is roughly true that all these variants derived from (or were buttressed by) interpretations or misinterpretations of Plato, especially but not only of the *Timaeus*.

The notion that primary evil is to be located in an ultimate evil soul (deriving in part from the two souls of *Laws* 10) is to be found in Plutarch; such dualism, popular in Gnostic circles, was beyond the pale for orthodox Christians and need not be discussed here. Certain passages of the *Phaedo* suggest that evil comes from the association of the soul with the body and the physical world more generally, but (as Plotinus recognized) Plato himself rejected that view in the *Timaeus*, where the physical world is itself the product of the Demiurge, necessarily inferior to the world of Forms but still ordered by the Demiurge "because he is good" (*Tim.* 30E). Plato, however, seems to have no interest in the notion that evil is just an unfortunate accident of matter, as Aristotle (in *Meta.* 7.9, 1051a17–21) and more specifically the Stoics suggest. Evil is like sawdust in a carpenter's workshop: a view at times also given too much credence by Plotinus. Nevertheless in the *Timaeus* Plato does imply that somehow there is a connection between evil and the physical universe;[35] it does not exist among the gods or Forms. The question is, "What is that connection?"—and this involves the complex matter of what Plato thinks "matter" is, and what he was considered to have thought about this in early Christian times.[36]

Plato's original theory of matter is constructed on a false biological model:[37] the Demiurge is the father who provides the seeds of the physical world, the Receptacle is the "space" in which the seed is deposited. Although this was eventually recognized by Philoponus, in the early centuries of the Christian era the *Timaeus* was interpreted via Aristotle's critique and Aristotle's theory of four causes. The Receptacle was read (as can be seen in the discussion of *creatio ex nihilo*) as a "pre-existing" material substrate which is "formed" by the Demiurge. Thus God is not responsible for matter but, somehow, the latter is "responsible" for evil: at least if there were no matter, there would be no evil. But with *creatio ex nihilo* matter must be created by God, and if it is evil it cannot be created by a good God. Hence matter cannot simply be the cause of evil—that must somehow be introduced by the fall of a soul—but it may be the condition of evil, perhaps that to which the soul is attracted. The soul is thus attracted to the lesser good (matter) as distinct from the greatest good (God).

If matter is created by God, it cannot be evil as such, and if its "problem" for the soul is that it is a lesser good, then the problem of evil, in Christian circles, should (and eventually did) resolve itself into the problem of why the soul is liable to choose a lesser good.[38] Dualism apart, matter is only a condition, not a cause, of the fall. Given *creatio ex nihilo,* omnipotence, and free will (with the possibility of "falling"), when did Christian philosophers face the last of our set of problems, namely what precisely is "wrong" with the soul, and why did an omnipotent God have to allow that "wrongness"? Or did they *never* see the problem clearly?

Tertullian is not alone in insisting (*De an.* 3.1) that the philosophers are at the root of all (heretical) evil. But as we have seen, Christian puzzlement about the origin of evil in the soul, though perhaps prompted by pagan philosophical reflection, was not resolved by it. Pagans might say that matter is the cause of moral evil, thereby confusing conditions with causes, or they might say (cf. *Enn.* 5.1.1) that τόλμα (recklessness) is the problem. But then why did God have to create souls with τόλμα? Doubtless to make them responsible for evil, but how is this not ordering them to vice and then blaming them for the sins they commit? God did not create material souls, but they still fell. Everything that God makes rational can enjoy what is unlawful, as Augustine later put it (*C. Faust* 22.18). But why?

Clearly the problem could only exist in this form once Christianity had committed itself to some sort of (Hellenic) body-soul distinction, but even without that distinction it must have arisen at some point, because even if "man" (as distinct from "soul") falls, the same problems occur: why does God allow either "man" or "soul" to fall?

Plotinus offers as one of the factors explaining why souls "forget their father" what he calls "primary otherness": there is something inadequate, that is, in being "other" than the One. But how "other" are we, for Plotinus or for the early Christians? When looked at in this way, it becomes clear that any adequate Christian solution to the problem of evil must be closely connected with a strong doctrine both of omnipotence and of *creatio ex nihilo* (and will therefore appear as a *consequence* of the emergence of these problems). That being so, we should not expect to find, nor do we find, any satisfactory attempt to explain the problem of evil before Augustine.

A glance at Clement of Alexandria and Origen will confirm this. Clement not merely "speaks with an ambiguous voice on *creatio ex nihilo*";[39] rather he neglects Theophilus of Antioch and follows Justin and the earlier Christian tradition that matter pre-exists the universe. He is old-fashioned in not raising the question of whether it is created by God.[40] Hence there is little in Clement about the nature of evil in a providential universe which cannot be accounted for in more or less typical Middle Platonic terms.[41] Clement contents himself with regularly asserting that it is free will, not God, which causes evil, without asking why God could not—logically—do better than that. God does not wish evil; he himself has no part in choosing it, and he turns it to good.[42]

With Origen we might expect something better: he is unambiguous about *creatio ex nihilo;* he cannot understand how distinguished thinkers have thought matter uncreated (*De Princ.* 2.1.4). But any effects of this on his account of evil are masked by his "platonizing" belief in the fall of a pre-existent soul. He does have to face the question of why such a soul could fall, but his answer still fails to come to grips with the hard question of *why* the soul (created, though eternal) gives way to temptation.[43] For give way it does; it gives way to "satiety" (presumably κόρον λαβεῖν, *De Princ.* 1.3.5, to "wilful negligence and pride" 1.5.4–5).[44] Yet this is merely to name the immediate cause of wrongdoing, not to face the problem of why souls must be liable so to behave. Origen's doctrine of *creatio ex nihilo* rules out the notion that matter as such is a subsistent *cause* of wrongdoing: it may allow him to claim that souls are tempted by matter, but still fails to explain—especially as they are pre-material—why they are tempted: by it, or by anything else.

Although, as we have seen, even Augustine did not recognize many of the problems associated with omnipotence as such, he did grasp the need to explain the metaphysical possibility of evil. His new moves, in a pattern which we should now easily recognize, were probably provoked by yet another (Platonic) philosopher, this time Plotinus. We can only deal with the matter quite briefly, noting that it has been helpfully discussed by Bonner.[45] Plotinus, following and deepening the Middle Platonic tradition (accepted by Clement and Origen) held evil to be a loss or "privation" of good. This is helpful, but the problem is to explain, how much loss and what kind of good? For Plotinus the One or Good generates all things (including matter); matter is not independent of the Good. Insofar as it exists, it derives from the Good. Thus matter is where God's creativity runs out: it cannot create; it is dead, a "corpse adorned" (*Enn.* 2.4.5). And insofar as it cannot "create" or "produce," it is evil. But it is not absolute nothingness, whereas "evil" is absolute privation; hence the unresolvable problem for Plotinus of the relationship between the two.

For Augustine matter is created *ex nihilo*,[46] while moral evil (*iniquitas*), the only sort with which he is seriously concerned, appears in rational beings (fallen angels, Adam, etc.). Moral evil has no *necessary* connection with matter. Souls are immaterial, so that, as we should now expect, the problem (insofar as matter may be an occasion but not a cause of *iniquitas*) is why the immaterial soul is liable to sin. A traditional answer (recall *tolma* in *Ennead* 5.1.1) is available, and certainly for Augustine pride— the self-loving creature wishing to be the creator—is the basic flaw of the fallen soul. But the *philosophical* question of "getting God off the hook" as responsible for that vice remains unsettled.

Augustine's solution depends on *creatio ex nihilo*. For if all is created from nothing, all will tend to return to nothing unless maintained in existence by God.[47] This must be taken strictly: there is a tendency in each of us towards ceasing to exist, though with- out some destructive act of God's—the counterpart of his original creative act—such a tendency could not be fully realized: a created being can only become more or less formless.[48] What would that mean for a rational being? Clearly for Augustine it would mean being "attracted to nothingness." But that too needs explication. Normally at least the soul is not directly attracted to absolute nothingness; rather it is attracted to a lesser goal by an attraction which is in fact leading it toward the (impossibility of) extinction; in the most extreme version that might take the form of destructiveness as such, of a kind of practical nihilism. Yet for Augustine these claims are philosophically dependent on the fact that rational souls (like other beings) are "from nothing"—but also that it would be a mistake to suppose that this "nothing" is, by mere virtue of our referring to it, some kind of (Heideggerian) thing (*De Mag.* 2.3).[49] To say that it is the fact of "nothingness" in things which makes them tend to destruction, and in rational beings toward the destruction which is sin, is to substitute a more plausible *condition* (their original non-existence) for a less plausible one (the existence of matter), to explain the origin of sin. For the real problem was always not that (good) matter dis- tracts, but rather why non-material souls are distracted by matter.

Augustine had long abandoned his more Tertullianesque view that the soul in some sense *is* material. Now he is saying that it is a condition of the immaterial itself, i.e., its "from nothingness," which allows for the possibility of sin. That is clearly an advance, but a philosophical advance always generates new problems. And here the new prob- lem is a much discussed one: if Satan's or Adam's sin is now philosophically possible, why is it not necessary?[50]

We may leave it at that for the present, noting only that Augustine is certainly not committed to the logical necessity of the fall. What he is committed to is that God's omnipotence must (as we have seen) be modified in that he knows that in fact Satan (and Adam) will fall and he is "logically" unable to do anything about a fall in the "free" nature he has created. Let us, however, be content with the more modest historical conclusion that once again a Christian (this time Augustine) is propelled at least partially by a philosophical challenge (in this case the confusion of Plotinus and the Neoplatonists on matter and evil) to advance the cause of Christian philosophy. Presumably it will always have to be so—unless Christian philosophers can put themselves in the shoes of skeptics in order to advance counterarguments adequate to advance the debate.

———

What more general conclusions can be drawn? More narrowly, that the study of the origins of Christian philosophy is best approached through identifying the emergence of specific philosophical questions and the *reasons* why such questions (whether new or revised) begin to appear in Christian texts. But a more general conclusion has also emerged. Constructive Christian philosophy in antiquity turns out to be largely the adoption, correction, or rejection of Platonism (in various forms), sometimes in a masterful, sometimes in a servile fashion. Other philosophical traditions, especially Stoicism, were sometimes put to use, but turned out to be helpful only within a broadly Platonic framework. Was that appropriation of Platonism merely a function of the prevailing conditions of an age, or does it have a deeper significance? I believe that the latter assessment is correct. But that—together with a historical scrutiny of the fate of the non-Platonic alternatives—is yet another story.

Notes

1. For the Platonically-transformed Aristotle with whom the medievals were familiar see especially R. Sorabji, ed., *Aristotle Transformed* (Ithaca: Cornell University Press, 1990).

2. Though he debated Stoics and Epicureans in Athens (Acts 17:18).

3. For a recent example see E. F. Osborn on Pannenberg in *The Emergence of Christian Theology* (Cambridge: Cambridge University Press, 1993), 309–13.

4. For somewhat exaggerated reaction to the danger see C. Stead, *Philosophy in Christian Antiquity* (Cambridge: Cambridge University Press, 1994).

5. Cf. my discussion of "Faith and Reason," in *The Cambridge Companion to Augustine*, ed. E. Stump (Cambridge: Cambridge University Press, 2001).

6. S.R.C. Lilla, *Clement of Alexandria: A Study in Christian Platonism and Gnosticism* (Oxford: Oxford University Press, 1971), 51.

7. P. Fredriksen, "Judaism, the Circumcision of Gentiles and Apocalyptic Hope: Another Look at Galatians 1 and 2," *Journal of Theological Studies* 42 (1991): 562.

8. Especially helpful is E. F. Osborn, *Justin Martyr* (Tübingen: Mohr [Siebeck], 1973), 28–43, 68–71.

9. Note the misleading character of the debate about certain apparently "Stoic" passages on providence in Clement of Rome: W. C. van Unnik, "Is I Clement 20 So Purely Stoic?" *Verbum Caro* 4 (1950): 181–89. Van Unnik rightly observes that the antithesis Jewish/Hellenistic is often too rigid to be of much hermeneutical help.

10. See M.. Edwards, "On the Platonic Schooling of Justin Martyr," *JTS* 42 (1991): 17–34; Osborn, *Justin;* J.C.M. van Winden, *An Early Christian Philosopher: Justin Martyr's "Dialogue with Trypho,"* Chapters 1–9 (Leiden: Brill, 1971); N. Hyldahl, *Philosophie und Christentum* (Copenhagen: Munksgaard, 1966); C. Andresen, "Justin und der mittlere Platonismus," *Zeitschrift für die Neutestamentliche Wissenschaft* 44 (1952–53): 157–95.

11. Cf. 1 *Apol.* 3, a reference to *Rep.* 5, 473C11 ff. (the text is disputed) where Justin may suggest that, unless the rulers *and subjects* become philosophers, it is impossible for states to become happy. On Plato and Moses more generally see J. M. Dillon, *The Middle Platonists* (Ithaca, NY: Cornell University Press, 1977), 143, and J. Whittaker, "Moses Atticizing," *Phoenix* 21 (1967): 196–201; M.J. Edwards, "Atticizing Moses? Numenius, the Fathers and the Jews," *VC* 44 (1990): 64–75. Cf. Theophilus of Antioch, *Ad Autol.* 2.12, 3.16.

12. Other divine attributes (one, simple, etc.) might be discussed philosophically, but omnipotence, as we shall see, introduces peculiarly new and interesting philosophical features.

13. Stead, *Philosophy,* 86, is right to object to the "broad" sense of philosophy employed by H. Chadwick, "The Beginnings of Christian Philosophy," in *The Cambridge History of Later Greek and Early Mediaeval Philosophy,* ed. A.H. Armstrong (Cambridge: Cambridge University Press, 1967), and by E. F. Osborn, *The Beginnings of Christian Philosophy* (Cambridge: Cambridge University Press, 1981). Philosophy is more than a way of life and more than just thinking: at the very least it must be, as Socrates said, an "examined/scrutinized" way of life. On the other hand, Stead's account of philosophy as an autonomous discipline is of limited hermeneutical value for our period; it cannot help us understand how Christian philosophy began, but at best what it strives to become. Our problem is to identify not Christian philosophers, but rather how bits of Christian philosophy, in something of the sense required by Stead, emerged simultaneously from more or less exegetical and pastoral requirements. Naturally Stead's list of "original" Christian philosophers is short (and "late"): Marius Victorinus, Augustine, Boethius, plus a little epistemology in Clement (83–84).

14. For fuller discussion see especially G. May, *Schöpfung aus dem Nichts: Die Entstehung der Lehre von der Creatio ex Nihilo* (Berlin–New York: de Gruyter, 1978). For a more recent introduction, N.J. Torchia, *Creatio ex Nihilo and the Theology of St. Augustine: The Anti-Manichaean Polemic and Beyond* (New York: Lang, 1999), 1–64.

15. See J.M. Rist, *The Mind of Aristotle* (Toronto: University of Toronto Press, 1989), 191–205.

16. Cf. 2 *Apol.* 10, where use of a "doctored" text of the *Timaeus,* also found in Alcinous (*Didask.* 27), is an interesting indicator of Justin's familiarity with parts of the contemporary philosophical scene. Cf. J.M. Dillon, "Tampering with the *Timaeus,*" *American Journal of Philology* 110 (1989): 50–72, especially on *Tim.* 28C.

17. Torchia, *Creatio,* 6.

18. Such possibilities seem to have impressed Tertullian's opponent Hermogenes, who argued that since the world could not have been created from God's substance, it must be eternal.

19. For the history see particularly J. Lebreton, "ἀγέννητος dans la tradition et dans la littérature chrétienne du IIe siècle," *RSR* 14 (1926): 431–43.

20. Cf. τὴν ὕλην τρέψας πόσμον ἐποίησε, 1 *Apol.* 67.

21. Note that Philo too thinks of the shift from chaos to cosmos as τὰ μὴ ὄντα εἰς τὸ εἶναι, *Spec. Leg.* 4.187; cf. D. T. Runia, *Philo and the Church Fathers* (Leiden: Brill, 1995), and particularly *Philo of Alexandria and the Timaeus of Plato* (Leiden: Brill, 1986), 140–57, 425–26, 453–55.

22. Torchia, *Creatio;* J. M. Rist, *Augustine: Ancient Thought Baptized* (Cambridge: Cambridge University Press, 1994), 104–08.

23. There is a certain amount of (muddled) discussion of God's "omnipotence" in Philo, who sometimes seems to hold (or at least to imply) that moral norms are created by God (*Op. mund.* 16); cf. Rist, *Augustine*, 264.

24. Cf. J. N. D. Kelly, *Early Christian Creeds* (London: Longmans, 1960), 133.

25. But note Clement of Alexandria, *Stromateis* 7.6 and 3.6.19, cited by E. F. Osborn, *The Philosophy of Clement of Alexandria* (Cambridge: Cambridge University Press, 1957), 69.

26. Cf. J. F. Ross, *Philosophical Theology* (Indianapolis-Cambridge: Bobbs-Merrill, 1980), 198; Rist, *Augustine*, 262–66.

27. Rist, *Augustine*, 262–66.

28. Cf. the remarks of J. Burnaby, *Amor Dei* (London: Canterbury, 1938), 230: "Augustine never realized that his own conception of grace required nothing less than a revolution in his thought of the divine omnipotence."

29. Cf. also the interesting discussion in *C. Faustum* 26.5 of the view that God cannot undo the past.

30. Still, as we have seen, denied (or at least not clearly asserted) by Origen; see H. Crouzel, *Origène et Plotin* (Paris: Téqui, 1991), 379–81.

31. See the groundbreaking article of W. Telfer, "Autexousia," *JTS* 8 (1957): 123–29.

32. God knew that it was good so to act, cf. *Dial.* 102.4.

33. Note the looser προαίρεσις ἐλευθέρη (for τὸ αὐτεξούσιον) at 1 *Apol.* 43.3–4.

34. See recently S. Bobzien, *Determinism and Freedom in Stoic Philosophy* (Oxford: Clarendon, 1998), especially chapters 6 and 7. In 2 *Apol.* 7.3 Justin argues that because the Stoics do not know about the actions of the fallen angels they fall back on the "necessity of fate," a theme later developed by Origen.

35. For the sake of simplicity I leave aside the question of intelligible matter; for discussion see J. M. Rist, "The Indefinite Dyad and Intelligible Matter in Plotinus," *Classical Quarterly* 12 (1962): 99–107 = J. M. Rist, *Man, Soul and Body* XII (Aldershot: Variorum, 1996).

36. The problem still persists in Plotinus, whose views may ultimately be confused precisely because the Platonic tradition which he inherited was confused. For Plotinus see D. O'Brien, *Théodicée plotinienne, théodicée gnostique* (Leiden: Brill, 1993); K. Corrigan, *Plotinus' Theory of Matter-Evil and the Question of Substance* (Leuven: Peeters, 1996); J. M. Rist, "Is Plotinus' Body Too Etherialized?" *Prudentia* supplement (1993): 103–17 = J. M. Rist, *Man, Soul and Body* XV. For a Neoplatonic recasting of Plotinus and the Neoplatonic tradition more generally see recently C. Steel, "Proclus on the Existence of Evil," *Proceedings of the Boston Area Colloquium in Ancient Philosophy* 14 (1998): 83–102, ed. J. J. Cleary and Gary Gurtler.

37. Rist, *The Mind of Aristotle*, 191–205.

38. In this sense the problem of evil is viewed as the problem of the origin of *moral* evil; for souls really do suffer (often unjustly) and really do cause evil (however other souls may respond to that evil).

39. Chadwick, *Cambridge History*, 171.

40. So Lilla, *Clement of Alexandria*, 193–95.

41. Stoic influence (either direct or indirect) can also be detected in the trivializing analogy of a painting, where ugly parts contribute to the beauty of the whole.

42. Cf. Osborn, *Clement of Alexandria*, 71–78.

43. Chadwick, *Cambridge History*, 191, thinks that Origen's aim is to relieve God of responsibility for evil. A strong doctrine of *un*created pre-existence might do that, but for Origen the soul is still created. Thus with a fairly strong account of God's power to create, Origen raises a problem about the origin of moral evil, while he cannot resolve it by evoking a full-blooded (Middle) Platonic doctrine of the uncreatedness of the soul.

44. Cf. M. Harl, "Recherches sur l'origénisme d'Origène: la satiété (*koros*) de la contemplation comme motif de la chute des âmes," *Studia Patristica* 81, *TU* 93 (1966): 373–405; *De Princ.* 1.3.8. One of the sources of the idea is Philo, see M. Simonetti in *Studi sulla cristologia del 2°e 3°secolo* (Rome: Augustinianum, 1993), 253, 77.

45. G. Bonner, *St. Augustine of Hippo: Life and Controversies* (Norwich: Canterbury, 1986), 201.

46. See most recently Torchia, *Creatio*.

47. For massive documentation (often overloooked by English-speakers) see Solignac in Augustine, *Confessioni*, ed. Manlio Simonetti (Milan: Fondazione Lorenzo Valla, A. Mondadori, 1992), vol. 4, 605.

48. Much trouble is still created by misunderstandings of the Middle and Neoplatonic notion that evil is a "privation" of good. Difficulties can be eliminated roughly as follows—at least for Augustine and probably for others: (1) "evil" is an adjective and refers to a property; (2) properties, though discussible, can only *exist* in substances; hence (3) "pure evil" cannot exist (for it is privation of a property). But what can exist are very evil substances, Satan, Hitler, etc. There is nothing unfeeling or unsympathetic about such an analysis. It muddies the waters, however, to say with R. Williams, "Insubstantial Evil," in *Augustine and his Critics: Essays in Honour of G. Bonner*, ed. R. Dodaro and G. Lawless (London: Routledge, 2000), 105–23, that evil is "located" in the malfunctioning of "*relations* between subjects" (my italics). Augustine would say that it lies in the *voluntas* of the vicious agent and characterizes him. (For a recent, though still incomplete, reply to many misreadings of Augustine in this area, see D. A. Cress, "Augustine's Privation Account of Evil: A Defence," *Augustinian Studies* 20 (1989): 109–28.

The charge that on the privation account evil is inactive, ineffective, not really taken seriously, even illusory, depends on a misconstrual of Augustine's "grammar" of evil. Far from being ineffective, the evil will, backed by instrumental rationality, tries to destroy itself and others (and in the appropriate respects is often successful). Nazi examples are often helpful in such contexts: cf. the observation of Goering that "I joined the party because I was a revolutionary, not because of any ideological nonsense." J.C. Fest, *The Face of the Third Reich* (New York: Pantheon Books, 1970), 115.

49. Cf. the difficulty of redescribing the "nothing" in a statement like, "There is nothing between two stars," and the problem Plato had of describing his pre-cosmic "place," for which he had to resort to pseudobiological language. For the effects of this on Augustine see Solignac, *BA* 14, 601.

50. This is argued by R. Brown, "The First Evil Will Must be Incomprehensible: A Critique of Augustine," *Journal of the American Academy of Religion* 46 (1978): 315–29, who specifically associates the notion of a necessary fall with Augustine's appeal to *ex nihilo*. For further comment see Rist, *Augustine*, 104–8.

Chapter 2

Averroes

God and the Noble Lie

RICHARD C. TAYLOR

While Averroes has certainly been a central figure in Western reflections on the history of ideas since the nineteenth century—and before that in the scholastic tradition even if only to be often attacked and, as it were, "refuted" by Christian medieval thinkers—since the mid-nineteenth century he has also been regarded among Arabic writers as an important figure confronting the advancement of Western scientific culture with its attendant economic benefits, in contrast with the lack of such advancement in the Arab world, where religious fundamentalism in various forms has often played a central role in society. This latter use of the thought of Averroes by modern Arabic writers has been documented by Anke von Kügelgen in her work on twentieth-century "Arab Averroists."[1] Recently this sort of interest has allied itself with somewhat different goals of modern Western humanism to set forth the characterization of Averroes as an Enlightenment figure, that is, as prefiguring and perhaps contributing to the rise of the views central to the Western Enlightenment movement. Both modern Arabic writers and Western humanists praise Averroes for his stance on the connection between religion and philosophy which they view as "enlightened" and which philosophically might be considered a form of compatibilism.[2]

What Averroes is praised for, in this context, is his account of the compatibility of Islamic religion and philosophical rationalism as found in his famous *Faṣl al-Maqâl* or *Decisive Treatise*. There he sets out his understanding of human religious psychology in a way which allows for the reading of religious texts on multiple levels in accord with the capacities of the readers, some being of the rhetorical class who are only able to consider scripture literally, others of the dialectical class who are able to approach and understand scripture in the context of preconceived notions or assumptions, and finally a last group who are able to consider scripture in accord with truth in its highest form, demonstrative argumentation. The Qur'ân is taken as being suitable for all three classes but with the proviso that those expounding religious doctrine not confuse the masses by exposing them to interpretations which they cannot understand and which may consequently lead them astray in their religious belief so important to proper moral character and a fulfilling and happy human life.[3] Although groundwork for such a view can be found in the writings of al-Farabi[4] and Avicenna,[5] Averroes spells it out in detail and adds critiques directed at the literalists, who would have *all people* read scripture literally, and the Mutakallimun, dialectical theologians, who would have *all people* reason on the basis of assumptions about the nature of God and creation. For Averroes, such ways of proceeding not only have their own intrinsic problems but are deeply inappropriate because they fail to respect the abilities of the diverse intellectual classes and may lead to confusion on the part of simpler believers who are unable to understand that scripture is to be read differently by individuals of differing levels of insight and understanding. Some have characterized this as a view which highlights philosophical reflection in the context of "a plurality of rationalities,"[6] while others understand Averroes to be holding that

> there is no privileged access to the nature of reality which represents how things really are. The ordinary person has just as valid a grasp of how things really are as does the philosopher or religious thinker, provided that the ordinary person is able to use concepts which connect with that reality in a loose way.[7]

Although Arabist scholars have almost universally denied that Averroes' own teachings entail a doctrine of Double Truth, understood in this way Averroes might be held to have taught in fact what in the Latin West came to be called the doctrine of Double Truth.[8]

The present essay explores Averroes' understanding of God and in doing so employs a different methodological approach, one more traditional than the two cited above, one founded on Averroes' foundational statement in the *Faṣl al-Maqâl* on the nature of truth. There, in the religious context of that legal determination of "whether the study of philosophy and logic is allowed by the [Religious] Law, or prohibited, or commanded—either by way of recommendation or as obligatory,"[9] Averroes writes,

> Now since this religion is true and summons to the study which leads to knowledge of the Truth, we the Muslim community know definitively that demonstrative study does not lead to [conclusions] conflicting with what Scripture [or Religious Law] has given us; for truth does not oppose truth but accords with it and bears witness to it.[10]

As I have shown elsewhere,[11] this remark that "truth does not oppose truth but accords with it and bears witness to it" is a paraphrasing quotation of Aristotle's *Prior Analytics* 1.32, 47a8–9; "For everything that is true must in every respect agree with itself."[12] In accord with this statement by Averroes, in the present article I assume that religion and philosophy *are* able to intersect and that propositions asserted about God, human beings, and the world *are* open to the possibility of contradicting one another in such a way that one is false and the other true. Averroes recognizes both this intersection and the methodological priority of philosophy when in his *Faṣl al-Maqâl* he asserts that scriptural interpretation which is in conflict with demonstrated truth must be set aside as incorrect and the text in question must be interpreted allegorically.[13] If that is the case for Averroes, it may well be that purportedly "true" statements in religion about God and purportedly "true" statements in philosophy about God should be ranked and compared with reference to their full truth since "truth does not oppose truth but accords with it and bears witness to it." Certainly this is in agreement with his view expressed in the *Faṣl al-Maqâl* where he argues that it is known that demonstrative philosophical arguments do not conflict with Scripture or Religious Law. And if that is so, it may be quite appropriate to consider in the thought of Averroes whether purportedly central principles and foundational pillars of religion concerning the nature of God are in fact compatible with truths about the deity grounded in philosophical argumentation.

In presenting Averroes' philosophical understanding of God I am making two assumptions. The first is the one to which I refer just above, namely the falsity of the notion that there are two truths, one for philosophy and one for religion. My second assumption is that truth in its fullest for Averroes is to be found in his philosophical writings. This is founded on his statement in the *Tahâfut at-Tahâfut* (*Incoherence of the Incoherence*) where he explains that the accounts and discussions in that work are dialectical in nature and that for a full account one must turn to his technical demonstrative works written for students of demonstration. I understand this to mean that the truth in the fullest sense is to be found in his philosophical works and particularly in his Aristotelian commentaries where he asserts there to be demonstrations.[14]

> All this is the theory of the philosophers on this problem and in the way we have stated it here with its proofs, it is a persuasive not a demonstrative statement. It is for you to inquire about these questions in the places where they are treated in the books of demonstration, if you are one of the people of perfect eudaemonia, and if you are one of those who learn the arts, the function of which is proof. For the demonstrative arts are very much like the practical; for just as a man who is not a craftsman cannot perform the function of craftsmanship, in the same way it is not possible for him who has not learned the arts of demonstration to perform the

function of demonstration which is demonstration itself: indeed this is still more necessary for this art than for any other—and this is not generally acknowledged in the case of this practice only because it is a mere act—and therefore such a demonstration can proceed only from one who has learned the art. The kinds of statements, however, are many, some demonstrative, others not, and since non-demonstrative statements can be adduced without knowledge of the art, it was thought that this might also be the case with demonstrative statements; but this is a great error. And therefore in the spheres of the demonstrative arts, no other statement is possible but a technical statement which only the student of this art can bring, just as is the case with the art of geometry. Nothing therefore of what we have said in this book is a technical demonstrative proof; they are all non-technical statements, some of them having greater persuasion than others, and it is in this spirit that what we have written here must be understood.[15]

And, following Aristotle closely in his *Long Commentary on the Posterior Analytics*, Averroes asserts that a demonstration is a syllogism proceeding on true premises to produce knowledge and which is such that the very grasp of the syllogism is that knowledge. In his *Long Commentary on the Posterior Analytics* Averroes stresses that, without true premises known to be such and the other conditions of the premises required by demonstration, the syllogism will not be a demonstration.[16] He says that such an argument will be a dialectical syllogism, a rhetorical syllogism or a sign[17] and will not be *al-yaqîn alladhî fî al-ghâyah / secundum maximam veritatem*.[18] I understand this to be in accord with my first assumption.

AVERROES ON GOD

While Avicenna proceeds to indicate the existence of God or the Necessary Being on the basis of the mind's grasp of the notion that all reality is divided into the possible and the necessary,[19] Averroes follows Aristotle in beginning his philosophical account from the physical world and its need for an ultimate cause of motion. For Averroes it is the science of physics, which includes cosmology, that establishes the ground of the eternal motion of the heavens. Aristotle's requirement of eternal motion which as necessary cannot be otherwise led him to assert the existence of a plurality of unmoved movers with one among them understood to be first. Working within a conceptual framework affected by the mixture of Aristotelian and Neoplatonic thinking together with religious thought on the nature of God, Averroes followed and expanded on Aristotle. For Averroes the celestial bodies have an indestructible matter free of contraries and contain potency only for movement. Herbert Davidson explains this by saying,

The heavens must instead be construed as a body of a completely different type, consisting in the association of a simple matter-like substratum in motion, and an independently existing immaterial form moving the substratum. The matter-like substratum exists *necessarily by virtue of itself,* and the form is a source of infinite power whereby the substratum moves eternally.[20]

The form to which Davidson refers is the immaterial and incorporeal soul which is associated with the celestial body. This soul has in turn a separate intellect as its extrinsic final cause. In his Aristotelian philosophical context, Averroes continues to hold that the immaterial intellects as such are not efficient causes of the motion in the celestial bodies. This, however, is as far as the science of physics can proceed in this investigation since physics has as its subject matter bodies and their accidents of motion. Physics is concerned with what has in itself its own principle of motion and rest (*Physics* 2.2, 192b14) and hence cannot then have as its subject matter incorporeal and immaterial substances which are not subject to motion and rest.

Aristotle, in *Metaphysics* 6.1, argues that unless the existence of immaterial entities is established, first philosophy will be physics. But Aristotle and Averroes do consider that they have shown the necessity of the existence of immaterial entities and so proceed to consider what we call metaphysics to be first philosophy. Now, while Aristotle quickly moved in *Metaphysics* Lambda to assert that the plurality of unmoved movers must each be immaterial and consequently intellectual, Averroes is apparently aware of the necessity of another step in this account. For Averroes, psychology, a branch of physics which bridges to metaphysics, must play a role here.[21]

In both his *Long Commentary on the De Anima* and in his *Long Commentary on the Metaphysics,* Averroes asserts the necessity of the use of the science of psychology to make possible the understanding of the natures of the immaterial entities to which physics ultimately points.[22] What are the essential elements in his arguments for this position? First, it must be assumed that human beings do have knowledge, that is, an actuality somehow in them for classifying particulars in groups, something we call a grasp of the universal. Such an actuality existing as a power in human beings is for Averroes and Aristotle an immaterial actuality. Second, Averroes understands (a) that the universal nature of this requires that it not be such as to take place in an individual entity, since, as particularized by the individual in which it exists, it would not be an intelligible in act, that is, an understood universal, and also (b) that discourse and interpersonal communication on intellectual issues would not be possible unless there is a single shared science or a thesaurus[23] of forms in which all human beings share or to which all refer in thought and discourse. On the basis of this, then, Averroes asserts that there must be a separate Material Intellect and a separate Agent Intellect actualizing it, shared by all human beings, and that these separate intellects, although immaterial

entities, nevertheless must be considered as part of human nature by way of an operational linking rather than as ontological parts of human beings.[24]

Additionally entailed in this understanding are four conclusions relevant for consideration of Averroes' understanding of God which can be drawn from this discussion.
First, in this demonstrative account there is no basis for asserting personal immortality for individual human beings, that is, there is no provision in his metaphysical
account of human beings and their relationship to the separate Material Intellect and
Agent Intellect for individual human beings to have any existence after earthly life.[25]
In the penultimate discussion of the *Tahâfut at-Tahâfut,* Averroes does provide arguments for the continued personal existence of the soul after death by way of a trans-
migration of individual souls to celestial matter. But such a view contradicts basic
Aristotelian principles of psychology to which Averroes adheres and is clearly only a
dialectical argument the conclusion of which is not known to be necessary or true.
That is to say, Averroes in the dialectical context of the *Tahâfut at-Tahâfut* does not take
that argument for personal immortality seriously but rather merely sets it forth for
those who wish to find some grounds for believing in personal immortality.[26]

Second, for Averroes only the human species is argued to be eternal and that argument is asserted on the basis of the eternality of the separate intellects. The separate
intellects as immaterial and therefore incorruptible are understood to have no beginning and no end to their existence. While the existence of the Material Intellect is
asserted by Averroes on the basis of human knowledge understood as indicated
above, once it is established as separate and eternal, its existence as such is used to
argue that its eternal nature as recipient of intelligibles in act also entails the eternality
of the human species. This works as follows. The senses affected by sensible objects
provide the imaginative powers of the soul with images which, while always essentially
particular, are then refined with as much particularity removed as possible. The results
are denuded intentions (which are nevertheless still particular intentions) then presented to the Agent Intellect for transformation by its "light" into universal intentions
now constituting knowledge. In that process these are impressed upon the separate
Material Intellect which is the thesaurus which all human beings share in the unity of
science.

Third, this establishment of the existence of the separate Material Intellect and
Agent Intellect as immaterial entities, which are intellectual in nature, proves that
immateriality and intellectuality coincide. This is something Averroes could have
argued from the general Aristotelian account of the relationship of form and being,
since for Aristotle substantial form and substantial being as investigated in Book Zeta
of the *Metaphysics* are shown to coincide and to be mutually entailed in any actually
existing entity.[27] This entails that all that has form has intelligibility, that is, is an intelligible object. On this basis it could be further argued speculatively that any actually

existing separate form must, as existing in act, be an intelligible not in potency but in act and that it must be so in virtue of itself, that is, its essence. Hence, any actually existing separate form must be both intelligible and intelligent in virtue of itself. This is what Aristotle asserts in Book Lambda of the *Metaphysics*.[28] For Averroes it is psychological theory which provides the evidence for such a position. In this way Averroes is able to assert that psychology is essential to the explication of the nature of metaphysics and its assertion of immaterial unmoved movers as intellectual entities.

Fourth, on his understanding of the Material Intellect as an intellectual substance into which are deposited forms derived from sense perception and purified by the light of the Agent Intellect, Averroes establishes that it is possible for there to be some sort of potency in separate immaterial intellectual entities. This is a doctrine which he cites in his *Long Commentary on the De Anima*:

> . . . as sensible being is divided into form and matter, intelligible being must be divided into things similar to these two, namely into something similar to form and into something similar to matter. This is [something] necessarily present in every separate intelligence which thinks something else. And if not, then there would be no multiplicity [410] in separate forms. And it was already explained in First Philosophy that there is no form absolutely free of potency except the First Form[29] which understands nothing outside Itself. Its being is Its quiddity (*essentia eius est quiditas eius*). Other forms, however, are in some way different in quiddity and being.[30] If it were not for this genus of beings which we have come to know in the science of the soul, we could not understand multiplicity in separate things, to the extent that, unless we know here the nature of the intellect, we cannot know that the separate moving powers ought to be intellects.[31]

These conclusions, which he understands as demonstrative, allow Averroes to assert that among the plurality of separate immaterial unmoved movers established by physics, there can be understood to exist a hierarchy of intellectual entities having less or more potency in them. At the pinnacle of the hierarchy is the first of these entities, God or the First Cause and First Form, who has no need in any way of anything outside Himself and is in complete actuality without potency in any sense. All the other intellects in the hierarchy, however, while being substances per se eternal and incapable of destruction, nevertheless are understood by Averroes to have some potency in them and to be classified in the hierarchy according to their intellectual powers. There are two considerations to be noted here. The note of potency found in all but the First, for Averroes, seems to be tied to the fact that in all below the First there is contained a reference to something outside themselves, namely a reference to the perfect and completely actual First Cause. That is to say, the separate intellects other than the First are not absolutely simple and have some sort of composite—albeit still intellectual and immaterial—nature as a consequence of their need to think something outside themselves. They are "composite things [which] surpass one another by the lack of composition and their proximity to the simple and the first in this genus."[32] Averroes uses this to explain that in comparison with the First they are of a lower ontological status and that their intellectual powers are proportional to their "proximity" to the First. But for my purposes here I will focus on the nature of this First, known as God.

Averroes follows Aristotle in asserting that the First Principle or God is self-thinking thought, a conclusion which is also suitable in regard to all other immaterial intellects in the hierarchy. But God's case is unique in that He does not have within His nature any comparison to anything outside Himself. All other entities have a relation to God while God has no relation or comparison to other entities. But does this mean that God has no knowledge of anything outside of Himself, no knowledge of particulars or, for that matter, of universals? If such is the case, of course, God would per se have no particular providence and perhaps also no universal providence, at least in the meaning which those words have in a religious understanding which entails divine intention in regard to creatures for their benefit.

In his *Long Commentary on the Metaphysics*, Averroes asserts that God has knowledge which is properly understood as neither of particulars nor of universals. He writes,

> The truth is that because it knows only itself, it knows the existents through the existence which is the cause of their existences. . . . [T]he First . . . is He who knows absolutely the nature of being *qua* being, which is His essence. Therefore, the word "knowledge" is said of His knowledge and our knowledge by homonymy. For His knowledge is the cause of being and being is the cause of our knowledge; and His knowledge cannot be described as universal, nor as particular, for he whose knowledge is universal knows potentially the particulars which are in actuality and the object of his knowledge is of necessity knowledge in potentiality since the universal (knowledge) is only knowledge of particular things; if the universal (knowledge) is knowledge in potentiality and there is no potentiality in His knowledge, then His knowledge is not universal. A clearer (argument) is that His knowledge is not particular, because the particulars are infinite and no knowledge encompasses them; He is not characterized by the knowledge which is in us, nor by the ignorance which is its opposite, just as that which is not fit to possess any of these two (knowledge and ignorance) is not characterized by the knowledge which is in us, nor by the ignorance which is in us, and whose existence is not distinct from his knowledge has thus become evident.[33]

In this context it is worth recalling that the attribution of knowledge to God in the first place is a consequence of the assertion that immaterial entities are necessarily intellectual entities, something I have shown is based on Averroes' arguments in psychology.

As an intellectual entity which cannot be merely in potency but must necessarily exist as an actuality of activity, God must then be exercising in complete actuality, eternally, an intellectual activity. Since intellectual activity is knowing, God is eternally active in knowing with the object of His knowing being Himself. Hence, it is clear that God's activity should be characterized as knowing on the basis of the view that any immaterial activity must be an intellectual activity of knowing. But, as Averroes himself indicates in the quotation just cited, the predicate "knowing" when said of God does not have the conceptual content which it does in the two forms of knowing of which we have experience. That is to say, we do not know the predicate to assert anything more than that God has an immaterial activity which should be intellectual and thereby should be classified as knowledge, since every intellectual activity is suitably called knowledge. The predicate asserted of God is true, but we do not have sufficient understanding of the conceptual content of the predicate so as to apply it with any more meaning than "God has an immaterial activity which should be intellectual and thereby should be classified as knowing."

Critical consideration also has to be given to his assertion that God "knows the existents through the existence which is the cause of their existences. . . . [T]he First . . . is He who knows absolutely the nature of being *qua* being, which is His essence."[34] If we can talk about God's knowledge in any meaningful sense, something which is highly questionable on this account, we have to say that God's knowledge of His essence does not necessarily involve his knowledge of what is per accidens consequent upon His essence.[35] When he writes, "The truth is that because it knows only itself, it knows the existents through the existence which is the cause of their existences," Averroes is stressing not that God knows the world and its many parts or even that God knows anything outside himself. Rather, God, who is final cause for the universe and all its beings, knows only Himself, as Averroes repeatedly stresses in the *Long Commentary on the Metaphysics*. When Averroes asserts that God "knows the existents" this must not be taken literally but must be understood in conjunction with the rest of the sentence, "through the existence which is the cause of their existences." For Averroes the predicate "Creator" is said of God not because of a divine activity of creation ex nihilo by some form of efficient creative causality, something rejected by Averroes on philosophical grounds, but because of a relation of final causality on the part of the world relative to God.[36] But, while it makes sense in Averroes' account to hold that final cause and formal cause coincide in the being of God, God's role as final cause of the universe does not entail that He know the forms of things in the universe in any direct way or even in any indirect way. That would perhaps be possible if God were the efficient cause of those things and if this efficient causality in the emanative creation of things—something completely unknown in the thought of Aristotle—were properly established to be understood along the lines of Aristotle's account of the causing of motion in *Physics* III[37] where he asserts that the actuality of the agent as cause (the mover) is in the patient (the moved) and traceable to the agent which possessed actually what the patient possesses only potentially prior to the action.[38] Indeed, that might open the door to a doctrine of naming of God as cause through a doctrine of analogy asserting that the effect is revelatory of its cause. In knowing Himself God could perhaps be argued to know what emanates from Him or what is created by Him. But such cannot be the case for Averroes since his philosophical account of God identifies God only as final cause for other things.[39] For a doctrine of analogy to function here, the actuality of the agent would have to come about in the patient, something which occurs only in efficient causality. God does not pre-contain the forms of the world for Averroes. Rather, the beings of the world are drawn to God as final cause of all and so God's role as extrinsic final cause draws them toward the perfection possible for them in virtue of the forms already present in them. God does not create the forms of the world but rather only draws them toward their perfection.[40]

Thus, God does not know the world since His activity is fully and totally self-contained. What is more, it makes no sense to say that by His self-knowledge God has either universal or particular intention in relation to the world if intention requires knowledge. Does this mean that God has no providence in relation to the world? On this notion Averroes holds that all that exists below the celestial bodies is receptive of the providence of the celestial bodies responsible for guiding the world.[41] He then writes,

> It must be known to you that this is Aristotle's view concerning providence, and that the problems arising about providence are solved by (his view); for there are people who say that there is nothing for which God does not care, because they claim that the Sage must not leave anything without providence and must not do evil, and that all his actions are just. Other people refuted this theory through the fact that many things happen that are evil, and the Sage should not produce them; so these people went to the opposite extreme and said that therefore there is no providence at all. The truth in this is that providence exists, and that what happens contrary to providence is due to the necessity of matter, not to the shortcomings of the creator.[42]

God's providence in reference to the world means nothing more than what is consequent upon His nature as most perfect being toward which all reality strives by final causality. God has no relation to and no knowledge of the world, but the world is related to God on the principles which Averroes employs in his demonstrative accounts. This does not mean that there is no providence in any sense, but only that providence in behalf of the changing world below the sphere of the moon is constituted in the effects of the celestial bodies and movements on the world. They have no intention in relation to the world; rather, their intention is in relation to their final causes. Providence, when said of the activity of the celestial bodies and their motions, means the reception of beneficial influence from a higher cause to the extent that this influence is not hindered "due to the necessity of matter." In this account providence and intentional action are fully distinct. If the concept of providence necessarily entails intentional action, God is not in fact providential. However, Averroes can assert that the predicate "providential" can be said of God insofar as the effects of God's final causality provide benefit to the world by drawing the world and all its beings toward the perfection of God, the most perfect being in the universe. This is all that his demonstrative account of Divine "providence" will allow. If others understand "providence" to entail other meanings on the basis of the religious views which they bring to their consideration of the notion, that is because of their philosophically unfounded assumptions based on religious beliefs.

Averroes' discussion of religion in the *Tahâfut at-Tahâfut* seems to proceed in accord with this. There he explains that in the case of human beings who, like all the rest of the universe, are related to God, God's final causality involves religious activity on the part of human beings for whom

> the religions are, according to the philosophers, obligatory, since they lead toward wisdom in a way universal to all human beings, for philosophy only leads a certain number of intelligent people to the knowledge of happiness, and they therefore have to learn wisdom, whereas religions seek the instruction of the masses generally.[43]

The value of religion, then, is to be found in the intrinsic fulfillment to which it leads all human beings, namely, happiness. This is why

> all the learned hold about religions the opinion that the principles of the actions and regulations prescribed in every religion are received from the prophets and lawgivers, who regard those necessary principles as praiseworthy which most incite the masses to the performance of virtuous acts.[44]

These two quotations taken from his *Tahâfut at-Tahâfut* emphasize the importance of religious duties and activities as contributing to human perfection and the attainment of happiness, the human version of the perfection which each entity seeks in its striving in final causality toward the perfection of God. These dialectically argued views are in accord with those found in his demonstrative accounts of these matters as just discussed.

————

Averroes' philosophical account of God follows upon Aristotelian principles and reaches a conclusion fundamentally the same as that of Aristotle. This can be discerned if one takes his methodological suggestions seriously and looks to the demonstrative arguments of his commentaries on Aristotle for the philosophical account. This entails setting aside the literal understanding of the rhetorical and dialectical accounts of religions when truth is sought in its fullest sense, *al-yaqîn alladhî fi al-ghâyah/secundum maximam veritatem*. Those religious accounts are not without value since they serve the practical function of leading human beings to the moral virtue which is necessary for human happiness and which is necessary for the perfection of the intellectual virtues by which human happiness in its fullest can be attained.[45] The fullness of moral virtue requires the involvement of the community and so too intellectual virtue in its fullness also requires the support of the community insofar as moral excellence is presupposed by intellectual excellence. In this sense religion, in supplying for the community "necessary principles as praiseworthy which most incite the masses to the performance of virtuous acts . . . " makes intellectual fulfillment possible. In this sense the principles of religion can be regarded as "true" insofar as they contribute to the welfare and happiness of human beings, something quite in accord with Aristotle who holds that practical truth involves "truth [which] is in agreement with right desire."[46] In accord with this, the religious proposition asserting God's providential interest and involvement can be regarded as "true" in the sense of being practically valuable in guiding human beings toward moral virtue, while it is in fact not proven true since the demonstrative philosophical account has no provision for providential action of an intentional nature by God in relation to the world. Taken literally the religious proposition may be false and certainly is insufficiently grounded in demonstrative philosophical argumentation for its truth to be asserted. But, of course, the consequences are stronger than that. The common religious proposition which asserts God to have an interest in the world and to have a providential relation to the world is in fact false for Averroes because demonstrative argument about God's nature and providence shows that God knows only Himself. While the world is related to God in a relation of dependence, the philosophical account holds that God is not related to the world and has no intentionality in relation to the world with the consequence that providence cannot be predicated of God as *al-yaqîn alladhî fi al-ghâyah/secundum maximam veritatem*. For Averroes, then, this would be a situation in which a religious proposition is in contradiction with a demonstrated philosophical proposition.[47] Thus, just as he holds that there cannot be correct interpretation of Scripture which is in contradiction to demonstrated philosophical propositions,[48] so too religious propositions derivative on Scripture or generally accepted religious belief cannot be true if they are in contradiction with demonstrated philosophical propositions.

The philosopher Averroes' support of religious statements in Scripture and Religious Law which affirm such common doctrines as universal and individual providence may in some sense be an acknowledgment of a plurality of rational ways to approach reality but surely is not an instance of a genuine support for a theory of double truth. Averroes' views on the priority of demonstrative argumentation in the interpretation of Scriptural statements makes it clear that religion and philosophy *are* intersecting disciplines and that propositions common to both can be evaluated with a view to their truth. And when there are conflicting propositions, the principle which comes into play is, "Truth does not oppose truth but accords with it and bears witness to it." What is more, the one best in the position of evaluating truth is the philosopher whose concern is with the truth of propositions which are characterized as *al-yaqîn alladhî fî al-ghâyah / secundum maximam veritatem.*

Nevertheless in the *Tahâfut at-Tahâfut* he asserts that " . . . the religions are, according to the philosophers, obligatory, since they lead towards wisdom in a way universal to all human beings, for philosophy only leads a certain number of intelligent people to the knowledge of happiness, and they therefore have to learn wisdom, whereas religions seek the instruction of the masses generally."[49] To this he later adds that philosophers are not to express doubt about religious principles or to contradict the sayings of prophets when he writes,

> For it belongs to the necessary excellence of a man of learning that he should not despise the doctrines in which he has been brought up, and that he should explain them in the fairest way, and that he should understand that the aim of these doctrines lies in their universal character, not in their particularity, and that, if he expresses a doubt concerning the religious principles in which he has been brought up, or explains them in a way contradictory to the prophets and turns away from their path, he merits more than anyone else that the term unbeliever should be applied to him, and he is liable to the penalty for unbelief in the religion in which he has been brought up.[50]

What, then, is the best way to understand Averroes' assertions about the intersection of religious propositions and philosophically demonstrative propositions?

As already indicated, Averroes wrote a paraphrasing *Commentary on the Republic* of Plato. Unlike middle commentaries, however, this work is not merely a paraphrase but rather a thoroughly Aristotelian interpretive work deeply imbued with his study of Aristotle's *Nicomachean Ethics.*[51] It is in the *Commentary on the Republic* that Averroes recounts Plato's famous "noble lie" (*Republic* 414B–C). This "noble lie" is put forward to forestall any dissension among the different classes and to unify the community for its own benefit. Averroes also adds,

> And it is due to his care [for the city] that the prophet announced that the ruin of this city will only come to pass when its chief who guards it is of iron or bronze.

This story will be transmitted to them through music from youth, just as other stories are transmitted to them. When he finished this he said that the settlements of these chiefs and guardians of the city ought to be raised above the city and that if there is one of them who does not wish to accept the Law he will be smitten.[52]

In light of this, of the texts from the *Tahâfut at-Tahâfut,* and of his remarks in the *Faṣl al-Maqâl,* it appears most reasonable not to give up the principle of truth ("Truth does not oppose truth but accords with it and bears witness to it") nor to assert that religious propositions are without practical value, nor to embrace Double Truth, but rather to hold that Averroes, like Plato, understands the practical necessity and value of the "noble lie" for the attainment of the human end which is, following Aristotle, the attainment of intellectual virtue and excellence founded on moral virtue.[53]

Notes

1. Anke von Kügelgen, "A Call for Rationalism: 'Arab Averroists' in the Twentieth Century," *Alif* 16 (1996): 97–132. This receives more comprehensive treatment in her *Averroes und die arabische Moderne: Ansätze zu einer Neubegründung des Rationalismus im Islam* (Leiden: Brill, 1994). Also see Abed al-Jabri, Mohammed, *Introduction à la Critque de la Raison Arabe,* trans. Ahmed Mahfoud and Marc Geoffroy (Paris: Editions La Découverte, 1995). This French translation of a collection of essays by Mohammed Abed al-Jabri has been translated into English recently as *Arab-Islamic Philosophy: A Contemporary Critique,* trans. Aziz Abbassi (Austin: University of Texas Press, 1999).

2. See *Averroes and the Enlightenment,* ed. Mourad Wahba and Mona Abousenna (Amherst, NY: Prometheus, 1996) and the contributions of Paul Kurtz and Timothy Madigan there. The view that the contradictory views of religion and philosophy can be reconciled by merely respecting each as a contribution to the discussion is just as unsatisfactory as the philosophical concept of compatibilism which holds that determinism is true and is compatible with human freedom. Such a view functions well only if human freedom itself is understood to be nothing more than liberty from external restrictions and restraints and to be compatible with internal psychological determinism. Similarly, religion and philosophy can be understood as reconcilable even when asserting incompatible propositions if one holds that each is true in its own sphere and that those spheres are non-intersecting.

3. Ibn Rushd, *Kitâb faṣl al-maqâl with its appendix (Damîma) and an extract from Kitâb al-kashf fî al-manâhij al-adilla,* ed. G. F. Hourani (Leiden: Brill, 1959), 18–26 (hereafter: Hourani Arabic 1959); *Averroes: On the Harmony of Religion and Philosophy. A translation, with introduction and notes, of Ibn Rushd's Kitâb Faṣl al-Maqâl with its appendix (Damîma) and an extract from Kitâb al-kashf fî al-manâhij al-adilla,* trans. G. F. Hourani (London: Luzac, 1967), 63–71 (hereafter: Hourani English 1967).

4. See, for example, *Taḥṣil al-Sa'âdah,* 29–36, in *Rasâ'il al-Fârâbî* (Hyderabad 1926/1345 H.); "The Attainment of Happiness," in *Alfarabi's Philosophy of Plato and Aristotle,* trans. Muhsin Mahdi (Ithaca, NY: Cornell University Press, 1969²), section iii, 34–41. Cf. *Al-Farabi on the Perfect State,* 17, trans. Richard Walzer (Oxford: Clarendon, 1985), 276–85.

5. See Dimitri Gutas, *Avicenna and the Aristotelian Tradition* (Leiden: Brill, 1988), 299–307.

6. Alain de Libera, *Averroes: Discours décisif*, ed. and trans. Marc Geoffroy (Paris: Flammarion, 1996), 10–11, writes, "L'intention, la destination, la nature du texte comptent autant, voire davantage, car le sujet n'est rien si l'on ignore le but poursuivi, le public visé, l'enjeu réel. Il faut le dire sans détour, le *Faṣl al-Maqâl* n'est ni un livre de philosophie ni un livre de théologie. Inde-pendammant même des thèses soutenues, son titre ne pourrait être ni le *Fides quaerens intellec-tum* d'un Anselme ni le *De reductione artium ad theologiam* d'un Bonaventure. Est-ce un texte 'rationaliste'? Le thème a fait florès depuis les travaux pionniers de L. Gauthier, alimentant des débats acharnés. Nous le croyons sans objet, car foundé sur l'assimilation ethnocentrique du rationalisme à la raison philosophique grecque—la *falsafa*—et la méconnaissance de la plural-ité des rationalités: philosophiques, juridiques, théologiques, scientifiques, religieuses. Le *Faṣl al-maqâl* n'est pas un manifeste du 'rationalisme', mais la mise en oeuvre d'une réflexion sur la philosophie au sein d'une certaine rationalité discursive. Le *Faṣl al-maqâl* est une *fatwâ*. C'est un avis légal."

7. Oliver Leaman, *A Brief Introduction to Islamic Philosophy* (Cambridge: Polity, 1999), 170. The complete paragraph is worth quoting: "This is a crucial aspect of ibn Rushd's theory of meaning, stemming perhaps from Aristotle's observation that the degree of precision which we should employ in language is a function of the context within which we are working. The impli-cations which ibn Rushd draws from this theory are radical. First, it means that there is no privi-leged access to the nature of reality which represents how things really are. The ordinary person has just as valid a grasp of how things really are as does the philosopher or the religious thinker, provided that the ordinary person is able to use concepts which connect with that reality in a loose way. Let us take as an example here the notion of an afterlife. For the philosopher, this should not be understood, ibn Rushd argues, as the individual survival of the person after his or her death in an environment rather like the environment of the world of generation and cor-ruption. Once our body perishes, there is no sense in thinking of the continuing existence of the individual soul, since the soul is just the form of the material body, and once the latter disinte-grates, there is no longer any matter to be informed by the soul."

This view is in accord with what Leaman wrote in his 1988 *Averroes and His Philosophy* (Oxford: Clarendon Press), 195–96: "Rather like Aristotle, Averroes respects a whole gamut of different views on a common topic, refusing to select some as more privileged or accurate than others." "We must respect the different uses of the same word because they represent different points of view, different points of view of the same thing. It is an error to represent some uses as essen-tially more accurate than others. . . . In his philosophical methodology Averroes tries to show how it is possible for one thing to be described in a variety of ways. The arguments which have subsequently arisen concerning his 'real' views fail to grasp the philosophical approach he has constructed. When he tries to reconcile apparently contradictory views his strategy is to argue that all these views are acceptable as different aspects of one thing. The Averroist movement pro-vides a useful focus for this idea, the precise nature of the apparent conflict between reason and religion. In his tentative remarks on language Averroes suggests that this conflict comes down to stress upon different aspects of one thing, namely, the way the world really is. This is an intrigu-ing interpretation of a longstanding philosophical dilemma, and may well be Averroes' most important contribution to philosophy itself." Cf. n. 8 below.

8. "According to this doctrine, a proposition could be both true philosophically and true theologically, even though the philosophical understanding of it is contrary to the theological one. This is sometimes seen as far too radical a notion to be identified with ibn Rushd, but I have

come to think that this is probably wrong. Certainly no proposition could be both true and false at the same time, but it is clearly possible for a proposition to be true when taken in one way, and false when taken in another. This is surely what the doctrine of double truth came to mean in medieval Europe, and this also explains how radical it is. Some commentators have spoken of a thirteenth-century European renaissance, and if there was one, then the principles of Averroism played a large part in it. According to those principles, neither religion nor philosophy has the last word to say on the issue of truth (Leaman, 1991). Both are equally valid views of the same truth, so neither the philosopher nor the theologian is in a superior position when it comes to determining the nature of reality. We tend to see this as the view that religion does not have priority over reason, but we could equally well take it that reason has no priority over religion. Both are valid and have appropriate uses; the problems arise only when one tries to mix them up and insist that one has priority over the other or that one form of argument may be assessed according to the criteria appropriate to the other." Oliver Leaman, *A Brief Introduction to Islamic Philosophy*, 171–72. The embedded reference to Leaman 1991 is a reference to his article, "Averroes, le *Kitâb al-nafs* et la révolution de la philosophie occidentale," in *Le Choc Averroes* (Paris: Maison des Cultures du Monde, 1991), 58–65. Also see O. Leaman, "Ibn Rushd on Happiness and Philosophy," *Studia Islamica* 52 (1980): 167–81. Regarding the issue in the Latin West, see Richard C. Dales, "The Origin of the Doctrine of the Double Truth," *Viator* 15 (1984): 169–79.

9. Hourani, Arabic 1959, 1; Hourani, English 1967, 44. I add [Religious] to his translation here and elsewhere.

10. Hourani, Arabic 1959, 8; Hourani, English 1967, 50.

11. Richard C. Taylor, "'Truth does not contradict truth': Averroes and the Unity of Truth," *Topoi* 19.1 (2000): 3–16.

12. Aristotle, *Prior Analytics* 1.32 (47a8–9), trans. A. J. Jenkinson. Averroes comments on this in his *Middle Commentary*, writing, "[Aristotle] said: It remains for us after this to say how we are able to reduce syllogisms used in books and addresses to these figures and to resolve them to these, since they are not used in books and speeches in the way mentioned. This is the third issue which remained for us to investigate regarding syllogisms. For if we know the kinds of syllogisms and are able to use them and able to reduce all that occur in discourse and in speech to the forms which we mentioned, then indeed we would have our first goal in the knowledge of the syllogism. For we find whenever we speak regarding the resolution of syllogisms to the forms mentioned that we grow in certainty regarding what was said about the fact that every syllogism exists only in one of the forms mentioned. For, when we find all the syllogisms used in books and speeches reduce to these forms, then we infer by way of induction that these syllogisms are the elements of all syllogisms. And this is the nature of the reality on which demonstration rests, namely, that it is found to be true in every way in which it is regarded and it is found to be consistent in each and every way. For truth, as Aristotle says, is a witness for itself and is consistent in every way , i.e., it bears witness to it in every way." My translation of the Arabic of Ibn Rushd (Averroes), *Middle Commentary on Aristotle's Prior Analytics*, Arabic, ed. Mahmoud M. Kassem, with Charles E. Butterworth and Ahmad Abd al-Magid Haridi (Cairo: The General Egyptian Book Organization, 1983), § 216, 226.1–15.

13. " . . . [W]e affirm definitely that whenever the conclusion of a demonstration is in conflict with the apparent meaning of Scripture [or Religious Law], that apparent meaning admits of allegorical interpretation according to the rules for such interpretation in Arabic. This proposition is questioned by no Muslim and doubted by no believer. But its certainty is immensely increased for those who have had close dealings with this idea and put it to the test, and made it

their aim to reconcile the assertions of intellect and tradition. Indeed we may say that whenever a statement in Scripture [or Religious Law] conflicts in its apparent meaning with a conclusion of demonstration, if Scripture [or Religious Law] is considered carefully, and the rest of its contents searched page by page, there will invariably be found among the expressions of Scripture [or Religious Law] something which in its apparent meaning bears witness to that allegorical interpretation or comes close to bearing witness." Hourani, Arabic 1959, 7–8; Hourani, English 1967, 51.

14. Regarding the nature of demonstration Averroes follows closely Aristotle's account: "By demonstration I mean a syllogism productive of scientific knowledge, a syllogism, that is, the grasp of which is eo ipso such knowledge. Assuming then that my thesis as to the nature of scientific knowing is correct, the premisses of demonstrated knowledge must be true, primary, immediate, better known than and prior to the conclusion, which is further related to them as effect to cause. Unless these conditions are satisfied, the basic truths will not be 'appropriate' to the conclusion. Syllogism there may indeed be without these conditions, but such syllogism, not being productive of scientific knowledge, will not be demonstration." *Posterior Analytics* 1.2 (71b18–24), trans. Mure. Cf. Ibn Rushd, *Sharḥ al-Burhân li-Aristû* in ed. 'Abdurrahmân Badawî, *Ibn Rushd, Sharḥ al-Burhân li-Aristû wa-Talkhîṣ al-Burhân* (*Grand Commentaire et Paraphrase Des Second Analytiques d'Aristote*) (Kuwait: al-Majlis al-Watanî lil-Thaqâfah wa-l-Funûn wa-l-Âdâb, Qism al-Turâth al-'Arabî, 1984), 180 ff. (hereafter cited as *Sharḥ al-Burhân*); *Aristotelis Stagirite Posteriorum Resolutionum Libri Duo cum Averrois Cordubensis Magnis Commentariis* in *In Aristotelis Opera Cum Averrois Commentariis* (Venetiis Apud Iunctas, 1562; reprint Frankfurt am Main: Minerva, 1962) vol. 1 part 2: 29ff. (hereafter cited as LCPA, *Long Commentary on the Posterior Analytics*). The published Arabic text of the *Sharḥ al-Burhân* extends from the beginning through Book I, chapter 23 (85a12).

15. Averroès, *Tahafot at-tahafot*, ed. Maurice Bouyges, S.J. (Beirut: Imprimerie Catholique,1930), 427–28; *Averroes' Tahafut al-Tahafut (The Incoherence of the Incoherence)*, trans. Simon Van Den Bergh (London: Luzac, 1969), 257–58. In his *Averroes and the Metaphysics of Causation* (Albany: SUNY, 1985) Barry Kogan is aware of Averroes' assertion that the *Tahafut at-Tahafut* argues dialectically but Kogan makes great use of it together with the *Long Commentary on the Metaphysics* to establish an understanding of Averroes' teachings on God and metaphysics (9). Kogan, however, is well aware that "Averroes designed the *Tahafut al-Tahafut* primarily for 'philosophers-to-be,' with a view toward preparing them to study strictly 'scientific' or demonstrative works. But the *Tahafut* itself, he openly admits, was not intended to be such a work" (255–56). Oliver Leaman regards the *Tahafut at-Tahafut* as a reliable source for understanding the thought of Averroes. In his *Averroes and His Philosophy* he writes, "I am taking it to be the case that he [Averroes] presents a broadly similar line of argument in all his works, whether commentaries or essays, and that analysis of his arguments will establish that this is the correct approach to take" (11). Kogan's book is clearly one of the most sophisticated and detailed attempts to understand Averroes' thought on God. The final chapter of Leaman's *Averroes and His Philosophy*, "Averroes' Philosophical Methodology" (179–96), is a similarly challenging albeit less penetrating account of Averroes for contemporary interpreters. The methodological approaches of both of these interpreters of Averroes are different from the one I employ here, with the result that the conclusions reached here are quite different from those of Kogan or Leaman. For discussion of an example of a dialectical account in the *Tahafut at-Tahafut* which is clearly contradicted by his account in a Long Commentary, see Richard C. Taylor, "Averroes' Philosophical Analysis of Religious Propositions" in *What is Philosophy in the Middle Ages? Proceedings of the 10th International Congress of Medieval Philosophy of the SIEPM, 25–30 August 1997 in Erfurt*, Miscellanea

Mediaevalia, bd. 26, ed. Jan Aertsen and Andreas Speer (Cologne: Walter De Gruyter, 1998), 888–94. This issue of Averroes' methodology is one I will take up elsewhere at greater length.

16. See n. 14 for those conditions.

17. *Thumma qâla: Awa-qad yakûna qiyâs min ghaira ijtimâ'i hâdhihî al-shurût"—yurîdu: imma qiyâs iqnâ'i aw jadalî aw dalîlun. Sharḥ al-Burhân*, 184; *Mox dixit: syllogismus enim erit etiam sine his conditionibus, hoc est vel syllogismus dialecticus vel rhetoricus, vel apparens* (Mantinus). The other two Latin translations in this volume have *dialecticus aut persuasivus aut apparens* (Abram) and *dialecticus aut tentativus aut apparens* (Burana). LCPA Book 1, Comment 9, 1.2:31rF. On demonstration by way of sign in Averroes, see Abdelali Elamrani-Jamal, "La démonstration du signe (*burhân al-dalîl*) selon Ibn Rushd (Averroès)," *Documenti e Studi sulla Tradizione Filosofica Medievale* 11 (2000): 113–31.

18. *Sharḥ al-Burhân*, 184; LCPA Book 1, Comment 9: 1.2:32rA. Note that at 32vD he quotes Aristotle's text that it is possible to make true conclusions from false premises, as is discussed in the *Prior Analytics*, but then those conclusions are *per accidens*. In his following comment he stresses that the conditions for demonstration must be fully met. If premises are known through something intermediate (*per medium*), then the demonstration is not absolute or simpliciter (as mentioned at 31vF) but only equivocally called a demonstration.

19. Ibn Sina (Avicenna), *Al-Shifâ': Al-Illâhiyyât*, 1.5, ed. G.C. Anawati and Sa'id Zayed (Cairo: Organisation Générale des Imprimeries Gouvernementales, 1960), 29–36; *Avicenna Latinus: Liber de Philosophia Prima sive Scientia Divina*, 1.5, ed. S. Van Riet (Louvain: Peeters; Leiden: Brill, 1977), 31–42.

20. Herbert A. Davidson, *Alfarabi, Avicenna, and Averroes on Intellect* (Oxford: Oxford University Press, 1992), 325.

21. This is discussed more fully in Richard C. Taylor, "Averroes on Psychology and the Principles of Metaphysics," *The Journal of the History of Philosophy* 36 (1998): 507–23. The account given here follows what was established in that article.

22. Averroes, *Tafsîr mâ ba'd al-ṭabî'ah*, Book Lâm c. 36, ed. Maurice Bouyges, S.J. (Beirut: Dar al-Machreq Editeurs [Imprimerie Catholique] 1967²), 2:1593–94; Charles Genequand, *Ibn Rushd's Metaphysics: A Translation with Introduction of Ibn Rushd's Commentary on Aristotle's Metaphysics, Book Lam* (Leiden: Brill, 1984), 149 (hereafter Genequand); *Aristotelis Metaphysicorum Libri XIIII cum Averrois Cordubensis in eosdem commentariis et epitome*, XII c. 36, in *In Aristotelis Opera Cum Averrois Commentariis* (Venice: Iunctas, 1574), 8: f. 318rv F–G (hereafter Latin); *Averrois Cordubensis Commentarium Magnum in Aristotelis De Anima Libros*, III c. 5, ed. F. Stuart Crawford (Cambridge, MA: Medieval Academy of America, 1953), 410 (hereafter LCDA). For discussion of these texts see Taylor, "Averroes on Psychology and the Principles of Metaphysics." Averroes also holds that ethical science accepts principles about the nature of human beings from physics (of which psychology is a branch) in his *Commentary on the Republic* of Plato. See *Averroes on Plato's "Republic"*, trans. Ralph Lerner (Ithaca-London: Cornell University Press, 1974), 82 (hereafter Lerner).

23. This term is used by Themistius. See Themistius, *In Libros Aristotelis De Anima Paraphrasis*, ed. R. Heinze (Berlin: 1899) [*Commentaria in Aristotelem Graeca*], 5:99.20. *Themistius, On Aristotle's On the Soul*, trans. Robert B.Todd (Ithaca: Cornell University Press, 1996), 123. Cf. *An Arabic Translation of Themistius' Commentary on Aristotle's De Anima*, ed. M.C. Lyons (Columbia, SC: University of South Carolina Press, 1973), 180.2.

24. Arthur Hyman discusses operational presence in "Aristotle's Theory of Intellect and Its Interpretation by Averroes," in *Studies in Aristotle*, ed. Dominic J. O'Meara (Washington: Catholic University of America Press, 1981), 190. The metaphysics of Averroes' epistemology

is discussed in Richard C. Taylor, "*Cogitatio, Cogitativus* and *Cogitare:* Remarks on the Cogitative Power in Averroes," in *L'élaboration du vocabulaire philosophique au Moyen Age,* ed. J. Hamesse and C. Steel, Rencontres de philosophie médiévale 8 (Turnhout: Brepols, 2000), 111–46.

25. See Richard C. Taylor, "Personal Immortality in Averroes' Mature Philosophical Psychology," *Documenti e Studi sulla Traduzione Filosofica Medievale* 9 (1998): 87–110.

26. See Richard C. Taylor, "Averroes' Philosophical Analysis of Religious Propositions," 888–94.

27. *Metaphysics* 8.2 (1043a19–21). The cause of actuality in a composite thing is the form. See Averroes *Tafsîr mâ ba'd al-ṭabî'ah,* Book Hâ' c. 7: 1055; Latin 8.7, 8: f. 215v K. Cf. *Metaphysics* 8.6 (1045b22–24) and Averroes *Tafsîr mâ ba'd al-ṭabî'ah,* Book Hâ' c. 16: 1102; Latin 8.16, 8: f. 225rF.

28. This account is a key element of my argument in Taylor, "Averroes on Psychology and the Principles of Metaphysics." At the time of writing that article, it had escaped my notice that this point had been made by Barry Kogan in his 1985 *Averroes and the Metaphysics of Causation* (Albany: State University of New York Press, 1985), 232. It is worth noting that Al-Farabi comes close to an account similar to this in his work on the *Opinions of the People of the Virtuous City,* Arabic: "6. Because the First is not in matter and has itself no matter in any way whatsoever, it is in its substance actual intellect; for what prevents the form from being intellect and from actually thinking (intelligizing) is the matter in which a thing exists. And when a thing exists without being in need of matter, that very thing will in its substance be actual intellect; and that is the status of the First. It is, then, actual intellect. The First is also intelligible through its substance; for, again, what prevents a thing from being actually intelligible and being intelligible through its substance is matter. It is intelligible by virtue of its being intellect; for the One whose identity is intellect is intelligible by the One whose identity is intellect. In order to be intelligible the First is in no need of another essence outside itself which would think it but it itself thinks its own essence. As a result of its thinking its own essence, it becomes actually thinking and intellect, and, as a result of its essence thinking (intelligizing) it, it becomes actually intelligized. In the same way, in order to be actual intellect and to be actually thinking, it is in no need of an essence which it would think and which it would acquire from the outside, but is intellect and thinking by thinking its own essence. For the essence which is thought is the essence which thinks, and so it is intellect by virtue of its being intelligized. Thus it is intellect and intelligized and thinking, all this being one essence and one indivisible substance—whereas man, for instance, is intelligible, but what is intelligible in his case is not actually intelligized but potentially intelligible; he becomes subsequently actually intelligized after the intellect has thought him. What is intelligible in the case of man is thus not always the subject which thinks, nor is, in his case, the intellect always the same as the intelligible object, nor is our intellect intelligible because it is intellect. We think, but not because our substance is intellect; we think with an intellect which is not what constitutes our substance; but the First is different; the intellect, the thinker and the intelligible (and intelligized) have in its case one meaning and are one essence and one indivisible substance. 7. That the First is 'knowing' is to be understood in the same way. For it is, in order to know, in no need of an essence other than its own, through the knowledge of which it would acquire excellence, nor is it, in order to be knowable, in need of another essence which would know it, but its substance suffices for it to be knowing and to be known. Its knowledge of its essence is nothing else than its substance. Thus the fact that it knows and that it is knowable and that it is knowledge refers to one essence and one substance." Trans. Richard Walzer in *Al-Farabi on the Perfect State,* 70–73.

29. This "First Form" is God for Averroes.

30. For Averroes God is pure actuality, *fa-inna-hu fi'lun maḥdun, Tafsîr mâ ba'd al-ṭabî'ah*, Book Lâm c.37: 1599.7; Genequand trans. 151. Note, however, that the Latin translation apparently omits this phrase. See Latin 12.37, 8: f.319v G–H.

31. LCDA 3.5, 409–410. My translation.

32. I modify Genequand's rendering of *qillah at-tarqîb*, "the insignificance of the composition." *Tafsîr mâ ba'd al-ṭabî'ah*, Book Lâm c. 51, 1704.16; Genequand tr. 196; Latin, 12.51, 8: f. 336v I. Averroes' discussion here (Book Lâm c. 51, 1703–7; Genequand tr. 195–97; Latin, 12.51,8: f. 336rE–vK) is drawn on by thinkers of the Latin West for the hierarchy of immaterial intellects up to God.

33. *Tafsîr mâ ba'd al-ṭabî'ah*, Book Lâm c. 36, 1707–8; Genequand trans. 197–98; Latin, 12.36, 8: 337A–C. At LCDA 3.36, 501, Averroes cites Themistius in this regard: "In this way, therefore, human beings, as Themistius says, are made like unto God in that he is all beings in a way and one who knows these in a way, for beings are nothing but his knowledge and the cause of beings is nothing but his knowledge. (1) How marvelous is that order and how mysterious is that mode of being!" In his paraphrase Themistius writes, "That is why it also most resembles a god; for god is indeed in one respect [identical with] the actual things that exist, but in another their supplier (*khorêgos*). The intellect is far more valuable insofar as it creates than insofar as it is acted on; that is because the productive first principle is always more valuable than the matter [on which it acts]. Also, as I have often said, the intellect and the object of thought are identical (just as are actual knowledge and the very object of knowledge)." Greek (1899), 99.23–28; Arabic (1973), 180.6–10; English tr. (1996), 124–25.

34. Kogan, drawing heavily on the *Tahafut at-Tahafut*, works hard to make sense of Averroes' statements that God does know the world and creates the world by his knowledge but ultimately finds Averroes' account sorely lacking. Averroes "bases his account of Divine causation on an inadmissibly ambiguous use of the verb 'to know.'" *Averroes and the Metaphysics of Causation*, 264. Druart remarks regarding Averroes' account of Divine understanding of the world through understanding Himself that "this seems to be a clever but rather unsatisfactory answer to the problems raised by God's Knowledge of anything outside himself. Even if God is a metaphysician, and therefore metaphysics is the divine way of knowing, it still does not ensure true knowledge of things here below." Thérèse-Anne Druart, "Averroes on God's Knowledge of Being Qua Being," in *Studies in Thomistic Theology*, ed. Paul Lockey (Houston: Center for Thomistic Studies, 1995), 175–205. An inferior printed version of this is found in *Anaquel de Estudios Arabes* 4 (1993): 39–57. My references are to the 1995 version. For the present quotation, see 198. Both Kogan and Druart are correct on this point.

35. Cf. Harry A. Wolfson, "The Plurality of Immovable Movers in Aristotle and Averroes," *Harvard Studies in Classical Philology* 63 (1958): 233–53, 248–49. "[A]ccording to the mediaeval explanations there is some kind of distinction of prior and posterior in the immaterial movers themselves, whereas according to our explanation [of Aristotle] there is no distinction at all in the immaterial movers themselves; the distinction between them is only a distinction in their relation to things outside themselves—a distinction of external relation which, as we have shown, does not affect their nature. Now the assumption on the part of the mediaevals of a distinction of prior and posterior, whether that of cause or that of nobility, in the immaterial movers themselves has led to those endless questions as to whether that distinction does not after all imply a relationship of matter and form and also as to whether that relationship of matter and form is compatible with the initial assumption that these immovable movers are immaterial. But to assume, as we do, that the distinction between the immaterial movers is

only a distinction in their relation to things outside themselves does not lead to any of those questions."

36. Creation ex nihilo is denied by Averroes in his discussion at *Tafsîr mâ ba'd al-ṭabî'ah*, Book Lâm c.18, 1497–1505, Genequand trans.108–12; Latin, 8: 304rD–305vI. For Averroes creation consists in "bringing what is in potentiality into actuality. What becomes actual is destroyed in potentiality and all potentiality becomes actuality when that which is in actuality brings it out. If potentiality did not exist, there would be no agent at all. Therefore it is said that all proportions and forms exist in potentiality in prime matter." 1505; Genequand trans. 112; Latin 305vH–I.

37. *Physics* 3.2–3 (201b24–202b21). See particularly c. 3 where Aristotle asserts that the actuality of the agent takes place in the patient.

38. Ibid., 3.3, (202b9–10).

39. Cf. the lengthy account of Divine causality by Kogan in his chapter on "Divine Causation and the Doctrine of Eternal Creation" in *Averroes and the Metaphysics of Causation*, 203–65.

40. I want to thank my friend Prof. Thérèse-Anne Druart for a stimulating and valuable critical comment on this issue following my presentation of a related paper at the University of Chicago Islamic Philosophy Conference held April 27–28, 2001.

41. "He means: the actions of the celestial bodies in their sharing one with another in the maintenance of the world are like the actions of the freemen in the maintenance of the house; for just as the freemen are not allowed to perform all the actions which they desire, all their actions being due to the help which they give to one another, the same holds for celestial bodies. As for the existents which are below them, their condition is like that of the slaves and the animals which guard the houses: just as the actions of the slaves which share in (those of) the freemen are few, and even more so those of the animals, so is the case with that which is below the celestial bodies with regard to the celestial bodies." *Tafsîr mâ ba'd al-ṭabî'ah*, Book Lâm c. 52, 1714; Genequand trans. 200; Latin, 8: 338rB–D.

42. *Tafsîr mâ ba'd al-ṭabî'ah*, Book Lâm c. 52, 1715; Genequand trans. 200–1; Latin, 8: 338rD–F.

43. *Averroès: Tahafot at-tahafot*, 582; Van Den Berg trans. 360.

44. *Averroès: Tahafot at-tahafot*, 584; Van Den Berg trans. 361.

45. "As for the moral virtues, it appears from their case too that they are for the sake of the theoretical intelligibles." Lerner, trans. 88. "But this kind of perfection, i.e. the moral, is laid down [in relation to] theoretical perfection as a preparatory rank, without which the attainment of the end is impossible. Hence, this perfection is thought to be the ultimate end because of its proximity to the ultimate end. It appears from this, then, that the human perfections are four classes and that they are all for the sake of theoretical perfection." Lerner trans. 92.

46. *Nicomachean Ethics*, 6.1 (1139a31), trans. W. D. Ross, revised by J. O. Urmson.

47. For another example of this sort of thing see the article mentioned in n. 26.

48. See n. 13.

49. *Averroès: Tahafot at-tahafot*, 582; Van Den Berg trans. 360.

50. *Averroès: Tahafot at-tahafot*, 583; Van Den Berg trans. 360.

51. Averroes also wrote a *Middle Commentary on the Nicomachean Ethics*. The surviving Hebrew translation of this work has recently been published. See *Averroes' Middle Commentary on Aristotle's Nicomachean Ethics in the Hebrew Version of Samuel Ben Judah*, ed. Lawrence V. Berman (Jerusalem: The Israel Academy of Sciences and Humanities, 1999). Also see Averroes, *In Moralia Nicomachia Expositione in Aristotelis Opera Cum Averrois Commentariis*, III (Venetiis Apud Iunctas, 1552; reprint Frankfurt am Main: Minerva, 1962). Regarding Averroes' *Middle*

Commentary on the Nicomachean Ethics, see Jerzy B. Korolec, "Mittlerer Kommentar von Averroes zur Nikomachischen Ethik des Aristoteles," *Mediaevalia Philosophica Polonorum* 31 (1992): 61–188; and L. V. Berman, "Excerpts from the Lost Arabic Original of Ibn Rushd's *Middle Commentary on the Nicomachean Ethics,*" *Oriens* 20 (1967): 31–59, and "Ibn Rushd's *Middle Commentary on the Nicomachean Ethics* in Medieval Hebrew Literature," in *Multiple Averroes,* ed. J. Jolivet et al. (Paris: Les Belles Lettres, 1978), 287–321.

52. Lerner trans. 37 (41.1–7).

53. See n. 45. I am pleased to express my thanks to Peter Adamson, Dimitri Gutas, Wayne Hankey, Steven Harvey, John Jones, and James South for reading this paper and offering valuable suggestions, some of which are incorporated here and others which will significantly enhance my future work on this topic.

Chapter 3

Undoing the Past

Fishacre and Rufus on the Limits of God's Power

R. JAMES LONG

Peter Lombard's assertion, *free choice does not refer to the present or the past, but to future contingencies,*[1] provides the Dominican master Richard Fishacre, commenting on this text, with the occasion to ask a question which to the best of our knowledge no one at the Oxford studium had yet asked,[2] namely, whether God is free to alter the past.[3] The treatment, which takes the form of a *quaestio,* is concise and nuanced, but not without its difficulties. As was not infrequently the case, moreover, it drew the fire of his contemporary, Richard Rufus.[4]

Any restriction of God's power over the past, of course, would entail a denial of the divine omnipotence.[5] But the authority to the contrary, from the Gospel of Luke, affirms that *no word shall be impossible with God.*

The solution for Fishacre lies in a distinction: power over the past is of two kinds. The first is the power to reconstitute in being something that had ceased to be; the other is the power to cause that which in fact had being not to have been, to make it such, for example, that Caesar, having crossed the Rubicon, did not cross the Rubicon. The latter is not within God's power according to Fishacre,[6] and on this point Rufus concurs.[7]

However, with respect to the former, there is another distinction that needs to be made: there are three different kinds of things that could conceivably be caused to be again. The first are those beings which, when corrupted, pass into profound nothingness (*in penitus nihilum*), and Fishacre counts in this group time, light, every "successive" or series, and the souls of plants and animals.[8] To restore these things such that they are the same in number is within the power only of God, not of creatures.[9]

A second kind, when corrupted, is reduced to "pure matter," which lacks any seminal natures (*rationes seminales*), such that this matter possesses only a passive power.

But a third kind, when corrupted, is released into matter that does retain seminal natures.[10] In one sense the reestablishment of this kind is within nature's power, but the reconstituted being is the same only in species, not in number, and at a time determined beforehand. Fishacre has in mind, for example, the regeneration of a tomato plant from last year's seed or the ubiquitous dandelion from seed propagated by an earlier plant. The due season for such regeneration cannot, however, be altered except perhaps by a saint performing a miracle or by an angel.[11]

But to restore the same in number from among the last class of things belongs to God alone, because this is in a manner of speaking creation. Moreover, it is a much greater miracle and bespeaks greater power to restore the same in number from matter in which there is not a residual seminal nature. But only the highest power can restore that which was reduced to absolute nothingness to the same in number.[12] If there is a possibility of this, God can do it, since he is able to do whatever is possible. Although Fishacre admits that he is unaware of any case where God has so acted, all of these modes are within God's power, but not within ours.[13]

Quite different is the question of undoing the past, that is, of making what was, like Caesar's crossing of the Rubicon, not to have been. Fishacre is clear that in his view neither human nor divine will is free to undo what has been done. Furthermore, the sentence *Caesar crossed the Rubicon,* having once been true, cannot be rendered false even by God. As to where this truth resides, Fishacre says it is in the human soul; but even should this historical memory be lost, that is, should this truth cease to exist in any human mind, the truth of this sentence would continue to live in Truth itself. On the strictly verbal level, therefore, God cannot undo a true proposition, whatever be its status in the souls of whomsoever.[14]

Such is Fishacre's brief exposition of the problem of God's power—or, more precisely in this context, God's freedom—over the past. Though Raedts is correct in his claim that "Richard Rufus . . . develops [this question] far beyond Fishacre's rather short treatment,"[15] he admits his perplexity over Fishacre's third class of things, those namely that are reduced to their seminal natures.[16] The setting for this question must be sought in Fishacre's notion of *ratio seminalis.*

The potentiality of matter, claims Fishacre, is twofold: a passive potency, which is simply receptivity to form; and an active potency, which is something of form latent in matter. This latter was called by Augustine a seminal nature or seminal reason (*ratio seminalis*) and corresponds to causal natures in God.[17] Matter in the sense of passive potency is one in number, whereas matter in the sense of active potency is plural; there are in other words as many active potencies as there are forms.[18]

Furthermore, there are two ways in which seminal reasons can be brought from potentiality into actuality. The first is through causal reasons immediately, and when something of this kind, which is deemed unusual, happens through the prayers of a saint, it is called a miracle. The second is when something is educed into act through the mediation of other agents. This mediation in turn is either through nature alone— in which case the event is called *natural* and not miraculous—or through nature along with the principle which is the will; the co-principle of the will may be either that of a good angel or a bad, and the agency of the latter accounts for what is called magic.[19]

Fishacre's point here seems to be that the angel, good or bad, cannot solely by willing it effect a change which is contrary to nature; however, the angelic will can speed the process of maturation so as to reduce from potency to act more quickly than nature alone would dictate. Such marvelous and unwonted (*mira et insolita*) happenings do not differ greatly from those produced by the magical arts. Miracles, on the other hand, in the true and proper sense are effected immediately from the causal reasons, absent nature and created will.[20]

The greatest miracles are those in which there is no *ratio seminalis* in the matter corresponding to the *ratio causalis* in the divine mind: the first woman, for example, did not have a seminal nature in the rib of the first man. Nature has no part to play in this kind of miracle.[21]

Other miracles, which are called *lesser,* likewise reduce from potency to act through causal reasons alone, but these are actualities which nature would also be capable of producing: the multiplication of the loaves, for example, or the changing of the water to wine, both from the gospel of John.[22] The lowest grade of miracles is that which takes place with the help of nature, namely (as above) those which can speed the natural process of maturation so as to reduce from potency to act more quickly than nature alone would dictate.[23]

What is worrying Fishacre in this passage are the astonishing feats recorded in the book of Exodus: the rods that were turned into serpents by the Pharaoh's magicians and the plague of frogs produced by the same.[24] In a subsequent chapter Fishacre adds the blossoming rod of Aaron and the ass that spoke to Balaam, both examples from the book of Numbers. Though in any given case the question whether the cause be created or uncreated cannot be answered, the principle for Fishacre is clear: of those things wherein dwell seminal reasons, angels as well as saints can effect the kinds of changes listed above; of those without such natures, only God can.[25] He thinks Adam's rib is an example of the latter; the remainder are *probably* examples of the former.[26] However, if Aristotle is correct that we can know only what is actual, it is not within our power to discern potencies, and hence we cannot assert which changes are within the power of the created will (that is, which things contain seminal reasons) and which are reserved to God's power alone.

With the remainder of Fishacre's taxonomy, however, Rufus has considerably greater difficulties. Of those things which, when corrupted, pass into absolute nothingness, namely time, light, every "successive" or series, and the souls of plants and animals, Rufus doubts (*de his forte est dubitatio*) that time and light pass into nothingness and flatly denies (*puto simpliciter esse falsum*) that animal and vegetable souls do.[27]

With respect to the last example, animal and vegetable souls, Fishacre had followed Grosseteste—perhaps uniquely among thirteenth-century scholastics[28]—in holding that animal souls were created *ex nihilo,* not generated by sexual transmission.[29] Furthermore, Fishacre provides four reasons in support of Grosseteste's view[30] and even extends the class to include vegetable souls as well. If therefore animal and vegetable souls were *ex nihilo,* they would have no pre-existent matter to which they would return when corrupted, and hence this is an apt example for Fishacre to use.

Much closer to Aristotle's conception of nature than to Grosseteste's (and Fishacre's), Rufus opposes the immediate creation of animal life, wishing instead to limit the direct intervention of God in the world, and in fact devotes considerable space to the question in his Oxford commentary.[31] If then, in Rufus's view, animal souls are produced from their seminal principles, they would not be reduced to absolute nothingness upon corruption, but to matter.

Rufus's *dubitatio* regarding time and motion and light also betrays very different concepts of these phenomena. The last of these, light, evoked from Fishacre a special *quaestio,* composed in the last years of his life and extant in only two manuscripts.[32] Though Grosseteste devoted considerable attention to light, Fishacre's question had never been asked by Grosseteste, namely, is light a substance or an accident?

Conflating the questions of whether light is body or spirit and whether substance or accident, Fishacre in the end decides that *light* is used equivocally of substance and accident, difficulties arising only when we fail to distinguish between the two usages. Sometimes *light* is the name given to the subtlest of bodily substances; sometimes the same name designates the accident caused by light, namely lighting up or illumination.[33]

However, in his most novel (and most vulnerable) position, Fishacre contends that the matter of light-as-substance neither emanates from the sun nor is bestowed by the air, but is unceasingly created by God on an as-needed basis. A parallel case is the soul, whose matter[34] is created *de novo,* though this does not entail a creation of a new nature that was not a part of the six days: indeed the matter of the soul (and of light) now being created is generically the same as the soul (and light) created in the beginning. There is, however, this difference between the two cases: the components of the entire soul—form and matter—are created together and simultaneously; when light is made, only the matter is created, the form being generated by the luminous body. Thus the sun confers light on the matter which is the ongoing effect of the creative action of God.[35]

Indeed, some things that have been generated have only their matter from their *generans,* as is the case with human progeny, who receive only their matter, not their form, from their parents. Other things, namely angels, emanate as form-matter composites[36] directly from the Creator. The principle of plenitude, therefore, would demand the existence of the only remaining possibility: beings whose matter is supplied by the creative act of God and whose form is provided by another creature, namely the sun.[37] If then light is totally form, its corruption leaves no matter to which it can be reduced. Its corruption, therefore, according to Fishacre's analysis, is into complete nothingness.

Here too Rufus is critical of Fishacre's views (*ista non placent*), especially his theory that God immediately creates the matter for the form which is light. Neither is it the case, he says, that matter is created without form, nor conversely.[38] They both need rather to be con-created by God.[39] In fact, Rufus turns Fishacre's plenitude argument on its head: since there is a being which has neither form nor matter from a creature (the angel), and a being which has only matter from a creature (the human being), receiving its form immediately from God, the *Timaeus* principle would suggest a third category to fill out the possibilities, namely one which has form only from a creature, that is, light which receives its form from the sun.[40]

Light, whose path is intercepted by a solid object, either suddenly returns to its source or is preserved in some manner or other, but is not reduced to absolute nothingness, claims Rufus.[41]

Concerning Fishacre's view of time, there is nothing unusual, nothing unusual that is for the reader of Aristotle. Time is the measure of motion,[42] and is caused by motion.[43] Time is a *successio*,[44] passing from the future through the present into the past.[45] Finally, time is an accident that inheres in the *mobile*, and like the *mobile*, its only reality is the present.[46]

Rufus's view by contrast is, to say the least, odd. Citing Augustine, Rufus finds matter to be the mutability of all mutable things, and thus matter is also the cause of change. But whatever lies within the potentiality of matter, God can restore; thus also time and motion.[47] Furthermore, if God can reconstitute every substance the same in number, a fortiori is he able to restore every accident (that is, time).[48] So far Rufus's arguments fall well within the harbor of traditional understandings.

However, at this point Rufus sets sail into the speculative deep. What if not even the present were real? What if the nature of time and of motion were sheer becoming? Though he admits his puzzlement, especially in the face of the authority of St. Augustine,[49] he concludes that if becoming and succession were the very essence of time, then not even God could recover the past, just as he could not render the following statement true: that what is not, is.[50] If becoming is the very essence of time, then time would recede into absolute nothingness.[51]

Rufus's next gambit is to consider time as a privation of eternity: more precisely, the prior and posterior of time is a privation of the simultaneity of eternity in Boethius's famous definition. Every privation, however, takes its origin from nothingness and is not incongruously returned to nothingness.[52]

The question of God's power over the past, as engaging as the issue is in itself, serves also to reveal more fundamental positions, especially as they highlight the degrees of engagement with the new science introduced by the Aristotelian translations. Rufus's years of experience in the Arts faculty at Paris had brought him a more intimate acquaintance and consequent sympathy with the natural philosophy of Aristotle than his Dominican colleague enjoyed. To the extent that Rufus has managed to understand and follow Aristotle's lead, his criticisms of Fishacre's views are well placed; to the extent that he ventures off on his own, which he does not infrequently, he ends in muddle and confusion.[53]

Finally, in contrast to Rufus, Fishacre is willing to ascribe more to divine intervention, thereby granting more to God's power. Though he stops short of affirming a *potentia absoluta* doctrine, he is paradoxically closer to that view, which will later be associated with the Franciscans, than his Franciscan colleague, Rufus.

NOTES

1. Petrus Lombardus, *In Sent.* 2. d. 25.1 (ed. Quaracchi 1:461).

2. We date the Fishacre Commentary between 1241 and 1245; see R. James Long and Maura O'Carroll, *The Life and Works of Richard Fishacre OP: Prolegomena to the Edition of His Commentary on the "Sentences"* (Munich: Bavarian Academy of Sciences, 1999), 39–42. For a complete bibliography see pp. 225–28.

3. The question itself dates back to Peter Damian (1007–1072), who had argued in his *De divina omnipotentia* that God can bring it about that a past event did not happen, the principle being that what is impossible in time is possible in eternity (PL 145:612); see Etienne Gilson, *History of Christian Philosophy in the Middle Ages* (New York: Random House, 1955), 616; David Knowles, *The Evolution of Medieval Thought* (London: Longmans, 1962), 96–97; and F. C. Copleston, *A History of Medieval Philosophy* (London: Methuen, 1972), 67.

4. Peter Raedts was the first to call attention to this question, and I derived much profit from reading his study; see *Richard Rufus of Cornwall and the Tradition of Oxford Theology* (Oxford: Clarendon Press, 1987), 217–20. Raedts also remains the most authoritative source for the life and works of Richard Rufus; see especially ibid., chapter 1, 1–13. Raedts dates the Rufus Commentary c. 1250 (5).

5. This question invites the celebrated distinction between God's ordained power (*potentia ordinata*) and his absolute power (*potentia absoluta*), but there is mention of such a distinction neither in Fishacre's treatment nor Rufus's rebuttal thereof. For an exhaustive treatment of the origin and development of this distinction, see Lawrence Moonan, *Divine Power: The Medieval Power Distinction up to Its Adoption by Albert, Bonaventure, and Aquinas* (Oxford: Clarendon, 1994). Though Moonan has identified the Distinction in Rufus's Balliol Commentary at book 1, distinction 42 (317–18), he has found no such usage in Fishacre's Commentary.

6. See Appendix A §8.

7. Appendix B §2.

8. Appendix A §4.

9. Appendix A §6.

10. Appendix A §4.

11. Appendix A §5. Examples of such miracles abound in the *Vitae fratrum,* compiled by Gerard Fracheto, OP, at the request of Humbert of Romans, the Dominican Master General. Though Fracheto's collection postdates Fishacre, he certainly would have heard many of the stories recorded there. For another collection of *exempla,* compiled by a younger contemporary of Fishacre's, see Stephen L. Forte, "A Cambridge Dominican Collector of Exempla," *Archivum Fratrum Praedicatorum* 28 (1955): 115–48; note especially no. 32.

12. Appendix A §6.

13. Appendix A §7.

14. Appendix A §8–10.

15. Raedts, 217.

16. Ibid., n. 66.

17. "Duplex est materiae potentia: scilicet potentia passiva, quae est receptiva formae; et activa, et haec est aliquid formae latitans in materia. Et haec ab Augustino vocatur *ratio seminalis.* Haec autem ratio seminalis in materia habet rationes causales in Deo sibi correspondentes." *In Sent.* 2. d. 7.6. In a subsequent chapter Fishacre explicitly connects the Augustinian and Aristotelian doctrines: "Et tertia [opinio] media, quae est Aristotelis, quae ponit nec formas omnino latere nec omnino esse ab extrinseco, sed aliquid eius latere (et hoc est potentia activa materiae, quam hic Augustinus vocat *rationem seminalem*) et aliquid eius esse ab extrinseco agente, scilicet complementum et actus." *In Sent.* 2. d. 7.8.

18. "DISTINCTIONES FORMARUM, ut sint res actualiter distinctae, sicut eorum potentiae erant distinctae in materia, scilicet eorum potentiae activae, quae tot sunt quot sunt et formae in materia. De potentia autem materiae passiva patet quod haec est unica et non plures." *In Sent.* 2. d. 7.8.

19. "Possibile est igitur rationes seminales educi de potentia in actum dupliciter. Vel per rationes causales immediate; et cum aliquid oratione sanctorum sic fit insolitum fieri, *miraculum* vocatur. Cum autem educatur in actum mediantibus aliis agentibus, hoc potest esse dupliciter: scilicet ut hoc agat natura tantum media, et tunc *naturale* dicitur, non *miraculosum;* aut natura cum principio quod est voluntas, et hoc vel bona, ut angeli, vel mala, ut diaboli, ut fiunt haec magica a diabolo et natura educentibus rationes seminales materiae de potentia in actum." *In Sent.* 2. d. 7.6.

20. Ibid., "Si qua autem educant boni angeli de potentia in actum, non immerito dubitatur. Simul dico *cum natura,* ut sicut mali adhibitis quibusdam maturantibus rationes seminales educunt aliquid de potentia in actum citius quam hoc consueverit facere natura, similiter hoc faciant angeli. Constat enim si hoc facere possunt mali, multo potentius et excellentius possent et boni. Quod si aliqua mira et insolita sic fierent, non multum distarent ab his quae magicae fiunt; utrobique enim agit voluntas creata et natura. Quae autem educuntur de potentia ad actum inconsuete ab ipsis rationibus causalibus immediate, talia vere et proprie miracula sunt."

21. Ibid., "Sunt enim plures rationes causales quae non habent seminales sibi correspondentes in materia, sicut mulier habuit rationem causalem in mente divina, sed non habuit seminalem in costa forte. Et talia cum fiunt, ita fiunt a Deo quod a natura nullo modo fieri possent. Et haec sunt maxima miracula."

22. Ibid., "Sunt autem aliqua quae educuntur de potentia seminali in actum per rationes causales tantum, quae tamen posset natura producere, ut fuit panum multiplicatio et aquae in vinum mutatio. Et haec sunt minora miracula." In what sense nature would be able to effect these results is not clear to me.

23. Ibid., "Minima autem si adiutorio naturae haec fiant, scilicet adhibitis aliquibus maturantibus citius quam natura faceret. Quorum si aliqua fiant a bonis angelis, nescio; scio tamen quod fieri possent. A malis, quia talia fiant, non dubito, Deo tamen cum voluerit permittente."

24. Exodus 7:12; 8:7. The apocryphal literature produced its own examples: Fishacre mentions Simon Magus, who made dogs sing, from the Acts of Peter, and Merlin, who was generated from an incubus, from a source I have not been able to discover.

25. Here, as elsewhere (e.g. *In Sent.* 2. d. 8.3), Fishacre exhibits a fondness for the distance metaphor: there is a finite distance between an active potency and act, and therefore the traversing of that distance requires only a finite power; whereas there is an infinite distance between pure matter (or pure nothingness) and act, and therefore, etc. "Sed producere de potentia activa in actum non est potentiae infinitae, quia inter talem actum et talem potentiam non est infinita distantia. Sed potest hoc potentia finita voluntatis bonae, ut angeli, vel malae, ut diaboli; tamen simul cum natura." *In Sent.* 2. d. 7.8.

26. "Cum enim ex virga magorum et Moysi fiebant serpentes, huius causa non fuit tantum in Deo, sed et fuerunt rationes seminales serpentium in materia virgae. Igitur multo fortius rationes seminales fructus fuerunt in virga Aaron. Et etiam ubicumque aliquid fit in materia non habente rationes seminales illius quod fit in ea, necessario est creatio. Sed quis dicat virgam Aaron fructificasse per creationem? vel asinum locutum per novi alicuius creationem? Si etiam ministerio daemonum agentium virgae mutatae sunt in serpentes, quomodo non ministerio eorum possent virgae fructificare? Et ita non solus Deus potest illas rationes seminales in actum educere. Solutio. Eorum quae praeter naturam fiunt in natura duo sunt genera: quorumdam enim rationes seminales sunt in materia; quorumdam vero non. Et haec tantum potest Deus; alia vero possunt ad minus angeli. In costa vero, ut aestimo, nec fuerunt rationes seminales ad corpus mulieris. Et ideo hoc potuit solus Deus. In virga vero fructificante, ut aestimo, fuerunt rationes fructus. Et ideo licet natura tunc non possunt educere de potentia in actum, tamen Deus et angeli hoc poterant. Immo quod per angelum hoc factum non sit quis sciat? Quod ergo supra dixit: QUORUM CAUSAE SUNT TANTUM IN DEO, intellige non causa qua fiant, sed qua tam repente fiant. Si dicas *immo*, et in angelis et in daemonibus. Credo quod ipsi rationem causae efficientis in naturalibus non habeant proprie, sicut nec agricolae vel medici; nec floruit virga vel loquebatur asinus quibusdam appositis, sicut per daemones virgae mutatae sunt in serpentes." *In Sent.* 2. d. 18.5.

27. Appendix B §3.

28. Raedts first claims the uniqueness of Grosseteste's view on the creation of animal life (*Richard Rufus of Cornwall*, 162), then admits that Fishacre also held this view, but that "he is dependent on Grosseteste" (n. 32).

29. "Salva tamen pace maiorum videtur mihi quod creatur et non educitur brutalis anima vel vegetabilis, cum sint spiritus, de potentia in actum." *In Sent.* 2. d. 15.1. Cf. Robert Grosseteste, *Hexaemeron,* ed. R. C. Dales and S. Gieben (Oxford: Oxford University, 1982), 200. See also Dales, *The Problem of the Rational Soul in the Thirteenth Century* (Leiden: Brill, 1995), 57.

30. "Cuius est multiplex ratio. Prima: si enim hi spiritus essent seminaliter in corporibus in quibus fiunt et inde in actum producerentur, videtur quod multo fortius rationalis esset seminaliter in anima sensibili et vegetabili et per consequens in corpore. Substantia enim genus generalissimum primo dividitur in corpoream et in incorpoream, id est in spiritum et corpus. Igitur hae duae naturae minime conveniunt prae ceteris in eodem genere, quia in solo genere generalissimo; alia vero in generalissimo et subalterno, et ideo haec differunt maxime. Igitur si haec ex se invicem producerentur et sibi invicem inessent seminaliter, multo fortius et alia minus

distantia, scilicet omnia. Item, cum brutalis anima forma sit et tamen aliter quam igneitas, quae tantum est forma—anima enim componitur ex materia et forma—si ipsa educitur de corpore in actum, utrumque accipit a corpore. Sed si materiam accipit a corpore, necessario fieret corpus minus, per hoc quod ab ipso esset anima. Quod nemo dicit. Item, si mediante corpore caelesti educeretur in actum, sicut et corpora, igitur proficeret et senesceret per motum corporum caelestium, sicut corpora. Quod non est verum, quia ut dicit Aristoteles: 'Si senex acciperet oculum iuvenis, videret sicut iuvenis.' Item, quanto aliquid nobilius, tanto simplicius, et econtrario. Igitur cum omnis spiritus omni corpore sit nobilior, ut dicit Augustinus, necessario erit et simplicior et per consequens indivisibilioris essentiae. Sed nobilissimum corpus, scilicet lux, est tam simplicis essentiae ut non distet in eo actus et potentia. Non enim educitur lux de potentia in actum. Sed quam cito aliquid est eius, perfectum est in genere lucis. Nec est aliqua materia ante hanc lucem in qua sit haec lux in potentia vel seminaliter, sicut est in aliis corporibus. Igitur multo magis similiter est in spiritibus." *In Sent.* 2. d. 15.1.

    31. See Raedts, *Richard Rufus of Cornwall*, 163–69, for a good summary.

    32. The question has been edited and published: see R. James Long and Timothy B. Noone. "Fishacre and Rufus on the Metaphysics of Light: Two Unedited Texts," in *Roma, magistra mundi: Itineraria culturae medievalis. Mélanges offerts au Père L.E. Boyle à l' occasion de son 75e anniversaire*, Textes et Études du moyen âge, 10, ed. Jacqueline Hamesse (Louvain-la-Neuve: Fédération Internationale des Instituts d' Études Médiévales, 1998), 517–48. The *quaestio de luce* is not found in any of the remaining seven manuscripts which contain the second book of the Fishacre Commentary.

    33. Ibid., 533–34, §19–20.

    34. Fishacre, like the majority of his contemporaries, embraced a doctrine of spiritual matter (or universal hylomorphism); see R. James Long, "Richard Fishacre and the Problem of the Soul," *The Modern Schoolman* 52 (1975): 267–69.

    35. Long and Noone, "Fishacre and Rufus," 535, §24–25.

    36. Angels, like human souls, are for Fishacre composed of form and matter: see R. James Long, "Of Angels and Pinheads: The Contributions of the Early Oxford Masters to the Doctrine of Spiritual Matter," *Franciscan Studies* 56 (1998): 239–54.

    37. Long and Noone, "Fishacre and Rufus," 535–36, §26–28.

    38. Ibid., 543, §43.

    39. Ibid., 542–43, §41–42.

    40. Ibid., §42. I omit mention here of an equally strange theory on Rufus's part, namely, light as *forma-habitus*. This odd hybrid, which did not survive its creator, was dubbed by Noone a "metaphysical novelty," 525.

    41. Ibid., §27.

    42. "Tempus est mensura motus," *In Sent.* 2. d. 2.5.

    43. ". . . in primo instanti temporis non fuit tempus, quia mutatio est causa temporis; et ideo cum non fuit mutatio, non fuit tempus." Ibid. Cf. idem: " . . . tempus sit mensura motus praecipue corporum caelestium, erit tempus aut mensura revolutionis imperfectae aut perfectae." *In Sent.* 2. d. 14.11.

    44. See Fishacre, *De creatione vel inchoatione mundi*, ed. R. James Long, in "The First Oxford Debate on the Eternity of the World," *Recherches de théologie et philosophie médiévales* 65,1 (1998): 85–86.

    45. "Uno enim modo tempus dicitur tantum quod a futuro per praesens transit in praeteritum." *In Sent.* 2. d. 14.10.

46. "Tempus est mensura motus primi mobilis per se et primo; et est in illo motu vel in illo mobili tamquam in subiecto. Alioquin quomodo esset tempus unum accidens numero, nisi haberet unum subiectum numero?" *In Sent.* 2. d. 3.4.

47. See Appendix B §12.

48. Ibid., §13.

49. Ibid., §15. He recalls Augustine's taxonomy: the present of past events (memory), the present of present events (contuition or simultaneous awareness), and the present of the future (anticipation).

50. Ibid. §14–15.

51. Ibid. §22. Raedts summarizes the position as follows: "But if time's essence is becoming, then it is reduced to nothing, because 'becoming' is contrary to 'being.' On the other hand, if the substance theory of time has any justification, then it looks as if time cannot be reduced to nothing. So far the argument is clear" (*Richard Rufus of Cornwall*, 219).

52. Appendix B, §24.

53. At least two years in the grave when Rufus's Commentary appeared, Fishacre never had the opportunity for rebuttal. One can well imagine, however, that, as Anselm did to Gaunilon, he would have pointed out some of the confusions of his fellow Oxonian.

APPENDIX A
RICHARD FISHACRE, *IN 2 SENT*. D. 25.1

The following text[1] was edited from the following six manuscripts:[2]

Bologna, Biblioteca Universitaria MS 1546, f. 162^{ra-b} (=*B*)

Cambridge, Gonville & Caius College MS 329/410, ff. 228vb–229ra (=*C*)

Oxford, Oriel College MS 43 (B 4.3), f. 206^{ra-b} (=*O*)

Paris, Bibliothèque Nationale MS 15754, f. 118vb (=*P*)

London, British Library MS Royal 10.B.VII, f. 158va (=*R*)

Vatican City, Biblioteca Apostolica Vaticana, Ottob. lat. MS 294, f. 252vb (=*V*)

I have followed the convention of numbering paragraphs for ease of reference. Spelling has been standardized for ease of access, and punctuation follows modern norms.

1. HOC AUTEM SCIENDUM, hic determinat respectu quorum actuum exteriorum dicatur *liberum arbitrium;* AD PRAESENS VEL PRAETERITUM NON REFERTUR, non enim[a] est liberum non fieri quod factum est vel quod sit. Quaeritur autem an liberum arbitrium Dei possit in praeteritum.

2. Quod si non, videbitur aliqua eius impotentia.

a. quia O.

3. Contra. *Luc.* 1: "Non erit impossibile apud Deum omne verbum."[3]

4. Solutio. Posse in praeteritum est dupliciter, scilicet posse ut res quae praeteriit iterum sit, et hoc variatur sicut et res. Rerum autem tria sunt genera. Quaedam enim cum corrumpuntur, cedunt in penitus nihilum forsitan non assero, ut tempus, lux, et omne successivum, et anima sensibilis et vegetabilis brutorum et plantarum. Quaedam vero cum corrumpuntur, resolvuntur in materiam[b] puram carentem omni ratione seminali, ut tantum sit in ea potentia passiva. Quaedam vero resolvuntur in materiam habentem rationes seminales.

5. Et tale praeteritum potest natura reparare, idem quidem specie, non numero, et tempore determinato ante, quod tempus non potest illud homo reparare, nisi sanctus aliquis per miraculum vel angelus.

6. Sed[c] idem numero reparare solius Dei est, quia hoc est secundum aliquid creatio. Multo maius autem miraculum et maioris potentiae est reparare de materia, in qua non est residua ratio seminalis idem numero. Sed summae potentiae est redactum in penitus nihilum in idem numero reparare.

7. Quod si posse est, potest Deus, qui[d] potest omne quod posse est. Quod Deum nusquam fecisse reperi, nec si uspiam hoc fecerit, nescio. Secundum hos ergo, ut patet, modos potest Deus in praeteritum, nos vero non.

8. Sed aliter est posse in praeteritum, scilicet ut quod fuit non fuerit. Et in hoc nec liberum arbitrium creatum nec increatum potest. Unde Augustinus, *Contra Faustum* lib. 2: " Quidquid praeteritum est, iam non est, quod si de ipso aliquid fieri potest, adhuc est, de quo fiat, et si est, quomodo[e] praeteritum est?" [4] Non est ergo quod vere dicimus *fuisse*. Sed ideo verum est illud *fuisse*, quia in nostra sententia verum est, non in ea re quae iam non est. Hanc sententiam Deus falsam facere non potest, quia non est contrarius veritati.

9. Quod si quaeras ubi sit haec sententia vera, prius invenitur in animo nostro, cum id verum scimus et dicimus.[f] Sed si de animo nostro ablata fuerit, manebit in ipsa veritate. Semper enim verum erit fuisse illud quod erat et non est.

10. Et ibi verum erit iam fuisse quod erat, ubi verum erat antequam fieret futurum esse, quod non erat. Huic veritati Deus non potest adversari, in quo est ipsa summa et incommutabilis[g] veritas. Qua illustratur ut sit, quidquid in quorumcumque animis verum est.

---

b. omnino *add.* O.

c. nota ex gravo corrupto producit natura aliquid gravum idem specie; sed illud idem numero iam corruptum impossibile est naturae reparare; reparat autem idem specie *add. marg.* C.

d. quia R.

e. quo O.

f. *corr. ex* dominus O.

g. immutabilis C.

Notes

1. Book Two of Fishacre's Commentary, from which this text is excerpted, will shortly be published by the Bayerische Akademie der Wissenschaften in Munich.

2. For a complete description of these manuscripts see Long and O'Carroll, *Life and Works* 57–197.

3. Luke 1:37.

4. Augustine, *Contra Faustum* 26.5 (CSEL 25:732).

Appendix B
Richard Rufus, *In 2 Sent.* d. 25.1

The following text was edited from Oxford, Balliol College MS 62, ff. 166^(va)–167^(ra) (=*Ba*). Direct and *verbotenus* citations from the Fishacre Commentary are italicized and enclosed in quotation marks. As in Appendix A, paragraphs are numbered, and spelling has been standardized.

1. AD PRAESENS VEL AD PRAETERITUM REFERTUR. In secunda[a]

parte est. Et quaeritur an liberum arbitrium Dei possit in praeteritum. Quod si non, videtur Deus esse impotens.

2. Respondetur quod " *posse in praeteritum dupliciter est, scilicet vel posse facere ut id quod fuit non fuerit, vel posse facere ut res quae praeteriit iterum sit.*" Primum non potest Deus facere. Nam hoc non est posse, quod satis docet Augustinus, *Contra Faustum* lib. 25, dicens: Hoc idem est ac si diceres: "faciat Deus, ut ea quae vera sunt eo ipso, quo vera sunt, ut falsa sint. . . . '*Quidquid praeteritum est, iam non est: quod si de ipso fieri aliquid potest, adhuc est, de quo fiat, et si est, quomodo praeteritum est?*'"[1] Quis ergo dicat ut id quod iam non est, faciat non esse. Ergo nec quod factum est nec quod praeteritum est, potest facere quod non sit praeteritum. Nec potest facere quod sit praeteritum, quia iam factum est praeteritum. "Huic veritati (quod praeteritum est praeteriit) Deus non potest adversari, in quo est summa et incommutabilis veritas, qua illustratur ut sit quidquid in quorumque animis verum est."[2]

3. Hoc modo ergo non potest Deus in praeteritum, sed secundo modo potest. Distinguitur tamen ibi quod " *rerum tria sunt genera: quaedam enim cum corrumpuntur, cedunt in pure nihil, ut anima vegetabilis et sensibilis in plantis et brutis.*" Quod pure falsum est. Iterum, " *ut tempus, motus, et lux, et omne successivum.*" De his forte est dubitatio.

4. "*Quaedam vero cum corrumpuntur, resolvuntur in materiam puram, carentem omni ratione seminali, ut solum remaneat in ea potentia passiva.*" Et istud puto simpliciter esse falsum. Nam

a. A *add. marg.* Ba.

secundum hoc redigerentur omnes formae generales in materia in pure nihil, de quarum numero sunt rationes seminales, nihil sic corrumpitur.

5. "*Quaedam iterum resolvuntur in materiam habentem rationes seminales, et tale praeteritum dicunt posse naturam reparare; idem quidem specie, non numero.*"

6. Sed intellige quod quidquid corrumpitur, hoc modo corrumpitur. Et non potest universaliter tale praeteritum natura reparare; nec idem specie nec numero.

7. "*Idem numero reparare solius Dei est,*" et de materia in qua non est residua ratio seminalis ut dicunt idem numero reparare, magnum est miraculum. Sed valde maius est in penitus nihilum redactum, idem numero reparare. Quod si posse est, potest Deus qui potest omne quod posse est.

8. Sed non est dubium quin Deus hoc possit eadem ratione qua primam creaturam de pure nihilo creavit.

9. His ergo modis potest liberum arbitrium Dei in praeteritum, scilicet de materia in qua est residua ratio seminalis, idem numero reparare et etiam in pure nihilum redactum sine omni materia. Et primo modo istorum forte faciet in resurrectione.

10. Et quaeritur hic in primis qua /Ba 166ᵛᵇ/ de causa non potest natura facereᵇ redire idem numero per viam generationis: verbi gratia, ex A igne generetur B aer. Quare non potest ex B aere generari A ignis, sed alius numero.

11. Ecce ignis qui generabit ex B aere ignem generaret si possibile esset ignem sibi numero eundem. Generat autem quantum possibile est sibi propinquum, et aliquid sui, scilicet formam communicat generato. Ergo quia A nihil est ipsius generantis—nam A non est in actu—ideo iste generans, alium numero generat ab ipso A. Et etiam a seipso generante. Generans enim generat aliud propter materiam; et non generat aliud nisi propter materiam. Unde si esset agens nullo modo patiens, et faceret de B aere ignem, posset indifferenter vel A ignem vel alium de ipso B facere. Hoc ergo potest Deus et natura non, quia generans physice partem suae substantiae communicat generato.

12. Utrum autem Deus possit quodcumque praeteritum idem numero redire facere posset quaeri. Et videtur quod sic. Nam sive illud quod corrumpitur cedat in pure nihil—potest enim illud Deus ex pure nihilo creare, sicut et prius fecit—sive illud cedat in aliquid ens et manens. Nam sic est ipsum ens in potentia. Facilius autem est de ente in potentia facere ens in actu. Quaeritur ergo de motu et tempore an possit facere idem numero redire. Et videtur iterum quod sic. Nam omnia accidentia causantur in substantia ex materia, ut vult Philosophus,³ et praecipue quantitas.

13. Et idem videtur per Augustinum *Confessionum* lib. 12: Materia est ipsa "mutabilitas rerum mutabilium."⁴ Tempora autem fiunt rerum mutationibus dum variantur et vertuntur species. Ergo materia ipsa causa est temporis. Et de hoc dictum est alias. Quidquid autem est in potentiis materiae potest Deus idem reparare. Ergo tempus et motum.

b. *corr. ex* non facere Ba.

14. Item, omnem substantiam eandem numero potest reparare. Ergo et omne accidens. Nam si eandem causam numero, et eundum effectum.

15. Contra: quidditas et substantia motus et temporis est ipsum fieri. Ergo si non potest Deus facere praeteritionem esse praesentialitatem, non poterit facere praeteritum praesens. Nec est tempus aliqua natura subiecta his rationibus: praeteritum, praesens, futurum.

16. Contra istud videtur quod vult Augustinus *Confessionum* lib. 11: "Tempora sunt tria . . . praesens de praeteritis memoria, praesens de praesentibus contuitus, praesens de futuris expectatio."[5] Nescio. Sed si est tempus aliqua natura subiecta his rationibus, sicut velle videtur etiam Philosophus: signum idem est quod semper fertur secundum esse solum differens, sicut idem in foro et in theatro.[6] Et si instans est tota substantia temporis, non solum hoc potest Deus, sed et facit ut idem numero sit semper secundum esse solum fore et praeteritum esse. Si autem ipsum fieri et succedere sit substantia et quidditas ipsius temporis, non potest Deus facere praeteritum redire, sicut non potest facere ut istud sit verum: quod non est, est. Nec potest facere ut eo sit aliquid falsum, quo ipsum est verum. Non est enim veritati contrarius.

17. Ait Augustinus, *Contra Iulianum* lib. 6: "Actus est qui opere ipso peragitur, et non erit; et si iterum fit, alterum fit."[7]

18. Non potest autem Deus facere ut duo tempora sint simul. Nam hoc esset duo tempora esse unum tempus. Unde si potest Deus idem tempus numero reparare, hoc fieret alio tempore non exsistente.

19. Item, quaeritur[c] si ista possint cedere in pure nihil. Et videtur quod nulla creatura omnino cedat in pure nihil per Augustinum in libro *De immortalitate animae:* Deus "praesenti potentia tenet universum. Non enim fecit atque dicessit effectumque deseruit. . . . Et item illa effectoria vis vacare non potest quin id, quod ab ea factum est, tueatur. . . . Quod enim per se non est, si destituatur ab eo <per> quod est, profecto non erit."[8]

20. Item, de corpore loquens ait. Non enim eius pars ad nihilum redigi sinitur, cum totum capescat vis illa effectoria /Ba 167ʳᵃ/ nec laborante nec deside potentia, dans ut sit omne quod per ipsam est in quantum est.

21. Sed hic posset responderi quod Augustinus intelligit de eis quorum esse est in factum esse.

22. Unde dici posset quod si substantia et quidditas temporis et motus est ipsum fieri et succedere, transit praeteritum in nihil, quia ipsum quidquid est ratio opposita enti est. Si autem aliquid subiectum est his rationibus illud non cedit in pure nihil.

23. Sicut autem dictum est: si ipsum fieri est tota substantia temporis, tunc cedit tempus in pure nihil.

24. Sed posito quod Deus vellet auferre omne tempus, numquid istud redigeretur in pure nihil?

c. B *add. marg.* Ba.

25. Dicendum quod mutabilitas non maneret, potentia tamen materiae maneret, nec est mutabilitas creatura nec natura, sed privatio. Quod patet sic. Aeternitas est integra vitae possessio, tota simul.[9] Huius simultatis privatio est prius et posterius temporis vere et formaliter tam tempus quam motus mutatio vel mutabilitas est et privatio est. Nam immutabilitas verissimus habitus, verissima firmitas et stabilitas est. Ergo mutabilitas privatio. Omnis autem privatio originem ducit ex nihilo. Unde privationes in pure nihil redigi non est inconveniens. Sed natura, scilicet aliquid et ens numquam in pure nihil redigitur.

26. Futurum et futuritio videtur aliquid esse in potentia materiae et praesens aliquid in actu et forma materiae. Praeteritum vero videtur dicere non aliquid et ens in actu materiae, sed forte aliquid in potentia materiae.

27. De luce autem in medio et in obiecto interposito aliquo umbroso inter visum et obiectum, quocumque deveniat sive subito in suam originem redeat, sive alio quocumque modo salvetur, non credo quod cedat in pure nihil.

NOTES

1. Augustine, *Contra Faustum Manichaeum* 26.5 (CSEL 25:732–33).
2. Ibid., (733).
3. See Aristotle, *Physics* 1.9 (192a15–16).
4. Augustine, *Confessiones* 12.6 (CCL 27:219).
5. Augustine, *Confessiones* 11.20 (CCL 27:207).
6. Vide forsitan Boethius, *In Categorias Aristotelis* 1 (PL 64:172).
7. Augustine, *Contra Iulianum Pelagianum* 6.19 (PL 44:860).
8. Augustine, *De immortalitate animae* 8.14 (CSEL 89:116).
9. Boethius, *De consolatione philosophiae* 5, 6, 4. Cf. *Auctoritates Aristotelis*, ed. J. Hamesse (Louvain, 1974), 293, § 86.

Chapter 4

The Real Distinction and the Principles of Metaphysics

Avicenna and Aquinas

R. E. HOUSER

It is well recognized that Thomas Aquinas held the metaphysical doctrine of the real distinction between essence and existence in creatures from the beginning of his writing career, and that he took it from Avicenna.[1] Aquinas's *mode of arguing* for this truth, however, has occasioned dispute. One reason for this is the way that Aquinas made use of the difficult text of Avicenna. E. Gilson said, "What Thomas attributes to Avicenna is always found there, but Thomas cites more ideas and doctrines than passages."[2] The passages can be found, but Aquinas's way of summarizing and simplifying Avicenna—for "his brothers and companions when he was not yet a Master" as Tolomeo of Lucca described his writing *De ente et essentia*—has made it difficult to see how much he depended on the Vizier.[3]

The place essence and existence hold within the structure of metaphysical science sets the argumentative strategy for establishing the real distinction between them. If the real distinction is a conclusion, Aquinas should offer a demonstration of it; if a principle, then dialectical argument seems in order. Avicenna had treated the real distinction in the course of presenting his metaphysical principles in Book 1, chapters 5–7, of the *Metaphysics* of his *Shifâ*. Br. Thomas used these chapters in treating the real distinction in *EE*. Comparing the two shows, I believe, that Avicenna held the real distinction between essence and existence in creatures to be a metaphysical principle for which he argued dialectically, not a demonstrated conclusion or an unargued thesis. Young Br. Thomas then followed the Vizier's mode of argument as well as adopting his doctrine.[4]

Aristotle had said that every science has three parts—subject, principles, and demonstrated conclusions—to which neoplatonizing Aristotelians like Avicenna added a fourth, an end distinct from its subject. Before the demonstrative part of his metaphysics (Books 2–10), Avicenna devoted Book 1 to clarifying these four points. The only subject universal enough for metaphysics is being, which "immediately is impressed in our soul in the first impression"[5]; while God is the end of metaphysics, not its subject (1.1–2). After outlining the range of conclusions as a kind of table of contents (1.3–4), Avicenna devoted chapters 5–8 to the principles he would use in subsequent demonstrations. Aristotle had distinguished three kinds of principles: common or universal axioms and two sorts of principles proper to each science, hypotheses and definitions. As a kind of reasoning, demonstration presupposes notions and propositions, and therefore takes its principles from these two prior acts of the mind.[6] So Avicenna understood definitions to be principles that are *notions,* while hypotheses are principles that are *judgments* or *propositions.* He presented the fundamental notions of metaphysics at 1.5, its fundamental propositions at 1.6–7, and the common axioms at 1.8.

In *EE,* young Br. Thomas focused on the principles of metaphysics, as he also did for natural philosophy in *De principiis naturae.*[7] He therefore set aside the subject and conclusions of metaphysics, opening his little work thus:

> Since a slight error in principle (*in principio*) grows to great proportions in the end (*in fine*), as the Philosopher says in *On the Heavens* 1, being (*ens*) and essence (*essentia*) are what the intellect first conceives, as Avicenna says at the outset of his *Metaphysics.*[8]

Principle and *end* here allude to beginning and end in time, to be sure, but more important is their scientific meaning. Following Avicenna, Br. Thomas set out the end of metaphysics in the last sentence of the work, a prayer to the God who is its "end and consummation."[9] But his little treatise is mainly devoted to the *principles* of metaphysics, since ignorance about them prevents one from reaching that end.

Br. Thomas's presentation of those principles in *EE* closely follows Avicenna. He devoted *EE* 1 to the fundamental *notions* of metaphysics, parallel to Avicenna, *Metaphysics* 1.5. He then devoted *EE* 2–4 to arguments supporting its fundamental *hypotheses* or basic propositions, with EE 4 parallel to Avicenna, *Metaphysics* 1.6–7. Aquinas summarized his results about substance at *EE* 5, which is parallel to the last part of Avicenna, *Metaphysics* 1.7. He completed his little treatise with some conclusions about accidents, not found in Avicenna, *Metaphysics* 1, but based upon his Book 3. To understand Aquinas's dependence upon Avicenna, and thereby his own arguments and doctrine, it is helpful to change slightly the order both philosophers follow. Let us look first at the fundamental notions and hypotheses of metaphysics before turning to the dialectical arguments used by Avicenna and Aquinas in support of them.

THE PRIMARY *NOTIONS* OF METAPHYSICS FOR AVICENNA (*MET.* 1.5)

Since Avicenna thought of metaphysics as a universal science, no lower branch of a Porphyrian tree—a species—nor even a higher genus-branch—the ten categories—is universal enough to be one of its *proper* notions. But once a metaphysician steps back to gaze on the categories, he sees even higher branches, which constitute the lofty realm of metaphysics. The categories now seem "like species." There must be *some* primary notions wider than the categories, because humans know through definitions which resort to higher and higher genera. "But if every notion required a higher notion there would be an infinite regress or circularity," which would undermine knowledge by basing it on unknown terms.[10] But what are they?

The easiest way to identify them is to look for the *concepts* presupposed by the *proposition* Aristotle said was the very first principle of all thought, now called the principle of non-contradiction. "If the *terms* signifying" such a principle "are not understood," then the principle itself would be lost.[11] The principle says that *some thing cannot both be and not be,* which clearly presupposes the notions of *being, thing, impossible,* and *not.* Since negatives are secondary to positives, Avicenna listed three fundamental notions:

> We say: Being (*al-mawjûd; ens*) and thing (*al-shay'; res*) and necessary (*al-darûrî; necesse*) are those <whose notions are> impressed on the soul in a first impression, which are not acquired from others more known than they are.[12]

This is the text of Avicenna to which Br. Thomas referred at the outset of *EE.* Here Avicenna lists the three absolutely universal notions that are proper principles of metaphysics. He recognized other transcendental notions—*one, true,* and *good*—but these are primary, since every proposition presupposes them because it presupposes the principle of non-contradiction.

Defining them through higher genera is impossible, but Avicenna argued for these primary notions in two ways. The first is to look back down the Porphyrian tree, using lesser notions as "signs" of them. Categories like action and passion illustrate what *being* means, while lower species, such as triangle and white, are Avicenna's examples of *thing.*[13] *Being* and *thing* are thus understood on the model of genera, which stand over the categories conceived as "quasi-species."

Avicenna's second technique was to substitute synonyms for these terms. *Being* is illustrated by the notions of the *established* and *realized,* which point to actuality. *Thing* has for synonyms *true nature,* which signifies determinate intelligible content, and *quiddity,* which points to definition.[14] *Established* and *realized* are not in point of fact notions separate from *being,* any more than *true nature* and *quiddity* are separate from *thing.* Such definitions might seem nugatory, but they can lead the mind to insight into the meaning of fundamental notions. They also allow us to use one of these notions to define another. Such definitions, while circular, open up a kind of reduction where claims can be translated from one language to another. Avicenna defines *necessity* this way, as the "assuredness of existence."[15]

Avicenna's two argumentative techniques produce an important analogy involving the language of *being.* To render the Greek language of being into Arabic, the translators turned to the verb "to find (*wajada,* he found)." The concrete and substantive notion of "a being," captured in Greek by the active participle ὄν, was rendered by the passive participle *mawjûd* (lit., "the found"), while the verbal noun *wujûd* signified more abstractly the aspect of a concrete thing that is its "being" or "existence." When translating Avicenna into Latin, Dominicus Gundissalinus turned *mawjûd* into the Latin active participle *ens,* which corresponds exactly to ὄν. The verbal noun *wujûd* was sometimes translated by an abstract noun like *entitas,* but Gundissalinus perceptively chose the infinitive *esse.* Avicenna's analogy compares these universal terms for being with being in an individual. When being is considered universally it includes the categories of passion and action. Likewise, each individual being (*mawjûd; ens*) includes two principles analogous to passion and action: a potency for being "realized," which is quiddity and is signified by the term "thing" (*shay'; res*), and an act analogous to the category of action, signified by the term "existence" (*wujûd; esse*).

Avicenna listed only two of these three terms among the primary notions: *being* and *thing* are there but *existence* is omitted. Existence is implicit in *being* but it is not listed because Avicenna's task is to present the primordial *notions* falling into the mind through its first act, apprehending *concepts.* But *existence* is peculiar, since it is understood through the mind's second act, the act of making judgments. Since he is concerned only with concepts, Avicenna listed only the terms appropriate to treating concepts. By the end of Avicenna's *Metaphysics* 1.5, one critical point at least is clear: "the *notion* of being and the *notion* of thing are conceived in the soul (and are) *two notions.*"[16] At this point, then, Avicenna has established dialectically a *conceptual* distinction between essence and existence, though not yet a *real* distinction.

THE PRIMARY *NOTIONS* OF METAPHYSICS FOR AQUINAS (*EE* 1)

When young Br. Thomas mentioned the primary notions of metaphysics in the first sentence of *EE,* he himself tells us he had borrowed the notions of *being* (*ens*) and *essence* (*essentia,* a term more familiar to his audience than *thing, res*) from Avicenna. He also omitted *esse,* presumably for the same reason Avicenna had done so. In order to simplify Avicenna's complicated thought for his confreres, he dropped the modal term *necessary*. But Avicenna himself had authorized restating *any* of his metaphysical claims in terms of essence and existence alone, when he defined necessity as the "assuredness of existence."

Br. Thomas also followed Avicenna when it came to *arguing* for the fundamental notions. He used both of Avicenna's modes of argument—division and synonyms—though he used his own examples. Being he divided into intentional being and real being, which in turn is divided into the ten categories. *Essence* follows real being: "And since, as has been said, *being* in this sense is divided into the ten categories, *essence* must mean something common to all the natures by which different beings are put into different genera and species."[17] This division by no means *demonstrates* that essence follows real being, and some commentators have thought that Br. Thomas confused metaphysics and logic here.[18] But he is simply following the mode of argument that Avicenna and Aristotle had used to offer insight into fundamental notions. Br. Thomas made more use in *EE* 1 of Avicenna's other mode of argument. Several synonyms are offered to explain *essence. Form, certitude,* and *quiddity* he borrowed from Avicenna; *nature* comes from Boethius and Aristotle; and *quod quid erat esse* from Aristotle.[19]

Comparison of Aquinas's prologue and *EE* 1 with Avicenna, *Metaphysics* 1.5, shows that Br. Thomas followed the Vizier closely about the end and principal notions of metaphysics, with the exception of *necessary*. He also took his two modes of argument from the Vizier. Reasoning by division or synonyms can lead to but cannot ensure the mind's grasp of the fundamental notions of metaphysics through insight. Such arguments are dialectical, not demonstrative.

THE PRIMARY HYPOTHESES OF AVICENNIAN METAPHYSICS
(*MET.* 1.6 – 7)

After setting out the fundamental notions of metaphysics at 1.5, Avicenna presented its other proper principles, its hypotheses, in chapters 6 and 7, which form a tightly organized unit. Al-Juzjani noted it was Avicenna's custom to set out theses to be proven as a kind of rubric heading each chapter.[20] The rubric for chapters 6 and 7 begins by dividing the fundamental notion of being, here expressed not as *mawjûd/ens* but as *wujûd/esse*, because Avicenna is looking at being qualitatively, focusing on two different *kinds* of existence:

> We say: necessary existence and possible existence each have their own properties. We say: things which enter existence can be divided by the mind into two: one of these is what, when considered in itself its existence, is not necessary. Now it is

clearly not impossible, otherwise it would not enter existence, while this thing is possible. The other is what, considered in itself, its existence is necessary.[21]

Here existence is treated like a genus divided into necessary and non-necessary existence, the non-necessary in turn divided into possible and impossible. Since impossible existence is self-contradictory, what results are two sub-genera: necessary existence and possible existence.

Avicenna then finishes the rubric by laying out theses that contain certain "properties" of these two kinds of existence. Chapters 6 and 7 consist in dialectical arguments for these "properties" and at the end of chapter 7, based on these arguments, Avicenna enunciated the hypotheses of metaphysics. There he further divided possible existence, producing three categories: fully necessary existence, possible but eternal existence, and possible but generated existence. These three kinds of existence have other names—God, intelligences, physical things—but these are their metaphysical names.

About necessary existence he says:

Therefore, necessary existence is one entirely, but not as a species under a genus; one in number, but not as an individual under a species; rather a notion whose name belongs to it alone, and its existence is not shared with another. We shall add an explanation later. These are the properties peculiar to necessary existence.[22]

The focus here is on the ontological unity of God, so Hypothesis 1 of Avicennian metaphysics is: *Necessary existence is ontologically simple, existence alone.*

Then he turns to the two levels of possible existence:

Of possible existence, its property is clear from what has been said: it necessarily requires another which makes it exist in act. And everything whose existence is possible, when considered in itself, is always something whose existence is possible. But when existence comes to it, this is necessary through another. And this comes to it always *or* <necessary existence from another does not happen always but> at some time or other. . . . And that whose existence is necessary through another always, its quiddity is not simple, because what it has in itself is *other* than what it has from another; and from both of these it acquires its individual existence. Therefore, nothing at all is free from being clothed with potency and possibility in itself, except necessary existence. <It is singular; what is not it is dual and composed.>[23]

While Avicenna distinguished eternal possible things from temporal possible things, Hypothesis 2 of Avicennian metaphysics focuses on what they have in common: *All possible existences are ontologically composite, made up of existence and quiddity.* In the text he describes that composition in terms of possibility and necessity, but possibility comes from the nature of a *thing* "considered in itself," while necessity resides in the *existence* that comes to it "from another." The conceptual distinction between essence and existence of chapter 5 has become a real distinction in all creatures. That Avicenna accepted this doctrine as a principle is clear on every page of his ontology, for he invariably analyzes every topic in terms of the real composition of essence and existence in creatures.

THE PRIMARY HYPOTHESES OF THOMISTIC METAPHYSICS (*EE* 5)

As he had done for its primary notions, young Br. Thomas followed Avicenna when he set out the fundamental hypotheses of metaphysics. He states them formally at *EE* 5, using Avicenna's three-fold division into God, "created intellectual substances," and "substances composed of matter and form." His hypotheses are introduced as conclusions flowing from the dialectical arguments of *EE* 2–4. "*From* what has been seen it is clear how essence is found in different things."[24]

Aquinas's hypothesis about God comes directly from Avicenna:

> There is something, namely God, whose essence *is* its own existence. This is why we find some philosophers [namely, Avicenna] who say that God does not have a quiddity or essence, because his essence is not *other* than his existence. From this it follows that he is not in a genus, for everything in a genus must have a quiddity in addition to its existence.[25]

Aquinas's three points were made by Avicenna: God's essence is his existence; God's essence is not "other" than his existence, which is the reason why Avicenna said that God does not have an essence; and God is not an individual confined within the limits of a genus. So Hypothesis 1 of Thomistic metaphysics is this: *Divine essence and existence are one and the same.* Aquinas has dropped the complicating factor of necessity, but it is otherwise identical in content with Avicenna's Hypothesis 1, for the simple reason that Aquinas took it from the Vizier.

Following Avicenna, when he comes to creatures Br. Thomas distinguishes two levels of creatures but his hypothesis underscores their metaphysical similarity.

> Essence is found in a second way in created intellectual substances. Their existence is *other* than their essence, though their essence is without matter. Consequently, their existence is not absolute but received, and therefore limited and restricted

by the capacity of the recipient nature; but their nature or quiddity is absolute, not received in some matter.[26]

Aquinas has carefully excised all references to the erroneous Avicennian doctrine that intelligences exist eternally, but the two claims he makes are precisely those Avicenna had made: their existence is ontologically "other" than their essence; and their existence is "received," that is, caused.[27]

Aquinas ends with material substances:

In a third way essence is found in substances composed of matter and form. In these too existence is received and limited because they have *existence from another.* Likewise, their nature or quiddity is received in designated matter. Therefore, they are limited from above and below.[28]

Here Aquinas repeats two points Avicenna had made: the existence of material things is "received" (*receptum*) since it comes "from another," namely, from their cause; and it is "limited" (*finitum*) because it is "other" than their essence.

Hypothesis 2 of Thomistic metaphysics, then, is the same as Avicenna's: *All creatures are ontologically composite, made up of essence and existence.* Again, the only significant change is to simplify by dropping necessity, thereby reducing Avicenna's three terms to two. Where Avicenna had said God is *existence necessary in itself* and a creature is *existence possible in itself,* Aquinas says God *exists in himself* because ontologically simple, while creatures do not, because they are ontological composites of *essence* and *existence.*

How Avicenna Argues for Metaphysical Principles

Simple induction is not normally sufficient to establish principles, so Aristotle had noted the need for dialectical arguments to move the mind from induction to insight.[29] Such arguments are deductive and consist in setting out consequences: either the negative consequences of denying a principle or the positive consequences of assuming one, in hopes that such consequences will open the mind to insight into principles.

Negative arguments for principles are *reductio ad absurdum* arguments that deny the principle, then deduce consequences of this denial until an "absurdity" is reached, in order to force the mind to deny the denial and affirm the principle. Formally, such deductions are valid *modus tollens* arguments.[30] They work well on behalf of general axioms, since they are usually the *only* way to account for certain facts of experience, such as Aristotle's claim that non-contradiction is the only way to preserve the meaningfulness of language. Such arguments do not demonstrate the axiom but lead a mind chastened by the dead end of contradiction back to it, in hopes that the principle will then be grasped by insight.

Reductio arguments are less effective for proper principles, because they can consistently be denied, even when axioms cannot. A principle thought true may imply some consequence (P1 ⊃ C), but it is also *possible* that a different principle can cover the same fact (P2 ⊃ C). It is notoriously difficult to establish the counterfactual premiss (~P1 ⊃ ~C) needed to mount a *reductio* argument. So Avicenna turned to affirmative arguments, which proceed by deducing consequences from the principle thought true (P1 ⊃ C), then reflecting on whether these consequences are consistent with the facts. Such a deduction argues by "saving the appearances." This is how Avicenna read Aristotle's arguments for the proper principles of his metaphysics. Logically such arguments affirm the consequent and so are formally invalid,[31] but the "fit" between principle and consequent offers insight into a principle that cannot be deduced.[32] While Avicenna used both types, "saving the appearances" arguments captured his imagination.

Avicenna chose the rubric of *Metaphysics* 1.6–7 with the audience of the *Shifa'* in mind. No abstraction, it consisted in the "you" Avicenna repeatedly addressed in the text, his secretary al-Juzjani, along with the small circle of ministerial subordinates who came to the Vizier for intellectual culture,[33] a culture that was Islamic. So Avicenna picked a rubric based on a theme from the *Qur'an* familiar to those in his circle: "Praise be to Allah, who *created* the heavens and the earth, and made darkness and light. Yet those who disbelieve set up *equals* to their Lord."[34] When recast in metaphysical language, Allah becomes *necessary existence*, while creatures are *possible existences.* The Quranic passage so understood asserts that necessary existence is uncaused while possible existence is caused, and necessary existence has no equal, while possible existences are equal to each other. These metaphysical renderings of a familiar religious truth constitute the rubric Avicenna sets out for chapter 6:

> So we say: [Thesis 1] Existence necessary in itself does not have a *cause,* while [Thesis 2] existence possible in itself does have a cause. [Thesis 3] And existence necessary in itself is necessary <existence> in all its aspects. [Thesis 4] And it is impossible that the existence of that which is necessary existence is *equal* to the existence of another, so that one of them is equal to the other with regard to necessary existence.[35]

Avicenna then completes his rubric with the "properties" of necessary existence that will be argued for in chapter 7:

> Moreover, [Thesis 5] it is impossible that the existence of necessary existence be composed, from multiplicity. And [Thesis 6] it is impossible that the true nature of

necessary existence is shared in any way at all. And from this it follows that necessary existence is not relative, changing, many, and does not share its proper existence.[36]

Avicenna then set out dialectical arguments for these theses, arguments that introduce the hypotheses of metaphysics as premises or presuppositions. In this way, a plausible case for the proper principles of metaphysics is made by showing how they "save" the properties of possible and necessary beings. This is why the conclusions listed in the rubric at the outset of chapter 6 are by and large different from the metaphysical hypotheses listed at the end of chapter 7.[37]

AVICENNA'S "SUFFICIENCY ARGUMENT" FOR THE REAL DISTINCTION IN CREATURES (*MET.* 1.6)

If this was Avicenna's argument strategy, what were his actual arguments? There are explicit arguments for all but Thesis 3. He employed *reductio* arguments for Theses 1 and 4, but since Aquinas passed over them, so shall we. Aquinas made use of Avicenna's arguments for Thesis 2 and Thesis 5.[38] The Vizier's long argument for Thesis 2, set out in *Metaphysics* 1.5, proceeds analytically from conclusion to premises:

> Furthermore, whatever is possible, when considered in itself, has both its existence and its non-existence from a cause. *For* when it has existence, existence as distinct from non-existence *has been acquired* by it; and when it ceases to exist, non-existence as distinct from existence has been acquired by it. . . . Now each of these two can only have been acquired from another or not from another. If acquired from another, that is its cause. . . . This is so because its quiddity either is sufficient (*yakfi; sufficiens*) for this determination or is not sufficient. Now if its quiddity is sufficient for one of these two, then it is a quiddity necessary through itself. But it was posited that it was not necessary, so this is a contradiction. If, however, <the existence of> its quiddity is not sufficient, but something else bestows its existence upon it, then its existence is from another, and this is its cause. Thus the thing *has a cause.* In sum, one of these two attributes becomes <necessary> for it, not through itself, but through a cause. The attribute of existence comes from a *cause of existence,* while the attribute of non-existence comes from a cause which is the absence of a cause for the attribute of existence.[39]

Avicenna begins by putting the Quranic claim that "the heavens and the earth are created by God" into metaphysical language: possible beings are caused to exist (or not exist). He then proceeds analytically to explain why this is so, his explanation gradually uncovering the metaphysical hypothesis that creatures are composed of essence and existence. He first isolates the precise attribute at issue in creation—existence. Articulating the claim in this way introduces the notion that existence is a distinct attribute of the creature. At "For" he explains the reason why a creature needs a cause: existence "has been acquired by it." Now this explanation might seem less clear than the thesis it is supposed to prove, since in normal parlance something must exist *before* acquiring anything. In order to proceed further, Avicenna moves from the predicate of the thesis—existence—over to its subject—possible being.

That subject is initially described as "whatever is possible, when considered in itself." A possible being is whatever can exist but does not have to exist. In order to understand the acquisition of existence Avicenna adds that such a being is "considered in itself," pointing to some intrinsic cause within the thing. In chapter 5, he used the term *thing* to point out that cause, here he calls it *quiddity:* the nature a being can have in common with others of the same type. Quiddity so understood includes *any* internally coherent content, not limited to what can be actually proven to exist. Actual substances have quiddities, but so too do actual accidents, and the metaphysician also can understand possible substances and accidents, even imaginary ones like Aristotle's goat-stag.[40]

Having thus isolated the two fundamental terms at issue—quiddity and existence—at "This is so because," Avicenna then asks a question that would have made no sense to Aristotle: Is the quiddity of a possible being *sufficient* to determine existence? *Sufficient* here refers to quiddity's strength, so to speak, to *necessitate* existence. A quiddity that is sufficient produces a necessary existent; a quiddity that is not sufficient is a principle of a being that exists contingently. These are the only two options. Avicenna focuses on the insufficient quiddity in order to bring the reader to entertain the metaphysical hypothesis toward which the argument has been moving all along: a being whose quiddity is not sufficient to necessitate existence must be composed ontologically of that quiddity and existence, an existence "acquired" from elsewhere.

Since the focal point of this argument is whether the quiddity is *sufficient* to necessitate existence, let us call it Avicenna's "sufficiency argument," a dialectical argument in the analytic mode. In sum, it is this: creatures are caused because their existence is acquired, and their existence is acquired because their quiddities are insufficient to entail existence, and those quiddities are insufficient because quiddity is really other than existence. But there is one more point that needs clarification: what kind of cause bestows existence on such a quiddity?

Its existence comes from "something else," its cause. Since this is not a cause of the *quiddity* of the thing produced, but a cause of its *existence,* Avicenna calls it simply the "cause of existence." Such a cause is similar to Aristotle's moving cause, since it is extrinsic and produces an effect in a subject. But it is different, since the subject at issue, namely, the quiddity, is not a pre-existing entity but an intrinsic principle within a creature that comes into being through this cause; and what is introduced is existence, which all subsequent acts of the being presuppose. Thus, what "existence" (*wujûd; esse*) adds to quiddity produces an actual being (*mawjûd; ens*). If this addition contained *any* quidditative content, then the subject-quiddity would change its nature, as a number is changed by adding one to it. Existence must change the quiddity from possible to actual *without* adding anything to its nature. What is added, therefore, can be nothing in the quidditative order, yet must be real.

Since existence is divided into the possible and the necessary, Avicenna added a clarification to Thesis 2. Thus far he has argued only for a "cause of existence." But "whatever is possible existence does not have existence unless its existence is necessary in relation to its cause." Actual existence is necessary, at least relatively speaking, so that by virtue of coming to exist a being also comes to be necessary. The "cause of existence," then, must introduce necessity into the effect, since necessity and existence are intrinsically linked together.

Avicenna's argument for this point is a *reductio.* Suppose the cause of existence did not also cause necessity: "For *if* it were not a necessary existent owing to the presence of the cause and in relation to it, *then* it would be possible. . . . But again this would require, along with the cause by which it has existence, some third thing by which it is determined to existence after non-existence or non-existence after existence. And that third is another cause, and so on to infinity." The infinite regress is created by separating the cause of existence from the cause of necessity, so that if the cause of existence were not also the cause of necessity, then to produce a real effect would require a third cause of existence, and then a fourth, and so on. The solution to the infinite regress is simply to identify the two kinds of causes, for to produce an actual rather than merely a possible effect requires the concatenation of all the causes required for the real effect.[41]

This clarification of Thesis 2 can be called Avicenna's "infinite regress argument." While young Br. Thomas will ignore necessity as a distinct feature of Avicenna's account, he will not ignore Avicenna's "infinite regress argument." Nor will he ignore Avicenna's "sufficiency argument." As presented by Avicenna, neither argument is demonstrative. They are dialectical arguments offered in support of his metaphysical hypothesis about creatures: all possible beings are composed of two metaphysical principles, quiddity and existence.

AVICENNA'S "PREDICABLES ARGUMENT" FOR THE UNITY OF ESSENCE AND EXISTENCE IN GOD (*MET.* 1.7)

Avicenna devoted chapter 7 to defending Thesis 5—"necessary existence" cannot be multiple—and its corollary Thesis 6—its "true nature" (*haqiqa; certitudo*) cannot be "shared in any way at all." Both serve to uncover the fundamental metaphysical hypothesis that essence and existence are absolutely identical in God. These theses are fully in accord with the logic of Avicenna's "sufficiency argument." A quiddity that suffices to require existence is a "quiddity necessary through itself" and, since necessity is the "assuredness of existence," must exist due *only* to itself. But how could a quiddity be "sufficient" to necessitate its own existence? There is only one way: on condition that there is absolutely no difference between quiddity and existence. For any difference between them would undermine the necessity whereby actual existence comes from the quiddity *alone*. In short, for quiddity to *necessitate* existence, quiddity and existence must be *one and identical*.

The argument Avicenna uses in chapter 7 is a *reductio* set up in terms of the five predicables—genus, species, difference, property, and accident—so let us call it his "predicables argument" for the unity of essence and existence in God. Assuming *per impossible* there were two necessary existences, they would have to differ in some way. Aristotle's predicables allowed Avicenna to locate all possible points of difference and to reject them all. His argument is long and complicated, but in outline is as follows.

The point of differentiation between two necessary existents could not be located in the two non-essential predicables. It could not be a *property*, because two necessary beings would have the same properties, since they have the same quiddity. Nor could the differentiating character be an *accident*. Accidents "occur from extrinsic causes, not from its own quiddity,"[42] which means that a necessary existent would be necessary both through itself and through another.

Neither could necessary existents be differentiated through the parts of the essence: genus, species, and difference. Differentiation here would have to take the form of dividing a genus "through differentiae" into species or dividing a species into individuals "through accidents." Why necessary being cannot be a genus multiplied into species through differentiae, can be seen through an analogy. The species *human* is constituted by the genus *animal* and the difference *rational*. The genus *animal*, "even though it exists with something other than itself, can be considered in itself," but it needs the difference *rational* to provide animal with "existence in actuality" as a certain species of animal. By analogy, if necessary being were a genus, its differentiae would add to it "existence in actuality." But this is impossible, since then it would not exist through itself. Nor can necessary being be divided like a species into individuals, which "differ through accidents." For this would entail composition of substance and accident and the presence of matter within a necessary existent.[43]

The net result of Avicenna's "predicables argument" is that necessary existence cannot be multiple in any way. Avicenna's metaphysical principle identifying essence and existence in necessary being can "save" God's absolute unity. In *Metaphysics* 1.6–7, therefore, Avicenna justified the two fundamental hypotheses of his metaphysics—the composition of essence and existence in creatures and their unity in God—by showing how they "save" two teachings at the heart of Islam: God is one; and God is the creator of all. A more attractive dialectic for his actual audience is difficult to conceive.

How Aquinas Argues for
Metaphysical Principles at *EE* 2 – 3

Young Br. Thomas followed Avicenna's argumentative strategy throughout *EE* 2–4. In *EE* 2–3, he offers deductive dialectical arguments "saving the appearances" of certain metaphysical conclusions about creatures and God. The arguments repeatedly point to the composition of essence and existence in creatures and their unity in God, as *principles assumed,* not as conclusions demonstrated. The theses Aquinas "saves" are as Avicennian as the principles used to "save" them, the hypotheses laid out at *EE* 5. But since Aquinas's actual arguments are not drawn directly from Avicenna's *Metaphysics* 1, let us consider them only long enough to verify the Avicennian style of dialectical argument they contain.

At *EE* 2, Br. Thomas first defends the thesis that "the term essence in composite substances signifies that which composed of matter *and* form" by appealing to authority, that of Boethius and Averroes, but especially Avicenna, who "says that the quiddity of composite substances is the very composition of form and matter."[44] Aquinas then adds an argument whose premisses reveal his metaphysical hypothesis about creatures.

> This is also in accord with reason, for the existence (*esse*) of a composite substance is not the existence of the form alone, nor the existence of the matter alone, but of the composite. Now the essence is that *by which* a thing is said to exist (*esse*). Therefore, it is necessary that the essence, by which a thing is called a being (*ens*), is not the form alone, or the matter alone, but both, though in its own way the form alone is the cause of this sort of existence.[45]

The conclusion that essence in material substances includes both matter and form comes from two premisses. First, existence is an attribute of the composite, not of matter or form by themselves. Second, essence is a kind of cause of existence. The argument moves deductively *from* existence as a middle term *to* a conclusion about essence. It is based on the fundamental assumption that material creatures are composed of existence and essence. This assumption is not a conclusion Aquinas *deduces,* but a principle he *uncovers* as a presupposition of his premisses. His argument, in short, is designed to open the minds of his confreres to this assumption, by showing how it resolves a metaphysical difficulty: whether matter is part of the essence of material substances.

At *EE* 3, Br. Thomas defends universal knowledge. His argument is built upon the distinction between essence and existence. What makes knowledge possible is that "essence can be considered in two ways." *Absolute* consideration focuses on the quidditative content of an essence, without regard to existence or number, while in what we might call *existential* consideration, the essence "is considered according to the existence (*esse*) it has in this or that thing." This existence is "two-fold: one in singulars, and the other in the soul."[46] The key to avoiding hyper-realism is the fact that the essence, *considered in itself,* is not a mode of existence, nor does it entail some mode of existence, as must happen in a metaphysics where existence is reduced to essence. The existentially neutral essence can be clothed, as it were, with real existence in singulars or intentional existence as a universal in the mind. Consequently, the essence absolutely considered unites an individual like Socrates with universal human nature in the proposition "Socrates is a man."[47]

This solution to the problem of universals is not without its assumptions. Indeed, Aquinas presents it in this way in order to highlight those assumptions. Aquinas's argument then, is this: *If* individuals are composed of essence and existence, *then* knowledge can be "saved" without attributing real existence to universals. Such reasoning does not *demonstrate* the real composition of essence and existence in composite substances, but it does argue for this metaphysical principle, as a way of preserving knowledge. The actual arguments Aquinas employs in *EE* 2–3, then, "save" the essences of material things and knowledge about them by assuming the real distinction in order to show its power as a metaphysical principle.

How Aquinas Argues for His Metaphysical Hypotheses in *EE* 4

There was no reason for Br. Thomas to change the argumentative strategy he learned from Avicenna in the much-controverted chapter 4, devoted to "the way essence exists in separate substances"—the human soul, angels, and God. And he did not do so. His thesis about God's essence Aquinas takes to be so uncontroversial that he need but state it and move on: "everyone admits the simplicity of the first cause." The rest of the chapter focuses on angels or, to use the Avicennian term Aquinas favors, intelligences, since they are a test case for the doctrine of universal hylomorphism in creatures espoused by Franciscan thinkers like Bonaventure. Angels are ontological composites, but not of form and matter, as Bonaventure said; they are composed of "form and existence," as Avicenna held.[48] Aquinas begins with a *reductio* of hylomorphism, then turns positive.

The *reductio* starts with an argument from authority: the Franciscan doctrine goes back only as far as Ibn Gabirol, author of the *Fons vitae,* while the great "philosophers"—

by which Br. Thomas meant Aristotle, Averroes, and Avicenna—held that "every intellectual substance must be completely free from matter." This conclusion they "demonstrated" from the fact that intellection is a completely immaterial act.[49] Then comes a brief *reductio*. Universal hylomorphism entails that "not all matter prevents intelligibility, but only corporeal matter." If so, however, by causing matter to be bodily the "form of corporeity" would cause matter both to be unintelligible, as corporeal, and to be intelligible, since it is a form, an impossible contradiction.[50]

Br. Thomas devotes the rest of *EE* 4 to the kind of positive, "saving the appearances" arguments he learned from Avicenna and preferred. He offers three arguments showing how the Avicennian view that there is a composition of "form and existence" in angels "saves" certain important facts about them. The first argument, which contemporary commentators have lost sight of, contains the main argument of the chapter, one designed to show that the composition of essence and existence ensures that angels can be completely immaterial while also being created. In the second stage Aquinas draws two important corollaries of his view of angels, corollaries he took from Avicenna himself. Finally, in the third stage Br. Thomas sets out a lengthy defense of potentiality in angels, also drawn from Avicenna.[51]

Aquinas says his first positive argument is "easy to see":[52]

> Whatever things are related to each other so that one is the cause of the existence of the other, the one having the nature of cause can have existence without the other, but the reverse is not true. Now matter and form are so related that form gives existence to matter. Therefore, it is impossible that matter exist without some form; but it is not impossible that some form exist without matter.[53]

Here Br. Thomas assumes without proof that form makes matter to exist. The major premiss makes the wider point that *any* cause of existence in another (*causa esse alterius*) has a kind of ontological priority that allows it to exist without the effect, though the effect cannot exist without its cause. *Esse* in both premisses has the technical Avicennian sense Aquinas had employed in previous chapters. Consequently, both premisses draw attention to the same underlying presupposition: the real distinction between essence and existence in creatures. The argument seems designed to offer Aquinas's confreres an opportunity to accept this hypothesis by showing, as before, what follows from it: *If* there is a real distinction between essence and existence in creatures, *then* form can exist on its own, without matter—in angels and human souls.

Young Br. Thomas was well aware that there are other ways to argue for this conclusion than by using existence (*esse*). Understanding form as act and matter as potency, for example, allows form to be separate from matter but not matter from form, because of the priority of act over potency. Bonaventure had reasoned this way and so had Aristotle. But Aquinas chose *not* to do so for a very good reason: an argument based on the general notions of act and potency, rather than specifically on existence, would *not* allow him to introduce his metaphysical hypothesis concerning essence and existence. His syllogism is carefully designed to focus attention on existence.

In the second positive argument in *EE* 4, Aquinas deduces two corollaries of the composition of "form and existence" in angels, both attributed explicitly to Avicenna. First, "as Avicenna says, 'the quiddity of a simple substance is the simple entity itself,' because there is nothing else that receives it." Second, "there are as many species among [the angels] as there are individuals, as Avicenna expressly says."[54]

Aquinas then turns to his third argument—the final and longest part of the chapter. Many interpreters have taken this to be the focal point of the chapter, because they have thought it contains *demonstrations* of the real distinction or of the existence of God. But in reality it is devoted to another point entirely—potency in angels. Hylomorphism can only preserve the ontological gap between God and creatures at the cost of positing a peculiar kind of matter that explains potentiality in angels. To attack this weak point, Br. Thomas again turns to Avicenna, who had explicitly addressed this very issue.[55] As we have seen, the Vizier had said that intelligences, though completely immaterial, also include potentiality, because all creatures, without exception, are composed of quiddity and existence: "nothing at all is free from being clothed with *potency and possibility* in itself, except necessary existence."

Aquinas's argument for potency in angels in *EE* 4 is a reprise of arguments Avicenna had offered in *Metaphysics* 1.6–7 in favor of his two metaphysical hypotheses, and consists in four steps. At Step 1, Aquinas adopts Avicenna's metaphysical hypothesis that creatures are composed of essence and existence and defends it with a simplified version of Avicenna's "sufficiency argument" that he found in al-Ghazali. At Step 2, Aquinas adopts Avicenna's other metaphysical hypothesis—that essence and existence in God are one—and he defends it as Avicenna had, with his "predicables argument." At Step 3, Aquinas combines Avicenna's "infinite regress argument" with his "predicables argument" to defend the Avicennian thesis that the existence of immaterial substances is caused by a "cause of existence" that Br. Thomas says is God. At Step 4, Aquinas repeats Avicenna's claim that there is potentiality in angels, though his argument is his own.[56]

POTENTIALITY IN ANGELS: STEP 4

Let us begin at the end, as a reminder of the context that contemporary commentators have forgotten. Aquinas's fourth and last step in reply to hylomorphism in angels is short, deductive, and put at a high level of generality:

Everything which receives something from another is in potency with respect to that, and what is received in it is its act. Therefore, it is necessary that the quiddity or form, which is the intelligence, be in potency with respect to the existence (*esse*) which it receives from God, and that existence (*esse*) is received as an act. And so potency and act are found in intelligences, but not form and matter, except equivocally.[57]

The conclusion offers a clear alternative to hylomorphism: quiddity or form, not matter, is what gives potentiality to angels. The argument assumes that intelligences are forms without matter, composed of essence and existence. The middle term— *something received from another*—that Aquinas uses to link *intelligence* and *potency*, assumes that in angels the quiddity or form *receives existence from God*.[58] Consequently, in order to prove that the source of potency in angels and human souls is not matter but quiddity or form, Br. Thomas had *first* to show that quiddity receives existence from God. But to show this, he turned to his two fundamental metaphysical hypotheses concerning essence and existence, in Steps 1 and 2.

The fourth step in Aquinas's argument for potency in angels, then, illuminates his overall argument strategy: *If* essence and existence are distinct in creatures and unified in God, *then* all creatures "receive" their existence from "another," namely, from God; and if so, *then* in turn intellectual creatures have potentiality by reason of their essences, which are potential in comparison with their existence. The metaphysical hypotheses Br. Thomas adopts from Avicenna "save" potency in angels in a way more plausible and intelligible than Franciscan hylomorphism.[59]

The "Understanding Essence" Argument for the Real Distinction: Step 1

Br. Thomas took the first step leading to potency in intelligences by tying his two metaphysical hypotheses together and presenting them in words that clearly echo Avicenna. "Therefore, it is clear that *existence* is *other* than essence or *quiddity, unless* perhaps there is some thing whose *quiddity* is its very *existence.*" Aquinas here simply reduces to its essentials this cumbersome description: "what it has in itself [i.e. essence] is *other* than what it has from another [i.e. existence]; and from both of these it acquires its individual existence (*esse id quod est*). Therefore, nothing at all is free from being clothed with potency and possibility in itself, *except necessary existence.*"[60] These two hypotheses supply the premises Br. Thomas needs to argue that creatures receive their existence from God, their "cause of existence" (at Step 3), and that there is potency in angels (at Step 4). But his longterm goal is to move the mind of his reader in the opposite direction, to accept the hypotheses themselves by seeing how they "save" potentiality in angels. To do so, Br. Thomas here offers one argument for each hypothesis: the argument for the hypothesis about creatures immediately precedes this statement (at Step 1), the argument for the hypothesis about God immediately follows it (at Step 2).[61]

We saw above that Avicenna's "sufficiency argument" for the hypothesis about creatures proceeded *deductively but analytically,* uncovering the distinction between essence and existence as an ultimate premiss. In the *mode of discovery* human reason normally proceeds this way, because it moves from what is more well known to us to what is less well known to us but intrinsically more intelligible. An argument that follows the *mode of exposition,* however, need not follow the same order. Would it not be easier for his confreres to understand a deductive argument proceeding syntheti-cally from premises to conclusion?

Aquinas accordingly presents the metaphysical hypothesis of the real distinction in creatures as a conclusion following from a syllogism that contains two premisses with a "proof" for each premiss.

[1] Whatever does not come from understanding essence or quiddity comes from outside it and produces a composition with essence, [1a] because no essence can be understood without those things that are parts of the essence. [2] Now every essence or quiddity can be understood without understanding anything about its existence, [2a] for I can understand what is a human or phoenix and yet not know whether it has existence in reality. Therefore, [3] it is clear that existence is other than essence.[62]

Twentieth-century scholars thought this argument original with Aquinas and dubbed it his "*intellectus essentiae* argument," from the phrase *de intellectu essentiae vel quid-ditatis* in the major premiss. In reality, however, it is not original but derives from Avicenna.

When viewed broadly, an argument attempts to answer a question by offering evi-dence of a conclusion. In this respect, Aquinas's syllogism accomplishes the same task as the Vizier's argument. Aquinas asks Avicenna's question: does quiddity entail exis-tence? He gives the same answer: quiddity does not. And he gives the same reason: the "otherness" of existence and quiddity in creatures.

When we turn to details, Aquinas's major and minor premisses are similar to but not identical with two sentences in Avicenna's "sufficiency argument." When initially considering possible quiddities, Avicenna noted: ". . . it is evident that *whatever* after non-existence has existence, it is determined through something else that *comes from another.*" Avicenna's "whatever" and "comes from" occur in Aquinas's major premiss, which enunciates the same claim: "[1] *Whatever* does not come from understanding essence or quiddity *comes from outside* it and produces a composition with essence."[63] The main difference is that Avicenna focused objectively on the quiddity itself, while Aquinas's middle term introduces a cognitive perspective: "understanding (*intellectus*) essence or quiddity." Avicenna also limited himself to existence and non-existence; Aquinas makes a broader claim.

A bit later in his "sufficiency argument" Avicenna said: "If, however, the *quiddity* is *not* sufficient, but *something else* bestows its existence upon it, then *its existence* is from another." Aquinas's minor premiss simplifies Avicenna's claim: "[2] Now every essence or quiddity can be understood without understanding anything about its existence."[64] Here again Aquinas's main addition is to insert the cognitive aspect of "understanding quiddity."

Such parallels cannot be happenstance, but they are not the whole story. Aquinas's syllogism is not just a simpler version of Avicenna's "sufficiency argument," because they are different modes of argument. Avicenna's is deductive but analytic, Aquinas's is deductive but synthetic.[65] The premisses Aquinas needed were not lying there ready to hand in Avicenna's text, so he turned to another thinker, a man also deeply influenced by the Vizier. His name was al-Ghazali. We now know that the philosophy circulated in the medieval Latin West under his name, the *Maqâsid al-falâsafa* (*The Aims of the Philosophers*), which was translated as *Liber philosophiae Algazalis*, was really an epitome of the philosophy of Avicenna composed by al-Ghazali in order to attack it. The Latins, however, were not privy to the attack so they thought he was a follower of Avicenna. In its logical section, al-Ghazali took up the topic of universals in a way that provided Aquinas with precisely the premisses he used.

Al-Ghazali explained universals with a famous Aristotelian example:

> When we say *This human is animal and white,* we apprehend the difference between comparing *animal* with him and comparing *white* with him. For when the comparison is the comparison of *animal* to the subject it is called essential, but when it is the comparison of *white* to the subject it is called accidental.[66]

Universals are here divided into the essential (where the example is a genus) and the non-essential (the example is an accident).

Al-Ghazali then notes how different it is to "*understand* the essential" from understanding the "accidental." Understanding an essence necessarily includes understanding *all* the components of the essence. The point is not original. Avicenna had said the same thing in his own logic: "I say that if you consider constituents and what is constituted, it will not be possible to remove what is constituted from what constitutes it in such a way that it would be true that what is constituted would have existence in the intellect but what constitutes it would not."[67] Al-Ghazali put the same point this way:

[1] . . . when you *understand* the *essential* and that of which it is essential, *you are not able* to imagine or to understand the subject unless you understand the essential present in it. [1a] The subject cannot in any way be understood without that. For when you understand what is human and what is animal, you are not able to understand human without understanding animal.[68]

Understanding *human* entails understanding the genus *animal* and the difference *rational* as parts of the human essence, while understanding *human* does not entail understanding *white*, which it is not part of that essence. Al-Ghazali's broad claim at [1] became the major premiss of Aquinas's "understanding essence" argument, while his point at [1a] became Aquinas's "proof" of the major:

[1] Whatever does *not* come *from understanding essence* or quiddity *comes from outside* it and produces a composition with essence, [1a] because *no essence can be understood without* those things that are *parts of the essence.*[69]

Aquinas borrows the framework of the predicables and the middle term (*understanding essence*) from al-Ghazali. He says "essence or quiddity" because he took *essentia* from al-Ghazali's *essentiale* and *quidditas* from Avicenna's "sufficiency argument," mentioning both to avoid equivocation. His major premiss and its proof are extracted from al-Ghazali in his normal way of dealing with an Avicennian text, by simplifying with an eye to his own purposes. In this case, however, he may have been too succinct. If he had included al-Ghazali's example (knowing the *human* essence necessarily includes *animal*) his own point might have been clearer. Aquinas's proof of the major [1a], like its exemplar in al-Ghazali, focuses on the mind's inability to understand essence without its components.

When he turned to non-essential universals, al-Ghazali added to the standard Aristotelian example of *white* another, peculiarly Avicennian example. Avicenna had used the predicables to describe *existence* as a kind of accident, though unlike a predicamental accident such as *white, existence* does not presuppose a previously existing subject. Al-Ghazali incorporated into his abridgement of logic this Avicennian example, one that attracted Aquinas's attention.

[2a1] Likewise, when you understand *what is a human* it is not necessary that you understand him to *exist* or to be *white*, but you are not *able to understand* him unless you understand what is an *animal*. Now this example you may not find satisfying,

because you and all the others who now exist are human. So take another example: [2a2] as is true of the *phoenix* or some other external thing, it will be manifest to you that existence is accidental to all the things that are.[70]

Aquinas's proof of the minor in his syllogism incorporates both of al-Ghazali's examples: "[2a] for I *can understand what is a human or phoenix* and yet not know whether it has *existence* in reality."[71] This claim is based upon the difference between two of Aristotle's four questions: "Is it?" and "What is it?" One can understand what *human* and *phoenix* mean, at least in a minimal way, without knowing whether or not they exist in reality. The two examples are meant to be taken in tandem. It is tempting to think the difference between the two is that humans have real existence but the phoenix is a mythical bird and therefore exists only in the mind. But in the Islamic version the phoenix (*'anqa'*) was huge and mysterious but real, probably a heron. It was originally created by God as a kind of Platonic ideal of bird, but fell from grace and had to be killed. For late antique and Islamic philosophers, the important fact was that it was one of a kind, a story Aquinas knew. The relevant difference, then, is that *human* is actually predicated of many subjects, but *phoenix* of one at most, making the phoenix a particularly apt example, since Aquinas's angels, like Avicenna's intelligences, are also one of a kind.[72]

Are al-Ghazali and Aquinas reasoning dialectically, as Avicenna did in his "sufficiency argument"? Al-Ghazali put his claims in terms of "understanding" essences rather than essences themselves, and Aquinas followed him in this. Al-Ghazali did not try to prove anything deductively, since he was concerned only to explain the distinction between essential and accidental universals by appealing to what he expressly calls "examples," a form of inductive reasoning, as he well knew. His examples (*animal* and *white* in relation to *human*, *existence* in relation to *human* and *phoenix*) illustrate the two general claims that Aquinas will repeat. Though al-Ghazali's focus is on *knowing* essences and accidents, in his own mind this knowledge is such a clear sign of their *reality* that the cognitive claim easily elided into the corresponding metaphysical claim. So he says "existence is accidental to all things that are." There is not a hint, however, that al-Ghazali thought the real distinction in things could be *demonstrated* from the fact that knowledge of one does not entail knowledge of the other. His reasoning, then, is thoroughly dialectical.

Aquinas's reasoning is more complicated because he takes a step beyond al-Ghazali and formulates a deductive syllogism, one that involves two inferences: the inductive inference from the examples *human* and *phoenix* to the minor premiss, and the deductive inference from the two premisses to the conclusion that "existence is other than essence." Aquinas's "proof" of the minor follows the same line of thought as al-Ghazali's. But Al-Ghazali had jumped directly from the fact that one can know what human or phoenix are without knowing whether they exist to the metaphysical claim that *in re-*

ality there is a real distinction between essence and existence. Aquinas more modestly and more logically breaks this inference into two parts. From the examples *human* and *phoenix* he generalizes to the minor premiss, an epistemological claim that for *every* quiddity knowledge of that essence does not entail knowing it exists. He then reasons to the metaphysical conclusion of the real distinction deductively. But this deduction is not a demonstration, because the inference runs from *knowing* essences to the *reality* of essences. No necessary inference is to be had here, a fact Avicenna, al-Ghazali, and Aquinas all knew very well. By breaking al-Ghazali's one-step inductive inference into two, however, Aquinas seems to have opened the door for some of his twentieth-century followers to think that the second, deductive inference purports to be demonstrative, simply because it is a syllogism. But this is to confuse deductive form with demonstrative content.

To avoid such confusion it is helpful to recognize that Aquinas's middle term— understanding essence—can be taken both objectively and subjectively. When considered objectively, that is, in terms of the natures of things understood, *intellectus* into an essence refers to the intelligible content found in a definition, as distinct from the subjective act of grasping that definition. This objective sense of "understanding" is nothing other than the essence understood, which is why al-Ghazali moved so quickly from understanding the human essence and its existence to the reality so understood, namely, the accidentality of existence. Aquinas is more careful, sharply distinguishing knowing essence (in both premisses) from the reality of the essence in relation to existence (in his conclusion).

When considered subjectively, that is, in terms of interior mental acts by which we understand things, the term *intellectus* has two distinct meanings, and Aquinas takes advantage of both. In relation to the three acts of the mind, it means the first act— apprehension of concepts—as opposed to judgment and reasoning. Maurer's translation, "the *concept* of an essence or quiddity," captures this sense of the term. But in the context of the principles of science, *intellectus* has another meaning: it is the technical term used to signify *insight* into principles as distinct from reasoning or proof of demonstrated conclusions, variously signified by *ratio, demonstratio,* and other terms. By employing *intellectus* in this sense, Aquinas tries to let his reader know that insight (*intellectus*) into the essences of creatures never entails insight into their existence. This fact about the cognitive order that is contained in Aquinas's premisses functions as a sign of the relation between essence and existence in the order of reality that is contained in his conclusion. But it could never *demonstrate* that conclusion. Insight into the real otherness that existence has in relation to essence can never be deduced, it can only be "seen" in the way all principles are seen.

The dialectical character of Aquinas's syllogism is reinforced if we consider how both Avicenna and Aquinas looked back at their common ancestor—Aristotle. No argument that moves from knowing to being can *demonstrate* the real distinction, for a very simple reason. There are *other* metaphysical principles, Aristotle's for example, which could account for this same fact of our experience while denying the real distinction. Aristotle knew that the questions "Is it?" and "What is it?" are different questions, but he never used the difference between them to draw an inference that there are two different principles in things corresponding to them. What the "understanding essence" argument can do, however, is to lead the mind to the point of being able to *see* this truth.

The "Predicables Argument" for the Unity in God: Step 2

Having made use of Al-Ghazli's simplified language in Step 1 of his argument for potentiality in angels, Aquinas returned to Avicenna's *Metaphysics* 1.6–7 for the rest of his argument, because that text provided all the materials he needed. In Step 2, Br. Thomas presents his other metaphysical hypothesis as an assumption, not a conclusion: "Now *if* one posits that there is some thing which is existence alone, so that existence itself is subsistent."[73] This expression could not be clearer. The reasoning that follows assumes this hypothesis and in no way demonstrates it. His line of argument follows the Avicennian approach used earlier in *EE:* arguing *for* a principle by showing how it "saves" conclusions deduced from it. The argument Br. Thomas presents is an extremely simplified version of Avicenna's "predicables argument" for the unity of necessary existence. As we saw above, in that argument Avicenna had assumed more than one necessary existent, then used a *reductio* to show it would be impossible to discover some trait that would serve to distinguish many necessary existents, because such a trait would fall nowhere within Aristotle's five predicables. Br. Thomas again prefers an argument that is positive and synthetic, using the predicables to move from his metaphysical hypothesis to divine unity.

Now unity has two aspects, for everything "one" is internally undivided and externally divided off from other things. Aquinas begins by *assuming* the fullest sort of internal indivision—that divine essence is undivided from divine existence—and then deduces two consequences. A thing "whose quiddity is its very existence" must be both "one and first." The essential predicables—genus, species, and difference—show that assuming his metaphysical hypothesis leads to the consequence that God is *one in number,* at Step 2 of the argument; the non-essential predicables—property and accident—show that God is the *first* being, the "cause of existence," at Step 3 of the argument.

If God's essence is existence, there are only a limited number of ways this essence, that is, existence itself, could be multiplied over several beings. The essential predicables uncover two possibilities, which Aquinas rejects. Some essences can be multiplied in the way a genus is extended to its species. But existence cannot be multiplied in this way, because existence would then require "the addition of a form," a differentia that would be added to existence alone. But this would violate the initial hypothesis that God's essence simply is existence. Second, existence cannot be multiplied in the way a species is extended to individuals, because this takes place through "the addition of matter," the principle of individuation. This would also violate the initial hypothesis, since "subsistent existence" is not "material existence." Aquinas then adds a third alternative—one not found in Avicenna—that the *nature* of existence is not shared, but existence is shared by some sort of participation. But in this case, there would only be *one* being whose very nature is existence, the existence of all creatures would be participated existence. This new option, of course, is the truth, which means there is only one being in which essence is identical with existence—God.[74]

This argument does not *demonstrate* that there is a being whose essence is existence or that there is only one such being, for the simple reason that the reasoning *assumes* there is such a being. The reasoning assumes the meaningfulness of the essence-existence distinction and, assuming further that there is a being whose essence is its existence, the argument deduces that, under these conditions, there would be only one such being. The identity of essence and existence is a hypothesis that "saves" the unity of God, just as Avicenna had said. The argument, in short, is dialectical.

THE CAUSE OF EXISTENCE: STEP 3

Aquinas then turns to creatures and combines in a new way two arguments from Avicenna. In arguing that necessary existence is one, Avicenna used the two non-essential predicables—property and accident—and in his "sufficiency argument" he invoked the impossibility of infinite regress to support the claim that the "cause of existence" is also a necessary cause. At Step 3 of his argument for potency in angels, Br. Thomas puts these Avicennian arguments together in order to show that God is the "cause of existence" for creatures.

Immediately after concluding dialectically that there is unity of essence and existence in God, he turns to creatures. "Hence the result that the kind of thing that is its own existence can only be one. Hence it is necessary (*unde oportet*) that in everything other than it, its existence is *other* than its quiddity or nature or form."[75] *Unde oportet* does not mean that Aquinas *deduces* the real distinction merely from the premise that in only one being is essence identical with existence. There is an implicit assumption here—that all beings *either* have essences identical with their existence *or* their essence is composed with their existence. But this assumption is nothing other than a restatement of Aquinas's two metaphysical hypotheses in disjunctive form. Both Avicenna and Aquinas think of them paired together. Br. Thomas then moves from the real distinction in creatures to God as "cause of existence" using the predicables property and accident, since they cover the dialectical possibilities when essence and existence are really distinct.

About property, Aquinas uses a *reductio* argument drawn from Avicenna. Existence could not be a kind of property caused by the essence of any being in which existence and essence are distinct, for a very simple reason. Such an essence would already have to exist in order to cause anything, including its own properties. This essence would then have to create itself by causing its property of existing, which is impossible.

The only other alternative left is accident. On the hypothesis that existence is other than essence in creatures, existence must be like a predicable accident, at least in one important respect: existence must be caused by some extrinsic efficient cause, *because existence is really distinct from the essence.* Existence, in short, must either be identical with the essence of a thing, as is true for God alone, or an accident caused by God. There are no other options.

At this point, Br. Thomas has part of the conclusion sought—existence in creatures is received from a cause. Sensitive to the fact that Avicenna had maintained a doctrine of mediate creation, with many causes of existence, Br. Thomas needs to add still another *reductio* argument, this one also taken from Avicenna. An infinite regress of causes of existence subordinated to each other is impossible. Aquinas does not state the reason why, but it is not far to seek. An infinite series of subordinated causes could never be brought together to work in unison to produce an effect, precisely because the series is infinite. Such an infinite series of causes would be inoperative. The alternative to infinite regress is a "first" in the series of causes. But in order to make clear that he does not subscribe to the Avicennian doctrine that intermediate causes would be creative causes, Br. Thomas is careful to point out that the "first cause" is "the cause of existence for *all* other things, because it is pure existence."[76] God alone directly bestows existence on intelligences and on all other creatures. Of course, this is precisely the premiss required to show that the locus of potentiality in such intelligences is essence, not matter, in Step 4.

The text of *EE* 4, when read historically by looking at the way young Br. Thomas incorporated Avicenna and al-Ghazali into his little work, gives no hint that Aquinas is attempting to mount a demonstration of the real distinction in creatures or a demonstration of the existence of God. The argument he uses is deductive, to be sure, but it is hypothetical and dialectical. From the *assumption* that there is a subsistent existence, it follows that there is only *one* such being. Our empirical ability to know what something is without knowing that it exists is a *sign* that there is a composition of essence and existence in all other beings, that is, in all creatures; it does not demonstrate this truth. From this *assumption* it follows that their existence is similar to a predicable accident, that it is caused by the being who is *first* as well as *one,* and that all creatures, even spiritual creatures, combine potency and act. All these conclusions are only as good as Aquinas's initial assumptions. Indeed, it is to help his confreres accept those initial assumptions—the two great hypotheses he had "spoiled" from the metaphysics of Avicenna—that Br. Thomas argues in the way he does.

Two Parallels from Aquinas's *Sentences* Commentary

At two different points in Book 2 of his commentary on the *Sentences*—written about the same time as *EE*—Br. Thomas set out in miniature the argument in *EE* 4:94–146. The topic of the first text is the unity of the first principle, God; the argument contains in outline Steps 1–3 of the *EE* argument. The deduction begins with the real distinction assumed as a hypothesis, it does not demonstrate it:

> Secondly, this is clear from the nature of things. For the nature of entity is found in all things, in some finer, in other less; yet so that [= Step 1 of *EE* 4] the natures of these things are not the very existence (*esse*) which they have. *Otherwise,* existence would be part of the *understanding* of any quiddity. But this is false, since the quiddity of anything can be understood without understanding whether it exists. [= Step 3] Therefore, it is necessary that they have existence from something, and it is necessary to arrive at something whose nature is its very existence. Otherwise, we would proceed to infinity. Now this is what gives existence to *all* things, [= Step 2] and can only be one, since the nature of entity is analogically one nature in all. For unity in the caused inherently demands unity in the cause. Now this is the way of Avicenna.[77]

The initial premiss is Aquinas's metaphysical hypotheses of the real distinction in creatures. It is supported by the same argument found in Step 1 of *EE,* here cast as a *reductio* and clearly dialectical. The infinite regress argument of Step 3 of *EE* then follows. After that comes Step 2 of *EE* concerning the unity of God. The parallel between the two texts is quite extraordinary. What is most important here is that Aquinas explicitly attributes the whole "way" to Avicenna, including Step 1 which uses the *understanding essence* formulation of al-Ghazali. Here we have it on the highest authority that Aquinas drew his dialectical arguments in *EE* 4 from Avicenna, for he himself has said so.

The second text concerns angels. It gives in summary form the argument of *EE* 4. Aquinas begins by arguing against matter in angels based upon the immateriality of the act of understanding, as he did in *EE* 4, then argues for the composition of essence and existence in angels and the consequence that potency is present in angels, due to their quiddity, not matter.

Now existence (*esse*), in so far as a thing is said to exist in act, is related in different ways to different natures or quiddities. [= Step 1 of *EE*] For one kind of nature is that whose *understanding* does not include its existence, as is clear from the fact that its nature can be understood while whether it exists is not known, for example, a *phoenix* or an eclipse or something of this sort. [= Step 2] Another kind of nature is that whose understanding does include its existence, indeed, its existence is its nature. Now existence of this sort does not have existence acquired from another, because what a thing has from its own quiddity it has from itself. [= Step 3] But everything that is other than God has existence acquired from another. Therefore, in God alone is his existence also his quiddity or nature; in all other things existence is other than the quiddity by which existence is acquired. . . . [T]herefore, the quiddity of an angel is that by which subsists its very existence, which is other than its quiddity and is that by which it is, as motion is that by which something is said to be moved. Therefore, an angel is composed of existence and what it is, or of that by which it is and what it is. . . . [= Step 4] And since everything that does not have something from itself but receives it from another is possible or in potency in relation to it, consequently that quiddity is like potency and its acquired existence is like act, and so there is then a composition of act and potency.[78]

This argument contains in outline all four steps of the argument for potency in angels from *EE* 4, including the unusual example of the phoenix. It begins with Aquinas's two metaphysical hypotheses, as do Steps 1 and 2 of EE 4. From these *undemonstrated assumptions* Aquinas concludes that angels are composed of essence and existence and that potency in them is due to their quiddities, not to matter.

———

Just as Avicenna before him had developed dialectical arguments to help his student al-Juzjani to gain insight into perennial metaphysical principles, so Br. Thomas filled his little treatise *On Being and Essence* with dialectical arguments appropriate for his fellow Dominicans living at the convent of S. Jacques. He borrowed the fundamental *notions* and the primary *hypotheses* of metaphysics from the Muslim master who had so much to teach Christian disciples. But perhaps the most important thing he took from Avicenna was a dialectical *mode of arguing* for those principles. After all, argument was absolutely necessary if he wanted his confreres really to understand the principles of metaphysics. And would it not have been contrary to charity simply to stuff their heads with philosophical opinions, either by foregoing argument altogether or by mounting arguments so difficult and obscure that the brothers for whom he wrote would have needed to be Masters in their own right to understand the words he put into his little introduction to the subject?

Notes

1. Cf. M.-D. Roland-Gosselin, *Le "De ente et essentia" de s. Thomas d'Aquin* (Paris: Vrin, 1948) 150–57; also J.-P. Torrell, *Saint Thomas Aquinas*, trans. R. Royal (Washington: Catholic University of America Press, 1996), 47–48; H.-F. Dondaine, introduction to ed. Leonina, 43:321.

2. E. Gilson, "Avicenne en Occident," *Archives d'histoire doctrinale et littéraire du moyen âge* 44 (1970): 10.

3. Tolomeo of Lucca, in Torrell, *St. Thomas Aquinas*, 47. *De ente et essentia* hereafter is *EE*.

4. For the literature, see A. Maurer, "Dialectic in the *De ente et essentia* of St. Thomas Aquinas," in *Roma magistra mundi: Itineraria culturae medievalis*, ed. J. Hamesse (Louvain: Fédération des Institutes d'Études Médiévales, 1998), 576–77. The parameters of the issue were set by E. Gilson, "La preuve de *Ente et Essentia*," *Doctor communis* 3 (1950): 257–69, who distinguished "two ways to attain the composition of essence and existence," (1) a demonstrative way, as in *ST*, where the real distinction is a conclusion demonstrated from the existence and simplicity of God, and (2) a non-demonstrative way in *EE*, "which discovers it at the end of a metaphysical analysis of finite being."

(1) Most subsequent interpreters have held that Aquinas attempted to demonstrate both the real distinction and the existence of God in *EE*. F. van Steenberghen, *Le probleme de l'existence de dieu dans les ecrits de s. Thomas d'Aquin* (Louvain: Éditions de l'Institut supérieur de philosophie, 1980), 34–42, said that *EE* 4 (ed. Leonina 43:376.94–103) was an attempted "demonstration" of the real distinction, independent of God's existence, but unsound because moving illegitimately from conceptual to real existence; and at 127–46 Aquinas then followed with an unsound demonstration of the existence of God. J. Wippel, "Essence and Existence in the *De ente* c. 4," *Metaphysical Themes in Thomas Aquinas* (Washington: Catholic University of America Press, 1984), 107–32, and *The Metaphysical Thought of Thomas Aquinas* (Washington: Catholic University of America Press, 2000), 132–76, thought the intervening text at 103–26 a sound demonstration of the real distinction, independent of God's existence, which makes his argument for God's existence at 127–46 also sound. J. Owens, "Quiddity and the Real Distinction in St. Thomas Aquinas," *Mediaeval Studies* 27 (1965): 19; *An Elementary Christian Metaphysics* 103–4; "Aquinas' Distinction at *De ente et essentia* 4.119–123" *Mediaeval Studies* 48 (1986): 264–87, said that 94–146 constitutes sound but highly enthymemic demonstrations, first of the existence of God by proceeding from a merely conceptual distinction between essence and existence, then of the real distinction in creatures based on the existence of God, akin to that found in *ST*. G. Rocca, *Speaking the Incomprehensible God* (Washington: Catholic University of America Press, 2004), 253–54, says "it is because we first know God as *ipsum esse subsistens* that we can conclude to the real distinction in creatures." But he then gives this view a rather fideistic interpretation: ". . . it is more by his *faith* than by his reason that he acknowledges the transcendent and free Creator as well as the radical contingence of creatures. . . . and *at the heart of that faith,* now philosophically interpreted, are the twin truths about God as subsistent being itself and about creatures as possessing a real distinction between their being and their essence" (emphasis added).

A minority of scholars have followed (2): J. A. Weisheipl, *Friar Thomas d'Aquino* (New York: Doubleday, 1974), 78, cf. ed. Leonina of *EE* 321, held that the real distinction is an unproven thesis, because *EE* is merely an "expository work in metaphysics." Gilson eventually opted for his second way, the real distinction being "the fundamental truth" of Christian metaphysics, a principle Thomists had tried and failed to demonstrate. The only kind of argument for it is dialectical meditation by a Christian philosopher on Ex. 3:14. *Introduction à la philosophie chrétienne* (Paris:

Vrin, 1960), trans. A. Maurer, *Christian Philosophy: An Introduction*, (Toronto: Pontifical Institute of Mediaeval Studies, 1993), 31, 56, 72–73. A. Maurer initially held that Aquinas offered no argument for the real distinction, in *St. Thomas Aquinas: On Being and Essence* (Toronto: Pontifical Institute of Mediaeval Studies, 1968), 21–26, but in "Dialectic in the *De ente et essentia* of St. Thomas Aquinas" has found in *EE* dialectical arguments. Scott MacDonald, "The *Esse/Essentia* Argument in Aquinas's *De ente et essentia*," *Journal of the History of Philosophy* 22 (1984): 157–172, carefully analyzed the steps of the argument in the manner of analytic philosophy, but did not definitively come down on one side or the other of the present issue. Avicenna, of course, was a philosopher but no Christian. I believe the parallels outlined here show the minority interpretation to be correct.

5. Avicenna, *Al-Shifâ'. Al-Ilâhiyyât*, ed. G.C. Anawati and S. Zayed (Cairo: Al-Hay'a al-ʿÂmma li-Shuʾûn al-Mutâbiʿ al-Amîrîya, 1960); *Avicenna Latinus. Liber de philosophia prima sive scientia divina*, ed. S. van Riet (Louvain, Leiden: Peters, 1977–83); *La Métaphysique du Shifâ'*, trans. G.C. Anawati (Paris: Vrin, 1978–85); Avicenna, *The Metaphysics of "The Healing,"* trans. M. Marmura (Provo, Utah: Brigham Young University Press, 2005), 1.5 (Ar: 29.5–6; Lat: 31.2–32.4; Fr: 106; Eng: 22, sec. [1]), hereafter *Met.*. All translations are my own unless otherwise indicated.

6. Aristotle, *Prior Analytics* 1.1 (24a10–b30).

7. J.-P. Torrell, *Initiation à S. Thomas d'Aquin* (Paris: Cerf, 1993), 70–72.

8. *EE* prologue (43:369.1–5).

9. *EE* 6 (43:381.170–1): finis et consummatio huius sermonis.

10. Avicenna, *Met.* 1.5 (Ar: 30.1–2; Lat: 33.22–24; Fr: 106–7; Eng: 23, sec. [4]).

11. *Met.* 1.5 (Ar: 29.7–8; Lat: 32.6–7; Fr: 106; Eng: 22, sec [1]).

12. *Met.* 1.5 (Ar: 29.5–6; Lat: 31.2–32.4; Fr: 106; Eng: 22, sec. [1]). < > indicates Arabic text not found in Latin and therefore unavailable to Aquinas.

13. *Met.* 1.5. Action and passion as species of being: Ar: 30.3–11; Lat: 33.25–36; Fr: 107; Eng: 23, sec. [5]. Triangle and whiteness as examples of thing: Ar: 31.5–9; Lat: 34.54–35.61; Fr: 108; Eng: 24, sec. [9].

14. Established: Ar: al-muthbat. Realized: Ar: al-muhaṣṣal. The Latin translation collapsed these two words into one: aliquid. Aquinas defines aliquid at *De veritate* 1.1 as the external side of transcendental unity—ens divisum ab aliis—which, when combined with its internal side—ens indivisum in se—yields transcendental unity. True nature: Ar: haqîqa, Lat: certitudo. Quiddity: Ar: mâhiyya, Lat: quidditas.

15. *Met.* 1.5 (Ar: 36.5; Lat: 41.80; Fr: 111; Eng: 28, sec. [24]). Assuredness of existence: Ar: ta'akkud al-wujûd; Lat: vehementiam essendi.

16. *Met.* 1.5 (Ar: 31.23; Lat: 34.5051; Fr: 107; Eng: 24).

Translations of "being" terms

Aristotle	ὄν	εἶναι	_____	τί ἦν εἶναι	τί ἔστι
Avicenna	mawjûd	wujûd	shay'	dhât	mâhiyya
Avic. Lat.	ens	esse	res	essentia	quidditas
Marmura tr.	existent	existence	thing	essence	quiddity
Aquinas	ens	esse	res	essentia	quidditas
Maurer tr.	a being	being	thing	essence	quiddity
My tr.	a being; being	existence	thing	essence	quiddity

I have rendered *mawjûd* and *ens* as "a being" or "being," as context requires, and in order to avoid ambiguity I have used a different term to translate *wujûd* and *esse*, namely, "existence," which has gained wide currency as a translation of *esse* in Aquinas. Since "being" and "existence" are not etymologically linked in English, this translation does not preserve such links in the Arabic and Latin terms they translate; but it avoids confusing *mawjûd/ens* with *wujûd/esse*. While he normally translates *wujûd* as "existence," at *Met.* 1.6–7 Marmura translates *al-wâjib al-wujûd* as "*the* Necessary *Existent*," namely, God, rather than as "necessary existence" (pp. 29–30), which translation undermines the argumentative character of Avicenna's text. For the terms in Greek, Arabic, and Latin, see: Avicenna, *Met.: Lexiques*, ed. S. van Riet (Louvain: Peeters, Leiden: Brill, 1983); and A.-M. Goichon, *Vocabulaires comparés d'Aristote et d'Ibn Sina* (Paris: Desclée de Brouwer, 1938).

17. *EE* 1 (43:369.20–25).

18. Cf. Introduction to ed. Leonina, 43:320: il est difficile de classer ce petit compendium où logique et metaphysique vont de pair.

19. *EE* 1 (43:369.31–52).

20. Gohlman, *Avicenna* (London: Routledge, 1992), 58–59.

21. *Met.* 1.6 (Ar: 37.6–10; Lat: 43.7–13; Fr: 113; Eng: 29–30, sec. [1]). Necessary existence: Ar: al-wâjib al-wujûd; Lat: necesse esse.

22. *Met.* 1.7 (Ar: 47.6–9; Lat: 54.38–43; Fr: 121; Eng: 38, sec. [13]).

23. *Met.* 1.7 (Ar: 47.10–19; Lat: 54.44–55.55; Fr: 121–22; Eng: 38, sec. [14]).

24. *EE* 5 (43:378.1–2), trans. Maurer.

25. *EE* 5 (43:378.3–10).

26. *EE* 5 (43:378.44–51). Aquinas's skill at simplifying Avicenna is clear in comparing them on intelligences. Avicenna: "And that whose being is necessary through another always, its quiddity is not simple, because what it has in itself is *other* (*aliud*) than what it has from another." Dropping necessity allows Aquinas to say simply: "Their existence is *other* (*aliud*) than their essence."

27. Cf. n. 23 above.

28. *EE* 5 (43:379.131–36).

29. Aristotle, *Posterior Analytics* 2.19: induction: 100a3–100b1; composing and dividing notions: 100b1–5; insight: 100b5–17.

30. [(~p ⊃ a) & ~a] ⊃ p, where "p" is the assertion of some principle and "a" the assertion of some absurdity.

31. [(p ⊃ c) & c] ⊃ p.

32. Cf. Aristotle, *Met.* 1.7 (988a20–23), where Aristotle says (P ⊃ C), then adds C. He does not fallaciously deduce P, but uses C to open his reader to admit the principle P, through *nous*.

33. L. E. Goodman, *Avicenna*, 28–29.

34. Qur'an 6.1, trans. Maulana Muhammand Ali.

35. *Met.* 1.6 (Ar: 37.11–15; Lat: 43.14–18; Fr: 113; Eng: 30, sec. [2]).

36. *Met.* 1.6 (Ar: 37.15–18; Lat: 43.19–23; Fr: 113; Eng: 30, sec. [2]).

37. The rubric in 1.6 (Ar: 37.11–18; Lat: 43.14–23; Fr: 113; Eng: 30, sec. [2]) contains the following *provable conclusions:* necessary being is uncaused, has no equal, shares neither its essence nor existence with anything, is not relative, changeable, or multiplied; possible being is caused. The additional thesis that necessary being is not composed of many parts is ambiguous. If understood to refer to essence and existence as parts, it is a hypothesis; but more likely it refers to other kinds of parts, making it a provable conclusion. The summary ending 1.7, (Ar: 47.6–19; Lat: 54.38–55.55; Fr: 121–2; Eng: 38, sec. [13]–[14]) contains the following *metaphysical hypotheses:*

necessary being is uniquely simple ontologically, while a possible being contains two fundamental parts, essence (making it possible in itself) and existence (making it necessary from another). The summary also contains provable conclusions: the possible is caused, and there are two sorts of possibles—eternal and perishable.

38. *Met.* 1.6. Arguments: For Thesis 1: Ar: 38.1–10; Lat: 44.24–37; Fr: 114; Eng. 30, sec. [3]. For Thesis 2: Ar: 38.11–39.16; Lat: 44.38–46.71; Fr: 114–15; Eng: 30, sec. [4]–32, sec. [6]. For Thesis 3: missing. For Thesis 4: Ar:39.17–42.7; Lat: 46.72–48.38; Fr: 115–17; Eng: 32 [7]–34 [13]. For Thesis 5: Ar: 43.1–46.12; Lat: 49.40–53.20; Fr: 118–21; Eng: 35, sec. [1]–37, sec. [9]. For Thesis 6: Ar 46.13–47.5; Lat: 53.21–54.38; Fr: 121; Eng: 37, sec. [10]–[12]. Avicenna summarizes the results of the first argument thus: "Therefore it is clear that if existence necessary in itself had a cause, then it would not be existence necessary in itself" ($\sim U \supset \sim N$). The consequent contradicts N, leading by *modus tollens* to the true thesis U. The contradiction, however, is only internal to the Avicennian system, and cannot demonstrate U or N, or, more importantly, the even more fundamental hypothesis from which p and q flow—the identity of essence and existence in necessary being. Sensitive to the limits of this way of arguing, Avicenna states his results in purely hypothetical form, and turns to a more positive mode of argument uncovering that hypothesis.

39. *Met* 1.6 (Ar: 38.13–39.4; Lat: 44.38–45.58; Fr: 114; Eng: 31, sec. [4]–[5]). "Illa al-wujûdiyya" has been rendered "cause of existence," following the literal and correct Latin: causa essendi (45.57). Quiddity: Ar: mâhiyya; Lat: id quod ipsum est.

40. Aristotle, *Posterior Analytics* 2.7 (92b3–8)

41. *Met.* 1.6 (Ar: 39.5–16; Lat: 45.59–46.71; Fr: 115; Eng: 31, sec. [6]).

42. *Met* .1.7 (Ar: 44.1–2; Lat: 50.59–60; Fr: 119; Eng: 35, sec. [2]).

43. *Met.* 1.7 (Ar: 43.4–46.5; Lat: 49.40–52.12; Fr: 118–20; Eng: 34, sec. [1]–37, sec. [9]).

44. *EE* 2 (43:370.45–47).

45. *EE* 2 (43:371.50–57).

46. *EE* 3 (43:374.26–54).

47. *EE* 3. On essence and existence in individuals: 374.55–56. On essence and existence in concepts: 375.102–7. Cf. *In Sent.* 2. d. 17.2.1 (ed. Mandonnet 2:429). "According to *Avicenna*, the species understood can be considered in two ways: either with regard to the existence (*esse*) it has in the mind, and in this respect it has individual existence; or as it is a kind of likeness of the thing known, producing cognition of it, and in this respect it possesses universality. For it is not a likeness of this thing in so far as this thing exists (*est*), but in relation to the nature in which it agrees with other things of its species."

48. *EE* 4 (43:376.36–37).

49. *EE* 4 (43:375.1–376.22).

50. *EE* 4 (43:376.23–36).

51. The three arguments are: (1) form exists without matter, 43:376.41–60; (2) two Avicennian corollaries, 43:376.61–89; (3) potency in angels, 43:376.90–378.201.

52. By contrast, J. Owens, "Aquinas' Distinction at *De ente et essentia* 4.119–123," *Mediaeval Studies* 48 (1986): 270, has described the argument he finds in this chapter of *EE* as "a *difficult reasoning process*."

53. *EE* 4 (43:376.42–49).

54. *EE* 4 (43:376.61–89).

55. *EE* 4 (43:376.90–378.201).

56. Step 1, about creatures: 43:376.94–103; Step 2, about God: 43:376.103–26; Step 3, existence as accident requires God as cause of existence: 43:377.127–46; Step 4, potentiality in angels, 43:377.147–59.

57. *EE* 4 (43:377.147–54).

58. *EE* 4 (43:377.162): "its existence received from God (et esse suum receptum a Deo)."

59. *EE* 4 (43:376.90–377.146).

60. *EE* 4 (43:376.102–4). The Leonine editor, following Roland-Gosselin, breaks the sentence in two, because the first clause flows from the argument at 94–103, while the second clause initiates the argument from 103–46. Avicennian doctrine as well as Latin syntax indicate that others were right to keep the sentence together. Cf. Baur ed. 40; Maurer trans. 55. For Avicenna see n. 23.

61. See n. 56.

62. *EE* 4 (43:376.94–103): *Quicquid* enim *non* est de intellectu *essentiae vel quiditatis,* hoc est *adveniens extra* et faciens compositionem cum essentia, quia nulla essentia sine his, quae sunt partes essentiae, intelligi potest. Omnis autem *essentia vel quiditas* potest intelligi *sine* hoc quod *aliquid* intelligatur de *esse suo:* possum enim intelligere quid est homo vel phoenix et tamen ignorare an esse habeat in rerum natura. Ergo patet quod esse est aliud ab essentia vel quiditate.

63. Avicenna, *Met.* 1.6 (Lat: 44.44–46; Eng: 31, sec. [5]): manifestum est autem quod *quicquid* post non esse habet esse iam appropriatum est per *aliquid* quod sibi *advenit ab alio a se.* For Aquinas, see n. 62.

64. Avicenna, Met. 1.6 (Lat: 45.52–54; Eng: 31, sec. [5]): si autem *id quod est non* est sufficiens ad acquirendum sibi utrumlibet, sed per *aliquid aliud adiunctum* est sibi esse id quod est, tunc *esse illius* est ex esse alterius a se, quo eget ad esse. For Aquinas, see n. 62; for Avicenna, see n. 39.

65. Aquinas's mode of argument is the main reason why many contemporary scholars have thought *EE* 4 a *demonstration* of the real distinction or the existence of God. But not all syllogisms set out in the synthetic mode are demonstrative.

66. Al-Ghazali, "*Logica Algazelis,* Introduction and Critical Text," ed. C. H. Lohr, *Traditio* 21 (1965): 246.5–247.9.

67. Avicenna, *Shifa', Logica,* c. 5, Lat. trans. (Venice: 1508, 4va–b): Iam autem scis quod hoc intelligere non volo dicere hoc, scilicet, ut cum intellexeris aliquid et consideraveris in effectu quod intelligeris etiam *partes* suorum constitutionum in effectu. Fortassis enim non considerabis partes in tuo intellectu. Set dico quod si consideraveris constituens et consitutum non erit possibile removere constitum a constituente se, taliter ut verum sit constitutum habere esse in intellectu non habente esse constituente se. Apart from *partes,* this text anticipates the doctrine but not the language of Aquinas's major premiss.

68. Al-Ghazali, "*Logica Algazelis,*" 247.15–19: cum *intellexeris essentiale* et id cui est essentiale, *non possis* imaginari subiectum vel *intelligere,* nisi intelligas essentiale existere in eo. Nec possit ullo modo subiectum intelligi sine illo. Cum enim intelligis, quid est homo et quid est animal, non potes intelligere hominem sine intellectu animalis.

69. Text at n. 62.

70. Al-Ghazali, "*Logica Algazelis,*" 247.26–32: Similiter cum intelligis *quid est homo non est necesse te intelligere* eum *esse* vel esse album. Nec tamen potes eum intelligere, nisi intelligas quod est animal; quamvis non satisfaciat tuo intellectui hoc exemplum, eo quod tu es homo et omnes alii qui nunc sunt. Pone ergo aliud exemplum: sicut de *phoenice* vel de aliquo alio extraneo—et ibi manifestabitur tibi, quia *esse* accidentale est omnibus quae est.

71. See n. 62.

72. Cf. Aquinas, *In 3 de caelo,* lec. 8, §4: nihil autem prohibet individuum quod est unum tantum in una specie, generari et corrumpi, sicut de Phoenice dicunt. On the phoenix in Avicenna, see: Deborah L. Black, "Avicenna on the Ontological and Epistemic Status of Fictional Beings," *Documenti e Studi sulla Tradizione Filosofica Medievale* 8 (1997): 425–53. Alain de Libera, *L'Art des*

généralités: Théories de l'abstraction (Paris: Aubier, 1999), 511–14, traces the phoenix in Porphyry, Simplicius, Avicenna *Metaphysics* 5.1, and Nicolas of Cornwall. In addition to al-Ghazali, Avicenna's three definitions of universal at *Met.* 5.1 may have served as a source for Aquinas's use of phoenix here. This text circulated in two versions. The version more faithful to the Arabic, called by Van Riet "texte ancien" (1:128*–130*; 2:82*) uses *human* as the example for universals actually predicated of many subjects, *seven-sided house* (domus heptangulae) for a universal not actually predicated of anything but potentially predicated of many, and *sun* and *earth* (not *moon*, as in de Libera 512) as actually predicated of only one thing. In the second version of the text, called by Van Riet "texte revu," the second and third kinds of universals were collapsed together because of a textual omission due to homeoteleuton. This second version reads: "Therefore, I say that universal is said in three modes. For that is called a universal as being actually predicated of many things, for example, *human;* and that intention is called a universal which can be predicated of many things, even though it actually has existence in none of them, for example, *seven-sided house,* which is a universal in that its nature can be predicated of many [textual omission], yet if something prohibits this, there is a cause owing to which it is prohibited, for example *sun* and *earth.*" In this version, sun and earth have ceased to be examples of a third kind of universal but have become the "cause" why the seven-sided house is not predicated. This conflation makes no sense, but sun and earth are the causes that explain the death of the phoenix through fire and its resurrection from ashes. At some point a clever clerk likely inserted the phoenix for the seven-sided house, a version of Avicenna's text known to Nicholas of Cornwall (ca. 1275): "Dicitur, sicut dicit Auiscenna, quod est quedam species que actu saluatur in multis, ut *homo;* quedam uero non actu set potencia, ut *fenix;* quedam uero nec actu, nec potencia, set intellectu, ut *celum.*" Cf. P. Osmund Lewry, "Oxford Logic 1250–1275: Nicholas and Peter of Cornwall," in *The Rise of British Logic,* ed. P. O. Lewry (Toronto: Pontifical Institute of Mediaeval Studies, 1983), 43. It is not known which is the version of Avicenna that Aquinas read.

73. *EE* 4 (43:377.113–15): Si autem ponatur aliqua res, quae sit esse tantum, ita ut ipsum esse sit subsistens.

74. *EE* 4 (43:376.105–377.119).

75. *EE* 4 (43:377.121–23). Unde relinquitur quod talis res, quae sit suum esse, non potest esse nisi una. Unde oportet quod in qualibet alia re praeter eam aliud sit esse suum et aliud quiditas vel natura seu forma sua. *Unde oportet* signifies a disjunctive syllogism whose major premiss is (I V D), highlighting the consistency of these hypotheses, and bringing forth the hypothesis relevant to the rest of the argument. It does not demonstrate one disjunct *from* the other. Following Avicenna, Aquinas does not hesitate to move deductively from one hypothesis to each other, as a way of illustrating (but not demonstrating) how all beings fit quite precisely within the stark alternatives his hypotheses set (I V D).

76. *EE* 4 (377).

77. *In Sent.* 2. d. 1.1.1 (ed. Mandonnet 2:12–3).

78. *In Sent.,* 2. d. 3.1.1 c (ed. Mandonnet 2:87–88).

Chapter 5

Faith and Reason

The Synthesis of St. Thomas Aquinas

LEO J. ELDERS, SVD

In a lecture delivered at the Sorbonne on November 27, 1999, Cardinal Joseph Ratzinger argued that the victory of Christianity over the pagan religions in the Roman Empire was made possible by its recourse to reason, by its reasonableness as well as by its moral doctrine. Christianity, indeed, does not rely on imagination or unverifiable events, but places itself at the junction of faith and reason. By its choice in favor of the primacy of reason in human life it continues to present a rational vision of the world and to encourage scientific research. In his encyclical *Fides et ratio* of 1999 John Paul II, dealing more *in extenso* with this theme, examines the relationship between faith and reason, the influence they have exercised on each other, and draws up the balance of the actual situation of the relation between philosophy and theology. As the pope explains, our reason is not imprisoned in the sensible world but, to a certain extent, it is able to go beyond it. Reason is universal and extends also beyond what is proper to particular cultures. On the other hand the rise and fall of often dangerous and frightening secular ideologies has shown the limits of reason, which can no longer pretend to master by itself alone nature, science, and progress.[1] The encyclical sketches some of the main events of the long history of the coexistence and collaboration of faith and reason to highlight the support and benefits each of them derived from it. In §43 it describes the particular place St. Thomas Aquinas occupies in this history, not only because of the high value of his theology and philosophy, but also because of the dialogue he conducted with medieval Arab and Jewish thought.

St. Thomas Aquinas on Faith and Reason

If we try to analyze the position of Aquinas, we must recall that Thomas was the first theologian to distinguish with great clarity between theology and philosophy. Their difference, he writes, derives from their different sources, from the way they proceed, and from their respective subject matters.[2] Indeed, differences in the source of knowledge and the way of knowing entail a diversity of disciplines.[3] Sacred doctrine receives its principles from divine revelation, namely, the fundamental truths of the faith as expressed in the articles of the creed. Philosophy, on the other hand, acquires its fundamental principles through evident insight into the structure of reality. It proceeds by gathering knowledge through experience—by analyzing and drawing conclusions from what is based on evidence. Sacred doctrine, on the other hand, proceeds in the twilight of the faith, without possessing evident knowledge about the truths it considers. While accepting the creed on divine authority, theologians use concepts, principles, and insights of everyday life and sound philosophy to penetrate further into the meaning of what has been revealed.

In addition to the source and basis of their respective sciences being distinct, the subject matter of sacred theology and that of philosophy also differ: philosophical disciplines study nature, man, and his actions in the light of his end, as well as being *qua* being, whereas sacred theology considers God insofar as he revealed himself and his design concerning man's supernatural salvation. Whatever God has revealed is the subject matter of sacred doctrine.[4] However, much of what has been revealed lies beyond the reach of natural reason, since it concerns infinite and transcendent divine being, wisdom, love,[5] and God's free decision, but God may also reveal certain basic truths which as such are accessible to reason, in order to make it easier for all to come to know them. As an example one may point to the revelation of the main precepts of natural law in the Ten Commandments.[6]

But St. Thomas does not stop short at the distinction between sacred doctrine and natural knowledge. He also insists on their harmony. There can be no contradiction between true natural knowledge and the doctrine of the faith, because both have their origin in God who, as the creator of the world and of man, places the principles of our knowledge in our minds, but has also given us revealed knowledge.[7]

Because of the patent incompatibility of certain positions of Averroistic Aristotelianism with the Christian faith (such as the theory of the eternity of the world), some masters of the faculty of arts in thirteenth-century Paris developed the theory of double truth: what is established in sacred theology sometimes contradicts what is true in philosophy, so that a Christian philosopher must accept simultaneously two conflicting theses. However, Aquinas strongly opposes this view. Since all truth comes from God, in whom there is no contradiction, such a position is impossible.[8] Apparent contradictions originate from erroneous reasoning or from false deductions from the doctrine of the faith.

GRACE BUILDS ON NATURE AND FULFILLS IT

Instead of opposition and conflict, Aquinas speaks of a harmonious collaboration where the supernatural order presupposes the natural order and fulfills it. In a considerable number of texts Aquinas confirms this position: "The order in which divine providence proceeds does not take away from things what is natural for them, but God takes care of each thing according to its nature."[9] The order of grace is not even possible without nature, since grace is a state or quality added to it. Thus the law of God presupposes natural law,[10] as faith presupposes man's natural knowledge.[11] Indeed, grace is not meant to do away with human nature, but to raise and accomplish it.[12] Grace renders nature more perfect. It does so in agreement with nature's basic characteristics. For this reason angels received their beatitude immediately after their initial choice of God, without having to go through the often long period of waiting in faith and hope which makes up the life of Christians on earth.[13] Likewise grace does not take away imperfections which are inherent to human nature itself, such as the fact that man is a creature.[14] Since nature proceeds from what is imperfect to greater fullness, grace was given first in an imperfect way but later in abundance.[15]

Thomas also indicates the manner in which grace perfects nature, namely, how the intellect and the will as well as the lower faculties of the soul can be controlled by reason.[16] "Since grace does not do away with nature but perfects it, natural reason must be subservient to faith as the natural inclination of the will follows charity."[17] This is so obvious for Aquinas that he even builds an argument on it: from the fact that by his natural inclination man loves God more than himself, it follows that supernatural charity also makes man love God above himself.[18] Sin, on the other hand, causes damage insofar as it obstructs the help of grace and the government of natural reason over man's faculties.[19]

What makes it possible for supernatural grace to bring about this effect is the presence in man of a certain potency toward a fulfillment and higher perfection, called the *potentia obedientialis* or *potentia obedientiæ*. This potency, as Thomas understands it, is man's very nature insofar as it lies open to God, who can bring about in it whatever he has decided.[20] One might describe this potency as a creature's nature being at the disposal of divine omnipotence.[21] Thomas states it even more explicitly: "In all created things there is a certain *potentia obedientialis* in so far as all created things obey God receiving whatever God has decided to give them."[22] The concept of *potentia obedientialis* is used in the first place to explain the occurrence of miracles. A miracle, such as the transformation of water into wine at the wedding in Cana, is not in conflict with the supreme law of physical nature according to which material things are subservient to spiritual realities. This subordination of created things to God's power is called their *potentia obedientiæ*. In a sense one might even say with Augustine that the nature of things is precisely the use God makes of them.[23] The potency to receive grace is different insofar as grace enhances nature and corresponds to man's most profound desires, whereas a miracle usually happens in discontinuity with the ordinary inclinations of natural things:[24] a dangerous tumor normally keeps growing and damages the organism and a blind person does not suddenly recover his vision. St. Thomas has given a most remarkable illustration of how grace completes nature and is meant by God to fulfill our every desire. He attaches much importance to this point: his use of convincing arguments illustrates how reason can be an aid to theology and how the Christian faith is in agreement with human nature.

THE SUPERNATURAL ORDER AS THE FULFILLMENT OF OUR DEEPEST NATURAL DESIRES

Assuming that the core of man's nature is reason, Aquinas argues in a number of texts that our natural desire to know the causes of things and events, and to reach ultimate explanations, can only be fulfilled by the vision of God himself. Since a natural desire cannot be in vain, man must have a certain capacity to be brought by God to this vision, as the Christian faith teaches.[25] Man's thirst to know the truth will be quenched when he is admitted into God's company.

Together with this desire, man seeks to exist forever and to avoid the destruction of his bodily being. What the Christian religion promises is precisely eternal life with God. To this may be added the following reflection: our soul exists by its nature in a body. It is against the soul's nature to be without a body. But nothing which is against nature can last forever. For this reason the soul must be united again to the body.[26]

A further natural desire disposes us to whatever we need to live rightly and to fulfill our tasks. This is actually a desire that our life be directed by right reason. In order to attain this goal one must possess the different virtues. A life according to the virtues will find its fulfillment in eternity, when right reason will direct our faculties.

Man desires to be understood by others and to have his merits acknowledged. As to this point St. Thomas observes that the blessed entering the glory of God will find complete satisfaction: their virtuous lives will lie open to others.

Connected to this is the desire to possess and to find delight in things. Now when we are united with God, we shall possess everything. Moreover, our joy will be predominantly spiritual and therefore much more intense than bodily pleasures. In this way grace fulfills our fundamental longings.[27]

In this connection one may also mention the desire to live together with other human beings. As Aquinas explains, the blessed in heaven constitute one community, which will be filled with delight, because everyone will have all goods together with all the blessed.[28] One will love others as oneself and therefore rejoice in the good of others as in that of oneself. For this reason the delight and joy of each will increase to become as large as the joy of all.[29]

St. Thomas's Confidence in Nature and in Reason

Aquinas has great confidence in the rectitude of nature as it has come from the hands of the Creator. Indeed, nature tends to what is fitting for each thing. We see that man seeks by nature the sort of pleasure which agrees with him. Since man is rational, the pleasure which is becoming for him, is that which is in agreement with reason. Thomas uses this principle to argue that the virtue of temperance is not contrary to the inclination of our nature, but is only opposed to lower tendencies which do not obey reason.[30] When an act is performed according to a natural inclination and is directed to our end, it is morally right.[31] Repeatedly Thomas asserts that man must execute the acts to which his nature moves him, but in conformity with right reason.[32]

This confidence in reason and the basic goodness of human nature gave rise to the humanism of Aquinas.[33] Man must live in accordance with what is highest in him and integrate the various inclinations, so that they are ordained to his true end. The different virtues bring about this harmony with nature and make human behavior wise, humane, just, and kind to others. Reason helps to establish rules for our conduct, in particular where faith does not go into details about our duties.[34] Basing himself on the need for relaxation, Thomas argues that one can set aside some of one's time for play.[35] It is even allowed, he writes, to devote oneself professionally to entertainment—within the limits of right reason—because of the relaxation one procures for others.[36] Reason has a positive role in theology and is essential for determining our moral duties.

The Use of Reason in Theology

When we speak of the use of reason in theology we do not mean so much the use of the concepts of natural knowledge—which is obvious and necessary—as recourse to analysis, reasoning, deduction, and arrangement of the contents of the doctrine of the faith. Our Christian faith is based on the authority of God who revealed himself to the prophets and, in the New Testament, revealed himself in Jesus Christ and then to the apostles and their collaborators in the redaction of the writings of the New Testament. We accept and believe the Christian message because of their testimony.

However, since this testimony is given to us by men, we must be convinced of their reliability. As Aquinas explains, the miracles wrought by Jesus and the apostles, as they surpass whatever nature can bring about, guarantee the supernatural origin of the message.[37] The greatest miracle of all (*maximum miraculum*) is that simple men were able to speak with so much wisdom and force and that people were converted to believe in what goes beyond human reason—disregarding temporal goods to gain the eternal.

He adds that there are also arguments tending to make the mysteries of the faith acceptable. But this kind of reasoning is weak and serves to comfort the faithful and to keep their minds fixed on the dogmas rather than to convince nonbelievers.

With regard to the use of philosophy in the elaboration of the science of theology, such Christian authors of the second century as Justin, Tatian, and Clement of Alexandria, who had received philosophical training, resorted to philosophy to defend the Christian faith and Christians against accusations such as atheism. But they knew that philosophers had often mixed truth with falsehoods. Tertullian even called philosophy the cradle of heresies and useless questions. He exclaimed: "Quid ergo Athenis et Hierosolymis? Quid academiæ et ecclesiæ?"[38] During the first centuries, the Christian authors used above all elements of Stoic thought, but always insisted on the distance which separated revealed doctrine from human wisdom. In the following centuries, Platonism exercised a strong influence. Plato's philosophy in its original form and as elaborated in Middle and Neo-Platonism constitutes a reservoir of philosophical theories which has accompanied Christian thought up to the Renaissance and beyond. It taught that things originate from a common, transcendent source and constitute a well-organized ensemble. The perfection of the First Principle is distributed in the universe according to a certain hierarchy. Furthermore, Platonism insists on the immateriality of the human soul and its kinship with God. The soul's real home is with God, and human life must be an effort to imitate God and to prepare for a new existence. Christians, however, corrected Platonism on certain points, such as the pronounced dualism of its doctrine of man, the theory of the pre-existence of the human soul, and an overly pessimistic view of the material world.

For various reasons, recourse to Aristotle was much more limited at first.[39] However, in the second half of the twelfth and in the thirteenth centuries Aristotle's writings attracted many theologians. This created some difficulties at first because they contained erroneous theories of man, the origin of the world, and moral life. At the University of Paris the use of the *libri naturales* of Aristotle was forbidden for a while, but later permitted, though with some restrictions at first. The chancellor Eudes of Chateauroux complained that certain theologians sell themselves to the sons of the Greeks and Robert Grosseteste admonished the masters of the faculty of theology in Oxford to remain faithful to the traditional way of teaching theology.[40] As a matter of fact, some theologians attempted to give theology a more scientific character and to arrange the various themes in a systematic order.[41] St. Thomas Aquinas was one of the first masters to present a rigorous organization of sacred theology as a science.[42] He sets out from the Aristotelian position according to which science is knowledge of what is necessary. In theology the different themes and their causal connections must be considered from the point of view of God's knowledge. Thus creation as well as the incarnation and redemption are studied as God knows them, rather than as willed by God, for God's will concerns the individual and contingent.[43]

The Biblical commentaries of St. Thomas contain some interesting remarks on the use of philosophy in the elaboration of theology. Philosophers distinguish themselves by their knowledge of the truth, even if the minds of some of them are obscured occasionally.[44] They have reached a certain knowledge of the truth, although not all are of the same opinion.[45] In an argument, based on social and juridical custom, used by St. Paul to show that the New Law has not done away with the Promise, Thomas sees proof that in matters of the faith one may use any truth from any science.[46] Thomas also refers to St. Jerome who, in a letter to the Grand Speaker of the city of Rome observed that all Christian doctors wrote *in ornatu philosophiæ* and enriched their works with the doctrine and wisdom of the philosophers, so that one did not know what to admire more in them, their profane knowledge or their acquaintance with the Scriptures.[47] In his systematic works and in several of the *Quæstiones disputatæ* Aquinas defends energetically the right of a theologian to make use of philosophy in the elaboration of sacred doctrine, even if resorting to philosophy is not without danger. The study of philosophy is legitimate and even praiseworthy because of the truth the philosophers have found, due to what God has made them understand, but because some philosophers misused their knowledge to attack the faith, the Apostle warns us: "Make sure that no one traps you and deprives you of your freedom by some second-hand, empty, rational philosophy, based on the principles of this world instead of on Christ."[48] If in the writings of the philosophers one encounters statements contrary to the faith, these are no longer philosophy but an abuse of philosophy.[49] Elsewhere Thomas speaks of the *vera philosophiæ principia quæ consideravit Aristoteles.*[50]

THE CONTRIBUTION OF PHILOSOPHY

The subject matter of philosophy coincides partially with the themes studied in theology. The faith presupposes and reason demonstrates that there is one God who is the origin and cause of all things.[51] Several rules of conduct which ethics formulates also fall under theology as, for instance, that fornication is a mortal sin. On the other hand, a good number of questions belonging to faith are of the domain of the philosophy of nature, e.g., the fact that the world is not eternal, or of first philosophy, such as the doctrine that divine providence is concerned with what people do.[52] Aquinas is convinced that almost all of philosophy is ordained to the knowledge of divine things.[53] It follows that certain theories can be refuted both by theological arguments and by philosophical demonstration. For this reason Aquinas writes repeatedly that certain opinions which contradict the faith, also contradict philosophy.[54] However, this does not mean that the mysteries of the faith are subordinated to philosophical reasoning. It would be a sign of great recklessness if one would undertake to discuss these mysteries at the level of philosophy.[55] Since grace perfects our faculties and presupposes nature, the Christian faith presupposes basic natural knowledge.[56]

In his *Expositio in Boetii De Trinitate*, St. Thomas develops his doctrine of the role of philosophy in theology. First he shows that in theology one may use arguments, that is, resort to the resources of reason. Next he deals with the question of whether an authentic science about God and revealed truth, based on revelation, is possible. Finally, he raises the question of whether in the doctrine of the faith which considers God, one is allowed to use philosophical arguments and refer to authors of acknowledged authority.[57]

With regard to the first point, some texts of the Church Fathers appear to reject the use of philosophy in theology: "Do away with arguments, when you want the faith;"[58] "Faith has no merit, if one lets reason make its object known."[59] Aquinas answers that we must seek God with all our powers and live according to what is best in us. Our mind must try to learn more and more about God in conformity with its own way of proceeding.[60] In the elaboration of theology reason does not provide strict demonstrations of the object of the faith, but only presents some probable arguments.

In the second article of this question St. Thomas argues that the knowledge of God which we have received in faith can become a science. Although its starting point is not evident (contrary to the first principles in philosophy), its scientific character is warranted insofar as strict conclusions are drawn from what has been revealed. The difficulty of non-evident first principles is resolved by the subalternation of theology to divine science: the articles of the faith function as do first principles in philosophy.

Having shown the scientific character of theology, Aquinas explains the role of philosophy in theology. The third article begins by quoting some statements against the use of philosophy. St. Paul reminds us that Christ did not send him to preach according to "the wisdom of language" or "in the terms of philosophy," in which the cross of Christ cannot be expressed.[61] St. Ambrose comments: "The mysteries of the faith are free from philosophical arguments."[62] This denial of a role for philosophy finds support in the well-known text of *Letter XXII* of St. Jerome. In a dream Jerome is reprimanded by God for the fact that he has been an avid reader of Cicero, whose works he promises never to touch again. St. Augustine in his turn observes that if one finds errors in a publication, it loses its authority. The writings of the philosophers are full of errors and must be discarded.[63] One could also say that a science must proceed from its own principles and that, for this reason, theology has nothing to do with philosophy. On the other side, Aquinas quotes a number of texts of St. Paul, Jerome, and Augustine which seem to favor the use of philosophy in theology. In his solution of the question, he argues that the gifts of grace do not destroy the light of natural reason which God has given us. Therefore it is impossible that the truth which is communicated to us by God in the faith contradict our natural knowledge. It is true that the light of reason is imperfect, but even in what is imperfect there is a certain imitation of what is perfect. In what reason proposes there is some similarity with the knowledge given to us by faith. If philosophy tells us something contrary to the faith, it is no longer true philosophy, but error, and the result of defective reasoning. Thus it is possible to refute such errors on the basis of philosophical principles.

When one uses philosophy in theology there are two ways in which mistakes occur: (a) when one resorts to theories contrary to the faith; and (b) when one measures theological doctrines with the yardstick of philosophy. Rather, philosophy should be measured by the criteria of the faith. It is obvious that the role of philosophy in theology is only a secondary one. Divine Providence arranged things in such a way that at the beginning of the Church, preaching was done in great simplicity, but that later the wisdom of the world rallied to the cause of Christ. Those who use philosophical statements in theology do not add water to the wine, but transform the water of philosophy into wine.[64] Thus theology can avail itself of the different philosophical disciplines. It does not use them because of the authority of the philosophers whose words are quoted, but only because of the intrinsic merits of what they said.

THE TRIPLE FUNCTION OF PHILOSOPHY IN THEOLOGY

As Aquinas argues in the article we have just summarized, the things studied in philosophy bear a certain likeness to the realities which are the object of the faith and are sometimes a certain *præambulum* to them, as nature is to grace.[65] Consequently the function of philosophy in theology is as follows:

(a) To demonstrate the *præambula* to the faith which every Christian must know. Thomas means such truths as the existence of God, but also theses on the nature of man, free will, divine providence, and natural law. Judging according to what he does in the first books of the *Summa contra gentiles,* Thomas has a rather broad view of what belongs to these preambles.

(b) To provide a deeper knowledge of the dogmas of the faith by means of certain analogies (*similitudines*). This term includes such concepts as being, person, nature, essence, goodness, truth, unity, father, son, spirit, beatitude, virtue, love, law, etc. Philosophical reflection may also provide certain comparisons concerning the Trinity, grace, the Church, and the sacraments. In order to throw some light on many doctrines one must necessarily refer to the natural order.[66]

In many questions recourse to a principle drawn from philosophy helps to find the solution. To show how proper the incarnation is, St. Thomas uses the following principle of the natural order: "What is proper to something agrees with its nature. Since God's nature is goodness itself, it is proper that he communicate himself."[67] Sanctifying grace and the infused virtues are explained by analogies with the order of nature. To illustrate somewhat the eternal generation of the Son of God, Aquinas resorts to the following principle: "The nobler a nature is, the more united to it is what proceeds from it."[68] "With regard to the truth of the faith, which can only be known by those who see the divine substance, human reason is in such a position that it can approach it with the help of analogies. But these are not sufficient to allow the intellect to understand the truth of the faith by means of demonstration or directly by itself."

(c) To refute arguments and criticisms brought forward against the faith. The *Summa contra gentiles* is an admirable example of this task of philosophy at the service of the theologian. In this work St. Thomas wants to bring his readers to accept the presuppositions of the faith and to present the supernatural mysteries so as to make them plausible. He also refutes countless errors.

A theologian who resorts to philosophy can err in two ways, by using theories contrary to the faith or by subjecting the dogmas of the faith to the limits and criteria of reason.[69] Thomas vindicates the autonomy of philosophy while in theology he uses without any hesitation many philosophical concepts, definitions, principles, and analyses, which he recognizes as true. His certitude concerning their truth is based on their evidence and on their astonishing harmony with the doctrine of faith. Here he continues what such Fathers of the Church as Augustine, Gregory of Nyssa, Basil, and others had done before him. The great difference, however, is that Aquinas made use of a complete and coherent philosophy.

St. Thomas and Aristotle

This takes us to our final question. To what extent did Aquinas use Aristotelian philosophy in elaboration of the doctrine of faith? Could one use a different philosophy in the study of theology?

Thomas's attitude with regard to Aristotle is complex. Quite often he follows him, but on several occasions he goes beyond what Aristotle says or even corrects and refutes him. Until about the middle of the twentieth century most authors considered the identification of Aquinas's thought with Aristotle's as evident. Certainly, Thomists acknowledged that in certain fields Thomas had gone beyond Aristotle,[70] but they were convinced that he followed the tracks of Aristotle. Augustino Nifo even wrote: "Expositor Thomas raro aut numquam dissentit a doctrina peripatetica; fuit enim totus peripateticus et omni studio peripateticus et numquam voluit nisi quod peripatetici."[71] However, about the middle of the century certain Thomists began to draw attention to what they called Platonic elements in Aquinas's philosophy. In particular H.-A. Montagne, E. Gilson, and Cornelio Fabro stressed that the doctrines of being and of participation are alien to the theories of Aristotle.[72] Carried along by his "discovery" of Thomas's theory of the act of being, Gilson even went so far as to write that he felt inclined to think that the main obstacle for the diffusion of Thomism was the influence of Aristotle.[73] Gilson's disciple Joseph Owens believes that even the Aristotelian commentaries of Aquinas are tainted by his own theory of being and "a theological concern" which infects the interpretation of a good deal of Aristotle's texts.[74]

When one considers this debate more closely, it appears that Aquinas accepted a great number of basic positions of Aristotle, among which one may cite the following: the object of the sciences is the universal and the necessary, which is abstracted from concrete reality; real things and not *a priori* objects of the mind are the basis of knowledge. In addition to this realism, Aristotle proposed a division of the sciences and assigned the first place to the speculative sciences. His epistemology helped Aquinas to determine the nature of theology, while his logic provided the tools for scientific work.

Aristotle's philosophy gives priority to knowledge rather than to desire or feelings. Man's happiness consists essentially in knowledge. The Stagirite is optimistic with regard to man's capacity to acquire real knowledge of things: there is finality in nature and things are, at least to a certain extent, intelligible. The main task of philosophy is the study of the causes of becoming. In this connection Aristotle developed his doctrine of the four genera of causality. The gradual discovery of the different causes by his predecessors gives him a principle for the organization of the history of philosophy. Furthermore, the Aristotelian doctrine of act and potency became the key for deciphering the universe.

The Stagirite also developed the theory of first principles although he failed to apply it to the moral order. Opposing Plato and the Academy he taught the primacy of being with regard to the Good and the One and defined first philosophy as the study of being *qua* being. In this way he laid the groundwork for a theory of the transcendentals which, however, he did not elaborate. While Plato attempted to reduce all of reality to two contrary principles (the One and the Indeterminate Dyad), Aristotle worked out the theory of the categories of being as so many modes of being, irreducible to each other. This, in its turn, prepared the way for the theory of the different senses of being and of analogy.

Substance is the core of reality. The other predicaments as determinations of substance are beings in being or of being. Instead of seeking real being in a world of Platonic ideas, Aristotle asserts that substances, and not the world of the ideas, are the focal points of reality. In the field of the philosophy of nature, Aristotle combated atomism and monism. His definition of nature, the discovery of first matter, the concept of hylomorphism, the analysis of movement, place, and time, and his theory of generation and corruption are some of the highlights of his accomplishments. To this one may add the first steps on the road to a scientific cosmology, the study of living beings and of the soul, his theory of sense cognition and intellectual knowledge, and his biological work. Aristotle also made a tentative start in the study of metaphysics and reached the insight that all processes must be reduced to the First Unmoved Mover. The originality and the lasting contributions of the Stagirite to ethics, political philosophy, and aesthetics are no less important.

We need not dwell on the introduction of Aristotle's complete writings into the Latin West during the second part of the twelfth century. Thanks to the efforts of such translators as James of Venice, Roland of Cremona, and Michael Scot, Western academics were presented with an overwhelming mass of knowledge.[75] A reaction set in against certain positions of the Stagirite not in accordance with the doctrine of the faith.[76] But his writings offered so much insight and provoked such an admiration that they began to be used again with the somewhat restrictive approval of the Holy See. After 1260 new problems arose due to the spreading of Averroism. St. Bonaventure, who, when commenting on the *Sententiæ*, had been quite sympathetic towards Aristotle, despite his erroneous view of the eternity of the world,[77] bitterly attacked this and similar errors in his *Collationes*, addressed to the students in Paris between 1267 and 1273.[78] In his *Hexaemeron*, Robert Grosseteste warned against recourse to the Stagirite: "Non igitur decipiant et frustra desudent, neve inutiliter tempus suum et vires ingenii sui consumant ut Aristotelem catholicum faciendo, seipsos hæreticos faciant."

Aquinas was well acquainted with these difficulties and saw the two roads of philosophical speculation lying open before him, the way of Plato and that of Aristotle, and he chose the latter. The main reason for his choice is his certitude that Aristotle's theories are basically correct and his method valid. According to Thomas, Platonism consists essentially in the theory of ideas, which places their essences outside things, and in the second place in the doctrine of participation. Insofar as the Platonists reduced individual things to a bundle of participated forms, their position is erroneous, but understood as expressing the dependence of all beings upon God, it is true, as Aquinas stresses in several places.[79] Even in metaphysics, Aristotle followed a better road than Plato, one that allows us to reach certitude with regard to the existence of immaterial beings.[80] But Aquinas admits that despite its correct structure Aristotle's theories show a good number of defects.

The Platonists are mistaken because their reasoning starts from concepts (*ex rationibus intelligibilibus*) and considers man's attributes as many distinct realities. Aristotle, on the other hand, argues from sensible things and this position is correct.[81] In anthropology St. Thomas sees an irreducible opposition between Aristotle's doctrine and Platonic dualism. In metaphysics, however, he finds a broad convergence between the two, even if he has to elaborate their views in order to show this harmony. Both philosophers agree on the existence of a supreme principle upon which immaterial and material things depend; spiritual things are devoid of matter but are composed of act and potency. He even writes that both philosophers accept divine providence.[82]

Aquinas placed himself within Aristotelianism, but he did so entirely freely. He penetrated Aristotle's doctrine to its core and, using the Stagirite's basic principles, frequently went beyond the conclusions reached by Aristotle himself to establish a greater coherence between the different doctrines, especially in anthropology, ethics, and metaphysics. The thousands of quotations from the *Corpus aristotelicum*, in particular from the *Organon*, the *Physics*, the *De anima*, the *Metaphysics*, and the *Nicomachean Ethics*, are proof of the importance he attached to the doctrine of Aristotle, as are his commentaries on twelve of Aristotle's major works. The purpose of these commentaries is to present and to explain the doctrine of Aristotle, to analyze the arguments he uses, to discard interpretations which disagree with the letter of the text or the intention of the Stagirite, to draw attention to certain disagreements with the doctrine of the faith and, finally, to construct a true philosophy of nature, metaphysics, and ethics, fit to be used in the various institutions of learning.

Thomas places the text to be explained in the light of the principles and the entire philosophy of Aristotle. We encounter quite often the expression *secundum intentionem Aristotelis*, which signifies: the meaning of a text as it appears to the attentive reader; but it can also denote a deeper sense which one discovers by reflection and comparison.[83] It can also mean that Thomas assigns a sense to a text which is not found in it, but which he takes from what Aristotle says elsewhere.[84] Thomas discusses those passages which seem to contradict the faith. Sometimes he shows that when one reads them attentively, the opposition disappears, but in other cases a particular tenet may be irreconcilable with the Christian doctrine. Quite often Aquinas corrects or completes what the text says by means of observations introduced by *sciendum est autem, advertendum est autem*, or *considerandum est autem*.[85] The trend of these commentaries is to replace a Neoplatonic interpretation of Aristotle by a rigorous exegesis based on the principles of Aristotle himself. On the other hand, Thomas also rejects repeatedly the interpretations of Averroes in order to show that the *Commentator* is not always trustworthy.[86] Aristotle's philosophy is potentially open to what God has revealed.

Aquinas was keenly aware of the opposition of a good number of theologians and ecclesiastics against certain doctrines of Aristotle and a more or less pronounced distrust of him. To refute these interpretations and preconceived opinions, he mentions real or supposed disagreements and provides explanations. An example: In *De cælo* I Aristotle "demonstrates" the eternity of the world. Having explained the arguments of Aristotle, Aquinas concludes with the following remark: Aristotle does not show that the world does not have a beginning, but establishes only that the world did not begin to exist in the way other philosophers had described. He does show that the world did not begin by a process of generation and that it is not destined to disappear.[87] This is a benign interpretation, for the proof based on the circular movement of the celestial bodies aims at excluding any beginning. Thomas apparently felt that a simple rejection of these arguments would also have lost some valuable reasoning and might have brought with it the loss of valuable philosophical views and shaken confidence in Aristotle.

Aquinas discards the theory of the divine nature of the first heavens. He writes that in this respect Aristotle expresses himself in the manner Plato did, who used the term "god" for several things,[88] as if he wanted to say: one might as well stay with Aristotle despite this error, for Plato too was mistaken. In other texts as well, he associates Aristotle with Plato in order to protect him against unilateral criticisms. For instance, he writes that "Plato, Aristotle, and those who followed them" arrived at the consideration of the universal cause of all things, as Augustine says in the *City of God* (VIII, 4).[89] Thomas makes Augustine guarantee the fact that the principles of Aristotle's philosophy lead us to accept the creation of the world by God. When evaluating Thomas's statements about the Stagirite one must always keep in mind the addressees of a given treatise: in order to defend Aristotelianism in the universities Thomas may go to great lengths to justify a certain text or reconcile it with the faith.

On the first page of the *Physics*, Aristotle writes that we must always seek the first cause. Thomas uses this affirmation to note that we must indeed continue our analysis until we reach the highest cause. This "adaptation" of Aristotelian doctrine to a Christian philosophy is very remarkable in the commentary on the *Nicomachean Ethics*. According to the Stagirite, man himself is the cause of his happiness, a doctrine which will be condemned by the bishop of Paris in 1277. Thomas notes that Aristotle is speaking of the imperfect happiness of this life and adds that even according to him happiness is a gift of the gods.[90] In fact, one can read this remark at 1099b12, but Aristotle is perhaps making a concession to a popular way of speaking. However, Aquinas quotes the sentence and, assuming that there must be a perfect coherence between the various parts of Aristotle's philosophy, uses it to justify an interpretation which goes against the grain of some other texts. One finds several "corrections" of this type in the commentaries on the *Ethics* and the *Metaphysics*. Thomas attempted to remove as far as possible any appearance of opposition to the Christian faith. To give another example, Aristotle wonders if there is a plurality of first movers. Both in his preface and throughout his commentary Thomas maintains the plural form (*primas causas rerum*) and leaves the question of the unity of the First Principle open, apparently for methodological reasons. Only in his commentary on *Metaphysics* XII, c. 8, he observes that a series of several movers is not necessary to explain the movements of the celestial bodies.[91] He avoids any hasty correction and respects the need for a patient analysis, what has been called *reverenter exponere.*

In many places Aquinas goes beyond the text in order to reach a higher synthesis. One example is in his preface to the commentary on the *Metaphysics,* when he brings Aristotle's differing descriptions of the nature of first philosophy into a higher unity: its subject is being *qua* being, but it also studies the cause of being so that it extends its investigation to the first cause, God. Philosophical theology is part of metaphysics. Likewise Aquinas completes Aristotle's sketch of analogy in *Metaphysics* IV, c. 2, and weakens the Stagirite's stern condemnation of the Platonic theory of participation. He elaborates the doctrine of the real distinction between the act of being and the essence. He goes further than Aristotle had done in pointing out that the original and first sense of the verb "to be" is to be real in an absolute way.[92]

This "going beyond" Aristotle's doctrine is very much noticeable in anthropology: the soul of man, his substantial form, is immaterial, although it constitutes the body. It is *non totaliter immersa corpori* and it is *aliquid subsistens.* He also explains why the soul is united to the body and defends the doctrine of afterlife, about which Aristotle voiced some doubts.[93] With regard to ethics, Aquinas stresses more than Aristotle the scientific character of moral philosophy. Ethics is directed not only to action but also to knowledge. The science of morals is not a form of prudence but has its seat in the theoretical intellect. Moreover, he transposes the theory of the criteria of morality to make them depend on the first principles of the practical intellect. But like Aristotle's ethics, Aquinas's moral philosophy is aiming at man's last end, happiness or beatitude, and at the virtues required to reach and secure this end.

A further question is whether these commentaries present Aristotle's philosophy faithfully or whether they express the thought of Aquinas himself. A first observation is that for Thomas himself these commentaries were philosophical works: to the best of my knowledge there is not a single passage where revelation provides *directly* an interpretation or evaluation of what Aristotle wrote. There is nowhere any confusion between philosophy and *doctrina sacra.* This does not mean that while writing them Thomas was not guided by revelation. What is decisive for our purpose is that his arguments remain at the level of natural reason. The theological viewpoint remains present in the background and leads Thomas to interpret certain statements of Aristotle in such a way as to discover a certain openness toward the doctrine of the faith.

With the exception of a handful of small passages, the commentaries are a faithful, learned, and excellent interpretation of what Aristotle wrote. Even Joseph Owens must recognize this fact.[94] One could say that, from a doctrinal point of view, they are the best commentaries extant on the text of Aristotle. Aquinas succeeds as no one else in introducing us to the thought of Aristotle. Although he did not have the instruments of contemporary philology, his knowledge of the *Corpus aristotelicum* is without equal.

Thomas sometimes goes beyond the immediate context of a passage to base his interpretation on other texts or to argue with the help of principles that Aristotle acknowledged. For instance, he places the agent intellect within the individual soul of each person; he assumes that Aristotle accepts the immortality of the individual soul; he draws a far-reaching inference from such a statement as "the universe is suspended from the First Principle." While Aristotle himself is not always consistent and scholars such as Sir David Ross and Ingemar Düring speak of slightly diverging lines of thought in Aristotle, Thomas wants to establish total consistency.

In fact, Thomas reads the texts of Aristotle in the light of his own philosophy of nature, metaphysics, and ethics. In many cases the influence of this situation is minimal, because his philosophy is identical to that of the Stagirite. This is especially the case with regard to the *Physics,* and the *De cælo.* In anthropology, metaphysics, and ethics the influence of Thomas's own thought is more pervasive. Joseph Owens drew attention to Thomas's own view of being which determined certain passages of his commentaries. Harry V. Jaffa mentions some principles which influenced the commentary on the *Nicomachean Ethics.*[95] Must we conclude that Thomas transformed Aristotle? The central question is whether the framework in which Aquinas interprets Aristotle is an *alien framework,* foreign to the thought of Aristotle, as Owens claims.[96] Is there a question of non-Aristotelian principles, as Jaffa says? Our answer is a categorical "no." Thomistic anthropology, metaphysics of being, and ethics based on the natural inclinations of man are not developments which adulterate Aristotle's thought. These doctrines are derived from principles posited by Aristotle himself. Aquinas indicates this with regard to the metaphysics of being: those who followed Plato and Aristotle understood the dependence of all beings on God and the real composition of the act of being and the essence in created things.[97]

St. Thomas does not restrict his comments to the interpretation of the text *prout iacet,* but he delves deeper into its very roots and so connects it to the principles of Aristotle and the *veritas rerum.* The truth contained in a passage appears in its full meaning through being brought into relationship with a more encompassing ensemble.[98]

Aristotle's writings are intended to be a faithful reflection of our experience of reality and to avoid, as much as possible, subjective points of view. Consequently they possess a high degree of truth and that is why they lend themselves to the in-depth study which Aquinas carries out. Aquinas has no equal in penetrating the meaning of the text and all its implications. He accepts Aristotle's conclusions insofar as they are based on an exact analysis of reality. But he delves deeper into the intelligibility of things and uncovers structures which Aristotle has not discerned. So he is able to present a more coherent doctrinal ensemble. The truth present in the text is saved, but the doctrine is developed with the help of Aristotle's own principles.

Aristotle's philosophy shows a surprising capacity for this kind of systematization because of its basic conformity to reality. As John Henry Newman wrote, "While the world lasts, will Aristotle's doctrine on these matters last, for he is the oracle of nature and truth. While we are men, we cannot help, to a great extent, being Aristotelians, for the great Master does but analyze the thoughts, feelings, views and opinions of humankind. He has told us the meaning of our own words and ideas, before we were born. In many subject-matters, to think correctly, is to think like Aristotle; and we are his disciples, whether we will or no, though we may not know it."[99]

Is the doctrine of the commentaries still that of Aristotle? In the vast majority of those more than five thousand pages of comments, yes, we do find Aristotle's historical doctrine. In some passages, Thomas presents a doctrine *secundum intentionem Philosophi*, an expression which may mean that we have do to with conclusions drawn from Aristotle's principles, more or less removed from what is expressed in a particular text.

Can the commentaries be used as a source of St. Thomas's own philosophy? The answer to this question is also affirmative, because Thomas professes the same philosophy based on the *veritas rerum*. This applies above all to those texts where the exposé is attributed to the *Philosophus*. An analysis of a great number of texts where this title is used, shows that according to Aquinas we are dealing with a philosophical truth which is above individual opinion. On the other hand, when he writes *secundum opinionem Aristotelis* or *hic Aristoteles supponit*, etc., he intimates that we have to do with a particular opinion one may disagree with. By the same token, the numerous passages beginning with *considerandum est autem, sciendum est autem* or *advertendum est autem* contain critical remarks which correct or complement the exposé of Aristotle himself. Finally, to find out whether Aquinas subscribes to a certain point of doctrine, one must read the entire commentary. For instance, to know what he thinks of a plurality of first movers, one has to consult the last part of the commentary on the *Metaphysics*. This is not surprising, for one cannot consider a difficulty raised at the beginning of an article of the *Summa theologiæ* the definite doctrine of Thomas himself. If one keeps these methodological principles in mind, the Aristotelian commentaries become an inexhaustible deposit of wisdom containing the treasures of Thomas's own philosophy.

But what to think of the mass of mistaken theories about natural phenomena, in particular in physics and cosmology, which mar the works of Aristotle and which Aquinas seems to accept without hesitation? Because of the presence of these theories,

Aquinas's philosophy of nature has been depicted as totally antiquated and useless, with the exception of a number of conceptual analyses, such as those of place and time. As is known, in Aristotle's treatises on nature, elements of what for us is natural science go together with philosophical considerations and are almost inextricably combined with them. However, a careful study of the commentaries of Aquinas shows, at least in a number of cases, that Thomas was well aware of a distinction between both and considered the cosmological system of Aristotle a hypothesis which may be replaced by a new one which explains the observed phenomena differently: "Although the phenomena are accounted for with the help of these hypotheses, one should not say that these assumptions are true, for one can perhaps explain what is observed in the celestial bodies in a different way which has not yet been conceived by man."[100] Aquinas writes that one may use these hypotheses as long as they do not run into difficulties.[101] He even felt the theory of the *four* elements to be an assumption, whereas the fact that there must be elements is definitely true. The philosophy of nature, however, aims at indubitable knowledge. The task ahead of us is to search the commentaries for indications of this distinction and of the hypothetical character of certain theories.

CAN ONE USE JUST ANY PHILOSOPHY
IN ELABORATING THEOLOGY?

The explanations given above show that, contrary to an opinion fairly widely held after the Second Vatican Council and advocated by Karl Rahner, one cannot use just any philosophy in the study of theology. If a main part of the task of a theologian consists in finding analogous structures in the natural order to explain and illustrate the mysteries of the faith, it is obvious that the theologian should have a correct grasp of reality. By means of created things, as they come forth from God, he must try to explain revealed truth, which has also been given to us by God. The more subjective, time-bound, and partial philosophical thought becomes, the less fit it is to function in theology. The history of theology shows how time and again orthodox interpretations were abandoned because theologians resorted to mistaken philosophical theories.[102]

This applies also to the task of demonstrating the preambles of the faith and refuting false interpretations of Christian doctrine. In his Apostolic Letter *Lumen Ecclesiæ*, Paul VI rejected the frequently proposed view according to which theologians should incorporate contemporary philosophical trends into theology, as Aquinas had done with Aristotle. Paul VI writes that this is impossible because one has to do with ways of thinking which cannot be compared at all.[103] In a remarkable discourse at the Pontifical University of St. Thomas Aquinas, on November 17, 1979, John Paul II reminded his audience that many dissenting views in theology are caused by a crisis of philosophical thought. He insisted that one cannot resort to just any philosophy: some philosophies are so limited and closed that they exclude the translation of revelation into human language.[104]

In conclusion we can say that the respect St. Thomas had for reality, the absence of personal views and preconceived ideas, and his concern to grasp reality as it is, make his philosophy the best and safest instrument to develop and to construct the science of theology.

NOTES

1. Cf. St. Thomas, *In Colossianos* 2, lectio 2, where he explains that secular philosophy may lead into error for two reasons: the mistaken views it defends and its faulty reasoning.

2. See *Summa contra Gentiles* 1.7–9.

3. *ST* 1.1.1 ad 2m: "Diversa ratio cognoscibilis diversitatem scientiarum inducit . . . Unde nihil prohibet de eisdem rebus, de quibus philosophicæ disciplinæ tractant secundum quod sunt cognoscibilia lumine naturalis rationis et aliam scientiam tractare secundum quod cognoscuntur lumine divinæ revelationis."

4. Thomas writes "whatever may be an object of divine revelation (*omnia quæ sunt divinitus revelabilia*)" instead of "what has been revealed," probably meaning whatever is somehow contained in what has been revealed, although not explicitly stated, as for instance the *convenientia* of many facts of the history of salvation, such as the time of the incarnation of Christ. Reflections on the *convenientia* make up a considerable part of the themes treated in the Third Part of the *Summa theologiæ*.

5. *ST* 1.1.5: "Ista scientia est principaliter de his quæ sua altitudine rationem transcendunt, aliæ vero scientiæ considerant ea tantum quæ rationi subduntur." In this connection Thomas lists as lying beyond the range of reason the dogmas about the divine trinity, the incarnation, grace, the sacramental order, the resurrection, glorification, and eternal beatitude (*SCG* 4.1).

6. Cf. *ST* 1.12.12; 1.32.1; *SCG* 3.47.

7. Cf. *In Boetii De Trinitate*, 2.3: "Impossibile est quod ea quæ sunt philosophiæ, sint contraria his quæ sunt fidei."

8. *SCG* 1.7: "Impossibile est illis principiis quæ ratio naturaliter cognoscit, prædictam veritatem fidei contrariam esse . . . Quæcumque argumenta contra fidei documenta ponantur, hæc ex principiis primis naturæ inditis per se notis non procedere . . . sed vel sunt rationes probabiles vel sophisticæ."

9. *SCG* 3.85.

10. *ST* 1-2.99.2 ad 1m.

11. *ST* 1.2.2 ad 1m.

12. *ST* 2-2.10.10: "Ius autem divinum, quod est ex gratia, non tollit ius humanum, quod est ex naturali ratione."

13. *ST* 1.62.5.

14. *In Sent.* 4. d. 49.2.3 ad 3m.

15. *In Sent.* 4. d. 2.1.4B.

16. *De malo* 2.11: "Gratia perficit naturam et quantum ad intellectum et quantum ad voluntatem et quantum ad inferiores animæ partes obaudibiles rationi."

17. *ST* 1.1.8 ad 2m.

18. *In Sent.* 3. d. 29.1.3.

19. *ST* 2-2.164.4.

20. *In Sent.* 4.d. 8.12.3 ad 4m: "Creaturæ inest obedientiæ potentia, ut in ea fiat quidquid creator disposuerit."

21. *De potentia* 6.1 ad 18m: "potentia obedientiæ secundum quod quælibet creatura creatori obedit."

22. *De virtutibus* 1.10 ad 13m.

23. Cf. *ST* 3.1.3: "divinæ potentiæ cui omnis creatura obedit ad nutum."

24. This point was stressed by L. B. Gillon, "Aux origines de la puissance obédientielle," *Revue thomiste* 47 (1947): 304 ff.

25. Cf. *ST* 1.12.1; *SCG* 2.55.

26. *SCG* 4.79.

27. For this list of basic human desires see *SCG* 3.63.

28. *In Symbolum Apostolorum*, art. 12: In the fourth place the communion of the saints "consistit in omnium beatorum iucunda societate, quæ societas erit maxime delectabilis quia quilibet habebit omnia bona cum omnibus beatis."

29. Ibid. "Diliget alium sicut seipsum et ideo gaudebit de bono alterius sicut de suo. Quo fit ut tantum augeatur lætitia et gaudium unius quantum est gaudium omnium."

30. *ST* 2-2.141.1 ad 1m.

31. *ST* 1-1.21.1: "tunc servatur rectitudo in actu."

32. *ST* 2-2.69.4 ad 1m.

33. See Leo Elders, "El humanismo cristiano de Santo Tomás de Aquino," in *Santo Tomás de Aquino, Humanista cristiano* (Buenos Aires: Sociedad Tomista Argentina, 1998), 9–22.

34. Cf. Leo Elders, "Bonum humanæ animæ est secundum rationem esse," *Lugano Theological Review* 4 (1999): 75–90.

35. *ST* 2-2.168.2.

36. *ST* 2-2.168.3: "ordinatur ad solatium hominibus exhibendum."

37. *SCG* 1.6: "quæ totius naturæ superant facultatem."

38. *De præscriptione hæreticorum*, VII.

39. See Leo Elders, "The Greek Christian Authors and Aristotle," in *Aristotle in Late Antquity*, ed. Lawrence P. Schenk (Washington: Catholic University of America Press, 1994), 111–42.

40. See M.-D. Chenu, *La théologie comme science au XIIIᵉ siècle* (Paris: Vrin, 1969), 28 ff.

41. On these attempts see L. Sileo, *Teoria della scienza teologica: Quæstio de scientia theologica di Odo Rigaldi e altri testi inediti (1230–1250)* (Rome: Pontificium Athenaeum Antonianum, 1984).

42. R. Heinzmann, "Der Plan der *Summa theologiæ* des Thomas von Aquin in der Tradition der frühscholastischen Systembildung," in *Thomas von Aquino: Interpretation und Rezeption*, ed. W. P. Eckert (Mainz: Matthias-Grünewald, 1974), 455–69.

43. *De veritate*, 14.8.

44. *In Job*, ch. 12.

45. *In I Timotheum* 3, lectio 3.

46. *In epistam ad Galataios* 3, lectio 6: "Ex quo quidem habemus argumentum quod ad conferendum de his quæ sunt fidei possumus uti quacumque veritate cuiuscumque scientiæ."

47. *In I Corinthos* 1, lectio 3.

48. *ST* 2-2.167.1 ad 3m. The quotation is from Colossians 2:8. At *In Colossianos* 2, lectio 2, Thomas explains that the wisdom of this world may deceive us in two ways: by incorrect philosophical theories and by sophistic arguments.

49. *Expositio in Boetii De Trinitate*, 2.3: "hoc non est philosophia, sed magis philosophiæ abusus ex defectu rationis. Et ideo possibile est ex principiis philosophiæ huiusmodi errorem refellere."

50. *De spiritualibus creaturis* 3.

51. *In Sent.* 1. d. 2.1.1.

52. *In Sent.* 3. d. 23.2.4B, arg. 3.

53. *In Sent.* 3. d. 24.1.3C: "cum fere tota philosophia ad cognitionem divinorum ordinetur."

54. See *De malo* 6.1, "non solum contrariatur fidei, sed subvertit omnia principia philosophiæ"; *In Sent.* 2. d. 27. 1.1, "a dictis sanctorum discordat et philosophiæ non convenit"; ibid., 2. d. 28.1.2, "nec fidei nec philosophiæ consonat"; *In Sent.* 4. d. 47.2.2B, "repugnat enim et philosophiæ"; *Quodlibet* 3.5.3, "contra rationem doctrinæ evangelicæ et contra rationem philosophiæ."

55. *De unitate intellectus* 5.

56. *In Sent.* 3. d. 24.1.3: "Fidei substernitur naturalis cognitio, quam fides præsupponit, et ratio probare potest."

57. *Expositio in Boetii De Trinitate* 2.1–3. The text dates to the beginning of St. Thomas's lecturing as a master in sacred theology in Paris. He may have chosen the first chapters of Boethius's otherwise not very important treatise, to have the possibility to develop an epistemology of theoretical sciences of unequaled depth. For more details see Leo Elders, *Faith and Science: An Introduction to St. Thomas' Expositio in Boethii De Trinitate* (Rome: Herder, 1974).

58. St. Ambrose, *De fide* 1.13.84.

59. St. Gregory the Great, *Homilia* 26.1, (PL 76:1197C): "Fides non habet meritum cui humana ratio praebet experimentum."

60. *Expositio in Boetii De Trinitate*, 2.1 ad 7m.

61. 1 Cor 1:17.

62. In reality the text is Peter Lombard's, but a similar statement is found in Ambrose's *De fide* 1.13.84, (PL 16:570D).

63. *Epistola* 28 *ad Hieronymum*, 3, 5.

64. *Expositio in Boetii De Trinitate* 2. 3 ad 5m. Philosophical terms and insights used in theology are transposed to the level of *doctrina sacra* and integrated into it.

65. *Expositio in Boetii De Trinitate* 2.3: "Continent tamen [ea quæ sunt philosophiæ] aliquas eorum [sc. quæ sunt fidei] similitudines et quædam ad ea præambula, sicut natura præambula est ad gratiam."

66. *ST* 1.91.1: "Unde in omnibus asserendis sequi debemus naturam rerum, præter ea quæ auctoritate divina traduntur quæ sunt supra naturam."

67. *ST* 3.1.1.

68. *SCG* 4.11.

69. *Expositio in Boetii De Trinitate* 2.3.

70. One may recall the ancient saying *Aristotele aristotelior*. In the following I make use of my article "Saint Thomas d'Aquin et Aristote," *Revue thomiste* 88 (1988): 255–76.

71. Quoted from Cornelio Fabro, *Enciclopedia Cattolica* 12:266. The quotation is from the 13th dispute on *Metaphysics* VII.

72. Some early voices in this choir were C. Huit, "Les éléments platoniciens de la doctrine de saint Thomas," *Revue thomiste* 19 (1911): 724–66, and P. Rousselot, *L'intellectualisme de saint Thomas* (Paris²: Beauchesne, 1924), with regard to the doctrine of the angels. See also, more recently, R.J. Henle, *Saint Thomas and Platonism: A Study of Plato and Platonic Texts in the Writings of Saint Thomas Aquinas* (The Hague: Nijhoff, 1956).

73. Etienne Gilson, "Cajetan et l'existence," *Tijdschrift voor Philosophie* 15 (1953): 267–86, 284.

74. Joseph Owens, "Aquinas as an Aristotelian Commentator" in *St. Thomas Aquinas on the Existence of God: Collected Papers of Joseph Owens, C.Ss.R.*, ed. J.R.Catan (Albany: SUNY Press, 1980), 16.

75. Roger Bacon writes: "Tempore Michael Scoti ... magnificata est Aristotelis philosophia apud Latinos." *Opus maius*, 2.13, ed. J.H. Bridges (Oxford: 1897), 1:55.

76. A council in Paris (1210) decreed: "Nec libri Aristotelis de naturali philosophia nec commenta legantur Parisiis publice vel secrete." In 1215 a legate of the Pope, Robert de Courçon, extended this prohibition to the *Metaphysics*.

77. See Leo Elders, "Les citations d'Aristote dans le *Commentaire sur les Sentences* de saint Bonaventure," in *San Bonaventura, maestro di vita francescana e di sapienza cristiana* (Rome: Pontificia facoltà teologica san Bonaventura, 1976), 831–42.

78. On whether one can speak of a critical attitude toward Aristotelianism, see J.F. Quinn, *The Historical Constitution of St. Bonaventure's Philosophy* (Toronto: Pontifical Institute of Medieval Studies, 1973), 854–78.

79. See the preface of the *Expositio in librum beati Dionysii De divinis nominibus* and *ST* 1.6.4: "Et quamvis hæc opinio irrationabilis videatur quantum ad hoc quod ponebat species rerum naturalium separatas per se subsistentes ... , tamen hoc absolute verum est quod aliquid est primum, quod per suam essentiam est ens et bonum, quod dicimus Deum." Cf. *De veritate* 21.4: "Quidditates et formæ rerum insunt ipsis rebus particularibus."

80. *De substantiis separatis*, 2.

81. *De spiritualibus creaturis* 1.3: "Harum autem duarum opinionum diversitas ex hoc procedit quod quidam ad inquirendam veritatem de natura rerum, processerunt ex rebus intelligibilibus, et hoc fuit proprium Platonicorum; quidam vero ex rebus sensibilibus, et hoc fuit proprium philosophiæ Aristotelis ... Consideraverunt Platonici ... quod quidquid est abstractum in intellectu, sit abstractum in re." Cf. *In Sent.* 2. d. 17.1.1: reality does not consist in a bundle of logical concepts.

82. *De substantiis separatis* 3: "In quo conveniunt positiones Platonis et Aristotelis." As he does elsewhere, Aquinas bases his assertion regarding Aristotle on some scattered texts of the latter.

83. Cf. *De substantiis separatis* 14: "Patet igitur prædicta verba philosophi diligenter consideranti quod non est intentio eius."

84. For example, in *Metaphysics* 12.9, Aristotle denies that the world is an object of divine knowledge since it would make God dependent on what is outside him. Thomas observes that this is not the case when God knows things in himself, which is the case if he is their creator. Aristotle himself acknowledges this, for he writes elsewhere that heaven and earth are dependent in their being on the First Mover.

85. Cf. *In VI Metaphysicam*, lectio 1, where Thomas contradicts the text by stating that the subject matter of metaphysics comprises also material beings.

86. See Leo Elders "St. Thomas Aquinas's Commentary on the *Physics* of Aristotle," in *Autour de saint Thomas d'Aquin*, (Paris: Vrin, 1983), 1: 28–35; "Averroès et saint Thomas d'Aquin," in *Doctor communis* 45 (1992): 46–56.

87. *In I De cælo et mundo,* lectio 6, §61–64.

88. Ibid., lectio 7, §75.

89. *De potentia* 5.3.

90. *In I Ethica* lectio 14, §165–76.

91. See Leo Elders, "St. Thomas Aquinas' Commentary on the *Metaphysics* of Aristotle," in *Autour de saint Thomas d'Aquin,* 1:134–38.

92. *In Peri Hermeneias* 1, lectio 5.

93. Cf. E. von Ivanka, "Aristotelische und thomistische Seelenlehre," in *Aristote et saint Thomas d'Aquin* (Paris: Publications universitaires de Louvain, 1957), 221–28.

94. Owens, "Aquinas as an Aristotelian Commentator," 16.

95. H.V. Jaffa, *Thomism and Aristotelianism: A Study of the Commentary by Thomas Aquinas on the "Nicomachean Ethics"* (Chicago: University of Chicago Press, 1952), 101. Jaffa means principles such as "perfect happiness is impossible in this life," "man is immortal," etc.

96. Owens, "Aquinas as an Aristotelian Commentator," 10.

97. *De potentia* 3.2: "Plato, Aristoteles et eorum sequaces pervenerunt ad considerationem ipsius esse universalis et ideo ipsi soli posuerunt aliquam universalem causam rerum, a qua omnia alia in esse prodirent." In the *Summa theologiæ* he restricts this breakthrough to a few later philosophers, excluding Plato and Aristotle (1.44.2): "Et ulterius aliqui erexerunt se ad considerandum ens inquantum est ens: et consideraverunt causam rerum, non solum secundum quod sunt *hæc* [Aristotle] vel *talia* [Plato], sed secundum quod sunt *entia.*"

98. Cf. W. Kluxen, *Philosophische Ethik bei Thomas von Aquin* (Hamburg²: Meiner, 1980), 104, states this as follows: "Es kann nur wiederholt werden, daß Thomas den Aristoteles nicht historisch, sondern in der wahrheitsgebenden Offenheit des Verstehenshorizontes orten will, in dem erst die eigentliche Wahrheit seiner Aussage hervortritt."

99. John Henry Newman, *The Idea of a University* (New York: Longmans, Green, 1947), 97.

100. *In II De cælo,* lectio 17, § 451. See also *ST* 1.32.1 ad 2m; *In I De cælo,* lectio 3, § 28.

101. *In I Meteor.,* lectio 11, § 68.

102. See Leo Elders, "Le rôle de la philosophie en théologie: Aide nécessaire et abus. L'Influence de catégories philosophiques sur l'expression de la foi," in *Nova et Vetera* (1997): 34–68.

103. *Lumen Ecclesiæ* (Città del Vaticano: Libreria editrice vaticana, 1974), § 29.

104. *Insegnamenti di Giovanni Paolo II* (Città del Vaticano: Libreria editrice vaticana, 1979), IV 2, 1418 ff.

Chapter 6

St. Thomas and Analogy

The Logician and the Metaphysician

LAWRENCE DEWAN, OP

The late Charles De Koninck, certainly someone to be revered,[1] said that "analogy is primarily a logical problem, to be used eventually in analogical naming by the metaphysician."[2] Ralph McInerny, in many works over the years, and most recently in *Aquinas and Analogy*, has undertaken to spell this out.[3] It is then with considerable hesitation that I propose a criticism of the latter's position.

McInerny's book takes the form of a rejection of the system of analogical naming proposed by Cajetan, together with a proposal for a much simpler approach. Because Cajetan used in an important way, among other texts of Thomas, a lengthy reply to an objection in *Sent.* 1.19, McInerny's first chapter consists largely in a rereading of this text, in order to show, against Cajetan, that it is not a classification of types of analogy of names at all, but merely a proof that consideration of named things from the viewpoint of their being is incidental to analogy of names, properly so called.

It is not my purpose to defend Cajetan in this matter. However, I do wish to affirm that the *Sent.* 1.19 text—a text which was used very effectively by Johannes Capreolus to combat the metaphysical errors of Duns Scotus and Peter Auriol—is truly meant as a classification of types of analogy of names.[4]

I am quite happy to say that the analogy of names pertains to logic. For example, we see Thomas treat the modes of unity presented in *CM* 5.8 (876–80): numerical, specific, generic, and *analogical,* as a logical presentation, i.e., in function of logical notions (*secundum intentiones logicales*). Analogy is thus presented as one of the logical *intentiones.*[5] Nevertheless, I wish to discuss the idea of logic and the relation of logic to metaphysics (and, to a certain extent, to other sciences of things).

There is another extremely important feature of the relation between the *intentiones* of logic and the science of metaphysics which should be considered. It is mentioned by Thomas in connection with Boethius's definition of the person. An objector, criticizing the Boethian definition, points out that "individual" is not the name of a thing outside the mind, but is rather a logician's consideration; not the name of a *res,* but merely of an *intentio;* and yet the person is a *real* thing. Boethius's definitional procedure is thus, he claims, unsuitable.

Thomas replies, explaining carefully the meaning of "individual" in the definition. We read:

> Because substantial differences are not known to us, or else are not named, it is necessary sometimes to use accidental differences in place of substantial [differences], for example, if someone were to say: "fire is a simple, hot, and dry body"; for proper accidents are the effects of substantial forms, and reveal them. And similarly the names of logical notions [*intentiones*] can be accepted in order to define real things [*res*], inasmuch as they are accepted in the role of some names of real things, which [names] have not been invented. And thus this name "individual" [*individuum*] is inserted in the definition of the person in order to signify the mode of subsisting, which belongs to particular substances [*modum subsistendi qui competit substantiis particularibus*].[21]

That the logical intention called "analogy" is used in this way by Thomas is clear. For example, consider *ST* 1.4.3, whether some creature can be like God.[22]

THOMAS'S PRESENTATION OF ANALOGY IN THE *SENTENCES*

The text which McInerny interprets, *Sentences* 1.19.5.2 ad 1m,[23] occurs in a discussion of the point: whether all things are true (*vera*) by virtue of the uncreated truth (*veritate increata*). Thomas's general answer will be that, just as there is the one divine *esse,* the efficient exemplar cause by virtue of which all things *are,* and yet each thing has its own *esse* by which formally it *is,* so also there is one divine truth by which all are true, as by an efficient exemplar cause; and yet there are the many truths in created things by which formally they are called "true." In ad 2m it is clear that it is the created *things,* taken in their own being, which are viewed as measures of our intellect and so are viewed as formally containing "truths."[24]

The first objector bases himself on the doctrine of the preceding article, that "the true" is said analogically. Using the standard model of "healthy," he argues that this means that truth is found only in God, and that other things are called "true" by reference to God.[25] Thomas replies:

... it is to be said that something is said according to analogy in three ways [*aliquid dicitur secundum analogiam tripliciter*]: either according to notion only and not according to being [*secundum intentionem tantum et non secundum esse*]: and this is when one notion [*una intentio*] is referred to several [things] through priority and posteriority, which nevertheless has being only in one: for example, the notion of health [*intentio sanitatis*] is referred to the animal, the urine, and the diet in diverse measures [*diversimode*], according to priority and posteriority; nevertheless, not according to diverse being, because the being of health is only in the animal.

Or else, [something is said according to analogy] according to being and not according to notion [*secundum esse et non secundum intentionem*]; and this occurs when many things are taken as equal [*parificantur*] in the notion [*in intentione*] of something common, but that common item does not have being of one intelligible character [*esse unius rationis*] in all: as for example, all bodies are taken as equal in the notion of corporeity [*in intentione corporeitatis*]; hence, the logician [*logicus*], who considers only notions [*intentiones tantum*], says that this name "body" is predicated of all bodies univocally; however, the being of this nature [*esse hujus naturae*] is not of the same intelligible character [*ejusdem rationis*] in corruptible and incorruptible bodies; *hence, for the metaphysician and the physicist, who consider things according to their being, neither this name, "body," nor any other [name] is said univocally of corruptibles and incorruptibles,*[26] as is clear from *Metaph.* 10, text 5, from [both] the Philosopher and the Commentator.[27]

Or else, [something is said according to analogy] according to notion and according to being [*secundum intentionem et secundum esse*], and this is when they are not taken as equal either in the common notion [*in intentione communi*] or in being; the way, for example, "a being" is said of substance and accident; and in such [cases] it is necessary that the common nature [*natura communis*] have some being in each of those things of which it is said, but differing according to the intelligible character [*rationem*] of greater or lesser perfection.

And similarly I say [*dico*] that "truth" and "goodness" and all such [items] are said analogically [*dicuntur analogice*] of God and creatures. Hence, it is necessary that according to their being all these be in God and in creatures according to the intelligible character [*secundum rationem*] of greater and lesser perfection; from which it follows, since they cannot be according to one being [*esse*] in both places, that there are diverse truths [*diversae veritates*].[28]

In this, it is quite clear that all three classifications are cases of *analogy*. The middle one is univocity, not analogy, for the logician; but it is not univocity, indeed it is analogy, for the metaphysician and the physicist. More is included in the metaphysician's notions of univocity and analogy than in the logician's notions of these *intentiones*.

The point of the objector was that since analogy was on the scene, one should conceive of it on the model of "healthy," and thus conclude that there is not truth in the creatures called "true." Thomas could have answered this by merely distinguishing between type 1 and type 3: he could have said that there are two sorts of analogy, one which is merely causal and one which is more essential—somewhat as he will reply to the objector in *ST* 1.13.6 ad 3m. Instead, he deliberately set out a threefold classification, and one in which the middle member makes the remarkable point that there is a type of term which a logician sees as univocal and a metaphysician sees as analogical. Of course, the middle position does help to make us think about the roles of *esse* and *intentio,* and the *ratio* that the common item has according to *esse.* But is there truly a systematic unity here?

Again, our interest is not in the question: did Cajetan read this text well? Nor: did Cajetan speak well about analogy? It is rather: what has McInerny done with the above text? Is he reading it as Thomas meant it?

McInerny's Reading of the *Sentences* Text

Having sketched my idea of Thomas's view of the difference between the logician and the metaphysician, and presented the key text for our present purpose, I come to how McInerny reads *Sent.* 1.19. His argument for its interpretation focuses on the *second* mode, which he holds is not meant as a sort of analogy of names at all. He even regards it as *showing* that the distinctions the reply mentions as between the first and third modes are *incidental* to analogy as such.

McInerny thinks he has shown that there is something wrong with Cajetan's division of analogy into types, based as it is on the text of 1.19. But, posing an objection to his own procedure, he asks whether Cajetan is not justified in using in the way he does a text which begins with the words: "something is said according to analogy in three ways." He then gives us his own reduction of Thomas's reply to its essential message:

> The response to the objection comes down to this. The feature *secundum esse* of things named healthy analogously is *per accidens* to their being named analogously. Other things named analogously have a different feature *secundum esse.* If some analogous names have feature X and other analogous names do not, feature X is accidental to their being analogous names. To underscore this point, Thomas notes that you can find the same variation *secundum esse* in univocal terms. (11)

The last sentence refers to the second mode passage, held by McInerny to be about "*univocal* terms." This is a remarkable rewrite of the answer to an objection. In doctrine it apes such a text as *ST* 1.26.1 ad 3m, on whether God has beatitude. The objector there argues that beatitude is the prize for virtue, and that neither merit nor prize befits a God. Thomas answers:

> ... to be the prize for virtue *happens* to beatitude or felicity inasmuch as someone *acquires* beatitude; just as to be the terminus of generation *happens* to a *being* inasmuch as [the being] issues forth from potency into act. Hence, just as God has being, though he is not generated, so also he has beatitude, though it is not merited.

Thomas knows how to make this sort of argument. One should wonder why he did not simply make it where McInerny wants to read it.[29]

McInerny wants us to reduce analogy to the issue of *secundum intentionem*. Thus, he says:

> There can be inequality, a relation *per prius et posterius*, both *secundum intentionem* and *secundum esse*. The *former* is what is in play when we talk of a term being used analogously. (12, my emphasis on *former*)

Now, of course, this is true for McInerny, the logician. Thomas Aquinas's *explicit* point is that this is not true for the metaphysician or the natural philosopher who say that the issue of *secundum esse* difference regarding a term such as "body" makes this an *analogous* term.

If we take the presentation of his argument from the beginning, I regret to note that what we first see is that McInerny, aiming to quote the crucial text of Thomas, *inadvertently leaves out the key passage in the middle case concerning the metaphysician and the physicist.* (6) This is alarming, since so much of McInerny's argument discourages the reader from seeing such things as univocity and analogy as having a peculiarly metaphysical interest. They are the proper preserve of the logician, he tells us. Still, this is just a very bad typographical error (one, nevertheless, which carries over from the Latin to the English translation, given in the footnote).

When he goes on to discuss what Cajetan has done with the text, McInerny provides his own analysis. He claims that the logician in the text is the dialectician, not the logician in the sense of the thinker who gives a definition of "genus" and "named univocally" and "named analogically" (8). This in itself is not clear to me. The basis for the discussed difference concerning "body" is the doctrine that the genus is a name for a thing taken from the side of the matter. The reason why "body" is different from a genus such as "animal" is that the things called "animals," though they have natures which are ordered according to more perfect and less perfect, nevertheless have at bottom the same sort of matter: the genus has a foundation in reality which is one. In the case of "body," the matter of the corruptible is of a different order than that of the incorruptible. Hence, the genus "body" is called "logical," in the sense that it does not have the sort of foundation in reality that genera of generable and corruptible things have. All of that sort of theory seems to me to pertain to the metaphysician (and the physicist), not to *any* logician. It has to do with that conception of the logical notion which includes the notion's foundation in reality: that is, it has to do with the *full* definition of those logical notions, not the sort of definition of them which satisfies the logician.[30]

I notice also that McInerny tells his reader that the metaphysician, faced with the "dialectician" calling "body" univocal, calls it "equivocal" (9). He seems not to want to let the reader face the fact that Thomas has said that this middle item is a case of something being "said according to analogy."

McInerny actually uses the (in this aspect, regrettable) doctrine of Cajetan, that the middle case is true of *any* genus, even, e.g., "animal," in order to argue that Thomas is not really teaching us about types of analogy at all in the text.[31] We read:

> The second member of Thomas's division of things said according to analogy makes it clear that inequality *secundum esse* is irrelevant to what is meant by an analogous name, just as inequality *secundum esse* is irrelevant to the univocal character of generic terms. In short, Thomas is noting that there are inequalities, orderings *per prius et posterius*, among things talked about that do not affect our way of talking about them. (9–10)

This is not true. The second member is a member of a group, each of which is a case of things said according to analogy. In that second member, though the logician sees only univocity, the metaphysician, Thomas is telling us, sees analogy *in the names.* This is because his mode of consideration of things is different from that of the logician. The metaphysician incorporates into the meaning of the *name* of the thing differences in the mode of being of the things given the common name. For him, "body" has two different meanings, as used of the natures of corruptible and incorruptible substances. A genus such as "animal," *pace* Cajetan and McInerny, is quite a different case.

Unless one thinks that Thomas is criticizing the metaphysician here, accusing him of a mistake (obviously this is not so), this is what is being said.

But we must not miss how far McInerny is willing to go in defense of his thesis. Still attempting to explain to us the threefold analogy text in the *Sentences*, he tells us:

> Why, then, does Thomas introduce these three accidental conjunctions with the remark that something is said according to analogy in three ways? It is already clear

that he cannot be taken to mean that there are three kinds of analogous name. When analogy is used to speak of a kind of naming, there is an inequality, an order *per prius et posterius*, among the intentions it signifies. Thus, when there is inequality *secundum esse*, the term "analogy" can be used to refer to it. Then we can say that talk of inequality can conjure up three different states of affairs (*aliquid dicitur secundum analogiam tripliciter*). Sometimes (1) there is inequality of meaning (and thus an analogous name), but the denominating quality is not multiplied in the things named so that it exists in them equally or unequally. Sometimes (2) there is inequality among things named univocally. We might put this as "proper inequality," or "specific inequality," or "*inaequalitas secundum rationes proprias*." Finally, sometimes (3) there is a conjunction of order and inequality among a plurality of notions of a common term *and* unequal, more or less perfect, existence of the denominating quality in the things talked about. (13)

If this is to be read as an answer to the question with which it begins, we must think that Thomas really meant to speak of three ways in which *inequality* is found (thus, McInerny's remarkable rewrite: ". . . talk of *inequality* can conjure up three different *states of affairs.*") McInerny, in his eagerness to convince us, even begins composing a Latin text that Thomas should have supplied us with: "*inaequalitas secundum rationes proprias.*" But Thomas Aquinas did not say that. He said "analogy," and even "something is *said* according to analogy. . . ."

To accept the "explanation" of McInerny, we must understand the middle item, the (2), as using "analogy" in a different sense: not about *naming*, but about inequality in the *being* of the things named. But this is an explanation which *flies in the face of the text.* The text does not say that the thing is spoken of univocally, but that what is being spoken of does not have the equality which the univocal way of naming (all that is seen by the logician) might lead one to believe it had. It says:

> For the metaphysician and the physicist, who consider things according to their being, neither this *word* [*nomen*] "body," nor anything else [i.e., any other name or word], is *said* univocally of corruptibles and incorruptibles.

Clearly, we are speaking about how people understand words. The *logicus* understands them in one way and the metaphysician and physicist in another. This is quite contrary to McInerny's reading.

Coming back to McInerny's argument to show that the threefold division in *Sent.* 1.19 is not a division of kinds of analogy, I would say that if we grant him his conception of defining the genus, analogy, etc., then what he says will follow. But we should not do so. The very text of 1.19, in the part on the middle mode, tells us that one thinker has a different conception of "univocity" than the other has: they agree that there is only one *intentio,* but they differ as regards the importance of the difference in the case. It is not enough, according to the metaphysician, to have one *intentio* for *univocity.* One must have the same kind of matter.[32] Or, if one will, we can say that the two do not speak one language as regards what is "one notion." But the reason they do not is that they have no agreement, either, on what "notion" means. "Being based on the matter" pertains to the *notion* of a genus, according to the metaphysician, but this is not in the "notion" of the genus, according to the logician. The net result is that the logician never has the last word, not even on "genus" or "univocity" or "analogy of names."[33]

Let us consider one last time the objection to which Thomas is replying. The objector wanted to locate truth in God alone, all other things being called "true" relative to God. His middle term was that it has already been established that "true" is said analogically concerning those things in which there is truth. This leads him to introduce the model of "healthy" and to conclude that truth is in God alone. Obviously Thomas could have answered that in some cases of things said analogously, what the objector says applies: but other cases exist in which what is said analogously is found in all the things spoken of, though according to more and less. Had he deigned to explain why this difference exists, he would have had to treat the modes of causality.[34] If he were McInerny, he would have gone on to say that whether or not the nature is found in all the things said by analogy is *per accidens* to analogy as such. Why did he rather give what has all the appearance of wanting to be a taxonomy of analogy of names?

Why does Thomas answer in the way he does? What is the lesson being taught by the answer? It is a little system, certainly mnemonically helpful, in terms of *intentio* and *esse.* It bears upon analogy, because that was the point of the objection, the objector's middle term. And it bears upon cases of analogy precisely as regards having a multiplication of the quality in being, or not. Thomas argues that it is *only in one sort* of analogy that one does *not* have the quality *distributed in the many things.*

Are these cases merely *per accidens* as regards analogy? No. It is the metaphysician who defines analogy, and does so in terms of *the foundations in reality* for the modes of discourse.[35] It is "dialectical" or "logical" to reduce analogy to the issue of *intentio* alone. This McInerny has done, but only by misreading the text.

Thomas, in the passage on threefold analogy, is not, in the middle item, merely interested in teaching us the difference between the logician and the philosopher. He is interested in *grading analogies from the viewpoint of being.* McInerny, looking at the whole thing from the viewpoint of the logician, does not see any point in looking at the analogy of names from the viewpoint of being. But that is to be expected. The metaphysician conceives of different modes of analogy as based on *the sort of real foundation* the logical intention has. We might say that it "happens" to the logician that he still recognizes analogy in the third type, this being because it does have a *secundum intentionem* dimension to it. What we should expect, however, is that he will not recognize it as significantly different, *qua* analogy, from the first type. And this is, of course, what happens to McInerny.

Notes

1. Cf. Plato, *Theaetetus* 183E. Abbreviations used include *ST* for *Summa theologiae*, *CM* for *Commentary on the Metaphysics*, *CP* for *Commentary on the Physics*, *SCG* for *Summa contra gentiles*, *DP* for *De potentia*, *In Sent.* for the *Commentary on the Sentences of Peter Lombard*.

2. Charles De Koninck, "Metaphysics and the Interpretation of Words," *Laval théologique et philosophique* 17 (1961): 33. Cf. Hyacinthe-Marie Robillard, O.P., *De l'analogie et du concept d'être* (Montréal: Les presses de l'Université de Montréal, 1963), 218–19: "Rappelons que le présent Traité [Cajetan's *De nominum analogia*] est un traité de *Logique*. Sans doute, en effet, métaphysiciens, théologiens, scientistes mêmes, font-ils usage de l'analogie, mais ils n'en dissertent point; du moins, s'ils se permettent à l'occasion d'en discuter et d'en fixer les règles, ils ne le font qu'à leurs risques et périls, s'engageant dans une discipline étrangère à leur spécialité. L'analogue, en effet, comme le genre, l'espèce etc. est un être de seconde intention, une construction de l'esprit qui intéresse, immédiatement, le Logicien."

3. Ralph McInerny, *Aquinas and Analogy* (Washington, DC: Catholic University of America Press, 1996). References to this work will be in the body of my text, simply noting the page number.

4. Capreolus, *Defensiones theologiae divi Thomae Aquinatis*, 1.2.1, ed. C. Paban et T. Pègues, (Turonibus: Alfred Cattier, 1900), 1:117–44, asks whether God is intelligible by us in the state of the way, i.e., in the present life. The ninth conclusion is that by the same concept by which the wayfarer conceives of the creature it can conceive of God, though the name signifying that concept is not said univocally of God and of the creature. Cf. 124B–125A for the use of the *Sentences* text.

5. Aristotle, *Metaphysics* 5.6 (1016b31–1017a3).

6. Cf. *ST* 1.14.6 ad 1m; 1.16.4 ad 2m; 1.16.2; 1.84.1. Thomas accuses Plato of failing to appreciate the possibility of our having a mode of knowing of material things different from the mode of being proper to the things themselves (*ST* 1.84.1): this suggests why in Platonism metaphysics and logic would tend to be identified.

7. Cf. *In Sent.* 1. d. 2.1.3 (ed. Mandonnet 1:67); also, *CM* 4.4, §572–77, especially §574; and 6.4, §1233. Cf. also *De ente et essentia* 3 (ed. Leonina 43:374.73–119).

8. Cf. *CM* 4.4, §577, concerning the "demonstrative part of logic," not to be confused with dialectic as demonstrative, §576.

9. Cf. *CM* 7.1, §1147. On the limits of physics as compared to metaphysics, cf. Lawrence Dewan, "St. Thomas, Physics, and the Principle of Metaphysics," *The Thomist* 61 (1997): 549–66.

10. *CM* 2.5, §335: "[Aristotle] shows what is the appropriate method of seeking truth; and . . . firstly he shows how man can know the appropriate method in the quest for truth. . . . He says . . . that diverse people seek the truth by virtue of diverse methods, therefore it is necessary that a man be instructed in what way [*per quem modum*] in each of the sciences [*in singulis scientiis*] the things said are to be taken [*sint recipienda ea quae dicuntur*].

"And because it is not easy for a man to grasp two things at once, but rather while looking towards two he can grasp neither, it is absurd for a man simultaneously to seek science and the method which is appropriate to science. And because of this, one ought to learn logic previous to the other sciences, because *logic treats of the common method of proceeding in all the other sciences. However, the method proper to each of the sciences ought to be treated in the individual sciences, towards the outset*" (my emphasis).

11. Cf. *CP* 2: Thomas presents the whole of book 2 of the *Physics* as treating of "the principles of natural *science*;" cf. 2.1 (ed. Maggiolo, §141), and he treats such questions as how the physicist and the mathematician differ (2.3) and on the basis of which sorts of cause the physicist demonstrates, cf. 2.5, §176. At 2.4, §175, we see a contrast between the physicist's interest in form and the metaphysician's interest in form.

12. Cf. *CM* prologue. Without a knowledge of the things metaphysics teaches, one cannot fully know the things proper to a genus or species; metaphysics is described as maximally intellectual and thus *regulative* of all the sciences. In *CP* 1.1, §4, we are taught that Aristotle's *Physics* is placed at the beginning of the study of natural science, just as *first philosophy*, i.e., metaphysics, is placed before *all* of the sciences; this is because it treats of what is common to beings as such.

13. Cf. *CM* 6.1, §1149: The geometer receives from the metaphysician the answer to the question: "what is magnitude?"—i.e., the very essence of the "subject genus" of the science of geometry. The example is not in Aristotle, but is supplied by Thomas.

14. Cf. *CM* 4.4, §587, concerning Aristotle at 4.2 (1005a13–18): "[The metaphysician] considers the prior and the posterior, genus and species, whole and part, and others things of this sort, because these also are accidents of that which is inasmuch as it is that which is (*accidentia entis inquantum est ens*)."

15. Cf. *CM* 10.12, §2137 [2], §2138–42, §2145). This doctrine figures in an important way later in this paper.

16. *In Sent.* 1. d. 2.1.3. This item is a disputed question, probably written about 1265–67, and inserted by Thomas in his *Sent.*; cf. James Weisheipl, *Friar Thomas D'Aquino: His Life, Thought, and Work* (Garden City, NY: Doubleday, 1974), 366 and 359. See especially A. Dondaine, O.P., "Saint Thomas et la dispute des attributs divins (I Sent., d. 2, a. 3): authenticité et origine," *Archivum Fratrum Praedicatorum* 8 (1938): 253–62.

17. Concerning logic, I have noted Aristotle's statement that it is the metaphysician who considers what genus and species are. In this respect, I would refer not only to *De ente et essentia* 2 and 3 (and especially 2, wherein we get the definitions of the genus and the species), but also to *De substantiis separatis* c. 6, §70, where, in criticizing the position of Gabirol, Thomas says that it does away with *the principles of logic,* doing away with the true notion of the genus and the species and the substantial difference, inasmuch as it changes all into the mode of accidental predication. Now, no particular science really provides the definition of its principles, not even logic. It seems to me clear that it is the metaphysician who provides the logician with the definitions of the principles. But the logician accepts them only in a limited way, by mere "logical consideration."

18. It is true that he is closer, in treating of names, to the concept's relation to things themselves than is the mere grammarian. Cf. *In Perihermeneias* 1.2, (ed. Leonina 1.1*: 10.49–55).

But because logic is ordered towards knowledge to be obtained concerning things [*de rebus sumendam*], the signification of vocal utterances, which is immediately related to the very conceptions of the mind [*inmediata ipsis conceptionibus intellectus*], pertains to its principal consideration, whereas the signification of letters, inasmuch as it is more distant [from our conceptions], does not pertain to its consideration, but rather to the consideration of the grammarian.

19. Cf. *CM* 4.5, §591, concerning the limited outlook the physicist has regarding the first principles of demonstration.

20. *CM* 7.13, §1576, on Aristotle, *Met.* 7.13 (1038b15–16).

21. *ST* 1.29.1 ad 3m. In *DP* 9.2 ad 5m, on the same point, we have: "'individual' is inserted into the definition of the person in order to signify the individual mode of being [*ad designandum individualem modum essendi*]." At *In Sent.* 1. d. 25.1.1 (ed. Mandonnet 1:601), the discussion of Boethius's definition of "person," note how different Thomas's handling of *individua* is than in *ST* 1.29.1 and *DP* 9.2; in the *In Sent.*, it is still merely the name of an *intentio*.

22. In McInerny's conclusion, "The Point of the Book," he says: "My second thesis is that Thomas never speaks of the causal dependence in a hierarchical descent of all things from God as analogy. That is, terminologically speaking, there is no analogy of being in St. Thomas" (162). A most prominent text, one that McInerny obviously knows well (*ST* 1.4.3), asks whether any creature can be like God. This is clearly a metaphysical question, a question about the intrinsic being of creatures. The notion of likeness involves community of form. Thomas answers the question on the basis of the doctrine that every agent causes something like itself, so that in any effect there must be a likeness of the form of the agent. He sketches degrees of such likeness using logical notions of species and genus; but obviously this is a use of logical notions as stand-ins for metaphysical conceptions (cf. 1.29.1 ad 3m). Ultimately he reasons to the case of the divine agent as "not contained in any genus." Here the similarity of the effect to the cause is called "according to some sort of analogy" [*secundum aliqualem analogiam*]. Notice that we proceed from the species to the genus to the analogously one. Thomas explains what he means:

. . . as being itself is common to all [*sicut ipsum esse est commune omnibus*]. And in this way those things which are from God are assimilated to him inasmuch as they are beings [*inquantum sunt entia*], as to the first and universal principle of being in its entirety [*totius esse*].

And one could cite many prominent texts in this line. McInerny is in error.

23. Aquinas, *In Sent.* (ed. Mandonnet 1:492).

24. *In Sent.*, 1: 492–93. Thus the doctrine is significantly different from that in the *ST* 1.16.6. See Lawrence Dewan, "St. Thomas's Successive Discussions of the Nature of Truth," in *Sanctus Thomas De Aquino: Doctor Hodiernae Humanitatis, Miscellanea offerta . . . al Prof. Abelardo Lobato, O.P.*, ed. Daniel Ols (Vatican City: Libreria Editrice Vaticana, 1995), 153–68.

25. *In Sent.*, 1:491.

26. The words which I have set in italics are omitted from the Latin and from the English translation by McInerny in his presentation on p. 6.

27. For examples of this sort of analogy, and the denial of its univocity, cf. *SCG* 1.32, §285 and *DP* 7.7 ad 6m.

28. *In Sent.*, 1:492.

29. This point of McInerny's, that the distinctions in *In Sent.* 1. d. 19 are *per accidens* as regards analogy of names, runs through his whole book. Thus, after telling us (erroneously) that Thomas does not use the terminology of "analogy of being," he says that, if he had, he would have made it clear that whether or not there is the same order in the *things* named, as regards their being, as there is in the *names* used about the things, is *per accidens*, having nothing intrinsically to do with the analogy of names or the analogy of being (162).

30. On this, cf. *CM* 10.12, §2137 [2], §2138–42, and §2145. In §2142 we read:

But no matter what genus be taken, it is necessary that corruptible and incorruptible be [intrinsic] to its notion. Hence, it is impossible that they communicate in any genus. And it is reasonable that this happen. For there cannot be one matter of corruptibles and incorruptibles. But *the genus, physically speaking,* is taken from matter. Hence, it was said above that those things which do not have matter in common are generically diverse. But, *logically speaking,* nothing prevents their agreeing in *genus,* inasmuch as they agree in one common notion [*in una communi ratione*] whether of substance or of quality or of something of that sort."

Obviously, it is the word "genus" which is *differently defined* by the physicist and by the logician. Hence, arise two different "ways of speaking." And we can expect the same thing with the word "analogy."

31. Cf. Thomas de Vio, Cajetan, *De nominum analogia,* c. 1, in Hyacinthe-Marie Robillard, O.P., *De l'analogie et du concept d'être* (Montréal: Les presses de l'Université de Montréal, 1963), §15 (corresponds to §5 in the edition of Zammit and Hering)]: "Omne enim genus, analogum hoc modo appelari potest." McInerny refers to this text on p. 9, n. 4.

Cf. Armand Maurer, "The Analogy of Genus," *The New Scholasticism* 29 (1955): 127–44, who notes that "[of late] the consensus of opinion is that the analogy of genus is not in the long run a true metaphysical analogy" (127). Fr. Maurer himself does not join this consensus. One should note, nevertheless, that his expression "analogy of genus" is itself somewhat Cajetanian by suggestion.

32. McInerny says: "The question must arise as to whether the *logicus* of the present text has a different conception of univocal or equivocal terms from the philosopher. Surely they agree on which such terms mean but disagree as to whether the things being talked about can provide a *ratio communis* which is found equally in them." I say: no, they speak different languages; hence, the need to qualify the word "genus" with the mode of consideration being used. For example, in *ST* 1.66.2 ad 2m we read: "si genus consideretur physice, 'corruptibilia et incorruptibilia non sunt in eodem genere,' propter diversum modum potentiae in eis, ut dicitur X *Metaph.* Secundum autem logicam considerationem, est unum genus omnium corporum, propter unam rationem corporeitatis." Cf. *ST* 1.88.2 ad 4m.

33. I note that *CP* 7.7, §936 [9], contrasts the "abstract consideration of the logician or the mathematician" with the "concrete conception of the physicist making applications to matter [*concretam rationem naturalis ad materiam applicantis*]," a text referred to by Maurer, "The Analogy of Genus," n. 16.

34. Cf. *ST* 1.13.6 ad 3m.

35. Cf. Aquinas, *In Ethica* 1.7, (ed. Leonina 47.1: 26.168–213; Pirotta ed., §95–96), on Aristotle, 1.6 (1096b26–29). We read in Thomas's paraphrase:

> Thus, therefore, he says that "good" is said of many things, not in function of meanings altogether different, as happens in those which are equivocals by chance, but inasmuch as all goods depend on one first source of goodness or inasmuch as they are ordered to one end. For Aristotle did not think that that separate good is the idea and *ratio* of all goods, but the source and end.
>
> Or else they are all called "good" according to analogy, that is, the same proportion, as sight is the good of the body and intellect is the good of the soul.
>
> He prefers this third mode for this reason, because it is taken in function of goodness inhering in things, whereas the first two modes [were taken] in function of a separate goodness, on the basis of which something is not named so properly. (ed. Leonina 27.198–213)

I note this because it shows the interest of the metaphysician in the *real* foundation for naming: naming is more truly naming when the foundation in reality is fuller.

Chapter 7

To Which "God" Must a Proof of God's Existence Conclude for Aquinas?

DAVID B. TWETTEN

The philosopher who would prove God's existence faces an uphill struggle in today's ecumenical and pluralistic context. Witness the exasperated reaction of a student in my graduate seminar on the medieval proofs for God's existence: "Even were I to grant the conclusion of Aquinas's 'five ways,' what does *that* have to do with the 'God of the Bible'?" When my student was asked which descriptions of God in which biblical passages would have to be proved for him to be satisfied with the conclusion, he answered without hesitation, "All of them!" Now, perhaps it is inevitable that the philosopher's "God" will seem cold and impersonal to the searcher for religious answers. When one approaches a proof for God's existence expecting from it an experience of a God such as is already familiar in one's reading or one's culture, one is bound to be unsatisfied with the conclusion of a syllogism. But the burden for the would-be proof of God is still heavier when, as today, few religious views can be presupposed in common and there is little shared discourse such as would help make acceptable the conclusion of a proof. Often, as in the case of my student, the very project of proving God's existence is deemed unfamiliar and suspect.[1]

Granted the project of a proof, though, under what philosophic understanding of "God" would a successful proof function? Again, there are different philosophies as well as different religions, and therefore disparate notions of "God." Einstein's "God," for example, would satisfy no believer—and perhaps few philosophers. Does the atheist reject the same "God" that the theist defends? In a pluralistic society one may wonder whether there will not be as many proofs of God's existence as there are different notions of God. Whose God, which rationality? Failing an answer, the proofs for God's existence could themselves appear to be but another argument for non-theism. Among competing and perhaps incompatible deities, who is to say which God is the right one?

I. THE RELIGIOUS STANDARD APPROACH:
AQUINAS CRITICIZED, AQUINAS DEFENDED

A growing number of contemporary philosophers of religion of a theistic bent have come to address this issue head on by insisting on a comprehensive argument for God's existence that would take as its inspiration "the God of the Judaeo-Christian-Islamic Scriptures." Such an argument, after all, arrives at perhaps the only God that Anglo-American theists are interested in affirming or that Anglo-American atheists are occupied with rejecting. Richard Swinburne, for example, tailors precisely such an argument to fit a proposal that could not be more straightforward or ambitious: "I take the proposition 'God exists' . . . to be logically equivalent to 'there exists a person without a body (i.e. a spirit) who is eternal, is perfectly free, omnipotent, omniscient, perfectly good, and the creator of all things.'"[2] For Swinburne, only an argument that meets these monotheist criteria can be accepted. I call this a "Religious Standard Approach" to the proof of God's existence; in this case, the religious standard is the "God of classical theism."

This Religious Standard Approach is reflected in many recent anthologies and introductory texts in the philosophy of religion. These often introduce readings and discussions on the nature of "the God of classical theism," considering such traditional attributes as omnipotence, omniscience, perfection, eternity, and necessity; and only then do they consider whether such a God exists.[3] As some of these texts make explicit, one needs to be able to answer the question, "What would anything have to be like to be God?" before examining evidence for the God thus described.[4] It is perhaps no accident that anthologies of this kind, though they normally include selections from Aquinas on the divine attributes, usually drop Aquinas's "five ways." Swinburne draws the consequence strikingly: "Aquinas's five ways, or rather the first four of his five ways, seem to me to be one of the least successful pieces of philosophy."[5] Swinburne asks, for example, why change is so surprising that we need to invoke *God* as its source (118n).

On the other hand, Aquinas himself has been associated with this Religious Standard Approach in the work of Norman Kretzmann. For Kretzmann, the first three books of Aquinas's *Summa contra gentiles* found a new discipline: natural theology or, better, the metaphysics of theism, the "top-down philosophy" in which the investigator systematically presents, on the model of an Aristotelian science, arguments through reason alone for as many as possible of the statements "about God" that have been revealed in the three monotheist religions.[6] Within such a discipline a proof establishing the existence of its principal theme must target "a being that theists would recognize as God" (65) and that therefore "must rely on traditional doctrinal accounts of God that have their source in putative revelation" (113).

Kretzmann admits that Aquinas, strictly speaking, fails to meet this religious standard by the end of the five purported "proofs of God's existence" in *Contra gentiles* 1.13, even though the proofs arrive successfully at a supreme explanatory being, the source of all things. It seems possible, observes Kretzmann, that such a breathtakingly extraordinary being exists, but that there be no God (85–86). Despite the fact that the fifth way in arriving at a providential being is "a little more nearly theological than merely cosmological" (89), and "does unmistakably describe *God*, a supernatural, knowing, universally governing person" (88), an atheist could still hypothesize, for example, an irreducible plurality of ultimate explanatory principles (86, 113). Subsequently Aquinas argues that this explanatory being is absolutely simple in its existence—in keeping with the "metaphysics of Exodus"—as well as absolutely everlasting, perfect, infinite, and unique. Nonetheless, for Kretzmann, traditional theists require more before they can agree that God's existence has been shown. All of these attributes, although increasingly more detailed, may be essential characteristics of God, yet none are "sufficient conditions for deity" (85, 112). Only by the end of Book I does the *Summa contra gentiles* make explicit the traditional divine attributes that unmistakably characterize a person: moral goodness, knowledge, will, and love (169).[7]

Should we agree with Swinburne, then, that Aquinas's project failed? Kretzmann believes to the contrary that were we to call the "primary, universally explanatory being" proved prior to the last chapters of Book I by the name "Alpha" rather than "God," we would capture Aquinas's spirit. For Aquinas, the word "God" is but a *placeholder* to be filled in by successively proved attributes until we reach that set sufficient for divinity (cf. 89). From the five ways on, Aquinas is careful never to defend attributes more God-like than are warranted by his purely philosophical premises, even though the "God of revelation" is, of course, in his sights from the beginning (88). Kretzmann's procedure of bracketing the question "whether God exists" in favor of the question "what God is" allows Aquinas's proof for God's existence to emerge gradually over the course of the entire metaphysics of theism, as Alpha gradually turns into the God of classical theism (86–89, 113).[8] Despite the occasional gaps in Aquinas's argumentation, Kretzmann proposes Aquinas's metaphysical system, instead of Swinburne's probable-inductive argumentation, as the best available theism.

Kretzmann's work may be the best available contemporary appropriation of Aquinas's thought, but does he succeed in bringing Aquinas under the Religious Standard umbrella of contemporary theism? Would it not be truer to both the contemporary project and to Aquinas himself to concede that he simply failed to uncover a satisfactory argument for God's existence? In one sense, Kretzmann "saves" Aquinas's proofs in a way already familiar to Aquinas scholars. The idea is that Thomas never intended to prove God's existence as such with his five ways, but only intended to prove various divine attributes that open the way to the complete discovery of God. I call this the "Total Package Defense" of Aquinas's proofs. William Rowe and William Lane Craig, for example, hold that Aquinas only arrives definitively at God's existence at the end of Question 11 of the *Summa theologiae*, for only there does he prove that there is but one God.[9] Kretzmann simply pushes back the arrival at God from question 11 to question 26, or from chapter 43 of the *Contra gentiles* to chapter 94. On the other hand, Kretzmann makes explicit that it is the complete set of questions 2–26 or chapters 13–94 that constitute Aquinas's proof of God. No one divine attribute, even a personal attribute, is alone a sufficient condition for deity; only the entire set will satisfy a classical theist.

Equally familiar to Aquinas scholars, however, is the rejection by Fernand Van Steenberghen of strained defenses of Aquinas's five ways like the Total Package Defense. According to Van Steenberghen, Aquinas failed in his project, and the sooner Thomists realize this fact, the better. Aquinas's failure in the five ways lies precisely in the uncritical definition of the term "God" that Thomas uses at the end of each argument, allowing him to conclude prematurely, "and this we call God."[10] For Van Steenberghen, definitions of "God" such as "prime mover," "first cause," or "necessary being" were justifiable in Aquinas's thirteenth-century context. Although such terminology was completely unknown to the average unlettered person, even anti-Christian intellectuals recognized it to belong to the best science, as warranted by the great pagan philosophers (291–93). The fact that these definitions fall short of describing the "God of monotheism" mattered little when the project of proving God was only an academic exercise, and widespread belief in God was based on religious experience, not argument. In the Middle Ages, proving God's existence was simply not a vital project.

Today the situation is completely different, observes Van Steenberghen. Given widespread atheism and agnosticism, it becomes imperative for believers to have a rational foundation for belief in the only God that they will take seriously, the God of monotheism. Hence, Van Steenberghen insists that the definition of "God" in a proof must be religious in character, must be borrowed from the core belief of the great monotheist religions. With the help of a philological and cultural analysis,[11] he argues for the following definition. A successful proof today must arrive at once at no less than: *the provident, creator of the universe*. A provident being would be both *personal* and concerned for us and for our destiny, and a creator of everything other than itself would have to be *unique* (293). Van Steenberghen finds it disconcerting that Aquinas does not begin each proof with a well-defended nominal definition (171–72, 184). As a result, with the exception of some flawed and partial reasoning in two of the proofs, Aquinas's five ways are valid but incomplete: they fail to arrive most obviously at the *unicity* of God, an essential part of any proof.[12] Aquinas, of course, knew this, hence he immediately proceeded to complete the proofs with a deduction of the traditional divine attributes. Unfortunately, subsequent Thomists have presented the five ways as if they could stand on their own. Alternatively, Van Steenberghen devises a new proof, one that utilizes reasoning for an infinite, absolute, causal being, and that begins with a systematic defense of the above definition—a definition to which no one, theist or atheist, will refuse the name "God."[13]

II. A NON-PRESCRIPTIVE APPROACH TO "GOD"

In my view, Van Steenberghen is correct to reorient the discussion of Aquinas's five ways on the definition of the term "God" prior to the proof. And, Kretzmann rightly trains our eye on the question, what condition or conditions are sufficient to merit the title "deity"? Insufficient is the standard Thomist response, traceable to Cajetan, that the five ways, even though they do not strictly prove God, prove an attribute that will turn out, in fact, to belong to God alone.[14] If the five ways do not *as such* conclude to a property already known in such a way as to be unique to God, then they fail, as Báñez insists.[15] Yet, I ask, must a proof of God target a specific set of conditions that alone would satisfy a given religious tradition—must it take what I call a "prescriptive" approach? Should the success of a proof be made to depend on a non-philosophical *religious standard*, as for Kretzmann, or on a cultural analysis of what would be accepted as "God" in the wake of the monotheist religions, as for Van Steenberghen? What if a proof proved "creator" but not "provident," and yet a culture accepted this to be God? Does not the absence of such an approach as part of the five ways suggest that Thomas has reasons for not regarding it as necessary? On my reading, Kretzmann and Van Steenberghen fail to take into account the systematic justification that Thomas himself gives for the use of a much less ambitious and prescriptive definition of the word "God" in a proof, a definition that is sufficient for Aquinas's project but that otherwise requires no more than is minimally necessary.[16] Notably absent from Aquinas's approach to defining "God" are such terms as "creative," "infinite," or even "unique": given Aquinas's non-prescriptive definition, even after having proved that "God" exists, one could still hold that there are many "Gods."[17] In fact, Aquinas's approach to God—which I call "non-prescriptive"—allows for a plurality of definitions and consequently for a variety of proofs, and Aquinas intentionally never attempts to reduce definitions *within the proofs* to one formula or specific set of sufficient conditions.

At the same time, Aquinas's logic contains a clear criterion to identify the sufficiency of a proof: it will target some causal attribute that can serve as a definition because that attribute is commensurate with and only with one *kind* of thing, God, as opposed to every other kind, like human or dog. Aquinas's clear-cut but minimal expectations, I suggest, are of particular value in a pluralistic society as a model for how to approach a proof of God's existence. The "God" of his proofs is not one that belongs to only one religious or philosophic tradition, but is one that most could acknowledge deserves a capital "G." In place of a highly prescriptive notion of "God," Aquinas in fact offers the most non-prescriptive notion possible, a notion that will be the lowest common denominator of a plurality of views, but which nonetheless singles out one kind of thing as distinct from all others: "a God." Aquinas places the burden for reconciling religious differences, not on the proof of God's existence, but on the subsequent discussion of the nature and operations of a God.

Instead of beginning, then, by criticizing Aquinas for failing to make a cultural investigation into the proper definition of "God," I ask, what grounds does Thomas himself offer for using a given notion of "God" as a target in his proofs? My question presupposes that we know what the word "God" means for Thomas. Hence, in Part III of this paper I direct attention to the only explicit, formal definition of "God" in Aquinas's works: "something that is existing above all things, which is the principle of all things and is removed from all things." This definition serves as a touchstone for my account of Aquinas's proofs and of the plurality of notions of "God" found there. In Part IV, I highlight the principal elements from Aristotelian logic that lie behind Aquinas's conception of the role of definition in a proof of God's existence. Aquinas is simply applying to the case of God the logic of existential arguments that he received through a living commentary tradition on the *Posterior Analytics.* Unless we appreciate this fact we will not be able to understand the project of his "five ways." Part V then lays out criteria for the definition of "God" formulated by Aquinas in light of the afore-mentioned logic. In Part VI, I argue that there are a plurality of definitions proper to the proofs of God's existence in Aquinas's thought, but that we can construct a formula that is common to all of them. This "definition" expresses formally what is found mate-rially in the five definitions implicit in the proofs. For Aquinas, every demonstration of God's existence begins from things in the world understood as effects and concludes *at least* to "a kind of thing that causes other things and that is either beyond all other kinds or is removed from all other kinds." It helps that there be a plurality of such demonstrations if some effects are more evident whereas others, since more perfect, tell us more about their cause. This minimal formula and this non-prescriptive approach could serve in today's pluralistic milieu even should Thomas's proofs themselves be found inadequate.

III.   AQUINAS'S *EX PROFESSO* DEFINITION OF "GOD" IN *SUMMA THEOLOGIAE* 1, QUESTION 13

In the context of the five ways Aquinas speaks in a general way of the kind of definition of "God" that his proofs employ, as we shall see. But nowhere there does he expressly propose to formulate a definition. Where, then, does Thomas offer an explicit, formal definition of the word "God" as part of a systematic presentation? The answer lies in an underappreciated passage in *ST* 1.13, where Aquinas reflects on how we name God, once he has completed his discussion of the divine "nature."[18] After first analyzing the divine names in general, question 13 takes up two particular names. The first is the name "God," to which Thomas devotes three of the twelve articles of question 13. In the first of these three articles, art. 8, Aquinas asks, does the term "God" name a nature? The second objection answers, no, since humans cannot know the nature or essence of God. In response Aquinas writes:

> [A]ccording as we know the nature of something from its properties and effects, we can signify [the nature] by a name. Hence because we can know the substance of stone (*lapis*) in itself from a property of stone in understanding *what* stone is, this name "stone" signifies the very *nature* of stone as it is in itself. For it signifies the definition (*definitionem*) of stone by which we know what stone is, since the notion (*ratio*) that a name signifies is the definition, as was said in *Metaphysics* 4.
>
> But from divine effects we cannot know the divine nature as it is in itself so that we know *what* it is; but [we can know it] only by way of eminence, causality, and negation, as was said above. And in this way the name "God" signifies the divine nature. For this is the name that has been imposed to signify *something that is existing above all things, which is the principle of all things and is removed from all things.* For, this is what they intend to signify who name God.[19]

This response is the only place in Aquinas's corpus where he explicitly presents, in the context of a systematic treatment of the topic, the signification—and therefore, as he says here, the definition—of the word "God." I have been able to find only one other explicit formula in Thomas's works for what *Deus* means. The *Sermon on the Creed*, explaining the Creed's first article, states: "We must consider what this name 'God' signifies: none other than the governor of and provider for all things."[20] But as Aquinas, relying on John of Damascus, explains several times, including here in question 13, the word *theos* or "God" is from the Greek word "to behold" as to its derivation, *not* as to its signification.[21] In Aquinas's technical language, "providence" belongs to "that *from which* the word 'God' is imposed for the sake of signifying (*id a quo imponitur ad significandum*)" as opposed to "that *for the sake of* signifying *which* the word is imposed (*id ad quod significandum nomen imponitur*)."[22] And so, we may say, the word "God" in Aquinas means "provident being" by etymology, but it properly signifies "something that is existing above all things, which is the principle of all things and is removed from all things."

One must ask, are we not reading too much into one isolated and unparalleled text in the corpus of Aquinas? In what follows I shall argue that this definition fits closely

Aquinas's Aristotelian logic on the definition of non-perceptible reality—except for the following strikingly non-Aristotelian feature. Question 13's definition is couched in three attributes—above all, principle of all, removed from all—which Aquinas expressly derives from Pseudo-Dionysius's "threefold way of knowing God," of which Aquinas often makes rich use: the ways of eminence, causality, and negation. The Dionysian character of Aquinas's definition of "God" allows us to discover the stages in which Aquinas gradually developed the definition. First, his *Exposition of Boethius's De trinitate* (ca. 1256–59) already links the way of defining "God" to the *triplex via* of Dionysius. Thomas explains there that in a definition of "God" *negation* takes the place of a genus, whereas relation to *effects* or comparison by way of *eminence* take the place of a specific difference.[23] Later, in the *Summa contra gentiles* (after 1259) and in the *Exposition of the Divine Names,* Aquinas formulates a triad of divine attributes that corresponds to the *triplex via,* the same triad found in the question 13's definition of God. He writes, "through effects we know that God exists, as well as that he is the *cause* of other things, that he is *supereminent* beyond other things, and that he is *removed* from all things."[24] It only remained for question 13 of the *Summa theologiae* (ca. 1266) to place these three attributes into an explicit definition. This definition, although unique, turns out to be a development of ideas that Aquinas had sketched in his earliest works as a master of theology.

What can we conclude from the definition of "God" in question 13? Can we conclude that this is the definition employed in the proofs of God's existence in question 2? I argue, no. First, if so, Aquinas should make explicit use of that definition in a syllogism, as Van Steenberghen does with his own definition. Aquinas should say, for example, " . . . there must be a first unmoved mover. But a first unmoved mover is an instance of 'what exists above all, which is the principle of all and is removed from all.' And, this we call God." It would be all the more necessary to make this step explicit because the definition is stated nowhere else in Aquinas's works and is only found buried in an objection some ten questions after the proofs themselves. Second, the definition as expressed prescribes more than what each of the five ways actually supply. The fourth way's conclusion to a "something that is maximally a being and the cause of all beings," for example, does not as such express a negative element or remove God from the quasi-genus "being." Third, and most importantly, the definition of "God" in question 13 uses a triad of attributes that are expressly linked to the *threefold way of knowing God* articulated only in question 12, articles 4c and 12c. The definition as stated belongs to the consideration of the divine names, which is precisely where Thomas places it. From here on, I argue, we should speak of two classes of definitions of the word "God" in Aquinas: one class proper to the proofs of God's existence, and another class proper to the discussion of what God is,[25] and therefore of how he is named. The need for this distinction will become clear after we examine the elements of the *Posterior Analytics* that lie behind Aquinas's way of defining "God."

IV. THE ARISTOTELIAN LOGIC OF EXISTENTIAL ARGUMENTS
AND THE NOMINAL DEFINITION

We have seen that question 13's explicit, formal definition of the word "God" is unique in Aquinas's works. Yet this fact is not as surprising, when we consider the unique-ness of the *Prima pars* itself in its use of Aristotelian methodology within the frame-work of revelation.[26] Aquinas in the *Summa theologiae* pursues, for the first time in an entirely "theological" *Meisterwerk*, the same systematic, philosophical approach to God that he had first tested in the philosophical part of the *Summa contra gentiles*, namely, in books 1–3. He applies to the case of God the method proposed by the *Poste-rior Analytics* for investigating the existence and nature of any thing. It is obvious that both *Summae* follow Aristotle in beginning with the question "does God exist?" then in asking "what is the nature of God?" (or rather, "what or how is God *not*?") But it is less often remembered how foreign is this approach to such standard expositions of sacred theology as the *Sentences* of Lombard. In fact, one looks in vain in Aquinas's *Scriptum on the Sentences* (1252–56) for an account of how the Aristotelian method might be applied to the investigation of God. Only in the subsequent *Exposition of Boethius's De trinitate*, which is itself unique in the thirteenth century, does Aquinas begin to ar-ticulate the method in detail that he then puts to work in the two *Summae*.[27] Thus, although both *Summae* present, for example, five ways of proving God's existence, it is not surprising to see considerable expansion in the later work, such as we in fact find in the discussion of the divine "nature" (qq. 3–11) and especially of the divine names (qq. 12–13).

1. *General Elements of Aristotelian Method.* I turn now to the major elements of the "scientific" methodology of Aristotle as understood by Aquinas in light of the commentators whom he directly or indirectly follows: Themistius, Grosseteste, and Aquinas's teacher Albert the Great.[28] This methodology underlies Aquinas's account of the definition of the word "God" proper to a proof of God's existence, which definition I take up in Part VI.[29] Aquinas inherited this logic from the Aristotelian commentary tradition as something alive and functioning in the thought of Albert and others, and as mediated through Grosseteste and Themistius (whose *Posterior Analytics* commen-tary had been translated into Latin and was known to Grosseteste). To avoid repeti-tion, I cite commentators other than Thomas only where they significantly deviate from or supplement the elements as found in Aristotle. Naturally, I cannot enter into the question here of the extent to which the commentary tradition inherited by Aquinas is an accurate portrayal of Aristotle's thought.

For Aristotle, "scientific knowledge" (*epistēmē*) in the highest sense results from a search for causes. Accordingly, Aristotle's work on "scientific" method famously item-izes four kinds of philosophical questions and seeks to reduce them to an investigation into the cause—or into what he calls the "middle term" of a syllogism (*PA* 2.1–2).[30] Here we are mainly interested, of course, in the first two questions in *Posterior Analytics* 2, "does *x* exist (*an sit*)?" and "what is *x* (*quid sit*)?"[31] According to Aristotle, the question to which the other three questions are principally reduced is "what is *x*?" (cf. *PA* 2.2–3, 89b36–90a15; 90a31–36). For this question asks for the essence of a thing, which is that thing's principal cause. The answer to this question is a "formula" or definition of the thing. For Aristotle, to know a thing's definition is to be able to have "science" about it: to be able to understand why it exists, or, at least, why it has the properties that it has (*PA* 2.2, 90a10–15; 2.8, 93a4–5).

Should one begin an investigation of something, then, by seeking out its essence? According to *Posterior Analytics* 2, one cannot investigate the essence of "nothing," that is, of something that is not already known to exist.[32] For Aristotle, it seems there is no point in engaging in a formal definitional analysis of a thing's essence if we are unsure whether it exists. In fact, properly we have no knowledge of a thing or of an essence unless we first know that it exists.[33] This claim seems to be central to Aristotle's realist methodology, and on it depends the rest of my account.[34] Of course, the claim itself depends on the prior realist claims that things have essences, that their essences can be known by us, and that they can be defined. Aquinas considerably qualifies Aristotle's confident realism, holding that we cannot directly know the essences of material things, and that we must define them by using in place of their differentiae— which are unknown to us—perceptible accidents, which as effects make known their causes.[35] The fact that definitions of species are less perfect than Aristotle suggests does not otherwise affect Aquinas's acceptance of the methodology of the *Posterior Analytics*.[36]

It follows that prior to the question "what is *x*?" is the question "does *x* exist?"[37] First one asks, does an eclipse of the Moon exist? Then one asks, what is an eclipse? First one asks, does god exist? Then one asks, what is god? The latter example, it is worth remembering, is that of Aristotle himself—and is followed by all of the commentators (*PA* 2.1, 89b32–35). Notice that contrary to many Thomists,[38] the question, does god exist? as well as the question, what is god? are *philosophical* themes and do not necessarily presuppose religious faith.[39]

2. *The Role of Nominal Definition.* Yet, what if, as in the case of a god, the thing whose existence is in question is not obvious from sense perception? In that case, the answer to the question "does *x* exist?" requires proof.[40] But how can we prove the existence of something if we do not know what it is? It must be that knowing "that *x* exists" presupposes some knowledge of "what *x* is," however partial.[41] Aristotle's answer is that one must use as a middle term a formula or definition at least of "what the term *x* signifies" to prove the existence of *x*[42]—one uses what Aristotle himself calls the "nominal formula" (*onomatōdes logos*).[43] The *Posterior Analytics* does not work through examples

of such proofs, but Aristotle appears to give several examples of the difference between preliminary and finished kinds of definition.[44] At the outset of an inquiry into lunar eclipses one must know minimally that an "eclipse" involves the absence of the Moon's light; later one comes to understand the essence of an eclipse, namely, the interposition of the Earth between the Sun and the Moon.[45] At the outset one knows that "soul" signifies the source of self-initiating activities of life, such as breathing, growing, and perceiving (*PA* 2.8, 93a24). Later one may determine that Aristotle is right: soul is the "first actuality of a body capable of life." In such cases, explains Aristotle elliptically, we first have "something of" the thing, which is sufficient to have "that it is" in an accidental sense (*PA* 2.8, 93a21–22, 24–28). Now, accidental knowledge of itself yields nothing regarding "what it is," for we do not yet know "that it is." But whatever we do have (of knowledge or of the thing?) makes the project easier than otherwise.

Based on these texts of Aristotle, the scholastic tradition distinguishes between a so-called "nominal definition" and a "real definition."[46] Aquinas does not use this terminology[47] but usually contrasts "*definition*" of an essence or "what *x* is" with "what is signified by its name."[48] By "nominal definition" is meant a formula that expresses at least what a given *word* means, as distinct from a "real definition," which is the formula for the essence of the actual thing itself. That Aquinas adopts Aristotle's methodology regarding nominal definition in proving God's existence is made explicit in *ST* 1.2.2, in the article immediately prior to the five ways. Aquinas writes: "For proving that something exists, it is necessary to take as the middle, not 'what *x* is' but *what the name signifies;* for, the question "'what is *x*' follows upon the question 'whether *x* exists.'"[49]

It is worth observing that a "nominal definition" is not necessarily a bad definition. On Aquinas's own principles, a name signifies, properly, a thing's definition (*ST* 1.13.1c; 1.13.8 ad 2m). Hence a "real definition" *could* be used to define a word, could be used for a "nominal definition."[50] A perfectly good definition of the *word* "eclipse" would be "interposition of the Earth between Sun and Moon," but it should not be taken as a real definition before this has been proved to exist. At the same time, a nominal definition at the beginning of an inquiry is typically preliminary and provisional, intended to be replaced by a subsequent "real definition," as in Aristotle's examples. As Aquinas spells out in the *Exposition of the De trinitate*, a nominal definition will describe a thing generically, through an immediate or remote genus, yet will use instead of a specific difference some perceptible accidents.[51] Similarly, Aristotle defines thunder in a preliminary way as a certain sound in the clouds (*PA* 2.8, 93a23).

The thirteenth-century theologians, applying the Aristotelian doctrine on method and definition to the case of God, drew special consequences for the role of nominal definition there. Revelation taught them that it is impossible in this life to behold the face of God or to comprehend the divine essence. Aquinas defends this claim philosophically, and some of his arguments are cogent even prior to the proof of God's existence.[52] Our intellect, because it gains all of its knowledge through the senses, cannot immediately conceive the essence of an imperceptible thing. Nor is it possible to conceive immaterial or spiritual beings mediately through the essences of perceptible things, since the former share no genus with the latter. For the same reason, it is not possible to have even confused cognition through a remote genus; and confused cognition through accidents is ruled out, since we do not know them. Hence, humans can never know the essence of an incorporeal being, such as is "God" or an "angel" (as will be subsequently be argued); we can never have a "real definition" of bodiless things. For Aquinas, when we speak of definition in the case of God, as throughout this paper, we are always speaking only of "nominal definition," of what the *word* "God" means. There may be better and worse definitions of "God," there may be definitions proper to proofs of God's existence and others proper to proofs about his "nature." But all of them are nominal.[53]

3. *Existential Proof through Effects in the Commentary Tradition.* As I have mentioned, *Posterior Analytics* 2 does not explain how a nominal definition will be used to prove the existence of some *x* in the first place. But the commentary tradition prior to Aquinas already uses parallel doctrines from elsewhere in Aristotle to draw consequences in general, as well as for the specific case of god. Most importantly, the commentators, following hints in Aristotle himself, draw on the distinction between knowing the fact that a subject has a given attribute versus knowing why; that is, between "proof of fact" and "proof of the reasoned fact" (*quia* v. *propter quid; PA* 1.13).[54] Aristotle will forgive me for suppressing his example of twinkling stars in favor of that of the Earth's revolution around the Sun. This theory was confirmed with certainty in the nineteenth century with the discovery of "stellar parallax"; that is, of the variation, corresponding to seasons of the year, in the apparent distance between stars. Stellar parallax, then, if we follow the *Posterior Analytics*, proves *the fact* that the Earth revolves, although it fails to explain *why,* fails to prove the "reasoned fact." Nevertheless, the Earth's revolution explains *why* stellar parallax is an observed fact; that is, it allows proof of the "reasoned fact" of stellar parallax.

What is the significance of this doctrinal link? It allows the commentators to draw connections between "proofs of fact" and "proofs of existence through nominal definition." According to Aristotle, even without a true cause one can prove a fact in two ways: by arguing from a remote genus, or by arguing from effects to their cause (*PA* 1.13, 78a22–b30). Indeed, Aristotle's proof of a prime mover epitomizes a proof of existence from effects.[55] Accordingly, the commentary tradition identifies existential proofs through nominal definitions in general as proofs through effects or "signs" of their cause.[56] Furthermore, Themistius, followed by Grosseteste, observes that there is no strict demonstration of god as of a reasoned fact, since god is without cause.[57]

Instead, according to Themistius, employing Aristotle's terminology (at *PA* 2.8, 93a22–23), the proof of god or gods is through "something of" god: namely, through the fact that there is healing, fulfilled prophecy, or everlasting motion (that is, through effects).[58] In this, as in all cases, the nominal definition is for Themistius the principle of all inquiry.[59] Grosseteste adds that the proof of the first uncaused is a "proof of fact" from effects, and that it belongs to metaphysics.[60]

Where there is need for a proof of the existence of some x, then, that proof will be made using the nominal definition of *x* as a middle term. One will misread Aquinas, however, unless one recognizes that on his reading of the *Posterior Analytics,* it will often be possible subsequently to formulate a second proof of the existence of the same *x.*[61] Once the real definition of x is known, this definition can be used as a middle term to show not merely the fact that x exists, as before, but now *why x* exists. For the essence of a thing is that thing's principal cause, that is, the formal cause of its existence.[62] Do eclipses exist? Initially, yes, because the Moon becomes dark (nominal definition)— and because when this happens our eyes have neither gone blind nor been obscured by clouds. Reasoning to this conclusion amounts to what I call a "*quia* existential proof." After further examination, a better answer can be given than before: yes, because the Moon's light is obstructed by the Earth (real definition). Reasoning to this conclusion amounts to a "*propter quid* existential proof."[63]

This doctrine of a twofold existential proof is not explicit in Aristotle although it is arguably warranted by his crabbed text. But it is explicitly maintained by Grosseteste:

> Aristotle has by now shown that knowing "what *x* is" precedes knowing "that it is," since through "what it is" it is demonstrated "that it is" . . . Nevertheless, this "what *x* is" does not state "what the thing in reality is (*quid est res*)" but only what the *term* signifies; and it is agreed that knowing "what a term signifies" precedes knowing "what *x* is." Aristotle has by now shown that knowing "what a term signifies" cannot demonstrate existence (*esse*). Indeed, it is absolutely impossible to know "what *x* is," *through which it is possible for existence to be demonstrated,* before knowing "that *x* is."[64]

Grosseteste here, like Aquinas, accepts two apparently contradictory guiding propositions:

(1) Knowledge of "what *x* is" precedes knowledge "that *x* is."
(2) It is impossible to know "what *x* is" before knowing "that *x* is."[65]

The contradiction is escaped by two different senses of "what *x* is," one of which precedes the other, as Grosseteste says. In Proposition (1), "what *x* is" means only "what the term signifies," as Grosseteste observes, that is, the nominal definition. By contrast, in Proposition (2), "what *x* is" means "what the thing in reality is (*quid est res*)," that is, the real definition. According to the two definitions, there are two existential arguments. First, the nominal definition can lead to knowledge "that *x* is," which, according to Proposition (2), precedes the real definition. Second, through the real definition, existence (*esse*) can be demonstrated, says Grosseteste. Thus, although definitions *of themselves* do not prove that the thing defined exists, as Grosseteste's Aristotle remarks (*PA* 2.7, 92b19–20), through definitions one can know, first, "that something is" as nominally defined, and second, why it exists (*propter quid sit*) as really defined.[66] The latter knowledge answers the question, on account of what cause does the thing in reality (*res*) exist?[67] The answer constitutes "demonstrative science that *x* is."[68]

In light of this doctrine on existential proof, it is possible to interpret in several senses the general rule that Aquinas sometimes formulates: "what a thing is" is the middle term for knowing "whether it is."[69] For Aquinas, the *propter quid* existential proof that results from this rule belongs properly to the science of metaphysics.[70] Of course, there can be no *propter quid* existential proof of God, since we cannot have knowledge of the essence of immaterial things, and God's existence is identical to, not caused by, his essence. It does not follow, however, that since we cannot know the *esse* of God which is identical to his essence, we cannot predicate "exists" of God: to say that "God is" is to use "is" in the propositional sense and "God" in the nominal sense.[71] Accordingly, we can, Aquinas proposes, have a *quia* existential proof "that God is." It must use as a middle term "what God is" as nominally defined. How, then, should the nominal definition be formed?

V. Aquinas's Three Criteria for the Nominal Definition in an Existential Proof of God.

Given the Aristotelian methodology for existential proof, I identify three criteria in Aquinas for a nominal definition of "God" in an existential proof.

1. *Drawn from Effects.* In light of the commentary tradition, it is a small though important step for Aquinas, who knows at least Grosseteste's commentary well, to infer that the nominal definition itself by which God is proved is to be drawn from effects. This inference is first made, again, not in his *Scriptum on the Sentences* but in the *Exposition of Boethius's De trinitate*[72]—which remains by far the most extended of the three discussions of nominal definition in Aquinas's personal works.[73] The same claim, that the nominal definition of God is drawn from effects, is defended in both *Summae*, twice in the first two questions of the *Summa theologiae*.[74] Both works open

with proofs of God's existence that are prefaced by formal discussions of whether and how such proof is possible. In each discussion Aquinas responds to the objection that God cannot be proved given that we cannot know the divine essence: for demonstration (of the reasoned fact) is through the essence as through a cause. I summarize Aquinas's response in the *Summa contra gentiles* 1.12, which is the more complete of the two responses.[75] In place of the divine essence, says Thomas, the proof of God's existence uses as a middle term an effect, as occurs in many proofs of fact (*quia*). From such an effect is derived the nominal definition of God. For, all divine names are formed from effects either being *removed from* or being *related to* God.

2. *Negation of or Relation to Effects.* The last sentence contains a second criterion that we may ascribe to Aquinas for how the nominal definition of God is formulated: not only is it drawn from effects, but it also involves negative and/or relational terms. Obviously, a cause cannot be defined as its effect; the effect must be denied or must be related to the cause. "God" is something *without* motion and is the *cause* of motion. The *Summa theologiae* makes no mention of this second criterion, but the criterion continues to apply to the nominal definitions that Thomas uses there, as I shall argue in the next part. The *Exposition of the De trinitate* contains an even more elaborate version of this criterion, which I have summarized above, in which the allusion to the *triplex via* of Dionysius is explicit. Since God shares no genus with creatures and has no accidents, says Thomas, a nominal definition of God must use in the place of a genus a broad *negation* of things in our experience, and must use narrower negations together with relations of *causality* or of *eminence* in place of perceptible accidents—which accidents normally characterize a nominal definition.[76] Aquinas's *Summa contra gentiles* drops this elaborate detail in its discussion of the nominal definition of God in a proof, but it retains the role of negative and relational terms.[77] We may think here, for example, of the negation "unmoved" and of the relations "prime" and "mover"—a thought to which I shall return in Part VI.

3. *Universally Commensurate with the Divine Nature or Essence.* I add here a third criterion for the nominal definition of "God," one which Aquinas repeatedly proposes, although not in the context of the proofs themselves. The word "God," he says, echoing Peter Lombard, and its abstract correlate "deity" ("Godhead"), "signifies" or "is imposed for the sake of signifying" the divine nature.[78] This statement could seem redundant in light of what we have said about definition in the context of Aristotelian methodology: a name and its definition signify the essence of a thing, according to Thomas.[79] The very project of definition suggests a species or kind that is being defined, that is, something that is being taken universally: we cannot define individuals. And if the definition succeeds—even a nominal definition—it picks out that and only that kind. Names and definitions are universally commensurate with what they signify, so that they can be substituted for the thing in sentences about the

thing. It might seem, then, that to specify "essence" as what is signified by the name "God" is either redundant or begs the question as to what God is by *prescribing* that God, whose essence is unknowable to us, must have an essence.

a. *There Must Be a Concrete, Affirmative, Substantival Name of the Divine Essence as Such.* This third criterion includes two main points that Aquinas makes about the *words theos* and *Deus*, for which a nominal definition is sought. The first is that these are *substantival* names of the divine essence as such. This point can be established through taxonomical considerations of language about the divine, even though such considerations belong properly to the treatment of the divine nature. For Thomas, the variety of divine predicates can be *broadly* divided into names said (1) absolutely and affirmatively versus (2) negatively, and (3) names signifying a relation to creatures.[80] Names said affirmatively and absolutely such as "wise" and "good," argues Aquinas, "are predicated substantially" or "essentially" and "signify the divine *substance*," as opposed to being predicated only causally or negatively, as for Aquinas's Maimonides.[81] By contrast, "one," "immobile," "incorporeal," "uncreated," "infinite," "simple," and "eternal" are negative names,[82] and "lord" or "king" signify a relation.[83]

In addition to this broad classification, Aquinas discovered in John of Damascus a classification of divine predicates, like creaturely predicates, into names about various features *in* a thing, about, for example, its substance, abilities, and activities—or as Aquinas puts it, into "names of essence, power, and operation."[84] Although, as Aquinas will eventually argue, none of these latter name features that can be actually distinct within God, such names are from beginning to end conceptually distinct even for God—a distinction that has a foundation in God himself considered as knowable to a human intellect.[85] According to this classification, then, "almighty" or "omnipotent" signifies God's power, just as "wisdom" and "will" name the principle of God's operations in relation to creatures, whereas "creator" and "savior" signify God's action.[86] Still, each of these names can also be understood to signify the divine essence, insofar as God's essence is identical to his power and action.[87]

Similarly, the name "good," although like other affirmative names it signifies the divine substance, introduces a *relation* of final causality, whereas essence is signified as remaining in that in which it is.[88] Hence, for Thomas, "good" is imposed for the sake of signifying, not the divine nature, but the perfection of "goodness" absolutely; or better, it signifies God not "from the side of the divine nature," but "under the *ratio*" of object of desire.[89] Furthermore, "good," like "being" (*ens*), "divine," or even "having divinity" (*habens deitatem*), signifies as an adjective rather than as a substantive.[90] According to Aquinas's logic of signification, although all concrete universal predicates affirm (or deny) a form of the thing signified by the subject,[91] substantival names carry in their signification also the supposit of the form, and hence they signify a thing absolutely, after the manner of a substance; whereas adjectival names signify only the form, and hence signify it *as inhering in* or *following upon* a substance, after the manner of an accident.[92] What, then, is the name that signifies concretely and substantively the kind of thing alone that "has divinity" as its form?[93]

"Nature" and "essence" name what God is abstractly, just as "thing" and even "substance" name God's essence concretely;[94] but each of these is a name of God's substance according to what it has analogously in common with all other substances. The same could not be said for "He who is" and "I am who am." They name God's essence, rather than his power or action, and their use of a relative pronoun and a verb ensures that they are substantival names, since "to be," like "to act" belongs properly to supposits.[95] Still, insofar as these names are "imposed from the act of being,"[96] which is common to many, do they not fail to name God properly? Aquinas argues to the contrary: since God is the only being in which there is no real distinction between its essence and its *esse* or "act of being," these are the most proper names of God— "because of their signification."[97] For they signify, not form, but the act of being, which is God's essence; they signify the same perfection, namely, "*from* which they are imposed."[98] Still, on this same basis, these names are not as proper to God as a name that signifies the divine essence in itself—which is entirely incomprehensible to us. As Aquinas might have said, "He who is" signifies the divine essence, not as such, but only under the *ratio* of the act of being.[99] As Aquinas does say, when we look at "that *to which* a name is imposed for the sake of signifying," as opposed to "that *from which* it is imposed," "He who is" is not the name most proper to God.[100] Only a concrete, affirmative, substantival name that is "imposed for the sake of signifying the divine nature" itself can be the most proper name of God. For Aquinas, this name is, by convention, "*Deus.*"[101] To speak of one name as "signifying the divine essence"[102] is thus a consequence of an analysis and classification of divine names. It does not commit Thomas to saying that God's essence is univocal with essences that we know, as if God must share a genus with them, any more than he must share in the genus "substance" because we can be said to "name his substance."[103] Nor is Aquinas committed to thinking of God, in the manner of Plotinus, as having an essence or form in the sense of being finite or fully graspable by a finite human concept. Aquinas speaks of God as having an essence or form,[104] which is nonetheless infinite and identical to his "to be." Since we cannot understand this essence in itself, we must understand it from effects (*ST* 1.13.8 ad 2m). Similarly, when we name this essence, we name it by conceiving of its relation to effects: as above, principle of, and removed from all of them. In fact, even material essences are understood and named from perceptible properties, actions, or effects. In sum, we can and must distinguish conceptually what God is—God's essence or nature—from the rest of God's "essential attributes" (*ST* 1.39.7c), powers, and operations. One name, in particular, names this essence: "God."

b. *"God" in the Primary Sense Is Not a Proper Name but a Kind-Name Excluding All Other Kinds.* The second point is that although there are several senses of the term

"God," the primary sense is a concrete name of a kind or species, like "dog," "frog," and "tree," not the name of an individual. As the *Summa theologiae* puts it, using terminology traceable to Priscian, Boethius, and others, "'God' is an appellative noun, not a proper [noun], because it signifies the divine nature as in what possesses it";[105] that is, as in a subject or "in the concrete," as a "subsisting thing,"[106] as opposed to by itself in the abstract, like "Godhead." Thus, for Aquinas, contrary to some interpreters, "God" is not the proper name of an individual, like "Achilles" (*ST* 1.13.9c).[107] In the history of philosophy and religion, we may add, "god" is predicable of many, unlike a proper name. As philosophers, we can ask or have asked, are there many gods? or even, are there many Gods? Are there many things of this kind? But we do not ask, are there many Achilles? Aquinas will in the end argue that there is only one God—precisely because of the kind of thing that God is *in reality;* that is, because of what it turns out God must be once it has been shown that God exists.[108] As a result, "God" in the proper sense identified by Aquinas could *legitimately* be used as a proper name, as seems to happen in monotheist practice in all languages, especially in prayer: "Dear God, why me?"[109] But if one considers merely the mode of being God has *in our cognition* as a kind of thing, as opposed to God's mode of being in reality, the word "God" can theoretically belong to many, like any kind-name (*ST* 1.13.9 ad 2m). Thomas understands a different term to be God's "proper name," "to signify God, not from the side of the nature, but from the side of the supposit," that is, as an individual rather than as a kind.[110] He calls this, following Maimonides, the *Tetragrammeton;* for us, יהוה, *Yhvh.*

As a consequence of these two points, one can already see that a proof of God's existence in Aquinas targets a *kind* of thing. We too often misread *his* project insofar as we take the project of proving God to be the proof of an individual, the object of our religious adherence and prayer, the singular protagonist of the Scriptures. The nominal definition that Aquinas targets excludes all individual attributes of God, like "the one who appeared to Moses in the burning bush," "who failed to stop World War II," "who refuses to answer my prayer, 'why me?'" In order to capture this point in English, it is helpful to use the indefinite article, to speak of a proof of the existence of "a God."[111] Does there exist an instance of this kind? Does there exist an "eclipse," a "soul," a "God?"

Why, then, use the word "God" with a capital "G," which suggests a proper name? Or, if a "kind" of thing is predicable of many individuals, should we not use the lower case so as not to prescribe in advance that there is only one God or that God is a person? Aquinas discusses the multiple senses of "god" in question 13 of the *Summa theologiae.* He holds that *deus* is an "analogous" name, what Aristotle calls a "*pros hen* equivocal": a name said in many senses but all in relation to one proper, primary sense (*ST* 1.13.10c). The primary sense of "god" in question 13, as we have seen, names a *nature* "that exists above all, which is the principle of all and is removed from all" (*ST*

1.13.8 ad 2m). Such a definition names only one *kind* of thing, even if putatively there could be many individual instances of such a kind. Do we need an argument to show this point? Could one maintain that there can be many *kinds* of things that are above all, the principle of all, and removed from all, such that Aquinas's nominal definition fails? If so, these kinds would have to be pluralized by a kind-term that would not in itself make them below another, from another, or part of another non-god. Consider a term like "beach-dwelling."

(1) Suppose there are two kinds of things that are above, principle of, and removed from all, but only one has the property of "beach-dwelling."

(2) Still, the beach-dwelling variety would be *above* the other in time spent on the beach, whereas it would be surpassed by the other in time spent away from the beach.

(3) Therefore, Step (1) involves a contradiction.

Hence, I conclude, Aquinas's nominal definition of "God" in the primary sense succeeds in picking out all and only one kind.

But the word "God" is used in secondary senses as well, explains Aquinas. As always, the primary signification is contained in the definition of the secondary (*ST* 1.13.6c). Thus, according to *ST* 1.13.9, "god" is used in a secondary sense of "*what is believed* to be" "God," that is, what is believed to be above all, the principle of all, and removed from all; as in the monotheist's statement, "the Egyptians made gods of bronze."[112] In the same place, Aquinas adds another sense of "god": "*what shares in* or *has a likeness to*" God, that is, to what is above all, the principle of all and removed from all, as in, "that actor is a god." Similarly, Aquinas recognizes elsewhere that "*theos*," "*deus*," or "divine" may signify, according to their etymology, something provident, or some source of the order in the world, such as in the general and confused conception of all humans.[113] Consequently, the pagans ascribed "divinity" to eternal substances;[114] that is, to many things that could not deserve the primary signification of the term. Still, insists Thomas, even many pagans would say that there is one highest god by whom the others are caused (*SCG* 1.42.19); that is, they would recognize, in practice if not in speech, "God" in the primary sense.

Accordingly, the English translation of *ST* 1.13.10 can help distinguish this primary from the secondary senses by reserving the upper case for the former. In a similar way, English conventionally capitalizes such words as "Lord," "Almighty," or "Father" as divine names, each of which admits a plurality when used in the lower case. At the same time, the upper case terms are *not* in the first instance proper names, and by themselves they do not preclude there being many "Lords," etc. I argue, then, that "God" with a capital is helpful in discussing Aquinas and the proof of God's existence only insofar as it prevents us from thinking of "god" in one of the secondary senses, directing our attention, instead, to the primary sense. We do not mean, "the Egyptians made Gods," or "that actor is God." We do not discuss proofs of the existence of *a god* whom the Egyptians made of bronze or whom movie-goers worship. Otherwise, the upper case use of "God" is misleading: it may make us think of a proper name. Hence, it is helpful to use it together with the indefinite article, as I shall prefer to do in what follows.

VI. THE NOMINAL DEFINITION OF "A GOD" FOUND IN THE FIVE WAYS

We have seen Aquinas's criteria, based on his understanding of Aristotelian methodology, for how to form the definition of "a God" in an existential proof: "a God" names one kind of thing substantively through that thing's effects by employing negative and/or relational terms. We are now in position to answer the question, what is the nominal definition of "a God" to which a proof of a God's existence must arrive, for Aquinas? Again, there is only one explicit, formal definition of "a God" in Aquinas's corpus, the definition of question 13: "what exists above all, which is the principle of all, and is removed from all." This definition, of course, fits to the letter Aquinas's three criteria: drawn from effects; negative or relational terms; and universally commensurate with the divine nature. But I have argued that it includes more than what the proofs of a God need, and more than what Aquinas's five ways supply. It is a definition proper to the consideration of the divine "nature," as the presence of the Dionysian triad indicates.

What, then, is the nominal definition of "a God" that for Thomas Aquinas is proper to the proof of a God's existence? Most readers who have addressed this question, like Van Steenberghen, have answered that "God" means precisely that to which the five ways conclude: prime mover, first efficient cause, per se necessary being, etc.[115] Thus, each of the five ways concludes "and this is a God," "and this all understand to be / all name a God," or "and this we call a God."[116] I argue that this common opinion is correct. Otherwise, Aquinas needs to offer an intermediate syllogism to relate the attributes concluded in the five ways to the statement "and this we call a God."

Furthermore, each of the five sets of attributes concluded in the five ways fits the criteria for a nominal definition that Aquinas presents prior to the proofs. I focus on the second criterion—the employment of negative and/or relational terms; for, the use of effects, as the first criterion requires, is evident in each of the five ways' conclusions to an efficient cause. There is also good evidence that the second criterion is met. The first and the third ways in the *Summa theologiae* explicitly conclude to negative terms: "*unmoved* mover," "*uncaused* being that cannot be otherwise but that is the *cause* of necessity and contingency in other things." But what about the other three ways? Aquinas observes in the *Summa contra gentiles* that we can only name a God's mode of "eminence" by using negations or by using relations, such as in "*first cause*" or "*highest good*."[117] In light of this clarification, we find "relations of eminence" explicitly concluded in the first, second, and fourth ways of the *Summa theologiae*: "*first* unmoved mover"; "*first* efficient cause"; "something that is *truest, best,* and *most* noble, and consequently *maximally* a being (*ens*)," and so "the cause of being (*esse*), goodness, and any perfection whatever in all beings."[118]

A good case can be made, then, that there is a different nominal definition of "a God" targeted in each of the five ways. Problems arise at this point, however. Does "a God" mean all of these definitions together, or are there many "Gods"? Van Steenbergen among others puzzled over the fact that Thomas, having arrived at five different "names" of a God, is not concerned to unify these, is not worried over whether there does not result a polytheism rather than a monotheism.[119] Gilson in his late thought wrestled extensively over the dilemma that either the first two ways are redundant, or they differ because of their origin—because each is drawn from a philosopher who would not, perhaps could not, have accepted the conclusions of the other way.[120] The exclusively final first cause of Aristotle and Averroes is irreconcilable with Avicenna's efficient first cause of being. How, then, can the "prime mover" of the first way also be the "first efficient cause" of the second way? For Gilson, only by seeing that Thomas writes as theologian can we explain why he presents five otherwise disparate conclusions.[121]

In my view, however, Aquinas did not need to worry about such a disunity, because he already conceived the five nominal definitions as fitting certain criteria, criteria whose unity can be expressed by a single nominal definition.[122] The criteria are provided by the Aristotelian logic of existential arguments—not without a Dionysian influence, as we have seen. "A God" must be defined in the only way that it could be known to us: through effects by using negative or relational terms to pick out substantivally a kind of thing other than those effects. That a single nominal definition could be derived from these three criteria is suggested by the definition of "a God" that is proper to the consideration of the divine "nature" at *ST* 1.13. Of course, Aquinas himself never expresses formally the definition of "a God" that is proper to the proof of a God's existence in Question 2. Yet the project of constructing a "formal" definition has the advantage of letting one see the pattern in the five "material" definitions of "a God" present in the five ways.

I take some inspiration for this project from the development in Aquinas's thought on the nominal definition of "a God." Question 13's Dionysian nominal definition drops the elaborate doctrine of the *Exposition of Boethius's De trinitate* on *negations* in the place of a genus and on *relations* of causality and supereminence in the place of a *differentia.* Negation is no longer given primacy in the nominal definition of "a God" in the *Summa theologiae,* and Aquinas no longer employs quasi-generic or quasi-specific parts of the definition. I argue, nonetheless, that some primacy is maintained, and that causality should be prior to negation in a nominal definition of "a God" proper to an existential proof in Aquinas.[123] This primacy corresponds to the criterion for the nominal definition that Aquinas does not fail to express in his three personal treatments of the theme: that the definition is derived from effects. A God's existence can only be known by arguing from effects. A late text in Aquinas (ca. 1272) that presents the threefold Dionysian way of knowing a God supports this conclusion. It associates the way of causality alone, which is placed first among the three ways, with the way of knowing the answer to the question "does a God exist?"[124]

But "a God" cannot be defined merely as "a cause." The difference between a God as one kind and other kinds of things needs to be expressed. It can be preserved *either* by negation, as in "unmoved" and "uncaused," *or* by eminence, as in "maximal being" and "first cause." To express both negation and eminence, as question 13's definition does, although possible, seems unnecessary in question 2. I conclude that the formal definition of "a God" proper to the five ways would be:

> a kind of thing that causes other things and that is either beyond all other kinds or is removed from all other kinds.

This "definition" expresses formally what is found materially in the five different nominal definitions actually present in the proofs. My contention is that because each of the five ways proves something that materially fits this formal definition, each concludes, in effect, "and this we call a God."

Nonetheless, it must be admitted that Aquinas seems reluctant to isolate or codify a precise formula as a target for his proofs. Were we to have one formula, would we not expect to have only one proof of a God's existence? Would we not end up with what I have called a "prescriptive" approach? This result would be contrary to the "Aristotelian" project of proving *a God* from effects. If one follows Aquinas's method, one gladly takes as a starting point *any effect* that can arrive at "a kind of thing that causes others and that is either beyond all or is removed from all other kinds." There is no reason to expect that there be only one proof or only five. There is nothing fixed in the number five, since one finds many more "ways" in Aquinas's corpus.[125]

At the same time, Aquinas's two most systematic treatments of the proof of a God's existence agree on his preferred presentation. Both begin with a way from motion or change, which the *Summa theologiae* calls the "most manifest"—manifest, he adds, because its effects are most certain to the senses. Indeed, the fact that Thomas does not end with the way from motion suggests that it is the least manifest in its conclusion; or at least, another way is more "effective" than the first, as the argument of the fifth and final way is elsewhere described by Aquinas.[126]

We are fortunate to have a passage from the *Exposition of the De trinitate* which shows that Aquinas is conscious of the advantages of his non-prescriptive method in the proofs. According to Thomas, one person can know that a God exists better than another.[127] For one person can know better than another the relation of a God to effects: whether by knowing better the progression of effects from their cause, or by knowing higher effects as requiring a more eminent cause, or by knowing the cause to be more and more distanced from the effects. Given a plurality of proofs through a plurality of effects, in other words, some like the first way will indicate best a God's causality, some like the fourth and fifth ways will indicate best a God's eminence, whereas some will indicate best a God's otherness, like the second and third ways in comparison to the first. Can there be any question that Aquinas prefers a plurality of ways in which a God is proved to exist and in the process is known better, and better as a cause that is beyond or removed from all?

It is best that there be a plurality of ways to a God. The nominal definition of a God, however, does allow one to identify a false path. It allows one to exclude any effect that will not pick out one kind of thing as distinct from all others. If a given effect leads only to a cause that is the same in kind as effects, like the "divine" statue of bronze, or that is a part of a whole that includes effects, like a world-soul, that effect cannot be used to arrive at a God: it will not lead to what is a sufficient condition for deity. Thus, critics of the "first way" from motion are right to attack the argument if it arrives at no more than the "outermost sphere" or a "celestial soul."[128] Only those effects can be used as ways which can be traced to a cause commensurate with all and only with one kind of thing: a cause beyond all or removed from all.

———

It is not necessary, in my view, to prove the existence of a personal, providential being, or of a creator, or infinite being in order that the conclusion "God exists" be drawn. In fact, for Aquinas, it is not even necessary to prove the existence of the *one* God. For him each of these claims can be shown, and to the extent that they are deducible from a God's "nature" as "a cause beyond all or removed from all," they can be said to be already implicit in the proof of a God's existence. But they need not be explicitly concluded in a proof in order that it arrive at God. In this sense, I call Aquinas's nominal definition "non-prescriptive," since it establishes only a necessary minimum and allows for a number of proofs of or "ways of arriving at" the being thus defined. It is immediately evident how this definition puts in a new light the project of Aquinas's five ways. In my view, we have misread them by looking at the outcome that we as theists desire to prove—or that we as atheists desire to disprove—the God of classical theism, instead of at the systematic logical standards for existential arguments and their corresponding nominal definitions, especially as the Aristotelian tradition conceived them.

The central project of philosophical theology is to establish through reason alone as much as is possible about the nature of God: to prove, for example, that God is creative, provident, all-powerful, all-knowing, love. When we take all of these attributes together, we will have what most monotheists can identify with what their religion teaches. If one could hold all of the requisite reasoning in one's mind at once, one would indeed have a very promising proof of God. At the end of the day, Aquinas would insist that knowing all of this, we still have not the slightest *comprehension* of the *essence* of God—and that we still have nothing more than a highly complex *nominal* definition of God. Now, since one could insist on knowing every last property before one has proved God, it is legitimate to ask whether the bar has been raised too high. The first task of philosophical theology, and arguably the most challenging, is to "get one's foot in the door" by showing the existence of a "cause beyond or removed from all other things." This nominal definition, as non-prescriptive as possible, is nonetheless subject to correction, for example, based on a deepened understanding of reality as effected. Aquinas's project of targeting a non-prescriptive nominal definition, then, does not depend on faith and is correctable: it simply proposes the most minimal standard necessary to distinguish the nature of a God from all other things.[129]

NOTES

1. Perhaps instead a sophisticated objection like that of Barth is at issue, one directed against the very possibility of identifying the "God of natural theology" with the God of Scripture; see Brian Leftow, "Can Philosophy Argue God's Existence?" in *The Rationality of Belief and the Plurality of Faith: Essays in Honor of William P. Alston*, ed. T. Senor (Ithaca, NY: Cornell University Press, 1995), 40–70.

2. Richard Swinburne, *Existence of God* (Oxford: Clarendon Press, 1979), 8.

3. See *Philosophy of Religion*, 1st ed., ed. J. Hick (Englewood Cliffs, NJ: Prentice Hall, 1963); *Philosophy of Religion: Selected Readings*, 1st ed., ed. W.L. Rowe and W.J. Wainwright (San Diego: Harcourt Brace Jovanovich, 1973), 2; William J. Wainwright, *Philosophy of Religion* (Belmont, CA: Wadsworth, 1988), 47; *A Companion to Philosophy of Religion*, ed. P.L. Quinn and C. Taliaferro (Cambridge, MA: Blackwell, 1997); *Philosophy of Religion: Selected Readings*, 2nd ed., ed. M.L. Peterson (New York: Oxford University Press, 2001); James F. Harris, *Analytic Philosophy of Religion* (Dordrecht-Boston: Kluwer, 2002), ch. 3. Cf. also *Readings in Religious Philosophy*, ed. G. MacGregor and J.W. Robb (Boston: Houghton Mifflin, 1962).

4. *Philosophy of Religion: The Big Questions*, ed. E. Stump and M.J. Murray (Oxford: Blackwell, 1999). Cf. Michael Peterson, William Hasker, Bruce Reichenbach, and David Basinger, *Reason and Religious Belief: An Introduction to the Philosophy of Religion*, 1st ed. (New York: Oxford

University Press, 1991), 9, 49; Richard M. Gale, *On the Nature and Existence of God* (Cambridge-New York: Cambridge University Press, 1991), 3; Charles Taliaferro, *Contemporary Philosophy of Religion* (Malden, MA: Blackwell, 1998), 6–7.

5. Swinburne, *Existence of God*, 119.

6. Norman Kretzmann, *The Metaphysics of Theism: Aquinas' Natural Theology in "Summa contra gentiles" I* (Oxford: Oxford University Press, 1997), c. 1, esp. 40–42, 49–52; cf. Thomas Hibbs, "Kretzmann's Theism vs. Aquinas's Theism: Interpreting the *Summa Contra Gentiles*," *Thomist* 62 (1998): 603–22.

7. Cf. David Braine, *The Reality of Time and the Existence of God* (Oxford: Clarendon, 1988), ch. 8, esp. 266: "A proof of the existence of a cause of continuance in existence as such is not yet a proof of the existence of God until it has been shown that such a cause is personal."

8. For Kretzmann, *Metaphysics of Theism*, 87, Aristotle's *Metaphysics* similarly allows evidence for the existence of its subject matter, the universal first source of being, to emerge in the course of considering what its nature would have to be.

9. William L. Rowe, *The Cosmological Argument* (Princeton: Princeton University Press, 1975), 5–6, 11–12; William Lane Craig, *The Cosmological Argument from Plato to Leibniz* (London: Macmillan, 1980), 159, 170–71; Edward Sillem, *Ways of Thinking about God: Thomas Aquinas and Some Recent Problems* (London: Darton, Longman, and Todd, 1961), 72–78, 140, 172–75. For Anton Pegis, in "Four Medieval Ways to God," *The Monist* 54 (1970): 341–47, the five ways truly arrive at God, though not as he is in himself, but only relationally, as the highest explanatory being; whereas qq. 3–44 prove God's existence absolutely, as the unitary subsistent existence from which all other existents proceed.

10. Fernand Van Steenberghen, *Le Problème de l'existence de Dieu dans les écrits de s. Thomas d'Aquin* (Louvain-la-Neuve: Editions de l'Institut Supérieur, 1980), 287–96. Frederick Copleston, *A History of Philosophy* (Westminster, MD: Newman, 1950), 2:342–43, admits that the conclusion of each of the five ways of the *Summa theologiae*, "and this all understand to be God," would be "over-hasty" were it not found in a summary textbook directed to theists—since what is proved has not yet been shown to be personal (or even immaterial). Copleston sees in each conclusion only the expression of the fact *that believers recognize that* God is the first cause, necessary being, etc. Similarly, for Leo Elders, insofar as the five ways are taken to reason in a purely philosophical way to "God" in the theological sense, the conclusion can appear hasty, and it must be completed by subsequent reasoning on the divine attributes; Leo Elders, "Les Cinq Voies et leur place dans la philosophie de saint Thomas," in *Quinque sunt viae: Actes du Symposium sur les cinq voies de la Somme théologique, Rolduc, 1979*, ed. L. Elders and B. Lakenbrink (Vatican City: Libreria Editrice Vaticana, 1980), 133. Nonetheless, the conclusion to "God" may be understood not in the Christian sense, but at the purely philosophical level of common human understanding, the level corresponding to the spontaneous human insight, defended by Aquinas, that there is an overarching cause of things; thus, the five ways' identification of what they conclude as "God," though imperfect, is provisionally justifiable, though needing correction by questions 3–11; Leo Elders, *The Philosophical Theology of St. Thomas Aquinas* (Leiden-New York: Brill, 1990), 131.

11. See Fernand Van Steenberghen, *Dieu caché: Comment savons-nous que Dieu existe?* (Louvain-Paris: Nauwelaerts, 1961), 27–44.

12. Van Steenberghen, *Le Problème de l'existence de Dieu*, 179, 235–36, 287–87, 295; *Dieu caché*, 183–84.

13. Fernand Van Steenberghen, *Ontologie*, 2nd ed. (Louvain: Publications Universitaires, 1952), 157–67; *Dieu caché*, ch. 9.

14. Thomas de Vio (Cajetan), *Commentaria in Summa theologiae* 1.2.3, n. III, in Aquinas, *Opera omnia* (ed. Leonina 4).

15. Domingo Báñez, *Scholastica commentaria in Primam partem Summae theologiae s. Thomae Aquinatis*, ed. L. Urbano (Madrid: Editorial F. E. D. A., 1934), on 1.2.3, 115a.

16. Van Steenberghen, *Le Problème de l'existence de Dieu*, 295–96, likewise ascribes to Aquinas the view that any of the attributes concluded in each of the five ways serves as an adequate definition of "God"; he explicitly rejects such *minimal* definitions.

17. Cf. the non-prescriptiveness in the notion of God that, for Aquinas, is understood by all in a general and confused way: *SCG* 3.38.1.

18. O'Rourke and Ewbank have each noticed, independently of one another, that this passage is unique in Aquinas's corpus for the order of the presentation of the *triplex via;* Michael Ewbank, "Diverse Orderings of Dionysius's *Triplex Via* by St. Thomas Aquinas," *Mediaeval Studies* 52 (1990): 99; Fran O'Rourke, *Pseudo-Dionysius and the Metaphysics of Aquinas* (Leiden: Brill, 1992), 40. Thus far I have found only two authors who link the formula of *ST* 1.13.8 ad 2m with the proof of God's existence or with the nominal definition of "God": Jan Aertsen, "Der wissenschaftstheoretische Ort der Gottesbeweise in der *Summa theologiae* des Thomas von Aquin," in *Medieval Semantics and Metaphysics: Studies Dedicated to L.M. De Rijk*, ed. E.P. Bos (Nijmegen: Ingenium, 1985), 180; and Timothy McDermott in Aquinas, *Summa Theologiae* (Cambridge: Blackfriars, New York: McGraw-Hill, 1964), 2:186–87, Appendix 4. For Aertsen (181), the word "God" signifies "principle of all things," whereas for McDermott (187) "God" means "a providence at the causal beginning of the world we see"; or "first origin" and "font of being."

19. Thomas Aquinas, *ST* 1.13.8 ad 2m: Sed ex effectibus divinis divinam naturam non possumus cognoscere secundum quod in se est, ut sciamus de ea quid est; sed per modum eminentiae et causalitatis et negationis, ut supra dictum est. Et sic hoc nomen Deus significat naturam divinam. Impositum est enim nomen hoc ad aliquid significandum supra omnia existens, quod est principium omnium, et remotum ab omnibus. Hoc enim intendunt significare nominantes Deum.

20. *In Symbolum Apostolorum expositio* 1 (*Inter omnia*). Other formulas can be found which are not expressly offered as definitions; cf. *De veritate*, 21.4c (ed. Leonina 22.3:601.131–33); *ST* 1.12.12c.

21. *ST* 1.13.8c and ad 1m; 13.9 ad 3m; *Sent.* 1. d. 2.5 *expos.* ad 1m; d. 18.1.5 ad 6m. Cf. *SCG* 1.44.10; *Compendium theologiae* 1.35 (ed. Leonina 42:92.611); *In Divinis nominibus* 12, lect. 1, §948. According to *Sent.* 1. d. 22.1.4 ad 4m, following John of Damascus, "*Deus*" names the operation of God; but see *Sent.* 1. d. 18.1.5 ad 6m; *ST* 1.13.9 ad 3m. For other etymologies of *theos* based on Damascene, see *Sent.* 1. d. 2.5 *expos.* obj. 1; *De veritate* 4.1 ad 11m (22.1:119.379–83); *ST* 1.13.8 obj. 1; *In Psalmos* 13.1 (*Sed sciendum*); *In De caelo* 2.1, §3. See also John of Damascus, *De fide orthodoxa: Versions of Burgundio and Cerbanus*, c. 9, ed. E. Buytaert (St. Bonaventure, NY: Franciscan Institute, 1955), 49.20–24, 50.29–30. For formulas that relate etymology and proper signification, see *Sent.* 1, d. 34.1.2 ad 2m; *Super Librum de causis*, ed. H.D. Saffrey (Louvain: Nauwelaerts, 1954), lec. 3, 18.13–14.

22. For the distinction between imposition *a quo* and *ad quod*, whose roots seem to lie in Gilbert of Poitiers, see, besides *ST* 1.13.8c: *Sent.* 1. d. 23.2 ad 1m; *ST* 1.13.2 ad 2m; 13.11 ad 1m; Ralph McInerny, *The Logic of Analogy: An Interpretation of St Thomas* (The Hague: Martinus Nijhoff, 1961), 54–57; Jennifer Ashworth, "Signification and Mode of Signification in Thirteenth-Century Logic: A Preface to Aquinas on Analogy," *Medieval Philosophy and Theology* 1 (1991): 45–49; Irène Rosier, "*Res significata* et *modus significandi:* Les implications d'une distinction

médiévale," in *Sprachtheorien in Spätantike und Mittelalter,* ed. Sten Ebbesen (Tübingen: G. Narr, 1995) 152; Seung-Chan Park, *Die Rezeption der mittelalterlichen Sprachphilosophie in der Theologie des Thomas von Aquin: mit besonderer Berücksichtigung der Analogie* (Leiden-Boston: Brill, 1999), 93–98.

23. Aquinas, *Super Boetium De trinitate* 6.3c (ed. Leonina 50:168.156–68, 172–81).

24. *SCG* 3.49.8. A parallel expression is also found among the deletions in Aquinas's autograph of the same chapter; see Aquinas, *Opera omnia* (ed. Leonina) 14: 16b. Cf. Anton Pegis, "*Penitus Manet Ignotum,*" *Mediaeval Studies* 24 (1962): 217–19.

25. Technically, we cannot know what God is. Hence, the *Summa theologiae* describes the inquiry that corresponds to a discussion of the divine nature as a consideration of "*how* God exists in himself*" (*ST* 1.12 prol.) in order to know what he is; or rather of "how God is not" in order to know "what he is not" (*ST* 1.3 prol.). In early works Aquinas adopts the formula from John of Damascus that at present we can only know that God is or whether God is, not what God is; *Sent.* 1. d. 8.1.1c; *Sent.* 3. d. 23.1.2c; *Super Boetium De trinitate* 1.2c (50:84.93–95, 105–07); 6.3c (50:167.109–13, 168.177–84); *De veritate* 2.1 obj. 9 (23.1: 43.61–63); *De potentia* 7.2 obj. 1; John of Damascus, *De fide orthodoxa,* c. 4 (19.3–5); Albert, *Super Dionysium De divinis nominibus* 1, c. 7 (ed. Cologne 37.1:356.40–65). Unlike Dionysius, Aquinas thinks that in the highest human *expression* of what God is, God is *properly* said to be "a being," "good," "wise," etc., in fact, more properly than creatures—at least with respect to the "thing signified" by these names; see Aquinas, *ST* 1.13.2c, 3c, 6c, 11c. For Thomas, it would be false to say that ultimately God is "a being" only in the sense of "beyond being." On the other hand, Aquinas' definition of "God" in *ST* 1.13.8 ad 2m by itself does not seem to commit him to one or the other interpretation of the *via negativa.*

26. On the theological context of *ST* 1.1–13, see Mark F. Johnson, "The Theological Character of Aquinas's Five Ways," in *Studies in Thomistic Theology,* ed. Paul Lockey (Notre Dame, Ind.: University of Notre Dame Press, 1996), 137–73; J. Aertsen, "Der wissenschaftstheoretische Ort," 171–84; and Victor White, *God the Unknown, and Other Essays* (New York: Harper, 1956), 3–61. For Aertsen, Van Steenberghen's error is to treat the five ways as if they can be divided from their theological context and can stand on their own as metaphysical proofs (184–85). Instead, they serve no more and no less than to answer the question, does the subject of the science of theology, God, exist (175, 180, 184–85)? This question can then be followed by the question: *what is* the subject of theology (Aquinas, *ST* 1.3, prol.)? One problem with this reading arises from the principle that no science can prove its own subject matter. The question that must be addressed is, what is the relation between God as revealable (*ST* 1.1.3c, 7c) and God as knowable through natural reason? For Aquinas, the two can be neither identical nor entirely diverse.

27. Jean-Pierre Torrell, *Initiation à saint Thomas d'Aquin: Sa personne et son oeuvre* (Fribourg: Editions Universitaires, 1993), 98–99, also applies to the *Exposition of Boethius's De trinitate* R.-A. Gauthier's theory as to why Aquinas began when he did such works as the *Disputed Questions on the Soul* and *On Evil,* and the *Commentaries on Aristotle's De anima* and *Nicomachean Ethics:* to help prepare for the composition of his magisterial works; 235, 252–53, 298, 337.

28. See Gauthier's introduction to Aquinas, *Expositio libri Posteriorum*(ed. Leonina 1.2*: 55*–58*); Themistius, *Paraphrasis Analyticorum posteriorum,* ed. M. Wallies (Berlin: Reimer, 1900); and the Latin Themistius in J. R. O'Donnell, ed., "Themistius' *Paraphrasis of the 'Posterior Analytics' of Aristotle,*" *Mediaeval Studies* 20 (1958): 239–315.

29. For other accounts of Aquinas's appropriation of Aristotelian method in the proof of God's existence, see especially Van Steenberghen, *Le Problème de l'existence de Dieu,* 96–97,

162–64, 291–94; Aertsen, "Der wissenschaftstheoretische Ort," 175–81; Thomas C. O'Brien, "Reflexion on the Question of God's Existence in Contemporary Thomistic Metaphysics," *Thomist* 23 (1960): 375–82; C. F. J. Martin, *Thomas Aquinas: God and Explanations* (Edinburgh: Edinburgh University Press, 1997), 15–109.

30. Aquinas, *In Post.* 2.2 (on 89b37–90a1), lect. 1 (1.2*:175.111–176.165). Aquinas observes that the middle term, the first and major topic of *Post. An.* 2, is introduced by an investigator in response to a question or doubt (ibid. 2.1, lect. 1, 1.2*:174.1–9, 23–30).

31. Linguistic studies reveal an existential sense for *einai* in classical Greek and in Aristotle, although Aristotle does not articulate a concept of existence or distinguish it carefully from other senses of *einai;* A. C. Graham, "'Being' in Linguistics and Philosophy: A Preliminary Inquiry," *Foundations of Language* 1 (1965): 223–24; Charles Kahn, "The Greek Verb 'To Be' and the Concept of Being," *Foundations of Language* 2 (1966): 247–48, 265. Still, some scholars have refused to Aristotle any existential notion of "*einai,*" holding that "to be" always means "to be so and so," as in the statement of the principle of non-contradiction: Joseph Owens, "An Aristotelian Text Related to the Distinction of Being and Essence," *Proceedings of the American Catholic Philosophical Association* 21 (1964): 164; cf. G. E. L. Owen, "Aristotle on the Snares of Ontology," in *New Essays on Plato and Aristotle* (New York, 1965), 69–95; Alfonso Gomez Lobo, "The So-Called Question of Existence in Aristotle, *An. Post.* 2.1–2," *Review of Metaphysics* 34 (1980): 71–90.

32. Aristotle, *Post. An.* 2.7 (92b5–8); 2.8 (93a16–20, 27); 2.10 (93b33). Aquinas holds that if something does not exist, its essence cannot be known, and as corollaries, that if something's essence is known, it must already be known to exist, and that it is impossible to know *what* something is if one does not know *that* it exists; Aquinas, *In Post.* 2.7, lect. 6 (1.2*:194.14–26). Cf. *In Met.* 7.17 (on 1041a11–16), lect. 17, §4 (1651).

33. Cf. Aristotle, *Post. An.* 1.1 (71a27–71b5); 2.8 (93a20–21). That it is impossible to know *what* something is if one does not know *that* it exists, see Aquinas, *In Post.* 1.1, lect. 2 (1.2*:11.63–65); 2.7, lect. 6 (1.2*:194.83–86); and 2.8, lect. 7 (1.2*:199.112–24); *In Metaph.* 7.17, lect. 17, §18–19 (1665–66). See Robert Grosseteste, *Commentarius in "Posteriorum analyticorum" libros,* ed. P. Rossi (Firenze: Olschki, 1981), 2.2, 323.417–19; 325.452–54, on 2.7 (92b2); 326.486–87; Albert, *Post. Analytica* 2.1.5, on 92b4–14 (ed. Jammy 1:623ab); cf. Themistius, *In Post.* 2.8, on 93a15, 49.13–14; Al-Ghazali in Charles Lohr, "*Logica Algazalis:* Introduction and Critical Text," *Traditio* 21 (1965): 282.25–26. By contrast, Joseph Owens, "The Accidental and Essential Character of Being in the Doctrine of St. Thomas Aquinas," in *St. Thomas Aquinas on the Existence of God: Collected Papers of Joseph Owens, C.Ss.R.,* ed. J. Catan (Albany: SUNY, 1980), 59, takes the Understanding of Essence Argument of *De ente* 4 to mean that for Aquinas, contrary to Aristotle, one can know what something is, such as a phoenix or eclipse, without knowing first that it is in reality.

34. Not all agree. For Owens, the question "whether something is" in *Post. An.* 2 in fact asks about a thing's generic or quasi-generic character; Joseph Owens, *The Doctrine of Being in the Aristotelian Metaphysics,* 3rd ed. (Toronto, 1978), 289–94; or about its logical possibility, "The Accidental and Essential Character of Being," 59. In any case, *esti* in an existential sense requires a defense, since Aristotle often means by *to einai* essence. For Graham, "'Being' in Linguistics," 224–25, *einai* in the existential sense in *Post. An.* 2 is a great exception in the *corpus* (2.1–2, 89b33; 90a5, 10–12, 33; *De Sophisticis Elenchis* 5, 166b37–167a7); elsewhere in *Post. An.* 2, *einai* may include existence but cannot merely be translated by "exists" since it also may imply a predicate, whether a thing's essence or properties (2.7, 92b20–25). Similarly, Hintikka, "On Aristotle's Notion of Existence," *Review of Metaphysics* 52 (1999): 785–87, ascribes to Aristotle the valid

inference from "Homer is human" to "Homer is" in a jointly existential and essential sense—a fused Aristotelian sense supported by Riek Van Bennekom, "Aristotle and the Copula," *Journal of the History of Philosophy* 24 (1986): 1–18. For Kahn, "The Greek Verb 'To Be,'" 248–89, 263–65, although *einai* has an existential sense, there is no universal concept of existence, such as would allow it to be a subject of predication, either in classical Greek or in Aristotle, and such a concept is not found in or required by Aristotle's conceptual scheme, as is indicated by *Metaphysics* Delta 7. Suzanne Mansion, *Le jugement d'existence chez Aristote* (Louvain: Éditions de l'Institut Supérieur de philosophie, 1976), 253–74, explains that the question "whether x is" plays a central role in Aristotle's scientific method, since scientific knowledge, though of the universal, does not merely attain abstract universals, but real essences of things already judged to be. Yet she admits that "that x is" in Aristotle's example of geometrical objects really means "that x can be constructed based on the principles of geometry" (263); whereas for Charles, the point is that a triangle can be proved to exist; David Charles, *Aristotle on Meaning and Essence* (Oxford: Oxford University Press, 2000), 58–75.

35. Aquinas makes this point at least seventeen times throughout his career. See especially *De spiritualibus creaturis* 11 ad 3m (ed. Leonina 24.2:121.333–39); *In Post.* 2.12, lect. 13 (1.2*: 222.118–31). As the Leonine editors have shown, Aquinas's source is not, as alleged, Aristotle's *Metaphysics* 7–8, but Averroes's *In libros Metaphysicorum Aristotelis* 8.2 (on 1042b25), t.c. 5, 8: 212A–213B. See also Joseph Owens, "Our Knowledge of Nature," *Proceedings of the American Catholic Philosophical Association* 29 (1955): 73–76.

36. Aquinas has this issue in mind in his early works, such as *De ente et essentia* 5 (ed. Leonina 43: 379.72–84), and it seems to affect his remarks on methodology. The effects of material essences, he says, unlike the effects of God, are proportionate to their cause and therefore sufficient to produce genuine knowledge of those essences; *Super Boetium De trinitate* 1.2c (50:84.47–52, 81–85); 6.2c (50:164.81–94, 165.117–32); cf. 6.3c (50:167.55–113); *Sent.* 3. d. 23.1.2c. Thus, Aquinas can still hold that the essence of material things is the proper object of our knowledge; *Sent.* 3. d. 23.1.2c; *ST* 1.85.1c; 5c.

37. Aristotle, *Post. An.* 2.1 (89b32–35); 2.2 (89b37–90a9); 2.8 (93a17–22). For the formula, see Aquinas, *Sent.* 2. d. 35.1.2 obj. 1; cf. *ST* 1.2.2 ad 2m; *In Phys.* 4.7, lect. 10, § 2 (507); *In Post.* 1.1, lect. 2 (1.2*: 11.58–71).

38. Vincent Edward Smith, "The Prime Mover: Physical and Metaphysical Considerations," *Proceedings of the American Catholic Philosophical Association* 28 (1954): 86–89; cf. M.-D. Philippe, *De l'être à Dieu: topique historique* (Paris: Téqui, 1977), 315, 428–29; Stéphane-Marie Barbellion, *Les "Preuves" de l'existence de Dieu: pour une relecture des cinq voies de saint Thomas d'Aquin* (Paris: Cerf, 1999), 278–80. For some, the use of the nominal definition of "God" to initiate a proof begs the question in philosophy and belongs exclusively to revealed theology; Antonin Finili, "Is There a Philosophical Approach to God?" *Dominican Studies* 4 (1951): 80–101; O'Brien, "Reflexion on God's Existence," 384–99. I use "god" in the lower case here because it is not clear in which of several possible senses Aristotle intends the word in *Post. An.* 2.1. I would argue, however, that the sense of the word *theos* that Aristotle, *Met.* λ.7 (1072b28–30), applies to the prime mover is at least consistent with the upper case sense that I ascribe to Aquinas below, even if Aristotle normally understands the term in a wider sense than Aquinas—such as in the sense of what is "immortal and incorruptible," as in Aristotle, *Phys.* 3.4 (203b13–14).

39. Joseph Owens, *An Elementary Christian Metaphysics* (Milwaukee: Bruce, 1963), 335.

40. Cf. Aristotle, *Post. An.* 2.2 (90a24–31). Aquinas, *Sent.* 3. d. 23.1.2c, speaks of three ways of knowing "whether x is" corresponding to three ways of knowing "what x is": through the

senses, through effects known through the senses, and through reflection on one's own inner activities.

41. See Aquinas, *Super Boetium De trinitate* 6.3c (50:167.114–123).

42. Aristotle, *Post. An.* 2.7 (92b12–25); 2.8 (93a22–31). See Aquinas, *In Post.* 2.7, lect. 6 (1.2*:194.71–86); *In Physica* 4.7, lect. 10, §2 (507); and *ST* 1.2.2 ad 2m. He formulates this statement into a principle that grounds an objection in *SCG* 1.12.4; cf. *SCG* 1.12.8.

43. Aristotle, *Post. An.* 2.10 (93b30–35); Aquinas, *In Post.* 2.10, lect. 8 (1.2*:203.92–114). For the proposition that one cannot know whether something is without knowing it nominally, see *In Post.* 1.1, lect. 2 (1.2*: 11.67–69). Cf. *De veritate* 10.12 sc 4 (22.2: 340.84–85).

44. See Aquinas, *In Post.* 2.8, lect. 7 (1.2*: 199.126–54).

45. Aristotle, *Post. An.* 2.8 (93a23–25, 93a38–b7). The example of the soul is better than that of an eclipse and of thunder. Aristotle's language seems to bear out that an eclipse is a property of the Moon, just as thunder is a property of a cloud (cf. *huparchei tōi; ibid.* 2.8, 92a39, b3–10). Hence, he appears to use these properly to illustrate the difference between proving facts and proving reasoned facts, that is, to illustrate the distinction between the third and fourth kind of philosophical question. Nonetheless, just as he elsewhere links these questions to the first and second, so he speaks of "whether the eclipse exists" and "what it is" (93b2–3).

46. For the dispute about whether to ascribe the notion of "nominal definition" to Aristotle, see Robert Bolton, "Essentialism and Semantic Theory in Aristotle: *Posterior Analytics* 2.7–10," *Philosophical Review* 85 (1976): 514–44; Joseph Koterski, "Aristotle on Signifying Definitions," *New Scholasticism* 54 (1980): 75–86; Richard Sorabji, "Definitions: Why Necessary and in What Way?" in *Aristotle on Science: The Posterior Analytics,* ed. E. Berti (Padua: Antenore, 1981), 205–44; J.L. Ackrill, "Aristotle's Theory of Definition: Some Questions on *Posterior Analytics* II.8–10," in *Aristotle on Science,* ed. Berti, 359–84; Demoss and Devereux, "Essence, Existence, and Nominal Definition," *Phronesis* 33 (1988): 133–54.

47. In one place Aquinas uses the term "real definition" for a definition that leads to the demonstration of proper accidents of a thing, as opposed to a "remote and dialectical definition"; *In De anima* 1.1 (on 402b21–403a2), lect. 1 (ed. Leonina 45.1:7.268–73).

48. For example, Aquinas, *In Post.* 1.1, lect. 2 (1.2*:11.58–71). In the primary sense, there is no "definition" just as no "essence" of what does not exist. Such analogous words, however, are used in a secondary sense of imaginary things; cf. *Sent.* 2. d. 35.1.2 ad 1m; d. 37.1.1c.

49. *ST* 1.2.2 ad 2m.

50. Grosseteste, *In Post.* 2.2, on 92b13 (326.481–87), makes this observation, explaining that what is introduced in geometry only as a nominal definition turns out to serve in demonstrations as a real definition.

51. Aquinas, *Super Boetium De trinitate* 6.3c (50:167.114–26, 156–76); cf. Aristotle, *Posterior Analytics* 2.8 (93a22–30). Elsewhere Aquinas contrasts a nominal definition of the word alone, perhaps like an etymology (as of "goat-stag"; cf. Aquinas, *In Post.* 2.7, lect. 6, 1.2*:194.14–26), with a nominal definition based on "something of" the thing, such as an accident; *In Post.* 2.10, lect. 8 (1.2*:203.100–14); cf. also *In Post.* 2.8, lect. 7 (1.2*:199.126–54).

52. Aquinas, *Super Boetium De trinitate* 6.3c (50:167.60–82, 168.133–59). Cf. *De ente* 5 (43: 379.74–104); *ST* 1.12.12c; *Quaestiones de anima* 16c (24.1:145.318–146.345).

53. Thus, I argue, Aquinas puts all positive knowledge of God's "essence" at the level of the questions "*quid significatur per nomen?*" and "*an sit?*," rather than "*quid sit?*" Thus, our cognition of the divine essence is distinct from that of the blessed, which is also non-comprehensive; cf. Hyacinthe-F. Dondaine, "Cognoscere de Deo 'quid est'," *Recherches de Théologie ancienne et*

médiévale 32 (1955): 72–78. For other readings, see John Wippel, "Quidditative Knowledge of God," in *Metaphysical Themes in St. Thomas Aquinas* (Washington, DC: Catholic University Press, 1984), 239–40. According to Van Steenberghen, *Dieu caché,* 43, the conclusion of a proof of God's existence affirms a "définition réelle." For David Burrell, in "Aquinas on Naming God," *Theological Studies* 24 (1963): 187–92, and *Analogy and Philosophical Language* (New Haven: Yale University Press, 1973), 231–36, the meaning of "God" for Aquinas, namely, "principle of all things" or "beginning and end of all things," can be taken as either a nominal or real definition, depending on whether "God" is merely the result of common usage, based on the inborn desire for total explanation, or is uttered within the framework of a law-like ontology.

54. The Latin tradition, following Aristotle, refers to knowledge "that *x* is" (*quia est*) as equivalent to knowledge "whether *x* is" (*an sit*) versus "what *x* is." Out of context, it is sometimes difficult to tell whether "knowledge *quia*" refers to existential knowledge or knowledge of the fact (*quia*) versus of the reasoned fact (*propter quid*). The same ambiguity is found in Aristotle's own use. In fact, Aristotle intends to line up the two pairs of philosophical questions and to show that they can be answered through two different kinds of proof, each using a middle term; see Aristotle, *Posterior Analytics* 2.1 (89b34–35); 2.2 (90a3–15); 2.7 (92b1–18); cf. *Met.* Z.17 (1041a15).

55. Cf. Aquinas, *In Meta.* 7.17, lect. 17, §24 (1671).

56. See Albert, *Post.* 2.1.3 (1:614b); Themistius, *In Post.* 2.2 (43.30–44.2); Grosseteste, *In Post.* 2.2 (325.460–71 and 331.589–333.617).

57. Themistius, *In Post.* 2.9 (50.29–51.1); Grosseteste, *In Post.* 2.2 (325.460–71).

58. Themistius, *In Post.* 2.8 (49.21–16), on 93a22–23; 2.9 (50.29–51.2). Note Themistius' definition of "god" here: "everlasting, living thing that does good things for humans (*zōon aidion eupoētikon anthrōpōn*)." Yet, "giving assistance" or "always moving" are only signs of the *fact* that god exists, not the cause of god's being.

59. Themistius, *In Post.* 2.7 (48.11–17).

60. Grosseteste, *In Post.* 2.2 (325.460–71, esp. 464–66).

61. See also Ralph McInerny, *Being and Predication: Thomistic Interpretations* (Washington, DC: Catholic University of American Press, 1986), 206–10.

62. See Aquinas, *In Post.* 2.8, on 93a4–12, lect. 7 (1.2*:198.27–48, 74–75). His use of the four causes to explain Aristotle's text is inspired by Grosseteste, *In Post.* 2.2 (329.539–331.580), whose comments are also paraphrased and rejected by Albert. Aquinas's remarkable reliance on Grosseteste here as opposed to Albert is not noted in the Leonine preface.

63. Aquinas spells out examples of *"propter quid* existential proof" in the course of explaining how definitions might be "demonstrated," or better, "made known"; Aquinas, *In Post.* 2.8, on 93a4–15, lect. 7 (1.2*:198.27–92). He turns into a principle a formula of *Posterior Analytics* 2.8 (93a28): we stand in the same relation to "what *x* is" as we stand to "that *x* exists"; that is, according as a thing's essence is known, so is its existence. Cf. *Super Boetium De trinitate* 1.2c (50: 84.89–92); Grosseteste, *In Post.* 2.2 (332.599–606). In the example, the fact that "virtue as a habit of right reason" (definition expressing the essence of virtue) exists follows after it is shown that virtue as a "habit leading to happiness" (nominal definition through the final cause) must exist; Aquinas, *In Post.* 2.8, lect. 7 (1.2*:198.46–58). Similarly, that "houses made of stones and wood" (definition expressing the material cause) exist follows after it is understood that "houses as artifacts to shelter humans" (nominal definition through the final cause) exist (cf. ibid. ll. 73–82). Cf. also *In Metaph.* 7.17, lect. 17, §20–21, 24 (1667–68, 1671).

64. Grosseteste, *In Post.* 2.2 (326.488–327.496), on 2.7 (92b15–25). See ibid. 327.496–511.

65. See also Grosseteste, *In Post.* 2.2 (332.606–08). For Aquinas, cf. n. 33, 37, 41–44. For al-Ghazali, see Lohr, *"Logica Algazalis,"* 282.22–26.

66. See also Grosseteste, *In Post.* 2.2 (332.593–333.619), which lays out the methodological sequence in detail, and especially ll. 616–17. Grosseteste there apparently identifies knowledge of a thing through an accident in *Post. An.* 2.8 (93a17–21), as an instance of nominal definition; see especially Grosseteste, *In Post.* 2.2 (331.589–332.595), on 2.8 (93a17–21). For Grosseteste on existential proof, see also ibid. 327.511–328.519, 329.539–47, on 2.8 (93a4–12); cf. Albert, *Post.* 2.1.5, on 2.7 (92b15–25), 1: 624a, 625a.

67. Grosseteste, *In Post.* 2.2, (327.510–11).

68. Grosseteste, *In Post.* 2.2 (332.600–01).

69. See Aquinas, *Sent.* 3. d. 23.1.2c; 3. d. 24.1.1; *Super Boetium De trinitate* 6.3c (50: 167.114–19). Cf. ibid. 1.2 obj. 5 (50: 83.32–35), where the objector argues that since one uses *quid est* as the middle in demonstrating *an est* and all of the other properties of x, one can know nothing about God, whose *quid est* is unknowable. This appears to be the earliest instance of the objection in *ST* 1.2.2 obj. 2; cf. also *De veritate* 10.12 sc 4 (22.2:340.84–88).

70. Aquinas, *In Meta.* 6.1, on 1025b8–16, lect. 1, §8 (1151).

71. See *ST* 1.3.4 ad 2m; *SCG* 1.12.7; *De potentia* 7.2 ad 1–2m.

72. Aquinas, *Super Boetium De trinitate* 1.2c (50:84.81–99), and especially ad 5m (85.183–86); also 6.3c (50:167.109–17, 168.172–80).

73. Aquinas, *Scriptum on the Sentences,* although it recognizes nominal definitions (*Sent.* 2. d. 35.1.2 ad 1m; *Sent.* 3. d. 24.1.2 *quaestiunc.* 1 ad 3m), does not witness to their use in an existential proof. Further, the *Scriptum,* like *De ente* 4, holds *without qualification* that one can understand the essence of a thing without understanding about it whether it is; *Sent.* 1. d. 8.3.3 *expos.*; d. 8.4.2c; *Sent.* 2. d. 2.1.1c; d. 3.1.1c; *De ente* 4 (43:376.97–101). It seems clear, then, as Harm Goris has helped me to see, that the *Exposition of Boethius's De trinitate* marks an early stage in Aquinas's methodology: it quotes Dionysius more than the *Posterior Analytics,* and its terminology shows little influence of the Aristotelian commentary tradition. Thus, Aquinas speaks of a "confused cognition" as preceding the "perfect definition"; *Super Boetium De trinitate* 6.3 (50: 167.114–23). Still, the same passage does expressly witness to nominal definition (*quid hoc nomen "homo" significat*) as a necessary condition for knowledge of *an sit,* which is the question treated in *Super Boetium De trinitate* 1.2c and ad 5m (50:84.81–99, 85.183–86).

74. *ST* 1.1.7 ad 1m; 2.2c, ad 2m; cf. *In Meta.* 7.17, lect. 17, §24 (1671).

75. *SCG* 1.12.8.

76. *Super Boetium De trinitate* 6.3c (50:167.114–26, 168.133–68, 172–81).

77. The discussion of the divine "nature" in the *Summa contra gentiles* retains a trace of the doctrine of the *Exposition of the De trinitate.* Aquinas speaks there of distinguishing God from all things, not through definition, but through successively narrower negations; *SCG* 1.14.2–3; 3.39.1. This project gives order to Thomas's subsequent account in the *Summa contra gentiles* of what God is: God is not material, not corporeal, etc. Cf. *Super Librum de causis expositio,* lect. 7 (49.28–50.2, 50.5–7); *In Metaph.* 10.3, lect. 4, §7 (1990).

78. *ST* 1.13.8c and ad 2m; 13.9c, ad 2–3m; 13.11 ad 1m; also *Sent.* 1. d. 2.5, *expos.* (*Deus enim*), and ad 1m, where Ambrose's purported statement in the *De fide,* that "God" is the name of a nature, is the misquoted *lemma* from the *Sentences* on which Aquinas comments; and *Sent.* 1. d. 18.1.5 ad 6m. For "deity" see *Sent.* 1. d. 23.3c; *In Ad Romanos* 1, lect. 6 (*Tertium cognitum*). Cf. Albert, *Super De divinis nominibus* 12 (ed. Cologne 37.1: 428.10–14). Of course, Aquinas is making not only a philosophical but also a theological claim, as the texts from the *Scriptum on the Sentences* show. That "God" names a nature or essence is implicit in Creeds in the wake of the Councils of Nicaea and Constantinople, and it allows the essence to belong to or to be the form of distinct individual "supposits" or persons (*ST* 1.39.2). By contrast, for Klaus Müller, *Thomas*

von Aquins Theorie und Praxis der Analogie: der Streit um das rechte Vorurteil und die Analyse einer aufschlussreichen Diskrepanz in der "Summa theologiae" (Frankfurt am Main–New York: Peter Lang, 1983), 123–25, the "divine nature" named by the word "God," since it is unknown to us, merely indicates that the word, though lacking content, can stand as a "logical subject" in propositions. Accordingly, *"aliquid . . . supra omnia existens, quod est principium omnium, et remotum ab omnibus,"* although it is the concrete meaning of "God" in theological discourse, merely repeats in objectivized form the foundation for knowledge about God; 125.

79. Aquinas, *Sent.* 1. d. 43.1.1c; *SCG* 1.22.10.

80. *ST* 1.13.2c. For the background in John of Damascus of this division, see *Sent.* 1. d. 22.1.4 obj. 4; John of Damascus, *De fide orthodoxa,* c. 4 (21.40–49); c. 9 (48.8–12, 50.29–40). Other divisions of names reflect Dionysius even more closely than does this one: Aquinas, *De potentia* 7.5 ad 2m; *In Divinis nominibus* 1, lect. 3, §79–104; c. 2, lect. 1, § 126.

81. Aquinas, *De potentia* 7.5c, ad 5m; 7.6c; *ST* 1.13.2c; 13.4c; 13.6c. Aquinas always qualifies his position by insisting that nevertheless such positive names do not "define," "comprehend," or "circumscribe" the divine essence as though they represent it adequately; see also *De potentia* 7.5 ad 1m, 6m, 9m; *ST* 1.13.5c. See Lawrence Dewan, "St. Thomas and the Divine Names," *Science et Esprit* 32 (1980): 24–30. According to John Wippel, "Thomas Aquinas on What Philosophers Can Know About God," *American Catholic Philosophical Quarterly* 66 (1992): 288, only the mature works claim that some names are predicated of God essentially or substantially, apparently so as to counter Maimonides. For Aquinas on divine names generally, see McInerny, *Logic of Analogy,* 153–65; *Being and Predication,* 273–78; Harry Austryn Wolfson, "St. Thomas on Divine Attributes," in *Mélanges offerts à Étienne Gilson* (Toronto-Paris: Vrin, 1959), 673–700. Names "predicated substantially" are elsewhere usually opposed to names "predicated relationally," such as names proper to the persons of the Trinity; similarly, names are "predicated essentially" as opposed to "personally" or "notionally," so that "essential attributes" are opposed to "personal attributes" or "properties." See Aquinas, *Sent.* 1. d. 10.1.1 ad 4m; d. 22.1.4 *expos.* (*Quod ad aliquid*); *Contra errores Graecorum* 1.6 and 1.10 (ed. Leonina 40:76.7–12; 78.91–96). So also, "names said of God" or "pertaining to the divine essence" are distinguished from "discrete names," that is, "pertaining distinctly to the persons"; *In Divinis nominibus* 2, lect. 1, §126–27.

82. *Sent.* 1. d. 22.1.3c; *SCG* 1.30.4; 3.39.1; *ST* 1.3 prol.; 11.3 ad 2m.

83. At the same time, relation presupposes essence and power, which are affirmatively and absolutely named; *ST* 1.13.7 ad 1m; *Sent.* 1. d. 2.5 *expos.* ad 2m; d. 22.1.3c; d. 22.1.4 ad 3–4m.

84. Aquinas, *Sent.* 1. d. 22.1.4 ad 4m. See John of Damascus, *De fide orthodoxa,* c. 9 (48.3–12, 50.29–38).

85. See Aquinas, *Sent.* 1, d. 2.1.3, a question inserted into the text over ten years after the composition of the *Scriptum on the Sentences.* On this question, cf. B. Lemaigre, "Perfection de Dieu et multiplicité des attributs divins," *Revue des Sciences Philosophiques et Théologiques* 50 (1966): 198–236. See also Aquinas, *Sent.* 1. d. 22.1.3 ad 3m; 1.4 ad 4m; d. 35.1.1 ad 2m.

86. *ST* 1.13.7 ad 1m; *Sent.* 1. d. 8.1.1 ad 2m; d. 20.1.3 *expos.;* d. 22.1.4 ad 3–4m; d. 30.2c.

87. See *Sent.* 1. d. 30.2c; *De potentia* 8.2 ad 7m; cf. *Sent.* 1. d. 22.1.4 ad 4m.

88. Cf. *De potentia* 7.5 ad 7m; *Sent.* 1. d. 8.1.3c.

89. *ST* 1.13.4; 13.9c and ad 3m. Aquinas lacks the precise logical system and terminology to make readily the distinctions that he intends, as is evident in his alternating use of *"res significata," "perfectio significata,"* and *"id ad quod significandum imponitur nomen."* What does the name "good" in "God is good," for example, signify? Does it signify God, the divine substance (*ST* 1.13.2c), the divine essence (*ST* 1.13.7 ad 1m), not the divine essence, but the perfection of

goodness absolutely (*ST* 1.13.9 ad 3m; cf. 13.3c; *In Divinis nominibus* 2, lect. 4, §180), or rather "the principle of all things according as 'good' preexists in it in a more eminent way than can be understood or signified" (*ST* 1.13.2 ad 2m)? The answer is: all of the above, depending on the level of precision of the question; but the last is the most precise answer, just as "*id ad quod significandum imponitur nomen*" in the most precise sense is apparently the best term available to Aquinas to signify the target of a name as opposed to the content of the concept used to target it, the "*res significata.*" Cf. also *Sent.* 1. d. 22.1.2c; d. 30.2c; *ST* 1.13.3c; 13.7 ad 1m; 13.8 ad 2m; 13.11c, ad 1m; *De potentia* 7.4 ad 1m. Cf. the remarks of Dewan, "St. Thomas and the Divine Names," 22, 30–31; C. Martin, *Thomas Aquinas: God and Explanation* (Edinburgh: Edinburgh University Press, 1997), 40–46; Park, *Die Rezeption der Sprachphilosophie in Thomas*, 124–26, 280–83, 431–36.

90. Aquinas, *De potentia* 8.2 ad 7m; *ST* 1.39.3 ad 1m; *Sent.* 1. d. 25.1.4 ad 1–2m.

91. *ST* 1.13.12c; 16.2c; for concrete versus abstract, see *ST* 1.13.1 ad 2m.

92. *Sent.* 1. d. 9.1.1 ad 2m; d. 9.1.2c, ad 4m; *Sent.* 3. d. 5.3.3 *expos.*; *ST* 1.39.3c; 39.5 ad 5m; *De potentia* 9.6c; cf. *ST* 1.13.2 ad 3m. Hence, Aquinas cites the grammatical tag: substantival names have supposition, whereas adjectives do not "suppose," they "couple with" another (*ST* 1.39.5 ad 5m; cf. 39.4 ad 4m; *Sent.* 3. d. 12.1.1c). Consequently, predications of substantival names can be true because of an identity of supposit ("deity is a man"), and not only through a form in the subject ("deity is not human"; *Sent.* 3. d. 5.3.3 *expos.*; *Contra errores* 1.18, 40: 86.21–37). One can overstate the difference between substantives and adjectives, however, since substantives can be taken adjectivally, such as "father" (*ST* 1.36.4 ad 7m; *Sent.* 1. d. 5.1.1 ad 3m), and adjectives can be taken substantivally, such as "a being," "the good" (*ST* 1.39.3c; *Sent.* 1. d. 4.1.3c; d. 9.1.1 ad 2m; d. 9.1.2c, ad 1–2m; d. 25.1.4c, ad 1–2m).

93. For "*Deus*" signifying a "form" in the grammatical sense, see *Sent.* 1. d. 4.1.3 ad 5m; d. 4.2.2 ad 4m; d. 21.2.2c; d. 32.2 *expos.* But the grammatical form in this case is founded on an ontological form that cannot be multiplied; *Sent.* 1. d. 23.4 ad 4m.

94. *Sent.* 1. d. 2, *expos.* (*Deus enim*); d. 5.1.3 *expos.*; d. 24.1.1 ad 4m; d. 25.1.4c; d. 26.1.1 ad 3–4m; *Sent.* 3. d. 5.2.2 ad 3m; *ST* 1.29.3 ad 4m; 39.5c.

95. *Sent.* 1. d. 22.1.4 ad 3–4m; d. 36.1.3c; *Sent.* 3. d. 8.1.2c, ad 3m; *SCG* 1.32.7.

96. *Sent.* 1. d. 8.1.1c; see *ST* 1.13.11 ad 1m.

97. *ST* 1.13.11c; see also *Sent.* 1. d. 8.1.1c (*Quarta ratio*); *Super Evangelium s. Ioannis lectura*, on 8:24, lect. 3.5, §1179. Thomas gives other reasons for the primacy of these names: as regards their "mode of signification," since as the most universal, they add the least determination possible; *ST* 1.13.11c; *Sent.* 1. d. 8.1.1c; *De potentia* 7.5c, ad 1m; *Contra errores* 1.1 (40:72.57–67). Cf. *Sent.* 1. d. 8.1.3c. As regards their consignification, since they name God according to the present tense that indicates atemporal eternity; *ST* 1.13.11c; *Sent.* 1. d. 8.1.1c. Also, because they signify the first perfection presupposed by all other perfections, and therefore the perfection that is caused first by and found first and eminently in its cause; *Sent.* 1. d. 8.1.1c; d. 8.1.3c; *In Divinis nominibus* 5 lect. 1, §632–39. Cf. Émilie Zum Brunn, "La 'Métaphysique de l'Exode' selon Thomas d'Aquin," in *Dieu et l'être: exégèses d'Exode 3, 14 et de Coran 20, 11–24* (Paris: Études augustiniennes, 1978), 245–69; Lluís Clavell, *El nombre propio de Dios: según Santo Tomás de Aquino* (Pamplona: Universidad de Navarre, 1980).

98. Aquinas, *ST* 1.13.9 ad 3m; 13.11c, ad 1m; see *ST* 1.13.3c; *Sent.* 1. d. 8.1.1 ad 2m; d. 22.1.2c; *De potentia* 7.5c, ad 1m, ad 3m.

99. See n. 89.

100. *ST* 1.13.9 ad 3m; 13.11 ad 1m. There is no affirmation in Aquinas that "*qui est*" is *not* imposed for the sake of signifying God or the divine nature. Furthermore, *ens* is not included

among the list of names that signify the perfections proceeding from God and are not imposed for the sake of signifying God or the divine nature; *ST* 1.13.9 ad 3m. Still, *ens* is elsewhere included among those names that signify perfections absolutely; *ST* 1.13.3 ad 1m. And, *ens* and *qui est* are in some texts equated; *Sent.* 1. d. 8.1.1c; *In Divinis nominibus* 5, lect. 1, § 632, 635–36.

101.   *ST* 1.13.8c; 13.9c, ad 3m; 13.11 ad 1m. Still, one other name is even more proper than the one signifying God from the side of the divine nature (*ex parte naturae*): the Tetragrammaton; see below at n. 110.

102.   *ST* 1.13.7 ad 1m; 39.3c; 39.4c; 39.5c; *Sent.* 1. d. 4.1.2c, ad 2m; d. 32.2.2 *quaestiuncula* 1 ad 1m.

103.   *ST* 1.3.5c. "Substantia vero convenit Deo, secundum quod significat existere per se"; *ST* 1.29.3 ad 4m. Cf. *De potentia* 7.3 ad 7m; *Sent.* 1. d. 8.4.2 ad 1m, ad 3m; *Sent.* 2. d. 37.1.1c. For predications of "substance" of God, see *Sent.* 1. d. 26.1.2c; d. 26.2.2 ad 3m.

104.   See, for example, on form, *ST* 1.3.2c, ad 3m; 3.7c; 13.11c; 39.4 ad 3m; *Sent.* 1. d. 22.1.1 ad 2m; d. 25.1.4c. Aquinas ascribes to Boethius, *De trinitate* 2, that God is *"forma simplex"*; *ST* 1.3.6 sc 1; 29.2 ad 5; *De potentia* 7.4 sc 1; 9.1 ad sc 1. According to *Sent.* 1. d. 24.1.1 ad 3m, God must be something determinate in himself, otherwise no negations could be made regarding what he is not; cf. *Sent.* 1. d. 8.1.4 ad 1m.

105.   Aquinas, *ST* 1.13.9 ad 2m. The statement there that God in reality is not a particular (see also *De potentia* 7.3c) hints at the theological dimension of Aquinas's doctrine. Elsewhere Aquinas affirms, of course, that the divine nature is one in number and cannot be multiplied in multiple supposits (*Sent.* 1. d. 4.2.1 ad 3m; d. 19.4.1 ad 2m; d. 19.5.3 *expos.;* d. 24.1.1 ad 4m; *De potentia* 9.5 ad 13m), and that divine *esse* is divided from all others or individuated of itself; *Sent.* 1. d. 8.4.1 ad 1m; *In De causis* 9 (65.10–13, 66.5–7); *De potentia* 8.3c. Still, although Aquinas also affirms that "God" is not a universal, three persons share the same essence, and so *"Deus"* signifies a form that, unlike any created form, is one and common *in reality,* not only in the mind (*ST* 1.39.4 ad 3m). Accordingly, although *in divinis* there is nothing properly universal or particular (*Sent.* 1. 4.2.2c; d. 19.4.2c; d. 23.2 ad 4m; d. 26.1.1 ad 3m; *Sent.* 3. d. 6.1.1 *quaestiunc.* 1c; *ST* 1.30.4 ad 3m; 40.3c, with the reference to John of Damascus, *De fide orthodoxa,* 50, 186.6–7), there is something common and something proper (*Sent.* 1. d. 13.3c; d. 23.3c; d. 34.1.1c, ad 4m; *De potentia* 7.3 ad 1m; but cf. *Sent.* 1. d. 8.4.1 ad 1m). The term "God," then, says Aquinas, is *like* a species in that it is predicated substantially of many in number, but *unlike* a species in that what is common to the many is itself one in number; *De potentia* 7.3 ad 1m; cf. *Sent.* 1. d. 4.2.1 ad 3m; *ST* 1.39.4 ad 1m. Consequently, it is no accident that Aquinas does not speak of God as a singular or particular: the word "God" cannot be the name of a particular (*Sent.* 1. d. 23.2 ad 4m). But "individuation," or "individual," or *hoc aliquid* does belong to God insofar as he is indivisible and incommunicable (*Sent.* 1. d. 25.1.1 ad 6m; *ST* 1.13.9c; 29.3 ad 4m): thus, God is undivided in essence, even while being common to the persons; and the persons are individuated as relations without the principle of their subsistence thereby being pluralized, as in the individuation of creatures (*De potentia* 9.5 ad 13m; *Sent.* 1. d. 34.1.1 ad 4m; *Sent.* 3. d. 6.1.1 *quaestiunc.* 1c). Cf. Franz Manthey, *Die Sprachphilosophie des hl. Thomas von Aquin und ihre Anwendung auf Probleme der Theologie* (Paderborn: F. Schöningh, 1937), 215.

106.   *Sent.* 1. d. 36.1.3c.

107.   For the opposite view of Aquinas, see Frank Harrison, "God as a Definite Description," *Sophia* 4 (1965): 11; Lubor Velecky, *Aquinas' Five Arguments in the "Summa Theologiae" 1a 2, 3* (Kampen, Netherlands: Kok Paros, 1994), 3, 30, 39; Hampus Lyttkens, "Die Bedeutung der Gottespraedikate bei Thomas von Aquin," in *Philosophical Essays Dedicated to Gunnar Aspelin on the Occasion of His Sixty-fifth Birthday,* ed. H. Bratt (Lund: Gleerup, 1963) 94.

108. See Aquinas, *ST* 1.13.9c. The arguments for divine unicity are in *ST* 1.11.3. They depend on premises established only after the five ways, like simplicity and perfection, as has been shown by Van Steenberghen, *Le Problème de l'existence de Dieu*, 298–300.

109. Then, again, it does not seem accidental that Aquinas does not recognize such a use. He is well aware of such invocations of God as in the Psalms: "O Deus." But one can call on a person through a common name: "Waiter, I need another drink." If Aquinas needs to, he can explain the singularity in the predication of such terms through supposition rather than signification. As Aquinas would put it, because "God" through its mode of signifying suggests a supposit that "has deity," it can "stand for (*supponit*)" a person; *ST* 1.39.4c; *Sent.* 1. d. 4.1.2c; *Sent.* 3. d. 7.1.1 ad 5m; see above, n. 92. For three possible suppositions of the name "God," see *Sent.* 1. d. 21.2.2c; d. 24.2.2 ad 2m. For "God," were there no Trinity, as signifying person, see *Sent.* 1. d. 23.3c; *De potentia* 8.3c; cf. ST 1.29.4c. In sorting out Aquinas, Cajetan affirms three significations of "*Deus*" in Aquinas, one of which is "*hic Deus*"; see Joshua Hochschild, "A Note on Cajetan's Theological Semantics," *Sapientia* 54 (1999): 368, 375–76; Timothy Smith, "The Importance of Order in Theological Discussion," *Sapientia* 54 (1999): 227–31.

110. Aquinas, *ST* 1.13.9c; see *ST* 1.13.11 ad 1m. Cf. Armand Maurer, "The Sacred Tetragrammaton in Medieval Thought," *Actas del V Congreso Internacional de Filosofía Medieval* (Madrid: Editora Nacional, 1979), 975–83; "St. Thomas on the Sacred Name Tetragrammaton," in *Being and Knowing: Studies in Thomas Aquinas and Late Medieval Philosophy* (Toronto: Pontifical Institute of Mediaeval Studies, 1990), 56–69.

111. I adopt the suggestion of Lawrence Dewan. One can find this use in English: for example, "Do you believe that there is a God?"

112. Aquinas, *ST* 1.13.10c. The answer to the fifth objection is relevant for understanding these secondary senses. The Egyptians may mean that the bronze statue is "God" in the primary sense. A secondary sense is used by the person who believes, for example, that the Egyptians are mistaken but who nevertheless admits that the Egyptians worship "gods." For the several senses of "*deus*," see also *In Ioannem*, 1:1, lect. 1.3, §57; 10:34, lect. 6.3, §1459. For another discussion, see Manthey, *Die Sprachphilosophie des hl. Thomas*, 215–16. Jennifer Ashworth, "Equivocation and Divine Language in Some Theology Texts from the Twelfth and Early Thirteenth Centuries" (forthcoming), points out that Aquinas's explanation of the senses of "*deus*" closely reflects a traditional one, found in William of Auxerre but also traceable to a twelfth-century reflection on the *Glossa ordinaria* on I Corinthians 8.5; see Propositinus of Cremona, *Summa "Qui producit ventos"* 1.8.6, in Giuseppe Angelini, *L'ortodossia e la grammatica: Analisi di struttura e deduzione storica della teologia trinitaria di Prepositino* (Roma: Università Gregoriana, 1972), 252–53; William of Auxerre, *Summa aurea*, ed. J. Ribaillier (Paris: Éditions du Centre national de la recherche scientifique, Rome: Editiones Collegii S. Bonaventurae ad Claras Aquas, 1980–), 1.4.5 (1:50.2–10).

113. See *ST* 2-2.85.1c; *In Meta.* 1.2, lect. 3, §13 (64), in addition to n. 21.

114. *SCG* 1.42.19. Cf. the ancients' use of "divine"—although it, unlike "*deus*," is denominative; *Sent.* 1. d. 29.4.1 *expos.; In Ad Romanos* 1, lect. 6 (*Tertium cognitum*); *In Physica* 3.4, lect. 6, §10 (335). By contrast, the natural philosophers who thought that all substances were corporeal may have applied to the many heavens the term "God" in the primary sense; see *Sent.* 2. d. 15.1.2c; *SCG* 3.38.3.

115. See Van Steenberghen, *Études religieuses* (Paris: Editions O.E.I.L.; Longueil, Québec: Le Préambule, 1991), 24; *Le Problème de l'existence de Dieu*, 97, 164, 295; O'Brien, "Reflexion on the Question of God's Existence," 379, 382; C. Martin, *Thomas Aquinas: God and Explanation*, 104–05;

Geo Siegwart, "*Et hoc dicimus Deum:* eine definitionstheoretische Betrachtung zu SthIq2a3," in *Klassische Gottesbeweise in der Sicht der gegenwärtigen Logik und Wissenschaftstheorie,* ed. F. Ricken (Stuttgart: W. Kohlhammer, 1991), 87–110. But Siegwart does not distinguish between nominal and real definition, and so he can criticize the five definitions for failing to satisfy the requirements of definitional theory that arise from, for example, biconditionality (102–8).

116. The five successive conclusions in the two *Summae* are as follows. Aquinas, *ST* 1.2.3c: (1) "aliquod primum movens, quod a nullo movetur: et hoc omnes inelligunt Deum"; (2) "aliquam causam efficientem primam: quam omnes Deum nominant"; (3) "aliquid quod sit per se necessarium, non habens causam necessitatis aliunde, sed quod est causa necessitatis aliis: quod omnes dicunt Deum"; (4) "aliquid quod omnibus entibus est causa esse, et bonitatis, et cuiuslibet perfectionis: et hoc dicimus Deum"; (5) "aliquid intelligens, a quo omnes res naturales ordinantur ad finem: et hoc dicimus Deum." *SCG* 1.13: (1) "aliquod movens immobile. Et hoc dicimus Deum"; (2) "motorem separatum omnino, qui est Deus. . . . primum motorem separatum omnino immobilem, qui Deus est"; (3) "unam causam primam: et hanc dicimus Deum. . . . oportet ponere primam causam efficientem esse. Quae Deus est"; (4) "aliquid quod est maxime ens. Et hoc dicimus Deum"; (5) "aliquem cuius providentia mundus gubernetur. Et hunc dicimus Deum." Siegwart's investigation is founded on the discrepancy he sees between Aquinas's proposal to prove "that God exists" and the actual conclusions, "that what *we call* God exists"; Siegwart, "*Et hoc dicimus Deum,*" 87, 95–96. But notice that two of the proofs in the *Summa contra gentiles* conclude "that God exists."

117. Aquinas, *SCG* 1.30.4; cf. also *In Divinis nominibus* 2, lect. 1, §126.

118. I find the fifth way to be parasitic on the reasoning of prior ways, to borrow the expression of Scott MacDonald, "Aquinas's Parasitic Cosmological Argument," *Medieval Philosophy and Theology* (1991): 119–55. For, the fifth way's conclusion contains relation and causality, but not eminence. Notice that in both *Summae* the fifth proof concludes successfully to "a God" understood according to the etymology of the term, to "a God" as defined, for example, in the *Sermon on the Creed;* see above, n. 20.

119. See Van Steenberghen, *Le Problème de l'existence de Dieu,* 235–36; cf. *Dieu caché,* 183.

120. See especially the article whose title is inspired by Van Steenberghen: Etienne Gilson, "Trois leçons sur le problème de l'existence de Dieu," *Divinitas* 5 (1961): 30–34, 52–62; also *Le Thomisme,* 6th ed. (Paris: Vrin, 1965), 91–97; *Elements of Christian Philosophy* (Garden City, NY: Doubleday, 1960), 81–86.

121. According to Gilson, "Trois leçons," 61, the explicit unification of the conclusions is appropriate not to the question *an sit Deus?* but only to the subsequent question *quid sit?*

122. I believe that McDermott, in Aquinas, *Summa theologiae* (Blackfriars) 2:186–87, proceeds in a way similar to mine in unifying the five different, admittedly highly philosophical conclusions of the five ways under the formula of "a providence at the causal *beginning* of the world we see," a formula that summarizes *ST* 1.13.8c and ad 2m. For McDermott, this is the same as the "ordinary person's" conception of the word "God," and to start from ordinary experience and ordinary language is part of what *ST* 1.2.2c recommends in "an effect takes the place of a middle term in the case of proving God." Still, although McDermott is correct to relate Aquinas' project to the "common and confused cognition" of God found naturally in all people, as for *SCG* 3.38.1, this latter consideration can be more general and more vague than the primary sense of the term "God" with a capital "G," the sense identified in *ST* 1.13.9c and 10c and targeted in the nominal definitions of the five ways. See *ST* 1.2.1 ad 1m; and at n. 113 above.

123. In summarizing Aquinas's approach to God through natural reason, *ST* 1.12.12c emphasizes the role of causality in knowing both that God is and what he is through the *triplex via.* By

contrast, the definition of *ST* 1.13.8 ad 2m gives primacy to eminence and suggests that *both* causality and negation be expressed. Again, I argue that this definition is more prescriptive than one finds or needs in the five ways, although its prescriptiveness may be very appropriate to the discussion of the divine "nature." I have only perceived the force of this point thanks to Lawrence Dewan. For the ascription to Aquinas of a nominal definition from effects, "cause of the world," that also gives priority to causality, see C. Martin, in *Thomas Aquinas: God and Explanation*, 85, 94, 104–05.

124. Aquinas, *In Ad Romanos* 1, lect. 6.

125. See Jules Baisnée, "St. Thomas Aquinas's Proofs of the Existence of God Presented in Their Chronological Order," in *Philosophical Studies in Honor of the Very Reverend Ignatius Smith, O. P.*, ed. John K. Ryan (Westminster, Md.: Newman Press, 1952), 29–64. To have a plurality of nominal definitions and therefore of proofs of existence is not something unique to the case of a God. This may occur whenever one uses accidental qualities in place of a difference, for they stand as effects to their causes (Aquinas, *Sent.* 2. d. 3.1.6c). According to many texts in Aquinas, again, we never completely know essences in themselves, but only through their accidents.

126. Aquinas, *In Ioannem*, prol., §3.

127. *Super Boetium De trinitate* 1.2c (50:84.89–85.117).

128. See David Twetten, "Clearing a 'Way' for Aquinas: How the Proof from Motion Concludes to God," *Proceedings of the American Catholic Philosophical Association* 70 (1996): 259–78.

129. I am very grateful to a number of people for help on and reactions to previous versions of this paper: Enrique Alarcón, Jennifer Ashworth, Steven Brock, Lawrence Dewan, Harm Goris, Joshua Hochschild, Sebastián Kaufman, Alejandro Llano, Garreth Matthews, Scott MacDonald, Cyrille Michon, Timothy Noone, Janet Smith, and Henk Schoot.

Chapter 8

Defense and Discovery

Brother Thomas's Contra impugnantes

MARY C. SOMMERS

Almost from the first moment of assuming his chair in sacred theology at the University of Paris in spring of 1256, Thomas Aquinas engaged in a public defense of the fitness of non-secular masters, like himself, to hold such chairs. The origins of the conflict between the religious and secular masters at Paris are a complicated and explosive mix of politics, patronage, and apocalypticism.[1] However, the very presence of *religiosi* at universities as teachers and students was a sign of an altered ecclesiological landscape, full of promise or dangers depending on one's point of view. For William of St.-Amour and his followers, religious who assumed public duties such as teaching in the consortium of masters were like the *gyrovagues,* monks without stability, whom Benedict had warned against in his *Rule,*[2] as well as portents of the "last days,"[3] i.e., they were both a perversion as old as monasticism itself and a dangerous "novelty."

The conflicting nature of the charges against religious masters must have presented a problem for anyone mounting a defense. Does one defend religious teaching in universities as consistent with the tradition of religious life or as a desirable innovation? Does one defend the right of religious generally to teach or the propriety of having teaching orders? Aquinas's *De opere manuali religiosorum* defends the "itinerant mendicity" of new orders, like the Dominicans, who did not support themselves either through ownership of land and property or manual labor, in order to free themselves for teaching and preaching, and for study, as enabling the first two. This work was the fruit either of one of the questions Aquinas disputed as part of the ceremonies surrounding his *inceptio* as a master or part of the first *Quodlibet* VII argued by Aquinas after becoming a master.[4]

However, it is not so clear whom Aquinas is defending in his *Contra Impugantes Dei cultum et religionem,* begun sometime after his inception and probably finished by

October of the same year, 1256. In his introduction to the critical edition, Hyacinth Dondaine has this to say about the "character of the work": "A polemical work, the *Contra Impugnantes* of St. Thomas is pitched entirely towards the defense of his endangered order."[5] Michel-Marie Dufeil, who has written a major work on this phase of the anti-mendicant controversies, does not agree. "But not for a moment does Thomas defend the Mendicants alone specifically; he covers as well their 'allies,' the Cistercien *studium*, for example, and the college of Cluny, which is located at the gates of St.-Jacques. It is religious in general who are fitted for ministry and teaching."[6]

Both Ulrich Horst, the German Dominican who writes on poverty and mendicancy issues, and Jean-Pierre Torrell, OP, author of the recent biography of Aquinas, adopt positions between these extremes. According to Horst, "In the *Contra Impugnantes*, Thomas is mainly concerned with establishing a secure position for the new orders in the Church, and—less noticed by scholars—with securing the right of members of monastic orders to teach and give pastoral care within the universities."[7] Torrell divides the first seven chapters of the work, which are the heart of its argument into those which are concerned with religious orders (1–3) and those "which energetically defend the mendicant ideal" (4–7).[8]

This paper will defend Dufeil's contention that the *Contra Impugnantes* is a defense of "religious in general," as the title *Against those who attack religion (dei cultum) and religious orders (et religionem)* suggests. Both the types of arguments Aquinas uses and the relative numbers of each type lend support to Dufeil's position. However, while Dufeil is correct that this "generic" defense has its origins in the historical contours of the *famosa querella*, it is also a function of Aquinas's "conservative" approach to his apologetic project, which cloaks the innovative character of mendicant religiosity within a traditional conception of religious life. While this approach has obvious polemical utility, it also reveals the extent to which Aquinas himself has not yet come to grips with the "novelties" which are the subject of this bitter debate. This paper will consider only the first seven chapters of the *Contra Impugnantes*, which include the introductory chapter on the nature of religion and religious orders and the six chapters in defense of the various activities, which the anti-mendicants thought should be forbidden to religious. These chapters complete parts one and two of the program laid out by St. Thomas in the "Prologue." The third part, chapters 8–26, treats "slanders," which have been advanced against religious who engage in the disputed activities.

THE ARGUMENTS: THEIR CHARACTER AND DISTRIBUTION

Aquinas adopts a consistent approach to the attacks of the anti-mendicants, as evidenced by the historical introductions that preface his defenses in five of the six chapters under consideration here (chapters 2–7). The attacks are revivals, although sometimes with novel twists, on ancient heresies. Aquinas positions himself in relation to the "mean" in his debate with the anti-mendicants in three of these introductions by recalling how extreme positions, adopted to avoid the "opposite error," have resulted in heresy. In chapter two, he recalls how "Sabellius, while avoiding the division of essence introduced by Arius, as Augustine says, fell into the error of confusion of persons." The same analysis can be applied to Nestorius, the Pelagians, Manichaeans, and "many other heretics," who "do not hold fast to the mean."[9] So "certain perverse men in our own time," Aquinas says, twist the prohibitions against "presumptuous monks," who thought that just because they were monks they had a right to teach, into a prohibition against any religious whatsoever exercising the office of teacher.[10]

Aquinas reiterates this analysis in chapter four, quoting Boethius, that the "way of faith 'between two heresies is the mean, just as virtues are means, for every virtue is found in the appropriate mean in things.'" There are two extremes to be avoided, both heretical: one claims that the power of ministry in the church depends on sanctity of life, and so, "certain presumptuous people, especially monks" take upon themselves offices, like preaching and absolving sinners. The "contrary error" is to assert that "monks and religious are not fit for these offices even when they perform them through Episcopal authority."[11]

Again, in the introduction to his defense of the exemption from manual labor in chapter 5, Aquinas speaks of those, who "again, on this issue, leaving the way of truth, while they have avoided one error, have fallen into the opposite one." Although "there was, in ancient times, an error among certain monks who said that religious were not able to work with their hands without detriment to their pursuit of perfection," it is also erroneous to hold that "religious are in a state of damnation unless they work with their hands."[12]

The theme of extremes is also sounded in the defense of conventual mendicity in chapter 6, where, in their revival of ancient heresies, some people, as can be expected, "go from bad to worse." Jovinian's apparently moderate position that marriage and virginity are of equal merit, though really an extreme since it involves the rejection of a divine counsel, when revived by Vigilantius involved the rejection not only of virginity but of the counsel of poverty as well.[13] Finally, Aquinas's opponents, "not content to equate wealth and poverty, like Jovinian, or to prefer wealth to poverty, like Vigilantius, totally condemn poverty, saying that it is not licit to give up all one's possessions for Christ unless one enters a religious order which has possessions or unless one intends to live by manual labor."[14]

In the introductory section to the defense of religious living on alms and especially those gotten from begging, Aquinas states that these "adversaries of the poverty of Christ" are proponents of an error "dating from the time of the early church."

Diostrephes (3 John) refused his responsibility for the "care of humanity" and would not extend hospitality to "pilgrims separated from their own possessions." This heresy was revived by Vigilantius and reproved by St. Jerome on the authority of the apostles, who tell us to "remember the poor." Diostrephes, indeed, was "teaching new things," i.e., lacking apostolic authority; his successors, "who cruelly attempt to deprive [religious] paupers of their subsistence," however, only seem to have a *positio novella.*

Only the third chapter, which concerns religious joining secular colleges, lacks reference to an ancient heresy. Rather, without historical prologue, the arguments of the anti-mendicants are said to be "damning, false and frivolous." Here, certainly, is a "novelty," although Aquinas rejects the position that it is one of those "dangers of these new times" against which William of St. Amour warns. Instead, he finds support for religious and seculars belonging to the same college in the unity of the church, which is one body, though of many members;[15] in the need to protect the unity of faith, since divisions among its teachers could cause it to be "cut up into different heresies";[16] in the unity of the "gift of knowledge"[17] and, indeed, of the universal search for knowledge;[18] and in the unity of those of the same craft or profession, a unity which comes from their common goal.[19]

We can conclude, then, that whenever possible Aquinas contextualizes his polemic as part of the perennial struggle against resilient heresies, a technique well suited to minimizing the innovations in religious life made by the mendicant orders. Further, moving from these historical prefaces to a consideration of Aquinas' defenses and his replies to the objections of his adversaries, we find relatively few arguments which identify or single out new orders or innovative practices.

The major sources of Aquinas' defensive arguments are the scriptures, predominantly the New Testament, the *Glossa Ordinaria,* Peter Lombard's *Glossa* on the Pauline epistles, the *Decretum,* the patristic sources on monastic life, particularly Augustine, Jerome, Pseudo-Dionysius, and Gregory the Great, and Aristotle's *Nicomachean Ethics.* Dufeil holds that the breadth and numbers of Aquinas' battery of authorities indicate a stable of researchers, rather like Supreme Court clerks locating precedents.[20]

Whatever resources he might have employed, the grasp of ecclesiology, the profound experience of religious life, and the understanding and respect for goals of the university and the community of scholars are all clearly Aquinas' own. So, too, are the vigor, cogency, and inventiveness of the arguments. Among the forms of argument that Aquinas uses are, unsurprisingly, analogies. He argues, for example, that just as "in mechanical trades, it is not only those who work with their hands who live by the trade, but the architect who directs their labor" also, so likewise "the man who teaches morals," i.e., the preacher, who is "the architect of all human duties" has a right to live by preaching, even though he does not work with his hands.[21] In another place, he defends mendicant orders who live "on the edge" by comparing them with soldiers who do not "tempt God by going to battle, even though uncertain as to the issue of the fight." He offers a further analogy:

> Neither does he tempt God who renounces, for His sake, all that he possesses, trusting both in Divine Providence and in the charity of the faithful for the supply of his necessities. Rather, does he resemble a man, who, seeing a bear approach, for some reasonable motive resigns his weapon of self-defense to armed men, whose duty and desire it is to defend him.

Aquinas also makes liberal use of *a fortiori* reasoning. He argues that if a parishioner is bound to obey his priest, so much the more stringently is he bound to obey his bishop, since obedience is proportional to rank. Conversely, the bishop is more responsible for the parishioner than is the priest, since he is invested with superior power. Therefore, it befits bishops, even more than parish priests, to hear the confessions of the parishioners.[22]

Aquinas uncovers an equivocation on the term "teaching" in one argument[23] and the fallacy of composition in another, because that which is "specific is extended to the whole," i.e., the prohibition against someone belonging to "two congregations" refers specifically to two ecclesiastical congregations, without dispensation or just cause. "Whence, since a *collegium scholasticum* is not an *ecclesiaticum collegium*, nothing prohibits a person from belonging to some secular or religious ecclesiastical community and at the same time belonging to a scholastic community."[24]

Another useful argument is that regarding the distinction among precepts between those which are always binding and those which are not binding except *sub conditione et in casu*. Therefore, religious and those in secular society who are able to obtain food (1) without theft, (2) without desiring the goods of others, (3) and without underhanded activities, are not held to the apostolic precept of manual labor.[25]

The authoritative sources and logical resources Aquinas employs in his defense can only be mentioned in passing here. For the purposes of this paper, we focus on the general lines of argumentation that can be discerned in these chapters from the *Contra impugnantes* and the thematic unity they create. The arguments that Aquinas uses to prove that religious may engage in the seven activities that the anti-mendicants claim are forbidden to them—teaching, belonging to a secular society, preaching, hearing confessions, living off alms, begging, and not engaging in manual labor—seem to fall into six categories. However, not all categories are used in relation to every topic and there are subcategories and variations on these basic types. (1) The first category might be called the argument from "imitation," namely, that the words and deeds of Christ, the apostles, the early Christians, the fathers of the Church, and the saints offer patterns of life and action which, if followed, should put a person beyond reproach.

(2) The second category is drawn from the nature of religious life, its vows—particularly the evangelical counsels—and its practices. This category also includes arguments from the variety of religious orders, and a small number for the utility of founding an order that "specializes" in teaching, preaching, etc. (3) A third category is comparative arguments, where religious life and activities are compared to those of persons in holy orders—deacons, priests, and bishops—and to those of persons in the secular world. (4) The fourth category contains arguments drawn from the unity and diversity of the Church, which diversity of states and functions, according to Aquinas, gives it perfection and beauty as well as serving its needs. This category maps the ecclesiastical hierarchy from the Roman pontiff and the bishops, who have the authority to commission confessors, to the penitent who has the right to be believed in the confessional. (5) A fifth kind, found chiefly in the chapter on mendicancy, argues from virtue theory, particularly from the requirements of justice and charity. (6) Lastly, there are arguments about the common good and the characteristics and activities of well-functioning organizations.[26]

I have distinguished 320 arguments in chapters 2–7, which constitute Aquinas's defenses and his answers to the contrary arguments.[27] Wherever an argument was significantly dependent on more than one category, it was counted in each of these, adding up to 397 usages of types of arguments.[28] For the purposes of this paper, category (2)[29] has been divided into three subgroups: (2a)[30] arguments based on what religious have in common; (2b)[31] arguments from the diversity of religious orders; and (2c)[32] arguments for establishing a teaching/preaching order. Similarly, category (4)[33] has been divided into three subgroups: (4a)[34] ecclesiological arguments which are not drawn from (4b) episcopal power[35] or (4c) papal power.[36] There are further divisions that could be deployed; e.g., in category (5),[37] one could specify arguments relating to virtue in general or to specific virtues, like charity, justice, humility, etc. In category (1),[38] arguments could be specified as those relating to the imitation of Christ, the apostles, the early church, etc. Category (3),[39] which contains comparative arguments for the legitimacy of religious performing certain actions, could be divided into those which compare secular, clerical, or episcopal activities. These divisions, while interesting, do not directly affect the thesis of this paper. Category (6)[40] is too small for useful subcategories, although it contains some of Aquinas's most important discussions on the nature of society.

Using the relative percentages of types of arguments and their distribution in the six chapters at issue, we can produce some tentative conclusions. First, one could, without significant distortion, summarize the argument of the central chapters of the *Contra Impugnantes* as follows: the disputed activities, such as preaching, are not inconsistent with the nature, vows, and practices of religious life (27%); they are compatible with justice, charity, or virtue in general (24.1%); indeed they are modeled by Christ, the apostles, etc. (18.5%); they are comparable to activities approved in others (12.9%); and therefore they can be done by religious either *qua* religious or when commissioned to do so by a bishop (12.2%), by the pope (6.3%), or when required for the common good (6.3%). Second, the defense of these activities in terms of the utility of "specialized" orders, like the Order of Preachers (4%), or simply a diversity of orders based on a diversity of ends (2.5%), is *insignificant* in the overall argument.

If we constructed separate narratives for each chapter, we could conclude that *university teaching* (chapter 2) is allowable primarily because of its compatibility with religious life and secondarily because it was modeled by Christ, etc., and is comparable to activities approved in others.[41] *Belonging to a secular teaching society* (chapter 3) is permissible because of the common good and the good of the church.[42] *Preaching* (chapter 4) is compatible with religious life, but it is the ecclesiological arguments which dominate in this defense, and primarily those having to do with the authority of the bishops and popes to commission preachers.[43] No other chapter makes use of these authorities. Teaching and preaching are the activities most associated with a diversity of religious orders and specialization, but these types of argument still represent a very small part of the overall argumentation of each chapter.[44]

In three related activities—*exemption* from manual labor (chapter 5), conventual *poverty,* (chapter 6) *and mendicancy* (chapter 7)—we find themes of imitation and compatibility with the general character of religious life in the latter two chapters, although the dominant argument for mendicancy is compatibility with the requirements of justice and charity, which is a tertiary theme for conventual poverty.[45] There is no dominant narrative with respect to exemption from manual labor.[46] Diversity and specialization arguments play a very small part in chapters 5 and 7 and do not appear in chapter 6.[47]

While these numbers support Dufeil's characterization of the *Contra Impugnantes* as a defense of "religious in general," they require some qualification. Despite the relatively small number of references to a "teaching/preaching order" as opposed to "religious teaching/preaching," two of the six chapters are structured so as to climax in defense of an order dedicated to preaching (chapter 4) or mendicancy (chapter 7). In chapter 4, Aquinas describes his procedure as first showing "that bishops and higher prelates have the authority to preach and to perform absolution on those subject to parish priests without permission from those priests; second, to show that the bishops have the authority to commit [these offices] to others; thirdly, that to commit them to non-parish priests promotes the salvation of souls; fourthly, that, in addition, religious are appropriate persons to exercise these offices . . .; and fifthly, that it would be a worthwhile thing to found a religious order to perform these offices . . ." In short, the bishops *can* appoint others to preach and hear confessions, they *should* appoint others, should appoint religious, and, better still, members of a religious order founded specifically for this purpose.

In chapter 7, Aquinas outlines this procedure: "First, we will show that the person without means, who has given away everything for Christ's sake, can live on handouts; secondly that preachers, even if they are not prelates, as long as they are sent by prelates of the Church, are able to accept their livelihood from those to whom they preach; thirdly, that it is permitted for those who preach to seek handouts through begging, even when they are physically capable [of work]; and fourthly, that they [preachers] should be the primary objects of charitable giving." While all the "holy poor" can accept charitable support, duly licensed preachers may also ask for such support and should be preferred by donors. We can conclude, at least, from the programmatic statements in chapters 4 and 7, that the relatively few references to a preaching order are, nevertheless, not random. Whatever judgment one comes to about the general program of the *Contra Impugnantes*, it is not unconcerned with the legitimacy of the Order of Preachers and with the appropriateness of its activities for a religious order.

The "Generic Defense"

Nevertheless, given that there is at least a plausible case for Dufeil's position, we can proceed to the next question: Why would Aquinas choose a "generic defense"? Dufeil's explanation involves the historical circumstances surrounding the crisis which precipitated Aquinas' polemical treatise. The hostility of the secular masters was not only aimed at the "new orders," like the Dominicans and Franciscans, but at the presence of all "regular" clergy, i.e., those living under a rule, in the consortium of masters. Indeed, it seems to have been the addition of the Cistercian Guy l'Aumône to their number which moved the secular masters to resist the further accession of religious masters.[48] So, if it were religious who were under attack *as* religious, this would seem to call for a defense of religious as such. Aquinas may also have considered that there were risks involved in stressing the "special" nature of Dominicans, similar to the elimination of a "vision" concerning Dominic in the abbreviated hagiography of the order, for fear that it would be associated with the apocalyptic pronouncements of William of St. Amour.[49]

There are also reasons to be found for the "generic defense" in what one might call the polemical contours of the debate. First of all, William of St. Amour, to whose *De periculis novissimorum temporum* and university sermons Aquinas is replying, does not distinguish among orders.[50] All religious who teach publicly, whether Cistercian or Dominican, are doing something at variance with religious life, which he understands as cloistered and contemplative. For William, since the monastic order or rank cannot assume a position of power over others in the ecclesiastical hierarchy, "monks and other religious, who are bound by the law concerning monks, are not allowed to preach or teach."[51] His solution would send them all back to the monastery, whether or not they were orders whose way of life was "monastic."

Indeed, the polemical problem is much deeper than a failure on William's part to recognize an historical, developmental character to religious life. The monk is the proto-religious and so becomes the prototype of religious *life*. But in the thirteenth century, monastic life did not exhaust religious life. Consequently, the term "monk" as understood through the writings of the Church Fathers, Ps.-Dionysius, the great monastic founders like Benedict and Bernard, the Rules, and canon law, has a complicated rhetorical role in the *Contra Impugnantes*. For example, when Dionysius speaks of monks, he is speaking of a group who, in the primitive church, were not clerics. Anyone, therefore, like William of St. Amour, who does not take this distinction into consideration will be arguing, according to Aquinas, "*ex malo intellectu Dionysii.*"[52] Aquinas uses terminology which invokes the distinctions within religious life—such phrases as *monachi et alii religiosi*[53] and *monachi clerici*[54]—as well as terms which categorize or name specific orders, such as *canonici regulares*,[55] *templariis*, or *religio specialiter ad hoc statuta*.[56] Nevertheless, Aquinas constructs an argument where "monk" is the subject of the minor premise, but "religious" is the subject of the conclusion.[57] Consequently, monks are a distinctive form of religious life while at the same time the characteristics and activities of monks are the *standard* for all religious life.

Aquinas, therefore, must sort through the disputed activities, measuring them according to their fitness for monastic life and accounting for all deviations from this traditional pattern. There are things religious do *qua* monk and those they do because, unlike in the primitive church where monks were lay, some monks now are clerics; there are things religious do because they are commissioned to do so by the bishops or pope; and finally there are things religious may do because such activities are not bad in themselves nor forbidden by their rule, although more commonly done by lay people. Although Thomas pitches most of his arguments toward the permissibility of any religious engaging in the disputed practice, such as begging, teaching, or preaching, he does argue that what might be forbidden to one group would not be forbidden to another.

One can see these categories of argument at work in chapter 2, where religious engaging in teaching is defended. Aquinas calls up the image of monastic scholars and *scriptoria* when he argues that religious have always worked to instruct the Church, "since there are libraries full of works and the books" they have made. If they have always taught, when absent, through such books, they may also teach when present in the classroom.[58]

If monks *qua* monk can teach, they can also *qua* cleric perform the Eucharistic consecration and other "holy rites." If so, then "so much the more so can they exercise the office of teaching, for which sacred orders are not required."[59]

Teaching in itself cannot be a bad deed. On the contrary, it is "a matter both of precept and of counsel," that is, something all Christians are required to do—"Go, therefore, teach all nations"—and which some Christians are specifically required to undertake.[60] Nor does the prohibition against seeking to be called "masters" apply only to religious; not to desire a high position out of "ambition" is a "precept by which *all* are bound."[61] Besides, Aquinas says, on a personal note, "that we are called doctors or masters, is not our doing, but that of those who give us these titles."[62]

If it is a good thing for a secular master to teach, it cannot be a bad thing for a religious to teach, unless it is inconsistent with his renunciation of the world and the vows defining that act. Aquinas argues that "religious do not renounce the world in the sense that they can make no use of the things of the world," but rather renounce "a worldly life," which is done even by some people who live in the world rather than the cloister. If they did renounce the things of the world, then they would sin by making any use whatsoever of riches or pleasures, including the occasional feast, a conclusion Aquinas clearly finds excessive.[63]

Nor do religious have to renounce all honors because they may be open to abuse. Honor as the reward of virtue follows the pursuit of virtue. "If religious do not, by their vows, renounce the priesthood, then they need not renounce the office of teaching," since both, although having worldly honors attached to them, are "spiritual" rather than "worldly." The devil may deceive "those who are puffed up with the honor of being a master," but this should not deter a person from teaching or any other good work.[64]

It could be objected that the rigors of religious life—its fasts, vigils, and the *horarium*—would interfere with teaching or would be neglected if a religious assumed a teaching office. Aquinas replies that religious who "are obliged to do daily ministry in the Church" are still considered as abiding by the monastic restrictions, and those who are elevated to the episcopacy receive a dispensation from certain daily practices, presumably because the good of the Church requires it. This would hold for those serving in a teaching office, even though "some religious remaining in the cloister and preserving the strictness of their order hold the office of teacher because their order requires it of them."[65] So, even though the monk *qua* monk has as his primary office doing penance, he may accept the office of "scholastic teaching" without becoming thereby a bad monk.[66] "Indeed, if a religious does something not prohibited by his Rule, even though the thing is not mentioned in the Rule, he is not acting excessively." Adding good things to a Rule cannot deform it.[67]

Aquinas, then, finds that traditional monastic religious life admits of sufficient elasticity to allow its members to become teachers even outside the cloister, providing they are competent. Nor should they or any religious be discriminated against in a competition for a teaching position. The "most suitable candidate should be preferred, whether religious or secular, without respect of persons."[68] Indeed, "it would have to be regarded as a punishment, if someone, after he had become qualified through study, were denied a teaching position" simply because he was a religious. This would amount to being punished for some good quality, which is reprehensible.[69]

Nevertheless, even if one granted, for the sake of argument, that those adhering to the rules of monastic orders should be excluded from teaching, this would not mean that no religious could teach. If every religious congregation were bound to every counsel of Christ or every work of supererogation just because another religious congregation had so bound itself, "there would follow a confusion of religions . . . and so no distinction among them would remain."[70] Aquinas thinks that, beyond the common adherence to the evangelical counsels of poverty, chastity, and obedience, religious orders take on more specific contours through additional vows and practices, such as "stability" for monastic orders and "begging" for the mendicant ones. So, even if it were not licit for a monk to teach, this would not constitute a prohibition against, for example, canons regular teaching.[71]

> As to the objection that the canons regular and monks are bound to the same [practices], this should be understood as referring to those things which are common to all religious life, such as living without private property, abstaining from commerce, not serving as an advocate in legal cases, and things of this sort. Otherwise one might similarly conclude that canons regular were bound not to wear linen clothes because the monks are so bound. So much the more, then would it be licit for those religious to teach whose order was especially instituted for this purpose, even if it were not licit for monks, as the Templars are permitted to use arms, although monks are not.[72]

Aquinas' defense of a *de facto* diversity of "religions" also produces some arguments for how this diversity arises and how it functions. Since any work of mercy is a fitting purpose for a religious order; and "teaching is an act of mercy, since it is listed among the acts of spiritual charity; therefore, it is possible for a religious order to be established specifically to teach."[73] Indeed, appealing again to *de facto* diversity, Aquinas argues that a *corporalis militia* like the Templars, who protect the Church through "force of arms," seems further removed from a general notion of religious life than a *militia spiritualis* which combats error using "spiritual weapons." Indeed, if an argument against religious masters can be mounted on the grounds that there exist secular masters, a stronger argument could be mounted against the military orders, since "there is no lack of secular rulers, who are bound to defend the Church in virtue of their office." The existence of military orders, therefore, constitutes an argument for the even greater need for an order to "fight against errors" through its teaching.[74]

This argument occurs again in chapter 4 of the *Contra impugnantes*, as Aquinas addresses the question of whether an order might be founded for the specific purpose of preaching and hearing confessions, since it has been established that bishops, whose charge this primarily is, may commission others, particularly religious, to preach.

It is the fourth in a series of seven arguments, which culminates in a clear reference to the Dominican order, as one established for the purpose of preaching, as "its very name manifests."[75] This short, tightly organized sequence follows six arguments that "others" besides parish priests should be allowed to preach and hear confessions and eleven arguments that religious in general would be "fitting" candidates. The seven arguments begin with an argument that the common life practiced by the Apostles was adopted in order "that they might be able to go throughout the world evangelizing and preaching." The common life of religious orders, therefore, is clearly suited to preaching, and it would be "most fitting" to establish one for that purpose.[76]

The next two of the seven arguments establish the appropriateness of religious orders engaging in the works of mercy, and, since "there already exist religious orders . . . to aid the poor in obtaining physical food and other bodily necessities," it is even more appropriate that there should be an order founded to visit those afflicted in soul, rather than body, and to provide spiritual necessities.[77]

In the fourth argument, this spiritual militia, made up of "the preachers of the word of God" is said to be "more religious than secular. Yet there exist religious orders which were founded to fight in the same way as secular armies." The existence of the spiritual militia, therefore, is even more appropriate.[78]

The fifth argument concerns the characteristics of an order which could constitute a "spiritual army," namely one made up of "learned men and with time for study," who can supply the shortage of priests "known for the excellence of their life and knowledge."

Finally, in arguments six and seven, Aquinas delivers a warning to opponents of such an order: the effects of this order's activities have already been significant, since "in many parts of the world the corruption of heresy has been rooted out through their ministry, the unfaithful have returned to the faith, and many throughout the world have been instructed in the law of God and moved to penitence." Because of these visible fruits and because "such orders have been established by the Apostolic See," anyone condemning them deserves condemnation in return.[79]

The "Diversity" Defense

Although polemically subordinate to the generic approach, we have seen that Aquinas does mount a defense of the disputed activities of teaching, preaching, etc., as "specializations," arguing that not only is there no "irregularity" in religious doing them, but they even provide the rationale for a distinct kind of religious order. Are the historical and polemical contours of the controversy the only reasons why this "diversity" defense constitutes such a small part of Aquinas' overall strategy? Or is it rather the case that he has not fully worked out a defense of the Dominican order as a distinct type of religious life with a distinct purpose? Or, to put it another way, at the time of the writing of the *Contra Impugnantes,* has Br. Thomas not yet fully recognized the "novelty" of the Order of Preachers, one that has so inflamed its opponents. There are good reasons to think so, the most basic of which is that the opening chapter of the *Contra Impugnantes* does not lead us to expect a "generic defense" of religious engaging in the activities of teaching, preaching, etc., but instead outlines a defense grounded in the diversity of modes of religious life. Why does Aquinas not deliver on the "diversity defense," a defense that would presumably include a substantial description and defense of his own order? Let us look at the terms of this derailed project.

In the opening chapter of the *Contra Impugnantes,* devoted to the "perfection of religion," Aquinas distinguishes between religion as it pertains to any Christian who "binds himself [*se ligat*] to God" through faith from the proper worship (*cultus*) and the religion of one who, renouncing the world, "pledges himself [*se obligat*] to some works of love by which God is specially served."[80] This second sense refers not to the virtue by which human beings fulfill their just debt to God, but to a state of life undertaken only by some of them. Charity, however, renders service to God according to the works of the active and contemplative lives, and in the works of the active life in diverse ways according to the different works of love, which are devoted to one's neighbors.[81] Religious orders, then, can be specifically differentiated according to the diverse works to which they are ordained within the two species of life. The examples which Aquinas gives here are instructive: "monastic and eremetic religion," which is instituted to "be free for the contemplation of God," and those religions which are instituted *ad serviendum Deo in membris suis per actionem,* e.g., to take in the sick, redeem captives, and perform the other works of mercy. They suggest a traditional understanding of the contemplative and active lives, with a clear division between interior activity, on the one hand, and exterior activity, on the other.[82] Nevertheless, there is no *opus misericordiae* "to the pursuit of which a religious order may not be instituted, even if it has not yet been instituted," a clear mandate for innovation.[83] No mention is made, however, of new mendicant orders or the offices of teaching and preaching, which are precisely the activities at issue in the controversy. We are promised a comparison of "religions" "in utility and dignity" based on the active and contemplative lives.[84] This is not executed, perhaps from "discretion," i.e., in order not to divide religious at a time when they are under attack, or perhaps from "confusion" about where one would place the teaching orders. Are the Dominicans a contemplative order, like the Benedictines or Cistercians, or are they an active order, like the Templars or the Trinitarians?

This question reflects the hybrid character of the Dominican founding. Unlike the Franciscans, the Dominicans did not create their rule from scratch. They adopted a version of the Augustinian rule, used by canons regular. This was necessitated by the declaration *Ne nimia religionum diversitas* of the Fourth Lateran Council, which closed off the period of innovation in the governing rules of religious life. Dominic himself had lived as a canon before founding his Order of Preachers. Like some historians of the order, Vicaire has claimed that "il n'y a pas dans la vie de saint Dominique, ni dans l'histoire de son Ordre un discontinuité entre las vie contemplative du chanoine d'Osma et la générosité apostolique du Prêcheur."[85] While there may have been a *practical* continuity, there were, nevertheless, difficulties at the *theoretical* level which would not have been lost on a thinker like Thomas Aquinas. "From Carolingian times, the life of the canon was recognized as being primarily contemplative," not essentially involving teaching or itinerant preaching.[86] By the time Humbert of Romans comments on the fitness of the Augustinian Rule for the Order of Preachers, he includes among his six reasons that "Augustinian canons are not bound to a single cloister as are monks. They are free to practice the *active* life, as preachers must, and they may have the cure of souls in their own parishes."[87] Later John Pecham, OFM, infuriated by Robert Kilwardby's claim (in a letter of 1270) that the Dominican way of life was closest to that of the Apostles, "denies that the Dominicans even have a right to be called the *Ordo Praedicatorum* on the grounds that their life is not in conformity with that of Christ and the apostles, but is in fact monastic," i.e., contemplative.[88]

How are the claims of the two types of life to be adjudicated, not just in practice but also in dialogue with a hermeneutic tradition which is both classical and Christian? It is the claim of many scholars, including Weisheipl, that Aquinas favored the so-called mixed life, but as I have argued elsewhere, this is a misunderstanding of Aquinas' position, which is that every life is defined by its predominant activity, not by the mix of activities. Each life, in some sense, is "mixed."[89] The notion of a "mixed life," then, does not produce a resolution. Jean Pierre Torrell speaks of Aquinas's "well-known theory of the superiority of the apostolic life over the solely contemplative life."[90] But this language begs the question. As M.-H. Vicaire makes clear in his book *L'Imitation des Apôtres,* monks, canons regular, and mendicants all modeled themselves on the life of the apostles and understood and explained themselves as their successors.[91] And, as Aquinas himself says: "Every religious order is formed according to the example of the apostolic life."[92] For Aquinas, it is the *active* life that is to be contrasted with the contemplative life and in the *De perfectione spiritualis vitae* he specifically states that it is the "contemplative life to which the religious state is ordained."[93]

Given these considerations, if we return to the arguments of the *Contra Impugnantes,* it is striking that not only do the vast majority of arguments constitute part of a "generic defense," as was discussed above, but this defense does *not* include any sustained consideration of the *active* life as valid for religious. Nevertheless, it is the abandonment of the cloister for the universities and pulpits which leads William of St. Amour to label the religious masters as "pseudo-apostles" and harbingers of the

Antichrist, i.e., precisely insofar as they are leading the active life, which had been the province of the secular clergy.[94]

It would seem that just as the controversy between secular and religious masters at the University of Paris was in some part a conflict between tradition and innovation, so the *Contra Impugnantes* reflects unresolved theoretical dimensions of this conflict in Aquinas's own thinking. Both sides in the struggle recognize the practical fact of innovation in religious life. But Thomas Aquinas, a practitioner and polemicist of this innovation, has not worked out the theoretical ramifications of this innovation for the traditional identification of religious orders with the life of contemplation.

Teaching is said to be an *actus misericordiae,* which would seem to place it as a work of the active life.[95] Aquinas also argues that "one can follow Christ, not only by doing the works of the contemplative life, but also the works of the active life; so that those who, giving away everything, free themselves for contemplation fulfill the counsel of Christ and, likewise, those who give up everything in order to do corporal works of mercy or spiritual works, for example, preaching or teaching."[96] It is, however, the association of religious with the contemplative life and contemplative activities that has a consistent and significant polemical function in the *Contra Impugnantes.* The contemplative nature of religious life is used to argue the fitness of religious for almost all of the contested activities—teaching, preaching, and hearing confessions, and being exempted from manual labor—while they relinquish all property, private and communal, and therefore necessarily live off alms and begging.[97]

Those are "most fit to teach who through contemplation are capable of understanding divine things to the highest degree."[98] The quiet of the human heart induced by religious vows creates "a greater facility for study and learning," as avoiding the obstacles on the track makes for a better runner.[99] The same way of life, which, in the past, has produced "libraries of books . . . for the instruction of the Church" can now produce teachers in the classrooms of the universities.[100]

The same relationship is argued between the contemplative life and the aptitude for preaching. "It is necessary that a preacher of the word of God be free from all other occupation," unlike the "parish priests [who] are constantly engaged in good works and in ecclesiastical business," that is, who live the "active life."[101] Emblematic of the parish priest's lack of leisure for study is that "many are so ignorant that they do not even know how to speak Latin," which leads to an ignorance of the sacred scriptures, which are at the core of the ministry of preaching, and of knowing "how to bind and to loose," which is at the core of hearing confessions.[102] "Thus, it is highly expedient, that a religious order should be founded of literate men, with leisure for study to help secular priests, who are not up to the task."[103]

Nevertheless, at times Aquinas's polemic displays a tension between the traditional alignment of religious with the contemplative life and the novel charism of the Order of Preachers. Religious who follow the Benedictine Rule take vows of stability. The task of preaching, on the other hand, needs to be entrusted to some who "can, by traveling from one place to another, spread the knowledge of the truth."[104]

The exemption from manual labor is also linked to the contemplative life in Aquinas's argumentation, despite the fact that manual labor was traditional to both eremitic and coenobitic monasticism.[105] Aquinas repeats the admonition of scripture to learn from "the birds of the sky" who, according to the *Glossa* on Matthew, are the saints "who seek heaven, certain of them being so far from the world that already on earth they do nothing, work at nothing, but live in contemplation alone as if already in heaven."[106] Gregory the Great, in the *Homilies on Ezechiel*,[107] argued that in the contemplative life, "the soul burns to see the face of her creator," having put all other desires, concerns, and actions aside. Aquinas, therefore, concludes that "those perfect in contemplation withdraw from any exterior action."[108] Again, Gregory wrote in the *Regula pastoralis* that because "those who have the office of preaching must never slack from the study of sacred scripture," they "ought to refrain from manual labor so that they be free for study."[109] Indeed, those who do so are following the example of St. Jerome, who was attacked by the wicked for substituting scriptural study for manual labor.[110]

There is no injustice here, since those who have other means to live do not need to live through manual labor, "otherwise all rich persons, whether cleric or lay would be in a state of damnation, which is absurd." If religious can live by means of possessions given to them by the faithful, or by preaching or serving in some divine office, then they need not work with their hands. The same is true of those whose lives are devoted to the study of sacred scripture: if the means of life come to them through this activity, they need not do manual labor in addition.[111] Another approach is to acknowledge that those whose business it is to keep the temporal peace, i.e., the military, are paid to render that service. However, since "spiritual utility is greater than temporal utility," then "those who serve the common utility by preaching, studying sacred scripture, or praying for the salvation of the whole church may licitly accept the means of life from the faithful and so need not work with their hands."[112]

Nevertheless, those who study and pray need not serve the common utility to be exempted from labor. A person can become "free" for spiritual acts in two ways: (1) as serving the common utility in a public act; or (2) as serving a private good with a private act. Examples are numerous: singing the divine office versus the private prayer of the laity; *lectio* in the schools for learning and teaching versus *lectio* as a private act, e.g., seeking the comfort of the scriptures like a monk in the monastery; proclaiming the word of God in public by preaching versus as a private act, like the monks in the desert, speaking to their brothers for edification. Those who perform such acts for public reasons legitimately receive support for this work and thus do not need to engage in manual labor. Further, those who perform these acts privately, not as fleeing a laborious life but with an *abundantia divini amoris*, withdraw from all exterior activities in order to be free for contemplation and do not transgress the apostolic precept on manual labor.[113] Finally, those who would have all religious work with their hands are "speaking in the voice of Martha," which advocates for love of neighbor in the active life. However, "the leisure of Mary is excused by the Lord," because she is consumed with love of Him alone.[114]

Aquinas also uses the requirements of the contemplative life to defend the mendicant constitutions, which not only forbade the ownership of private goods by individual religious, as did the *Rule* of St. Benedict, but also imposed corporate poverty.[115] The person who wants "space" for contemplation needs to "be free from worldly things": this is true of those who wish to pursue philosophy, like the immensely rich Theban Socrates who, when he went to Athens, threw away a huge quantity of gold as being incompatible with the life of virtue. *A fortiori* those who wish to contemplate divine things need to "relinquish everything";[116] as St. Jerome wrote to Lucinus (590–96), possessions only get in the way of turning the mind to God.[117]

Further, the very counsel of poverty was given in support of the contemplative life, as the Gloss on Matthew 19, *Si vis perfectus,* indicates.[118] However, if the counsel is understood as requiring manual labor, in the absence of possessions, to provide food, etc., religious will be "very much hindered in the act of contemplation"[119] and not free to pursue "prayer and other spiritual goods."[120] Therefore, following the counsel of poverty would "more impede than promote the end for which it was ordained; thus it would be a counsel lacking in discretion: which is an oxymoron."[121]

The defense of mendicancy in chapter 7, through the requirements of contemplation, employs arguments similar to those in the chapters on manual labor and corporate poverty in religious life. It is argued that a healthy person should abandon any pursuit, however good, if it necessitates living on "handouts." Aquinas counters with a text from Augustine's *De opere monachorum,* which argues that even those who ordinarily work with their hands "ought to have some time set apart, in which to rest from labor and to commit to memory that which they ought to know. They also ought to be assisted by the good works of the faithful who supply necessities, in order that, during the time freed for educating the mind, they may not be oppressed by need."[122] When Jerome says that, while he lived in the desert, he never took any thing from another person, "seeking food through his own sweat," rather than being "at leisure";[123] he was alone there, "neither teaching nor preaching." Aquinas implies that these activities, at least, may be supported through begging, although he argues further that no contemplative is bound to work, except through "his own dictate" or unless it should be enjoined by some "rule for hermits."[124]

Aquinas again uses the analogy between those who devote leisure to philosophical pursuits and those who devote it to divine contemplation. Since some "do, without sin, live for awhile on what is given to them, in order to have the time to study philosophy, therefore, others may do the same, in order to devote themselves to divine contemplation." However, since to live for divine contemplation is "more praiseworthy" than to live for philosophy, and to do so "at all times" is better than doing it for a certain period of time, it is a good thing that "some should, without doing manual labor, live on what others give them in order to give all their time for the whole of their lives to contemplation."[125]

Chapter 3, again, provides the exception. Unsurprisingly, there are no arguments here based on the contemplative nature of religious life. For a religious to belong to a secular, professional *collegium* may not be incompatible with membership in a religious order, but it cannot be explained as either facilitating or being facilitated by contemplation. But with the exception of this departure, the traditional identification between religious and contemplative life provides a broad-reaching defense of the disputed activities, tying them tightly to the nature of religious life itself and deflecting any argument about innovations or novelties.

———

It appears, then, that in the *Contra impugnantes* Thomas Aquinas does not make a comprehensive case for a new model of religious life, primarily active rather than contemplative, and therefore engaging in classroom teaching (chapter 2), membership in professional organizations (chapter 3), being "on the move" in order to fill the needs of the Church for preachers and confessors, as determined by the bishops and the pope, and thus supplementing the active ministry of the secular parish clergy (chapter 4), their wandering facilitated by conventual poverty (chapter 6) and mendicancy (chapter 7), in contrast to the stability of the monastic cloister, supported by *ora et labora* (chapter 5). Indeed, although the treatise begins by outlining a program for explaining and defending the full range of orders, differentiated by the various works of love of God and neighbor, which they pursue, it is the commonalities of religious life, grounded in ancient models and ancient practice, which predominate. While avoiding the imputation of dealing in "novelties" is a medieval commonplace, and well suited to a rebuttal of anti-mendicant attacks, the strategy delays a moment of discovery and clarification for its author. The monastic model of religious life, which in the course of the *Contra Impugnantes* is called upon to accommodate university teaching, faculty unions, parish work, and itinerant begging, does not remain unaltered in the process. One effect of the "generic" defense is indeed to produce a "genus," with multivalent possibilities, in place of the single monastic prototype. However, this effect is unlikely to have been part of Aquinas' polemical plan. His is a strategy intended to unite rather than divide, to address the historical primacy of the monastic model and its status in the anti-mendicant polemic, while grafting onto that model a set of activities, the pursuit of which will, in turn, justify the foundation of orders whose overall character is quite different from the monastic original.

That character, however, does not become a matter of direct discussion in the *Contra Impugnantes.* Aquinas famously states that "operation follows being." It is the operations of the mendicant orders which he investigates in this work, passing over the question of their distinctive character. He argues convincingly against the anti-mendicants that a diversification of activities need not produce a deformation of religious life and, beyond the diversity of "activities," he recognizes a diversity of "lives" undertaken by religious. However, while Aquinas categorizes certain religious orders as following the active life, namely, those which take in the sick, redeem captives, and perform the other works of mercy, both he and the anti-mendicants accept the traditional identification of religious life with the *vita contemplativa* in contrast to the *vita activa* of the secular clergy—deacons, priests, and bishops. This position creates a theoretical impasse in Aquinas's defense of his order as specifically different. It is not, therefore, surprising that he does not categorize teaching and preaching orders as either active or contemplative in the first chapter of the *Contra Impugnantes,* where he is giving examples of each type, nor elsewhere in this work.

That this is his position is certainly implied by the polemical use he makes of the properties of contemplation in the *Contra impugnantes.* It is explicit in his apologetic tract *De perfectione spiritualis vitae* (1269–70), written during the second anti-mendicant controversy. There he argues that religious are in a state of perfection because their vows embrace the "triple way" to the perfection of divine love. Bishops, analogously, are in a state of perfection with respect to the perfection of love and neighbor, the two love precepts being identified, respectively, with the contemplative and active lives.

Thomas Aquinas will not leave the lists in the struggle of the mendicant religious to teach, preach, hear confessions, etc., without solving the problem of reconciling innovations in religious life with the traditional understanding of religious life. In his final treatment of religion and religious orders at the end of the *Secunda Secundae,* he will "discover" a new type of active life, one which "flows from the fullness of contemplation"[126] and which parallels his explanation there of the twofold act of teaching, which has both contemplative and active components.[127] This innovation will allow Aquinas to identify the Order of Preachers as religious living an *active* life of this sort. The comparison of "religions" "in utility and dignity" based on active and contemplative lives, promised in the prologue of the *Contra Impugnantes,* is finally performed, giving pride of place to the new orders.[128] Nevertheless, in his first major polemical work Aquinas lends support to the notion that invention frequently outstrips our ability to explain and control it.

Notes

1. Thomas Aquinas, *Contra impugnantes Dei cultum et religionem,* c. 10 (ed. Leonina, 1970, 41:A130.3–7), hereafter, *CI.* For an exhaustive and stimulating account of the conflict, see M.-M.

Dufeil, *Guillaume de Saint-Amour et la polémique universitaire parisienne 1250–1259*, (Paris: Éditions Picard, 1972).

2. *The Rule of St. Benedict in English*, c. 1, ed. Timothy Fry, OSB (Collegeville, MN: The Liturgical Press, 1982), 10–11. "Fourth and finally there are the monks called gyrovagues, who spend their entire lives drifting from region to region . . . Always on the move, they never settle down, and are slaves to their own wills and gross appetites."

3. *CI*, c. 25 (41:A162–3.3–7; A164.167–177).

4. During Lent, 1256. See J.-P. Torrell, *Initiation à Saint Thomas d'Aquin: Sa personne et son oeuvre* (Paris: Iditions Universitaires, Fribourg: Éditions du Cerf, 1993), 117–18. English translation, Robert Royal, *St. Thomas Aquinas*, Vol. 1, *The Person and His Work*, (Washington: Catholic University of America Press, 1996), 81.

5. "Ouvrage de polémique, le *Contra Impugnantes* de saint Thomas est tout tendu vers la dJfense de son Order en danger," in the editor's introduction to the Leonine text (ed. Leonina 41: A13).

6. M.-M. Dufeil, *La Polemique Universitatire*, 254: "Mais pas un instant Thomas ne défend spécifiquement les Mendiants seuls; il couvre aussi ses alliés, le *studium* cistercien, par exemple, et le collège de Cluny qui se prepare aux portes de Saint-Jacques. Ce sont les religieux en général qui sont aptes au ministère et à l'enseignment."

7. Ulrich Horst, O.P., "Christ, *Exemplar Ordinis Fratrum Praedicantium*, according to Saint Thomas Aquinas," in *Christ among the Medieval Dominicans*, ed. Kent Emery, Jr., and Joseph P. Wawrykow (Notre Dame, Ind.: University of Notre Dame Press, 1998), 256.

8. Torrell, *Saint Thomas Aquinas*, 82 (English); 119 (French).

9. Thomas Aquinas, *CI*, c. 2 (41:A56.100–114).

10. Ibid., 115–135.

11. C. 4 (A72.335–364).

12. C. 5 (A87.143–180).

13. Aquinas finds this error alive and well in his own time among the Cathars.

14. C.6 (A96.197–A97.257).

15. C. 3 (A64.104–122).

16. C. 3 (A65.152–173).

17. Ibid., 174–191.

18. Ibid., 192–200.

19. Ibid., 217–231.

20. Dufeil, *Polémique*, ch. 4, 257–259, commenting on St. Thomas's "arsenal."

21. C. 7 (A113.727–735).

22. C. 4 (A74.506–527).

23. C. 2 (A60.422–451), where he distinguishes between *doctrina praedicationis*, which is the province of the bishop or those designated by him, and *doctrina scholastica*, which is the type of teaching at issue.

24. C. 3, ad 3m (A67.359–372).

25. C. 5 (A88.271–A89.313).

26. Examples of (1) imitation are: c. 6 (A97.278–289): "Evangelical perfection consists in the imitation of Christ. But Christ was a pauper in fact, not only in desire. . . . Therefore, it is poverty in fact which is relevant to evangelical perfection"; c. 7 (A110.463–483): "That the paupers who give up everything for Christ can live on alms, is proved first by the example of St. Benedict, of whom St. Gregory tells us, that while dwelling in a cave for three years, he lived on what the

monk Romanus provided . . . He was in good health, but we do not read that he sought his food through manual labor." (2) Re practices: c. 5 (A92.635–653): "In response to the argument that manual labor . . . is not practiced [by religious] only to seek food, but also to repress empty thoughts, which arise from leisure: leisure can be effectively filled not only by manual labor but also by spiritual exercises, by which the desires of the flesh are reined in." Re diversity: c. 2 (A60.406–421): "Were all religious orders bound to obey every counsel and to perform every supererogatory act, a great confusion would follow . . . and there would be no distinction among them." Re specialization: c.4 (A78.831–839): "While preachers of the word of God ought to be free from all other work, parish priests are very often engaged in other holy works and church business. . . . Therefore, it is clear that it is sufficiently necessary that they have others to help them." (3) Re comparison of religious life to the episcopate: c. 2 (A58.243–256): "Now a religious, even if he does not belong to an order founded to teach, is able to assume the office of prelate . . . since, therefore, the office of prelate is greater than the office of 'professor,' which masters teaching in the schools exercise, and since the office of prelate has the teaching office joined to it, it is not inappropriate that a monk, with the proper authority, should assume the office of teacher." Re comparison of religious life with secular life: c. 2 (A60.480–A61.494): "For religious by religious vow do not renounce 'the world' so that they do not use worldly things, but they renounce a worldly life, namely, being preoccupied with worldly activities. Likewise there are persons who live in the world insofar as they use the things of the world, but they are not in the world insofar as they are free from worldly activities." (4) Re unity of the Church: c. 3 (A64.104–122): "whence it is clear that whoever impedes one person from serving another, in any office he is competent to hold, damages the unity of the Church. . . . Therefore, whoever impedes religious either from teaching others or from learning from them, damages the unity of the Church." Re hierarchy: (A74.495–505): "He who performs something through another can also do it by himself. When, however, priests give absolution to their parishioners, the bishops are said to do it through them. . . . Therefore, the bishop is able, should he wish, to absolve those parishioners or to preach to them himself." (5) Re virtue theory: c. 6 (A102.705–754): "Therefore, we see that the mean of virtue is not destroyed, when one circumstance is taken to its limit, so long as it is moderated by other circumstances. . . . he who gives away all that he has, in order to fulfill the counsel of Christ is not prodigal, but performs a perfect act of virtue." (6) Re common good: c. 3 (A68.472–484): "Just as the ruler, whose charge is the commonwealth, can compel citizens to accept someone into their organization, so an ecclesiastical society can be forced to accept someone as a canon or brother."

27. This is a slightly larger number than that suggested by the numbering and paragraphing of the critical edition.

28. For example, the following argument depends both upon an argument about what constitutes a well-functioning society and a comparison between military and teaching organizations: "Again, any person who is competent to perform some special function has a right to be admitted to the society of those who are selected for the exercise of that function. For an association means the union of men, gathered together for the accomplishment of some specific work. Thus, all soldiers have a right to associate with one another in the same army; for an army is nothing but a society of men, banded together for the purpose of fighting. Hence religious of a military order, do not exclude from their society secular soldiers, and vice versa. Now, an association of study is a society, established with the object of teaching and of learning; and as not only laymen, but also religious, have a right to teach and to learn, there can be no doubt that, both these classes may lawfully unite in one society." C. 3 (41: A65.217–231).

29. (2) 107 usages found in 33.5% of the 320 arguments.

30. (2a) 86 usages found in 27% of arguments.

31. (2b) 8 usages found in 2.5% of arguments.

32. (2c) 13 usages found in 4% of arguments.

33. (4) 88 usages found in 27.5% of arguments.

34. (4a) 29 usages found in 9% of arguments.

35. (4b) 39 usages found in 12.2% of arguments.

36. (4c) 20 usages found in 6.3% of arguments. Cf. Dufeil, *Polémique*, 257: "Le sens de nouveau et l'autorité romaine sont au milieu du xiii siècle une seule et même chose aux yeux de Thomas d'Aquin."

37. (5) 77 usages found in 24.1% of the arguments.

38. (1) 59 usages found in 18.5% of arguments.

39. (3) 41 usages found in 12.9% of arguments.

40. (6) 25 usages found in 7.8% of arguments.

41. (2a) 20 usages in 51.3% of 39 arguments. (1) and (3) 8 usages each in 20.5%.

42. (6) 13 usages in 68.4% of 19 arguments. (4a) 7 usages in 36.8%.

43. (2a) 17 usages in 20.5% of 83 arguments. (4) 74 usages in 89.1% of 83 arguments. (4a) 16 usages in 19.3%. (4b) 38 usages in 45.8%. (4c) 20 usages in 24.1%

44. C. 2: (2b) 4 usages in 10.3% of 39 arguments. (2c) 2 usages in 5.1% = 15.4%. C.4: (2b) 2 usages in 2.4% of 83 arguments. (4c) 8 usages in 9.6% = 12%.

45. C. 6: (1) 20 usages in 35.7% of 56 arguments. (2a) 26 usages in 46.4%. (5) 14 usages in 25%. C. 7: (1) 18 usages in 18.9% of 95 arguments. (2a) 17 usages in 17.9%. (5) 50 usages in 52.6%.

46. C. 5: (2a) and (3) 6 usages each in 22.2% of 27 arguments. (5) 5 usages in 18.5%. (1) 4 usages in 14.8%.

47. C. 5: (2a) 2 usages in 7.4% of 27 arguments. (2b) 1 usage in 3.7% = 11.1%. C.7: (2b) 2 usages in 2.1% of 95 arguments.

48. Dufeil, *Polémique*, 106–7, 113.

49. This point was made by Stephan Müller, Technische Universität, Dresden, in the question session following his paper, "*Exemplum* and *Disputatio:* The Public Argument between Mendicants and the Secular Clergy on Poverty and the Story of the Jackdaw in the Episode of *Aurons Pfenning* in the *Wartburgkrieg*," Texas Medieval Association, Trinity University, 1 September 2001. "One day, before the institution of the Order of Preachers, a certain monk was rapt in ecstasy and saw the Blessed Virgin kneeling, with clasped hands, praying to her son for the human race. Several times he seemed to resist his loving mother, but she insisted, and he said: 'Dear Mother, what more can I do or ought I to do for them? I have sent them patriarchs and prophets, and little have they amended their ways. I came to them myself, and then sent my apostles, and they put me and them to death. I sent them also martyrs, doctors, and confessors, and they paid no attention to them. But it would not be right for me to refuse you anything. Therefore, I shall send them my preachers, through whom they can be enlightened and cleansed. If they are not, I shall come against them.' Another monk had a similar vision about this time, when twelve abbots of the Cistercian order had been sent to Toulouse to combat the heretics. In this vision, when the Son had given the above-mentioned answer to his mother, the Virgin said to him: 'Dear Son, you must not deal with them in accordance with their evil deeds, but as your mercy dictates.' Conquered by her prayers, he replied: 'At your appeal I shall grant them this mercy, that I send them my preachers to instruct and admonish them. If then they do not change their ways, I shall spare them no longer.'" *Legenda Aurea* (ca. 1260), in Jacobus de

Voragine, *The Golden Legend,* trans. William Granger Ryan (Princeton: Princeton University Press, 1993), 2:47.

50. Dufeil, *Polémique,* c. 4, 255.

51. *CI,* c. 4 (A69.79–86). The authority for this argument is Ps. Dionysius.

52. C. 2, §4 (A61.558–569).

53. C. 4 (A69.24, 84; A70.95, 149–50.)

54. C. 2 (A61.578).

55. C. 2 (A60.453, 468, 473).

56. See n. 17, A60.476–478. See also A58.226–227.

57. C. 4 (A71.194–99).

58. C. 2 (A58.285–292).

59. C. 2 (A62.558–581).

60. C. 2 (A59.313–319).

61. Ibid., 357–375.

62. Ibid., 350–352.

63. C. 2 (A60.480–61.494).

64. C. 2 (A60.480–A61.529).

65. C. 2 (A62.582–603).

66. C. 2 (A60.422–451).

67. C. 2 (A62.604–620).

68. C. 2 (A65.680–697).

69. C. 2 (A62.621–647).

70. C. 2 (A60.406–421).

71. Ibid., 452–467.

72. Ibid., 468–479.

73. C. 2 (A58.222–227).

74. Ibid., 228–242.

75. C. 4 (A78.875–A79.948).

76. C. 4 (A78.880–889).

77. C. 4 (A78.890–A79.906).

78. Ibid., 907–914.

79. C. 4 (A79.930–943).

80. C. 1 (A53.46–55).

81. Ibid., 55–68.

82. See *ST* 2-2.181.1 resp.; 182.1 resp.

83. *CI,* c. 1 (A54.66–68). Cf. c. 2 (A58.222–227).

84. C. 1 (A54.135–145).

85. M.-H. Vicaire, "Saint Dominique Chanoine d'Osma," *Archivum Fratrum Praedicatorum* 63 (1993): 38. M Michèle Mulchahey repeats this position in her excellent book *"First the Bow is Bent in Study": Dominican Education before 1350* (Toronto: Pontifical Institute of Mediaeval Studies, 1998), 13: "Dominic . . . had found no incompatibility between his ministry as a preacher and the clerical life he practised as a canon-regular. Dominic's positive experience and his sense of the possibilities offered by this life may be owing in part to a local evolution of the *ordo canonicorum* in Spain. . . . There, during the twelfth century and in contrast with the north, the canon's life had been given a clear pastoral orientation."

86. Mulchahey, 13.

87. Ibid., 14.

88. Simon Tugwell, OP, "Christ as a Model of Sanctity in Humbert of Romans," *Christ among the Medieval Dominicans*, ed. Kent Emery, Jr., and Joseph P. Wawrykow (Notre Dame, Ind.: University of Notre Dame Press, 1998), 93–94.

89. M.C. Sommers, "Thomas Aquinas' Polemic of Perfection", *Atti del IX Congresso Tomistico Internazionale* V, Studi Thomistici 44 (Rome: Libreria editrice vaticana, 1991), 371–72. See also *Albert and Thomas: Selected Writings*, ed. Simon Tugwell (New York: Paulist Press, 1988), 538–39.

90. Torrell, *Saint Thomas Aquinas*, 89 (English); 129 (French).

91. *L'Imitation des Apôtres: Moines, chanoines mendiants*, 11: "Il est donc particulièrment intéressant d'examiner comment les grands hérauts du mouvment monastique, en instituant, développant, réformant un type de vie auquel était promis un très fécond avenir, se sont explicitement proposé de reproduire la formule de vie qu'avait voulue Jésus, que les apôtres avaient acceptée et déterminée par leur vie aussi bien que leurs paroles, et dont un certain nombres de textes du Nouveau Testament transmettent encore aujourd'hui le message." Ibid., 66: "[L]es Chanoines de la réforme grégorienne, parcequ'ils sont des clercs par définition et possèdent un ministère propre, s'estiment plus proches des apôtres que les moines, si parfaits que ceux-ci puissent être dans la rigeur et la pauvreté de leur vie de communauté." According to a liturgical office, composed before 1242: *Tandem virum canonicum auget in apostolicum* (67).

92. *CI*, c. 4 (A78.880–81).

93. E.g., *DPSV* (20.3–11).

94. C. 22 (A156.4–21, A157.109–127); c. 24 (A159.3–10).

95. *CI*, c.2 (A58.222–227).

96. C.5. (A92.570–576).

97. There are 24 occurrences of forms of *contemplatio* (20) and *contemplativus* (4) in the *CI*. However, there are numerous other references to things associated with contemplation, e.g., study, prayer, etc.

98. C. 2 (A57.193–199).

99. C. 2 (A57.199–A58.211).

100. C. 2 (A58.285–292).

101. C. 4 (A78.831–839).

102. Ibid., 840–858.

103. C. 4 (A79.915–929). Cf. c. 11 (A132.90–133.154).

104. C. 4 (A78.820–830).

105. Aquinas, however, includes examples of monks who do not work: "There is the example of Benedict, who lived in a cave for three years without working and many other examples in Gregory's *Dialogi* and in the *Vitae patrum* who lived their lives without manual labor." C. 5 (A88.217–228).

106. C. 5 (A87.184–192).

107. Gregory, *Homilia in Hezechielam*, 2, n. 8 (PL 40:577–78).

108. C. 5 (A87.193–A88.200).

109. C. 5 (A90.394–406).

110. Ibid., 407–426.

111. C. 5 (A89.314–352).

112. Ibid., 353–364.

113. C. 5, ad 11m (A92.700–A93.765).

114. C. 5 (A88.201–216). Aquinas employs the traditional exegesis of the Mary-Martha story, which aligns the sisters with the contemplative and active lives respectively. See my article, "Imaging the Contemplative Life in Thomas Aquinas" in *Semiotics 2001,* ed. John Deely and Scott Simpkins (Toronto: Legas, 2002), 40–53.

115. E.g., Dominican *Constitutiones Antiquae* (II.26, 360; Preambulum, 309–10).

116. C. 6 (A98.412–426).

117. C. 6 (A99.486–491).

118. C. 6 (A98.424–6): "Ecce contemplativa quae ad evangelium pertinet."

119. C. 6 (A100.548–559).

120. Ibid., 560–586.

121. Ibid., 556–59.

122. C. 7 (A111.484–504).

123. C. 7 (A107.139–144). *Epistula* 17, § 2 (PL 22:360).

124. C. 7 (A119.1238–1244).

125. C. 7 (A111.533–543).

126. *ST* 2-2.188.6 corp. "Sic ergo dicendum est quod opus vitae activae est duplex. Unum quidem quod ex plenitudine contemplationis derivatur, sicut doctrina et predicatio."

127. *ST* 2-2.181.3 corp. "Dicendum quod actus doctrinae habet duplex obiectum: fit enim doctrina per locutionem; locutio autem est signum audibile interioris conceptus. Est ergo unum obiectum doctrinae id quod est materia sive obiectum interioris conceptionis. Et quantum ad hoc quandoque doctrian pertinet ad vitam activam, quandoque ad contemplativam . . . Aliud vero obiectum doctrinae est ex parte sermonis audibilis. Et sic obiectum doctrinae est ipse audiens. Et quantum ad hoc obiectum omnis doctrina pertinet ad vitam actvam."

128. See Prol. (A54.135–145). *ST* 2-2.188.6 corp. "Sic ergo summum gradum in religionibus tenent quae ordinantur ad docendum et praedicandum. Quae et propinquissimae sunt perfectioni episcoporum."

Chapter 9

A Note on Love and Governance

JAMES P. REILLY, JR.

In two passages of his commentary on the *De divinis nominibus,* St. Thomas considers the relationship of governance and love.[1] The intent of this "Note" is twofold: (1) to examine in a preliminary way the relevant texts; and (2) to propose some conclusions suggested by this examination.

In the first passage, chapter 10, lectio 1, §855–858, Thomas distinguishes two kinds of governance, limited and unlimited. Human governance is limited governance, because there is a certain reciprocity between the ruler and those subject to his rule.[2] Consequently, justice is a mutual requirement. Rulers must enact laws that promote peace and virtue in society; subjects must obey all such laws.[3]

On the other hand, there is no reciprocity between the Creator and creatures. Divine governance is unlimited. As sovereign ruler and providential Creator, God holds all things, as it were, in his grasp. Therefore, unlike human governance which is limited and temporal, divine governance is absolute and eternal.[4]

But how may governance be exercised? Again, Thomas distinguishes. Governance, he says, may be exercised in one of two ways: either by fear or by love. The former, governance by fear, is an ineffective way of governing. Persons subject to governance of this kind are unwilling subjects. Given the opportunity, they will cast off the yoke of servitude that results from this kind of rule.[5]

The second way of governance, governance by love, is the most effective form of governance, because persons subject to such a rule subject themselves to it with complete voluntariness. This way of governing is proper only to God, the Supreme Good, Whom every creature necessarily, but willingly, desires.[6] Nevertheless, human rulers must try to emulate this kind of governance. However, even the usually just ruler may fail to do so. When he does fail, the result is oppressive laws that do not bind those subject to his rule.[7]

God's governance never fails; nor are his laws ever oppressive.[8] Rather, God wills to share His goodness with creatures. Not only does He give being to every creature, but also the natural inclinations necessary for the perfection of its being. These natural inclinations, or natural laws, are the effects, or in the Dionysian expression appropriated by Thomas, the sweet offspring (*dulces partus*) of the love with which the divine goodness is loved.[9] This love may be understood in one of two ways: either of the love with which God loves his own goodness necessarily; or of the love divinely implanted in every creature, namely, the love that governs its being as a creature. As a consequence of this implantation, every creature loves God of necessity, at least in his effects.[10]

This latter love, the love divinely implanted in creatures, is a direct manifestation of God's governance through love. Motivated solely by the love of his own goodness, God bestows on every creature not only being, but also a concomitant desire for the perfection of its being. This desire for perfection is the sign of every creature's participation in the *Summum Bonum*.[11] It is, therefore, the *Summum Bonum* to which all governance is ordained.

In the second passage, chapter 4, lectio 9, §401–402. Thomas examines the relationship of love to appetite and, implicitly, the role of the natural inclinations in governance.

It is evident, Thomas argues, that love pertains to appetite.[12] Accordingly, love is the first and common root of every appetitive operation.[13] Therefore, love takes its meaning from that which is the common object of appetite, namely the good.[14] And so, something is said to be loved, which the appetite of the lover relates to as to its good.[15] And when that good is attained, the object loved is present to the lover in some way, and the two are united according to some sort of likeness.[16] However, in any given instance, the degree of presence and union depends directly upon the quality of the appetite involved, as well as the quality of object loved.

Now according to the order of the appetites, there is a corresponding order of loves.[17] The least perfect is the natural appetite which is entirely non-cognitive. This corresponds to man's natural inclination, shared with every creature, to preserve the being that is possessed. More perfect is the sensible appetite which is consequent upon cognition, but not upon deliberation and choice. This corresponds to man's natural inclination, shared with sentient but non-rational beings, to seek whatever is necessary for the preservation of the species.[18]

The most perfect of the three is the rational appetite. This appetite is consequent, not only upon cognition, but also upon deliberation and choice, for this appetite moves itself in some way. In other words, this corresponds to man's distinctive natural inclination, namely, to act in accord with reason.[19] The love that pertains to this appetitive activity is most perfect, and is called *dilectio,* since by means of free choice man discerns what ought to be loved.[20]

Four conclusions seem to follow from this exposition. First, love and divine governance are intrinsically linked. For just as the existence of every creature is a witness to the love that governs its origin, so too the natural appetite of every creature for the perfection of its being is a witness to the love that governs its proper finality.

Second, because of the indeterminacy of the rational appetite, man has the potential for self-determination. No good of human experience, even the most exalted, can fully determine the rational appetite. The only adequate object of the rational appetite is the good itself, namely, the *Summum Bonum.*

Third, this capacity for self-determination, namely, the potential to elect those goods consonant with the perfection of his nature, is an evident sign of man's participation in divine governance. In other words, God leaves man free to love what he ought to love, and, in so loving, to become what he ought to be.

Finally, since the end of divine governance is the divine goodness, the only fitting end of the governance that man exercises by means of the rational appetite, that sweetest offspring of divine love, is the end to which divine governance itself is ordered.[21]

Notes

1. Cf. St. Thomas Aquinas, *In librum Beati Dionysii De Divinis Nominibus Expositio,* ed. Pera (Rome: Marietti, 1950), cap. 10, lect. 1, §855–857, et cap. 4. lect. 9, §401–402.

2. §855: Si autem aliquis aliquibus principetur, tamquam unus de numero eorum existens, tenet quidem eos inquantum est principans, sed et tenetur ab eis, inquantum eis permiscetur et sub eodem ordine includitur.

3. Cf. *ST* 1-2.95.1: Unde necessarium fuit ad pacem hominum et virtutem, quod leges ponerentur; and 98.1: Legis humane finis est temporalis tranquillitas civitatis. Cf. *In librum Beati Dionysii,* 11.1 §891.

4. §855: Deus autem sic omnia tenet quod a nullo tenetur <quia non permiscetur rebus, sed est supra omnia>; et hoc est quod dicit: *immixte gubernatis principans.*

5. §856: Contingit autem aliquem aliquibus principari, dupliciter: uno modo, per modum timoris et iste modus principiandi non est efficax ad subditos tenendum: qui enim contra propriam voluntatem subduntur, qui timore serviunt, data opportunitate, servitutis iugum excutiunt.

6. §856: Alio modo, per modum amoris et hic modus principandi est efficax ad tenendum subiectos qui voluntarie subduntur; et hunc modum principandi Deo attribuit, cum dicit: *et sicut omnibus desiderabilis,* omnia enim Ipsum desiderant, ut pluries dictum est.

7. §857: Posset autem iterum contingere quod aliquis principans, in persona sua desiderabilis esset, sed leges graves subditis daret, quas ipse non teneret et ideo subiecti non efficaciter sub ipso teneretur.

8. §857: Sed hoc a Deo excludens, subdit quod *omnibus* supermittit *voluntarias leges.*

9. §858: Sic igitur ipsae naturales inclinationes rerum in proprios fines, quas dicimus esse naturales leges, sunt quidam *partus,* id est effectus, *dulces,* idest consoni naturali appetitui, effectus dico vel *partus amoris* quo divina bonitas amatur.

10. §858: Qui quidem amor est divina et omnia tenens et insolubilis: sive hoc intelligatur de amore quo ipse Deus amat suam bonitatem, per quam omnia tenet et insolubilis est quia ex necessitate se amat; sive dicatur divinus amor qui est divinitus omnibus rebus inditus, per quem

omnia tenentur a Deo et qui solvi non potest, quia omnia ex necessitate Deum amant, saltem in Eius effectibus.

11. §857: Nihil enim est desiderabile, nisi inquantum habet aliquam participationem Summi Boni.

12. §401: Ad evidentiam autem eorum quae hic dicuntur, considerandum est quod amor ad appetitum pertinet.

13. §401: Est autem amor prima et communis radix omnium appetitivarum operationum; quod patet inspicienti per singula.

14. §401: Et ideo oportet quod ratio amoris accpiatur ex eo quod est commune obiectum appetitus. Hoc autem est bonum.

15. §401: Ex hoc igitur aliquid dicitur amari, quod appetitus amantis se habet ad illud sicut ad suum bonum.

16. §401: Omne autem quod ordinatur ad aliquid sicut ad suum bonum, habet quodammodo illud sibi praesens et unitum secundum quamdam similitudinem, saltem proportionis, sicut forma quodammodo est in materia inquantum habet aptitudinem et ordinem ad ipsam.

17. §402: Sic igitur patet in quo differt quod dicit: *desiderabile et amabile;* nam desiderium est quidam affectus amoris. Quod autem dicit: *diligibile,* determinat quemdam modum amoris: cum enim amor ad appetitum pertineat, secundum ordinem appetituum est ordo amorum.

18. §402: Est autem imperfectissimus appetituum, naturalis appetitus absque cognitione, quod nihil aliud importat quam inclinationem naturalem. Supra hunc autem est appetitus sensibilis, qui sequitur cognitionem, sed est absque libera electione; cf. *ST* 1-2.94.2.

19. §402: Supremus autem appetitus est qui est cum cognitione et libera electione: hic enim appetitus quodammodo movet seipsum; cf. *ST* 1-2.94.2.

20. §402: Vnde et amor ad hunc pertinens est perfectissimus et vocatur dilectio, inquantum libera electione discernitur quid sit amandum.

21. §858: Ultimus autem omnium finis est bona divinitas, ad quam sicut ad finem ordinantur omnes praevii et particulares fines in quos res naturaliter inclinantur.

Chapter 10

Godfrey of Fontaines and the Condemnation of March 7, 1277

JOHN F. WIPPEL

Beginning with the commemoration in 1977 of the seven-hundredth anniversary of the condemnation of 219 propositions on March 7, 1277, by the Bishop of Paris, Stephen Tempier, there has been a resurgence of scholarly interest in this event and its implications. Especially significant was the publication in 1977 of Roland Hissette's book on this topic and the many subsequent discussions occasioned at least in part by its appearance.[1] Most recently David Piché has published a new and critical edition of the text of the Condemnation itself, along with an extensive study of the same.[2]

It is not my purpose here to review these discussions but rather to concentrate on a more limited issue—the reaction of a well-informed eyewitness to the Condemnation itself and the events leading up to it, and of one who played an important role in the philosophical and theological life of the University of Paris during the final quarter of the thirteenth century, Godfrey of Fontaines. In another recently completed article I had the occasion to present Godfrey's career as a witness to the major philosophical issues which were being debated at the University during this time, that is to say, during his student days in Arts and then in Theology at the University of Paris in the 1270s and 1280s and then as Regent Master in the Theological Faculty from 1285 until ca. 1303/1304.[3]

There is considerable evidence in the library Godfrey left to the Sorbonne to indicate that he was keenly interested in a number of the figures directly touched by the Condemnation of March 7, 1277, including Siger of Brabant, Boethius of Dacia and other anonymous Masters in Arts from the 1260s or 1270s.[4] And whether one holds, as I do, that some of Thomas Aquinas's positions were also directly targeted by the Condemnation, or with Hissette that Thomas was only indirectly targeted by this prohibition, Godfrey was clearly interested in his writings as well.[5] More than this, he was also a persistent critic of one of the best known members of the commission assembled by Stephen Tempier to assist in drawing up the list of prohibited articles, Henry of Ghent. Because of this, and because Godfrey's own Quodlibets range from 1285 until 1303/1304, I attached to the other study which I have just mentioned an appendix which cites the various texts wherein Godfrey refers to this condemnation. In the present study I propose to examine in some detail Godfrey's reaction in each of these cases to the condemned articles and will consider them in chronological order. Hopefully this will provide the reader with a fuller appreciation of how one eyewitness viewed and reacted to the Condemnation itself and its aftermath.

I. *QUODLIBET* V, Q. 6 = ART. 212 / 74

In *Quodlibet* V, q. 6 of 1288 Godfrey refers to article 212/74 according to which an intelligence moves the heaven by its will alone (*Quod intelligentia sola voluntate movet caelum*).[6] Here he is considering the general question whether in angels there is some active principle distinct from the intellect and the will.[7] He comments that if angels were movers of the heavenly spheres in the way the philosophers maintained, namely so that it would be of their very nature or essence to move such spheres and so that without doing this they would not enjoy their full perfection, there would be nothing in them in addition to their substance by which they would move such bodies. Indeed, according to the philosophers, anything assigned to them in addition to their essence differs from that essence only conceptually (*secundum rationem*), just as we (Christians) hold to be true of God.[8]

But, counters Godfrey, to be moved is not a natural perfection of heavenly bodies in such fashion that their motion must not cease. Nor is the nature of angels so ordered to move such bodies that they (angels) would not enjoy their full perfection without actually moving them. Therefore there is no need to hold that angels move by reason of their essence, but rather by some active power that exists within them, and which does not necessarily have to be applied to the heaven. However, since they are spiritual and intellectual substances, there does not seem to be any power in them which can serve as the principle for such operation other than the intellect and the will. And indeed, just as there is only one passive apprehensive power in them—the intellect—so too, it seems that there is only one active power in them, which is virtually multiple in the sense that it can produce different effects, i.e., the will.[9]

But Godfrey now comments that an angel will not be said to move the heaven by its will alone, for this is rejected as one of the condemned articles, in an obvious reference to article 212. He explains that something is moved by the will alone of an agent if it is moved entirely according to the choice or at the pleasure (*ad libitum*) of the agent, and not according to some determination and relationship of that agent to some further end. But neither good nor bad angels move the heaven in this way by their will, since a good angel does not move except insofar as an end is presented to it by God, whose minister it is. And an evil angel does not move bodies except insofar as God permits this. After some additional discussion, Godfrey comments that it is clear that angels do not move themselves except by means of their will, and that they seem to move bodies by the same power whereby they move themselves. Thus for them to move themselves by their will is for them to enjoy being wherever they will, or to be joined to a corporeal body as a mover which they will to move and, once joined to such a body, to move it by their will in accord with the end given to them by God.[10]

But because he does not want to speak against the condemned article, and because it seems to be true of God alone that for him to will is to act, Godfrey observes that in an angel in some way the will (appetite) should be distinguished from its motive power just as it is distinguished from its apprehensive power (intellect). Just as it is the task of an angel's apprehensive power to grasp and regulate its extrinsic operation and to direct its appetite or will to such an operation, so it seems to be the task of its will to will or to desire that what is apprehended be done, and to command that it be done. But because to command that something be done is not yet to do it, it seems that in addition to the will in some way a motive power should be posited which is moved by the intellect and by the will to perform the external act, in this case, to move the heavenly body which the will, or the angel by means of its will, wants to move. One gathers the impression from this discussion that Godfrey would not have postulated this third executive power in angels, as he styles it, except for the condemned proposition.[11]

II. *QUODLIBET* VI, Q. 13 = ART. 204 / 55

In this *Quodlibet* dating from 1289 Godfrey is considering the question whether one instant of our time corresponds to many instants which measure many *mutata esse* in the successive motion of an angel.[12] Without pursuing in detail his complicated investigation of that issue, it will suffice for us to note that he begins this discussion by observing that one should speak of the motion of angels in place and of the measure of such motion in accord with the manner in which they are present in place. Therefore, if angels were not held to be present in place except by means of their external operation, that is, by moving or changing corporeal things, it would be easier to see how they are moved according to place and how their motion would be measured or not measured by time. But he comments that because they are held to be in place *diffinitive*, that is, so as to be here and not there at one and the same time and without any external operation on their part, he considers an alternative explanation proposed by some. According to this explanation, offered by Henry of Ghent in his *Quodlibet* IV,

q. 17, they are moved in terms of place solely through their internal operation insofar as by their acts of understanding and willing they apply themselves to place.[13]

Godfrey is very critical of this way of accounting for angelic presence in place. He counters that according to this explanation, whereby an angel would be present in place without performing any external operation in that place but merely by understanding or willing it, it cannot really be said that the angel is in place, but rather that the place is in the angel. For what is understood is present in the intellect of the one who understands, and what is willed is in the one who actually wills it, since as immanent acts these operations remain within the agent.[14] But if one requires some external operation on the part of the angel with respect to the place, then this explanation will not differ from one that has been judged insufficient according to the condemned article, i.e., article 204, which reads: "That separate substances are in place by their operation, and that they cannot move from one extreme to another, or through a medium, except insofar as they can will to operate either in the medium or in the extremes.—This is an error if it means that without operating a [separate] substance is not in place nor does it pass from place to place."[15] Somewhat farther on in this question, Godfrey comments that it is not pertinent to the present discussion to determine what suitable way there might be of holding that an angel is present in place and moved in terms of place apart from this view (Henry's) which he rejects, and apart from the one which is to be rejected in light of the condemned article. Nor does he know what any such explanation might be.[16] But as will be seen below, the condemnation of article 204 and of article 219 will continue to trouble Godfrey because he finds them mutually exclusive.

III. *QUODLIBET* VI, q. 16 = ART. 96 / 42 AND / OR 81 / 43

In this question Godfrey was asked to determine whether, if a human body should rise from the dead without quantity, it would be numerically the same as it was before.[17] Godfrey begins by seriously questioning the possibility of any such separation of quantity from a human body, since quantity seems to be included in one's understanding of a human being. But because he does not wish to detract from divine power, and even though he does not understand how this could be possible, he takes up the question nonetheless.[18]

He responds that in one way such a resurrected human being would be the same as before, and in another way he or she would not be. He introduces a distinction between the one or unity which is convertible with being (what we may call transcendental unity) and the one or unity which is a principle of number. He comments that in a way every kind of unity is a principle of some number, since every multitude is a certain number, i.e., it is based on a multiplication of units. But when he speaks here of the kind of unity that is a principle of number, he has in mind that kind of number which is discrete quantity, or which falls into the accidental genus quantity. Hence, for the sake of clarity, as I have proposed elsewhere in a fuller discussion of this, we may distinguish with Godfrey between numerical unity in the broad sense (the kind that is convertible with being) and numerical unity in the strict sense (the kind based on quantity).[19]

Accordingly, because unity or the one indicates that something is undivided in itself and divided from other things, whatever has a nature or entity that is undivided in itself and divided from other things is one in this broader sense, that is to say, it enjoys transcendental unity or unity of being. This will be true, however, only insofar as that thing exists or subsists in reality in such a way that it cannot be further divided in the way a genus is divided into species, or a species into individuals. Hence this kind of unity—transcendental unity—will apply to any subsisting substance and to all the accidents that exist in such a substance. Thus any subsisting angel will be numerically one in this broad sense, i.e., transcendentally one, even if it is identical with its entire species so that no other angel can be found within that same species; for it will be as undivided in itself and divided from everything else as it would be if another angel existed or could exist with it under the same species.[20] So too, if two angels are held to fall within the same species, as is clearly true of two souls which are multiplied in accord with the multiplicity of their bodies, they will be said to differ not in species but in number when this is taken broadly, since their form will be multiplied in such a way that it is undivided in itself and divided from all else.[21] And in this way, if two human beings should arise without accidents, they would differ in number when this is taken substantially or essentially, that is, according to the kind of unity that is convertible with being. And in this sense each of them would be numerically the same as it was before in terms of its numerical unity taken broadly, since it would still possess the same matter and the same substantial form which would constitute one and the same *suppositum* as previously.[22]

But the kind of numerical unity that is not convertible with being—numerical unity taken strictly—is present in substances only through something that is added, i.e., continuous quantity.[23] Consequently, it would have to be said that two human beings who arose from the dead without the accident quantity would not differ from one another numerically when this is taken in the strict sense, since they would lack quantity. Moreover, neither of them would be numerically the same as it was before, once again because of the absence of quantity. Thus while such a human being would retain the substantial or transcendental unity it previously enjoyed, it would not retain its strict numerical unity.[24]

In light of all of this Godfrey concludes that it seems that things that lack quantity can differ numerically (in the broad sense) insofar as they differ in species, but in order for them to differ numerically within one and the same species, they must be quantified. But after having said this, he comments that one must admit that there are many souls that do differ numerically from one another in the strict sense. One may explain this by appealing to the numerically diverse bodies of which they are forms and with which they also attain their strict numerical distinction. So too, opines Godfrey, one might perhaps hold that two human beings who rise from the dead without quantity would still differ numerically because they once enjoyed quantity or were of such a nature as to do so. But, he continues, it is difficult to understand how things which are actually separated from the quantity with which it was their nature to be united can still be numerically distinct from one another, as in the case of separated souls, and as in the case under discussion—two human beings who would arise without quantity. Nonetheless, one must hold this as regards separated souls. But, he concludes, it is still more difficult to understand how there can be many angels that differ numerically in this sense, i.e., within the same species. He comments, however, that this possibility must not be completely denied (*non est omnino negandum*) in accord with a certain article wherein the contrary position is condemned. Here he seems to be referring to prohibited article 81 ("That because intelligences do not have matter, God could not make many intelligences within the same species"), and probably also to the related article 96 ("That God cannot multiply individuals within a species without matter").[25]

IV. *Quodlibet* VII, q. 11 = Art. 36 / 9 and 215 / 10

In this question dating from either 1290/1291 or 1291/1292 Godfrey was asked to determine whether it is by the same knowledge that one knows of God that he is and what he is.[26] Before replying Godfrey spells out in some detail his understanding of the difference between knowing "what something is" and knowing "that it is" and draws upon Aristotle's *Posterior Analytics* for a distinction between preexistent knowledge or foreknowledge (*praecognitio*) and knowledge that must be established by investigation (*quaestio*). He then applies this distinction to knowledge *quid est* and knowledge *si est* or *quia est*. He sets up a sequence whereby one begins with merely nominal knowledge of a thing (*quid nominis*), which is purely foreknowledge. From this one advances to knowledge *si est* of it (awareness of it as belonging to one of the supreme genera, whether substance or one of the accidents, either potentially or actually). Depending on the circumstances, such *si est* knowledge may either be precognition, as in one's awareness of being or of mobile being (the subjects of metaphysics and physics), or it may be a *quaestio* and established by discursive investigation and reasoning. One may then move on to *quid est rei* knowledge of the thing, i.e., more precise knowledge of it in terms of its proximate species.[27]

In turning to the issue of *si est* and *quid est* knowledge of God in this life, Godfrey considers and rejects as inadequate the view of some who say that in this life we can know of God "that he is," but not "what he is." And when we know that God is, the "is" we discover is not that whereby God subsists in himself, but only that expressed in the proposition which states: "God is." Against this view, clearly that of Thomas Aquinas,[28] Godfrey argues that we must acknowledge the possibility of arriving at some kind of *quid est* knowledge of God in this life. He proposes a process whereby one moves from a very confused and general knowledge or nominal (*quid nominis*) knowledge of God which could apply to being and to nonbeing. From this, by appealing to philosophical argumentation such as Aristotle's argument from motion in *Physics* VII, one recognizes the existence of a First Mover, or God, presumably thereby recognizing him as a substance. Then one specifies this knowledge and thereby reaches a more particular and quasi-specific knowledge (*quid est*), for instance, by proving that he is an incorporeal and living substance, and then that he is intelligent. While maintaining that this provides some *quid est* knowledge of God, Godfrey recognizes that such knowledge is always imperfect and incomplete. Even so, and while also granting that God does not fall into any genus, including that of substance, he insists that by knowing such things about God in some way we know what he is.[29]

Finally he comments that it is in this way that certain propositions condemned by the Bishop of Paris are to be understood, which seem to be opposed to what he has just said. According to art. 36/9 it is prohibited to hold "That we can understand God in this mortal life through his essence." But according to art. 215/10 it is also prohibited to hold "That concerning God it can only be known that he is or that he exists (*ipsum esse*)."[30] Godfrey remarks that the first error cannot be reconciled with the second and, therefore, he implies, the simultaneous condemnation of the two cannot be defended, unless in some way we introduce some distinction into that knowledge whereby God is knowable through his essence. This distinction, Godfrey comments, is now sufficiently clear from what he has just said. But as we shall see, a few years later in his *Quodlibet* XII, he will simply dismiss the simultaneous condemnation of these two propositions as contradictory.[31]

V. *QUODLIBET* VII, Q. 18 = PROLOGUE TO THE CONDEMNATION

In this question Godfrey was asked to determine what position a *Magister* in theology should take if a question is proposed to him about which he firmly holds one side as true on the strength of reason or authority when that side has been condemned as false by the judgment of a Bishop together with the penalty of excommunication for anyone who asserts or teaches it. Godfrey responds by noting that affirmative precepts deal with good things that are to be done, including the obligation to teach the truth. These oblige *semper* but not *ad semper*. He contrasts these with negative precepts which deal with evils to be avoided and comments that the obligation not to teach falsehood falls under these. While falsity can never be taught, the truth does not always have to be proposed but only at the right time and place and under appropriate circumstances. He also distinguishes between truths that are necessary for salvation and others that are not but are indifferent with respect to faith and morals.[32]

If a Master is dealing with a truth which the Bishop has judged to be false and condemned as erroneous under penalty of excommunication and which is not essential for salvation, Godfrey concludes that the Master should defend neither side. In this case, so long as such a Prelate is tolerated by the Church, under such circumstances and within the territory over which he has jurisdiction, he should be obeyed. There is no obligation to teach the truth on every occasion, and this is neither the time nor the place to teach such a truth.[33] Godfrey does add, however, that in such a case, or even in a case where what the Bishop has condemned contains probable truth, such an excommunication and condemnation seem to be wrong (*erronea*) because thereby the search for truth and knowledge of the same are impeded. Again he remarks that in such a case an individual is not obliged to oppose such a Bishop openly by saying that he should not be obeyed. But Godfrey also comments that one should prevail upon the Bishop to have him revoke such a condemnation and excommunication. If an evil opposed to salvation of souls does not result from it, an evil against the perfection of the intellect does. Moreover, scandal arises among unbelievers and among many believers at the ignorance and simple-mindedness of such Prelates.[34]

On the other hand, if the condemned truth pertains to salvation and it is absolutely certain that it must be held on the authority of Scripture or on the basis of correct reasoning, then the condemnation and the prohibition are entirely erroneous and do not bind anyone. In such a case the doctor should teach that which he takes to be true even though some may be scandalized by what appears to be his lack of obedience. Finally, Godfrey also applies this conclusion to someone who mistakenly thinks that what has been condemned by a Bishop as false is certainly true and pertains to salvation. One who acts against an erroneous conscience sins more gravely than one who acts in accord with it. Hence such a person would sin more gravely if out of fear of excommunication he failed to teach that which according to his erroneous conscience he judges to be a truth necessary for salvation.[35]

Before concluding this section I should note that nowhere in this particular question does Godfrey explicitly refer to any of the articles prohibited by Bishop Stephen Tempier in his Condemnation of March 7, 1277. And neither the way the question is posed nor the way Godfrey responds necessarily restricts this discussion to that particular prohibition. Even so, it can hardly be doubted that the questioner, and Godfrey himself in his reply, and for that matter those in attendance, would have had this particular Condemnation in mind. Godfrey's ongoing concern with various articles explicitly prohibited by Tempier in March 1277 is one indication of this, as the present study illustrates. A second is the very language of Tempier's introductory letter to the Condemnation, especially where he threatens to excommunicate all who shall have taught or presumed to defend or support in any way whatsoever any of the errors he has singled out, along with those who shall have listened to them, unless they shall report to him or to the Chancellor of Paris within seven days.[36] As we shall see below, Godfrey would continue to take the penalty of excommunication for teaching any of the condemned articles very seriously throughout his career.

VI. *QUODLIBET* VIII, Q. 16 = 130 / 166, 163 / 163, 129 / 169

In this question dating from the 1292/1293 academic year, Godfrey was asked to determine whether the appetite of a brute is free and can therefore be described as a will.[37] In the course of preparing his negative reply to this question, he offers a very long presentation and defense of his highly intellectualist explanation of human freedom.[38] One of the contested issues had to do with whether the will can refuse to choose something that has been presented to it by the intellect in its (ultimate) practical judgment. Godfrey here defends his view that the will cannot choose against the ultimate practical judgment of reason in such a case. While different versions of this view had been defended by Thomas Aquinas and Siger of Brabant,[39] it also seemed to be prohibited by some of the condemned articles. Witness, for instance, article 130/166: "That if reason is correct, so too is the will.—This is an error because it is against Augustine's Gloss on this text from the psalm 'My soul longed to desire' [Ps. 119/20], and because according to this grace would not be necessary for rectitude of the will but only knowledge, which was the error of Pelagius"; art. 163/163: "That the will necessarily pursues that which is firmly accepted by reason, and that it cannot abstain from that which reason dictates. This necessitation, however, is not coercion but the nature of the will"; art. 129/169: "That while passion and particular knowledge remain in actuality, the will cannot act against them."[40]

In support of his position Godfrey cites a proposition which, he states, was granted by all the Doctors in theology as true and as to be held as its words indicate, namely "that there is no malice in the will unless there is error or lack of knowledge on the part of reason."[41] Known as the *propositio magistralis,* this proposition was agreed upon by the members of the Theology Faculty at the time they considered the case of Giles of Rome in March 1277, and may be seen as something of a concession to him. According to Wielockx, in all likelihood it was granted again at the time of Giles's reinstatement to the faculty in 1285.[42] Godfrey is more than pleased to cite it in support of his own view and comments that this proposition could not be true if the choice of the will could go against the judgment of reason. He concludes therefore that certain articles rejected by the Bishop before this proposition was approved, which seem to be opposed to it, must be interpreted in such a way that they agree with it—insofar as this can be done. While he does not here explicitly identify these particular articles, those such as we have mentioned seem to be on his mind. Indeed, he will cite all three of them in his discussion of the 1277 Condemnation in *Quodlibet* XII, q. 5.[43]

VII. *QUODLIBET* IX, q. 4 = 124 / 147, 187 / 146

In this question dating from the 1293/1294 academic year, Godfrey was asked to determine whether the human nature of Christ enjoyed the same degree of perfection as human nature in the state of innocence, i.e., in Adam.[44] He connects his discussion of this with a broader issue concerning whether a substance in terms of that which pertains to its very substance can admit of more or less so as to permit one instance of nature within the same species to be more perfect than another. After noting that opinions concerning this differ, he recalls a theory he himself had developed elsewhere (probably in his Disputed Question 18), according to which variation according to the more and less can be found in any nature only insofar as that nature is changeable. Because material substances may be viewed either in terms of their form and species or in terms of their matter, he had proposed that by reason of their material parts they allow for variation and therefore for more and less or the more and less perfect within the same species.[45] Because separate substances or angels are completely immaterial and therefore invariable in their substance, the more and less cannot be realized in them in terms of that which pertains to their substance so long as they remain the same in species. And the same would seem to apply to the human soul unless it can be said to be material in some sense, insofar as it is the natural perfection of matter.[46]

Consequently, continues Godfrey, the proposed question raises a difficulty both for those who hold that there cannot be differentiation according to the more and less within the same species in any substance whatsoever, and for others, such as Godfrey himself, who allow for this in the case of purely material substances; for the human soul is not material in the unqualified sense. According to the first opinion, which Godfrey describes as more common, human nature not only as realized in Christ but in any other human being could not be more or less perfect than as it was realized in Adam, nor could the converse obtain. This applies to that which pertains to human nature in terms of its form—the soul—and in terms of its matter. And even according to Godfrey's theory it does not seem that human nature can be diversified according to the more and less perfect with respect to that which pertains to its form or the soul. Hence it will be difficult for either position to avoid falling under the Parisian article.[47]

Godfrey immediately protests that he does not intend to contradict the article condemned by the Bishop, and comments that given its way of speaking, it is not really relevant to the question at hand. Whether or not there are degrees of more or less in that substantial form which is the human soul, this will have no impact on the question concerning whether Christ's soul is more excellent than that of Judas.[48] After developing more fully this point about the theological non-relevance of the question concerning gradation in human souls with respect to the issue of the perfection of Christ's soul, Godfrey acknowledges that nonetheless it would not (seem to) be permissible at Paris to hold that one human soul is not more or less perfect than another because of the condemned articles.[49]

But then, in order to show how one who wants to maintain this position concerning the human soul might respond to those articles which seem to assert the contrary, Godfrey turns to them. The first, art. 124/147, states: "That it is improper to hold that some intellects are more excellent than others because, since this diversity does not come from the side of bodies, it must come from the side of intelligences; and thus more excellent and less excellent souls would necessarily belong to different species, as do intelligences. This is an error because then the soul of Christ would not be more excellent than the soul of Judas." The second, art. 187/146, reads: "That we understand in worse or better fashion arises from the passive intellect, which is said to be [Piché: which he says is] a sensitive power. This is an error because this is to hold either that there is one intellect for all (human beings) or equality among all souls."[50] As the reader can see, common to the condemnation of both articles appears to be a rejection of the notion that souls are equal to one another in perfection.

Godfrey suggests that one way of not contradicting the prohibited articles without giving up the general theory that there can be no diversity between human souls in terms of their essential structure or substance is to emphasize the point that the soul is the form of a material body, and that different souls are of such a nature as to inform different bodies. Diverse bodily dispositions and organs will easily account for diversity in those properties and powers of the soul which inhere in the matter-form composite. But even in the case of those powers and properties which inhere directly in the human soul itself, i.e., the intellect and the will, diversity of the bodies to which particular souls are related will account for diversity in the degree of perfection of those properties or powers in individual souls as well. Thus we find different degrees in properties or characteristics, such as industry and intelligence (*ingenium*) in different souls, precisely because it is of the nature of each of these souls to inform differently disposed bodies.[51] Godfrey concludes that in this way the articles would be granted as they stand, since under this explanation it is not improper to posit different degrees of excellence and perfection in souls of the same species.[52] Whether this solution would have satisfied Bishop Tempier and his advisers is, of course, another matter.

Finally, in returning to the question initially raised here—whether human nature as realized in Christ was more perfect than human nature in Adam—Godfrey concludes that this is simply a question of fact. He sees no argument that proves necessarily that Christ's soul was more perfect. Nor can this be proved from the condemned articles, since they only hold that the soul of Christ was more excellent than the soul of Judas *simpliciter*, that is, without specifying how or in what way. Godfrey himself had earlier reasoned that the fact that Christ was without sin is enough to establish this. Nonetheless, for reasons of fittingness and appropriateness, he concludes that one should hold that it was more excellent.[53]

VIII. *QUODLIBET* XII, Q. 5 = 96 / 42, 81 / 43, 124 / 147, 36 / 9, 215 / 10, 204 / 55, 219 / 54, 129 / 169, 130 / 166, 160 / 101, 163 / 163

In this very sensitive and carefully structured discussion dating from the 1296/1297 academic year, Godfrey was asked to look back some twenty years or so to the Condemnation of 1277. The question posed for his resolution was this: Whether the Bishop of Paris sins by failing to correct certain articles which were condemned by his predecessor.[54] Godfrey opens his response with a syllogism. That which (1) impedes the advance of students and (2) is an occasion of scandal among them and (3) works to the detriment of useful teaching should be corrected. But such is true of the matter at hand, i.e., of the condemnation of certain articles.[55]

In support of the first point in his major premise Godfrey argues that if some issue is so undetermined and uncertain with respect to its truth that different views may be held without rash assertion of either side and without danger to faith and morals, to impose a bond forcing people to defend only one side of such a question is to impede knowledge of the truth. Truth will better be found by means of different disputations which defend each side in the pursuit of truth, conducted by learned and informed men. The purpose of those disputing such matters should be to arrive at that position which seems to be more in accord with right reason, not at that which is more pleasing. Therefore to impede this way of investigating and manifesting the truth seems to hinder the progress of students and understanding of the truth on the part of those seeking it.[56]

As regards the articles in question, continues Godfrey, it seems that there are many among them about which it is permissible to hold different opinions. Moreover, some seem to involve contradictory positions, so much so that no way of teaching with respect to them can be found whereby they can be understood, and thus the intellect is impeded in arriving at the truth concerning them. In addition, there are some which, when taken according to the letter of the text, seem to be completely impossible and irrational. Hence one can only give them an interpretation which is, as it were, violent and forced.[57]

Godfrey then lists a number of such articles to illustrate his point. He first cites art. 96/42, whereby it is condemned as an error to hold that God could not multiply individuals within a species without matter, and art. 81/43, which follows from it and states that God could not make many intelligences of the same species because they do not have matter. Godfrey comments that these would seem to be defensible opinions since these things have been said and written down by many Catholic teachers.[58] The same may be said of art. 124/147, where it is condemned as an error to say that it is improper to hold that some intellects are nobler than others because, since this diversity could not be from the side of the body, it must be from the side of the intellect, and thus more excellent and less excellent souls would belong to different species.[59] Godfrey comments that concerning these articles and many others condemned as erroneous, it seems to lettered and skilled persons that one could legitimately think otherwise.[60] He then cites art. 36/9 where it is condemned as an error to hold that we can know God in this mortal life through his essence, and art. 215/10, in which it is condemned as an error to say that we can only know "that God is" or his *esse*. Between these two there seems to be contradiction because there seems to be no intermediary position between knowing of something "that it is" and knowing "what it is" or through its essence.[61]

Godfrey next notes that it is also condemned as an error to hold that separate substances are "somewhere" or move from place to place by their operation, if this is understood to mean that without operating the substance of an angel is not in place nor does it pass from place to place (art. 204/55). It is also condemned to hold that separate substances are nowhere according to their substance if this is understood as meaning that the substance of the angel is not in place. If it is understood as meaning that the substance is the reason for its being in place, it is true that separate substances are not in place according to their substance (art. 219/54).[62] With respect to these Godfrey comments that again there seems to be contradiction because no middle position can be found between these two. If neither the substance of an angel nor its operation is the reason for its being in place, what can be?[63]

He then cites four more articles having to do with volition: that so long as passion and particular knowledge remain in actuality, the will cannot act against them (art. 129/169); that if reason is right, so is the will (130/166: he has omitted the remainder of the text); that no agent is open to alternatives, but each is determined [to one] (160/101); that the will necessarily pursues that which is firmly held by reason, etc. (163/163: he has omitted the remainder of the article).[64]

He comments again that these articles and many others seem to be so impossible and irrational that they cannot be reasonably supported unless they are interpreted in some other way than the letter of the text seems to indicate. In light of all this he repeats his point that the condemnation of such articles hinders students in their pursuit of studies.[65]

He then turns to the second point of his major premise—that the condemnation of such articles serves as an occasion of scandal among those pursuing studies, including both teachers (*doctores*) and students (*auditores*). Because it is necessary to explain some of them against what appears to be the letter of the text, although not against the truth and not against the intention those who issued them should have had in mind, some less skilled and simple souls think that those who do so explain them are thereby automatically excommunicated and denounce (lit. "delate") good and serious men to the Chancellor or the Bishop as marked (*notatos*) with excommunication and error. And as a result many unseemly situations and divisions arise among the students.[66]

And then, to seal his case, as it were, Godfrey turns to the third point in his major premise. He notes that the condemnation of such articles does no small harm to the extremely useful teaching of Brother Thomas [Aquinas] which is less justly defamed in some way by them. This is because the articles he has mentioned above and many others seem to have been taken from what Thomas has written in his so useful and solemn teaching. Godfrey laments that many simpler souls, seeing that such articles have been condemned as erroneous, hold Thomas's doctrine as suspect. And thus many could be led to withdraw from studying his teaching. Not only would this be injurious to that doctrine itself, but students themselves would thereby suffer the greatest loss. To support this point Godfrey then heaps words of highest praise on Thomas's teaching.[67]

Godfrey also criticizes a certain great Doctor who, in the course of determining a difficult topic and not finding other effective arguments for his position, attempts to strengthen his determination by citing such articles. Godfrey repeats his point that among those articles there are many about which it is not at all clear that they are erroneous and that it is permissible to hold contrary views concerning them. He also comments that these laws bind in only one place and should not be regarded as general laws which apply to the whole world and which might be used to determine such questions.[68]

And in finally answering the question directly posed for his determination, he responds that the current Bishop of Paris, while eminently learned in both canon and civil law and sufficiently so in theology, is not so expert in that field that he would not need to consult the Masters of theology about these articles. Since they themselves are not in agreement concerning them, the bishop can in some way be excused for not correcting them. But since he could now remove the penalty (excommunication) attached to these articles without endangering the peace and to the benefit of many, Godfrey does not see how he can be excused for not doing this. Still, Godfrey does not dare condemn him, but repeats the point that the articles in question should be corrected.[69]

Godfrey's response to the opening argument for the opposite position is worth mentioning. According to that argument, in an evident reference to Bishop Stephen's introductory letter, the Bishop had taken this action with the consent of wise men.[70] In responding Godfrey is somewhat conciliatory and grants that while the articles were drawn up by wise men, nonetheless, it seems that now they should be corrected. Those who originally produced the articles can be reasonably excused because at that time many, especially from the faculty of Arts, were involving themselves excessively with the subjects covered by the articles and without exercising restraint, so much so that their statements seemed to incline greatly toward errors. Because of that extreme situation, it was necessary to tend more toward the opposite extreme in correcting such excesses. Thus it was necessary to condemn certain things which can have a good and sound meaning but which can also be given another bad interpretation, so that the parties involved might strive all the more to withdraw from anything erroneous concerning such matters and to hold to what is true. But now, some twenty years later, Godfrey judges that things have changed and the truth concerning these matters has become more manifest. Therefore many of the aforementioned articles could now be corrected without impeding truth and without any negative reflection on those who originally produced them.[71]

IX. *QUODLIBET* XIII, Q. 3 = ART. 212 / 74

This question, dating from the following academic year (1297/1298), gives no indication that Godfrey's advice was heeded in any way by the Bishop. Indeed, all the evidence indicates that it was not, since it would not be until after Aquinas's canonization that a future Bishop of Paris, Stephen of Bourret, would in 1325 revoke the condemnations insofar as they touched on or were said to touch on the teaching of Thomas.[72] Godfrey refers again to the Condemnation in *Quodlibet* XIII on two occasions. In q. 3 he was asked to determine whether some created substance by itself and without the addition of anything else could be the immediate principle of some operation, and especially of a transitive operation. Godfrey begins by repeating his long-held position that no created substance can be immediately operative or, as he puts it here, the immediate principle of any operation or perfection that exists within it either by operating by itself or by means of something added to itself. Because the substance itself, even with something added to itself, lacks such an act or perfection, it serves as a subject and therefore as something in potency with respect to it. Therefore it cannot be the agent or the efficient cause of that act or perfection. Otherwise one and the same thing would be in act and in potency (simultaneously) with respect to the same thing, and would be active and passive with respect to itself.[73]

After considerable discussion and refutation of other positions concerning the more general issue, Godfrey returns to the question of angelic causality of transitive operations. He notes that he has previously considered whether the intellect and will of an angel are sufficient for production of this kind of operation, or whether it is necessary to posit some third and additional power, a *virtus motiva,* and that in that discussion he had touched on two different opinions concerning this. Nevertheless, here he concludes that, unless a certain article condemned by the Bishop of Paris eliminates this view, the intellect and will of an angel are sufficient to enable it to cause local motion or to move some body locally. And he adds that the article in question may be explained as he has done elsewhere.[74]

This is curious because, as we have seen above in section I, in *Quodlibet* V, q. 6 he was heavily influenced by the condemnation of art. 212/74, which asserts that an intelligence moves the heaven by its will alone. There Godfrey had concluded that because he did not want to speak against the prohibition of the article, and because it seems to be true of God alone that to will is to act, one should posit in angels a motive or executive power in addition to the intellect and the will in order to account for their moving heavenly bodies. Now he more openly favors the view that there is no need to postulate such a third power in angels, and suggests that the condemned article be dealt with as he had already done elsewhere. This final remark can hardly refer to his discussion in *Quodlibet* V, q. 6, since there he had ultimately simply deferred to the prohibited article. Perhaps he has in mind another discussion of this, one which has not survived or remains unknown to us. Or perhaps he is thinking of his more general view as expressed in *Quodlibet* XII, q. 5 to the effect that many of the condemned articles should be corrected and that, until that happens, some of them have to be given a quasi-forced and extorted meaning. In any event, his discussion here confirms what we had already sensed while examining his earlier discussion of angelic causation of local motion in *Quodlibet* V, q. 6. He really does personally prefer the view that would not assign a third and motive power to angels unless, as he puts it here, "a certain article condemned by the Bishop of Paris stands in the way."[75]

X. *QUODLIBET* XIII, Q. 4 = 204 / 219

In this question Godfrey was asked to determine whether an angel could in some way be present simultaneously in many places. An opening argument *sed contra* reasons that what is not of such a nature as to be in place at all cannot be in many places. But an angel is not in place at all because its operation cannot be its reason for its being in place, as a certain article states (art. 204/55). Likewise, according to another article (219/54), its substance is not its reason for being in place.[76]

After showing that an angel is not in place in the same way bodies are,[77] Godfrey comments that one might conclude from this with certain great *doctores* (i.e., Thomas Aquinas) that an angel is not in place *per se* but only *per accidens* by operating therein. But the present question does not ask how an angel is in place but rather, however it may be in place, whether it can be in many places simultaneously. Godfrey comments that certain articles seem to say that an angel is present in place *per se* since it is not present there by operating therein, but by its substance. Without attempting to resolve that issue, he proposes to show that however a body or an angel may be thought to be present in place *per se,* neither can be present *per se* in different places simultaneously. After establishing this at some length with respect to bodies,[78] he draws the same conclusion with respect to angels. If an angel is in place *per se,* it cannot be present in different places *per se* simultaneously.[79] And if it can be in place *per accidens* by operating therein, he concludes that it cannot be present in different places *per accidens* simultaneously by operating on different bodies located in place.[80]

Godfrey also considers the possibility that an angel might be in many places simultaneously *per accidens* in a different way, because different bodies that are present in place *per se* might be changed into the substance of the angel. As Godfrey recalls here, he had previously (in *Quodlibet* V, q. 1) considered the possibility of such a transubstantiation of a spiritual or angelic nature into a corporeal substance, or of a corporeal substance into an angel. Because Godfrey does not want to detract in any way from divine power, he does not absolutely rule out this possibility. But as in his earlier discussion of this, he does not understand how any such view can be supported and, without asserting anything absolutely, concludes that it is probable that this kind of change or transubstantiation is not possible. Hence it also seem probable that an angel cannot simultaneously be present *per accidens* in different places even in this way.[81]

As for the opening argument *sed contra,* Godfrey says this is of little concern to the present issue, since without determining whether or how an angel is present in place, the question can be answered adequately. Moreover, it is difficult to determine the issue concerning whether and how an angel is in place because of articles concerning this which have been condemned, which seem to be contrary to one another. Here again he is clearly referring to articles 204/55 and 219/54, and he concludes: "against which [articles] I intend to say nothing because of the danger of excommunication."[82]

This is his last word about the 1277 Condemnation, so far as I am aware. Even at this relatively late date, some twenty years or more after the event, Godfrey still takes very seriously the penalty of excommunication attaching to those who would violate the Paris prohibition by teaching the condemned articles.

———

From Godfrey's various discussions of and reactions to the Condemnation of 1277, we may draw some brief conclusions. First, it cannot be denied that the condemnation had an inhibiting impact on the teaching of theology at the University of Paris in the final quarter of the thirteenth century. The danger of excommunication for those who taught or even heard any of the condemned articles being taught was taken quite seriously.

Second, it is evident that Godfrey had particular difficulties with a number of the condemned articles. Thus he did not hesitate to point out inconsistencies and incoherences between some of them. With respect to those dealing with human volition, he was pleased to cite the *propositio magistralis* as carrying greater interpretative authority than any condemned articles that might be incompatible with it. And by the time of his *Quodlibet* XII, he was convinced that some of the condemned articles should be revised by the then ruling Bishop of Paris.

Finally, Godfrey states that a number of the condemned articles seem to have been taken from the writings of Thomas Aquinas. His usage of the term "seems" need not be taken as implying that he had any real doubt about this. He clearly regards the implication of Thomas's doctrine in the Condemnation as unjustified. He regrets that this has caused simpler souls among the students to regard that doctrine as suspect, and that it might deter them from studying it. If he had really doubted that Thomas's teaching was directly targeted by the Condemnation, he would have surely made that point in defending it. The fact that he did not make any such claim is telling.

NOTES

1. Rolande Hissette, *Enquête sur les 219 articles condamnés à Paris le 7 mars 1277* (Louvain: Publications Universitaires, 1977). Shortly before the appearance of Hissette's book I myself had completed an article on this topic, "The Condemnations of 1270 and 1277 at Paris," *The Journal of Medieval and Renaissance Studies* 7 (1977): 169–201. Subsequent book-length studies on this topic include Luca Bianchi, *Il vescove e i filosofi: La condanna parigina del 1277 e l'evoluzione dell'Aristotelismo scolastico* (Bergamo: Pierluigi Lubrina, 1990); K. Flasch, *Aufklärung im Mittelalter? Die Verurteilung von 1277* (Mainz: Dieterich, 1989). Bianchi also devotes considerable attention to this event in his recently published *Censure et liberté intellectuelle à l'université de Paris (XIIIe–XIVe siècles)* (Paris: Les Belles Lettres, 1999). For references to the many articles treating this topic which have appeared since 1977, see the bibliography in Bianchi's last-mentioned book, and that given by D. Piché (see n. 2 below).

2. David Piché, *La condamnation parisienne de 1277: Texte latin, traduction, introduction et commentaire* (Paris: J. Vrin, 1999).

3. John Wippel, "Godfrey of Fontaines at the University of Paris in the Last Quarter of the 13th Century," *Nach der Verurteilung von 1277: Philosophie und theologie an der Universität von Paris im letzten Viertel des 13. Jahrhunderts, Studien und Texte,* ed. J. Aertsen, K. Emery, and A. Speer, Miscellanea Medievalia 28 (Berlin-New York: Walter de Gruyter, 2001). For more details on Godfrey's life and writings also see my *The Metaphysical Thought of Godfrey of Fontaines: A Study in Late Thirteenth-Century Philosophy* (Washington, DC: Catholic University of America Press, 1981), xi–xxxiv. Also see M. De Wulf, *Un théologien-philosophe du XIIIe siècle: Étude sur la vie, les oeuvres et l'influence de Godefroid de Fontaines* (Brussels: Hayes, 1904).

4. See J. Duin, "La bibliothèque philosophique de Godefroid de Fontaines," *Estudios Lulianos* 3 (1959): 21–36, 137–160; and my "Godfrey of Fontaines at the University of Paris," as cited in n. 3 above.

5. In addition to my article cited above in n. 1, see my "Thomas Aquinas and the Condemnation of 1277," *The Modern Schoolman* 72 (1995): 233–72, and my *Mediaeval Reactions to the Encounter between Faith and Reason* (Milwaukee: Marquette University Press, 1995). In addition to his book, Hissette has returned to this issue on many occasions. See, for instance, his "Albert le Grand et Thomas d'Aquin dans la censure parisienne du 7 mars 1277," in *Miscellanea Mediaevalia* 15 (1982): 222–46; "L'implication de Thomas d'Aquin dans les censures parisiennes de 1277," *Recherches de Théologie et Philosophie médiévales* 64 (1997): 3–31; "Thomas d'Aquin directement visé par la censure du 7 mars 1277? Réponse à John F. Wippel," in *Roma, Magistra Mundi: Itineraria culturae medievalis. Mélanges offerts au Père L.E. Boyle à l'occasion de son 75e anniversaire* (Louvain-la-Neuve: Fédération Internationale des Instituts d'Études Médiévales, 1998), 425–37.

6. For the dating of Godfrey's *Quodlibets* see my *The Metaphysical Thought of Godfrey of Fontaines,* xxiii–xxviii. In citing the prohibited propositions I will follow the text just edited by Piché, *La condamnation parisienne,* 72–147. As regards the numbering of the propositions, he follows the order and numbering of the *Chartularium Universitatis Parisiensis* 1 (Paris, 1889), 543–58, and so shall I, although I will also list the corresponding numbers in the rearranged systematic version published by P. Mandonnet in his *Siger de Brabant et l'Averroïsme latin au XIIIe siècle,* 2nd ed., 2 vols. (Louvain: Institut Supérieur de Philosophie de l'Université, 1908–1911), 2:175–91.

7. *Les Quodlibet Cinq, Six et Sept de Godefroid de Fontaines,* ed. M. De Wulf and J. Hoffmans, Les Philosophes Belges 3 (Louvain: Institut Supérieur de Philosophie de l'Université, 1914), 21 (hereafter *PB*).

8. *PB* 3.22.

9. *PB* 3.22–23.

10. *PB* 3.22–23. Note his reference to this article as "inter articulos condemnatos."

11. *PB* 3.23–24. Note: "Sed quia contra articulum dicere non intendo" (*PB* 3.23). Also note his remark near the end of this discussion: "Sed ponetur talis virtus proxime et immediate motiva propter ordinem potentiarum, quia scilicet apprehendere et appetere motum vel rem movere vel imperare quod corpus aliquod moveatur non sufficit, sed requiritur tertia potentia executiva per eius actum sic apprehensi et imperati." (*PB* 3.24).

12. *PB* 3.238.

13. *PB* 3.238–39. For Henry see his *Quodlibet* IV, q. 17, in *Quodlibeta Magistri Henrici Goethals a Gandavo Doctoris Solemnis* (Paris: I. Badius, 1518), 1:132rv. Henry also refers there to his earlier discussion of angelic presence in place, for which see his *Quodlibet II,* q. 9, ed. R. Wielockx (Leuven: Leuven University Press, 1983), 58–72.

14. *PB* 3.239–240.

15. *PB* 3.240. Note in particular: " . . . si autem aliquid efficit per huiusmodi operationem non differret ille modus ab illo modo qui non sufficit articulo condemnato." For the condemned proposition see 204–55: "Quod substantiae separatae sunt alicubi per operationem; et quod non possunt moveri ab extremo in extremum, nec in medium, nisi quia possunt velle operari aut in medio, aut in extremis.—Error, si intelligatur sine operatione substantiam non esse in loco, nec transire de loco ad locum" (Piché, 140).

16. *PB* 3.244: "Qualis autem modus ponendi angelum esse in loco et moveri secundum locum praeter istum et praeter illum alium qui non sufficit secundum articulum episcopi sit conveniens non est praesentis speculationis; nec ego etiam scio illum." Even though he was a member of Tempier's commission charged with drawing up the list of prohibited propositions, Henry of Ghent also had difficulty in reconciling the prohibition of proposition 204 with that of proposition 219/54: "Quod substantiae separatae nusquam sunt secundum substantiam.— Error, si intelligatur quod substantia non sit in loco. Si autem intelligatur ita quod substantia sit ratio essendi in loco, verum est quod nusquam sunt secundum substantiam" (Piché, 146). See Henry's *Quodlibet II*, q. 9, 61–65 (an angel's substance cannot be the explanation for its presence in place); 65–67 (on its powers of intellect and will as a possible explanation); 67–72, esp. 70 (on his puzzlement as to what may account for its presence in place when it does not operate there). Also see his reference to proposition 204 in *Quodlibet* IV, q. 17 (1:232v).

17. *PB* 3.254: "Deinde circa naturam corporis humani quaerebatur unum, scilicet si corpus aliquod humanum resurgeret sine quantitate, utrum esset idem corpus numero quod prius fuit."

18. *PB* 3.255–56.

19. *PB* 3.256. See my *Metaphysical Thought of Godfrey*, 25–26, 353–55.

20. *PB* 3.256–57.

21. *PB* 3.258–59.

22. *PB* 3.258.

23. *PB* 3.258–59. Here Godfrey offers some additional precisions concerning the nature of quantity which are important for his theory of individuation. See my *Metaphysical Thought of Godfrey*, 353–54.

24. *PB* 3.259.

25. *PB* 3.259. Note: "Quantumcumque tamen sit difficile hoc intelligere, tamen de animabus simpliciter hoc est tenendum; sed magis est difficile intelligere quomodo possunt esse plures angeli numero differentes; quod tamen hoc sit possibile non est omnino negandum secundum quod dicit quidam articulus quo contrarium condemnatur." See art. 81/43: "Quod, quia intelligentiae non habent materiam, Deus non posset plures eiusdem speciei facere"; 96/42: "Quod Deus non potest multiplicare individua sub una specie sine materia." Also see his reference to this in *Quodlibet* VII, q. 5 within the context of his discussion of the individuation of material substances: "Ex his etiam patet quod in separatis a materia quantitati subiecta non potest esse individuatio sive divisio speciei vel formae specificae in plura individua solo numero differentia dicto modo. Si autem possit fieri alio modo non intelligo; sed tamen non nego" (*PB* 3.329). Because he has rejected matter-form composition of angels, he has eliminated the possibility of accounting for their multiplication within species by any appeal to matter and quantity. But his desire not to contradict the prohibited articles prevents him from absolutely denying that angels could be so multiplied. Cf. my *Metaphysical Thought of Godfrey*, 366–69.

26. *PB* 3.377.

27. *PB* 3.378–79, and for more details, 380–82. Here Godfrey has in mind *Posterior Analytics* 1.1 (on the need for precognition) and Bk 2.1–2 (on four kinds of questions which may be raised

about our knowledge of something). For discussion see my *Metaphysical Thought of Godfrey*, 106–10. For some similarities and differences between Godfrey's discussion and that found in Henry of Ghent's *Summae quaestionum ordinariarum*, a. 24, q. 3 (Paris: 1520), ff. 138r–138v, see 107, §19.

28. *PB* 3.383–384. Note that here Godfrey is considering the kind of knowledge of God that is available to us in this life. As regards that granted to those enjoying the beatific vision, it is by one and the same knowledge that they know that he is and what he is (see 382–83). For Thomas on this, see for instance, *ST* 1.3.4. ad 2m (ed. Leonina 4:42); *De potentia* 7.2. ad 1m, ed. P. M. Pession (Turin-Rome: Marietti, 1965), 191–92.

29. *PB* 3.383–86. Note: "Ergo manifestum est quod talia de Deo cognoscendo cognoscimus de eo quid est et cetera" (386). Cf. my *Metaphysical Thought of Godfrey*, 112–14.

30. *PB* 3.386. "Et ex praemissis patet quomodo intelligendi sunt quidam articuli ab Episcopo Parisiensi condemnati quae tamen praedictis contrarii videntur. Unus enim sic dicit: Deum in hac vita intelligere possumus per essentiam; error alius dicit: de Deo non potest cognosci nisi quia est sive ipsum esse." Compare with Piché's edition: "Quod de deo non potest cognosci, nisi quia <ipse> est, sive ipsum esse" (215/10); "Quod deum in hac vita mortali possumus intelligere per essentiam" (36/9).

31. *PB* 3.386.

32. *PB* 3.402–03. Note: " . . . dicendum quod praecepta affirmativa quae sunt de bonis faciendis sub quibus cadit actus docendi veritatem obligant semper, sed non ad semper" (403).

33. *PB* 3.403.

34. *PB* 3.404. Cf. N. Gaughan, "Godfrey of Fontaines—An Independent Thinker," *American Ecclesiastical Review* 157 (1967): 43–54, esp. 50–51. Also see De Wulf, *Un théologien-philosophe*, 40–41.

35. *PB* 3.404–05. See L. Bianchi, "Censure, liberté et progrès intellectuel à l'université de Paris au XIIIe siècle," *Archives d'Histoire doctrinale et littéraire du moyen âge* 63 (1996): 92; F. X. Putallaz, *Insolente liberté: Controverses et condamnations au XIIIe siècle* (Fribourg: Éditions universitaires/Paris: Éditions du Cerf, 1995), 168–70.

36. From Tempier's text note: " . . . districte talia et similia fieri prohibemus et ea totaliter condemnamus, excommunicantes omnes illos qui dictos errores vel aliquem de eisdem dogmatizaverint aut deffendere seu sustinere praesumpserint quoquomodo, necnon auditores, nisi infra septem dies nobis vel cancellario parisiensi duxerint revelandum, nihilominus contra eos processuri pro qualitate culpae ad poenas alias, prout ius dictaverit, infligendas" (Piché ed., 74–76). Both De Wulf (40–41) and Gaughan (48–49) take this question as referring to Tempier's Condemnation of March 7, 1277. However, Bianchi has also suggested that Tempier may not have intended to condemn the articles themselves, but merely to prohibit their being taught. He argues that in the text just cited the words "ea totaliter condemnamus" refer not to the articles themselves but to the "behaviors previously described." See his "1277: A Turning Point?" in *Was ist Philosophie im Mittelalter?* Miscellanea Mediaevalia 26 (Berlin-New York: Walter de Gruyter, 1998): 93–95, and 93, n. 12. He acknowledges that Tempier's action was interpreted as a condemnation by late-medieval philosophers and theologians, and mentions Richard of Middleton, Scotus, Bradwardine, Gerson, and "many others" (95–96). Godfrey clearly thinks that the articles were condemned by Tempier (see above, nn. 10, 15, 25, 30, and texts to be cited below). Tempier's introductory letter has already referred to certain "studentes in artibus" who dare to expose and dispute as debatable ("dubitabiles") in their schools "quosdam manifestos et execrabiles errores, immo potius vanitates et insanias falsas," meaning thereby the attached articles. To identify them as errors is not to approve of them and, it seems to me, is to condemn them at the very least as false. Moreover, on February 14, 1325, Bishop Stephen Bourret annulled the

"supradictam articulorum condemnationem et excommunicationis sententiam" insofar as they touch on or are asserted to touch on Thomas Aquinas's teaching (*Chartularium Universitatis Parisiensis* 2:281, §838). Hence I am inclined to think that Godfrey, those mentioned by Bianchi, and Bishop Stephen Bourret himself were correct in concluding that Tempier had *condemned* the prohibited articles.

37. *PB* 4.140.

38. Controlling much of Godfrey's thinking on this issue is his unbending acceptance of the Aristotelian theory of act and potency and his conviction that nothing can be in act and potency at the same time with respect to the same thing, or that whatever is moved is moved by something else. For his defense of this principle see my "Godfrey of Fontaines and the Act-Potency Axiom," *Journal of the History of Philosophy* 11 (1973): 299–37. For his application of this to volition see my *Metaphysical Thought of Godfrey*, 199–202; De Wulf, *Un théologien-philosophe*, 104–12; O. Lottin, "Le libre arbitre chez Godefroid de Fontaines," *Revue Néoscolastique de Philosophie* 40 (1937): 213–41; O. Lottin, "Le thomisme de Godefroid de Fontaines en matière de libre arbitre," 554–73; O. Lottin, *Psychologie et morale au XIIe et XIIIe siècles 1: Problèmes de Psychologie* (Louvain: Abbaye du Mont César and Gembloux: J. Duculot, 1942), 304–39 (substantially the same as the two articles just cited); F.X. Putallaz, *Insolente liberté: Controverses et condamnations au XIIIe siècle* (Fribourg: Éditions Universitaires/Paris: Cerf, 1995), 177–87, 198–08 (with special attention to the controversies on this between Godfrey and Henry of Ghent), 225–48 (on Godfrey's *Quodlibet* VIII, q. 16 and his critique of Giles of Rome, as well as on Siger of Brabant's influence on Godfrey).

39. See *PB* 4.149–50, 155–56, 160 (freedom in the formal sense is to be attributed to the intellect as well as to the will because of the soul's immaterial nature); the intellect, or that which is apprehended by the intellect, serves as a moving principle with respect to the will (150) or as the *per se* cause of the act of volition (169); the will cannot determine itself (151–53). See p. 164: "Similiter etiam deliberando de eo quod est volendum propter finem, facta conclusione et stante tali apprehensione, voluntas non potest illud non velle; et tamen dicetur quod illud velit libere et laudabiliter et meritorie non obstante tali immutabilitate voluntatis." In the immediatelly following context (164–65) he goes on to show: "Ex his ergo patet quomodo salvari potest libertas voluntatis in eligendo id quod est ad finem post conclusionem factam per consilium rationis deliberantis absque hoc quod oporteat ponere quod possit agere oppositum, stante dicta notitia determinata ex principio aliquo propter se volito. Semper enim electio voluntatis est conformis iudicio rationis deliberantis sive in bonum sive in malum." Cf. pp. 169–70 (in every act of the will the *per se* cause is the intellect or what is apprehended by the intellect). For discussion of Thomas's view on this see Lottin, *Psychologie et morale*, 226–43, 252–62; my "Thomas Aquinas and the Condemnation of 1277," 255–60; D. Gallagher, "Free Choice and Free Judgment in Thomas Aquinas," *Archiv für Geschichte der Philosophie* 76 (1994): 247–77. On Siger see Putallaz, *Insolente liberté*, 16–45, and the references given there.

40. Art. 130/166: "Quod si ratio recta, et voluntas recta.—Error, quia contra glossam Augustini super illud psalmi: 'Concupivit anima mea desiderare', etc., et quia secundum hoc, ad rectitudinem voluntatis non esset necessaria gratia, sed solum scientia, quod fuit error Pelagii;" Art. 163/163: "Quod voluntas necessario prosequitur quod firmiter creditum est a ratione: et quod non potest abstinere ab eo quod ratio dictat. Haec autem necessitatio non est coactio, sed natura voluntatis." Art. 129/169: "Quod voluntas, manente passione et scientia particulari in actu, non potest agere contra eam."

41. *PB* 4.165–66: "Et hoc patet etiam ex hoc quod ab omnibus doctoribus in theologia concessum est quod haec propositio est vera et tenenda secundum quod verba eius sonant et prae-

tendunt, scilicet quod non est malitia in voluntate nisi sit error vel nescientia in ratione. Haec enim propositio non posset habere veritatem si contra iudicium rationis posset esse electio voluntatis. Propter quod etiam quidam articuli ab episcopo reprobati, ante approbationem tamen huius propositionis, qui videntur contrariari huic propositioni, sunt sic exponendi quod huic propositioni, prout fieri potest, concordent."

42. R. Wielockx, *Aegidii Romani Opera Omnia III.1. Apologia* (Firenze: Leo S. Olschki, 1985), 77–81, 91, 108. Also see Putallaz, *Insolente liberté,* 212–18; B. Kent, *Virtues of the Will: The Transformation of Ethics in the Late Thirteenth Century* (Washington, DC: Catholic University of America Press, 1995), 76–81.

43. For Godfrey's citation see n. 41 above. For *Quodlibet* XII, q. 5, see section VIII here.

44. *PB* 4.216.

45. *PB* 4.217. For some foreshadowing of this as applied to accidents (quantity and quality) see *Quodlibet* II, q. 10 (*PB* 2.145). For discussion see my "Godfrey of Fontaines on Intension and Remission of Accidental Forms," *Franciscan Studies* 39 (1979): 332–33. For Disputed Question 18 see the same, 333–34, 337–39 (as applied to substances), 339–41 (as applied to accidents), and 343 (on *Quodlibet* IX, q. 4).

46. *PB* 4.217. Note his remark concerning the human soul: "Et sic enim videretur de anima, nisi possit dici aliud de ipsa, quia scilicet aliquo modo materialis est in quantum est naturalis perfectio materiae secundum quam contingit transmutatio." For his earlier treatment in Disputed Question 18 see n. 45 above.

47. *PB* 4.217–18.

48. *PB* 4.218. "Circa hoc autem est intelligendum quod articulo ab episcopo condemnato non intendo contradicere, tamen propter modum eius loquendi non videtur debere facere aliquam fidem in proposito, quia sive sint gradus secundum magis et minus in forma substantiali etiam quae est anima humana, sive non sint gradus, nihil ad hoc quod possit concludi animam Christi esse nobiliorem anima Iudae."

49. *PB* 4.218–19.

50. *PB* 4.219: "Primus dicit sic: inconveniens est ponere aliquos intellectus nobiliores aliis, quia cum ista diversitas non sit [Piché: possit esse] a parte corporum, oportet quod sit a parte intelligentiarum; et sic animae nobiles et ignobiles essent necessario diversarum specierum sicut intelligentiae. Error: quia sic anima Christi non esset nobilior anima Iudae" (art. 124/147); "Alius dicit sic: quod nos peius vel melius intelligimus, hoc provenit ex intellectu passivo, qui dicitur [Piché: quem dicit] esse potentia[m] sensitiva[m]. Error: quia hoc ponit intellectum unum in omnibus aut aequalitatem in omnibus animabus."

51. *PB* 4.220–21.

52. *PB* 4.222.

53. *PB* 4.222. See 218.

54. *PB* 5.100. Also see *PB* 5.95, where this question was already announced. On this see De Wulf, *Un théologien-philosophe,* 42–47; M.-H. Laurent, "Godefroid de Fontaines et la condamnation de 1277," *Revue thomiste* 5 (1930): 273–81 (for another edition of the text); Gaughan, "Godfrey of Fontaines," 53; Wippel, *Metaphysical Thought of Godfrey,* 382–85; S. Brown, "Godfrey of Fontaines and Henry of Ghent: Individuation and the Condemnations of 1277," *Société et Église: Textes et discussions dans les universités d'Europe centrale pendant le moyen âge tardif* (Turnhout: Brepols, 1995), 193–07; Putallaz, *Insolente liberté,* 217–23.

55. *PB* 5.100.

56. Ibid.

57. Ibid. Note concerning the last point: "Item sunt aliqui qui secundum quod superficies literae sonat, videntur omnino impossibiles et irrationabiles, propter quod oportet illos exponere expositione quasi violenta et extorta."

58. *PB* 5.101: "Articulus enim quo pro errore condemnatur quod Deus non posset multiplicare plura individua sub una specie sine materia. Item alius qui ex isto sequitur quod Deus non posset facere plures intelligentias eiusdem speciei, quia non habent materiam, viderentur posse pro opinabilibus reputari cum haec a pluribus catholocis doctoribus sint dicta et scripta." For the original articles see n. 25 above.

59. Ibid. See n. 50 above for the original version.

60. *PB* 5.101: "De istis et de pluribus aliis inter dictos articulos pro erroneis condemnatis videtur literatis et peritis quod posset licite opinari."

61. Ibid. Note Godfrey's comment: "Sed in istis videtur esse contradictio: quia inter cognitionem de aliquo quia est et quid est vel per essentiam medium non videtur." For the original version of these two articles, see n. 30 above.

62. *PB* 5.101–02. In citing these two articles, Godfrey has abbreviated them considerably. For the original texts, see nn. 15 and 16 above.

63. *PB* 5.102. Note: "Hic etiam apparet contradictio quia non bene potest assignari medium inter ista duo, scilicet quod nec substantia angeli sit angelo ratio essendi in loco nec etiam eius operatio, quia si substantia angeli non sit ratio essendi in loco, eadem ratione nec potentia angeli vel quaecumque proprietas eius in ipso formaliter existens poterit esse ratio essendi in loco." Then Godfrey generalizes: "Consimiliter etiam de pluribus aliis articulis praedictis potest dici quod in ipsis et inter ipsos videntur incompossibilia implicari."

64. Ibid. The full text of art. 160/101 reads: "Quod nullum agens est ad utrumlibet, immo determinatur" (Piché ed.). For the original texts for the others see n. 40 above.

65. Ibid.

66. Ibid. Note especially: ". . . aliqui minus periti et simplices reputant sic exponentes excommunicatos, et formant sibi conscientias quod tales male sentiunt; et tales simplices bonos et graves tanquam notatos de excommunicatione et errore cancellario vel episcopo deferunt."

67. *PB* 5.102–3. Note: "Sunt etiam in detrimentum non modicum doctrinae studentibus perutilis reverendissimi et excellentissimi doctoris scilicet Fratris Thomae, quae ex praedictis articulis minus iuste aliqualiter diffamatur. Quia articuli supra positi et quam plures alii videntur sumpti esse ex his, quae tantus doctor scripsit in doctrina tam utili et solemni. Et ideo in hoc quod tales articuli tanquam erronei reprobantur, dicta doctrina etiam suspecta a simplicioribus habetur, quia tanquam erronea et reprobabilis innuitur. Propter quod plures possent habere occasionem retrahendi se a studio in tali doctrina, in quo non solum ipsa doctrina laederetur, sed ipsi studentes vere damnum maximum sustinerent, quia, salva reverentia aliquorum doctorum, excepta doctrina sanctorum, et eorum quorum dicta pro auctoritatibus allegantur, praedicta doctrina inter ceteras videtur utilior et laudabalior reputanda, ut vere doctori qui hanc doctrinam scripsit, possit dici in singulari illud quod Dominus dixit in plurali apostolis, Matth., quinto: 'Vos estis sal terrae'; et cetera, sub hac forma: 'Tu es sal terrae, quod si sal evanuerit, in quo salietur?' Quia per ea quae in hac doctrina continentur quasi omnium doctorum aliorum doctrinae corriguntur, sapidae redduntur et condiuntur; et ideo si ista doctrina de medio auferretur, studentes in doctrinis aliorum saporem modicum invenirent."

68. *PB* 5.103.

69. Ibid.

70. *PB* 5.100.

71. *PB* 5.103–4. Note especially: "Nunc autem circa illa magis est veritas declarata. Et ideo posset fieri correctio circa praedictos articulos quantum ad plures absque impedimento veritatis et absque confusione illorum qui eos ediderunt."

72. *Chartularium Universitatis Parisiensis* (2:281): ". . . supradictam articulorum condemnationem et excommunicationis sententiam, quantum tangunt vel tangere asseruntur doctrinam beati Thomae praedicti . . . totaliter annullamus, articulos ipsos propter hoc non approbando seu etiam reprobando, sed eosdem discussioni scolasticae libere relinquendo" (281). As Brown has pointed out, "Godfrey finally got what he wanted" ("Godfrey of Fontaines," 207). Unfortunately, he had already died in 1306/1309.

73. *PB* 5.191. For fuller discussion of Godfrey's general position on this see my *Metaphysical Thought of Godfrey*, 184–202.

74. For his discussion of the general issue concerning see *PB* 5.191–205. For his response to the question concerning angelic causation of local motion see 206. Note his concluding remarks with reference to this: "Ergo videtur quod in angelis sufficient etiam intellectus et voluntas ad movendum localiter aliquod corpus suae virtuti proportionatum. Et potest exponi dictus articulus sicut alibi est expositus."

75. *PB* 5.206: "Videretur tamen quod, nisi obstaret quidam articulus a Parisiensi Episcopo condemnatus, posset dici quod ad causandum motum localem sufficit intellectus et voluntas in angelis."

76. *PB* 5.213–14.

77. *PB* 5.214–15.

78. *PB* 5.215–17.

79. *PB* 5.220.

80. *PB* 5.220.

81. *PB* 5.220. For discussion of his earlier treatment of this in *Quodlibet* V, q. 1, see my "Some Issues concerning Divine Power and Created Natures according to Godfrey of Fontaines," in *Diakonia: Studies in Honor of Robert T. Meyer*, ed. T. Halton and J. P. Williman (Washington, DC: Catholic University of America Press, 1986), 160–70. Cf. *Quodlibet* V, q. 1 (*PB* 3:6): "Super hoc tamen nihil assero, quia quae divinae potentiae sunt subiecta, non potest humanus intellectus perscrutari."

82. *PB* 5.221: "Hoc etiam est difficile determinare propter articulos circa hoc condemnatos, quia contrarii videntur ad invicem; et contra quos nihil intendo dicere propter periculum excommunicationis."

Chapter 11

Franciscan Attitudes toward Philosophy

1274–1300

TIMOTHY B. NOONE

Franciscans figured prominently in the events leading up to the condemnation of 1277: St. Bonaventure's delivery of the series of *Collationes* on the gifts of the Holy Spirit, the ten commandments, and the work of creation was a precursor in many ways of the views that were to triumph in the condemnatory documents; John Peckham's writings on the eternity of the world as well as his interchanges with St. Thomas regarding the plurality of forms were also telling indicators of what was to come. Yet the effect of the condemnation upon all parties, including Franciscans, was mixed and complicated.

The recent publication of a set of specialized studies devoted to the condemnation of 1277 shows that there is little general agreement as to what the positive and negative effects of it were.[1] Pierre Duhem, the leading historian of science in the first third of the twentieth century and a trained physicist, proposed that the condemnations of 1270 and 1277 were—however repressive—ultimately beneficial in their consequences since they encouraged philosophers and scientists to develop a non-Aristotelian account of the natural world and thus paved the way, indirectly, for modern science.[2] The recently published studies are nearly unanimous in rejecting either the entirety of Duhem's thesis or substantial parts of it.[3] But, to the extent that recent historical study has shown the persistence of "Latin Averroism" at Paris and its environs after 1277, the views of de Libera and Bianchi regarding the repression of intellectuals and the suggestion that the freedom that philosophy requires for its proper development was absent there seem to be in need of qualification also.[4] Furthermore, Msgr. John Wippel's study of Godfrey of Fontaines indicating the latter's occasional disregard of certain of the condemned articles as well as his efforts to reinterpret others (or call their juridical force into question) leads one to wonder just how repressive the atmosphere could have been in the Paris of the 1280s and 90s.[5] Perhaps most curious of all, Henry of Ghent, who sat on the commission that drafted the condemned articles for consideration by Bishop Etienne Tempier, is now known to have felt the ill consequences of its aftermath himself since shortly after the condemnation he was put under ecclesiastical pressure to redact his first *Quodlibet* in a manner that more clearly supported the plurality of forms, a thesis in some sense promoted by several of the condemned articles.[6]

If such complications are to be found in the effects of the condemnations upon secular masters of theology, even more are to be found among the Franciscans. In many ways one would expect that the Franciscans were the beneficiaries of the condemnations and that their doctrinal views would be unaffected by the events of 1277. But, as we have seen, matters were not so simple, even for a partisan such as Henry of Ghent. For one thing, the articles—there were 219 of them—did not form any coherent system or express a single viewpoint; thus, one could fall afoul of them relatively easily without meaning to do so. In general I would suggest that, in the case of the Franciscans in whom we are interested, there was a tendency for the condemned articles to encourage them to become more vocal in their opposition to doctrinal currents, especially those in theology, that in any way seemed to be akin to the ideas that were included in the condemnation. What this meant was that the Franciscans increasingly tended to become sharper in their critique of philosophy, at least that found in the arts faculty in Paris, and more strident in the tone they adopted toward philosophically minded theologians such as St. Thomas Aquinas. Or perhaps a better way to state the situation would be to say that, for the most part, the condemnation caused them to veer even further from the philosophy associated with the condemnations—what might be termed integral Aristotelianism—and prompted them to develop, mainly from elements in the Augustinian tradition, alternative views. To the extent that such views led, in turn, to thought turning in creative new directions, the effect upon the Franciscans might be adjudged beneficial, but the period of intellectual confusion that ensued in the decades immediately following was real, and doubtless disturbing, to many contemporaries.

I would like to examine the attitudes of two Franciscan theologians, Matthew of Aquasparta and Peter John Olivi. Though both were influential, the more original and more interesting one is Olivi and it is upon his thought that I would like to spend the most time. Olivi, like Henry of Ghent, opposes many of the ideas associated with the Aristotelianism of the arts masters and Thomas Aquinas; yet, despite this, he falls under ecclesiastical suspicion, not least of all from his Franciscan *confrères*.

I.

Let us begin with Matthew of Aquasparta. Matthew was born in Italy ca. 1240 and educated primarily in Italy before coming to Paris in the 1270s. He became a regent master at Paris, where he taught from 1277 until 1281. He was then assigned as a theologian to the papal palace in Rome, succeeding John Peckham, who had just been named the archbishop of Canterbury. Master General of the Franciscan order from 1287 until 1288, Matthew spent the rest of his life in Rome functioning as cardinal priest and titular bishop and advising Boniface VIII in the early days of the growing crisis with the French monarchy. The works that we shall consider are his disputed questions, dating to the late 1270s and all written shortly after the condemnation of 1277.[7]

In the *QDF*, Matthew poses a number of questions that allow him to express his attitude toward philosophy, both the Aristotelian and Arabic inheritance in philosophy and its use by Latin philosophers. What is most curious in this regard is the second question of the series: "Whether we need to believe for the sake of our salvation something that is neither perceptible by sense nor able to be proven by reason." The question follows upon the first question that treated of Academic skepticism as it had been argued for by Cicero in the *Academica,* the *De natura deorum,* and elsewhere, and attacked by Augustine in the *Contra Academicos.* Hence the question might just be read as a continuation into the area of religious belief of the concern to justify belief in general against stock, ancient objections. And in many ways that is just what it is. In the body of the question the first opinion mentions the "philosophers" who posited that nothing should be believed, whether the belief is presented with reasons or without reasons, since assent should be witheld in all matter wherein we may be misled. As Matthew tells us, this is just an application of the Academic skepticism discussed and rejected in the first question to contingent matters, though Matthew tries to update the genealogy of this opinion by suggesting that it was also shared by Heraclitus, as reported in Aristotle's *Metaphysics.* In any event, this first opinion is attributed to the philosophers, i.e., ancient philosophers. What is surprising to discover, however, is the contemporaneity of the references that Matthew gives for the second, erroneous opinion he presents:

> Others say, *and many still say,* that, though we ought to assent to matters based on reasoned argument, we should not assent to matters unless they are either perceived by sense or comprehended by reason; otherwise assent is bold and dangerous. And these men posit that nothing is true unless it can be reached by rational investigation and proven by reason. Peter Abelard fell into this error, as St. Bernard tells in several of his letters to Pope Innocent and Henry, the archbishop of Sens. But this error is most absurd to anyone who considers it carefully. For it renders

null every human act, every contract, every bond of piety and society, every effort to show the truth, and thus undermines the entirety of human life.[8]

In the apparatus for this text, Fr. Gedeon Gál directs our attention to the fact that Matthew is getting the reference to Peter Abelard from St. Bonaventure's *Commentary on the Sentences* 1 d. 43, as may be inferred from the spelling of Abelard's name in the corrected autograph copy of the *QDF*.[9] Now what is even more telling for the meaning of this passage is that Bonaventure makes no mention of "many" who "still say" in his text. For Bonaventure, the position described is historical, bearing upon discussions then a century old; for Matthew it is contemporary and apparently threatening.

Thereafter, Matthew proceeds to detail the many ways in which such a severely guarded approach to belief is irrational. Of course, the opinion itself reminds any modern reader of the views of David Hume in eighteenth-century philosophy and the replies by Matthew, nearly all *reductio ad absurdum* in form, are reminiscent of some of Hume's early critics, particularly figures such as Thomas Reid and Richard Whately. Regarding living one's everyday life, Matthew notes that, taking such a strict standard for credibility seriously, will mean not believing physicians regarding medicine whose value we do not understand, not planting fields that we do not independently know are fertile, not sailing to places that we are not sure have ever been found, and so forth. Contracts will soon become impossible on this score since no one will have the certainty of demonstration regarding the veracity and trustworthiness of the other party. Likewise, the bond of society will break down since, armed with this criterion of belief, we shall not be reasonable if we trust our friends; we cannot, after all, peer into their souls. If such a strong and natural bond as friendship could be broken, the weaker ties will readily dissolve even more quickly than friendship: serfs will no longer trust their lords, nor lords their serfs. Even family bonds will become untenable since children cannot know who their parents really are by demonstration and thus should, presumably, not trust them. Finally, ordinary teaching in schools will break down since students, at least beginners, need to trust the teacher at the beginning of the educational process but should not do so, if they use the criterion adopted here.[10]

Of course, Matthew then goes on in the text to suggest that, if the employment of the "do not believe anything unless it is a matter of perception or demonstrative reasoning" rule is unworkable in the case even of human affairs, how much more is it necessary to depend on authority in the case of divine matters. But to delineate his reasoning proposing a defensible basis for religious belief is not my purpose here. Rather, my purpose is to indicate how Matthew viewed contemporary thinkers who attempted to live out a philosophical life bound solely by perfectly formed and tested philosophical ideas; their convictions would lead to the undoing of Christian society in the long run, or any society for that matter. And Matthew's very concern with them shows first that they existed and second that the attempt to live out a life devoted exclusively to philosophy was what disturbed many—especially Franciscan philosopher-theologians—during this period.

Before leaving Matthew, I wish us to note three things: First, he takes a relatively mild attitude (for the most part) toward philosophy if practiced properly or under conditions of indefeasible ignorance, as was the case with Aristotle and other ancient thinkers. Second, he takes an equally mild (for the most part) attitude toward St. Thomas Aquinas. Examples of the same may be found throughout the *QDF* and the *QDC.* Typically, Matthew simply mentions Aquinas as someone of some stature (*QDF,* q. 5: "*Ista positio, licet sit magnorum . . .*") and usually, though not always, rejects his views as too close to the Aristotelian view or too distant from the opinions of Augustine. About the worst thing that Matthew has to say about St. Thomas is in the *QDC* where, commenting on Aquinas's rejection of divine illumination, he contends that in following Aristotle's views regarding the intellect Thomas has played the part of a philosopher (*QDC* II; 231:23, *quidam philosophantes*). Third, the only area in which philosophical opinions are cast aside as totally worthless is another one that touches upon the moral or practical sphere: opinions on human beatitude. In his response to the question whether the rational creature's good may be located in any other good besides an uncreated good, Matthew simply announces that the philosophical views are unsuited for discussion owing to the inability of the philosophers to reach the true good since they relied on natural reason and not divine authority, which is the only solid guide in such an area.[11]

II.

On each of these points, where the attitude of Matthew tends to be mild and his response measured, despite the intensity of the conflict at Paris during the late 1270s, the manner of our other author, Peter John Olivi, is much more extreme. Born in southern France in 1248, Peter John Olivi studied in Paris during the time of Bonaventure's return to Paris to deliver the *Collationes* and pursued, at the recommendation of his superiors, the doctorate in theology. Suspected for novelties and unusual opinions during the first years of the 1280s, Olivi was investigated by a commission numbering among its members the famous Franciscan theologian, Richard of Mediavilla. After making replies to the masters and being put under silence, he was forced to submit his writings to them; his work was confiscated, and Olivi was reassigned outside of Paris. Thereafter, Olivi spent most of his remaining years in friaries in his native southern France, save for a brief teaching position as lector to the Franciscan convent in Florence, where he taught another well known Franciscan, Peter de Trabibus. Though he was rehabilitated in the late 1280s, Olivi was once again under suspicion toward the end of his life; he died in 1298 and his opinions remained under some stricture until long after his death.[12]

Olivi considered himself first and foremost a theologian who preserved the integrity of the Gospel message as expressed in the life of the Poverello. As he instructs those about to begin their life of contemplative study in the Franciscan order, he advises that they avoid any unnecessary disputation and apply themselves steadily to the Holy Scriptures. What is particularly striking is the manner in which he appropriates many of the recommendations in St. Bonaventure's *Itinerarium* and the *De reductione* but so changes their emphasis as to make them say entirely different things. He writes that we should follow the correct order of learning both in coming to know the subject of theology and in judging the results of what we learn, not becoming bogged down in questions beyond our abilities. We should rely on the principles of faith, i.e., the articles and the authority of the Sacred Scripture, more than our own reasoning, that of another human being, or any human authority. There are those, Olivi tells us, who overturn the proper order of judgment by relying more upon the sayings of Aristotle or those of other pagan and worldly philosophers than upon the sayings of Christian teachers, preferring in similar fashion the sayings of the modern teachers (of theology) to those of the saints, and the *dicta* of the saints outside the canon of Scripture to the canon of Scripture itself.[13] The proper order of reliance is: (1) the Scriptures, (2) the Saints, (3) the theological masters, and (4) the "marshes and swamps" (*et sic deinde ad stagna vel paludes mundanorum philosophorum deflecti*) of the philosophers.

Note that here by the philosophers Olivi has in mind the ancient philosophers primarily, though others may be included under this rubric to the extent that they are themselves embedded in the intellectual tradition of such philosophers. Olivi acknowledges that the order of learning requires that we reverse the order of reliance since the sayings of the masters are initially easier for us to follow than those of the saints and likewise the sayings of the saints easier to grasp than the text of the Scriptures; yet even here the Occitan master cautions that we need to bear in mind the proper authoritative order so as not to become misled by the texts we must perforce study initially. What is most interesting in this regard is that in Olivi's recommended approach the philosophers should only be studied so as to understand aright the sayings of the theological masters and only then by those of keener intelligence (*solis subtilioribus*); first, the philosophical teachings should be studied so as to examine them critically for errors and refute them; second, they should be turned to good use, i.e., taken from the philosophers as unjust possessors and applied to the benefit of the faith. This second use is, of course, the one so emphasized by Bonaventure and before him Hugh of St. Victor and St. Augustine, but Olivi does not think much of it—*In hoc autem secunda causa non magnum haberet locum*—since he does not hold philosophy to be all that important to begin with, compared to prayer and spiritual discipline.[14]

The last point is emphasized again and again by Olivi, as Prof. David Burr pointed out in a classic article,[15] as Prof. Putallaz confirmed in his recent survey of late thirteenth-century Franciscans,[16] and as the textual evidence provided by the even more recently published Acts commentary of Olivi indicates. As might be expected, Olivi deals with the philosophers in his Acts commentary at the point in chapter 17 where Paul attempts to convince the Athenian philosophers that they should accept his teaching about Christ crucified and raised from the dead. Explaining the drama of the Biblical encounter to what must have been a young audience of rustic friars somewhere in southern France, Olivi recounts a brief history of ancient philosophy, employing, curiously enough, Augustine's *De civitate Dei* as his source rather than the much more detailed, if doctrinally slanted, history of philosophy given by Aristotle in book A of the *Metaphysics*, a text with which Olivi was certainly acquainted. Thereafter, two methods of adducing philosophical texts in theological teaching are described. The first is the method actually used by Paul whereby the writings of philosophers are appealed to so as to persuade an audience that is more accustomed to yielding to philosophers and poets on important matters than to religious texts; such a manner of using philosophical teaching makes evident in the manner of its appeal that the authority of the faith and the Scriptures is vastly superior, but, even in such cases, the use of philosophical texts should be infrequent and, to some extent, involuntary, being rooted in the needs of the audience and not the nature of the subject presented. The second way of using philosophical doctrines is cast in the following terms:

> Secondly, someone can use the philosophers in a different and opposed manner, such as the one that modern teachers and their students employ abusively, pompously, and ever more often in their schools of theology, books on theology, and disputes and lectures on theology. From this practice, arises much vice and danger for the Christian religion and its study.[17]

One notes immediately that the use of philosophy by theologians is what is at stake in Olivi's mind and that it is the frequent use of philosophical teaching within theological instruction which is inherently objectionable. Furthermore, the contemporary use of philosophy on the part of the theologians is what remains the focus of attention as Olivi lists the four major vices forthcoming from the abuse of philosophy: (1) the vice of pride and empty glory in philosophical study, leading to dismissal of those unlearned in philosophical matters no matter how advanced the latter are in Christian wisdom—*Et reliquos, quantumcumque Christi et sanctorum sapientiae plenos, reputant nihil scientialiter scire et quasi syllogisticae seu philosophicae rationis expertes;* (2) the vice of excessive curiosity, distracting people from devotion to the Scriptures; (3) the vice of unwittingly mixing pagan errors with Christian teaching, just as the pagan philosophers themselves mixed the views of pagan culture in with what the natural light of reason told them and were unaware of the difference between the two; and (4) the worst vice of all, the self-conscious, faithless, and erroneous worship of philosophical authority within the body of theological doctrine. The last is not only evil in itself, but leads to the most disastrous social consequences: in ancient times, Origen led the Eastern Church astray using Platonic philosophy and the effect of that ill-mixture was still perceptible centuries later. So, too, Olivi assures his younger *confrères,* the modern study of theology will yield to disastrous results since it is so strongly fermented and poisoned with the philosophy of Aristotle; the modern theological trend will usher in the reign of the Antichrist, though the true Christian stem will be preserved in the ark of Noah, that is, tropologically speaking, the ark of St. Francis or the Franciscan order and its associates.[18]

There can be no doubt about the persons to whom Olivi is referring by the phrase "the modern study of theology (*studium theologicum modernorum*)": contemporary Scholastic theologians and, chief among them, St. Thomas Aquinas. In one of his few major works of systematic theology available in modern critical edition, his *Quaestiones in secundum librum Sententiarum,* edited by Fr. Bernard Jansen, SJ, in the 1920s, Olivi shows his disdain for Aquinas in many ways, ones that make for colorful reading. Since space does not permit me to mention more than a couple, let me describe the pattern one detects in these and many of the others: Thomas's view is introduced as closely associated with that of the philosophers, generally Aristotelians (who, in Olivi's eyes are often mistaken and not to be trusted); and Thomas's view is framed within the body of the question in such a way as to have Aquinas's opinion on the one side and the common, safer, and more Catholic view on the other. Here are two examples. In q. 16, the matter at stake is whether angels are composed of matter and form. Before sketching out his own position, Olivi says the following:

> To this question, we must say that, though some people have held and hold that there is neither matter in intellectual substances nor any composition of matter and form, I believe nonetheless, in line with the more common opinion, that there is a composition of matter and form in them and I believe furthermore that this opinon is safer and sounder in terms of the faith and that the other comes quite close to the error of philosophical and pagan infidelity.[19]

Notice the rhetorical effect Olivi has created: Aquinas is isolated and, practically speaking, a philosopher. Another example is q. 33, again on the angels, "whether in an individual angel the whole species is found in such a way that there cannot be another individual of the same species":

> Certain people, following in this matter the pagan philosophers and the Saracens, have said and say that each one of the angels encompasses in itself the whole of the

species according to its full expression in such a way that nothing belonging to that species can either be or be understood outside of that individual any more than the species itself can. They base themselves chiefly upon two claims, the complete lack of matter in the angels and the source of the multiplicity of individuals within a species or division of the species into many individuals; the latter source they think is matter and material accidents, which accidents they believe cannot occur in the angels. Hence, on their account, the species in the angels cannot be multiplied into individuals at all. But, following in this matter the sounder teachers and the more Catholic ones, I believe that this position [i.e. Aquinas's] not only is contrary to reason and truth but very much dangerous for the faith.[20]

Here are, for our consideration, just some of the numerous places wherein the Occitan lector rails against the Philosopher and the cult of idolatry that is associated with his name: "Though I do not care what Aristotle thinks here or elsewhere, for his authority and that of any other infidel and idolater are of no bearing for me, especially in matters that concern the Catholic faith or touch closely upon it."[21] "These claims are false in their own right, but I have deliberately added these arguments against them so that the empty and false philosophy of Aristotle and that of the people who follow him in this and other errors may be avoided."[22] "Averroes in these matters, as in so many others, is quite mad."[23] And, quite characteristically, "Aristotle proves his statement with no sufficient reason, nay with almost no reason at all, but people believe him without reason as if he were the god of the age."[24]

The sayings of Olivi in this vein could be multiplied and could fairly compete with the anti-Aristotelian *dicta* of any fifteenth-century humanist, sixteenth-century Protestant or Catholic reformer, or seventeenth-century philosopher. But what are we to make of Olivi? Is he anti-philosophical as well as anti-Aristotelian? For that matter, is he really anti-Aristotelian in light of his appropriation of so many doctrines of the Stagirite?

To answer any of these questions is difficult; Olivi, in many ways, is an enigmatic figure. As David Burr asserted in the article mentioned earlier, Olivi opposes any effort to make of his anti-Aristotelian stance itself a standard or canon of theological orthodoxy:

> Thus Olivi's harangues against Aristotle cannot lead him into the sort of coercive anti-Aristotelianism which would call for a total elimination of his views from Christian theology. Any attempt to eradicate Aristotelianism in favor of some other view would be almost as idolatrous at the attempt to deify Aristotle. . . . Militant anti-intellectuals are no more palatable than militant Aristotelians.[25]

Yet I believe the situation is more complicated. Two features of Olivi's outlook strike me as being of overarching importance: first, he likes to play with philosophical and theological ideas in a Socratic manner, however much he may suggest that philosophy is dispensable for the friars and should be pursued only by a few and then only the most gifted; second, he does have certain philosophical and theological theses that he defends vigorously, as if those theses at least are part and parcel of any respectable philosophical outlook. The first feature is evident in the numerous places in which Olivi plays off one opinion against another, leaving no clear indication of which view he ultimately favors. Though one might suspect a certain degree of disingenuousness, as Fr. Bettoni did, and a subtle effort—worthy of a Straussian analysis—to disguise his own opinion since there are undeniably cases in which Olivi's opinion is the view introduced by the phrase "certain people say," on balance I am inclined to think that there is a genuine Socratism in Olivi, as Puttalaz suggests. We must remember, however, that Socrates's own Socratism was capable of generating, as Cicero tells us, diametrically opposed philosophical schools such as the Stoics, the Epicureans, and even the Cynics. Olivi's Christian Socratism shares, in its second feature, something else found in the attitude of the great Athenian philosopher: underneath all the dialectical interplay there are firm philosophical commitments that must be maintained. To see that this is so, let us turn to what is one of most sensitive areas for Olivi in philosophy or theology: the freedom of the human will.

III.

In q. 57 of his questions on the second book of the *Sentences*, Olivi asks whether human beings have free will (*liberum arbitrium*). Many of the arguments listed to show that we do not have free choice are based on metaphysical considerations impinging on act and potency and cause and effect, but some are also expressive of the deterministic psychology found in Aristotle and the Islamic commentators. There must be a determining factor that causes a power to act or a person to act in one way rather than another, or else there is no causal source of the action taken by the person. If there were no determining factor causing a power to be related to actual effects rather than to its potential effects, we would not be able to distinguish between actual and potential effects, though we actually do so.[26] Any power that had opposite effects in its power at one and the same time would either have to produce both or cease from doing both since it is equally related to both, but the power cannot do both simultaneously and obviously does not refrain from doing both since a given act is performed; hence the power is determined at the time that it acts to a given effect.[27] In one argument, Olivi even approaches a formulation of the principle of sufficient reason: there must be for every actually existing effect some greater reason for it to be than for it not to be; otherwise there would be no reason at all for it to exist when it does exist. Such a reason must be located in the efficient cause of that effect. Hence the efficient cause must have some reason to give being to the effect when it does so rather than not. But that could only mean that the effect must happen when it does and thus no action, as an effect of the will as efficient cause, could fail to happen when it does.[28] Among the psychological arguments we might mention one that argues for a kind of internal determination. Every person acts rationally by taking counsel with himself, but the intellect presents only one object at a time as preferable after deliberating. Hence the will may only elect that option at the time it acts since only that object is presented at the time it acts.[29] Finally, even the social and political arguments that tend to be used to argue that free choice must be presumed to exist are countered in the opening arguments of Olivi's question by the suggestion that complete indetermination is not required to make sense of punishment or reward; all that is required is a kind of relative degree of indetermination so that the will may be determined in many different ways and is not related to its effect in the straightforward manner in which, say, fire produces heat.[30]

Olivi does not balance this seemingly persuasive case for determinism, composed of twenty-nine arguments, by listing authoritative arguments on the other side. Instead he launches directly into his solution by asserting, in what comes as a surprise to the reader, that the libertarian position is true beyond the shadow of a doubt—*absque omni dubitationis scrupulo est tenendum in nobis esse liberum arbitrium.*[31] The evidence that he will adduce on behalf of this assured conviction is the internal experience we have of our own actions and their properties and the manner in which free choice functions.

The properties or affections that belong to us as rational beings indicate clearly that they spring from free choice for the very good reason that they do not make sense without the supposition of free choice. Altogether Olivi lists seven of them—a typically Franciscan number—but we may get some idea of what his reasoning is by examining one pair of them. Before presenting his arguments on the affections, however, Olivi lays down two maxims or principles that he thinks no one of sound mind will deny: (1) it is impossible for all the affections of a rational nature to be utterly false and perverse and based on some false and perverse object; and (2) it is equally impossible for human beings to become better and better and advance in goodness by following as a guide to an ever greater degree something incorrect and without foundation in fact. With these principles in place, Olivi commences his list of seven affections, which come in pairs: zeal and mercy, pride and shame, etc. Let us look at the first two: zeal and mercy.

No one gets angry, Olivi observes, with zeal against the deeds of the lower animals or any person, such as a child, who lacks the full use of reason, in the way that everyone gets angry at the action of a person in possession of their reason and at the person themselves. Why? Because only in such a case are we convinced that the person had the ability to avoid their action. The perception that such is the case and the emotion itself would be based on something utterly false and perverse were the person against whom we got angry unable to control their conduct. Yet we think that someone who grows angry at a person's deliberate act of malice and wrongdoing is acting rightly, and the greater the injustice, the more righteous the zeal and anger in a good person. Hence, if there is no free choice a person gets better and better by getting more and more zealous based on convictions completely false and perverse since they are entirely out of keeping with the way things are; but this is utterly absurd and contrary to the maxims laid down at the beginning of the discussion. Olivi conducts a similar argument based on our primitive experience of pity. We pity especially those who suffer through no misdeeds of their own, but the distinction between those suffering from no misdeeds of their own as opposed to those who bring their misfortune upon themselves breaks down in a world without free choice.[32]

One thing we should notice straightaway. When Olivi analyzes such emotions as zeal and mercy, he focuses on the specifically human form of those emotions. If you will, his analysis produces a phenomenology of human emotions as experienced concretely; he does not even attempt the kind of philosophical psychology found in Aristotle's *De anima* that begins with the lower animals and distinguishes powers, acts, and objects. His approach instead is to take something like the emotion of anger, that both he and we know is found in humans and lower animals, and argue that not anger but the way we get angry is peculiarly human and points to something uniquely human.

His analysis of emotions is furthermore the articulation of an internal experience that itself provides the positive basis for defending the power of free choice in human beings. To dispel the arguments taken from metaphysical principles such as act and potency, cause and effect, and so forth, Olivi provides a negative criterion: though such principles hold sway in non-rational natures, they do not apply straightforwardly in rational natures precisely because the latter are endowed with free choice.[33] Hence, Olivi proposes a modification of the model of contingency associated with the necessitarian reading of such metaphysical principles by introducing a notion of synchronic contingency in addition to the notion of diachronic contingency. For those interested in the history of these notions and their reformulation later in Scotus's writings, I recommend an excellent article by Prof. Stephen Dumont, as well as the introduction to the translation of Scotus's *Lectura* by Prof. Antoine Vos of the University of Utrecht.[34] The basic idea is that the will has the power of opposites at one and the same time and retains that power even when it elects one of the acts in which it could engage. Such an ability is not vacuous if the will is equally capable at one and the same time of producing either of two opposite acts, even though it cannot produce both acts simultaneously, since that involves a contradiction. For Olivi, as later for Scotus, this ability to act otherwise even at the time of the performance of a given act is the key meaning of freedom that underlies human responsibility.

Now I introduced this whole discussion in Olivi to show a fundamental point: he does argue philosophically and holds that such argumentation establishes claims that are undeniably true within the scope of natural reason. This is obvious from the way in which Olivi closes his reply to q. 57 prior to answering the opening arguments. He tells us that the view denying that we have free choice or free will (the terms "free choice" and "free will" seem interchangeable, for the most part, for Olivi) is so clearly false that it is tantamount to eliminating our personhood and making of us intellectual brutes without any autonomy: *personalitatem scilicet nostram a nobis tollit nihilque amplius nobis dat nisi quod simus quaedam bestiae intellectuales seu intellectum habentes.* No one, he thinks, of sound mind will believe something that so undermines the basis for human life. Furthermore, in the next question, where he establishes that free will is an active and not a passive power, Olivi points out that the confrontation over the issue of whether the will is active or passive is one that engages different parties, philosophers and Catholics, on the one hand, and different groups of Christians thinkers, on the other. Regarding the former conflict he states unequivocally that certain of the philosophers and many of the Saracens are really determinists, attributing to the will no more activity as power of the soul than they do to the intellect or the sense powers. But in the case of the latter disagreement, he describes opinions ranging from Aquinas's view that the will is not free with regard to all of its acts to his own view (hidden under the rubric of persons of lesser authority) which holds that the will is active and free in all of its proper acts, requiring the presence of the object as presented by the intellect only as a necessary condition for its activity. As he proceeds to argue for the activity of the will, he emphasizes that the will's activity is something attested by both faith and what he calls correct reason (*recta ratio*). *Recta ratio* is not, in this context, to be understood as the practical ability to judge moral matters correctly, as in Aristotle's *Nicomachean Ethics,* but rather as the facility of thinking correctly in matters philosophical. Hence we must conclude that Olivi, at least on some issues, is committed to philosophical arguments which are the underpinnings of theology and not quite so anti-philosophical as he makes himself appear in some of his writings.

––––––––

What should we conclude from our survey of these two Franciscans between St. Bonaventure and Duns Scotus? First, both authors are, to some degree, critical of philosophy and what they deem the inappropriate use of philosophy by theologians, though Olivi is much more strident in his criticism of philosophers and philosophically-minded theologians than is Matthew of Aquasparta. Second, neither author seems inclined to embrace the earlier Bonaventurean synthetic vision of the universe of discourse being structured so that knowledge in one department leads to knowledge in another as signs pointing to things beyond themselves. This is obviously the case with

Olivi, whose tendency to downplay any connection between philosophy and theology made us investigate the extent to which he himself advanced philosophical arguments at all. But even Matthew of Aquasparta does not subscribe wholeheartedly to Bonaventure's optimism; when discussing illumination, a theory that he does endorse, Matthew does not give it the semiotic Bonaventurean cast, while his concern for delineating the limits of philosophy, especially within the area of its impact upon conducting one's everyday life, shows that he is not so confident as Bonaventure was that philosophy will point even serious-minded inquirers to the higher discipline of theology rooted in faith. Finally, neither author shows symptoms of developing the attitude that is characteristic of Duns Scotus: the approach of carefully marking what is demonstrable in contradistinction to what is known only by dialectical arguments within the realm of philosophy, while simultaneously articulating the manner in which the claims of theology are grounded in faith even when theology employs sophisticated reasoning strikingly similar to arguments found in philosophy.

NOTES

1. Jan A. Aertsen, Kent Emery, Jr., and Andreas Speer, eds., *Nach der Verurteilung von 1277: Philosophie und Theologie an der Universität von Paris im letzten Viertel des 13. Jahrhunderts, Studien und Texte*, Miscellanea Medievalia, bd. 28 (Berlin-New York: Walter de Gruyter, 2001).

2. Pierre Duhem, *Études sur Léonardo de Vinci* (Paris: 1913), 3:v–vi. As Stephen Marrone points out in the article cited below (277), this view was trenchantly criticized by Alexandre Koyré, "Le vide et l'espace infinie au XIV siècle," *Archives d'histoire doctrinale et littéraire du moyen-âge* 17 (1949): 45–91; yet we should note that, despite not mentioning the condemnations, Alfred North Whitehead seemed quite sympathetic to locating in the late Middle Ages the intellectual attitude that leads to modern science: Alfred North Whitehead, *Science and the Modern World* (New York: Macmillan, 1925), 9–25.

3. The paper by Steven P. Marrone, "Aristotle, Augustine, and the Identity of Philosophy in Late Thirteenth-Century Paris: The Case of Some Theologians," in Aertsen, *Nach der Verurteilung*, 276–98, is a notable exception, but even he only wishes to redeem certain elements of Duhem's outlook.

4. Kent Emery, Jr., and Andreas Speer, "After the Condemnation of 1277: New Evidence, New Perspectives, and Grounds for New Interpretations," in Aertsen, *Nach der Verurteilung*, 9–11; Albert Zimmerman, "Ferrandus de Hispania—Ein Verteidiger des Averroes," in Aertsen, *Nach der Verurteilung*, 410–16, shows the continuing influence of Averroes on the shape of later thirteenth century thought.

5. John F. Wippel, "Godfrey of Fontaines at the University of Paris in the Last Quarter of the Thirteenth Century," in Aertsen, *Nach der Verurteilung*, 359–89.

6. François-Xavier Putallaz, *Insolente liberté: Controverses et condamnations au XIIIᵉ siècle* (Fribourg: Éditions Unversitaires de Fribourg, 1995), 172–75; Henricus de Gandavo, *Quodlibet* 1.16 (ed. Macken 5:98); for some later influences of the condemnation of 1277, see Edward P.

Mahoney, "Reverberations of the Condemnation of 1277 in Later Medieval and Renaissance Philosophy," in Aertsen, *Nach der Verurteilung,* 902–30.

7. For Matthew's life, see Matthaei ab Aquasparta, *Quaestiones disputatae de fide et cognitione,* BFS I, editio secunda, cura Patrum Coll. S. Bonaventurae (Quaracchi, Florentiae: Typographia Collegii S. Bonaventurae, 1957), 5*–9*; R.E. Houser, "Matthew of Aquasparta," in *A Companion to Philosophy in the Middle Ages,* ed. J. Gracia and T. Noone (Oxford: Blackwell, 2003), 423–31. Hereafter the *Quaestiones disputatae de fide* will be cited as *QDF* and the *Quaestiones disputatae de cognitione* as *QDC.*

8. Matthew, *QDF* 2 (ed. Gál 59.30–60.10). "Alii dixerunt, et multi adhuc dicunt quod, etsi alicui assentiendum sit cum ratione, nulli tamen assentiendum nisi quod aut sensu percipitur, aut ratione comprehenditur; alias assentire temerarium est et periculosum. Et ii ponunt quod nullum sit verum ad quod non possit pertingi investigatione et quod non possit ratione convinci. In istum errorem lapsus fuerit Petrus Baalardi, sicut refert beatus Bernardus in pluribus epistolis ad Papam Innocentiam et Henricum archiepiscopum Senonensem.—Sed iste error diligenter consideranti absurdissimus est. Evacuat enim omnem humanum actum, omnem contractum, omne vinculum pietatis et societatis, omne documentum veritatis, ac per hoc totam vitam subvertit humanam."

9. Matthew, *QDF* 2 (60, §1). For Bonaventure, see *In Sent.* 1. d. 43.4 (ed. Quarrachi 1:775a).

10. Matthew, *QDF* 2 (60.11–61.29).

11. Matthaeus de Aquasparta, "De anima beata," 1, in *Quaestiones disputatae de anima separata, de anima beata, de ieiunio et de legibus,* BFS XVIII, cura patrum Collegii S. Bonaventurae editae, ed. Gál (Quaracchi, Florentiae: Typographia Collegii S. Bonaventurae, 1959), 85–86.

12. Alain Boureau et Sylvain Piron, *Pierre de Jean Olivi (1248–1298): Pensée scolastique, dissidence spirituelle, et société* (Paris: Vrin, 1999), 9–10. Several of the studies in the volume cited deal with Olivi's later influence upon literature and religious movements within medieval society.

13. Peter of John Olivi, "De studio," in *On the Bible: Principia in Sacram Scripturam, Postilla in Isaiam et I ad Corinthios cum appendice in qua continentur 'Quaestio de oboedientia' et sermones duo de S. Francisco,* ed. David Flood and Gedeon Gál (St. Bonaventure, NY: Franciscan Institute, 1997), 27.3–13.

14. Olivi, "De studio," 27.18–30.

15. David Burr, "Petrus Ioannis Olivi and the Philosophers," *Franciscan Studies* 31 (1971): 41–71.

16. François-Xavier Putallaz, *Figures franciscaines à la fin du XIIIᵉ siècle* (Paris: Cerf, 1997).

17. Peter of John Olivi, *On the Acts of the Apostles* 17, ed. David Flood (St. Bonaventure, NY: Franciscan Institute, 2001), 342.11–15: "Secundo potest quis eis uti modo contrario, sicut utique multi moderni doctores et discipuli in scholis et libris theologiae et in eius lectionibus ac disputationibus pompatice ac saepe et saepius abutuntur. Ex quo multiplex vitium et periculum suboritur studio et cultui Christiano."

18. Peter of John Olivi, *On the Acts of the Apostles,* 17 (342.16–343.11), especially 343.8–11: "Sic et studium theologicum modernorum est per Aristotelis philosophiam ita fortiter fermentatum et venenatum quod suo tempore erumpet in regulum Antichristi, salvo semine in arca Noe, id est patris Francisci, servando."

19. Petrus Ioannis Olivi, *In secundum librum Sententiarum,* 16c, BFS IV, ed. Bernardus Jansen (Ad Claras Aquas [Quaracchi]: Typographia Collegii S. Bonaventurae, 1922), 304. "Ad quaestionem istam dicendum quod licet aliqui tenuerint et tenent in substantiis intellectualibus non esse materiam nec compositionem materiae cum forma, credo tamen iuxta communiorem opinonem in eis esse compositionem materiae cum forma et credo quod haec secundum fidem

sit sanior et securior et quod altera multum appropinquet errori philosophicae et paganicae infidelitatis."

20. Olivi, *In Sent.* 2. q. 33 (ed. Jansen 596–97): "licet quidam sequentes in hac parte paganos philosophos et Saracenos dixerint et dicant quod quilibet angelus comprehendit totam suam speciem secundum totum suum ambitum, ita quod nihil illius speciei potest esse vel intelligi extra ipsum sicut nec extra ipsam speciem, fundantes se praecipue in duobus, scilicet in omnimoda privatione materiae et in causa multiplicationis numeralis individuorum sub eadem specie vel speciei in plura individua, quam volunt esse materiam et accidentia materialia quae quia secundum eos nullatenus sunt in angelis, sic per consequens nullo modo poterit in eis numeraliter multiplicari species in plura individua: sequendo tamen doctores in hac parte saniores et magis catholicos credo quod haec positio non solum est rationi et veritati contraria, sed etiam in fide valde periculosa."

21. Olivi, *In Sent.* 2. q. 16 (ed. Jansen 337): "Aristoteles etiam hoc non videtur ibi sentire, licet mihi non sit cura quid hic vel alibi senserit; eius enim auctoritas et cuiuslibet infidelis et idolatrae mihi est nulla, et maxime in iis quae sunt fidei christianae aut multum ei propinqua."

22. Olivi, *In Sent.* 2. q. 16 (ed. Jansen 355): "Licet autem ista falsissima sint in se, ut tamen inanis et fallax philosophia Aristotelis et sequacium eius in iis et aliis erroneis evitetur, scienter ista apposui."

23. Olivi, *In Sent.* 2. q. 16 (ed. Jansen 336): "Averroes igitur hic, sicut et in multis aliis, insanit."

24. Olivi, *In Sent.* 2. q. 58 (ed. Jansen 482): "Aristoteles nulla sufficienti ratione, immo fere nulla ratione probat suum dictum, sed absque ratione creditur sibi tanquam deo huius saeculi."

25. David Burr, "Petrus Ioannis Olivi and the Philosophers," 70.

26. Olivi, *In Sent.* 2. q. 57, §1 (ed. Jansen 305).

27. Ibid., §2 (ed. Jansen 305–6).

28. Ibid., §6 (ed. Jansen 306–7).

29. Ibid., §15 (ed. Jansen 310).

30. Ibid., §22 (ed. Jansen 313–14).

31. Ibid., q. 57c (ed. Jansen 316).

32. Ibid., q. 57c (ed. Jansen 317–319).

33. Ibid., q. 57, ad 10m et 11m (ed. Jansen 348–53).

34. Stephen D. Dumont, "The Origin of Scotus's Theory of Synchronic Contingency," *Modern Schoolman* 72 (1994/95): 149–167; John Duns Scotus, *Contingency and Freedom: Lectura I 39*, ed. A. Vos, H. Veldhuis, A. H. Looman-Graaskamp, E. Dekker, and N. W. Bok, The New Synthesis Historical Library 42, (Dordrecht-Boston-London: Kluwer, 1994).

Chapter 12

Peter of Candia's Portrait of Late Thirteenth-Century Problems concerning Faith and Reason in *Book I of the Sentences*

STEPHEN F. BROWN

Peter of Candia, a Franciscan from Crete, lectured on the *Sentences* of Peter Lombard at Paris during the years 1378–1380. Following the statutes of the university, he gave an inaugural sermon for each of the four books of Lombard's *Sentences*. After each sermon, he debated before the university community a question that was linked to the theme of his sermon. The overall theme of the four sermons is announced by a text from the Acts of the Apostles 10:30 that Peter cited: "*Stetit ante me in veste candida* (He stood before me in a dazzling garment)." This Scriptural citation was in reality a signature theme, since the Scripture account was a story about the Apostle Peter (thus linked to the author Peter), who had an angel appear before him in a shining white garment (*in veste candida*), linked to Candia, i.e. Crete, the birthplace of the inaugural preacher. In imitation of the Scripture story, our author's sermons envisioned Peter Lombard standing before him and his audience, showing himself in each semester as a dazzling or shining white model for the beginning scholar, then for the bachelor, next for the master, and finally for the bishop.[1] In the questions that followed each sermon, Peter of Candia worked in the *veste candida* theme by asking:

1. Utrum candida christianae religionis professio sit a qualibet perceptiva potentia rationabiliter imitanda? (Book I)
2. Utrum candida lucis aeternae simplicitas sit secundum rationes intrinsecas creaturarum omnium causaliter effectiva? (Book II)
3. Utrum candida Redemptoris humanitas fuerit ex unione hypostatica ad Verbum immensum beatifice quietata? (Book III)

4. Utrum candida beatorum societas in finali gloria aequaliter obiectum beatificum speculetur? (Book IV)

Peter of Candia's sermons show he is an author who is familiar with Thomas Aquinas, John Duns Scotus, Peter Aureoli, Gregory of Rimini, and John of Ripa.[2] However, his inaugural questions show us different sources: his immediate teachers at Paris. He refers to their own *Commentaries on Lombard's Sentences* and the positions they sustained therein. Peter's first inaugural question thus introduces to us four masters (Malivus a Sancto-Adomaro [Saint-Omer], Gerardus de Calcar, Lambertus de Marchia, and Franciscus de Sancto-Michaele [Saint-Michel]) and two unnamed bachelors (a Carmelite and a Dominican).[3] These formal inaugural questions present us with the positions they held and the arguments they garnered to support them.

The text we will edit and study here is the first inaugural question that Peter debated in the Fall of 1378: whether the open profession of the Christian faith should be matched by a reasonable effort to attain understanding of it by our knowing powers? The teachers just mentioned all held that it should not. Malivus of Saint-Omer argued that the profession of the Christian faith which more depends on the will than on the intellect could not be matched by a rational justification. Gerard of Calcar contended that the profession of faith that asserts that there is a unique distinct intellectual species for two contradictories, such as the essential divine light that represents in itself all things that are specifically distinct and also those that are individually distinct, could not be defended rationally. The Carmelite bachelor, likewise, held that perfect faith that sets as an end or goal for someone what is beyond his ability to attain could not be rationally confirmed. Lambert of Marches, for his part, claimed that one could not provide a rational explanation of a teaching of faith that holds that a natural agent is superior to a free agent. Taking a different angle, Francis of Saint-Michel stated that we could make no successful rational effort to justify a belief in the case where an absolute reality cannot be conceived without relations. Finally, according to the Dominican bachelor, a Christian faith which declared that merits or demerits are distributed in a manner showing partiality, could not be rationally defended.

In contrast to these immediate negative voices influencing him at Paris, Peter brings the weight of the argument of the Oxford Franciscan, Richard Brinkley, to the affirmative side. Brinkley explains his position by citing the opening words of St. Augustine in Book XI of *The City of God:* "The city of God we speak of is the same as that to which testimony is borne by that Scripture which excels all the writings of all nations by its divine authority, and has brought under its influence all kinds of minds, and this not by any chance efforts of men, but clearly by an express providential arrangement." Divine revelation, Richard contends, excels all human authorities and measures their reasons. We should, therefore, consider all human arguments opposed to the profession of the Christian faith and judge their worth. So, the profession of Christian faith, and indeed its perfection, should be matched as reasonably as possible by our knowing faculties.

In pursuit of a more detailed picture justifying the pursuit of understanding and defense of the Christian faith, Peter reverses the order of his presentation and begins with the position of the Dominican bachelor. This Dominican author who initiated Peter into the study of the *Sentences of Lombard* contended that the Christian law hands out merits and demerits in an unequal way. In conferring awards and punishments it does not follow the rule of justice that Aristotle sees as the guide for merits and demerits. The Dominican bachelor used a number of examples to establish his point: merit and demerit should be distributed according to an equal measure for all. Yet, the Christian law does not operate in this way. It demands more of religious who have taken vows and priests who have embraced a more demanding way of life than the ordinary believer. So, for him, the difference between the strict demands of the Gospel and the supererogatory demands of the counsels of poverty, chastity, and obedience show that more is expected of some than of others. Peter of Candia, following Richard Brinkley, argues that the Gospel itself does not impose the vows of poverty, chastity, and obedience, but demands a way of life that binds all equally. If some Christians follow a higher kind of life, that is due to the Gospel counsels offering a special calling and those who have responded to it have taken upon themselves further obligations. They are not imposed by the Gospel, but are taken up by the religious and priests on their own, and are thus not unfair, though they are more demanding.

The second position Peter criticizes is represented by Master Francis of Saint-Michel. Francis argues that the good news of the Gospel teaches those who accept it that there corresponds to the absolute divine nature a proper concept formally distinct from the concepts of the divine relations. This suggests that we have to verify contradictory things—that our proper concept of God is a concept of one God and our proper concept of God is also of three persons. Francis believes that a corollary of this observation is that since each of the divine persons is distinct, each can be seen in the beatific state without any of the others. Peter of Candia differs with this conclusion and also with its corollary. For him, no divine relation is formally taken to be connected to the formal character of beatitude. Someone, then, can be blessed without the vision of any divine relation. When, for example, St. Augustine tells us in *De doctrina christiana* that "the things that make us blessed and that we must enjoy are the Father, the Son, and the Holy Spirit, the same Trinity, the one highest reality that is common to all who enjoy it," Peter points to the intention of Augustine: "He wishes that the three supposits produce blessedness in us, so that they are the efficient cause, not the formal object of our blessedness." That formal object is the divine essence, which in reality is triune, but the proper formal object of our blessedness is the divine essence.

Lambert of Marchia, as the third opponent, charges that the Christian faith makes a natural agent more perfect than a free agent, and thus cannot be reasonably explained. He bases himself on the premiss that formal beatitude is found in acts of the intellect and will, but more properly in an act of the intellect than an act of the will. As John's Gospel affirms: "This is eternal life, that they may *know* you," etc. Aristotle points in the same direction when he argues that human happiness consists in the *contemplation* of separate substances. Now, if beatitude consists in knowledge and contemplation, then the intellect is the higher faculty and it is also a natural faculty that is forced to assent when evidence is presented to it. It is thus superior to the will which is a free faculty. Peter of Candia argues to the contrary that the highest perfection of the Christian religion is grounded in and perfected more fully in the burning acts of love belonging to the will. To be rewarded with eternal life follows upon meriting it with persevering love, for it is because of such love that we find final perseverance. Man's complete and highest perfection is thus found in love, which is a free activity. Thus, freedom is a good more lofty than the knowledge that is marked by the natural, and therefore necessary, assent associated with the intellect's necessary assent to the true.

The fourth opponent Peter refutes is the Carmelite bachelor who affirmed that when the Gospel (or any teaching) promises a certain goal or end that people cannot attain directly, then such teachings cannot be reasonably justified. However, Peter argues that what the Carmelite claims as impossible is not impossible. This is so since God can represent himself to the human mind more perfectly than any indirect means that represents him. Also, from the side of man's ability to know, he can be elevated to the vision of the divine essence by God. So, it is not impossible, but rather absolutely possible, that the divine essence can be for our created intellects the object of our beatific vision and also the enjoyment fulfilling our created will.

Gerard Calcar, in his position as the fifth opponent of Peter of Candia, focused on the divine ideas and the Christian portrayal of them. The multiplicity of these ideas, he imagined, presented a problem. It is this: the divine light, which is an essential and thus a unified light, represents things that are different specifically and individually. How can this be? How can multiplicity be avoided in God as he represents in his knowledge all the various species and individuals? If God, for example, knows eternally that "a man is not a donkey," what is the object of his knowledge? Are the very existing men and donkeys the objects of his knowledge? This cannot be so, since the existing men and donkeys are not eternal, but temporal, so they cannot be the objects of God's eternal knowledge. Can it be explained by a Platonic appeal to a world of ideas distinct from God? Not really; this would impoverish God's knowledge, since he would be cognitively perfected through things distinct from himself. Besides, there are no eternal entities distinct from God that could cause his perfect knowledge. Thus, God's eternal knowledge must have as its object the divine essence. According to Peter of

Candia, to posit a plurality of really distinct ideas in God in order to explain things that are different specifically and individually in creatures would take away the divine simplicity. Thus, he will admit only a formal distinction in the divine ideas, a distinction which denies that there are distinct *rationes* in the divine mind that account for the diversity of species and individuals in creatures.

Malivus of Saint-Omer argued that the profession of Christian faith depended more principally on the will than on reason. His view of reason comes from the portrait given of it by Peter Lombard in the prologue to his *Sentences.* It is a view of reason as presented by St. Hilary at the beginning of Book X of his *De trinitate*—one that sees reason as what the will employs in defense of its own prejudices rather than as a faculty that begins to lead it to what is true. Peter of Candia appeals to Richard Brinkley for a more nuanced view of reason in the sixth and final conclusion of his inaugural question, when he argues that firm adherence to the law of Christ depends more principally on reason rather than on will. When Malivus argues that reason is not sufficient for faith, Brinkley and Peter of Candia contend that the Christian tradition indicates that reason is to be understood in different ways. Hugh of Saint-Victor in the *Sacraments of the Christian Faith* and Augustine in *On Free Will* give a more elevated view of reason as the image of God. There is also the philosophers' view of reason, that of syllogistic reason and deduction; and when he later presents his view of theological study Peter of Candia will stress the importance of deductive theology. In this case, he will be stressing the theological method of Gregory of Rimini, which legitimately goes from revealed but implicit Biblical teaching to revealed and explicit truths, as happens in the Church councils and in the more explicit credal statements. There is also a further portrait of reason, as found in chapter 10 of Cassiodorus's *Treatise on the Soul,* where reason is portrayed as intellectual imagination. One begins from the known and through analogy goes to the hidden or unknown truths of the faith. This is what Peter of Candia calls declarative theology, following Peter Aureoli. The declarative function of *ratio* is the basis for saying that reason, that is, declarative reason, establishes the confirming intellectual grounds for faith. Faith is not pure will; it is a rational affirmation. This rational affirmation is not such that the reasons themselves demand our belief. It is rather an affirmation that is a confirmation: it is the fulfillment of the *fides quaerens intellectum.* Faith is an intellectual assent.[4]

When one examines the references Peter of Candia makes to the positions of his Parisian teachers, one sees the specific character of his footnotes. When Peter refers to the opinion of Malinus of Saint-Omer, it is to the third corollary that belongs to the second part of the first conclusion of Malivus's first article in his *Commentary on Book I of the Sentences.* In the case of Gerard of Calcar, his reference is to the fifth conclusion of the second article of his *Commentary on Book I.* The position of the Carmelite bachelor is recited from his second conclusion of the third article of the *Commentary* of this author. Lambert of Marchia's position focuses on the third conclusion of the second article of his *Commentary*. It is in the fourth proposition of the fourth conclusion of the first article of his *Commentary on Book I* that Peter finds the position of Francis of Saint-Michel. The opinion of the Dominican bachelor is borrowed from the second part of the first conclusion of his *Commentary on the First Book*.

Commentaries on the *Sentences* of Lombard varied very much in the Middle Ages. In general terms, when Alexander of Hales at Paris and Richard Fishacre at Oxford initiated such commentaries in the Scriptural faculties in the first half of the thirteenth century, these were assimilating tools used to teach the Patristic views on the whole sweep of theological questions. Authors were not producing original creative works as a rule, but were learning and advancing the tradition. Often their commentaries were expositions of the letter of Lombard, followed by related questions that updated the debate. At the turn of the fourteenth century, commentaries were much more personal achievements and signs of new organization and focus. For the most part, they stayed with the framework of Peter Lombard, but the patristic tradition, while present, was less literally cited. Contemporaries became the chief opponents, since they were the masters who set the parameters for the ways in which the tradition could be interpreted. By the third decade of the fourteenth century, we find that authors focus more on the burning questions of the time. They tend not to cover all the various distinctions of Lombard and earlier commentators. Peter of Candia in his inaugural question on *Book I of the Sentences,* and throughout the whole of his *Commentary on Lombard's Sentences,* shows the basic framework of *Sentences* commentaries at Paris in his era at the end of the fourteenth century. At least that is what his inaugural question on Book I suggests. It has to be confirmed by the commentaries of these lesser known authors, in the cases in which such commentaries on Lombard's *Sentences* exist.

NOTES

1. A detailed introduction to the inaugural exercises is found in F. Ehrle, "Der Sentenzenkommentar Peters von Candia," *Franziskanische Studien* 9 (1925): 39–56. The texts of the inaugural sermons for all four books were edited by S. F. Brown, "Peter of Candia's Sermons in Praise of Peter Lombard," in *Studies Honoring Ignatius Charles Brady, Friar Minor,* ed. R. S. Almagno and C.L. Harkins (St. Bonaventure, NY: Franciscan Institute, 1976), 141–176.

2. Cf. S. F. Brown, "Peter of Candia's Hundred Year 'History' of the Theologian's Role," in *Medieval Philosophy and Theology* 1 (1991): 156–190.

3. F. Ehrle, "Der Sentenzkommentar," 49–51.

4. Cf. S. F. Brown, "Peter of Candia's Hundred-Year 'History.'" It is strange that in dealing with the nature of theology in the prologue to the *Sentences,* and specifically with the deductive and declarative aspects of it, Peter of Candia gives due credit to Gregory of Rimini (for deductive theology) and Peter Aureoli (for declarative theology), but never mentions Richard Brinkley.

This present inaugural question might well indicate that Peter of Candia will mention the "bigger" names in his *Sentences* commentary, but that behind the cited authors in his commentary are these lesser known personages that show up in his inaugural questions and are the more immediate authorities with whom he is dealing in the audience immediately before him.

APPENDIX

The *Sentences* commentary of Peter of Candia exists in whole or in part in thirty-seven manuscripts.[1] In the judgment of Ehrle the best manuscript is that contained in the Bibl. Apostolica Vaticana, cod. Lat. 1081.[2] Emmen also used the same manuscript as the base for his edition of Peter's question on the Immaculate Conception and demonstrated its undeniable superiority.[3] We have used this manuscript for our present edition of this inaugural question on Book I of the *Sentences*. Any alterations we have made to the text are found between angle brackets < >.

<*Quaestio collativa pro primo principio in Sententiarum lectura per venerabilem fratrem et magistrum Petrum de Candia ordinis minorum, compilata anno Domini mccclxxviii Parisius in scholis fratrum minorum.*>[4]

Incipit quaestio primi principii. Iuxta thema collationis talem formo titulum quaestionis: Utrum candida Christianae religionis professio sit a qualibet perceptiva potentia rationabiliter imitanda.

[Opinio Magistri Malivi de Sancto-Adamaro]

Et arguo ad negativam sex mediis, et primo sic: nulla professio principalius dependens a voluntate quam a ratione est ab aliquo rationabiliter imitanda. Sed candida Christianae religionis professio est principalius dependens a voluntate quam a ratione; ergo quaestio falsa. Consequentia est nota et maior apparet per Magistrum in prologo,[5] redarguentem contrarium asserentes: Talem, inquit, opinionem "*deus huius saeculi operatur in illis diffidentiae filiis* (II Cor. 4:4 et Eph. 2:2) qui non rationi voluntatem subiciunt, nec doctrinae studium impendunt, sed his quae somniarunt sapientiae verba coaptare nituntur: non veri, sed placiti rationem sectantes." Ex quibus apparet maior. Minor vero sequitur ex tertio correlario subsequente ex secunda parte primae conclusionis primi articuli venerabilis magistri mei, Magistri Malivi de Sancto Adomaro de venerabili collegio Navarrae, qui dicit quod in assensu articulorum fidei imperium voluntatis principalius concurrit quam ratio vel apparentia; ergo minor vera.

[Opinio Magistri Gerardi Calcar]

Praeterea, nulla professio asserens duorum contradictoriorum fore unicam numero distinctam speciem est ab aliquo rationabiliter imitanda. Sed candida Christianae religionis professio est asserens duorum contradictoriorum fore unicam numero distinctam speciem; ergo quaestio falsa. Consequentia est nota, et minor declaratur, quoniam distincta et propria specie alicuius rei semper idem iudicium provenit; ergo si esset praecise unica species duorum contradictoriorum, sequitur quod habens illam de quolibet illorum idem haberet iudicium, et per consequens falleretur, et ita non esset consonum rationi. Minor vero sequitur ex quinta conclusione secundi articuli venerabilis magistri mei Magistri Gerardi Calcar, qui dicit quod divinum essentiale lumen absque distinctione in se omnia repraesentat specifice et individualiter distincta; quare propositum.

[Opinio Bachelarii de domo beatae Mariae de Carmelo]

Praeterea, nulla professio praestituens alicui certum finem quem non potest immediate consequi est ab aliquo rationabiliter imitanda. Sed candida Christianae religionis professio est praestituens alicui certum finem quem non potest immediate consequi; ergo quaestio falsa. Consequentia est nota, et maior declaratur: quod ordinatum ad finem ex intrinseca naturae inclinatione absque aliquo alio, nisi fuerit impedimentum, sequitur suum finem, sicut apparet in singulis rebus naturalibus tendentibus in proprium finem. Ergo ponere tale medium non videtur consonum rationi. Et minor sequitur ex secunda conclusione tertii articuli reverendi patris mei bachelarii de domo beatae Mariae de monte Carmelo, qui dicit quod sicut ex esse beatifico agminis seraphici non resultat perfectio infinita, ita ei maius bonum correspondere non potest perfectione finita, et per consequens, cum Deus sit infinitus, et ipsum non attingit nisi per finitam perfectionem, sequitur quod non immediate attingit suum finem; quod erat probandum.

[Opinio Magistri Lamberti de Marchia]

Praeterea, nulla professio indicans naturale agens fore perfectius libero est ab aliquo rationabiliter imitanda. Sed candida Christianae religionis professio est indicans naturale agens fore perfectius libero; ergo quaestio falsa. Consequentia est nota; et maior apparet, quoniam vox omnium <est> vox naturae. Sed omnes ex hoc se putant perfectiores quia liberiores; ergo propositum. Minor vero sequitur ex tertia conclusione secundi articuli venerabilis magistri mei Magistri Lamberti de Marchia, qui dicit quod quamvis beatitudo formalis sit in duobus actibus, scilicet intellectus et voluntatis, principalius tamen et proprius consistit in operatione intellectus quam in actibus ipsius voluntatis. Cum igitur beatitudo sit maximum bonum et ab effectu valor esse indicatur, sic quod intellectus est naturalis potentia, voluntas vero libera, sequitur intellectum esse nobiliorem voluntate; quod est propositum.

[Opinio Magistri Francisci de Sancto-Michaele]

Praeterea, nulla professio asserens absolutum non posse concipi sine respectu est ab aliquo rationabiliter imitanda. Sed candida Christianae religionis professio est asserens absolutum non posse concipi sine respectu; ergo quaestio falsa. Consequentia est nota et maior apparet, quoniam recta ratio dictat priora sine posterioribus posse concipi. Absolutum vero ut sic quolibet respectu est prius; ergo indicans contrarium indicat dissonum rationi. Minor vero sequitur ex quarta propositione declarativa venerabilis magistri mei Magistri Francisci de Sancto-Michaele suae quartae conclusionis primi articuli, qui dicit quod quamvis quaelibet divinarum personarum distinguatur ab alia, nulla tamen potest complete videri beatifice sine reliqua; et per consequens propositum.

[Opinio Bachelarii de domo Praedicatorum]

Praeterea, et ultimo, arguo sic: nulla professio ex ratione propria partialiter distribuens merita vel demerita est ab aliquo rationabiliter imitanda. Sed candida Christianae religionis professio est a ratione propria partialiter distribuens merita vel demerita; ergo quaestio falsa. Consequentia est nota, et maior declaratur, quoniam partialiter agere est iniuste agere, cum iustitia secundum Philosophum, V *Ethicorum*,[6] sit medium inter iniustum facere et iniustum pati, et per consequens quod partialiter agit non tenet medium, et per consequens nec imitatur iustitiam; quare nec imitandum Minor vero sequitur ex secunda parte primae conclusionis reverendi patris mei bachelarii de domo Praedicatorum, qui dicit quod lex Christi non omnes homines ratione utentes ad sui observantiam aequaliter obligat, et per consequens cum distributio praemii ratione meriti proveniat ex obligatione legis, sequitur quod lex quantum est ratione sui inaequaliter praemiabit.

[Opinio Magistri Richardi Brinkel]

Ad oppositum tamen arguo unico medio: quaelibet professio cunctas alias leges praecellens est a qualibet perceptiva potentia rationabiliter imitanda. Sed candida Christianae religionis professio est cunctas alias leges praecellens; ergo quaestio vera. Consequentia et maior patent. Et minor est beati Augustini, XI *De civitate Dei*, capitulo primo,[7] dicentis: "Civitatem Dei dicimus, cuius ea Scriptura testis est, quae non fortuitis motibus animarum, sed plane summae dispositione providentiae super omnes omnium gentium litteras, omnia sibi genera ingeniorum humanorum divina excellens auctoritate subiecit"; et per consequens propositum.

[Opinio Auctoris]

Pro decisione quaestionis huius iuxta materias sex auctorum ad oppositum quaestionis deductorum sex erunt conclusiones principaliter decisivae mere et collativae cum dictis patrum meorum venerabilium, cum quibus me indignus concurro ad bravium capescendum.

[Prima Conclusio—contra opinionem Bachelarii de domo fratrum Praedicatorum]

Similiter, igitur ista prima conclusio: regularis Christi professio indifferenter et communiter fuit iniuncta singulis viatoribus ad aeternam beatitudinem consequendam. Haec conclusio probatur tribus mediis, et primo sic: quaelibet lex in cuius promulgatione non est expressus determinatus gradus obligationis est indifferenter et communiter imposita illis quibus est iniuncta. Sed regularis Christi professio est huiusmodi lex; ergo conclusio vera. Consequentia tenet. Maior apparet, et minor declaratur per id quod habetur *Marci* ultimo, <15–16>: "*Euntes,*" inquit Salvator, "*in mundum universum praedicate evangelium omni creaturae.*" Ecce promulgatio: "*Qui crediderit et baptizatus fuerit salvus erit; qui vero non crediderit condemnabitur.*" Constat autem quod in huiusmodi promulgatione non exprimitur quod unus sub uno gradu obligetur et alius sub alio; ergo propositum.

Praeterea, quaelibet lex cuius observatio non obligat servatores sub aliquo gradu determinatae observantiae est iniuncta indifferenter et communiter. Sed regularis Christi professio est huiusmodi; ergo conclusio vera. Consequentia est nota, et maior declaratur exemplo familiari, nam si rex praecipiat quod quilibet exsistens Parisius vadat ad sanctum Dionysium, non aliter specificando ex tali praecepto, nullus astringitur ire potius die lunae quam die martis, nec peditando potius quam equitando, sed praecise quod vadat ad sanctum Dionysium, et per consequens, lex non specificans modum particularis observantiae obligat solum indifferenter et communiter. Et minor probatur, quoniam lex Christi continet consilia et praecepta, et non plus artat sub uno gradu observantiae consiliorum vel praeceptorum quam sub alia; ergo propositum. Probo antecedens: signo per imaginationem latitudinem observantiae. Et signo gradus in ea *a b c.* Tunc quaero: aut omnes tenentur observare legem huiusmodi sub *a* vel non. Si non, habetur propositum. Si sic, contra: servando sub *b* gradu adhuc servatur praeceptum, et similiter sub *c;* ergo cum ex quolibet gradu observantiae solvatur debitum et ad nullum talem quis obligatur, sequitur quod talis lex est iniuncta communiter.

Praeterea, radix Christianae religionis maxime consistit in dilectione, iuxta illud *Matthaei,* 22, <39–40> "*Diliges*" etc. "*In his duobus <mandatis> universa lex pendet et prophetae.*" Cum igitur nullus gradus dilectionis obliget aliquem, sed praecise tenetur quis diligere, ergo praecise praeceptum de dilectione est omnibus indifferenter et communiter traditum. Consequentia est nota. Probo antecedens, quia nullum tale obligat sub cuius observantia non minus solvitur debitum. Sed quocumque gradu in latitudine dilectionis assignato, sine illo stat solutio debiti; ergo propositum. Minor patet, nam signantur *a b c* gradus dilectionis. Sine *a* possum servare praeceptum, et sine *b,* quia cum *c,* et sic de singulis; ergo propositum.

Ex ista conclusione taliter probata, sequitur correlarie contradictorium secundae partis primae conclusionis primi articuli reverendi patris bachelarii de domo fratrum Praedicatorum, videlicet quod lex Christi omnes homines ratione utentes ad sui observationem aequaliter obligat. Patet, cum omnibus sit indifferenter et communiter imposita. Ipse vero tenet quod lex Christi non omnes homines ratione utentes ad sui observationem aequaliter obligat. Et pro suae conclusionis confirmatione habet tres rationes. Arguit primo sic: non omnes homines ratione utentes sub aequali poena ad legis observationem et debitam observationem obligatur; ergo conclusio vera. Consequentiam dicit patere. Sed antecedens probat de religiosis, quia praeter mundum commune sunt etiam ex voto ad legem Christi servandam strictius obligati.

Praeterea, sacerdotes magis tenentur ad observantiam legis Christi quam alii Christiani; ergo conclusio vera. Consequentia apud ipsum est manifesta, et antecedens apparet sic, quia ipsi tenentur ad castitatem servandam, ut habetur XXVII et XXVIII,[8] et in multis locis; ergo propositum.

Ultimo arguit sic: voto et praecepto obligati ad utriusque impletionem tenentur sub poena peccati mortalis; obligatus vero solo praecepto non tenetur nisi ad impletionem unius; ergo conclusio vera. Consequentiam dicit patere. Et probat antecedens per illud *Psalmi* 75:<12>: "*Vovete et reddite,*" ubi dicit *Decretalis, Extravagantes* 'De voto et voti redemptione'[9]: "Consulit vovere et praecipit redimere." Ergo sicut homo sub poena peccati mortalis tenetur ad unius praecepti impletionem, sic etiam ad veram et licitam voti impletionem. Haec est sua positio breviter recitata.

Sed salva reverentia sua, istae rationes non probant intentum. Arguo igitur contra conclusionem in se primo, et secundario ostendam motiva fore minus valida. Contra quam arguo tribus mediis. Primo sic: quaelibet lex cuius praeceptio vel prohibitio, consiliatio vel promissio non exprimunt certum gradum punitionis vel praemiationis aequaliter sibi subiectos obligat. Sed lex Christi est huiusmodi. Ergo conclusio, cum reverentia, falsa. Maior ex hoc apparet, quoniam obligatio qua legis conditor per legem obligat sibi subiectos oritur ex notificatione propositi voluntatis condentis legem. Sed talis notificatio non habetur nisi per praeceptionem, prohibitionem, consiliationem, vel promissionem; ergo quantitas obligationis est penes illas realiter attendenda. Si ergo prohibitio, praeceptio, etc. non exprimunt certum gradum sed generaliter dantur, sequitur quod et obligatio est generaliter data. Et per consequens, sicut omnibus aequaliter prohibetur vel praecipitur, ita omnis talis lex aequaliter obligabit. Minor vero apparet textum evangelii discernenti ubi nullus gradus exprimitur particulariter sed generaliter tantum.

Praeterea, si lex Christi magis obligat unum quam alium, aut hoc est ratione sui aut ratione differentiae personarum suscipientium legem. Non primo modo, quia lex quae ratione sui non plus specificat unam personam quam aliam non plus obligat unam personam quam aliam. Cum ergo lex Christi nec in moralibus, nec in caeremonialibus, nec in iudicialibus plus specificat unam personam quam aliam, ut sic patet in evangelio, sequitur quod ratione sui non consurgit illa inaequalitas obligationis. Nec secundo modo, quia tunc unusquisque tantae obligaretur a lege quantae esset. Sed hoc est falsum et contra eum, quia tunc nullus posset nova obligatione obligari nec aliquod votum obligatorium emittere. Quod probo, quia quantae est tantae obligatur a lege. Sed non potest plus obligari quam sit. Ergo tantae obligatur quantae potest obligari, et per consequens per votum emissum nulla accrescit obligatio.

Praeterea, data conclusione, sequitur, cum aliquibus veris additis, istae conclusiones quae videntur impossibiles, videlicet Sortes in duplo magis peccat quam Plato, et sic quilibet eorum decedit, et tamen aequaliter praemiatur. Similiter, Sortes et Plato aequaliter peccant et quilibet eorum taliter decedit, et tamen Sortes in duplo plus punitur quam Plato; ergo conclusio falsa. Probo antecedens. Ex quo lex per conclusionem inaequaliter obligat sibi subiectos, sic, gratia argumenti, quia obliget Sortem in duplo plus quam Platonem, tunc volo quod Plato eliciat actum demeritorium in duplo peiorem uno alio actu demeritorio quam elicit Sortes; et sic ambo decedant. Tunc arguo sic: Sortes obligatur a lege in duplo plus quam Plato, et quilibet eorum transgressus est legem; ergo Sorti correspondet in duplo maior poena quam Platoni et hoc ratione transgressionis legis. Et ex alia parte Plato elicuit actum in duplo magis demeritorium quam Sortes, et sic decesserunt; ergo Platoni correspondet in duplo maior poena quam Sorti ratione talis commissionis. Cum igitur poena correspondens Sorti ratione obligationis sit aequalis poenae correspondenti Platoni ratione commissionis, et poena correspondens Platoni ratione obligationis sit aequalis poenae correspondenti Sorti ratione commissionis, sequitur quod ipsorum poenae sunt simpliciter aequales. Consequenter posset et alia conclusio probari quam gratia brevitatis dimitto.

Nec sua motiva, cum reverentia, probant intentum suum, quoniam per hoc quod religiosus facit votum et sacerdos suscipit ordinem, non sequitur quod lex ipsum plus obligaret, sed bene quod ipse se plus obligavit ad observantiam legis, sicut non sequitur: si Sortes mihi accommodavit centum francos et ego iure liberalis donationis promisi sibi ultra illos alios centum quod Sortes me obligavit ad ducentum. Sed hic sunt duae obligationes ex diversis radicibus ortae, sic et ibi. Unde ex suo motivo haberet concedere quod in potestate mea est facere quod lex Christi plus me obliget quam obligabat, et similiter quod lex me obligat sub praecepto ad aliquid quod in lege sub praecepto minime continetur, quae non videntur vera. Quare nec motiva, cum reverentia, exsistunt valida.

Ex quibus omnibus inferendo, offero patri meo quattuor propositiones correlarias, quarum prima est haec: non plus lex Christianae religionis ad sui observantiam obligat verum catholicum quam schismaticum vel paganum; patet ex quo lex huiusmodi omnibus indifferenter et communiter est iniuncta. Secunda: quilibet vivens gentiliter ad quem pervenit sufficiens notitia talis legis iugiter praevaricatur legem huiusmodi omissione; patet ex quo quilibet tenetur ad observantiam talis legis. Tertia: stante obligatione communiter sumpta non potest obligatus exsequi servitium debitum nisi faciat aliquid quod facere non tenetur; patet ex quo per legem tenetur Deum diligere et sub certo gradu signato, et quandoque diligit sub certo gradu signato diligit; igitur propositio vera. Quarta: eligibilius est sub *a* gradu legem evangelicam observare quam sit eligibile simpliciter legem evangelicam observare; patet, quia ex quocumque gradu observantiae legis evangelicae sequitur observantia talis legis.

[Secunda Conclusio—contra opinionem Magistri Francisci de Sancto-Michaeli]

Secunda conclusio est haec: salutaris evangelii lectio sibi subiectos rationabiliter instruit naturae divinae correspondere conceptum proprium a divinarum relationum conceptibus formaliter condistinctum. Haec conclusio tribus mediis declaratur, et primo sic: impossibile est de unico conceptu simplici proprio et distincto contradictoria inter se contradicentia verificari. Sed nostra professio nos instruit de divina essentia et divinis relationibus contradictoria inter se contradicentia verificari; ergo necesse est naturae divinae correspondere conceptum proprium a divinarum relationum conceptibus formaliter condistinctum. Consequentia et maior patent. Et minor apparet, nam per fidem concedimus divinam essentiam esse Patrem, quod praedicatum a Filio removemus, et sic de multis aliis praedicationibus; quare propositum.

Praeterea, ex nostra regula evangelica instruimur septem fore articulos divinitatis essentiam concernentes, quattuor videlicet ad intra et tres ad extra, quos doctrinaliter sic distinguunt doctores, quia aut respiciunt divinam essentiam absolute consideratam, et sic habetur unus de deitatis unitate, aut tres personas, et sic sunt tres ex attributione ad quamlibet personam, aut eius operationem, quae cum sit triplex, videlicet naturae collatio, gratiae infusio et gloriae retributio. Consimiliter, alii tres articuli constituuntur, et ita per consequens sunt quattuor quae concernunt divinam essentiam et personas. Si ergo respectu deitatis in se et trium personarum non esset nisi unicus proprius et distinctus conceptus, frustra poneretur articulorum distinctio, cum idem penitus formaliter per unum quod per alium in esse ponitur. Ergo oportet de necessitate quod eis distincti conceptus formaliter correspondeant; quod erat probandum.

Praeterea, ex fide habemus has propositiones concedere: "Pater non est trinitas" et "Divina essentia est trinitas." Tunc quaero: aut idem conceptus proprius correspondeat in mente subiectis illarum propositionum aut non. Si non, habetur propositum. Si sic, ergo sequitur quod istae propositiones erunt synonymae: "Pater est trinitas" et "Divina essentia est trinitas." Et per consequens, negatione praeposita alteri illarum, essent aequivalentes contradictoriis, sicut patet ex istis propositionibus vocalibus "Ensis est de ferro," "Mucro est de ferro," idem penitus conceptus ipsarum subiectis correspondet, et praedicata, ut suppono, sunt similia, sequitur ipsas propositiones esse synonymas. Et ideo istae aequivalent contradictoriis "Ensis est de ferro" et "Mucro non est de ferro." Ergo pariformiter in proposito, quod est falsum; quare propositum.

Ex ista conclusione taliter declarata, sequitur corollarie contradictorium quartae propositionis declarativae quartae conclusionis primi articuli magistri mei Magistri Francisci de Sancto-Michaeli, videlicet quod licet quaelibet personarum distinguatur ab alia, quaelibet tamen potest complete videri beatifice sine reliqua, cuius contrarium ipse asserit. Et ad hoc ponendum movet ipsum Christi auctoritas dicentis. *Ioannes* 14:<7 et 9> *"Si cognovissetis me, et patrem meum utique cognovissetis."* Et sequitur, respondendo Philippo: *"Philippe, qui videt me, videt et patrem meum."* Ex qua dicit suum patere propositum.

Similiter, beatus Augustinus, I *De doctrina Christiana*, capitulo primo,[10] dicit quod res quae nos beatos faciant et quibus fruendum est, sunt Pater et Filius et Spiritus sanctus. Ex qua similiter infert suum propositum. Adducit ad hoc unicam rationem ubi non obviat relationis operatio nec auctoritas ecclesiae. Contrarium manifestat ratione infinitae identitatis inter divina supposita: quidquid de uno supposito conceditur est et de alio concedendum. Sed ita est in proposito, ut patet inspicienti; ergo propositum.

Sed salva reverentia magistri mei, motiva non inducunt suum propositum sufficienter. Arguo ergo contra conclusionem in se, et deinde contra motiva. Primo sic: sta aliquem esse beatum, circumscripto quocumque quod non est de ratione formali beatitudinis. Sed nulla divina relatio formaliter sumpta est de ratione formali beatitudinis; ergo stat aliquem esse beatum sine visione alicuius relationis divinae. Consequentia est nota, et maior ex hoc apparet, quia posita causa necessaria ad inductionem alicuius effectus, quocumque alio circumscripto, ponitur ille effectus. Sed beatitudo potentiae volitivae debite applicata est causa sufficiens ad hoc quod volitiva dicatur beata; ergo circumscripto quocumque alio quod non est de ratione beatitudinis concurrentis in esse causae, non minus tale erit beatum. Minor vero probatur, quoniam quidquid est de ratione formali beatitudinis est formaliter immensum. Sed nulla relatio divina formaliter sumpta est formaliter immensa; ergo propositum. Consequentia et maior patent, et minor ex hoc, quia tunc essent tria formaliter immensa, et per consequens, aliquam perfectionem simpliciter includeret unum suppositum et non aliud. Patet, videlicet, relationem proprii esse constitutivam quae, ut ponitur, est immensa formaliter; quod non est consonum veritati.

Praeterea, nulla ratio beatificans paternum suppositum est ratio trinitatis formaliter sumpta. Sed quaelibet ratio beatificans creaturam est ratio beatificans paternum suppositum; ergo nulla ratio beatificans creaturam est ratio trinitatis formaliter sumpta, et per consequens nullam includit repugnantiam creaturam beatificari absque visione vel fruitione trinitatis formaliter sumptae. Consequentia est nota, et minor ex hoc, quoniam unica est beatitudo cuiuslibet potentiae beatificabilis, aliter si essent duae, vel creatae, vel increatae, vel una creata et alia increata. Non primo modo, quia tunc aliquod limitatum posset volitivam obiective quietare; quod non est tutum. Nec secundo modo, quia tunc essent plura increata, contra *Symbolum*.[11] Nec tertio modo, quia idem inconveniens sequeretur quod prius; ergo minor vera. Maior vero probatur, quia si in ratione beatificante paternum suppositum caderet ratio trinitatis formaliter sumpta, cum in tali ratione ratio filiationis formaliter includatur, sequitur quod in ratione Filii Pater formaliter esset beatus. Consequens est falsum, ergo et antecedens. Cuius falsitas sic probatur, quoniam ratio formalis beatitudinis est de ratione formali Patris. Si ergo de ratione formali beatitudinis esset ratio Filii suppositalis, sequitur quod de ratione formali Patris esset ratio suppositalis Filii, quod est absurdum, quia tunc Pater non esset a Filio distinctus ut sic. Possit ratio confirmari: nullum posterius est de ratione formali sui prioris. Sed quaelibet ratio suppositalis est posterior quacumque ratione essentiali; ergo nulla talis est prior ratione beatitudinis quae est ratio essentialis, et per consequens, nec de eius ratione formali; quod est probandum.

Praeterea, si non stat aliquem esse beatum sine visione trium personarum, vel hoc est quia tria supposita simul includunt maiorem beatitudinem quam quodlibet per se sumptum, vel propter identitatem divinorum suppositorum, vel propter ipsorum mutuam coexigentiam. Non primo modo, quia tantae perfectionis est praecise Pater quantae quodlibet illorum simul, cum omnis perfectio quae sit in eis sit ratione divinae naturae, et cum divina essentia aeque perfecta sit in uno illorum sicut in tribus simul, sequitur propositum. Nec secundo modo, quia non obstante identitate essentiali inter divina supposita, Verbum terminat dependentiam naturae humanae quam Pater et Spiritus Sanctus non terminant. Ergo pariformiter, non obstante tali identitate possit unum suppositum terminare actum visionis vel fruitionis creaturae sine alio. Nec tertio modo, quia mutua coexigentia divinorum suppositorum est ratione relationum originis quae non requiritur ut rationes beatificantes, ut dictum est; ergo propositum.

Nec motiva, cum reverentia, probant conclusiones, nec auctoritates. Prima non, videlicet, "*Si cognovissetis me,*" quia <si> ibi ly 'si' diceretur faciliter, non est nota consequentiae formalis. Sicut non semper ubicumque ponitur ly 'si' denotat consequentiam formalem, et ideo oppositum consequentis est absolute possibile cum suo antecedente, licet forsitan sit nota legalis consequentiae. Quo dato, non concluditur suum intentum.

Similiter, secunda auctoritas, quae est propositio de inesse, "*Qui videt me videt et Patrem meum,*" non concludit quod oppositum sit impossibile, sicut non sequitur: "Qui videt Sortem videt Martinum, ergo impossibile est videre Sortem sine Martino."

Similiter, auctoritas Augustini non infert suum propositum, cum sit de inesse. Unde non sequitur "Res quae nos beatos faciunt et quibus fruendum est sunt Pater et Filius et Spiritus Sanctus, ergo Pater non potest videri beatifice sine Filio." Consequentia nulla est. Sed ad mentem Augustini: vult quod in nobis beatitudinem efficiant tria supposita, ita quod sit habitudo effectiva et non obiectiva, ut verba praemissae auctoritatis sonant expresse.

Nec ratio, cum reverentia, est sufficiens, quia multae sunt veritates quas non determinavit ecclesia, et tamen non negatur esse possibiles, propter similitudinem quam habent cum veritatibus ab ecclesia determinatis. Et ideo sicut Verbum terminavit dependentiam naturae humanae absque aliis personis, ita videtur hic possibile. Ideo allegare ecclesiam non facit ad propositum, cum possibilitas vel impossibilitas veri a determinatione ecclesiae minime sit dependens.

Ex quibus omnibus inferendo, offero patri meo et magistro quattuor propositiones correlarias, quarum prima est haec: infinita identitas aliquorum ad invicem non infert formaliter in qualibet perceptiva potentia ipsorum mutuam visionem; patet ex quo habent distinctas conceptibilitates. Secunda: unica divinorum suppositorum immensa bonitas actum beatificum creatae perceptivae potentiae non infert ad ipsa supposita necessario terminari; patet per idem medium. Tertia: nulla divinae relationis formalis condicio est formaliter ratio beatificans obiective; patet per idem medium, supposita relationis condicione intrinseca. Quarta est haec: actus immediate ad divina supposita terminatus non est formaliter beatitudinis participans rationem; patet similiter ex praedictis.

[Tertia Conclusio—contra opinionem Magistri Lamberti de Marchia]

Tertia conclusio est haec: summa Christianae religionis perfectio in amoris ardoribus completive perficitur et fundatur. Haec conclusio tribus mediis declaratur, et primo sic: in actu illius potentiae maxime et completive consistit summa Christianae legis perfectio in cuius potestate principalius consistit meritorie operari. Sed in voluntate principaliter consistit meritorie operari; ergo conclusio vera. Consequentia et minor patent, et maior declaratur, quoniam potentia quae principaliter se habet respectu alicuius antecedentis similiter se habet respectu consequentis ex illo antecedente. Sed ad mereri cum finali perseverantia sequitur praemiari; ergo si voluntas se habet principaliter ad mereri, similiter se habebit ad praemiari. Sed non beatificatur ut potentia exsistens in habitu sed ut est in actu. Cum igitur actus voluntatis respectu appetibilis praemialiter adepti sit amor, sequitur quod in amore erit talis perfectio.

Praeterea, in actu nobilioris potentiae est summa Christianae legis perfectio rationabiliter ponenda. Sed voluntas inter potentias animae est nobilior; ergo conclusio vera. Consequentia patet, et maior ex hoc, quoniam actus nobilissimus est in potentia nobiliori ponendus. Cum igitur actus beatitudinis sit nobilissimus, sequitur propositum. Minor vero apparet, quoniam potentia quae aliis imperat nobilior est potentiis quibus imperat. Sed voluntas est potentia imperativa respectu aliarum; ergo est nobilior. Maior patet de se, et minor est omnium doctorum. Et etiam habetur ab experientia: unusquisque experitur in se per velle aliis potentiis imperare.

Praeterea, quaelibet virtus motiva alicuius mobilis ad aliquem terminum facit mobile quiescere in illo termino virtute propria. Sed actus amoris principaliter facit viatorem moveri ad terminum quam actus alicuius alterius potentiae; ergo conclusio vera. Consequentia et maior patent. Et minor declaratur, quia actus intellectus quantaecumque clarus stat cum fuga sui termini, ut patet, quia Dei clara visio stat absolute cum eius odio. Sed non sic est de actu voluntatis, quia ex ipsa dilectione habetur prosecutio talis termini; ergo per actum amoris rationalis creatura principaliter movetur ad Deum, et per consequens per ipsum similiter quiescit in ipso. Et hoc videtur expressa intentio beati Augustini, XI *De civitate Dei*, capitulo 28,[12] dicentis: "Ita enim corpus pondere, sicut animus amore fertur, quocumque fertur." Ad hoc est similiter Salvatoris auctoritas, *Matthaei* 22:<37>: "*Diliges dominum Deum tuum ex toto corde tuo*" etc.

Ex ista conclusione taliter declarata sequitur corollarie contradictorium secundae partis tertiae conclusionis secundi articuli magistri mei Magistri Lamberti de Marchia, videlicet quod beatitudo principalius consistit in operatione voluntatis quam ipsius intellectus, cuius contrarium ipse asserit. Ad quod probandum aliquas apparentias adducit. Prima: ille actus est perfectior quem solitarie positum sequitur perfecta delectatio quam ille quem non sequitur. Sed posito per imaginationem quod esset visio clara respectu Dei sub ratione infiniti delectabilis, consequitur delectatio, dato quod non sit aliqua volitio; et posita volitione, secluso omni actu intellectus, nulla sequitur delectatio; ergo propositum. Maior et minor apud ipsum sunt manifestae.

Praeterea, actus primo et immediate attingens ad ipsum Deum qui est obiectum beatificum est nobilior et perfectior quocumque non tali. Sed actus intelligendi attingit primo et immediate; actus vero volitivae non sic, nisi mediante cognitione; ergo propositum. Praemissae apud eum sunt manifestae.

Praeterea, ad hoc est auctoritas canonis, cui est maxime insistendum, *Ioannis* 17:<3>: "*Haec est vita aeterna, ut cognoscant te,*" ergo etc.

Praeterea, Philosophus, X *Ethicorum*,[13] dicit quod in speculatione substantiarum separatarum consistit humana felicitas; ergo propositum.

Sed salva semper reverentia magistri mei, motiva non inducunt suum propositum sufficienter. Arguo igitur contra conclusionem in se, et deinde contra motiva, et primo sic: in illo actu principalius consistit beatitudo ad quem omnes alii finaliter ordinantur. Sed in actu dilectionis Dei super omnia omnes alii actus ordinantur; ergo et in ipso principalius consistit beatitudo. Consequentia et maior patent. Sed minor declaratur, quia quaero: aut voluntas vult Deum diligere propter ipsum intelligere aut e converso, aut neutrum propter alterum. Non primo modo, quia absque hoc posset ipsius intellectionem adquirere, cum intellectio non praesupponat dilectionem. Et est etiam contra venerabilem Anselmum, II *Cur Deus Homo,* capitulo primo[14]: "Ordo," inquit, "perversus esset velle amare ut intelligeret." Nec tertio modo, videlicet, quod neutrum vult propter alterum, quia quandocumque aliqua per se ordinantur ad aliquem finem habent etiam ordinem inter se. Sed intelligere et velle ordinatur ad Deum; ergo et habent ordinem inter se. Si vero detur secundum, habetur propositum, videlicet quod voluntas vult Deum intelligere propter ipsum diligere, et per consequens propositum.

Praeterea, in illo actu principalius consistit beatitudo per cuius rationem formalem verius excluditur omnis culpa. Sed per formalem rationem dilectionis Dei super omnia verius excluditur omnis culpa quam per formalem rationem actus intellectus; ergo propositum. Consequentia patet, et maior ex hoc, quoniam ratio beatitudinis est omnis culpae formaliter exclusiva; ergo quod magis appropinquat ad istam rationem proximius est beatificae rationi. Et minor apparet, quoniam non videtur repugnantia aliquem intuitive Deum videre et exsistere in peccato. Sed quod Deum super omnia diligat maxime fruitive et sit in peccato multum videtur habere apparentiam repugnantiae; quare propositum.

Praeterea, in illo actu principalius consistit beatitudo cuius formalis ratio principalius respicit rationem beatitudinis. Sed actus dilectionis principalius respicit rationem beatitudinis quam actus intellectus; ergo propositum. Consequentia et maior patent. Sed minor probatur, quoniam ratio formalis beatitudinis potius respicit rationem boni quam veri, quia ipsum verum appetimus propter bonum. Propter quod Philosophus, II *Ethicorum,* capitulo 2,[15] dicit "Quid est virtus scrutamur, non ut sciamus, sed ut boni efficiamur." Cum igitur actus voluntatis respiciat ipsum bonum tamquam obiectum proprium, actus vero intellectus ipsum ens, vel secundum aliquos, verum, sequitur quod actus voluntatis principalius respicit rationem beatitudinis quam actus intellectus, et per consequens, principalius consistit beatitudo in voluntate quam in intellectu.

Nec motiva, cum reverentia, probant conclusionem suam. Primum non, quia quando imaginatur quod quilibet actus talis si solitarie poneretur, unus inferret delectationem, videlicet actus intellectus, alius vero non. Quia hoc non probat, ideo quaero ab eo: aut hoc habet actus intellectus ex ratione propria et formali, aut quia terminatur ad tale obiectum delectabile, aut quia intimius talis actus intellectus attingit et figitur in obiecto quam actus voluntatis. Primum non potest dari, quia tunc ex quolibet intelligere sequeretur delectatio; quod non est verum. Nec secundum, quia aeque immediate terminatur actus voluntatis ad tale obiectum sicut intellectus. Ergo, per hoc non plus sequeretur delectatio ex uno quam ex alio. Nec tertium, quia applicatio voluntatis in summe dilecto est ferventior, ideo diceretur faciliter et probabilius quod delectatio magis sequatur ex volitione quam ex intellectione, nam delectatio est formaliter bonum vel apparens bonum. Unde Aristoteles, I *Ethicorum,*[16] dividit bonum in utile, honestum et delectabile. Cum igitur obiectum voluntatis sit bonum vel apparens bonum, sequitur quod potius cadit sub ratione voluntatis quam intellectus. Et ideo, cum reverentia, non concludit.

Secundum vero similiter non concludit, quia per hoc quod proprius attingit obiectum intellectus quam voluntatis non sequitur quod actus intellectus sit perfectior, quia per idem probare-tur quod pro statu viae potentia sensitiva esset nobilior intellectiva, ut vult Philosophus in prima propositione I *Posteriorum.*[17] Ergo talis prioritas non infert maiorem perfectionem, sicut dicit Philosophus, IX *Metaphysicae.*[18] "Priora generatione sunt posteriora perfectione." Nec auctoritas evangelica concludit suum propositum, quoniam unum exprimitur et aliud tacetur. Inferre perfectiorem modum ex parte expressi vel totalem negationem ex parte taciti est modus Graecorum. Unde sic arguunt: "Spiritus Sanctus procedit a Patre et non est expressum in evangelio de Filio, ergo non procedit a Filio." Ita haec non valet: "Haec est vita aeterna, ut cognoscant te, ergo principalius consistit in intellectu, quia non exprimitur ibi voluntas." Dico igitur ad intellectum auctoritatis quod sicut sentire est sensibilis vita, intelligere est intelligibilis vita. Quia igitur cognitio illa quae erit in vita beata erit aeterna et est vita, de copulato extremo ideo et vita aeterna. Et per hoc vult Salvator illam huic vitae temporali praeferre. Nec auctoritas Philosophi cogeret multum, quia per similem modum diceretur quae fuerit intentio Philosophi inter doctores est controversia. Dico tamen quod vult quod felicitas, prout respicit partem intellectivam, consistit in speculatione substantiarum separatarum.[19] Ita dicit Augustinus, I *De Trinitate,* capitulo penultimo,[20] quod visio est tota merces, supple partis intellectivae. Et sic omnes auctoritates in consimili forma glossandae sunt.

Ex quibus omnibus inferendo, offerro patri meo et magistro venerabili quattuor propositiones corollarias, quarum prima est haec: susceptivum formalis beatitudinis adaequate consistit in ratione voluntatis completive; patet ex quo completa et summa perfectio in amore consistit. Secunda: habitus perficiens potentiam memorandi non est eandem formaliter beatificans inhaesive; patet ex quo non est in actu, cum felicitas sit actus et operatio, ut vult Philosophus, I *Ethicorum.*[21] Tertia: principalius in intellectu practico quam speculativo consistit actus formaliter beatificans perceptivam; patet, quia plus participat rationem voluntarii. Quarta: principalius tota regio intellectualis substantiae per actum productum libere quam naturaliter elicitum finaliter quietatur; patet ex quo felicitas principalius consistit in voluntate quam in intellectu.

[Quarta Conclusio—contra opinionem Bachelarii de domo beatae Mariae de Carmelo]

Quarta conclusio haec est: formalis increatae formae susceptio per observantiam legis seraphicae est absolute possibilis potentiae volitivae. Haec conclusio tribus mediis declaratur, et primo sic: actus creatus beatificus vel est intrinsece beatificus vel solum extrinsece. Non primo modo, quia tunc esset essentialiter beatitudo; quod non videtur verum. Si ergo extrinsece, sequitur quod ex aliqua habitudine: vel ergo ex habitudine ad suam potentiam ut activam, vel ex habitudine ad ipsam ut informativam, vel ex habitudine ad ipsam ut vitaliter immutativam. Plures habitudines non videntur ex parte actus ad suam potentiam. Non potest dici beatificus ex prima habitudine, quia tunc quaelibet qualitas a tali potentia producta esset beatifica; quod non est verum. Nec potest dici ex secunda, similiter propter eandem causam. Ergo praecise ex habitudine ad suam potentiam ut vitaliter immutativam, ad obiectum videlicet infinitum. Sed divina essentia potest perfectius vitaliter immutare, cum hoc sit perfectionis. Ergo si propter hoc talis actus creatus dicitur beatificus, a fortiori divina essentia potest esse perceptivae creatae visio et fruitio beatifica; quod est probandum.

Praeterea, divina essentia est sibi ipsi fruitio beatifica. Si ergo non possit esse fruitio beatifica voluntatis creatae, aut hoc est propter limitationem creatae potentiae, aut propter informationem quae requiritur ad potentiam beatificandam, aut propter hoc quod talis beatitudo debet esse a tali potentia elicitive. Primum non impedit, quia quamvis intellectus creatus in esse perceptivo et activo sit finitus, non tamen in esse receptivo. Et etiam quia divina essentia posset tantae talem intellectum elevare quantae per talem qualitatem creatam elevaretur. Nec secundum impedit, quia huiusmodi habitudo, ut dictum est, non est ad beatitudinem necessario requisita. Nec tertium impedit, quia tunc divina essentia non esset sibi ipsi beatitudo, cum respectu sui non se habeat elicitive; ergo absolute possibile est divinam essentiam esse formalem beatitudinem creaturae non per modum informationis sed vitalis immutationis.

Praeterea, possibile est intellectum creatum habere simplicem apparentiam de divina essentia mediante qua habeatur iudicium de immensitate et infinitate eiusdem; ergo possibile est divinam essentiam fore intellectui creato formalem apparentiam. Consequentia probatur, quia tantitas obiectivae apparentiae attenditur et mensuratur penes quantitatem formalis apparentiae, verbi gratia, in visione sensitiva obiectum mihi apparet tantum vel tantum secundum quod visio quae est formalis apparentia est tanta vel tanta. Ergo ubi haberetur simplex et obiectiva apparentia divinae essentiae de sua immensitate, et non discursive, formalis apparentia esset infinita, et per consequens, cum talis non possit esse aliud a divina essentia distinctum, sequitur quod erit ipsa divina essentia. Et antecedens probatur, quia possibile est beatos habere iudicium quod Deus est infinitus sine discursu, aliter non plus possent beati cognoscere vel habere iudicium de divina immensitate quam habeant viatores; quod non videtur verum.

Ex qua conclusione sequitur corollarie contradictorium secundae conclusionis tertii articuli reverendi patris mei bachelarii beatae Mariae de Carmelo, videlicet, quod agmini seraphico maius bonum correspondere potest perfectione finita, cuius oppositum asserit et confirmat motivo triplici. Primo, quia meritum et praemium habent ad invicem commensurari. Cum igitur quodlibet meritum creaturae rationalis sit finitum, sequitur quod et similiter erit et praemium. Et per consequens, non poterit unquam maiorem perfectionem habere perfectione finita.

Secundo, quia tunc creatura posset esse aeque beata sicut Deus; quod videtur absurdum. Et consequentia patet, quia si potest sibi correspondere maior perfectio quam finita, cum quaelibet talis sit infinita, sequitur quod sibi poterit perfectio infinita correspondere, et cum non maior Deo correspondeat, sequitur quod habebunt aequales perfectiones.

Tertio, quia tunc inaequaliter merentes, et sic decedentes, aequaliter de possibili praemiarentur. Patet possibilitas conclusionis. Ex quo est possibile infinitum praemium creaturae. Nec est maior ratio de una quam de alia. Sed ista sunt inconvenientia; ergo habet suum propositum.

Sed salva semper reverentia, nec motiva concludunt nec quod reputat impossibile est impossibile. Arguo igitur primo contra conclusionem in se, deinde contra motiva, et primo sic: actus creatus beatificus ex quo ponitur medius inter divinam essentiam et perceptivam potentiam vel requiritur ut medium repraesentativum divinae essentiae vel ut dispositivum et elevativum perceptivae potentiae. Si primo modo, cum divina potentia sit se ipsam perfectius repraesentans quam quodcumque ab ea distinctum, sequitur quod etiam cuicumque intellectui se ipsam potest perfectius repraesentare quam quodcumque ab ipsa distinctum. Et per consequens, cum talis actus sit ratione talis repraesentationis beatificus, a fortiori divina essentia per se et immediate poterit esse actus beatificus creatae potentiae. Si secundo modo, requiratur, cum divina essentia per se immediate possit perfectius elevare intellectum creatum quam quodcumque aliud creatum ad visionem divinae essentiae, quia per talem actum creatum non fit beatificanda potentia ita deiformis sicut per actum increatum, sequitur quod tam ratione elevationis quam etiam, ut deductum est, praesentationi, absolute possibile est divinam essentiam fore intellectui creato visionem beatificam vel voluntati creatae fruitionem; quod erat probandum.

Praeterea, aut talis actus creatus medius requiritur necessario ad hoc quod creatura sit beata aut tantummodo contingenter. Si secundo modo, habetur propositum: quod stat creaturam esse beatam sine talibus actibus creatis, et per consequens, eius bonum immediatum erit perfectio infinita. Si dicatur quod primo modo, contra: omnis actus ad esse alterius necessario requisitus causative se habet vel exigitur ad esse illius, vel igitur talis actus requiritur in genere causae materialis, formalis, finalis vel efficientis. Non primo modo, quia talis actus non requiritur ut materia, aliter si per imaginationem esset ab anima separatus, non minus esset susceptivum beatitudinis; quod videtur absurdum, et declaratur in exemplo secundum imaginationem ponentium quantitatem fore distinctam a substantia et qualitate. Tunc immediatum subiectum qualitatum est ipsa quantitas, et ita si separaretur a substantia, non minus esset susceptivum qualitatis, sicut nunc dicitur de accidentibus in sacramento Altaris, quae, secundum eos, albedo et aliae qualitates sunt subiective in quantitate, quamvis quantitas sit ibi sine subiecto; ergo similiter in proposito. Secundum etiam non potest dari, quia, ut dictum est, ratio informationis est indifferens ad esse beatificum. Si ergo dentur aliae duae causalitates, cum ipsas Deus se solo potest supplere, sequitur quod per se potest beatificare creatam potentiam, secluso omni actu creato, et ita bonum correspondens creaturae potest esse perfectio infinita.

Praeterea, imaginemur potentiam intellectivam fore pure passivam eo modo quo Aristoteles, II *De anima*, de sensitivis potentiis imaginatur, nam sensitiva suum obiectum percipit per speciem sive radium causatum et multiplicatum in medio usque ad talem potentiam, et sic percipit suum obiectum. Si igitur Deus faceret quod tale obiectum immediate moveret talem potentiam, non esset talis species media necessaria qua potentia sensitiva caperet suum obiectum, sed ipsummet immediate sufficeret et taliter potentia perfectius perciperet suum obiectum. Tunc similiter applico ad intellectivam: applicetur divina essentia in ratione obiecti potentiae intellectivae. Tunc intellectiva ex tali applicatione perciperet divinam essentiam. Vel ergo per aliquem radium causatum ad ipsam potentiam vel per ipsummet obiectum, aut per aliquem actum voluntarie causatum in tali potentia. Primum non est dicendum, quia sic divina essentia radiaret ut corpora faciunt, et esset error dicentium Deum videri in talibus theophaniis, id est, deificis radiis, ut quidam doctores Graecorum fuerunt imaginati. Si secundum, habetur propositum. Si vero tertium, adhuc habetur propositum, quia non videtur bene theologicum dicere quod per aliquid creatum Deus potest aliquid facere quod se solo non possit. Ergo absolute possibile est divinam essentiam esse perfectionem beatificam creaturae rationali, non solum obiective sed etiam formaliter, id est, per modum vitalis immutationis.

Nec etiam motiva, cum reverentia, probant aliquam impossibilitatem. Primum non, quia non oportet ex finitate meriti arguere finitatem praemii, quia praemium non comparatur ad meritum ut condigne aequaliter respiciat ipsum, quia tale praemium non respondet nostro merito de condigno sed solum de congruo, id est, secundum misericordiam promittentis. Unde non attenditur differentia praemiorum secundum istam rationem, videlicet, secundum differentiam meritorum, quia in tali casu unicum esset praemium, sed secundum differentiam vitalis immutationis ad tale obiectum. Et sic stat veritas formalis praemii cum diversitate motionum in beatificandis potentiis.

Similiter, secundum non movet, videlicet, quod creatura esset beata sicut Deus. Non sequitur, quia diversitas est in participatione talis boni, et in gradu participandi, nam Deus adaequate participat tale bonum. Nulla vero creatura potest sic adaequate participare. Similiter, Deus necessario et essentialiter participat; quod creatura minime facit, et igitur non sequitur quod intendit.

Consequenter etiam nec tertium movet, videlicet quod omnes essent aequaliter beati cum haberent <idem> praemium obiectivum et formale, nam sicut ponendo tales actus creatos obiectum beatificum non aequaliter ab omnibus beatis videtur, sed secundum varietatem formalis praemii est etiam participatio praemii obiectivi, sic etiam secundum istam positionem ex quo divina essentia supplet vices talium actuum secundum variam et variam participationem per vitalem immutationem, erit beatorum varietas. Et sic erunt in domo Dei mansiones plurimae.

Ex quibus omnibus inferendo, offero patri meo quattuor propositiones corollarias, quarum prima est haec: formale beatificum praemium non infert necessario in beata perceptiva potentia habitudinem inhaesivam; patet ex quo possibile est divinam essentiam esse tale praemium cui repugnat quaecumque informatio. Secunda: varia obiecti vitalis immutatio in obiecto nullatenus arguit latitudinem intensivam; patet per idem medium. Tertia: non est de per se ratione formalis praemii ut elicitive a potentia qua elevat aliquatenus producatur; patet per idem medium. Quarta et ultima: non est necessario consequens quamlibet denominationem concretivam formalis praemii correspondere potentiae per ipsum beatifice elevatae; patet per idem medium de divina essentia.

[Quinta Conclusio—contra opinionem Magistri Gerardi Calcar]

Quinta conclusio est ista: idearum pluralitas in divina substantia iuxta legem Christi mirabilem est rationabiliter asserenda. Ista conclusio tribus mediis declaratur, et primo sic: intellectus divinus aeternaliter ferebatur super istam veritatem "Homo non est asinus," quia aeternaliter intellexit hominem non esse asinum. Quaero igitur quid obiective terminabat intellectionem divinam? Aut rerum exsistentiae ad extra, videlicet hominis et asini, aut species aeternae hominis et asini obiective moventes divinum intellectum, aut ipsamet divina essentia. Primum non potest dari eo quod aeternaliter tales rerum exsistentiae non fuerunt. Nec secundum, quia tunc divinus intellectus vilesceret cum cognitive perficeretur ab alio a se; tum etiam quia non sunt aliae entitates a Deo aeternae. Ergo per sufficientem divisionem ipsa divina essentia terminabat, et per consequens terminabat ut ratio vel species intelligibilis hominis, et similiter asini. Cum igitur negatio removens hominem ab asino, et econtra, non sit in re, et tamen sic intelligit intellectus divinus, ergo sequitur quod cadit super rationes intelligendi, et per consequens una ratio non est alia. Ex quo habetur propositum.

Praeterea, signo divinam essentiam ut speciem intelligibilem hominis, et similiter ut speciem intelligibilem asini, et quaero: aut divina essentia ut species intelligibilis hominis est ipsamet ut species intelligibilis asini, aut non. Si non, habetur propositum. Si sic, contra: tunc videns divinam essentiam ut speciem intelligibilem hominis videret eandem ut speciem intelligibilem asini. Sed ex hoc beatus cognitione matutina videt asinum, quia videt divinam essentiam ut speciem intelligibilem asini; ergo, ex hoc similiter cognitione matutina videt hominem, quia videt divinam essentiam ut speciem intelligibilem hominis, et per consequens pari ratione ex visione divinae essentiae ut speciei intelligibilis hominis videret quodlibet in Verbo relucens; quod non est verum. Ergo necesse est varias rationes intrinsece divinae naturae correspondere, aliter qui videret divinam essentiam praecise intuitive videret eam et quodlibet in ea relucens.

Praeterea, signo divinam essentiam ut artem causalem hominis et eandem ut artem causalem asini. Et quaero, ut prius, aut divina essentia ut ars causalis hominis est eadem ut ars causalis asini aut non. Si non, habetur propositum, videlicet quod sint diversae rationes causales. Si sic, contra: divina essentia ex hoc est ars causalis hominis, quia est hominis causativa. Si ergo divina essentia ut est ars causalis hominis est ipsamet ut est ars causalis asini, ergo ex hoc quod est ars causalis asini est hominis causativa, et per consequens ex hoc quod est asini causativa est hominis causativa; quod videtur absurdum. Nec valet dicere quod hoc est propter diversas connotationes terminorum, unde concederetur quod non ex hoc quod est causativa asini est hominis causativa. Sed propter hoc non haberetur quod essent variae rationes ex natura rei sed praecise diversae terminorum connotationes. Sed contra: per nullum extrinsecum divinae essentiae divina essentia est hominis causativa, et similiter asini. Et est causativa utriusque, ergo hoc habet intrinsece et non ex hoc quod habet unum habet aliud; ergo de necessitate ex natura rei una ratio ab altera formaliter est distincta; quod erat probandum. Ista conclusio est expresse de mente altissimi theologi, Ioannis evangelistae, videlicet evangelii sui capitulo primo, <3–4>: "*Quod factum est in ipso vita erat,*" et beati Augustini, *LXXXIII quaestionum* quaestione 46,[22] et similiter venerabilis Anselmi in suo libello *De unitate divinae essentiae et pluralitate creaturarum,*[23] et fere omnium antiquorum et valentium modernorum doctorum, quorum dicta allegare gratia brevitatis dimitto.

Ex qua taliter declarata, sequitur correlarie contradictorium quintae conclusionis secundi articuli venerabilis magistri mei Magistri Gerardi Calcar, videlicet, quod per distinctas rationes divinum essentiale lumen repraesentat rerum species et ipsarum individua, cuius contrarium asserit et confirmat motivo triplici. Primum, quia sic repraesentare, videlicet per unicam rationem, est excellentius repraesentare quam per distinctas rationes exemplares intrinsecas. Ergo conclusio sua vera. Antecedens est sibi notum et consequentia patet. Secundum, quia ponendo distinctas rationes exemplares in divinis ad intra videtur aliquo modo diminuere a summa simplicitate, ergo propositum suum. Tertium, quia singula possunt salvari quae enuntiantur de Deo non ponendo tales distinctiones rationum exemplarium; ergo conclusio vera.

Sed salva reverentia magistri mei, nec motiva sunt valida nec conclusio sua videtur vera. Arguo igitur contra conclusionem primo et deinde contra motiva. Et primo sic: divina essentia est cuiuslibet effectus perfectionaliter contentiva; ergo non per unicam rationem formalem est cuiuslibet effectus perfectionaliter contentiva; et per consequens propositum. Antecedens est notum cuilibet theologo, et consequentiam probo: impossibile est duas rationes formaliter incompossibiles concurrere unitive ad unam rationem formalem, sicut impossibile est duas rationes essentialiter incompossibiles concurrere unitive ad unam rationem essentialem. Sed ratio hominis et ratio asini sunt duae rationes formaliter incompossibiles; ergo impossibile est ipsas concurrere unitive ad unam rationem formalem. Sed si divina essentia per aliquam unam rationem continet hominem et asinum, talis ratio est aequivalenter talis ac si illae duae concurrerent unitive. Ergo impossibile est divinam essentiam per aliquam unam rationem continere illas duas rationes incompossibiles, et per consequens, consequentia bona. Maior huius probationis est nota, et minorem probo, et est contra imaginationem magistri mei qui dicit se non videre incompossibilitatem quin illae duae rationes possint in unam concurrere. Radix distinctionis arguit formaliter incompossibilitatem. Sed radix pluralitatis sive multitudinis est prima radix distinctionis; ergo et ipsa arguit incompossibilitatem. Ergo si ponuntur duae rationes, participant rationem pluralitatis, et per consequens, distinctionis, et ita incompossibilitatis. Et ita videtur contradictio quod per rationem qua aliqua sunt plura possint esse unum, et ratio: quia unum et multa sunt formaliter opposita; nolo tamen dicere in ratione communi, sed in rationibus formalibus; ex quibus apparet propositum.

Praeterea, imaginemur quod sicut numeri constituuntur in esse per novam replicationem unitatis mathematicae, sic et species creaturarum per novam replicationem unitatis divinae. Tunc sic: si replicatio unitatis mathematicae esset praecise eiusdem rationis cum prima replicatione, nulla esset distinctio specifica numerorum, sed praecise omnes numeri essent eiusdem rationis. Ergo pariformiter, si species creaturarum recipiunt eandem replicationem unitatis divinae in suo esse formativo, sequitur quod omnes erunt eiusdem rationis. Ex quo ratio participata est unica; nec aliunde habent distingui. Sed ista sunt falsa et inconvenientia; ergo illud ex quo sequitur.

Praeterea, omnes duae rationes quarum una est formaliter contingens et alia formaliter necessaria sunt de necessitate ex natura rei distinctae. Sed aliquae tales sunt in divina essentia; ergo propositum. Consequentia et maior patent. Minorem probo: signo divinam essentiam ut notitiam sui et ipsam ut notitia contingentis. Et quaero: numquid una sit formaliter alia vel non. Si non, habetur propositum. Si sic, contra: ad divinam essentiam ut notitiam futuri contingentis necessario sequitur esse contingentis. Si ergo eadem esset formaliter divina essentia ut notitia sui et ut notitia futuri contingentis, sequitur quod ad divinam essentiam ut notitiam sui sequitur esse contingentis. Et per consequens, ex ratione absolute necessaria sequitur ratio contingentis; quod videtur impossibile. Istam rationem multum ponderaverunt metaphysici scrutatores. Ad quam obsecro magistrum meum taliter respondere non logice, quia fugit difficultatem. Nec motiva, cum reverentia, probant quod magister meus intendit. Primum vero quando dicit quod sic repraesentare est excellentius. Cum reverentia, hoc est simpliciter negandum. Et ratio est, quoniam sic repraesentare est impossibile, et ideo nullo modo excellentius. Quod autem ita sit declaratur, nam ratio idealis unius speciei nullo modo continet aliam, et ita quia denominationes perfectionum simpliciter in Deo sunt formaliter distinctae, nulla est alterius contentiva, sed omnes concurrunt unitive ad unitatem divinae essentiae. Propterea, non oportet quod aliqua una sit omnium repraesentativa, cum nulla talis formaliter sit omnium contentiva.

Nec secundum movet, videlicet, quia tunc diminueretur divina simplicitas, quia inter relationes originis est realis distinctio, nam Pater realiter distinguitur a Filio, et tamen ex hoc non tollitur divina simplicitas quinimmo sit summe simplex. Ergo a fortiori non tolleretur divina simplicitas per positionem talium idealium rationum inter quas non assignatur realis distinctio, sed potius formalis.

Tertium similiter non movet quando dicitur quod singula possunt salvari sine talibus distinctionibus exemplarium rationum. Hic dico quod 'salvari' potest intelligi duobus modis: primo modo, quod tenens oppositum potest se defendere a contradictione, et sic concedo. Et per hoc non concluderetur propositum, nam protervus posset tenere nullum orbem moveri sed praecise stellas moveri sicut pisces in aqua faciunt; et sic consequenter omnes apparentias salvare. Et tamen ex hoc non concluderetur, quoniam ad motum orbium stellae moventur. Secundo modo potest intelligi rationabiliter et satisfactive intellectui. Et hic dico quod non, quia difficile est quietare intellectum de quidditatibus obiectivis creaturarum sine talibus rationibus idealibus in divina essentia formaliter distinctis.

Ex quibus omnibus inferendo offero patri et magistro meo quattuor propositiones corollarias, quarum prima est haec: quaelibet ratio exemplaris in divina essentia est solum in creatura formaliter continens denominationis consimilis quidditatem; patet, ex quo sunt diversae secundum varias denominationes. Secunda, quasi sequens ex prima: nulla ratio idealis est eminenter vel formaliter rationis alterius contentiva; patet per idem. Tertia: quaelibet res cui ex variis rationibus essentialibus plures distinctiones formaliter correspondent est absolute perfectior qualibet alia non tot distinctionum formalium inclusiva; patet, per idem. Quarta: nulla divina suppositalis ratio exsistit formaliter idealis ratio creaturae. Patet, ex quo nulla talis dicit denominationem perfectionis simpliciter.

[Sexta Conclusio—contra opinionem Magistri Malivi de Sancto-Adomaro]

Sexta et ultima conclusio est haec: firma Christi legis adhaesio a rectae rationis dictamine dependet potius quam ab imperio voluntatis. Haec conclusio tribus mediis declaratur, et primo sic: impossibile est aliquem actum alicuius potentiae excedere obiectum sibi adaequatum. Sed apparens verum est obiectum adaequatum actus assensus. Ergo impossibile est actum assensus ferri super aliquo non habente apparentiam veri. Et per consequens, per nullum voluntatis imperium quis assentit contentis in lege Christi. Maior est de se nota, et minor probatur, quia quam naturaliter intellectus dissentit falso apparenti sibi falso tam naturaliter assentit vero apparenti sibi vero. Sed tam naturaliter dissentit falso apparenti sibi falso quod ipsum impossibile est alicui alteri dissentire. Ergo tam naturaliter assentit vero apparenti sibi vero quod impossibile est ipsum alicui alteri assentire. Et per consequens, apparens verum est obiectum adaequatum actus assensus; quod erat probandum.

Praeterea, posito imperio volitivae ut intellectiva assentiat alicui sibi non apparenti vero, quaero: aut stat intellectivam vero assentire, aut non. Si sic, igitur praeter volitivae imperium requiratur alia causa. Qua posita, non stat intellectivam non assentire, et per consequens, diminuta aut superflua fuit causa primaria assignata. Si vero detur secundum, sequitur quod intellectiva sit a volitiva necessitabilis, et per consequens haec esset consequentia naturalis: volitiva imperat intellectivae ut assentiat alicui propositioni; ergo intellectiva assentit eidem, et ita respectu cuiuscumque staret imperium volitivae respectu eiusdem esset assensus intellectivae. Cum igitur volitiva possit velle contradictorium alicuius propositionis per se notae, cum voluntas sit impossibilium, ex III *Ethicorum*,[24] sequitur quod si imperaret intellectivae quod ipsa assentiret cuicumque impossibili quod mox assentiret propter naturalem connexionem imperii praecedentis; quod est manifeste falsum.

Praeterea, quam repugnat volitivae illibertari tam et intellectivae libertari; sed tam repugnat volitivae illibertari quod impossibile est ipsam volitivam esse et non esse liberam. Ergo, similiter tam repugnat intellectivae quod impossibile est ipsam esse et esse liberam. Maior apparet, quia liberum et naturale ex suis rationibus formalibus ex opposito distinguuntur. Minor est de se nota. Cum igitur intellectiva sit potentia mere naturalis, sequitur quod impossibile est ipsam alicui assentire nisi iuxta modum suae naturae et nulli iuxta modum suae naturae assentit nisi sibi appareat verum; ergo cuicumque assentit non per imperium volitivae assentit, sed per hoc quod tale sibi verum apparet. Ex quibus concluditur quod assensus articulorum potius dependet a ratione quam ab aliquo imperio voluntatis; quae est conclusio principaliter probanda.

Ex qua conclusione taliter declarata sequitur corollarie contradictorium tertii corollarii sequentis ex secunda parte primae conclusionis venerabilis magistri mei Magistri Malivi de Sancto-Adomaro, videlicet quod in assensu articulorum fidei principalius concurrit ratio vel apparentia quam voluntas. Cuius contrarium asserit et confirmat tali motivo: ratio inducens quantum est ex se non sufficit nisi superveniat imperium voluntatis imperando intellectui quod assentiat. Quia posito quod infidelis videat hominem bonae vitae praedicantem Christum, in nomine eius miracula facientem, et multa talia, adhuc est in potestate voluntatis eius imperare intellectui quod assentiat, quia aliter non esset meritorium credere vel assentire articulis fidei; quod est falsum. Et ad hoc est auctoritas beati Augustini vulgata,[25] quod caetera potest homo nolens, credere autem non nisi volens. Nunc vero imperans, cum sit nobilius imperato, principalius concurrit quam imperatum. Et per consequens, voluntas principalius, quia tamquam imperans concurrit ad assensum talem quam ratio vel apparentia quae ex se agere non possunt in intellectu pro assensu tali contra imperium voluntatis.

Sed salva reverentia magistri mei, istud motivum non est sufficiens pro sua conclusione. Contra quam primo arguam; deinde contra motivum. Arguo igitur tribus mediis, et primo sic: quilibet actus principalius dependens a voluntate quam a ratione est potius volitio quam iudicium. Sed per conclusionem patris mei assensus articulorum fidei est principalius dependens a voluntate quam a ratione; ergo est potius volitio quam iudicium. Consequentia est nota. Maior probatur, quia effectus dependens a duabus causis quarum una principalius concurrit, altera potiorem denominationem sortitur a praedominante, ut patet in singulis effectibus productis taliter. Si ergo ad eundem actum concurrant voluntas et ratio, et principalius concurrit voluntas quam ratio, sequitur quod talis actus potius est volitio quam iudicium. Sed hoc consequens est falsum; ergo et antecedens. Non maior, ut probatum est; ergo minor, et per consequens, conclusio falsa. Cuius consequentis falsitas sic probatur: ille actus potius est iudicium quam volitio qui immediate respicit veritatem vel falsitatem. Sed assensus articulorum fidei immediate respicit veritatem vel falsitatem. Ergo potius est iudicium quam volitio, et per consequens potius dependens a ratione quam ab imperio voluntatis; quod erat probandum.

Praeterea, signo illam rationem quae per se non est sufficiens ad causandum assensum nisi concurrat imperium voluntatis. Et capio istam propositionem mere creditam "Resurrectio erit." Tunc arguo sic: nullum istorum est per se sufficiens ad causandum assensum respectu articulorum fidei, sed ambo simul concurrentia. Tunc sic: ista duo integrant unam sufficientem causam ad talem assensum. Ergo in quocumque essent ista duo simul, illae sufficienter assentiret. Consequens est falsum; ergo et antecedens. Et per consequens oportet aliam causam assignare. Cuius consequentis falsitas sic probatur, nam cuicumque infideli philosophice illustrato sunt fere notae rationes quas faciunt Christiani pro tali articulo inducendo "Resurrectio erit," et quilibet habet velle respectu illius, quoniam quilibet naturaliter appetit immortalitatem, et tamen nullus talis assentit. Ergo oportet aliam causam assignare.

Praeterea, sit *a*, gratia exempli talis articulus "Resurrectio erit," et arguo sic: qualitercumque *a* primo significat, scit philosophus naturali lumine illustratus *a* significare et non scit *a* esse verum nec scit *a* esse falsum, ergo dubitat *a* esse verum. Ista consequentia est bona, isto supposito, quod omnis propositio de qua considerat aliquis, quoniam nescit esse veram nec scit esse falsam, sit illi eidem dubia, ut admittunt communiter tractantes de scire et dubitare. Ergo cum quocumque stat veritas antecedentis cum eodem stat veritas consequentis. Sed cum omni actu imperativo voluntatis stat veritas antecedentis, quoniam non sequitur: voluntas imperat intellectui ut sciat *a* esse verum vel sciat *a* esse falsum; ergo intellectus scit *a* esse verum vel scit *a* esse falsum, et per consequens oppositum consequentis stat cum antecedente, videlicet quod voluntas imperat intellectui ut credat *a*, et tamen intellectus dubitat *a*, et per consequens non credit *a*.

Non ergo ex imperio voluntatis assensus articulorum fidei principalius quam a ratione causatur; quod erat probandum.

Nec motivum, cum reverentia, concludit suum propositum: cum enim arguit quod ratio non est sufficiens, hic dico pro materia rationis et fundamento positionis iuxta imaginationem fratris Richardi Brinchil, cuius positionem sustineo, quod ratio solet multipliciter accipi: quandoque pro illa parte hominis quae ad Dei similitudinem est formata, ut capit Hugo, *De sacramentis*, libro I, parte 3, capitulo 6,[26] et similiter Augustinus, *De libero arbitrio*, libro I, capitulo 12.[27] Quandoque pro forma syllogistica seu discursu ex quo nata est causari notitia propositionis alias ignotae, et sic capiunt communiter philosophi cum dicunt "argumentum est ratio rei dubiae faciens fidem."[28] Quandoque pro quocumque tali quo immediate innotescit actu abstractivae intellectui veritas vel falsitas propositionis, alias incognitae. Et istum modum capiunt frequenter doctores, ut Cassiodorus in libro suo *De anima*, capitulo 10,[29] dicens quod ratio est "animi motus qui per ea quae conceduntur atque nota sunt ad incognitum perducit, deducens intellectum in veritatis arcanum." Dico igitur ad argumentum quod accipiendo rationem primo modo utique verum est. Si secundo modo, vel illative vel adhaesive. Si adhaesive, verum est; illative vero non, quia multae sunt veritates ex quibus possunt inferri articuli. Sed ex his non sequitur quod nulla ratio, quia dico: sicut phantasma irradiatum est causa copulationis ipsius cum intellectu possibili secundum imaginationem Commentatoris, III *De anima*, capitulo 5,[30] ita fides irradiata in intellectu est causa assensus articulorum fidei, ita quod voluntas hoc per se non facit sed illa irradiatio supra fidem in intellectu inclinat intellectum ad assensum quem approbans voluntas vel concommitans multum meretur. Et in hoc consistit meritum voluntatis secundum imaginationem istius auctoris.

Ex quibus omnibus inferendo, offero patri meo quattuor propositiones corollarias, quarum prima est haec: actus iudicativus perceptivae potentiae nullatenus subest imperio volitivae; patet per iam dicta. Secunda: intellectiva potentia non potest ex voluntatis imperio veritati sibi neutrae assentire; patet similiter ex dictis. Tertia: actus respectu veritatum fidei adhaesivus naturalis potius quam voluntarius est censendus; patet similiter. Quarta: assensus veritatum credibilium ex conditione elicitivi principii non suscipit meritoriam rationem; patet per idem.

Ad formam igitur quaestionis patet per conclusiones quod eius pars affirmativa est sustinenda, nam prima docet hominem legem perfectam, cum non sit partialis sed omnibus indifferenter tradita. Secunda ostendit obiectum complete sacians. Tertia, actum quo mens in obiecto figitur. Quarta, modum quo Deus illabitur. Quinta, rationes quibus illabitur. Et sexta, radium quo mens assentit in lege tradita.

Ex quibus correlarie sequitur quod candida Christianae legis perfectio est a qualibet perceptiva potentia rationabiliter imitanda.

Et ad rationes in oppositum patet quid per conclusiones positas est dicendum. Et sic sit finis huius collativae quaestionis ad Christi laudem, cui est honor et gloria per infinita curricula saeculorum. Amen.

Explicit quaestio primi principii.

Notes to Appendix

1. A. Emmen, "Petrus de Candia, O.F.M. *De immaculata Deiparae conceptione,*" in *Tractatus quatuor de immaculata conception B. Mariae Virginis,* Bibliotheca Franciscana Scholastica 16 (Quaracchi: Collegium S. Bonaventurae, 1954), 235–59.

2. Ehrle, *Der Sentenzenkommentar,* 21.

3. Emmen, "Petrus de Candia," 261–266.

4. Quaestio . . . Minorum] Explicit quaestio collativa pro primo principio in Sententiarum Lectura per venerabilem fratrem et magistrum Petrum de Candia ordinis Minorum compilata anno Domini millesimo, trecentesimo septuagesimo octavo Parisius in scolis fratrum Minorum per ipsum eodem anno studio recitata cod. P, *om.* V.

5. Petrus Lombardus, *Sententiae in IV libris distinctae,* prol., ed. I. Brady (Grottaferrata: 1971), 3. Cf. Hilarius, *De Trinitate,* 10.1–2 (PL 10:344).

6. Aristoteles, *Ethica Nicomachea,* 5.9 (1133b29–30).

7. Augustinus, *De civitate Dei,* 11.1 (CCSL 48:321).

8. Gratianus, *Decretum,* pars prima, dist. XXVII, c. l et dist. XXVIII, cc. 1 et 7, in *Corpus Iuris Canonici,* ed. A. Friedberg (Lipsiae: 1879–81), 1:98 et 102.

9. *Corpus Iuris Canonici,* 2:592.

10. Augustinus, *De doctrina Christiana,* 1.5.5 (CCSL 32:9.1–3): Res igitur, quibus fruendum est, Pater et Filius et Spiritus Sanctus, eademque trinitas, una quaedam summa res communisque omnibus fruentibus ea.

11. Symbolum 'Quicumque': increatus Pater, increatus Filius, increatus Spiritus Sanctus . . . et tamen non tres aeterni, sed unus aeternus; sicut non tres increati nec tres immensi, sed unus increatus et unus immensus. *Enchirdion Symbolorum,* §75, ed. 32, ed. H. Denzinger and A. Schonmetzer (1964).

12. Augustinus, *De civitate Dei,* 11.28 (CCSL 48:348).

13. Aristoteles, *Ethica Nicomachea,* 10.9 (1179a23–30).

14. Anselmus, *Cur Deus Homo,* 1.2.1 (ed. Schmitt 2:97–98).

15. Aristoteles, *Ethica Nicomachea,* 2.2 (1103b29).

16. Aristoteles, *Ethica Nicomachea,* 1.3 (1095b18–19).

17. Aristoteles, *Analytica Posteriora,* 1.1 (71a1–2).

18. Aristoteles, *Metaphysica,* 9.8 (1050a4–5).

19. Cf. Aristoteles, *Ethica Nicomachea,* 10.7 (1177a12–21).

20. Augustinus, *De Trinitate,* 1.13.28–30 (PL 48:841–42): Et ipsa visio est facie ad faciem, quae summum praemium promittitur iustis. . . . Haec vita aeterna est illa visio quae non pertinet ad malos . . . Deinde venit ad visionem suae claritatis, in qua venturus est ad iudicium; quae visio communis erit et impiis et iustis.

21. Aristoteles, *Ethica Nicomachea,* 1.6 (1098a13–15).

22. Augustinus, *De diversis quaestionibus octoginta tribus,* q. 46, §2 (CCSL 44a:71–73).

23. Anselmus, *Monologion,* 35 (ed. Schmitt 1:54): Verum cum constet quia verbum eius consubstantiale illi est et perfecte simile, necessario consequitur, ut omnia quae sunt in illo, eadem et eodem modo sint in verbo eius. Quidquid igitur factum est sive vivat sive non vivat, aut quomodocumque sit in se: in illo est ipsa vita et veritas.

24. Aristoteles, *Ethica Nicomachea,* 3.4 (1111b23).

25. Cf. S. Augustinus, *In Ioannem,* 26.2 (PL 35:1607).

26. Hugo de Sancto-Victore, *De sacramentis fidei Christianae,* 1.3.21 (PL 176:225).

27. Potius S. Augustinus, *De ordine*, 1.11.30 (CCSL 29:124).

28. Cicero, *Topica*, 1.2.8, ed. H.M. Hubbell (Cambridge, MA: Harvard University Press, 1949), 386: Itaque licet definire locum esse argumenti sedem, argumentum autem rationem quae rei dubiae faciat fidem.

29. Cassiodorus, *De anima*, 4 (CCSL 96:540).

30. Averroes, *In Aristotelis De anima*, III, tc. 5 (ed. Crawford 404–6).

Chapter 13

What Was Contingency?

CALVIN G. NORMORE

My concern in this paper[1] is not with what contingency is but with what it was at the beginning of the fourteenth century. This is, of course, an historical issue but it is a philosophical issue too if, as I believe, there are serious philosophical difficulties about what contingency is. So, to motivate interest in what contingency *was* I begin with some remarks about what the modal notions in its family *are*.

Twentieth-century modal theory revolved around various ways of understanding modality in terms of generality. One such way is commonly employed in thinking about *logical* necessity. Here there is an intuitive and a technical characterization. The intuitive characterization is that a claim is logically necessary if it *follows from* any premises whatever. This involves a notion of following from which seems to be understood thus: B follows from A just in case it is impossible that A be true and B be false. So a claim is logically necessary if it is impossible that anything be true while it is false. This account of logical necessity uses the concept of impossibility and logicians have tried to avoid this by talking instead about *form*. Here the idea comes from the method of counter-example. Suppose someone reasoned like this:

If it is a boy it is allowed to inherit.
Therefore: If it is not a boy it is not allowed to inherit.

I might claim that this is not very good reasoning because if it were, then so would be:

If it is a cat then it is a mammal.
Therefore: if it is not a cat it is not a mammal.

Here "boy" is replaced by "cat" and "allowed to inherit" by "a mammal" but the form of the argument is otherwise the same. I have implicitly appealed then to the idea that an argument is good only if no other argument of the same form has true premisses and a false conclusion. Logicians have built on this foundation to argue that a claim is logically necessary just in case every other claim of the same (suitably picked out) form is true.[2]

There is a twentieth-century philosophical conception of necessity: a claim is necessary just in case it would be true in all possible situations. This idea is different from the conception in terms of uniform substitution because it holds the claim constant and varies the situation whereas the other, so to speak, holds the situation constant and varies the claim. But the idea that necessity is truth in all possible situations is radically under-determined. What is a possible situation? A way the world *can* be? A way the world *could have* been? A way the world could be *consistently* described as being?[3]

It is this last idea, that a possible world is determined by a consistent (and complete) description in a first-order language which undergirds the model theory for contemporary modal logics. But almost nobody believes it because we recognize relationships, semantic relationships at least and perhaps others, which are not captured in such languages. Hence we rule out as impossible models which are perfectly acceptable models of QCB models in which things are red and green all over, for example.

One way in which one might restrict such models is to hold that what is possible at a time is restricted by the history of the world up to that time. One way of doing this is with a thesis of the necessity of origin—of the sort suggested by Kripke in *Naming and Necessity*. Such theses are powerful—they may well have, for example, the consequence that if the world has always existed then it necessarily has always existed. In any case what they force us to consider is the relationship between modality and time. If what is necessary depends upon how things came to be, then one might reasonably think that what is necessary varies over time—and that might lead to interest in conceptions of modality which tie modality and time more closely.

I. The Historical Thesis

Many historians of philosophy think that our ideas of possibility and necessity grew up in the late Middle Ages as a result of debates between *then* current conceptions of these concepts. But there is some disagreement about what the conceptions of modality available in the Middle Ages were and what the relation between them was. There has been, in particular, considerable debate about how the Middle Ages understood the relationship between time and modality, and there are several competing pictures

According to one influential picture, necessity is just truth at every time, possibility is truth at some time.[4] On this picture every genuine possibility is realized at some time or other. A number of historians of philosophy, especially Jaakko Hintikka, have suggested that in at least some texts (especially *De Caelo* 1,12) Aristotle had this conception in mind. N. Rescher has suggested that it was a common view in medieval Islam. S. Knuuttila suggests that it was a view we sometimes find in the Latin West—especially in early physics texts. This view explains easily, perhaps too easily, why nature is said to do nothing in vain.

The statistical picture has heretical consequences. For example it requires that God cannot do anything other than what God does. Although some thinkers held this view (Abailard was condemned for it) they are rare and so it is pretty clear that the statistical view cannot be the central medieval picture.

Suppose we take a notion of *power* as primitive and claim that for X to be possible is just for it to be in the power of some agent to bring about X. This approach has a notion some find mysterious—power—at its core but it certainly fits some texts. For example in *De Casu Diaboli* chapter 12 Anselm asks how it can be said that the world was possible before God made it. He is puzzled because before the world existed it obviously did not have power to come into existence—indeed it had no powers at all. He concludes that what makes it true to say that before the world existed, it could exist, is that God had the power to bring the world into existence. The claim looks like a claim about the powers of the world but turns out to be one about the powers of God. This also illustrates one consequence of the power picture. On this picture act precedes potency. Every possibility depends upon the state of something actual—notably upon the omnipotence of God.

The power picture suggests a thesis about the relation between time and modality. On an Aristotelian view, time is the measure of change and change is the actualization of potentialities. Hence time just is a measure of the passage from potency to act. This suggests that there is something very odd about the idea of power over the past. The power view makes very natural the idea that the past is somehow fixed in a way that the future is not fixed.

These considerations also raise issues of the relation between consistency and realizability—and suggest that many of our modal intuitions are really intuitions about realizability, that is, about the conditions under which things can be brought about. It is in the work of John Duns Scotus that the question of the relation between possibility and realizability is, perhaps for the first time, clearly faced. I have argued elsewhere (following others for the most part) that while Scotus distinguishes a logical power—an absence of *repugnantia* in the terms—and a real power capable of bringing the thing about, he does not think that these are unconnected. The logical power is the modal ground for the real power but it is the real power which is crucial for understanding what we usually think of as modality. And that real power involves time.[5]

II. AQUINAS'S SIMILE AND SCOTUS'S CRITIQUE

Most Platonists and many Christians maintain that God is outside time. This is not merely the claim that God's duration is not measured by time, a claim from which few

Christians would dissent, but involves the stronger claim that for God there is no past, future, or even, strictly speaking, present. God has no temporal *location*. This picture of God is encoded in the simile Boethius employs in his *Consolatio* of God as the centre of a circle with the times spread out around him like the points on the circumference of the circle. The simile is developed by Aquinas and seems to form the basis of another, that of the man on a rooftop or a mountaintop who can see all those on a path below even though they can only see those ahead of them. It may be Aquinas's development of this doctrine which Duns Scotus criticizes:

> There is another opinion which maintains that God's certain cognition of future contingents is thus: They say that all things are present to God in eternity according to their actual existence. For they say it should not be imagined that time and those things which flow in time are present in eternity as a stick is present to a whole river if it is fixed in the middle of the river. Such a stick is present to the whole river successively because it is present to each of its parts, but eternity is simultaneous with the whole of time and with all those things which flow in time, so that the whole of time and whatever is in time successively is present to eternity, so that eternity is supposed to be like a centre and the whole of flowing time like a circumference, it may be allowed that the circumference be moved continuously and part may succeed part yet in relation to the centre be uniformly related. They maintain another example of someone on the roof of a house. . . .
>
> But on the contrary. First, the opposite of the foregoing opinion is argued for from the example which is adduced. The divine immensity is not a reason for [God's] existing except in a place which exists, for if a place were able to be augmented to infinity successively (just as time flows to infinity), then God would not be simultaneous with the infinite place because that place would be only *secundum quid*—and what is not is not able to be the reason for something existing presently. Similarly therefore God will not be present to the whole of flowing time. The example therefore concludes the opposite.
>
> Besides, if all future things were present to God according to their actual existence, it would be impossible for God to cause something *de novo*. For that which is related to God as present according to its own actual existence is related to him as what has been caused, not as what is to be caused (because then it would not be as present). Therefore if a future contingent is related to God according to its actual existence he will not cause a future contingent unless he were to cause it twice over.[6]

Scotus has fundamentally two arguments here. One is that Aquinas's simile requires a space on which all the points of time exist—and there is no such space. The second is that the view that past and future are similarly related to God makes a hash of the doctrine of creation. On Scotus's understanding of it, creation requires that something be brought from non-existence to existence. But, if things are present to God in their actual existence then they do not need to be further brought into actual existence—and so creation is nugatory.

To the best of my knowledge Scotus never fully articulates the picture he wants to oppose to Aquinas's but we can assume it has at least the features for the lack of which he criticizes Aquinas. That is, we can suppose that while Scotus does not deny the immutability of God he holds that only the present is present even to God. We can also suppose that even if the divine creative act itself does not change, only those things which are now exist so that the effects of the divine creative act are genuinely different from time to time.

III. *Omne Quod Est . . .*

It is difficult to reconcile the eternalist view of God's relation to time with the view that what is necessary may change over time. One could, of course, hold that necessity is temporally indexed—there is the necessary at t_1 and the necessary at t_2 and . . .—but necessity, like existence, is not, intuitively, a relative notion. I can ask sensibly what existed or will exist at t and I can ask what was necessary or will be necessary at t, but that is not to ask either what is (tenselessly) at t or what is (tenselessly) necessary-at-t. It may be, as D. K. Lewis has suggested, that "now" and "actual" are indexical terms but, as Scotus might well have said, indexicals only pick out points from a field of which all the elements are or exist.[7] From that perspective, if I ask what exists the correct answer is the whole field and if I ask what is necessary the answer has to be given absolutely. If we agree that what is necessary changes over time, then the correct answer to what is necessary depends on what time it now is absolutely.

Ockham claims that the past is necessary. This is not the claim that what is past, relative to an arbitrarily chosen point of time, is necessary relative to that moment, but the claim that absolutely speaking what is past (what is *now* past) is necessarily so. Ockham also claims that the present is fixed in the sense that if something is genuinely present the claim that it *was* will always be necessarily true hereafter. It is less clear whether Scotus thinks that the past is necessary. For example in his Lectura I d. 40 q. Unica, he considers the objection that:

> what passes into the past (*transit in praeteritum*) is necessary—as the Philosopher wishes in Bk. VI of the *Ethics* approving the saying of someone who says that this alone is God not able to make, that what is past is not past.[8]

He replies:

> to the first argument, when it is argued that that which passes into the past is nec-
> essary, it is conceded. And when it is argued that this one's being predestined
> passes into the past it should be said that it is false. For if our will were always to
> have the same volition in the same immobile instant, its volition would not be past
> but always in act. And thus it is of the divine will which is always the same. . . .
> Hence [with respect to] what is said in the past tense—that God has predestined—
> there the "has predestined" joins (*copulat*) the now of eternity as it coexists with a
> now in the past.[9]

This is a bit gnomic but seems to say both that there is no past for God—whose
act is like an eternal present—and that while that act has coexisted with our past it
does not share the necessity of the past. On the other hand, the passage also seems to
say that what is genuinely past really is necessary. If what is genuinely past is what is
past for us, this raises a very delicate issue of whether what is in our past is really necessary or not.

However that may go (and it is not an issue to the bottom of which I yet see), it is
clear that Ockham and Scotus disagree about the necessity of the present and, that this
difference has consequences for their views about the relation of God to time, as we
shall see.

The source of Ockham's disagreement with Scotus about the present lies in a
deeper disagreement about the structure of powers. For Aristotelians, change is analyzed into various types of actualization of potencies. And time is *the measurement of
change with respect to before and after*, says Aristotle in the *Physics* (220a25–6). Although
it is, I think, very hard to get the doctrine out of the text of Aristotle, Ockham seems
to have followed Averroes and a substantial medieval tradition in thinking that the
motion of which time was most properly the measure was that of the outermost sphere.
Whether Aristotle held this or not, it has the advantage of giving a clear direction to
time. If time is the measure of the actualization of potencies as such, then the direction
of time is naturally given by the passage *from* potency *to* act but, in the absence of a
privileged change, there is always the question of what guarantees that all actualiza-
tions run in the same temporal direction. Privileging a particular motion also simplifies the problem of duration. Durations are strictly proportional to the distance
traveled by a point on the outermost sphere.

A complete theory of time uncontroversially requires an account of duration, an
account of temporal direction, and an account of simultaneity. I would add (more con-
troversially) that it requires an account of the difference between past and future. This
is controversial because there are some, Bas van Fraassen for example, who think that

simultaneity is an objective (if frame relative) physical relation but also think the distinction between past and future is not.

For Ockham it is the distinction between past and future which is basic and insofar as he considers simultaneity it is parasitic upon the notion of the present. Ockham never attempts to define the present but it is clear from his critique of Scotus's formal distinction that he thinks it intimately connected with the notion of existence. To say that something is present or *is* now, is just to say that it exists, period, with no tense or modal qualifiers. On Ockham's view, if I say truly that S is P and then go on to say truly that S is not P, I am speaking of two different times as present. Ockham regards Scotus's willingness to allow that sometimes S *qua* A is P and S *qua* B is not-P, as the ruination of any method for determining that time has passed. Given that to say that S exists is to say that S is now, Ockham could define simultaneity if he cared enough to do so. S's being P and T's being U are simultaneous if it was, is, or will be that S is P and T is U.

Ockham and Scotus agree that free choice requires at least a power to do and power to not-do. Now there is a thought experiment which goes back at least to Grosseteste in which one considers a rational creature, an angel for example, which exists only for an instant during which it is, let us suppose, loving God. The question posed is whether it could be loving God freely.

The argument that the angel could not be loving God freely is that for it to do so it has to have a power to do otherwise, for example, to hate God. But, the argument continues, there is no power to hate God if it is impossible to actualize that power and it is impossible to actualize a power if that power could not be actualized at any time. The angel in question exists only for an instant and cannot actualize its supposed power when it does not exist, so if it has the power to hate God it can actualize it at the very instant it exists.

Aristotle's definition of the possible is that which, when posited does not entail an impossibility. Suppose then that we posit that the angel hates God and see what follows. We have already hypothesized that the angel is loving God, and we did not take back that supposition. So we have now supposed that the angel is loving God and that the angel is hating God—and that is a contradiction.

It seems that if we are to suppose that the angel which is loving God can, nonetheless, hate God for that same instant we have to suppose that the angel *can* not be doing what it in fact is doing at the very moment it is doing it. The problem here is that it is very plausible that if something is actually one way and can be another it can change from the first way to the second. But time is the measure of change and so change takes time—even sudden change requires two times. Alas our angel has no time to change and so cannot change. If being other than you are requires change, our angel cannot be other than it is and so is not the way it is freely.

Scotus is moved by this argument to modify the principle that being other than you actually are requires change. Scotus's way of doing this is to take up a device used by thirteenth-century physicists to treat problems of the continuum and then extend it—as Stephen Dumont and Timothy Noone have argued—to problems in theology: the device of *signa* or *instants of nature.*

In this context, Scotus treats an instant of time as, or as containing, a sequence of instants of nature. The present instant can, at a minimum, be regarded as a pair of instants of nature ordered as before and after in nature and we can treat the prior one as that in which the angel has both the power to love God and the power to hate God and the posterior instant of nature as that in which the angel has actualized the power to love God. Since there is an instant of nature "in" the instant of time at which the angel has the power to hate God we can say that the angel has the power to hate God at that instant of time (and could, relative to that instant of nature actualize it at the posterior instant of nature) and so that the angel is now free.

Scotus thinks that it is because of this ordering of nature within the present instant of time that we can speak of the present as being only contingently the way it is. It is as if the past and future met in the present instant with the prior instant of nature belonging to the past (as its endpoint) and the posterior one to the future (as its beginning).

IV. Ockham's Argument That Scotus's Distinction between the Necessity of the Past and That of the Present Cannot be Maintained

Ockham is firmly convinced that one cannot consistently admit the necessity of the past and hold the present to be contingent and he has an argument designed to show it.

The argument depends on a principle which he thinks both Scotus and he will accept, that if an entirely singular sentence is entirely about the present *secundum rem* and it is true, then there is another sentence (usually but not always had by replacing the present tensed verb by the corresponding past tense of the same verb) which will be necessarily true hereafter. For example, if it is now true that Socrates is pale, then hereafter it will be true that "Socrates was pale" is necessarily true. The restrictions are all needed. Ockham argues in several places—notably in his *Tractatus de Praedestinatione*—that if the sentence is not singular or has a common noun as part of its subject or is not entirely about the present, the principle fails. Indeed the failure of this principle for such cases lies at the very heart of Ockham's own solution to the problem of future contingents. "Peter is predestinate" is true, he says, but contingently true and " '"Peter was predestinate" is necessary' will be true tomorrow" is simply false. For Ockham,

Peter is predestinate iff Peter will be saved and "'"'Peter will be saved' was true" is necessary' will be true tomorrow" is just as false.

Given the properly restricted principle Ockham argues as follows:

Suppose:
(1) "A wills X at t" is true where t is the present time.
Then   (2) "A willed X at t" will always be necessarily true after t.
Then   (3) " 'A willed X at t' is necessary" will always be true after t.
And   (4) " 'A nilled X at t' is impossible" will always be true after t.
Suppose further:
(5) "A can nil X at t" is also true.
Then   (6) "A nils X at t" is possible at t.
Then   (7) " 'A nilled X at t' is possible" will always be necessary after t.
So after t it will always be true that
(8) A nilled X at t is impossible and A nilled X at t is possible. [from 4) and 7)]
—And this is a contradiction.

The validity of the argument hangs, I think, on the inference from 6 to 7 and it is a tricky inference. No doubt it is true that if it is now possible that S is P, it will be true to say that it was possible that S is P, but does it follow from this that it will be true to say that it is possible that S was P? I think that the inference is invalid on Ockham's own tense and modal principles, but I can see that he might have thought otherwise. He accepts the equivalence of strictly singular composite and divided sense possible sentences, that is, he accepts "A can be B" iff " 'A is B' is possible." It is not far to accept "A could have been B" iff " 'A was B' is possible." But it is further than someone who thinks that what is possible changes with time should go.

V. Ockham's own Account of the Freedom of Creatures

Whether he is entitled to think so or not, Ockham does think that the contingency of the present entails the contingency of the past and he thinks the past is not contingent. Ockham thus cannot avail himself of Scotus's solution to the problem of how choice could be free for an agent which cannot change, and he takes a different tack. Ockham does not analyze freedom in terms of the ability to do otherwise-at-t than you are in fact doing at t. Throughout his work he explains it this way:

I call "freedom" the power by which I am able indifferently and contingently to hold (*ponere*) different things so that I am able to cause and not to cause the same effect, there being no difference existing anywhere outside that power.[10]

Now this is one of the three senses of contingency he introduces at the end of Question III of his *Tractatus de Praedestinatione,* right after rejecting Scotus's account of the contingency of the present on the ground of its incompatibility with the necessity of the past:

> But how then will the contingency of the will be preserved in respect of what is willed by it? I answer that God's will (as regards what is external) as well as the created will, acts contingently at the instant at which it acts. But this can be understood in three ways. In one way, that the will, existing for a time prior to the instant a in which it causes, is able freely to cause or not to cause in a. And this understanding is true if the will so pre-exists. It can be understood in a second way, so that at the same instant in which it causes, it may be true to say that it does not cause. This understanding is not possible because of the contradictories which follow, namely that it causes in a and does not cause in a. In a third way, "to cause contingently in a" can be understood [to mean] that freely and without any variation or change occurring to it or to any other cause, and without the ceasing of another cause, it is able to cease its act in another instant after a, so that in instant a this is true: "the will causes," and in another instant after a, this is true: "the will does not cause." And the will causes thus in a, however a natural cause does not cause thus.[11]

In a footnote (p. 75, n. 111) to their translation of the *Tractatus,* Adams and Kretzmann suggest that "Contingency in sense (3) is compatible with strict determinism. Contingency in sense (1), i.e., freedom of the will, is a necessary condition of sinning." Ockham very clearly employs sense (1) in his *ex professo* treatments of freedom, the very sense that Adams and Kretzmann quite plausibly thought too weak. What are we to make of this? We have become used in recent years to arguments by Douglas Langston and others to the conclusion that Scotus is a compatibilist who admits determinism by God's will—and indeed such arguments go back to Ockham—but that Ockham himself is a compatibilist seems hard to credit.

VI. The Application of This Account to the Contingency of a Beginningless World

The talk of beings existing only for an instant is Scotus's. Ockham does not think there are any instants of time any more than there are points of space—indeed given that the regular motion of the outermost celestial sphere is what time primarily measures, the two are interdependent. Nonetheless he is well aware that Scotus's problem could arise for any being which is unchangeable and he is convinced that God is such a being.

We have just seen him suggest that if a will did not precede its act in time, then the appropriate sense of contingency is the third—the "weak" one.

Ockham thinks it *probabile* though not demonstrable, that God could have created contingently a universe without a temporal beginning. He takes up the issue twice. In *Quodlibet* II q. 5, replying to the objection that God could not have made the world from eternity because "then God would have produced it of necessity, for everything eternal is necessary" and thus God's freedom would be undermined, Ockham writes:

> I say that had God produced the world from eternity he would have produced it from eternity of necessity because this sentence would, in that case, now be necessary: "The world was from eternity," since it would now be true and never could be false. However it would have been able to be false, just as a true proposition about the past is necessary and yet was able to be false.

Supposing such a sentence were true, when might it have been able to be false? Ockham's answer in his longer treatment of the issue—in his Disputed Question on the subject—is disturbing. Instead of saying when the sentence could have been false he claims that God's production of such a world would have been contingent because God is naturally prior to the world. In that longer discussion, he then turns to Henry of Ghent's arguments not against the possibility of an eternal world dependent on God but of an eternally created world and claims that the creation of an eternal world is possible, because for such a world creation and conservation come to the same thing. God would create and conserve such a world by a single act.

This suggests, I think, a startling answer to our query. When could God falsify the sentence "The world was from eternity"? Never! If his creating such a world is his conserving it, then God creates it contingently in the third of Ockham's senses, because he can at any time without any change outside his will cease from that very act by which he created. Thus that act is free and contingent even though it has always been too late to prevent its effect.

Is this an intuitively satisfying sense of "contingent" or of "free"?

Ockham thinks that God is able to create contingently even a universe with no temporal beginning because he is naturally prior to it and because the creation of such a universe is no different from its conservation. But Ockham thinks the past is necessary. Can we reconcile these?

VII. *PER ACCIDENS* NECESSITY AND OCKHAM'S MODAL MONISM

First then, what does Ockham mean by the claim that the past is necessary? Ockham draws at least two distinctions between necessities. On the one hand, something can be absolutely or suppositionally necessary. On the other hand, it can be simply necessary or necessary *per accidens*. The distinction between absolute and suppositional necessity really is a distinction between claims which are necessary and claims which are not themselves necessary but are the consequents of true conditionals—which are, for Ockham, necessary.

On the other hand, I claim, the distinction between *per accidens* and simple necessity is a distinction within the absolutely necessary between what is always absolutely necessary and what is absolutely necessary but was not always absolutely necessary. It follows, if I am right, that the difference between *per accidens* and simple necessity is not a difference between types of necessity but simply a difference in what accounts for the same underlying necessity.

Simple necessity is the kind of necessity by which the conclusion of a valid argument follows from its premises and there is textual evidence that Ockham thinks that the sense of necessity in which the past is necessary is the same sense which governs valid inference. He writes:

> This should be noted—that some such consequences are merely *ut nunc* and some are simple. When predicating the subject of the antecedent of the subject of the consequent [yields] a necessary predication the consequence is simple; however when the [resulting] categorical sentence is contingent and not necessary then the consequence is merely *ut nunc*. Hence this consequence is only *ut nunc:* "any divine person was from eternity, therefore something which is creating was from eternity," if the subject of the consequent is taken for what is, because this is contingent: "something which is creating is God." However, if the subject of the consequent is taken for what was, then the consequence is in a way simple, because this is necessary: "something creating was God," taking the subject for what was, just as this is necessary: "God was creating."[12]

Ockham is claiming that "God was creating" and "Something which was creating was God" are necessary in a sense strong enough for us to be able to accept that it is impossible for "Some divine person was from eternity" to be true and yet "God was creating" to be false. Since that is the sense of impossible he uses in evaluating inferences, I take it that the corresponding sense of "necessary" is that in which a consequence is, for him, necessary.

If the past is necessary in the same sense in which valid inferences correspond to necessary truths, then necessity and possibility are, I argue, notions closely connected in Ockham's thought with that of power. On Ockham's view necessity must be such that it can be acquired and some claims acquire it in virtue of things coming to be or ceasing to be. From this alone it follows that necessity for Ockham is not a logical or semantic notion, or even a matter of the real essences of things. None of these would allow what is necessary to change over time. What is left?

Once again, I think, the answer lies in the Aristotelian framework of potency and act. In brief, something is possible if there is a power to bring it about and necessary if there is no such power.

Why then is the past necessary for Ockham? The short answer is that there is no power with respect to the past. But why is that? The longer answer is that for Ockham the present consists of the actualities and powers there *are* and the future just is what will come into being through the actualization of those powers. Time is the measure of that actualization. For Ockham the actualization of any power either leaves us temporally where we are or takes us forward in time.

One important consequence of this is that God is as located in time as we are. God's power *is* exercised now just as it *was* in the past and *will be* in the future and the effects of that exercise are the future. God, of course, differs from us in substantial ways. He alone is such that quite generally his relational properties change without any change in his intrinsic properties.

Locating God in time in this sense is the natural outcome of Scotus's critique of Aquinas's account of God's relation to time and Ockham's critique of Scotus's account of the present. I would myself venture that it is the road a Christian should take, but it has consequences and the reaction to it leads the generation after Ockham to reject the connection between powers and time and to alter substantially the connection between powers and possibility. The result is a semantic conception of possibility which, though unstable as I would argue, has dominated most modal thinking ever since. The short-run effect of this in Ockham's own lifetime was the rejection of the necessity of the past and various attempts by Bradwardine, Rimini, and others to treat what is past as perspectival. But that lies in Ockham's future—and is another story.[13]

NOTES

1. This paper (like so much else of my study of Ockham and Scotus) began in a seminar which Fr. Maurer offered at the University of Toronto and the Pontifical Institute of Medieval Studies in 1970/71. Just two of us sat that seminar so it was really an extended tutorial in the thought of Ockham and Scotus by one of their most acute contemporary interpreters. I would like to take this opportunity to (very belatedly) thank Fr. Maurer for that seminal seminar and for his subsequent interest, help, and inspiration.

2. Christopher J. Martin has suggested that it is Ockham who introduces the notion of form here employed and that it is his notion of formal consequence which this picture makes to be the whole of consequence. Cf. Martin's Ph.D. dissertation, *Theories of Inference and Entailment in the Middle Ages* (Princeton University, 1999).

3. For Ockham's reflection on a rather different (but not unrelated) notion of possible world, cf. Armand Maurer, "Ockham on the Possibility of a Better World," *Mediaeval Studies* 38 (1976): 291–312.

4. This "Diodorean" or "statistical" picture owes its currency to work by Jaakko Hintikka particularly on ancient modal theory and Simo Knuuttila on medieval modal theory. Cf. S. Knuuttila, ed., *Reforging the Great Chain of Being: Studies of the History of Modal Theories* (Dordrecht, Holland and Boston: Reidel, 1981). For Knuuttila's more recent views, cf. *Modalities in Medieval Philosophy* (London: Routledge, 1993).

5. Cf. my "Scotus, Modality, Instants of Nature and the Contingency of the Present" in *John Duns Scotus: Metaphysics and Ethics*, ed. L. Honnefelder, R. Wood, and M. Dreyer (Leiden: Brill, 1996).

6. Duns Scotus *Lectura* 1 d. 39.1–5 (ed. Vaticana 17:481–510). The translation is my own.

7. Cf. D.K. Lewis, "Anselm and Actuality," *Nous* 4 (1970): 175–88, reprinted with a postscript in his *Philosophical Papers*, vol. 1 (Oxford: Oxford University Press, 1983), 10–25.

8. Scotus, *Lectura*, 1, d. 40.unica, §9 (17:511.7–10).

9. Ibid., § 9 (17: 512.27–513.9).

10. Ockham, *Quodlibet* I q.16, in *Opera Theologica*, 9:87.

11. Ockham, *Tractatus de Praedestinatione*, d. 3, in *Opera Philosophica*, 2:536.83–98. Translation mine after Adams and Kretzmann.

12. Ockham, *Summa logicae* III.3.6, in *Opera philosophica*, 1:608. 243–256. Translation mine.

13. I began this story in my "Future Contingents" in *The Cambridge History of Later Medieval Philosophy*, ed. A. Kenny, N. Kretzmann, and J. Pinborg (Cambridge: Cambridge University Press, 1982), 358–81.

Chapter 14

Francis Mayronis on Cognition

Abstractive and Intuitive-Abstractive

G I R A R D   J .   E T Z K O R N

In the process of cataloging "Franciscan" manuscripts in the Vaticanus Latinus collection, I happened upon a heretofore unnoticed treatise by Francis Mayronis, "On Intuitive and Abstractive Cognition."[1] The treatise, even though there is no attribution to Francis Mayronis (1288–1328), is followed in the manuscript[2] by copies of other treatises which are undeniably the work of Mayronis.[3] A comparison of the questions edited here to the *Conflatus* of Francis confirms their authenticity.[4] The questions here edited are a sequel to the question "On Intuitive Cognition" previously edited.[5]

Francis Mayronis is clearly in the intellectual lineage of John Duns Scotus, to whom he refers as "Our Doctor." Much of what he says about intuitive and abstractive cognition, often more clearly than the Subtle Doctor, is obviously dependent on Scotus. On the other hand, Francis is an independent thinker and does not hesitate, respectfully if you will, to disagree with his Franciscan predecessor.

In the two questions here edited, the objections raised against Francis's opinion seem to have come from the students who attended his lectures rather than his more famous fellow Franciscans, such as Peter Aureoli and William of Ockham. This seems true simply because the objections follow closely upon the conclusions and responses of Francis. While it may seem that Mayronis in these questions expresses his views tersely at times, this in no way diminishes from their insightfulness. It is possible, of course, that the present text is the result of a *Reportatio*. However, it is just as reasonable to suppose that Francis is prone to state his views clearly and distinctly.

It is not my purpose to go into a lengthy analysis of this French Franciscan's views on intuitive and abstractive cognition. My intent is rather to provide a text which can provide a basis for studies and translations of this important fourteenth-century thinker.

The text as we find it in Vaticanus Latinus 3026 is generally quite good. There are two exceptions to which we have alluded in the footnotes, namely in Question 3, paragraph 16, parts of the third and fourth examples are missing in the text. There likewise seems to have been an omission at the end of Question 3 paragraph 21.

It has been a privilege for me to have been invited to add a small part to this Festschrift in honor of Fr. Armand Maurer, CSB, who has done so much to retrieve and illuminate our intellectual heritage.

NOTES

1. Cf. G. Etzkorn, *Iter Vaticanum Franciscanum: A Description of Some One Hundred Manuscripts of the Vaticanus Latinus Collection* (Leiden: Brill 1996), 10–11.

2. Codex Vaticanus Latinus 3026, ff. 63ra–71vb.

3. Cf. B. Roth, *Franz von Mayronis O.F.M.: Sein Leben, seine Werke, seine Lehre vom Formalunterschied in Gott* (Werl: Franziskus Druckerei, 1936), 74–84, 322–25, 385–87, 487–88, 521–523); also H. Rossmann, "Die Quodlibeta und verschiedene sonstige Schriften des Franz von Meyronnes, O.F.M.," in *Franziskanische Studien* 53 (1971): 160–61; idem, *Franziskanische Studien* 54 (1972): 10–11.

4. Lengthy texts from Francis's treatment of intuitive and abstractive cognition, taken from the *Conflatus* as found in Vat. Lat. 894 and ed. Venice 1504, are cited in the insightful study of Katherine Tachau, *Vision and Certitude in the Age of Ockham* (Leiden: Brill, 1988), 327–32; the "Conflatus" is the title generally ascribed to Mayronis's commentary on Peter Lombard's Sentences, Book I.

5. Cf. G. Etzkorn, "Franciscus de Mayronis: A Newly Discovered Treatise on Intuitive and Abstractive Cognition," in *Franciscan Studies* 54 (1994–1997): 15–50.

APPENDIX A

[Franciscus de Mayronis]

[Quaestio 2: De notitia abstractiva]

Circa notitiam abstractivam[1] negotiando secundo principaliter occurunt hic plures articuli declarandi, quorum primus est: quid est notitia abstractiva.

[I.—Art. 1 Quid est notitia abstractiva
A.—Plures opiniones et argumenta in contrarium]

1. Dicitur quod illa quae est de re non in se ipsa, quia immediate distinguitur contra intuitivam quae per oppositum definitur.

2. Sed contra: quia per notitiam abstractivam cognoscitur quiditas rei; ipsa autem quiditas non meretur[2] extra rem cognitam formaliter.

3. Item, quiditas obiecti in alio non differt ab illo utpote a specie, et sic dum cognoscet obiectum in alio, illud aliud et non ipsum formaliter cognoscetur.

4. Ideo dicitur quod notitia abstractiva est de re in aliquo repraesentativo, licet non negetur in se ipsa quia ubi est notitia intuitiva, non est ibi repraesentativum.

5. Sed contra: quia angeli in Verbo notitia matutina cognoscunt creaturas intuitive et tamen sicut in quodam repraesentativo.

6. Ideo dicitur quod talis notitia est illa quae est per repraesentativum, non eminens, quia in tali repraesentativo non est vere res in se sicut in supereminenti est verius, ut docet Anselmus in *Monologion*.[3]

7. Sed contra: quia qualitas corporalis videtur supereminenter contineri a qualitati spirituali, sicut substantia, et tamen omnis qualitas corporalis cognoscitur abstractive per speciem intelligibilem quae est qualitas spiritualis.

8. Item, passio cognoscitur ex subiecto et tamen videtur supereminenter contineri in ipso, licet proprie talis continentia ad Deum pertineat.

9. Item, dicitur quod notitia abstractiva est quae immediate causatur a representativo aliquo, quantumcumque ad oppositum terminetur immediate.

10. Sed contra: quia quidquid Deus potest facere mediante causa secunda, potest immediate. Et ideo si mediante repraesentativo causat effectum poterit immediate causare talem notitiam.

11. Item, omnis respectus effectualiter ad causam secundam efficientem accipit fundamentum, et ideo potest definiri per ipsum.

12. Ideo dicitur quod notitia abstractiva est quae nata est causari immediate a repraesentativo effective, quantumcumque non causaretur de facto.

13. Sed contra: notitia intuitiva angelorum est nata esse in aliquo repraesentativo mirabili[4] et tamen non ponitur abstractiva.

14. Item, de notitia divina idem, cum omnia cognoscat in sua essentia.

15. Ideo dicitur quod notitia abstractiva [f. 67rb] est quae abstrahit ab omni praesentia quia obiectum quantumcumque praesens potest abstractive cognosci.

16. Sed contra: quia anima est sibi ipsi praesens et tamen non se cognoscit intuitive.

17. Item, eodem modo arguitur de praesentialitate divina, cum tamen Deus solum abstractive cognoscatur.

18. Ideo dicitur quod notitia abstractiva est quae abstrahit ab exsistentia, quia non-exsistentia non potest intuitive cognosci.

19. Sed contra: quia Deus dicitur ab aeterno omnia cognovisse antequam exsisterent, et non abstractive.

[B.—Solutio Francisci ad primum articulum]

20. Ideo dicitur quod notitia abstractiva est illa quae est de re in se ipsa secundum quod abstrahit ab omnibus quae conveniunt ei per accidens, quia cum omnis notitia, ut patuit, sit de re in se ipsa, ista et intuitiva dicuntur, quia illa est de re in se ipsa secundum quod etiam concernunt illa quae insunt per accidens. Ista autem abstrahit ab omni per accidens, et ideo dicitur abstractiva.

[1.—Obiectiones quattuor contra definitionem Francisci]

21. Sed contra istam definitionem arguitur quadrupliciter. Primo, quia sancti in patria possunt videre divinam essentiam, non videndo personam divinam,[5] secundum Doctorem nostrum,[6] et tamen non erit notitia abstractiva cum abstrahat ab omnibus quasi per accidens.

22. Secundo, quia divinus intellectus, per exemplaria quae habet apud intellectum, videtur noscere solum illa quae per se insunt, cum semper uniformiter repraesentent et tamen non dicitur abstractiva.

23. Tertio, quia per speciem hominis albi cognosco abstractive ipsum esse album quod tamen est per accidens.

24. Quarto, quia intuens albedinem visus non videtur cognoscere nisi eius naturam, et tamen non ex hoc dicitur notitia abstractiva.

[2.—Responsio Francisci ad obiectiones]

25. Ad primum:[7] quod illa notitia qua cognoscit solam essentiam, natum esse cognosci personam quae convenit ei quasi per accidens sicut naturae suppositum, nisi esset impedimentum.

26. Ad secundum:[8] quod, ut vulgo dicitur, illa exemplaria quamvis uniformiter se habeant, tamen repraesentant omnem difformitatem per accidens exsistentem.

27. Ad tertium:[9] quod talis non est certa notitia, cum specie uniformiter manente apud me poterunt denigrari.

28. Ad quartum:[10] quod intuens albedinem per talem intuitum dignoscit ipsam praesentem et exsistentem quae conveniunt ei per accidens.

[3.—Difficultas aliqua]

29. Sed remanet difficultas: quomodo talis notitia est de re in se ipsa, cum fiat plerumque per repraesentativum.

30. Dicitur autem quod talis notitia terminatur ad suum obiectum ut relucet in repraesentativo.

31. Sed contra: quia obiectum, ut in repraesentativo, non differt ab ipso, sicut nec creatura in Verbo, et tunc non cognosceretur nisi tale repraesentativum, ideo dico quod licet tale reprae-

sentativum se habeat in ratione moventis propter absentiam obiecti, obiectum ut in sua quiditate se habet in ratione terminantis, vel ut melius dicatur [f. 67va] secundum suam quiditatem,
et hoc est dicere de re in se.

[4.—Responsio Francisci ad difficultatem]

32. Intelligendum tamen quod talis notitia non arguit obiectum ut est in tali loco aut ut in
tali subiecto, aut in tali parydo[11] aut ut in actuali exsistentia, quia quiditas obiecti abstrahit ab
omnibus istis sicut ab his quae sunt per accidens.

[II.—Art. 2: Quot sunt modi notitiae abstractivae]

Secundus articulus: quot sunt modi notitiae abstractivae.

[A.—Solutiones aliorum]

33. Dicitur autem quod quadrupliciter dicitur de notitia abstractiva. Uno modo quod notitia abstractiva quandoque fit per repraesentativum deficiens sicut quando cognoscitur substantia per speciem, et quandoque per repraesentativum excedens sicut quando cognoscitur albedo
per speciem suam, quia accidens spirituale est species et ipsa sensibile, quandoque per repraesentativum adaequatum, sicut quando quis per habitum geometriae, quando habet, cognoscit
omnem geometriam, quia omnes sunt rationis eiusdem; quandoque fit per verum repraesentativum sicut si Deus crearet immediate supplendo effectivam causalitatem ipsius repraesentativi.

34. Alio modo dicitur quod alia est abstractiva quae abstrahit ab esse et fore sicut omnis
notitia abstractiva de eo quod est contingens esse quia esse convenit ei per accidens, alia quae
non abstrahit ab esse et fore, sed esse concernit sicut notitia abstractiva de Deo quia actualis
exsistentia per se convenit Deo non per accidens eo quod ipse sit necesse esse.

35. Alia quae ab omnibus per se praeter primum modum sicut cum quiditas alicuius rei
praecise consideratur per se.

36. Alio modo dicitur quod alia est abstractiva in qua fit abstractio realis, alia rationis sicut
quando intelligit quod non exsistit sine exsistentia, utpote angeli ante creationem specierum
sensibilium noverant eas, tunc est realis quia ita est in re; sed rationis tantum quando abstrahi-
tur unum a reliquo in quo est actu, ut homo a Sorte.

[B.—Opinio Francisci]

37. Sed contra: quia in ista regula abstractive intellectus intelligit naturam humanam esse sine
individuo, et tunc est falsus intellectus, secundum Augustinum,[12] quia intelligit rem aliter esse
quam sit. Aut intelligit naturam humanam, non quidem esse sine individuo, sed esse praecisam

ab eo, et istud est ex natura rei. Et ideo tales abstractiones non fiunt ab anima quantum est ex parte obiecti sicut nec anima mercat[13] principia prima. Et isto modo intelligitur "abstrahentium non est mendacium,"[14] quia ipsi nihil fingunt quin ita sit in se sicut concipiunt.

[II.—Art. 3: Quot sunt proprietates notitiae abstractivae]

Tertius articulus: quot sunt proprietates notitiae abstractivae.

[A.—De quattuor proprietatibus notitiae abstractivae]

38. Dicitur quod quattuor, quarum prima est quod ipsa est notitia secundaria quia, ut supra patuit,[15] intuitiva est prima quantum est ex parte obiecti nisi sit impedimentum in potentia.

39. Secunda est quod ipsa est notitia imperfecta quia cum quaelibet res verius sit in se ipsa quam in sua similitudine, numquam sua similitudo deminuta potest ita perfecte [f. 67vb] repraesentare veritatem obiecti, sicut quando ipsamet est praesens ut intuitiva numquam, ceteris paribus, potest ita esse.

40. Tertio, quia ipsa abstrahit a praesentia sui obiecti quia, secundum Augustinum *De Trinitate*,[16] per species absentia cogitantur.

41. Quarto est quia ipsa abstrahit ab omni sui exsistentia, per speciem non cognoscitur de re si exsistit vel non, quia exsistentia per accidens contingit cuilibet creaturae.

[B.—Difficultas
1.—Opiniones aliorum]

42. Sed obstat difficultas: si omnia quae cognoscuntur de aliquo obiecto per notitiam intuitivam possunt cognosci per abstractivam.

43. Dicitur autem quod sic: omnia quae insunt per se, et talia per speciem possunt repraesentari, non tamen illa per accidens, ut patuit. Sed numquid ita perfecte[17] cognoscit quiditatem cognoscens abstractive sicut intuitive? Dicitur autem quod non, licet eadem penitus cognoscantur, sicut in albedine eadem cognoscit sensus et intellectus, sed non aeque perfecte.

44. Sed contra: quia in proposito in eadem potentia et non ibi. Dicitur autem quod non sumitur hic ex parte potentiae, sed quia obiectum melius repraesentat se ipsum quam species eius, et ideo actum causat perfectiorem.

45. Sed contra: quia quandoque species perfectior obiecto, utpote species intelligibilis albedinis, et ideo videtur actum perfectiorem causare cum agat secundum totum conatum suae naturae.

46. Dicitur autem quod notitia abstractiva est actus secundarius speciei in intellectu, quia ipsa species in intellectu sibi proposito nata est causare prius de se notitiam intuitivam quam abstractivam de alio. Et tunc illa notitia abstractiva foret perfectior intuitiva albedinis.

[2.—Responsio auctoris ad difficultatem]

47. Intelligendum tamen sicut alibi dicitur,[18] quod notitia abstractiva abstrahit a quattuor condicionibus. Primo quidem ab exsistentia et non-exsistentia sui obiecti, quia tam exsistentia quam non- exsistentia possunt abstractive cognosci per aliquam eandem speciem et omne commune aliquibus oppositis abstrahit ab ipsis.

48. Secundo, abstrahit a praesentia et non-praesentia, quia tam praesentia quam absentia possunt intelligi per speciem cum anima cognoscat se sicut alia.

49. Tertio, a causatione et non-causatione sui obiecti, quia si obiectum sit praesens poterit eam causare, si absens non; sic clarius deducitur de exsistentia et non-exsistentia.

50. Quarto, a terminatione et non-terminatione, quia si obiectum est, terminat; si autem non est, non videtur posse terminare.

51. Intelligendum ulterius quod intuitiva concernit quattuor extrema istarum contradictionum.[19] Primo quidem exsistentiam, quia non-exsistens nullus potest intueri.—Secundo, praesentiam quia absens non potest cognosci nisi per speciem remanentem.—Tertio, causationem, quia de communi lege intuitiva ab obiecto causatur.—Quarto, terminationem quia omnis visio actualis terminatur ad rem visam; intuitio autem est visio quaedam.[20]

[C.—Contra positionem Francisci
1.—Quattuor instantiae]

52. Sed contra praemissa instatur quadrupliciter. Primo quia ratio exsistentiae est cognoscibilis abstractive, cum de ipsa formamus complexiones aliquas nunc quando omnia abstractive cognoscimus, et tamen ipsa non abstrahit a se ipsa.

53. Secundo, quia non videtur quod obiectum praesens possit causare nisi notitiam intuitivam.

54. Tertio, quia omnis notitia [f. 68ra] immediate ab obiecto causata sine praesente sive absente videtur intuitiva.

55. Quarto, quia nulla notitia videtur posse esse de aliquo obiecto nisi terminetur ad illud.

[2.—Responsio Francisci ad instantias]

56. Ad primum:[21] quod licet exsistentia alicuius rei possit discursive intelligi per effectus, ut exsistentia primae causae, non tamen abstractive per aliquod repraesentativum cum corrupta re species uniformiter repraesentatur.

57. Ad secundum:[22] quod immo, quando divina voluntas quando supplet vicem speciei quae ipsam repraesentaret. Et alibi esset difficile invenire exemplum.

58. Ad tertium:[23] quod instantia est in voluntate divina quando ipsa est obiectum cognitum.

59. Ad quartum:[24] quod ipsa notitia terminatur ad quiditatem quantum quae conveniunt ei per se; talia autem manent in esse essentiae quamvis exsistentia quae per accidens convenit, aufferatur. Et ideo remanet adhuc notitia terminata ad non-exsistens, quod tamen est ens. Talis autem terminatio quae fuit realis, nunc non est realis ex parte termini, licet forte extra animam.

[D.—Difficultas et responsio auctoris]

60. Sed obstat difficultas: qualiter intuitiva concernit illa quattuor extrema, cum tamen tam non-exsistentia quam non-absentia intuitive in Deo cognoscatur et per consequens tunc non causant nec terminant.—Dicitur autem quod illud refertur de lege communi in istis inferioribus.

[IV.—Art. 4: An intellectus in puris naturalibus constitutus
potest omnia cognoscere abstractive]

Quartus articulus est: si intellectus in puris naturalibus constitutus potest omnia cognoscere abstractive.

[A.—Quattuor conclusiones
1.—Concl. 1: Intellectus non potest cognoscere res supernaturales per proprias species]

61. Circa quem articulum praemittuntur quattuor conclusiones, quarum prima est quod intellectus noster non potest cognoscere res supernaturales per ipsarum proprias species, ex puris naturalibus semper loquendo, quia tunc ex puris naturalibus deveniret in notitiam supernaturalis obiecti quod implicat incompossibilia.

[2.—Concl. 2: Intellectus non potest cognoscere creaturas supernaturales
per proprias species]

62. Secunda conclusio: quod nec creaturas supernaturales, quia illae non habent species per quas intelligantur sensibiliter nec intelligibiles quas causent extra se in medio, cum non sit receptivum talium formarum.

[3.—Concl. 3: Intellectus non potest cognoscere substantias corporales]

63. Tertia conclusio: quod nec substantiae corporales, quia nullius rei species est in intellectu quin prius fuerit in sensu. [In sensu] autem nulla cadit substantia.

[4.—Concl. 4: Sola accidentia abstractive cognoscuntur per suas species]

64. Quarta conclusio: quod sola accidentia per suas species cognoscuntur abstractive quia, sicut docet Augustinus II *De Trinitate*,[25] non gignuntur species in memoria nisi ex sensu cernen-

tis nec intelligibilia nisi ex memoria. Et ideo cum sola accidentia sensibilia percipiantur per sensum, sola illa cognoscuntur sic per propriam speciem.

[B.—Contra conclusiones Francisci
1.—Quattuor instantiae]

65. Sed contra istas conclusiones instatur quadrupliciter. Primo, quia nos cognoscimus Deum secundum rationes proprias quibus distinguitur a creaturis, ut aeternitas et infinitas. Ratio autem propria non videtur cognosci nisi per speciem propriam.

66. Secundo, quia non habemus aliquam notitiam de substantiis spiritualibus prout a corporalibus distinguitur, et istud non videtur posse aliquas corporales species repraesentare.

67. Tertio, quia, ut dicunt aliqui,[26] sicut substantia stat sub accidentibus, ita sub ipsis suam speciem multiplicat per quam cognoscitur.

68. Quarto, quia tunc accidentia videntur esse [f. 68rb] primum adaequatum obiectum nostri intellectus, si omnes species esset accidentium, cum omnia communiter per species cognoscimus.

[2.—Responsio Francisci ad instantias]

69. Ad primum:[27] quod illa proprie quae de Deo novimus arguitive a rebus causatur quas decrevimus dependere ab aliquo et sic cum non sit processus in infinitum, nec idem a se ipso inferimus esse primum independens.

70. Ad secundum:[28] quod per species corporales illa argumentatur; eo enim quod intuemur corporaliter aliquam substantiam, arguimus quod melior esset si non corrumperetur. Et ideo condicionem incorruptibilitatis attribuimus nobilissimis substantiis.

71. Ad tertium:[29] quod illa fictio nihil valet. Quia si ibi esset species ducens in notitiam eius, tunc naturaliter cognosceremus quod in Eucharistia non est substantia, sicut cognoscimus quod ibi sunt accidentia.[30]

72. Ad quartum:[31] quod accidens est primum obiectum generatione, quia ab eo incipit nostra cognitio, non tamen adequatione, quia de ipso argumentamur substantiam.

[C.—Aliquae difficultates et responsiones Francisci]

73. Sed obstat difficultas: qualiter cognoscimus substantiam per speciem sensibilem accidentis.—Dicitur quod discursive sic quia per quiditatem sensibilis rei, cuius habemus speciem, cognoscimus quod ipsa nata est inhaerere quia talis aptitudo est eius passio et ideo inferimus quod inhaereat inhaerenti vel subsistenti. Si primo modo, procedimus donec perveniamus ad primum subsistens et illud vocamus substantiam.

74. Secunda difficultas: qualiter per species investigamus substantias spirituales.—Dicitur autem quod ibi incipimus ab intuitiva notitia eo quod experimur actum intelligendi vel volendi

et arguimus quod talis actus non potest esse a carne nec ab osse vel sanguine. Tunc enim posset esse, ubicumque ista sunt, arguimus quod est ab aliquo principio in nobis quod non percipitur sensu et illud vocamus animam.

75. Tertia difficultas: qualiter isto modo veniemus in notitiam intelligentiarum.—Dicitur autem quod per motum. Sicut autem ex motu corporis arguimus animam quia in eo non videmus aliquod principium corporale sufficiens ad talem effectum. Et isto modo philosophi per motum caeli investigaverunt intelligentias.

76. Quarta difficultas: qualiter per istum modum deveniemus in notitiam Dei.—Dicitur quod procedendo in causis, cum non sit processus in infinitum, oportet devenire ad primam incipiendo a motu caeli et investigaverunt eam philosophi.

77. Sed remanet difficultas: per quem locum fiunt omnes istae argumentationes?—Dicitur quod per locum a correlatis fit prima argumentatio, quia ex effectu non arguitur causa nisi per locum istum. Postea vero postquam habemus respectum causalitatis formalem vel fundamentalem arguimus quod ista passio debet convenire enti perfectissimo, et sic postea ex perfectione fiunt aliae deductiones et hoc tam in Deo quam in angelo quam in creata substantia.

78. Sed quomodo passio praecognoscitur subiecto?—Dicitur quod sic in notitia a posteriori, tamen statim habita passione utpote causalitate [f. 68va] activa intellectus arguit quod convenit alicui fundamento.

[V.—Art. 5: An intellectus ex puris naturalibus possit devenire a sensibilibus
in notitiam omnium rerum inferiorum]

Quintus articulus: si talis intellectus ex puris naturalibus potest devenire sic arguendo a sensibilibus in notitiam omnium rerum inferiorum.

[A.—Opinio contraria]

79. Dicitur autem quod sic quia inferiora sunt obiecta naturalia.

80. Sed contra: quia cum in istis inferioribus inveniantur habitudines ad superiora et per ipsum sic terminus cognoscatur, tunc naturalia omnia superiora essent nobis nota.

[B.—Quattuor conclusiones negativae
1.—Concl. 1: Intellectus noster non attingit ad proprias quiditates
generum generalissimorum]

81. Ideo ponuntur hic quattuor conclusiones negativae, quarum prima est quod non attingit ad proprias quiditates generum generalissimorum, quia definiens accidens quod est commune cum praedicamentis circumloquimur omnem quiditatem per 'inesse' quod est per se passio cuiuslibet praedicamenti, cum sit eius naturalis aptitudo eo quod in actu inesse ad minus quan-

titati accidit.—Item, definientes qualitatem circumloquimur per 'quale' quod est eius effectus formalis.—Item, definientes relationem ipsam describunt per referre quod est eius formalis effectus. Ideo patet quod ignoramus eorum quiditates cum per posteriora circumloquamur.

[2.—Concl. 2: Non arguimus ad proprias quiditates generum subalternorum]

82. Secunda conclusio: quod non arguimus ad proprias quiditates generum subalternorum quia definimus animal per sensibile quod est aptum natum sentire. Tale est passio ipsius potentiae sensitivae cum sit eius naturalis aptitudo ad accidens.—Item, habitus in praedicamento qualitatis definiuntur per qualitatem de difficili mobilem, cum tamen difficultas eo quod privatio facultatis non sit de quiditate cuiusquam.

[3.—Concl. 3: Non attingimus ad proprias quiditates specierum]

83. Tertio conclusio: quod non attingimus ad proprias quiditates specierum, quia in genere substantiae definimus hominem per animal rationale, cum naturalis aptitudo ad ratiocinandum sit eius passio.—Item, in genere qualitatis albedinem per disgregativum et nigredinem per aggregativum et tamen sicut rationale est aptitudo quae sunt utriusque aptitudines naturales.

[4.—Concl. 4: Intellectus noster non attingit ad haeceitates solo numero differentes]

84. Quarta conclusio: quod non attingimus ad haeceitates[32] per intellectum nostrum solo numero differentes. Quia quanto aliqua sunt magis propria, tanto sunt minus nota nobis cum ab universalibus ad particulare procedamus.—Item, sensus noster non cognoscit singularia, ut singularia sunt, igitur multo minus intellectus noster, cum sit abstractior potentia.

[—Intellectus non cognoscit singularia ut singularia
a.—Probatio prima]

85. Quod autem intellectus noster non cognoscat illa probatur dupliciter. Primo, quia illa potentia quae non cognoscit distinctionem inter aliqua, non cognoscit eorum principia distinctiva, cum per talia principia innotescat immediate distinctio. Sensus autem nescit distinguere inter duo individua penitus consimilia, sicut sunt duo ova aut duae apes, si unum ostendatur post aliud, ut patet ad sensum. Ergo non attingit ad eorum principia distinctiva quae sunt singularitates.

[b.—Probatio secunda]

86. Secundo probatur hoc idem quia potentia sensitiva nullam percipit difformitatem inter individua totaliter consimilia, cum conveniant in omnibus obiectis visus. Sed rationes singularium sunt primo diversae cum sint multae differentiae. Igitur non attinguntur [f. 68vb] a sensu.

[C.—Difficultates ulteriores et responsiones Francisci]

87. Sed obstant difficultates. Si quiditates transcendentes sunt nobis notae.—Dicitur quod non, quia de ipsarum rationibus est multiplex dubitatio, ut patet in desceptationibus de ratione boni, utrum sit absoluta aut respectiva vel[33] utrum realis aut rationis vel unius utrum positiva aut privativa.

88. Secunda difficultas: quomodo possumus naturam praedicamentorum cognoscere si ignoramus eorum quiditates.—Dicitur quod a posteriori per quasdam ipsorum passiones quia sic definimus ipsas.[34]

89. Tertia difficultas: quomodo poterimus investigare genera subalterna si ignoramus eorum quiditates.—Dicitur, ut supra.[35] Et signum huius est quia non bene possumus venire ad divisionem generum nisi per negationes et circumlocutiones.

90. Quarta difficultas: quomodo potest species specialissima sic nobis esse innota cum primo moveat intellectum, ut patet alibi.—Dicitur quod talis non est ignota sed non invenitur nisi habeat propriam speciem, et tunc non agnoscitur discursive.

91. Quinta: qualiter cognoscimus singularia si sensus non nuntiat eorum singularitates.— Dicitur quod numquam inter individua eiusdem speciei possumus distinguere nisi accidentia distincta specie, ut patet per figuram aut colorem aut 'ubi' etc. et quandoque per motum 'inter' ut inter album et nigrum.

[VI.—Art. 6: An intellectus noster possit per aliquod repraesentativum cognoscere divinam essentiam abstractive]

Sextus articulus: si intellectus noster potest per aliquod repraesentativum cognoscere divinam essentiam abstractive quantumcumque sit in via supernaturaliter electus.

[A.—Quattuor conclusiones
1.—Concl. 1: Intellectus non potest causare aliquam speciem intelligibilem de divina essentia]

92. Circa quem articulum sunt quattuor conclusiones. Prima est quod non[36] potest causare aliquam speciem intelligibilem[37] de divina essentia ipsam repraesentantem, quia quidquid possumus intelligere possumus recordari, cum intelligibilia et memoria sint adaequatae potentiae, ut patet conclusio, et II *De Trinitate*.[38] Sed aliquis potest intelligere divinam essentiam sicut fertur de Paulo in raptu. Igitur transeunte tali actu potuit recordari de viso et non nisi per speciem aliquam derelictam.

[a.—Solutio aliorum per quattuor rationes]

93. Ista autem quaestio solvitur primo quia negatur adaequatio illarum potentiarum. Secundo, quia dicitur quod intellectus et memoria non sunt duae, sed una potentia. Tertio, quia

poterit recordari talis quidquid vidit indistincte de eo quod vidit. Quarto quia poterit recordari per dispositionem aliquam derelictam in potentia intellectiva ex actu et non per speciem illam.

[b.—Contra hanc opinionem et pro conclusione prima per quinque rationes
i.—Prima ratio]

94. Sed prima non valet, quia est contra Augustinum, ubi supra,[39] et contra experientiam et contra veritatem, quia Paulus de viso recordabatur cum dicat se talia audivisse. Nec secunda, quia dato quod sic, una potentia tantum valet acsi essent duae, dum tamen concedatur quod de omni cognito possumus recordari quod non videtur posse negari rationabiliter. Nec tertia, quia nullum simpliciter simplex potest cognosci nisi distincte; talis autem est divina essentia. Nec quarta, quia sufficit illa dispositio ad notitiam abstractivam, sed species ipsa.[40]

[ii.—Secunda ratio]

95. Secunda ratio ad eandem conclusionem est quia maius est [f. 69ra] quodlibet obiectum cognoscere per actum quam per speciem repraesentare, cum actus de quolibet obiecto sit nobilior specie quae est propter actum, sed non repugnat per actum limitatum divinam essentiam cognosci. Igitur multo minus per speciem repraesentatam cum hic non ponatur impedimentum nisi quia creatura non potest tantum exaltari ut repraesentet, et maior fit exaltatio in notitia.

[iii.—Tertia ratio]

96. Tertia ratio: quia potentia intellectiva potest habere habitum de divina essentia quia ponitur lumen gloriae respectu obiecti beatifici. Sed habitus est perfectior omni specie de eodem obiecto, ut per se patet. Igitur multo magis poterit habere speciem cum superiora respectu Dei sint nobis difficiliora.

[iv.—Quarta ratio]

97. Quarta ratio: quia omnis potentia plus appropinquat ad perfectionem sui obiecti quam species de eodem cum species ponatur esse perfectior habitu; sed habet potentiam ad intelligendum divinam essentiam; igitur potest habere speciem, cum Deo propinquiora magis arguant illimitationem in creatura.

[v.—Quinta ratio]

98. Quinta ratio: quia quandocumque sunt aliqua duo essentialiter infinita, si uni ex illimitatione sua non repugnat habere speciem intelligibilem, nec alteri, ut per se patet. Sed divina entitas et propria ratio eius essentiae aequaliter sunt illimitata, alioquin alterum esset imperfectum.

Igitur cum divina entitas possit cognosci per speciem poterit et essentia, cum non ponant repugnantiam nisi propter illimitationem. Quod autem ratio entitatis, quae formaliter est in Deo, cognoscatur a nobis per species probatur: quia de entitate prima demonstramus causalitatem finalem, secundum omnes, et ideo ipsam praecognoscimus. Ipsa autem non est formaliter nisi in Deo.—Item, dividendo ens in creatum et in increatum, oportet nos[41] intelligere utrumque extremum, et alterum non est formaliter nisi in Deo.—Item, omne creditum est aliquo modo intellectum. Credimus autem aliquam infinitam entitatem quae formaliter non est in creatura.—Item, si non cognosceremus nisi ea quae formaliter sunt in creatura, nulla differentia creaturae repugnans esset nobis nota, ut necessitas autem actus prius cuius oppositum patet in complexionibus quas de eis formamus.—Item, nullus negat quin aliqua de Deo cognoscimus et omnia divina praeter respectum sunt aequaliter infinita.

[2.—Concl. 2: Deus potest speciem creatam animae nostrae infundere]

99.   Secunda conclusio: quod Deus talem speciem creatam potest animae nostrae infundere quia habitus, actus et species de eodem obiecto sunt nata esse in eadem potentia.—Item, omne accidens est propter subiectum; subiectum autem speciei intelligibilis non est nisi potentia intellectiva.

[3.—Concl. 3: Intellectus noster potest intelligere divinam essentiam per speciem infusam]

100.   Tertia conclusio: quia per talem speciem intellectus noster intelligit divinam essentiam sub propria ratione quia quodlibet obiectum per suam propriam speciem intelligitur secundum propriam rationem.—Item, quidquid potest aliqua species creata repraesentare potest potentia intellectiva in qua est per ipsam intelligere cum propter intelligere sit omnis species [f. 69rb] in intellectu.

[4.—Concl. 4: Intellectus noster intelligens divinam essentiam per speciem
infusam non erit beatus]

101.   Quarta conclusio: quod taliter intelligens sic divinam essentiam non erit beatus, quia non videt ipsam intuitive. Sola enim visio intuitiva ponitur in beatifica.—Item, notitia creata potest nos verificare; talis autem species est creata, et ipsa causa in intellectu agente concernente actum talem.

[B.—Difficultates circa solutionem et responsiones Francisci]

102.   Sed obstant difficultates. Qualiter species limitata potest repraesentare obiectum infinitae perfectionis secundum suam totam perfectionem.—Dicitur autem quod sicut actus potest ipsum attingere, ut patuit, non repraesentat ipsum totaliter secundum totum quod est

simplex. Istud autem repraesentare non est nisi compositum de ipso causare et istud pertinet ad limitatam veritatem.

103. Secunda difficultas: qualiter ita bene per speciem naturaliter acquisitam non cognoscimus divinam essentiam sub ratione propria sicut sub ratione entis.—Dicitur autem quod licet utrumque sit aequaliter limitatum, tamen rationes propriae rerum sunt nobis naturaliter ignotae, quamvis non communes, ut patet de differentiis propriis in genere substantiae.

104. Tertia difficultas: quia cum perfectius obiectum semper habeat perfectiorem speciem, species Dei excederet in infinitum quamcumque aliam speciem, quia si essent infinita obiecta se excedentia sub Deo non attingerent ad ipsum, et sicut nec aliqua eorum species speciem illam.—Dicitur quod ita concluderet de actu et habitu sicut de specie, ut patet intuenti. Unde diceretur quod excessus talium specierum fieret secundum proportionem sicut in continuo in infinitum antequam veniatur ad duplum. Cuius signum est, quia non tantum excedit species substantiae speciem accidentis sicut substantia accidens.

105. Quarta difficultas: quare talis non est beatus cum cognoscat obiectum beatificum sub propria ratione et perfectissima.—Dicitur autem quod ratio illa formalis non beatificat nisi sit cognita intuitive, quia illa sola est perfecta notitia simpliciter. Licet enim imaginatio et intellectus[42] sub eadem ratione attingat tamen notitia intellectualis est perfectio simpliciter et non imaginativa.—Sed contra: si per perfectius in eadem specie, sed in diversis.

[VII.—Art. 7: An intellectus noster per aliquod obiectum cognitum possit cognoscere divinam essentiam discursive]

Septimus articulus est: si intellectus noster per aliquod obiectum cognitum potest cognoscere divinam essentiam discursive.

[A.—Quattuor conclusiones
1.—Concl. 1: Intellectus noster in statu isto non potest cognoscere divinam essentiam per aliquod obiectum cognitum]

106. Circa quem articulum sunt quattuor conclusiones. Prima est quod intellectus noster in puris naturalibus constitutus et corpori coniunctus non potest per aliquod obiectum cognitum cognoscere divinam essentiam, quia cum cognito subiecto possint eius passiones non cognosci,[43] latent nos multa quae non possumus de Deo investigare.—Item, non possumus differentias rerum proprias per aliquod obiectum investigare, ut patet ex circumlocutionibus quae fiunt erga definitiones. Ergo multo minus divinam essentiam.

[2.—Concl. 2: Intellectus noster coniunctus et supernaturaliter electus non potest ita cognoscere divinam essentiam]

107. Secunda conclusio: quod intellectus noster coniunctus et supernaturaliter electus de lege communi quantum claret lumine[44] fidei non potest ita [f. 69va] cognoscere divinam essentiam

quia quidquid affirmat fidelis negat infidelis et non oportet ut cognoscatur eosdem terminos.—
Item, tunc possemus demonstrare omnia credita cum contineantur in essentia divina sicut in
primo subiecto theologiae.

[3.—Concl. 3: Intellectus noster separatus potest naturaliter cognoscere
divinam essentiam discursive sub propria ratione]

108. Tertia conclusio: quod intellectus noster separatus in puris naturalibus constitutus
potest cognoscere divinam essentiam discursive sub ratione propria. Quia quicumque intellectus potest cognoscere aliquam potentiam perfecte, potest cognoscere obiectum eius primum
ad quod est ordinata. Intellectus autem separatus perfectionem cognoscit potentiam intuitivam
et volitivam. Igitur ex ipsis poterit cognoscere tale obiectum.

109. Et confirmatur ista ratio, quia quaelibet istarum potentiarum habet ex natura sua
ordinem naturalem ad primum suum obiectum ordine perfectionis, cum quaelibet sit apta nata
elevari ad ipsum. Talis autem naturalis ordo potest cognosci, ut patuit, intuitive ab intellectu
creato.

110. Item sic arguitur: quicumque potest cognoscere aliquam potentiam, non solum secundum se sed in habitudine ad obiectum, potest cognoscere illud obiectum cum habitudo sive terminatio intelligi non possit. Sed talis intellectus, ut patuit, cognoscit potentiam in habitudine ad
obiectum sub ratione propria. Ergo id cognoscet sub tali ratione.

111. Item, quicumque intellectus potest cognoscere aliquam scientiam potest cognoscere
subiectum illius scientiae, cum conclusio scientifica constet ex subiecto illius scientiae cum passione, et cognita complexione impossibile est terminos eius ignorare. Sed talis intellectus potest
cognoscere scientiam theologiae sanctorum vel alicui revelatam cum sit quaedam qualitas naturaliter informans scientem. Ergo poterit in eius subiectum quod est essentia divina.

112. Item, quicumque intellectus potest intelligere aliquem actum, potest intelligere eius
obiectum ad quod primo terminatur. Intellectus autem separatus potest intelligere actum
beatificum sanctorum, ut cognoscetur sicut et potentiam beatificam. Igitur poterit cognoscere
obiectum beatificum ex eo discursive.—Sed quia negant, aliter probatur: quia intellectus beati
potest formare aliquam complexionem de obiecto quod videt et quaecumque intelligeret actum
illum complexum necessario intelligeret terminos illius complexionis.

113. Item, quicumque cognoscit aliquem effectum, non solum quantum ad suum absolutum
etiam in habitudine ad causam, necessario cognoscit causam, sicut exemplificatur in statua Herculis et in praemissis ad conclusionem comparatis, cum omnis habitudo det intelligere suum
terminum. Sed intellectus separatus perfecte cognoscens res creatas et eorum habitudines naturales cognoscit quod omnes sunt ordinatae ad divinam essentiam naturaliter sicut ad finem ultimum. Igitur cognoscet ipsam essentiam.—Dicunt autem quod cognoscit eam sub ratione
communi sub qua est causa. Sed reducitur ratio, quia sub eadem ratione cognoscitur sub qua [f.
69vb] creatura ad ipsam ordine refertur. Sed ad essentiam sub ratione propria ordinatur. Ergo
sub ea ratione cognoscitur.

114. Item, quicumque cognoscit aliquam relationem cognoscit eius terminum, cum quiditas relationis sit ad aliud, et illud aliud sit terminus. Sed, ut patuit, intellectui separato de se non repugnat intelligere unionem naturae humanae Christi ad Verbum. Ergo poterit intelligere eius terminum secundum illam rationem secundum quam terminat. Terminat autem sub ratione essentiae et tunc habetur propositum. Aut per proprietatem, et tunc cum cognita generatione passiva, quae est proprietas Verbi, cognoscatur activa per naturam relatorum et cognita activa cognoscatur eius terminus qui est divina essentia sub ratione propria, sic discursive erit a tali intellectu cognita.

[4.—Concl. 4: Intellectus separatus per revelationem divinam potest cognoscere divinam essentiam]

115. Quarta conclusio: quod intellectus sic separatus, licet nondum glorificatus, per revelationem[45] divinam potest noscere per divinam essentiam quia plura potest Deus revelare quam intellectus noster vel alicuius causae ex sua natura cognoscere.—Item, incarnationis sacramentum putatur beato Ioanni Evangelistae fuisse revelatum alioquin piscator sic eam descripsisse non valuisset. Tale autem sacramentum, ut patuit, ducit in notitiam divinitus et si hoc possibile coniuncto, multo magis separato.

[B.—Instantiae contra conclusiones auctoris]

116. Sed contra istas conclusiones instatur. Primo, quia intellectus noster cognoscit ex puris naturalibus res cum ordine quem habet ad ultimum finem, et sic ipsa divinitas cognosceretur.

117. Secundo, quia fide tenemus istam complexionem quod divina essentia est formaliter infinita et omnis qui intelligit per fidem aliquam complexionem oportet ut praeconcipiat terminos illius.

118. Tertio, quia divina essentia est obiectum supernaturale et ideo non videtur cognoscibile naturaliter nisi a potentia supernaturali.

119. Quarto, quia non videtur quomodo possit revelari divina essentia quin ipsa videatur et intellectus verificetur.

[C.—Responsio Francisci ad instantias]

120. Ad primum:[46] quod intellectus noster talem ordinem non cognoscit nisi arguitive in communi, et ideo termini non nisi sub ratione communi.

121. Ad secundum:[47] quod non formamus istam complexionem nisi de ente primo aut spiritu, quia illa ratio propria est nobis ignota.

122. Sed contra: quia notum est cuilibet quod illa ratio supernaturalis cognoscibilis est infinita.—Dicitur quod nulli est aliquid notum de ista nisi prout ipsam circumloquimur rationibus generalibus.

123. Ad tertium:[48] quod forsitan non est obiectum supernaturale quantum ad notitiam cir-cumcursivam[49] tamen aeternitatem quae par ei est, nullo dubitante discursive cognoscimus.

124. Ad quartum: quod illa revelatio potest quadrupliciter fieri: 1) Aut immediate osten-dendo divinam essentiam; 2) Aut quod Deus immediate per suam voluntatem causet actum talem supplendo causalitatem cuiuslibet causae secundae; 3) Aut quod infundat speciem intelli-gibilem, ut supra; 4) Aut quod ostendat aliquod obiectum quo cognito immediate fertur intel-lectus in ipsum.

[D.—Difficultates et responsiones Francisci]

125. Sed obstant difficultates, [f. 70ra] quia cum respectibus causae ad Deum, in Deo non respondeat nisi relatio rationis, tunc ex causarum cognitus in habitudine ad Deum non cogno-scemus nisi respectus rationis.—Dicitur autem quod omnis respectus realis necessario habet terminum realem, et ideo oportet quod ad absolutum in Deo terminet ipsum respectum.

126. Secunda difficultas: quia si cognita simpliciter relatione cognoscitur terminus, ita cognito respectu intuitive videtur quod respectu intuitive cognoscatur.—Dicitur autem quod ista deductio parum valet, quia licet praemissae cognoscantur sine discursu, non tamen conclu-sio quae ex ipsis cognoscitur. Item, licet experiamur actum intelligendi, non tamen cognoscimus eius principium productivum nisi abstractive. Item, cognoscens statuam Herculis in habitudine ad Herculem cognoscat Herculem ex hoc, non tamen intuitive.

[VIII.—Art. 8: An in notitia abstractiva obiectum causat actum intelligendi]

Octavus articulus: si in notitia abstractiva obiectum causat actum intelligendi.

127. Dicitur quod non ut est in se, sed ut relucet in specie intelligibili, aut in phantasmate secundum illos qui negant species.

128. Sed contra: quia nullum istorum continet obiectum, nec formaliter nec virtualiter, et sic non videtur ibi relucere, quia nulla res relucet ubi non est.

129. Sed contra: quia facies hominis dicitur relucere in speculo ubi non est formaliter nec virtualiter.—Item, Deus relucet in creaturis eodem modo, secundum Dionysium *De divinis nominibus*.[50]

130. Ideo dicitur quod obiectum aliquo modo relucet in sua specie, quia species est simili-tudo obiecti.

[A.—Quattuor conclusiones
1.—Concl. 1: Actus notitiae abstractivae non causatur totaliter ab obiecto]

131. Istis autem praemissis, pono quattuor conclusiones. Prima est quod actus notitiae abstractivae non causatur totaliter ab obiecto sic sumpto, quia omnis actus intelligendi est

nobilior specie a qua causatur, cum species sit in anima propter actus, et tamen nulla causa aequivoca totalis est ignobilior suo effectu.

[2.—Concl. 2: Potentia intellectiva non causat talem notitiam totaliter]

132. Secunda conclusio: quod potentia intellectiva non causat talem notitiam totaliter, quia talis notitia dependet a specie cum experiamur ablata specie non intelligere sicut prius. Talis autem dependentia non potest reduci nisi ad effectivam causalitatem.

[3.—Concl. 3: Tam potentia intellectiva quam obiectum requiruntur]

133. Tertia conclusio: quod potentia intellectiva et obiectum sunt duae partiales causae quia neutra ipsarum per se sufficit et nulla aliarum datur.

[4.—Concl. 4: Potentia intellectiva est causa principalior]

134. Quarta conclusio: quod principalius concurrit potentia quam obiectum, quia potentia est causa universalis respectum omnium notitiarum et obiectum causa particularis respectu suae notitiae; causa enim universalis semper videtur magis principalis.

[B.—Instantiae contra conclusiones et responsiones Francisci]

135. Sed contra istas conclusiones instatur. Primo, quia ignis generans dicitur causa totalis ignis geniti, licet ibi concurrat causa universalis, et ita erit de obiecto.

136. Secundo, quia licet talis notitia dependeat a specie, dicitur autem quod non a causa per quam sed sine qua non.

137. Tertio, quia quando in natura non videmus similem concursum duarum [f. 70rb] animarum disparatarum.

138. Quarto, quia principalius concurrit homo ad generationem hominis quam sol eo quod vivens est praestantius non-vivente,[51] et tamen sol est causa universalis.

139. Ad primum:[52] quod ignis non dicitur similiter totalis causa nisi in genere causarum particularium.

140. Sed contra: quia tunc nulla erit causa totalis in natura cum concurrat ibi divina influentia. —Dicitur quod verum est simpliciter. Dicitur tamen quod caelo non influendo ignis igniret ignem.

141. Ad secundum:[53] quod si concedatur dependentia, haberetur propositum quia dependentia est causari positive sicut positiva est dependentia, et per hoc quod effectus dependet a causa, causatur ab ipsa.

142. Ad tertium:[54] quod tali modo dicuntur concurrere pater et mater ad causandum prolem; si uterque active, aut sol aut ignis.

143. Ad quartum:[55] quod licet homo sit nobilior sole, tamen principium formale per quod homo generat, scilicet forma seminis est minus perfectus. Vita autem in genito non est a sole nec ab homine, sed ab influente primo, ut alibi patet.

[C.—Difficultates et responsiones Francisci]

144. Sed obstant difficultates, quia causa particularis magis assimilat sibi effectum quam universalis, et tamen actus, cum sit vitalis, est similior intellectu quam obiecto.—Dicitur quod actus est similior speciei quam potentiae cum utrumque sit qualitas et potentia substantia et ipsa species est vitalis quia, secundum Anselmum in *Monologion*,[56] arca in mente artificis vivit; in notitia autem intuitiva substantiarum sensibilium non est ista fuga. Ideo potest dici quod non est talis ordo in effectibus potentiarum obiectivarum sicut formarum mere naturalium.

145. Secunda difficultas, quia actus vitalis non videtur esse a potentia non-vitali elicitus.—Dicitur autem verum est assumptum totaliter sed non partialiter.

146. Sed contra: quia esse vitale est nobilissima condicio actus et talem habet effectus a causa particulari, ut patet in homine generante.—Dicitur quod homo non habet vitam a homine nisi dispositive quia forma per quam gignit non est vivens. Unde non ponimus unam condicionem ab una causa et aliam ab alia, sed omnes ab utraque partialiter, licet principalius a causa universali.

147. Tertia difficultas: quia effectus semper consequitur modum minus principalem causae et sic actus erit non-vitalem ab obiecto magis quam a potentia.—Dicitur autem quod non est vitalis ab obiecto nec a potentia effectiva quia est intellectus agens, sed a se intellectu possibili ipsum recipiente. Quia si effectus esset vitalis eo quod effective elicitus a potentia vitali, tunc omnis actus imperatus a voluntate esset vitalis, immo omnis effectus naturalis ad quem concurrit divina voluntas.

148. Quarta difficultas, quia ubicumque causa universalis et particularis, secunda non agit nisi mota a prima a qua etiam accipit virtutem agendi. Obiectum autem hic non movetur a causa universali, sed movet ipsam potentiam.—Dicitur [f. 70va] autem quod neque obiectum movet intellectum agentem qui est causa effectiva, nec etiam movetur ab agente sicut in effectibus naturalibus quia est potentia ad actiones immanentes.

[C.—Notabile de modis concursus duorum agentium
ad effectum producendum]

149. Intelligendum tamen quod quattuor modis inveniuntur concurrere duo agentia ad aliquem unum effectum: 1) Aut quod sint eiusdem rationis, ita quod unius actio possit tantum intendi quod totaliter efficiat effectum totum, ut patet in trahentibus navem; 2) Aut quod, cum sint rationis eiusdem, virtus unius non potest tantum intendi quod tenet totum effectum, ut patet in patre et matre; 3) Aut quod, cum sint diversarum rationum, unum recipit ab alio vir-

tutem,[57] ut in sole et homine generante; 4) Aut quod, cum sint diversarum rationum, unum non recipit ab alio aliquid ut causet, sicut quando sol et luna non-illuminata concurrunt ad aliquem effectum in inferioribus causandum. Et isto modo ponitur in proposito.

[IX.—Art. 9: An ad causandum notitiam abstractivam concurrant aliae causae praeter potentiam et obiectum]

Nonus articulus: si ad causandum notitiam abstractivam concurrunt aliae causae praeter potentiam et obiectum.

150. Dicitur autem quod non, quia istae sufficiunt, ut patet ex praemissis.

151. Sed contra: quia habitus est principium elicitivum actum cum comparetur scientiae ad considerare sicut actus primus ad secundum.

152. Item, quandocumque voluntas imperat in intellectu actum considerandi, ille actus dicitur liber, quia a potentia libera elicitus et nullus actus aliter est liber, ideo ibi voluntas videtur concurrere.

[A.—Responsio auctoris ad nonum articulum]

153. Ideo dico quod ad eundem actum intelligendi contingit concurrere quattuor causas effectivas et unam materialem. Intellectus enim possibilis est eius causa totalis in ratione subiecti. Quando vero actus scientiae imperatur a voluntate scienter,[58] tunc enim concurrit obiectum terminans. Intellectus agens ut universaliter causans notitias ut intellectum possibilem movens. Et scientia ut actum eliciens.

154. Intelligendum tamen quod quandocumque actus intellectus causatur ab una sola causa, scilicet quando intellectus separatus possibilis intulit agentem, tunc enim solum obiectum causat effective, sicut intellectus possibilis materialiter. Quandoque concurrunt duae sicut in prima cognitione quam voluntas non potest imperare nec habitus elicere. Quandoque a tribus sicut quando habitus elicit ante imperium voluntatis, aut voluntas imperat intellectui non habituato. Quandoque quarto [modo] ut supra patuit.

155. Intelligendum ulterius quod istae causae effectivae causant quattuor effectus: primo quidem speciem intelligibilem, secundo actum intelligendi, tertio dispositionem ad habitum, quarto ipsum habitum. Et istos quattuor effectus eodem ordine recipit intellectus possibilis, ut patuit supra de notitia intuitiva.[59] Sed in hoc differunt notitia intuitiva et abstractiva, quia intuitiva obiectum postquam causavit speciem [f. 70vb] intelligibilem immediate causat actum; in abstractiva immediate non causat nisi speciem. Et quia postea species facit sequentia omnia vice eius in intellectu separato, in coniuncto autem numquam obiectum causat speciem intelligibilem, sed illam quae est in sensu, et ista illam quae est in phantasia, et haec illam quae est in intellectu, concurrentibus semper potentiis.

[B.—Difficultas circa solutionem Francisci eiusque responsio]

156. Sed obstat difficultas: quare melius potest fieri notitia abstractiva sine repraesentativo quam intuitiva sine obiecto cum repraesentativum suppleat vicem obiecti in abstractiva.—Dicitur autem quod intuitiva includit respectum ad obiectum.

157. Sed contra: quia ita diceretur quod abstractiva includit respectum ad repraesentativum. Unde sicut non potest fieri intuitiva cum respectu ad obiectum sine obiecto, licet bene quantum ad suum absolutum, ita dicetur in proposito.—Sed non valet, quia notitia intuitiva, ut notitia, est obiecti; notitia autem abstractiva, ut notitia, non est repraesentativum quia per ipsam reprasentativam non cognoscitur.

[X.—Art. 10: An intellectus divinus possit aliquid intelligere vel agnoscere abstractive]

Decimus articulus: si intellectus divinus potest aliquid intelligere vel agnoscere abstractive.

158. Dicitur autem quod non, quia Deus cognoscit omnia perfectissime. Perfectissima autem notitia uniuscuiusque est intuitiva.

159. Item, cognoscit omnia quae insunt tam per se quam per accidens.

160. Sed contra: quia Deus per suam essentiam non cognoscit contingentia cum essentia omnia uniformiter repraesentet et notitia intuitiva est contingentium cum agnoscatur per ipsam illud quod inest per accidens.

[A.—Quattuor conclusiones
1.—Concl. 1: Deus cognoscit abstractive quiditates rerum per exemplaria]

161. Hic ponuntur quattuor conclusiones. Prima est quod Deus cognoscit abstractive quiditates rerum per exemplaria quae sunt apud intellectum suum, quia per talia examplaria non potest cognoscere illa quae insunt rei per accidens cum talia sint contingentia et exemplaria semper uniformiter repraesentent et necessario quidquid repraesentant. Talis autem est notitia abstractiva.—Item, notitia intuitiva attingit ad exsistens secundum quod exsistens; per illa autem exemplaria non potest cognoscere de re si exsistit vel non, cum illud contingat et illa necessario repraesentet; ergo est abstractiva.

[2.—Concl. 2: Deus intuitive cognoscit res per actum suae voluntatis]

162. Secunda conclusio: quod Deus intuitive cognoscit res per actum suae voluntatis et non abstractive, quia non solum cognoscit res quantum ad ea quae conveniunt per se, sed etiam per accidens cum omnia contingentia per suam voluntatem cognoscit.—Item, per suam voluntatem cognoscit exsistere uniuscuiusque rei et non exsistere opposito modo.

[3.—Concl. 3: Intellectus creaturae beatus cognoscit creaturas
abstractive per divina exemplaria]

163. Tertia conclusio: quod intellectus creaturae beatus cognoscit creaturas abstractive per divina exemplaria quae refulgent in mente divina quia non cognoscit nisi illa quae insunt ei per se sicut intellectus divinus eadem ratione.—Item, omnis notitia qua uniformiter cognoscitur res, sive exsistat sive non exsistat, est abstractiva. Sic autem intellectus beatorum novit res per talia exemplaria cum sint uniformiter, semper et necessario [f. 71ra] repraesentativa.

[4.—Concl. 4: Intellectus beatus cognoscit intuitive res in divina voluntate]

164. Quarta conclusio: quod talis intellectus cognoscit intuitive res in divina voluntate et non abstractive, quia per voluntatem cognoscit ea quae insunt per accidens, ut iustitiam in esse[60] vel iniustitiam.—Item, cognoscit etiam rem ut exsistentem.—Item, cognoscit etiam rem ut alicubi praesentetur ut aliquando cum abstractiva abstrahat ab hic[61] et nunc.—Item, cognoscit rem ut contingentem cum per abstractivam nulla contingentia attingatur ut contingit.

[B.—Quattuor instantiae contra solutionem et responsiones Francisci]

165. Sed contra istas conclusiones instatur quadrupliciter. Primo, quia melius repraesentatur creatura in exemplari divino quam in se ipsa et ideo videtur melius intueri, secundum Anselmum in *Monologion.*[62]

166. Secundo, quia non videtur melius cognoscere per voluntatem quam per intellectum, cum sint aeque perfecta et notitia intuitiva dicitur potior.

167. Tertio, quia notitia quae est per eminens repraesentativum dicitur intuitiva secundum doctorem nostrum.[63]

168. Quarto, quia cum notitia intuitiva sit exsistentis ut exsistens est, illa quae non exsistunt non potuerunt intueri per voluntatem divinam in qua uniformiter cognoscuntur futura contingentia et praesentia.

169. Ad primum:[64] quod non obstat Deo eodem obiecto clariorem et sublimiorem esse notitiam abstractivam propter repraesentati eminentiam.

170. Ad secundum:[65] quod Deus omnia perfectissime cognoscit, nec ideo dicitur intuitive per voluntatem quia sublimiori modo, sed quia alia de obiecto cognoscit, scilicet illa quae insunt per accidens.

171. Ad tertium:[66] quod ipse vocavit eam intuitivam propter primum obiectum intuitive cognitum in notitia matutina.

172. Ad quartum:[67] quod licet in re futura contingentia non exsistant, tamen ut exsistentia pro tali periodo cognoscuntur in voluntate divina.

[C.—Difficultas circa solutionem et responsio Francisci]

173. Sed obstat difficultas, quia Deus cognoscit omnia a se scita per suam essentiam sicut per primum et adaequatum sui intellectus obiectum, et ideo non per voluntatem et intellectum.—Dicitur autem quod ideo dicitur omnia cognoscere per suam essentiam quia actus unicus quem habet intelligendi prius terminatur ad essentiam et secundario ad intellectum et voluntatem et per ista cognoscit omnia exteriora.

[D.—Notabile de quattuor modis repugnantibus notitiae intuitivae]

174. Intelligendum tamen quod quattuor sunt genera obiectorum in quibus repugnare dicitur intuitive cognosci. Primo quidem entibus rationis, quia non conveniunt rei ut in se ipsa.—Secundo entibus prohibitis quia talibus repugnat exsistentia.—Tertio entibus privativis quia formaliter non dicunt aliquam entitatem.—Quarto negativis, sicut ponitur nihilitas ipsa, quia si intuitive eam Deus noscet, illud de quo creaturam facit, tunc esset illud subiectum, et ideo si Deus illa intelligit, oportet ut abstractive cognoscat.

Notes to Appendix A

1. Codex Vaticanus Latinus 3026, ff. 67ra–71rb; sigl. = V. The questions here edited are labelled "Questions 2 & 3" and constitute a sequel to "Question 1: De cognitione intuitive" edited by me in *Franciscan Studies* 54 (1994–1997): 15–50.

2. meretur] *lect. dub.* V

3. Anselmus, *Monologion* 36 (ed. Schmitt 1:54–55; PL 158:190).

4. mirabili] *lectio dubia* V

5. divinam] *add.* potentiam V

6. Duns Scotus, *Ordinatio,* 1 d. 1.1.2, §34–50 (ed. Vaticana 2:23–35).

7. Cf. supra §21.

8. Cf. supra §22.

9. Cf. supra §23.

10. Cf. supra §24

11. parydo] *lect. dub.* V

12. Non invenimus.

13. mercat] *lect. dub.* V

14. Aristoteles, *Physica* 2, text 18 (Aristoteles Latinus: VII[10] 1:50–51; 2.2, 193b35).

15. Cf. supra §20.

16. Augustinus, *De Trinitate* 11.3 (CCL 50:337; PL 42:988): "Sed pro illa specie corporis quae sentiebatur extrinsecus, succedit memoria retinens illam speciem quam per corporis sensum combibit anima, pro quae illa visione quae foris erat cum sensus ex corpore sensibili formaretur, succedit intus similis visio cum ex eo quod memoria tenet, formatur acies animi et absentia corpora cogitantur."

17. perfecte] perfectio V
18. Franciscus Mayronis, *Conflatus in I Sent.*, prol. q. 17 (ed. Venetiis: 1504, f. 10ra).
19. Cf. Franciscus Mayronis, *Conflatus in I Sent.*, prol. q. 17 (ed. Venetiis: 1504, f. 10rb).
20. Cf. Franciscus Mayronis, *Conflatus in I Sent.*, prol. q. 17, a. 1 (ed. Venetiis: 1504, f. 9va).
21. Cf. supra §52.
22. Cf. supra §53.
23. Cf. supra §54.
24. Cf. supra §55.
25. Augustinus, *De Trinitate* 11.9 (CCL 50:353; PL 42:996): "Ab specie quippe corporis quod cernitur ea quae fit in sensu cernentis, et ab hac ea quae fit in memoria, et ab hac ea quae fit in acie cogitantis."
26. Cf. Rogerus Bacon, *De multiplicatione specierum* 1.2, ed. D. Lindberg (Oxford: Clarendon Press, 1983): 22, 24: "Ergo substantia generat suam speciem in principio, sicut accidens . . . Substantia facit speciem sensibilem, non tamen a sensibus exterioribus quinque nec a sensu communi." Ioannes Pecham, *Quodlibet II*, 7–8, ed. G. Etzkorn, Bibliotheca Franciscana Scholastica 25 (Grottaferrata: 1989), 95: "Totum enim individuum multiplicat speciem suam in medio." Rogerus Marston, *Quodlibet I*, 19, ed. G. Etzkorn, Bibliotheca Franciscana Scholastica 26 (Grottaferrata: 1994), 58–59: "Emittuntur ergo radii per modum quo quaelibet res corporalis speciem suam multiplicat, et oculi plus quam aliqua alia pars corporis."
27. Cf. supra §65.
28. Cf. supra §66.
29. Cf. supra §67.
30. Similarly and frequently so argued Duns Scotus, *Lectura*, 1 d. 3.1.1–2, §111–13 (ed. Vaticana 16: 266); *Ordinatio*, 1 d. 3.1.3, §140 (ed. Vaticana 3:87–88); *Quaestiones in Metaphysicam* 7.3, §10, ed. G. Etzkorn, et al. (*Opera Philosophica* 4:116–117).
31. Cf. supra §68.
32. haeceitates] *lect. dub.* V
33. vel] *lect. dub.* V
34. ipsas] ipsa V
35. Cf. supra §82.
36. non] *spat. vac.* V
37. intelligibilem] intelligibiliter(?) V
38. Augustinus, *De Trinitate* 11.3 (CCL 50:351; PL 42:990).
39. Cf. supra §92.
40. There seems to be something missing or incorrect in the text at this point.
41. nos] non V
42. intellectus] *add.* albet(?) V
43. non cognosci] c. non V
44. claret lumine] *lect. dub.* V
45. revelationem] relationem V
46. Cf. supra §116.
47. Cf. supra §117.
48. Cf. supra §118.
49. circumcursivam] *lect. dub.* V
50. Ps.-Dionysius, *De divinis nominibus* 5 (PG 3:839).
51. Cf. Aristoteles, *Topica* 3.2 (Aristoteles Latinus, V[35], 1:56; 3.2, 118a 7).

52. Cf. supra §135.

53. Cf. supra §136.

54. Cf. supra §137.

55. Cf. supra §138.

56. Anselmus, *Monologion* 5 (ed. Schmitt 1:18; PL 158:150B); hardly verbatim; there are five occurences of "arca" in the authentic works of Anselm, all in his letters where he talks about the "arca mentis" in those to whom his letters are addressed.

57. virtutem] unitativam(?) V

58. scienter] *lect. dub.* V

59. Cf. G. Etzkorn, "Franciscus de Mayronis: A Newly Discovered Treatise on Intuitive and Abstractive Cognition," in *Franciscan Studies* 54 (1994–1997): 40.

60. esse] *lect. dub.* V

61. hic] hoc V

62. Anselmus, *Monologion* 36 (ed. Schmitt 1:54–55; PL 158:190).

63. Duns Scotus, *Ordinatio*, 1 d. 3.1.4 (ed. Vaticana 3:123–72); cf. S. Day, *Intuitive Cognition. A Key to the Significance of the Later Scholastics* (St. Bonaventure, NY: Franciscan Institute, 1947).

64. Cf. supra §165.

65. Cf. supra §166.

66. Cf. supra §167.

67. Cf. supra §168.

Appendix B

[Quaestio 3. De notitia intuitiva et abstractiva simul

Art. 1: An notitia intuitiva et abstractiva semper differant specie]

Circa tertiam partem istius sermonis, negotiando circa intuitivam et abstractivam notitiam simul, ponitur prima quaestio an notitia intuitiva et abstractiva semper differant specie.

1. Et videtur quod sic, quia quaecumque ex opposito dividuntur sub aliquo genere sunt principia disiunctiva specierum illius. Sic autem de notitia intuitiva et abstractiva in genere notitiae.

2. Sed contra: quia transcendentia secundum se non differunt specie; istae autem notitiae sunt transcendentes, cum ponantur in Deo formaliter.

[Responsio auctoris ad primum articulum: quattuor conclusiones]

3. Circa istam quaestionem pono quattuor conclusiones, quarum prima est quod istae duae notitiae non semper differunt numero, quia numero Deus non habet nisi unum actum intelligendi et tamen, ut patuit, cognoscit intuitive et abstractive.—Item, intuitiva notitia in quolibet beato est una numero et tamen per ipsam, ut patuit, cognoscunt sancti apud divinum intellectum abstractive et apud eius voluntatem intuitive, ut patuit.

4. Secunda conclusio: quod non differunt specie quia quaecumque differunt specie, differ-unt numero.—Item, in divinis ubi ambae collocantur non est specifica distinctio.

5. Tertia conclusio: quod non differunt realiter, quia tunc quilibet sanctus haberet duas matutinas notitias realiter distinctas.—Item, in divinis non meretur absolutorum realis distinctio.

6. Quarta conclusio: quod semper differunt formaliter, quia quandocumque aliquod com-mune dividitur per aliqua opposita, illa oportet esse formaliter distincta nisi sit modalis dis-tinctio quae non habet locum in proposito.—Item, aliquid convenit intuitivae, ut intuitiva est, quod non convenit alicui abstractivae in quantum abstractiva, ut cognoscere ea quae insunt per accidens. Et si aliqua intuitiva sit simul abstractiva, non convenit sibi in quantum abstractiva, ut patet ex definitionibus datis.

[Instantiae contra conclusiones auctoris]

7. Sed contra istas conclusiones instatur quadrupliciter. Primo, quia quicumque numer-antur, differunt numero. Istae duae notitiae semper numerantur quia ponuntur duae.

8. Secundo, quia licet sapientia et scientia collocentur in Deo, tamen differunt specie secun-dum se ipsas.

9. Tertio, quia per divinam potentiam potest quilibet sanctus videre quiditates creatas in intellectu divino non videndo earum exsistentias in voluntate, et sic ibi separabitur notitia abstractiva ab intuitiva; unde infertur realis distinctio.

10. Quarto, quia cum notitia in ista formaliter dividatur, videtur quod multiplicatis istis multiplicetur notitia ab inferiori ad superius et tunc erunt in Deo plures notitiae.

[Responsio Francisci ad instantias]

11. Ad primum:[1] quod numerantur sicut duae rationes formales unius notitiae in Deo, nisi sint duae notitiae. Ideo quando dicitur "istae duae notitiae" est intelligendum illae duae rationes formales pertinentes ad notitiam.

12. Ad secundum:[2] quod non differunt specie secundum suas rationes formales, sed per accidens in creatis scientia et sapientia et ita in istis.

13. Ad tertium:[3] quod eadem notitia remanet in substantia uno ablato respectu, scilicet ad voluntatem.

14. Ad quartum:[4] quod ista divisio non est sicut in differentias formales facientes aliud, sed sicut facientes alteratum, sicut ens dividitur in idem et diversum, et tamen una entitas [f. 71va] numero habet utrumque.

[Quattuor exempla in favorem conclusionis]

Intelligendum tamen quod quattuor exempla reperiuntur in Deo quae declarant proposi-tum istud.

15. Primum est quia actus intelligendi dividitur simpliciter in affirmativum et negativum et tamen, cum in Deo non sit nisi unus actus, per ipsum affirmat Deus vera et negat falsa.

16. Secundum exemplum: quia actus intelligendi dividitur per scientialem et sapientialem; Deus eodem actu[5] oportet quod natura fruatur.

17. Quartum exemplum: quia cum voluntas dividatur per signum et beneplacitum non est in Deo nisi una voluntas.

[Responsio Mayronis ad argumentum principale]

18. Et per ista patet ad rationem conclusionis,[6] quia non est talis divisio sicut generis in differentias essentiales.

[Art. 2: Utrum notitia intuitiva et abstractiva quandoque differant specie]

Quaeritur ulterius utrum notitia intuitiva et abstractiva quandoque differant specie.

19. Et videtur quod non, quia diversitas sola respectuum non facit diversitatem specificam; notitiae autem non videntur differre nisi in habitudine ad obiectum vel ad repraesentativum.

20. Sed contra: quia plus videntur differre intuitiva et abstractiva quam diversae abstractivae, et tamen multae abstractivae differunt specie ab obiectis.

[Responsio Francisci ad secundum articulum:
Quattuor conclusiones]

21. Circa istam quaestionem sunt quattuor conclusiones. Prima: quod intuitiva et abstractiva quandoque differunt plus quam genere, sicut intuitiva et abstractiva nostra, quia una est in genere, alia extra genus.—Item, divina notitia est transcendens et non abstractiva; in nobis.[7]

22. Secunda conclusio: quod quandoque genere [differunt] istae notitiae, quia notitia nostra intellectiva plus differt a sensitiva quam ab alia intellectiva. Ergo cum hic inveniatur distinctio specifica, erit ibi maior, cum tamen una sit intuitiva et alia abstractiva.—Item, plus videntur differre notitia intuitiva et abstractiva de diversis obiectis quam duae abstractivae de eisdem, quae tamen ponuntur distingui specifice.

23. Tertia conclusio: quod quandoque differunt sola specie, ut quando sunt de eodem obiecto et in eadem potentia. Sed una causatur immediate per obiectum et alia per repraesentativum, quia causae particulares diversarum rationum causant semper effectus diversarum rationum, ceteris uniformiter concurrentibus, ut patet inductive. Talia autem sunt in proposito obiectum et repraesentativum, ut patet ex discussis.—Item, quod non differant plus quam specie probatur: quia minor est distinctio actuum quam obiectorum, cum omnes actus sint de genere qualitatis, et non obiecta.

24. Quarta conclusio: quod numquam istae notitiae differunt solo numero, quia in istis inferioribus una causatur immediate a repraesentativo et alia immediate ab obiecto, et ideo semper plus quam numero.—Item, in superioribus quando ab eodem causantur, ut in notitia matutina [f. 71vb] non differunt numero, ut patuit.

[Instantiae contra conclusiones auctoris]

Sed contra istas conclusiones instatur quadrupliciter.

25. Primo, quia si transcendentia differunt a non-transcendentia plus quam genere, maior esset differentia inter relationem creaturae ad Deum—quae ponitur transcendens—et ipsam creaturam quam inter substantiam et qualitatem.

26. Secundo, quia licet plus differat ignis ab aqua quam ab aere ab ipsa specie differente, non oportet quod ignis et aqua propter hoc differant genere sicut inducit secunda conclusio.[8]

27. Tertio, quia calor eiusdem rationis videtur causari ab igne et motu differentibus specie sicut a causis particularibus.

28. Quarto, quia ubicumque est invenire extrema potest dari medium; aliqua autem intuitiva differt ab alia plus quam numero, et alia minus, ut deducit quarta conclusio.[9] Ergo quandoque numero solo.

[Responsio Francisci ad instantias]

29. Ad primum:[10] quod maior distinctio formalis est inter quodcumque absolutum et respectivum quam inter duo absoluta, sicut minus distinguuntur quae sunt eiusdem generis quam diversorum; sed realis identitas in illa relatione reformat pactum.

30. Ad secundum:[11] quod licet non sit via demonstrans, tamen evidenter ibi percipitur distinctio essentialis ulterior, et non in proposito nisi accidentalis.

31. Ad tertium:[12] quod motus, cum sit forma successiva, non causat aliquam formam permanentem, sed primo motu causa universalis causat calorem rationis eiusdem cum calore ab igne causato.

32. Sed contra: quia ignis et aer sunt causae particulares diversarum rationum, et tamen non causant calorem rationis eiusdem:—dicitur autem quod illud faciunt per principia rationis eiusdem.

33. Ad quartum:[13] quod instantia datur illi regulae de actu utendi et fruendi qui sunt idem numero in Deo. Et in creatura differunt specie et numquam inveniuntur solo numero differentes.

[Difficultates ulteriores et responsio auctoris]

34. Sed obstat difficultas: si istae differentiae sunt essentiales.—Dicitur autem quod non, quia tunc omnis intuitiva differrent a quacumque abstractiva essentialiter, sed sunt quiditativae prout quiditas abstrahit ab essentia et ideo semper distinguitur formaliter.

35. Contra: quia differentiae quiditativae unius sunt semper subalternatim positae. Sapientialis autem notitia, cum sit quiditativa differentia virtutis intellectualis, non est cum intuitiva vel abstractiva subalternata, cum alia sit sapientia intuitiva, alia abstractiva; et abstractiva aliqua sit essentialis, alia sapientialis.—Dicitur autem quod sapientiae formales transcendentes non semper sunt subalternatim positae sicut limitatae in genere, ut patet in substantia et accidente absoluto et relativo cum immediate dividunt ens.

[Responsio Francisci ad argumentum principale]

Ad rationem:[14] quod non differunt solis respectibus sed absolutis perfectionibus creatis, tamen a diversis agentibus particularibus.

Notes to Appendix B

1. Cf. supra §7.
2. Cf. supra §8.
3. Cf. supra §9.
4. Cf. supra §10.
5. actu] *sign.* cruc. *mg.* V. It is clear that part of the text has been omitted in this manuscript. Missing are parts of the second and third examples.
6. Cf. supra §1.
7. The text appears to be incomplete here. One would expect something like "in nobis autem differunt plus quam genere."
8. Cf. supra §22.
9. Cf. supra §24.
10. Cf. supra §25.
11. Cf. supra §26.
12. Cf. supra §27.
13. Cf. supra §28.
14. Cf. supra §19.

Chapter 15

Mastrius on *Esse Cognitum*

NORMAN WELLS

Given his Scotist heritage, the metaphysical issue of *esse cognitum* in Bartholemew Mastrius, OFM Conv (1602–1673), is embedded in a complex context that involves an ongoing historical dimension, a theological aspect, and a logical one.[1] All three fuse together on behalf of what has to be characterized as his defense of the significance and role played by *esse cognitum* in the teaching of his *Magister*, John Duns Scotus (1266–1308).[2] Mastrius's ongoing confrontation with the positions of Henry of Ghent (1217–1293), John Capreolus, OP (1380–1444), Francis Albertinus, SJ (1552–1619), et alii, are all part of his defense of his Scotist heritage; an apologia with no apologies.[3]

At the same time, Mastrius also defends Scotus's position against the alleged adversarial misunderstandings of the *Thomistae*[4] as well as against the outrageous misinterpretations of certain *Scotistae* for whom he appropriates the damning label, *Scotimastiges*, Scotistic scoundrels, worthy of scourging, as it were.[5] Moreover, on behalf of reinforcing his defense of Scotus, Mastrius is not averse to citing the testimony of non-Scotistic *magistri* such as Francisco Suárez, SJ (1548–1617) and Gabriel Vasquez, SJ (1549–1604).[6]

The theological as well as the metaphysical aspects of the issue of *esse cognitum* have to do with God's knowledge of creatures and the classical theological distinction between His *scientia simplicis intelligentiae*, on the one hand, and on the other, His *scientia visionis*.[7] The former is addressed in Mastrius's *Disputationes Metaphysicae*[8] as well as in his later *Disputationes Theologicae*.[9]

Mingled with these metaphysical and theological considerations of *esse cognitum* are Mastrius's allusions to his treatment of *esse cognitum* and *ens rationis* in his Logic on behalf of what he likes to characterize as the *recta intelligentia* and, at other times, the *major intelligentia* of such notions.[10]

I. Historical Background

The historical section is introduced in Disputation VIII by Question I: *An status essen-tiae creaturarum ut ab existentia praescindit sit solius possibilitatis, an etiam alicuius actu-alitatis?* wherein the old confrontation between the *antiqui,* Henry of Ghent and John Duns Scotus, is revisited and updated with Mastrius's confrontation with John Capre-olus and Francis Albertinus.[11]

Mastrius takes care at the outset to note that all parties to this dispute are in agreement that possibility is prior to actuality. Moreover, everyone acknowledges that possibles are distinguished from impossibles such as chimerae.[12] However, Mastrius indicates that there is a problem as to just what this *status possibilitatis* involves. Is this an instance of mere possibility or is it a case of some sort of actuality that is the foundation of such possibility?[13]

Given the statement of the initial question that introduces Question I, it should come as no surprise that Mastrius would cite Henry of Ghent as espousing the *Prima opinio.* He also cites Giles of Rome, John Capreolus, and *Recentiores* such as Francis Albertinus.[14] Another opinion is cited that disagrees with Henry's position on the eter-nal essences of creatures as possessed of a genuine actual *esse,* while acknowledging an *esse diminutum* that is in some fashion midway between *esse reale et rationis.* How-ever this position, as so stated, is not so much an authentic historical stand as it is an adversarial misunderstanding of Scotus's opinion by the *Thomistae.*[15] Mastrius is quick to remark that not only do all the *Scotistae* come to the defense of their *Magister* on this score, but others (*alii extra scholam nostram melius quam Thomistae Scotum intelligentes*), such as Vasquez and Suárez, join them.[16]

Still highlighting misinterpretations, Mastrius makes much of the position of John Punch, OFM (1599–1661), who claims that the Thomist misinterpretation is *de mente Doctoris.* In addition, Punch is alleged to go so far as to say that creatures *ab aeterno* have such an *esse diminutum* by themselves independently of God and independent of the divine intellect (*ait creaturas ab aeterno tale esse habere a seipsis independenter a Deo, & ab operatione divini intellectus*). Moreover, in Mastrius's view, Punch's claim attributes a worse error to Scotus, especially when he defends it as Scotus's position.[17]

Mastrius closes his historical record by stating what he insists is the *communis sen-tentia.*[18] It remains accordingly for Article I to spell out the classical arguments against the position of Henry of Ghent et al. that support the conclusion espoused by the *com-munis sententia* cited in the title of Article I: *Creaturas non ab aeterno habuisse aliquod esse reale actuale essentiae.*[19] Contrary to Henry et al., God knows *ab aeterno* both the existence and the essences of creatures, as Scotus insists.[20]

What is forthcoming in Article I is an initial recapitulation of Scotus's refutations of Henry's position on an eternal *esse essentiae* caused *ab aeterno* by way of divine exemplary causality, but not created by way of divine efficient causality.[21] As so framed, Henry's opinion raises the issues of creation *ex nihilo* and annihilation of creatures back into the nothingness (*in nihilum*) whence they came. These refutations, in turn, are refocused by Mastrius upon facets of the positions of Capreolus and Albertinus.[22]

If only the existence of creatures is genuinely created by a divine efficient cause, then creation *ex nihilo* is clearly threatened. For, in this instance, such an existence presupposes the priority of an actual eternal essence. Nor does it help to claim that creatures are forthcoming *ex nihilo existentiae,* but not *ex nihilo essentiae.* Such a perspective continues to confuse genuine creation *ex nihilo sui et subjecti* with a production that presupposes an extant subject-matter (*productio quae aliquid praesupponit*).[23] Mastrius notes that this perspective is fittingly rejected by everyone. It may be *ex nihilo sui,* but it is not *ex nihilo subjecti.*[24]

In a similar fashion, it is argued that there can be no annihilation since any resolution of creatures *in nihilum existentiae* would still leave intact the eternal essence of creatures. Hence there would be no reduction of a creature back into the nothingness whence it came.[25]

Further, Scotus had argued that the very coming to be of Henry's eternal and actual *esse essentiae* is tantamount to a genuine creation. For, contrary to Henry's position on the efficient creative causality of existence that presupposes an eternal essence, the coming to be of *esse essentiae* is genuinely *ex nihilo ut de termino a quo, & ad verum ens ut ad terminum ad quem.*[26] However, the untenable consequence of such a position is an eternal creation that denies the Biblical prescription on creation in time according to Genesis.[27]

This, in turn, poses the concomitant issue of whether that coming to be of an eternal *esse essentiae* is freely chosen by God or is a necessary offspring. The latter is unacceptable since God as a free agent (*agens liberum*) is able not to produce *ab aeterno* the *esse essentiae* of creatures (*si primum [agens liberum], ergo potuit non producere esse essentiae rerum*). But given the case that God has produced the essences of creatures *ab aeterno,* then he would have been unable to create in turn the world in time. This, however, is false (*quo dato casu non potuisset mundum deinceps in tempore creare, quod est falsum*).[28]

It is at this point that Mastrius makes a transition from his refutation of Henry of Ghent to the perspective of unspecified others (*Respondent proinde alii*). Here Mastrius confronts an outright denial that the essences of things are produced in any fashion *ab aeterno,* purportedly not even dependent upon divine exemplary causality, as Henry would have it. To characterize this feature these adversaries use such distinctive language as *ex seipsis, & a seipsis* to emphasize the independence of the essences of things in regard to any creative efficient causality.[29] In this fashion, creatures could gloat that they would have some *esse ex seipsis independenter a Deo* after the fashion of some demigods (*Semidii*) in their own demi-monde.[30]

Mastrius next moves to confront Albertinus, whose position he describes as not sufficiently daring (as was the preceding opinion) to claim some unparticipated *esse*, independent of God, and this, despite Albertinus's claim that the essences of creatures do not depend upon God as a creative efficient cause. Following Henry and Capreolus, Albertinus insists that the essence of a creature depends upon God as an exemplary cause in terms of which that creature is an *ens participatum*.[31]

In refutation, Mastrius turns back to Scotus's insistence upon the coincidence of exemplary and efficient causality when the latter is an omniscient efficient cause; what depends upon God as an exemplary cause, depends on that same source as an efficient cause.[32] In what has preceded, Mastrius had alluded to what apparently he takes to be the implicit separability of essence and existence in the doctrine of Henry of Ghent. He explicitly confronts this issue in what he characterizes as Scotus's destruction of the principal foundation of Henry's position. Herein, Scotus, following St. Augustine, insists that God's eternal knowledge of simple intelligence includes both the essence and existence of creatures (*Deus . . . praecognovit igitur esse existentiae, sicut esse essentiae*).[33]

Indeed, Capreolus had made the same contention when he conceded that God eternally knows both essence and existence. Yet, though both essence and existence are in the divine mind *ut intellectum in intelligente*, Capreolus acknowledged that only essences and their essential truths enjoy an intramental eternal essential being. Existence and existential truths, then, do not have any such intramental eternal essential being.[34] Such are the consequences of Capreolus's efforts to defend the real distinction between the essence and existence of creatures by embracing the position of Henry of Ghent on the caused, but not created, eternally actual and necessary *esse essentiae* of creatures, and their created and contingent *esse existentiae*.[35]

Mastrius notes that Scotus concedes this same point that no *esse existentiae creaturae* has been *ab aeterno* a true real *esse*. So he concludes, unlike Capreolus, that such a concession undermines any espousal on behalf of the priority of an actually eternal *esse essentiae*. This conclusion is reinforced by Mastrius's consideration of God's knowledge of simple intelligence as well as God's knowledge of vision (*per scientiam, quam visionis appellant Theologi*).[36]

For just as the existences of things *ab aeterno* are not said to have *esse reale existentiae ab aeterno* on this latter level of God's knowledge of vision, so given God's eternal knowledge of the essences of creatures on the level of simple intelligence, it does not follow that the essences of creatures have any eternal real *esse essentiae*.[37]

In view of this evidence, Mastrius is convinced that he can dismiss the positions of Capreolus and Albertinus who have maintained the priority of an eternal actual esse essentiae to a temporal *esse existentiae* and on behalf of a real distinction of the one from the other. Moreover, he is convinced as well that he can secure the possibility of creatures without presupposing any priority of an eternal non-repugnant actual *esse essentiae.*[38] For if the priority of an eternal actual *esse essentiae* must be presupposed in order to save the non-repugnance of the essences of creatures, then the same consideration must be presupposed in the case of the essence of existence. For the essence of such a mode as existence is distinguished by itself from a chimera and by itself is non-repugnant, not by something really distinct from it.[39]

II. *ESSE COGNITUM HUMANUM*

Before coming to grips with the *esse cognitum* enjoyed by creatures in the divine mind, one must be alerted to an enormous number of vexing linguistic twists and turns. Not that it is not a daunting task, in the first place, to entertain, much less pursue, an intramental analysis of the divine mind. But when the language used is fraught with ambiguities and equivocations, distinctions within distinctions, and more nuances than were ever entertained by the original coinage of that French term, it tends to bedazzle the mind and produce a sort of metaphysical vertigo that cries out for significant linguistic therapy.[40]

In any case, initial consideration must be be given to Mastrius's *divisio aequivoca* of being (*ens*) into *ens extra animam* or *ens reale* and *ens in anima* or *ens rationis* at the same time he rejects any sort of *ens transcendentissime* that is univocal or conceptually common to *ens reale* and *ens rationis.*[41] Heed must be given to Mastrius's insistence that *ens reale* is what exists, or at least is not repugnant to exist *in rerum natura nullo cogitante intellectu.* This is to say that *ens reale* comprehends *ens verbaliter* as well as *ens nominaliter.*[42] *Ens rationis*, for him, is accordingly what neither exists, nor can exist, save by the sole function of the intellect (*nisi per solam intellectus cogitationem*).[43] It is clear that any metaphysical discussion of *esse cognitum*, as the bulk of the above terminology attests, takes its point of departure from within the mind, both human and divine.

Moreover, on the human level, the mind-dependence of any *ens rationis* contrasts strikingly with the mind-independence of what is extramentally actual or what happens to be an intramental possible.[44]

In keeping with Mastrius's emphasis on the *ordo doctrinae*[45] in his discussion of *esse cognitum* and his frequent comparisons between the divine and human intellects, *esse cognitum divinum* and *esse cognitum humanum*, it is fitting first to introduce his position on the origins of *esse cognitum* in the human intellect.[46]

Mastrius declares that it is common to the human intellect when understanding something to endow it, as it were, with a certain *esse cognitum et intentionale* that denominates the thing in question "to-be-known" (*cognitum*). But he is quick to say that to be so denominated does not ascribe any *esse aliquod simpliciter ac extra animam* to the objects of that knowledge even though some terminal objects may well be extra-mental. On this score, the mere act of knowing in no way modifies what is known.[47]

This is clear from the examples he cites when he refers to the extramental wall that is being-seen on an obvious sensory level and denominated accordingly as *esse visum*.[48] Just so, as *videri* gives way to *cogitari*, he cites the example of Homer, now more intra-mental than extramental, out of sight, but not out of mind. Herein *esse cognitum* is akin to the *esse exemplatum & repraesentatum* ascribed to Homer when he exists *in opinione*. It is also akin to the *esse repraesentatum* ascribed to the extramental statue of Caesar, again on an initially sensory level.[49] Herein, what is in the mind objectively is also extramentally real.

Be the terminal object extramental or intramental, then, such denominations only have to do with a qualified intramental *esse,* an *esse diminutum,* or an intramental *esse secundum quid* indicating that such objects are "being known." For these objects "as known" are *in anima et intentionales.*[50] In order to appreciate Mastrius's claim that *esse cognitum, esse visum,* or *esse intellectum* on the part of the terminal objects represented to the human mind here is an *esse purum rationis* that is an *esse simplicis denominationis,*[51] consideration has to be given to Mastrius's later distinction between *esse rationis* as it is taken in a formal sense (*formale et fabricatum*) and *esse rationis* taken in a material sense.[52]

Here, Mastrius is addressing the human intellect as it is knowing things as they are (*sicut est*) such that it presupposes the thing in its *proprium esse.*[53] So, too, any extrinsic denomination that accrues (*advenit*) to the thing known equally presupposes that it enjoys its own being (*esse*) independent of any cognition.[54] On this level, the level of first intentions,[55] the human intellect is confronted by what Mastrius charac-terizes as both an extramental intrinsic motive intelligibility and a terminative intelli-gibility that is proper to real being.[56] As such, these are instances of mind-independent intelligibilities of real being that are prior to any intramental *esse intelligibile et intellec-tum, esse cognitum, esse exemplatum, esse opinatum,* or any *esse secundum quid ac diminu-tum.*[57] For them to be intelligible is not for them to be known by the human mind.

Still on the human level, then, Mastrius is intent on making the case that when the human mind knows something as it is, such intellection does not afford it its first and primary *esse.*[58] Consistent with the *tabula rasa* tradition on human intellectual cogni-tion with its external sensory origins and the above examples of the wall, Homer, and the statue of Caesar, the things of this world must causally impress themselves upon the human knower. Such things, when and as known as extramental terminal objects of human cognition, take on a second esse in virtue of an extrinsic denomination, an intramental *esse cognitum, esse diminutum,* or *esse secundum quid.* Such is the stuff of first intentions on this level of human knowledge.[59]

This level of human knowledge must be distinguished from another level of human knowing wherein something is not known as it is. Rather, it knows what it knows other than it is (*aliter ac est*) such that it produces its own intramental object; in no way does it presuppose it in any proper extramental fashion. Rather, it is the knowing that is pre-supposed to the known. Herein one is dealing only with a terminative intelligibility that, as we shall see, on the human level is attributed to formal *entia rationis*.[60]

What is at issue is an intramental object that is thoroughly mind-dependent such that the being of this terminal object is only the-being-of-being-conceived.[61] More importantly, on the metaphysical and theological level this terminative intelligibility is also attributed to possible creatures that are the terminal objects of God's *scientia simplicis intelligentiae*. This will be addressed explicitly in the context of *esse cognitum divinum*.[62]

Such a mind-dependent object is not *ens reale* after the fashion of what Mastrius describes as what actually exists or what is non-repugnant to so exist.[63] Rather, it is what does not actually exist, nor can it do so. It exists only *per solam intellectus cogita-tionem*.[64] Herein, the human mind is no longer subject to any form of motive intelligi-bility. It is functioning only in the context of intramental terminative intelligibility wherein an object does not causally motivate a human cognitive response. It merely serves to terminate intramentally the cognitive activity in question.[65]

What is at issue here has to do with what Mastrius calls an *esse rationis formale, & fabricatum*.[66] This concerns the classical catalogue of privations, negations, and rela-tions of reason along with figments and *entia prohibita* such as chimerae, goat-stags, hippogriffs, etc.[67] The latter are classified as *entia rationis non fundata*, while the former are labelled *entia rationis fundata*.[68] However, the formal being of reason comes into being in the human mind only when such considerations as privations, negations, rela-tions, and figments are conceived after the fashion of positive real being (*ad instar entis realis*). Thereby they are conceived of as other than they are.[69] Prior to this, such con-siderations are *entia rationis materialia* such that they only enjoy an intramental *esse cognitum* in virtue of "being known."[70]

To this list must be added extrinsic denomination. For it, too, can be conceived of otherwise than it is.[71] This occurs when we conceive of such an extrinsic denomination as *esse visum*, or what Mastrius characterizes as *visio passiva*, in the wall as a relation corresponding to the active vision in the human eye.[72] This does not mean, however, that an *ens rationis*, formally taken, consists in an extrinsic denomination.[73]

In this age of celebrity, another instructive classical example of extrinsic denomina-tion as it comes into being as a formal being of reason, and the language thereof, has to do with the all too frequent ascription of fame and honor allegedly conferred upon people as a qualitative disposition, as it were. However well-deserved, these are not intrinsic denominations at all. Rather they are extrinsic attributions that we conceive to be in the *res denominata* in a correlative fashion as a relation of the known to the initial knowing activity exercised by a human subject.[74]

In regard to another complexity of extrinsic denomination, heed must be given to the issue of extrinsic denomination and *ens rationis* taken formally (*inter auctores valde controversum sit, an denominatio extrinseca formaliter sit ens rationis*).[75] There is no question that denomination, both extrinsic as well as intrinsic, is an *opus intellectus*.[76] But does this indicate that every extrinsic denomination constitutes an intramental formal *ens rationis?* Fonseca and Vasquez et al. have said that it does.[77]

It may be granted that extrinsic denomination has also to do with intramental formal beings of reason as terminal objects such that it comes and goes with the exercise (or the lack thereof) of a cognitive activity just as the *res denominata* does if it is a formal being of reason.[78] But Mastrius is opposed to any facile identification of one with the other, if for no better reason than that extrinsic denomination concerns as well genuinely real extramental beings as terminal objects, e.g., the wall that is being-seen or being-known, etc.[79]

When it comes to beings of reason taken formally and second intentions, these presuppose no such extramental *esse* as the above-mentioned first intentions whose intrinsic intelligibility, as mind-independent, is prior to their being known on the human level.[80]

However, they do presuppose an intramental first intention attended by its *esse cognitum*.[81] Hence, the *esse cognitum* of beings of reason and second intentions in their absolutely first *esse*, and their intramental terminative intelligibility, is altogether mind-dependent such that for them to-be-known is for them to-be-intelligible.[82]

The sources of such extrinsic attributions as *esse cognitum, esse objectivum, esse intellectum, esse intelligibile, esse representatum, esse exemplatum, esse opinatum*, etc., are initially in an intellect formally and subjectively (rather than objectively) in virtue of the intramental formal and subjective cognitive activity.[83] *Esse cognitum*, etc., then, is nothing but (*non nisi*) the cognitive activity itself as terminated to an object.[84] As an extrinsic denomination, it is only in the intellect objectively by way of a reflexive cognitive activity that attains that object *ut cognitum*. On this reflexive level, *esse cognitum* is now apprehended as something intrinsic to the object.[85] On this level, then, the human mind is in the presence of an extrinsic denomination wherein the initial *esse cognitum* is apprehended as other than it is and after the fashion of a real being, an *ens rationis*, taken formally, that now exists objectively in the human mind.[86]

Considerable heed and critical care must be given to this last point because it is here that the specter of equivocation in the use of the language of *esse cognitum* comes to the fore. Heretofore, Mastrius has made use of *esse cognitum* as an extrinsic denomination. While this usage has to do with a *res denominata*, to be sure, it does so as an extrinsic denomination thereto. On the reflexive level of human knowing, however, the initial *esse cognitum* is now the *res denominata* wherein the *esse cognitum* is in some way intrinsic to the *res denominata*. The "thing known," the *res denominata* attended by its extrinsic denomination, is known again. This critical consideration will be revisited again in regard to *esse cognitum divinum.*[87]

Again on the human level, it remains to note Mastrius's above-mentioned distinction between an *ens rationis* taken formally and that taken materially.[88] This is where his metaphysics meets his logic. For, when Mastrius insisted above that the *esse cognitum, esse visum,* or *esse intellectum* on the part of objects represented to the human mind is an *esse purum rationis,* that is, an *esse simplicis denominationis,* it is not in the sense of *esse rationis formale & fabricatum;* it is to be taken in a material sense.[89]

At this juncture, with a consideration of the intramental *esse cognitum* of mind-dependent beings of reason taken formally and materially on the human level in hand, it is fitting to make a transition to the *esse cognitum* of mind-dependent creatures in the divine mind. To do so it must be recalled that both beings of reason and creatures in the divine mind are intramental terminal objects in the divine mind enjoying therein only a terminative intelligibility. At the same time, as insisted by Mastrius at the outset, one must distinguish between the non-repugnance of possible creatures and the repugnance and contradictory character that are part and parcel of beings of reason, taken formally.

But if creatures are possible because God knows them, what then to say of God's knowledge of beings of reason? Given that both possibles and impossibles are intramental terminal objects of the divine mind, how to explain the origin of the possibility of the one and the impossibility of the other in terms of divine cognition?

III. *ESSE COGNITUM DIVINUM*

Before considering Mastrius's explicit treatment of *esse cognitum divinum,* attention must be given briefly to his position on the *objectum primarium* and the *objectum secundarium* of the divine intellect. The former is the divine essence itself as both the motive and terminative object thereof.[90] The latter has to do with God's *scientia simplicis intelligentiae* whereby creatures are known *ab aeterno* as the terminative object.[91] On this latter score, to deny such knowledge of possible creatures and to deny that they have *esse cognitum* from eternity *in mente divina* is just as unreasonable as it is to grant that the human eye sees the wall and then to deny that the wall is seen (*deinde negare parietem esse visum*).[92] Moreover, his position on this issue is certain not only in faith, but also in true philosophy.[93]

Contrary to what was stated on behalf of *esse cognitum humanum,* when the divine intellect understands possible creatures, it produces their first being, an intramental *esse intelligibile, vel intellectum.* But prior to the coming to be of this *objectum secundarium,* creatures have *esse intelligibile proprium et formale* only virtually (*sed tantum virtuale*) or eminently in the divine essence.[94] For the divine essence is not an actual formal exemplar of creatures. Nor are creatures reflected in the divine essence as in a mirror.[95]

In light of these rejections, Mastrius concludes that the *esse cognitum* attributed to intramental secondary objects in and forthcoming from the divine intellect is altogether their first *esse*. For such objects to-be-intelligible is for them to-be-understood.[96] Just so, the intelligibility of such intramental objects is *terminativa* such that the object comes-to-be-intelligible as the terminus of a cognitive activity.[97] Wary here of a charge of anthropomorphism because the human mind is subject to the causal influence of extramental motive objects that are presupposed when seeing and knowing the extramental wall, etc., there is no such mind-independent *intelligibilitas motiva* prior to the divine intellect, save in the case of the divine essence.[98] On the divine level, possible creatures *as known* presuppose the divine knowing.

In the course of his analysis, Mastrius affords his reader what he characterizes as a better grasp of his position on *esse cognitum*.[99] It is here, now on the divine level, that the reader again confronts the problem of equivocation mentioned above in regard to *esse cognitum*. For one must acknowledge that *esse cognitum* formally received by possible creatures in virtue of the knowing exercised by the divine intellect. But one must distinguish this from the *res denominata* whose *esse* is attained by divine knowledge and constitutes the terminal secondary object of *divina scientia simplicis intelligentiae*.[100] This other *esse* is what is non-repugnant and in terms of which creatures are said to be *in potentia logica* as well as *in potentia objectiva*. This *esse* is also rendered as *esse reale potentiale*.[101] One must, then, be prepared to distinguish this *esse possibile* of the *res denominata*, possible creatures, from their only actual being, the *esse cognitum* that is their intramental being-of-being-conceived by the divine mind.

Mastrius insists that this first *esse cognitum*, derived from the termination of divine knowledge at possible creatures, is not to be understood as some real being midway between *ens reale* and *ens rationis* as the *Thomistae* mistakenly think.[102] Rather, it is a *purum esse rationis* as is the *esse visum* in the wall and the *esse intellectum* in the object represented to any intellect.[103]

But as noted on the human level, this *purum esse rationis* for Mastrius is not a full-blown *esse rationis*, formal and fabricated, (*esse rationis formale, et fabricatum*), as he would have it. It is to be classified as a material and residual *esse rationis* (*sed materiale, & derelictum*), not unlike Scotus's consideration of *esse exemplato & repraesentato* of Homer when *in opinione*. This pure *esse rationis* is akin to that *esse opinatum* that Scotus attributed to Homer.[104]

In order to appreciate the significance of what Mastrius is addressing here, it is important to recall again what he once remarked to the *Thomistae* in order to illuminate and to cure their failure to understand Scotus's position. He makes it clear that it is one thing to speak of creatures as eternally known (*cogniti*), their actual intramental being, a *quo;* it is another thing to speak of the *esse possibile* as that which is known by the divine intellect to be non-repugnant to creatures, the *res denominata* at issue, a *quod*. It is still another consideration to speak of the simple denomination (*esse simplicis denominationis*) that creatures are subject to because they terminate divine cognition—an extrinsic denomination.[105]

This latter consideration, on the divine level, is where Mastrius's use of the language of extrinsic denomination joins his position on material beings of reason in his claim that *purum esse rationis* is an *esse simplicis denominationis*.[106] This is to say that what is here characterized as *esse* is a *cognosci*.[107] It is that actual intramental being that is the-being-of-being-conceived on the part of intramental possible creatures. As such, it is not to be confused with any intrinsic actual extramental *esse* nor with an intrinsic intramental possible *esse*.

At this point in his discussion of *esse cognitum*, Mastrius confronts what he characterizes as "an ongoing problem" (*illud quaesitum quod hic proponi solet*) that is raised by some *Scotistae: an hoc esse cognitum positum a Scoto dicatur tale per extrinsecam, vel potius per intrinsecam denominationem?*[108]

While Mastrius cites two Scotists and attempts to mediate between them, as one opts for extrinsic denomination and the other embraces an intrinsic denomination, he is convinced that this is, for the most part, a disagreement about a name (*sed esse fere contentio de nomine*).[109] Nevertheless, speaking for himself, Mastrius acknowledges that the *esse cognitum divinum* does not belong to things by a denomination as extrinsic as that *esse cognitum* belonging to things in virtue of human intellection.[110]

This latter extrinsic *esse cognitum humanum* that is ascribed to extramental existents as a second *esse*, an *esse simplicis denominationis*, is altogether extrinsic and adventitious to such things (*sequitur esse illis omnino extrinsecam et adventitium*). By contrast, the fact that the intramental *esse cognitum divinum* forthcoming from the divine intellect is the first *esse formale* for possible creatures, leads Mastrius to infer that such an *esse*, even though it be an *esse diminutum & secundum quid*, is intrinsic in some fashion (*sequitur esse in illis aliquo pacto intrinsecum*).[111]

Following up on his examples of *entia rationis*, taken formally, and of second intentions in the course of his treatment of human cognition on the reflex level, Mastrius noted that the *esse* ascribed to formal beings of reason and to second intentions by our intellect is not extrinsic to them. Nor does it belong to them in virtue of that real extrinsic denomination that customarily presupposes the thing to which it happens.[112] This is the case with the *esse cognitum* forthcoming from the divine intellect; it is formal and intrinsic to possible creatures "as that which is known," even though diminished and qualified (*diminutum & secundum quid*).[113]

Yet, for Mastrius, it must be accepted as certain that the *esse cognitum* ascribed to things by the divine intellect is not so intrinsic as to posit something in creatures that they can be said to be *in seipsis* absolutely. For a *res in esse cognito,* as an intramental *esse diminutum & secundum quid,* can in no way be considered as something *per ipsum in seipsa* after the fashion of an actual extramental entity.[114] Rather, this is merely a case of something that exists in the divine mind as that which is known exists in a knower (*sed tantum in mente divina ut cognitum in cognoscente*).[115]

Adding to the terminological complexity of this issue wherein Scotus's intramental *esse cognitum* is characterized as *esse diminutum & secundum quid* is Mastrius's commentary on the text where his *Magister* indicated that *esse cognitum* is also designated to be an *esse rationis absolutum.* The purpose of this additional characterization is to point out that the intramental *esse cognitum* attributed to the possible essences of creatures, while forthcoming from the divine intellect, serves as the foundation of a relation of reason to that divine intellect.[116]

It is here that Mastrius directs his reader to his Logic, where he had explained that an *ens rationis,* since it is conceived and divided after the fashion of *ens reale,* is divided into *absolutum & respectivum* just as *ens reale* is. An *ens rationis absolutum* is what is conceived or what can be conceived after the fashion of an *ens ad se* (*ad modum entia ad se*); an *ens rationis respectivum* is what is conceived after the fashion of an *ens ad aliud,* as is the case with second intentions.[117]

Mastrius argues accordingly that, since the intramental *esse cognitum* enjoyed by creatures can be conceived as a foundation of a relation of reason to the divine intellect whence it originates, it is aptly designated to be an *ens rationis absolutum* since it fulfills the proper function of an absolute in founding a relationship.[118]

Further, it is important to note here that Mastrius adds (*Addo*) that what Scotus frequently understands by that intramental *esse absolutum creaturarum* is that *esse possibile* that formally constitutes the foundation of that relation to divine cognition. For this reason, *possibilitas logica* is customarily characterized as *possibilitas absoluta.* However, the *esse possibile* as the *res denominata* attained by that divine cognition is an *esse reale potentiale* or an *ens nominaliter* since the creature, taken precisely *secundum illud possibile,* is an *ens reale potentiale.*[119]

At this point, Mastrius finally comes to grips with the persistent claims of the *Thomistae* that the *esse cognitum* ascribed to possible creatures in the divine mind is midway between real beings and formal beings of reason. These adversaries correctly make the point that Scotus himself denies that *esse cognitum* is an *ens reale* properly taken. Moreover, he clearly rejects that it is an *ens prohibitum* or a formal being of reason such as a chimera. It must, then, come down between these two extremes. Further, intramental possible creatures are truly creatable by way of an efficient cause; formal beings of reason such as chimerae are not so producible. Indeed, the former is characterized by its non-repugnance to actual created existence; the latter embodies a repugnance thereto.[120]

Esse cognitum, then, in this interpretation, is that sort of *esse* that is akin to (*conveniens*) *esse rationis* in that it is not an *esse reale simpliciter.* It is also akin to *esse reale simpliciter* to the extent that, "as known," it is not repugnant for it to so exist. In short, it is more perfect than an *esse rationis* due to its non-repugnance; it is less perfect than *esse simpliciter* since it is an intramental *esse diminutum ac secundum quid.* It must accordingly be midway between these two extremes.[121] So much for this ongoing challenge to Mastrius.

It is interesting to witness Mastrius respond to this issue. Possible creatures are clearly *ens reale potentiale.* But when taken reduplicatively as subject to the denomination "as that which is known," possible creatures take on the character of an *ens rationis.* So these creatures themselves can be said to be partly real beings and partly beings of reason. Creatures here are real beings in terms of what is known by the divine intellect—that they are non-repugnant to actual created existence. When this *esse possibile* is considered "as that which is known", it is akin to an *ens rationis.* For, as so considered, creatures only have an *esse objectivum/esse cognitum in mente divina.*[122]

Lest Mastrius's position here be taken as a capitulation to the claims of the *Thomistae,* he distances himself from their claims by diagnosing wherein these adversaries go awry. Their shortcoming comes down to confusing the *esse cognitum* that is a *purum esse rationis* of simple denomination with the *res denominata* which they, too, must acknowledge to be possible creatures in the divine mind. Such a confusion on their part leads to the conclusion that this being of the *res denominata* is the-being-of-being-known after the fashion of an *ens rationis* taken formally. Hence, their untenable conclusion that this *res denominata* is partly real and partly an *ens rationis* (*ut illud ostendant esse ens partim reale, et partim rationis*).[123]

Mastrius refuses to acknowledge such a confusion since for him the *res denominata* that is the *objectum terminativum* is not the extrinsic denomination thereof. That terminal object as *esse possibile creaturarum* is an *ens reale nominaliter.* As such, it can in no way be confused with a formal *ens rationis* or an *ens prohibita* as a chimera or a goat-stag. However, Mastrius will concede that, if *esse reale* be taken *verbaliter,* then, of course, after a fashion (*dici quoque posset quodammodo*), a possible creature, as an *ens reale nominaliter,* could be something midway between *ens reale verbaliter* and a formal *ens rationis* repugnant to actual existence.[124]

IV. *TRES ARDUAE DIFFICULTATES*

In article three, Mastrius recapitulates what has preceded in order to set the stage for his explication of the real possibility of the essences of creatures. To do so, he has to confront three serious difficulties (*tres arduae difficultates*).

The first has to do with the nature of this possibility. The second raises a causal question: Are there causes of these possible essences? If so, what are they? The third query asks whether the essence of something possible can be truly characterized as a real being (*possit dici vere ens reale*).[125]

As to the first difficulty, Mastrius takes issue with those who explain the possibility of creatures in terms of divine omnipotence. On this score, something is denominated to be possible because God can produce it.[126]

Mastrius remarks that Scotus has rejected this because, in the absence of any active omnipotence (*Si per impossibile, Deus non esset*), many things are said to be possible in terms of *potentia logica*. This is to say that possibility in this latter sense is not an extrinsic denomination forthcoming from divine omnipotence. Rather, it is an intrinsic possibility independently of divine omnipotence (*independenter ab omnipotentia divina*). Further, Mastrius insists that this extrinsic denomination that is designated as objective possibility presupposes logical potency as its foundation.[127]

Logical potency is also characterized as *potentia absoluta*. This is because it consists only in the non-repugnance of the thing in question and prescinds from whether something be producible by another or were to exist *a seipsa*.[128]

But within this first difficulty arises a further difficulty that has to do with the correct understanding (*recta intelligentia*) of this intrinsic logical potency and its non-repugnance.[129]

Mastrius takes issue with the interpretation of some (*Aliqui*) who reject a positive appreciation of *non-repugnantia* and opt for a negative rendering of that non-contradiction. This is understood as a privative reality (*realitas privativa*) indicative of a mere negation of repugnance or contradiction. In keeping with the ongoing explication of logical potency in terms of the logical composition or connection of propositional extremes, the conclusion is drawn here that this only involves a negation of diversity between the subject and predicate.[130]

Mastrius finds this unacceptable because the objective concepts that constitute the terminal intramental objects of that *scientia simplicis intelligentiae* exercised by the divine mind are positive.[131]

To make his point, Mastrius turns to grammar to afford some linguistic therapy. Just as the negation of darkness is light and the negation of blindness is sight, so too the negation of repugnance, as a negation of a negation or a negation of impossibility, is indicative of something positive.[132]

The second serious difficulty referred to by Mastrius has to do with whether the possibility of things has a cause (*an possibilitas rerum causam habeat?*). Mastrius makes it clear, however, that he is not seeking a cause, strictly speaking. Since creatures have no eternal actual reality, a genuine efficient causal inquiry is literally out of the question. What is sought here is a *ratio*, rather than a *causa* (*sumitur ergo causa pro ratione*), of possibility as well as impossibility. Is the first "reason" that answers the whys and wherefores for the possibility and the impossibility of things to be found in God or in the things themselves?[133]

In response, Mastrius lists those who insist that possibles are, indeed, independent of God, both *ex se* and *a se*. Others conclude that possibles depend upon the divine will and divine omnipotence. Still others claim that possibles depend upon the divine intellect in virtue of the divine ideas.[134]

Scotus is assigned an intermediate position between the preceding extremes since he embraces both an intrinsic and an extrinsic source of the possibility and the impossibility of things. The divine intellect is the extrinsic and principiative source thereof, while possibility and impossibility are intrinsically and formally forthcoming from the formal features of the things themselves.[135]

Mastrius wastes no time in rejecting the extreme positions for their neglect of each other. Those who, such as Vasquez and Punch, emphasize independence and the intrinsic role played by the possible essences and the *impossibilia* themselves, fail to realize that these possibles and the impossibles do not have such a status totally *a seipsis & ex seipsis,* independently of God.[136]

To claim that the essences of creatures have their intrinsic possibility *a seipsis* is to conclude that it is not communicated from another and is independent of any extrinsic source. For Mastrius, the positive non-repugnance of the possible essence of creatures posited (*ponat*) by God's *scientia simplicis intelligentiae* is surely dependent upon God.[137]

At the same time that Mastrius insists upon the tethering of the possible essences of creatures *ex seipsis* to the divine intellect, he has to confront Vasquez and Poncius on another score. Both *Recentiores* have understood Scotus's position on the cognitive origins of *esse cognitum* to maintain that the essences of possible creatures are possible because God's knowing does not just represent them, but that it produces them and renders them intelligible. Divine intellection fuses with their intelligibility. They are possible and intelligible because they are known; they are not known because they are possible and intelligible, the position defended by both Vasquez and Punch.[138]

Since Mastrius has insisted that the divine intellect is also aware of *entia rationis* whose sole actual being is *esse cognitum divinum* or *esse objectivum divinum,* involving a terminative intelligibility akin to that enjoyed by intramental possibles, the tensions herein cannot be overlooked. If the essences of creatures are possible because God knows them, then *entia rationis* must be possible because God knows them as well.[139]

Mastrius's reply reaffirms the intermediate position noted above. If *potentia logica* and *possibilitas logica* is acknowledged to be a mode of composition produced by an intellect judging that a predicate belongs to a subject as in a proposition, in the absence of any repugnance, then logical possibility arises both from the formal features in things and the judgment of the intellect. One without the other is insufficient to explain any logical possibility or any logical impossibility for that matter.[140]

But there is a critical difference between the principiative intellectual origins of possibility and those of impossibility. Possibles and their intelligibility proceed from the divine mind proximately and immediately (*proxime & immediate*); impossibles and their intelligibility are forthcoming therefrom remotely and mediately (*remote & mediate*). This is to say that the divine mind produces two beings (*duo entia*) in such a way that they are each formally possible, but in themselves they are formally incompossible.[141]

Thus, this formal incompossibility is forthcoming both from the formal features themselves and principiatively from the extrinsic intellectual source that produced them, but in a mediate and remote fashion.[142]

As a consequence, Mastrius concludes that, whereas *esse possibile* is forthcoming from the *esse cognitum* that constitutes the intelligibility of creatures in the divine mind, such is not the case with chimerae and any other impossibles. For such impossibles are not imposed upon (*objici*) the divine intellect as an object, neither primary nor secondary, that is essentially one (*unum per se*) and immediately intelligible. Lacking, as they do, a proper unitary structure, impossibles do not have a proper intelligibility that is forthcoming from their intentional presence in the divine mind.[143]

When it comes to the third difficulty, Mastrius takes measures to reinforce his previous claim that the objective concepts of things in the divine mind are positive, indicating that the *esse essentiale rerum* is an *esse positivum*.[144]

In doing so, Mastrius again must take issue with those who, while denying that the logical possibility of things in the divine mind *ab aeterno* is an *esse positivum*, insist that this logical possibility is a mere negation of repugnance. As a negation of diversity, it is but a privative reality.[145]

In rebuttal, Mastrius calls upon what he characterizes as "the well-known distinction of the Schools." He refers to the twofold significance of *ens reale* such that a distinction is made between real being taken nominally and real being taken verbally or participially.[146] Indeed, Mastrius repeats Scotus's classic remark to the effect that he agrees that the divine intellection of the stone *ab aeterno* has not been logical, but metaphysical and real on the part of the object thereof. Hence, the possible stone as it prescinds from existence can, and must, be designated as *ens reale*. Otherwise the divine knowing of this stone *ab aeterno*, as something positively *creabilis*, could never be called objectively real.[147]

In further opposition to those who deny the positive reality of the likes of a possible stone, etc., Mastrius rejects any attempt to discredit his claim that his *ens possibile* signifies formally and directly that *ens positivum* that would exist, if it were produced *ad extra*.[148] Indeed, this *lapis possibile* and *lapis actualis* are not only generically and specifically the same, they are numerically so since the individual now in act is the same thing that was in potency.[149]

On this score, Mastrius refuses to entertain a traditional consideration wherein it is acknowledged that the predication of *ens possibile,* of both the possible and the actual stone, does not warrant the claim that they be positively the same. Negative identity is all that is called for.[150] Mastrius disclaims that there can be any identity between a negative and a positive term such as between *homo* and *non ens.* For it is false that *homo* and *non ens* are not diverse. On the other hand, it is true that the man who is now extant is not diverse from the man who was possible.[151]

———

It remains to reflect on a number of facets of Mastrius's perspective. Perhaps the most striking is his insistence upon, and defense of, the intrinsic reality of the logical possibility enjoyed by the essences of creatures as secondary objects of the divine intellect.

In light of a preceding and ongoing tradition wherein the non-repugnance of those essences of creatures in the divine mind is understood in a negative fashion as a negation of impossibility, Mastrius's rejection of that position tends to move him back into the orbit of Henry of Ghent's position. Granted that Henry's eternal essences have been reduced from an actual status to a possible status, the positive formal structure remains the same, not altogether unlike Kant's 100 possible thalers.

Granted also that such positive essential realities have been purged of their exemplary causal origins of any actual essential being (*esse essentiae actualis*) as in Henry, they are still intrinsically positive and each is an intrinsically positive *aliquid.*

As such, given the similarity of Mastrius's position to that of Henry of Ghent, the early criticism of the latter's position on creation *ex nihilo existentiae,* but not *ex nihilo essentiae,* comes back to haunt Mastrius. For his intrinsically positive *esse essentiae,* a positive *aliquid,* seems vulnerable to much the same critique. Granted this possible essence of Mastrius is purged of an actual *esse essentiae,* it is still a positive *ens possibile* and positively creatable. How, then, can this meet the standard of the traditional criterion of creation as *ex nihilo sui et subjecti* that Mastrius made so much of in his critique of Henry of Ghent?

Moreover, given the priority of the essential formal order involved in *possibilitas logica* or *potentia logica,* over the potential efficient causality at issue *in potentia objectiva,* the question of its causal origins cannot help but arise. This is inevitable because the notion of logical potency encompasses both God and creatures. Just as the deity does not call for any consideration of an efficient cause, it is not a pertinent issue for the possible creature under such a rubric as logical potency.

Further, even though the presence of *potentia objectiva* is inevitably pertinent to possible creatures, but not to the deity, it must be acknowledged that this has to do with a potential efficient cause, not an actual one. For the possible creature, then, to be related to a potential efficient cause is for it to be still causally underived.

On this last score, it is all very well to look to the divine intellect as an explanation and to indicate that the *esse cognitum, esse objectivum, esse diminutum,* and *esse secundum quid* of possible creatures is forthcoming from the divine intellect since every knowing involves something being known and every representation involves something represented. Granted, then, that possible creatures possess a mind-dependent being-of-being-known, it still remains to be seen if the divine intellect is the source of the logical possibility of such creatures. Creatures, then, may well be intelligible because known. But their logical possibility is forthcoming from themselves (*ex seipsis*).

To claim that creatures are possible because God knows them is to acknowledge as well that God also knows beings of reason. Any distinction, then, between these possibles and impossibles is not forthcoming from their intramental *esse cognitum* or *esse objectivum.* Again, the divine knowing may well be the source of their being known. But the possibility and impossibility here must be acknowledged to be forthcoming from themselves (*ex seipsis*).

In the matter of God's speculative knowledge vis à vis the possible essences of creatures, it must be recognized that the divine intellection involved in God's *scientia simplicis intelligentiae* has to do with the divine formal concept or idea that is representative of the divine objective concept. Like *esse cognitum,* etc., *conceptus objectivus* is also an extrinsic denomination. But it is an extrinsic denomination that designates a *res denominata* that is presupposed to its extrinsic denomination.

Once again there is an aspect of standing over and against the divine mind on the part of that *possibilitas logica.* For that gaze, as speculative and presupposing the possibility of a secondary object that awaits its representation in virtue of a divine formal concept, is never fully repudiated by Mastrius in his exchange with both Vasquez and Punch, save to say that their claim that such a speculative consideration is not operative does not repudiate that such a representative consideration is operative and productive of things in *esse cognito.*[152]

NOTES

1. See B. Crowley, "The Life and Works of Bartholemew Mastrius, OFM Conv, 1602–1673," *Franciscan Studies* 8 (1948): 97–152; C. H. Lohr, *Latin Aristotle Commentaries* (Firenze: Leo S. Olschi, 1988), 2:249–50. Mastrius's *Disputationes in Organum Aristotelis,* cowritten with his fellow Franciscan, Bonaventura Bellutus, OFM Conv, dates from 1639 (hereafter *DO*); his *Disputationes in XII libros Metaphysicae* dates from 1646–47 (hereafter *DM*); his *Disputationes in libros De Anima,* also cowritten with B. Bellutus, dates from 1643 (hereafter *DA*). He also wrote a *Disputationes Theologicae in primum Sententiarum* (hereafter *DT*) begun in 1655. I have used the Venice 1719 edition.

2. *DM* d. 8.1, §2 (ed. Venitiis 1719 2:51a): a qua gravissima calumnia nedum Scotistae omnes etiam Magistrum suum incunctanter defendunt, & vindicant sed alii extra schola nostram

melius, quam Thomistae, Scotum intelligentes. Mastrius refers explicitly here to Suárez and Vasquez. See n. 5 below for another use of *defendunt*. In view of the complexity of the Scotistic tradition, to much of which Mastrius is thoroughly privy, let it be said that it is beyond the scope of this effort to assess whether Mastrius is altogether faithful to the perspective of his master, Duns Scotus. It is sufficient to say that he intends to be.

   3. See nn. 14, 15, 21, 25, 29, 31, 33, 34 below referring to Henry, Capreolus, and Albertinus.

   4. See *DM* d. 8.1.1, §3 (2:51b) where Mastrius mentions the influence on Punch of Bañez, Cajetan, and Zumel.

   5. *DM* d. 8.1.2, §12 (2:57a): Conclusio est Scoti locis mox citandis, & communis inter Scotistas contra Poncium, & Herrera qui unice in schola nostra calumniam hanc a Thomistis Scoto impositam approbarunt, imo ut Scoticam opinionem defendunt hanc tenet Rada I. Part. Controvers. 29. Art. 3 ubi vocat Scotimastiges, qui hanc opinionem Doctori subtili adscribunt.

   6. See n. 2 above and *DM* d. 8.1.1, §18 (2:59ab): for other references to Vasquez. This is not to say that Mastrius is not also critical of both Suárez and Vasquez, as will be seen. See nn.130, 134, 138, 139 below.

   7. See *DM* d. 8.1.1, §2 (2:50b–51a) for the initial reference to scientia simplicis intelligentiae in regard to Henry of Ghent. This is followed by Mastrius's own reference thereto in §2, 51a. See n. 33 below. The distinction between *scientia simplicis intelligentiae* and *scientia visionis* is to be seen in §9, 55a. There are many other references to *scientia simplicis intelligentiae* in Disp. 8 as well as a few references to a *tractatus theologica de scientia Dei* (cf. *DM* d. 8,1.4 ad 1m, §57 (2:83b) that appear to be what Mastrius formally addressed in his *Disputationes Theologicae*. For another reference to this tract, see *DM* d. 8.1.4, §18 (2:61a). In order to understand the epistemological structure of *scientia simplicis intelligentiae,* heed must be given to the distinction between the formal and the objective concepts. This not only functions on the level of the divine intellect, but on the human level as well. See nn. 53, 55 below and *DM* d. 2.1, §2 (1:66ab):

> conceptus enim formalis est ipsa rei cognitio, vel actus ipse intelligendi, & dicitur conceptus, quia est proles mentis, formalis vero, quia per ipsum formaliter intelligimus; conceptus autem objectivus est ipsa res mente concepta, vel saltim menti repraesentata per speciem, diciturque conceptus denominatione extrinseca a conceptu formali, quo dicitur concipi, & dicitur objectivus, quia cum res concipitur non se habet ut forma inhaerens concipienti potentiae, sed ei ut consideranda objicitur, & obversatur . . . differunt autem hi conceptus non parum inter se, nam formalis est semper inter res positiva menti inhaerens; objectivus vero non semper, cum privationes, & non entia, ac etiam entia rationis menti objiciantur. Item conceptus formalis semper est res singularis in essendo, licet possit esse universalis in repraesentando, cum sit ipsemet intelligendi actus; sed objectivus esse potest universalis, & singularis, nam & singularia, & universalia intellectui objiciuntur, ut intelligantur.

   See n. 131 below citing *DM* d. 8.1.3, §32 (2:69a) where reference is made to *conceptus objectivi rerum in mente divina sunt*. See also where (§47, 78a) reference is made to *lapis possibilis* as *objective realis*. It must be noted here that the terminology, *conceptus objectivus,* as noted in the above text is an explicit example of an extrinsic denomination that designates the *res denominata*. This is certainly the case for Suárez as well in *Disputationes Metaphysicae* (Paris: Vives, 1866) (hereafter *DM*), 2.1.1 (25:64b–65a). See n. 12 below on the equivocal character of *esse cognitum*.

   8. See n. 7 above.

   9. See *DT* d. 3, q. 1, 1 (1:103a).

10. See *DM* d. 8.1.2 (2:59b, §17; 62a, §20). *Recta intelligentia* is referred to in §26, 66a, but does not allude to his Logic. Mastrius also devotes a section of his *Disputationes Metaphysicae* to a discussion of *ens rationis*. See *DM* d. 2.9.1 (1:234b–250a).

11. *DM* d. 8, q. 1, §2 (2:50–51). For the confrontation between Scotus and Henry, see Duns Scotus, *Ordinatio*, 1. d. 35 and d. 36 in *Opera Omnia*, ed. C. Balic et al. (Vatican City: Typis Polyglottis Vaticanis, 1954), 1:245–98.

12. *DM* d. 8.1.1, §2 (1:51a): per hoc enim res possibiles ab impossibiles secernuntur. It must also be recognized that this distinction between possibles and impossibles has to do with objective concepts (*conceptus objectivi*) and/or *res denominatae* (cf. n. 7 above). Since *esse cognitum* attends both intramental possibles, *entia rationis* and impossibles, and there are two kinds of terminative intelligibility, primary and secondary, such that the latter is attributed to *entia rationis* and to creatures terminating the activity of the divine mind (cf. *DM* d. 5.6.1, §135 [1:428b] cited in n. 56 below), considerable care is called for in distinguishing one from the other. Further, anyone dealing with the significance of *esse cognitum* on the human and divine levels at this period of Western thought must ponder and heed Francisco Suárez's caveat in regard to the problem of equivocation: Unde cavenda est aequivocatio, quando agimus de esse cognito, aut aliis similibus denominationibus intellectus. He acknowledges a twofold meaning to such terminology as *esse cognitum* and its synonyms, e.g., *esse objectivum*, etc. See *DM* 54.2.13 (26:1021). Mastrius knows this text because he cites it in *DO* d. 3.2.1 ad 3m, §22 (303b). Suárez had earlier referred to these two meanings as "esse cognitum quoad rem denominatam, seu quoad ipsum esse quod cognoscitur and esse cognitum quoad denominationem." See *DM* 25.1.32 (25:908). We shall have occasion to confront both meanings below in the twists and turns of the ongoing analyses of Mastrius on both the human and divine levels as it has to do with intramental possibles and *entia rationis*. So sensitivity is called for as to when and where *esse cognitum*, as an extrinsic denomination, is used to indicate the extrinsic denomination that is at issue. That same sensitivity is called for as to when and where the same terminology, *esse cognitum*, etc., as an extrinsic denomination, is used to indicate the *res denominata*. See N.J. Wells, "*Esse Cognitum* and Suárez Revisited," *American Catholic Philosophical Quarterly* 67 (1993): 339–48, and Sven K. Knebel, "The Early Modern Rollback Of Merely Extrinsic Denomination," in *Meeting of The Minds: The Relations Between Medieval And Classical Modern European Thought*, ed. Stephen F. Brown (Turnhout: Brepols, 1998), 317–31.

13. *DM* d. 8.1.1, §2 (2:51a): difficultas est, quid dicant [essentiae rerum] sub tali statu [possibilitatis], & an hic status sit merae possibilitatis, vel an etiam alicuius actualitatis, in qua talis possibilitas fundetur.

14. *DM* d. 8.1.1, §2 (2:50b–51a). The catalogue of texts attributed to Henry is the same catalogue listed in Suárez that has been attacked by Vasquez at the time and has been a source of criticism in our day as well. See *DM* d. 31.2.2 (26:229b) and N.J. Wells, "Suarez on the Eternal Truths, Part I," *The Modern Schoolman* 58 (1981): 90 n. 23 for evidence of the presence of a *maginista Scoti*. See n. 31 below. One must heed the citation of H.A. Burgus: "Tam multa . . . Henrico tribuuntur circa essentiarum aeterntatem falsa penitus et impossibilia, ut non possit Henricum damnare qui alibi quam apud ipsum ipsius sententiam quaerit," cited by R. Macken, "Le statut de la matiere premiere dans la philosophie d'Henri de Gand," *Recherche de Théologie ancienne et medievale* 66 (1979): 151 n. 87. In any case, it is clear that Henry, Capreolus, and Albertinus constitute a doctrinal trio for Mastrius. For the pertinent texts of Albertinus that manifest his sympathy for Henry and Capreolus, see Wells, "Suarez on the Eternal Truths," 90 n. 24. For Capreolus's sympathy for Henry, see N.J. Wells, "Capreolus on Essence and Existence," *The Modern Schoolman* 38 (1960): 21–23. The reference to Giles of Rome appears to derive from

Albertinus's reference thereto in his *Corollaria seu Quaestiones Theologicae*, d. 1.1 (Lugduni: 1616), in Wells, "Suarez on the Eternal Truths," 90 n. 24.

15. *DM* d. 8.1.1, §2 (2:51a): Alia quoque in hac quaestione solet referri opinio, quae quidem licet non tribuat essentiis rerum ab aeterno esse quoddam actuale verum, & reale, ut faciebat Henricus, admittit tamen quoddam esse diminutum medium quodammodo inter reale, & rationis, quam opinionem Scoto impingere solent Thomistae. Mastrius inveighs against this misinterpretation throughout Disp. 8.

16. See nn. 2, 6 above.

17. *DM* d. 8.1.1, §35 (2:51b): at Poncius concl. 5, §53: & seq. ait creaturas ab aeterno tale esse habere a seipsis independenter a Deo, et ab operatione divini intellectus, ex quo patet peiorem errorem Scoto tribuere, & velut eius defendere quam fecerint Thomistae. For Punch on this issue of independence and speculative knowledge, see *DM* d. 8.1.3, §39 (2:73b). See also Vasquez on this same issue, *DM* d. 8.1.3, §40 (2:74ab). Mastrius's encounters with Punch are ongoing in his Metaphysics and in his Logic. On this exchange, see Jeffrey Coombs, "The Possibility of Created Entities In Seventeenth-Century Scotism," *The Philosophical Quarterly* 173 (1993): 447–59, and S. Sousedik, "Der Streit um den wahren Sinn der Scotischen Possibilienlehre," in *John Duns Scotus: Metaphysics and Ethics*, ed. L. Honnefelder, R. Wood, and M. Dreyer (Leiden: Brill, 1996), 191–204. For the terminological origins of *esse diminutum*, see A. Maurer, CSB, "*Ens Diminutum*: A Note on its Origin and Meaning," *Mediaeval Studies* 11 (1950): 216–22.

18. *DM* d. 8.1, §3 (2:51b): Communis sententia docet statum essentiae creaturarum ab aeterno esse merae possibilitatis itaut nullum esse reale actuale habeant seclusa existentia, nec medium inter esse reale, & rationis, ita passim tenent Thomistae, Scotistae, & Neutrales omnes; Scotus autem addit, quod si aliquod esse actuale habent creaturae possibiles ab aeterno, hoc nequit esse aliud, quam esse rationis, seu esse cognitum, quod ab intellectu divino recipiunt eo ipso, quod cognoscuntur, ut possibiles, ut magis infra explicabit.

19. *DM* d. 8.1.1, §4 (2:52a) where Mastrius lists at some length the *magistri Recentiores* who oppose Henry's position. It must be acknowledged that many of the criticisms of Henry's position, prior to those of Scotus, are to be found in Godfrey of Fontaines. See John F. Wippel, *The Metaphysical Thought of Godfrey of Fontaines* (Washington, DC: Catholic University of America Press, 1987), 130–45. See Honnefelder, *John Duns Scotus*, and esp. S.P. Marrone, "Revisiting Duns Scotus and Henry of Ghent On Modality," 175–89, and Simo Knuuttila, "Duns Scotus and the Foundations of Logical Modalities," 127–43.

20. See n. 33 below where Mastrius presupposes that Henry maintains a separability between essence and existence.

21. See n. 31 below. In the initial text referred to in n. 14 above, Mastrius never refers to Henry's position on this twofold causality embraced thereafter by Capreolus and Albertinus.

22. *DM* d. 8.1.1, §4 (2:52a): Primo itaque probat [Doctor] quia ex opposita sententia sequitur nullam creaturam posse vere, & proprie creari, nec etiam annihilari. See Scotus, *Ordinatio* 1. d. 36.1, §17–18 (6:277).

23. *DM* d8.1.1, §4 (2:52a): creatio est productio totius entis ex nihilo, & hoc patet per differentiam ipsius creationis ab aliis productionibus, quae aliquid praesupponunt.

24. *DM* d. 8.1.1, §4 (2:52a): Sed haec solutio merito ab omnibus rejicitur, ut insufficiens; #4, 52b: si pariter existentia non fit ex nihilo essentiae, tanquam ex nihilo subjecti, non diceretur vere creari, quia etiamsi fieret ex nihilo sui, non tamen fieret ex nihilo subjecti.

25. See *DM* d. 8.1.1, §7 (2:54a) where Mastrius, oblivious to Henry's insistence upon an exemplary cause of essences, lacking an efficient cause (cf. n. 31 below), insists that the essences of creatures could "gloat" that they have some *esse ex seipsis*, independently of God: Tum gloriari

possunt creaturae, quod aliquod esse ex seipsis haberent, independenter a Deo. Cf. ibid., §14, 57b. Such criticisms as this do not prevent Mastrius from adopting Henry's terminology for his own purposes. See *DM* d. 8.1.4, §68 (2:89ab) where Mastrius indicates that *esse essentiae* has a twofold significance. It can be taken to indicate the *esse possibile* of things (ideo dupliciter sumi solet vel pro esse possibili rerum) or it can be taken actually (alio modo accipitur esse essentiae; ut actu convenit creaturis iam existentibus). See Suárez in *DM* 31.2.11 (26:232b), taking the same position on this.

26. *DM* d. 8.1.1, §5 (2:52b).

27. *DM* d. 8.1.1, §5 (2:52b): sequitur res fuisse ab aeterno creatas, & non in tempore, quod fidei adversatur, qua docemur Genes. I in principio temporis Deum creasse Coelum, & Terram.

28. *DM* d. 8.1.1, §6 (2:53b–54a).

29. *DM* d. 8.1.1, §7 (2:54a): Respondent proinde alii negando rerum essentias esse revera productas, quia essentiae rerum sunt ingenerabiles, & incorruptibiles, sed tales esse ex seipsis, & a seipsis, & in tali esse non dependere a Deo, tanquam a causa efficiente. Because of the anonymous *alii*, this seems to point to Capreolus's citation of a text of St. Albert that uses terminology similar to *ex seipsis* and *a seipsis* to indicate the independence of the essences of creatures in regard to any efficient causality. See this text in Wells, "Capreolus on Essence and Existence," 8 n. 20. It remains to be seen whether this is an early reference to Punch and Vasquez. See n. 17 above and n. 138 below.

30. See n. 25 above and *DM* d. 8.1.1, §7 (2:54a): sic creaturae essent quidam Semidii, quia portionem potiorem sui esse haberent a seipsis.

31. *DM* d. 8.1.1, §8 (2:54b): Albertinus loc. cit. non audens asserere illud esse imparticipatum, & a Deo independens, ait quod licet non dependeat a Deo, tanquam a causa efficiente, adhuc tamen dependet ab eo, velut a causa exemplari, quod sufficit, ut sit ens participatum, ac a Deo dependens, quae erat responsio Henrici, & Capreoli. See Albertinus embracing both Capreolus and Henry on this twofold causality in *Corollaria*, d. 1.1 ad 6m, §42 (2:9b); d. 1.2, §1–8 (2:10–12). However, it is here that Albertinus parts company with both Henry and Capreolus since he maintains that the exemplary causality terminates in an actual essence that is a *parte rei extra intellectum divinum*. See this text in Wells, "Suarez on the Eternal Truths," 91 n. 24. This same position is attributed to Henry in Mastrius's initial citation of the Prima opinio in n. 14 above.

32. *DM* d. 8.1.1, §8 (2:54b): unde idem est effectus causa exemplaris, ac efficientis, ergo quod dependet Deo in genere causae exemplaris, dependet quoque in genere causae efficientis. See Scotus, *Ordinatio* 1. d. 36.1, §23 (6:279–80).

33. *DM* d. 8.1.1, §9 (2:55a): arguit Doctor destruendo praecipuum Henrici fundamentum, tribuit enim hoc esse actuale creaturis ab aeterno, ut secundum hoc esse sint objecta divinae scientiae, quae vocatur simplicis intelligentiae; at instat Scotus *concedo conclusionem istarum*, quia Deus ab aeterno non minus cognovit rerum existentias, quam essentias, secundum enim August. 5 super Genes. cap. 7. non aliter Deus novit facta quam fienda, praecognovit igitur esse existentiae, sicut esse essentiae. See Scotus, *Ordinatio* 1. d. 36.1, §27 (6:281). The claim of the separability of essence and existence is made by Mastrius in *DM* d. 8.1.1, §5 (2:53a): unde si semel [essentia] ponitur separabilis ab existentia, ut aiebat Henricus, statim sequitur posse seipsa, absque existentia terminare creationem. Such a claim owes more to the positions of Capreolus and Albertinus as they assimilated Henry's position into their perspective on the real distinction of essence and existence as between *duae res*. It could also be due to Suárez's misinterpretation of Henry's position on this score. See N.J. Wells, "Suárez, Historian and Critic of the Modal Distinction Between Essential Being and Existential Being," *The New Scholasticism* 36 (1962): 427–28.

For Albertinus on essence and existence and Aquinas, see *Corollaria*, 1. 12; 2:4b. For Henry's intentional distinction, see J. F. Wippel, *Metaphysical Thought of Godfrey of Fontaines*, 79–89. When it comes to the significance of actual existence in Mastrius, it must be acknowledged that it indicates an actual essence rather than an *actus essentiae*. See 6:53b: sequitur creaturas ab aeterno productas esse etiam quoad existentiam, quia existentia non nisi essentia creaturae extra causas . . . esse essentiae extra causas est ipsum esse existentiae. See Suárez *DM* 31.10.18 (26:271b): At vero, juxta nostram sententiam, existentia ut in re ipsa invenitur, non tam actus essentiae quam ipsa essentia in actu.

34. See Capreolus, *Defensiones Theologiae Divi Thomae Aquinatis*, ed. Paban-Pègues, (Turin: Alfred Cattier, 1900), *In Sent.* 1. d. 8.1.1 (1:330ab): Sed conceditur quod tam essentiam quam ipsum ejus esse, Deus aeternaliter intellexit; ac per hoc, quodlibet eorum fuit in Deo aeternaliter, ut intellectum in intelligente. Ex quo provenit quod aeternaliter rosa est rosa, rosa est essentia; sed non aeternaliter fuit nec aeternaliter exsistebat. See N.J. Wells, "Jean Capreolus et Successeurs sur Les Vérités Éternelles," in *Jean Capreolus et son temps 1380–1444*, ed. G. Bedouelle, R. Cessario, and K. White (Paris: Du Cerf, 1997), 263 n. 21.

35. See Wells, "Capreolus on Essence and Existence," 1–24; Wells, "Jean Capreolus et Successeurs," 259–73.

36. *DM* d. 8.1.1, §39 (2:55a): non concedit [Scotus] aliquis esse existentiae creaturae fuisse verum reale esse ab aeterno, ergo pari ratione non est concedendum de *esse* essentiae, atque ita sicut ex eo quod cognoscit per scientiam quam visionis appellant Theologi, rerum existentias ab aeterno, non dicuntur res habere esse reale existentiae ab aeterno." See Scotus, *Ordinatio* 1. d. 36.1. §35 (6:284–85).

37. *DM* d. 8.1.1, §9 (2:55a): sic nec ex eo quod [Deus] cognoscit rerum essentiae ab aeterno per scientiam simplicis intelligentiae, dici non debet quod res habeat esse reale essentiae ab aeterno.

38. *DM* d. 8.1.1, §9 (2:55ab): & ita opus non est existentiam lapidis supponere esse actuale propriae essentiae ut supponatur formaliter non repugnansYquia inferius ostendam bene salvari possibilitatem rerum ab aeterno absque actuali esse essentiae praecedente.

39. *DM* d. 8.1.2, §9 (2:55b): "Tum quia si tale esse supponi deberet, id etiam de essentia ipsiusmet existentiae asserendum foret, quia essentia talis modi per seipsam a chimaera distinguitur, & per seipsam est non repugnans, & non per aliquid ab ipso realiter distinctum." See A. Santogrossi, OSB, "Duns Scotus on Potency Opposed to Act in Questions on the Metaphysics, IX," *American Catholic Philosophical Quarterly*, 67 (1993): 55–76, and A. Wolter, OFM, "Scotus on the Divine Origin of Possibility," ibid., 95–107.

40. As a case in point, witness a representative listing: esse cognitum, esse objectivum esse subjectivum, esse intelligibile, esse intellectum, esse intentionale, esse diminutum, esse secundum quid, esse exemplato, esse repraesentato, esse opinatum, esse possibile, esse rationis, esse rationis formale, esse rationis materiale, ens rationis, esse in anima, esse purum ens rationis, esse rationis absolutum, esse rationis respectivum, objectum primarium, objectum secundarium, prima intentio, secunda intentio, objectum terminans, objectum motivum, intelligibilitas terminativa, intelligibilitas motiva, potentia logica, potentia objectiva, denominatio extrinseca, denominatio intrinseca. On this last, dealing with the issue of denomination, one is considerably vexed and certainly bewitched to learn that there is such a linguistic etiquette of *esse* as *esse simplicis denominationis;* what Suárez once characterized as *ens extrinsecae denominationis.* See Suárez, *DM* 54.2.12 (26:102). See N.J. Wells, "*Esse Cognitum* and Suarez," 345 n. 22. Also see Suárez, *DM* 54.1.10 (26:1018): esse objective in ratione non est esse, sed est cogitari et fingi. See Mastrius,

DM d. 8.2, §72 (2:92a): Hinc primo deducitur existentiam esse quid reale intrinsecam rei existenti, quia res non dicitur existere per extrinsecam denominationem.

41. See Mastrius's rejection of an esse diminutum as midway between *ens reale* and *ens rationis* in *DM* d. 8.1.2, §12 (2:57a): "ens prima sui divisione aequivoca dividitur in ens in anima, & ens extra anima, seu in ens reale, & rationis, ut docet Doctor I, d. 36, qu. un., lit. F"; *DM* d. 8.1.2, §13 (2:57b): Tum quia admisso tali medio inter ens reale, & rationis, tunc dari posset ens transcendentissime sumptum commune univocum illis, cuius oppositum docet Doctor I d. 29, qu. un. & nos cum ipso disp. 2, q. On the issue of a common name, in the absence of any conceptual community, see *DM* d. 1.2, §23 (1:18ab). See Scotus, *Ordinatio* 1. d. 36.1, §36 (6:285).

42. *DM* d. 8.1.2, §12 (2:57a): ens reale dicitur illud, quod extat, vel saltim extare non repugnat in rerum natura nullo cogitante intellectu. For the use of *ens verbaliter*, see *DM* d. 8.1.3, §46 (2:77b); §47, 78a; §51, 80a; §55, 82b; *DO* d. 3.2, §24 (305a).

43. *DM* d. 8.1.2, §12 (2:57a): ens autem rationis dicitur illud, quod nec extat, nec extare potest, nisi per solam intellectus cogitationem; *DO* d. 3.2, §24 (305a): omnes enim communiter concipiunt ens rationis, ut quid distinctum ab ente reali; tum ratione, quia enti rationis nec convenit, nec convenire potest, nisi existentia tantum objectiva, ergo distinguitur ab ente reali tam existente, quam possibili, tum tandem quia quod possibile est in re, licet actu putetur esse, cum actu non sit, ut mons aureus, non est ens rationis sed vere ens reale, quia ad rationem essentialem entis realis per accidens est actu existere, sed eius essentia salvatur in hoc, quod sit aptum existere.

44. *DO* d. 3.1 ad 6m; §9 (295) on *ens* taken *in rigore* and *ens* taken *magis ample:* docet Doctor quol. 3. art. 1. vel nomen entis sumitur in rigore pro eo, quod vere, & proprie est, id est, realiter, vel saltim existere potest, & nihil, prout opponitur enti hoc modo sumpto, & sic ens rationis est purum nihil, quia nec realiter est, neque sic esse potest; vel nomen entis sumitur magis ample pro eo, quod est vel in re, vel saltim in apprehensione, nihil vero, prout opponitur enti in ista amplitudine, & in hoc sensu ens rationis non est purum nihil, sed aliquo modo ens; vel demum sumitur ens proprie, & in rigore, nihil sumitur ample pro eo, quod negat quodcunque esse, sive in re, sive in apprehensione, & sic ens rationis est medium inter ens, & purum nihil, quia ex una parte non est ens reale, ex alia non caret quocunque esse, quia habet esse saltim in intellectu, hinc tamen non sequitur esse medium inter contradictoria quia ens reale, & nihil hoc tertio modo sumptum non contradicunt. See also *DM* d. 8.1.4 ad 4m, §55 (2:82b); Scotus, *Quodlibetum* 3.1, ed. F. Alluntis, in *Obras del Doctor Sutil Juan Duns Escoto: Cuestiones cuodlibetales* (Madrid: Biblioteca de Autores Cristianos, 1968), 93–94.

45. See the text cited at the outset of the discussion in *DM* d. 8.1, §1 (2:50): Quoniam in praecedenti disp. diximus praecipuam entis divisionem esse in finitum, & infinitum, eius membra deinceps declaranda proponentur; Et quamvis ordini naturae insistendo prius de ente infinito agere deberemus, ut primo, ac praecipuo membro, as principali analogato, quod proinde disp. 1 statuimus Metaph. primarium objectum principalitatis; ordo tamen doctrinae, qui incipit a notioribus, & facilioribus, postulat, ut prius agamus de ente finito, quod nobis magis est obvium, & proximum sensibus, quam de ente infinito, quod est remotissimum, juxta illud Apost. ad Corint. I, invisibilia Dei per ea, quae facta sunt intellecta conspiciuntur.

46. In many of the following notes, the emphasis is obviously upon the divine intellect. But the comparisons and differences with the human mind must not be overlooked. For Mastrius's use of the term *esse cognitum divinum*, see *DM* d. 8.1.2, §19 (2:61b).

47. *DM* d. 8.1.2, §18 (2:60b): non tantum divino intellectui convenire, cum res intelligit, & cognoscit, in esse quoddam cognito, & intellecto producere, sed hoc ei commune esse cum intel-

lectu creato, qui etiam suo modo cum objecta intelligit, dicitur ea in esse quoddam cognito, et intentionali producere, sicut ait Doctor . . . ita in proposito cum denominatio cogniti, & intellecti objecto, cui advenit, non tribuat esse aliquod simpliciter, & extra animam, sed tantum secundum quid, & in anima, ac intentionales; *DO* d. 2.6, §90 (284a): quia denominatio extrinseca, etsi vera sit a parte rei, nihil tamen reale, & physicum ponit in termino, quem denominat.

48. *DM* d. 8.1.2, §17 (2:59b): tamen illud esse cognitum prius, quod in creaturas possibiles derivatur ex terminatione divinae cognitionis non est aliquod esse reale, vel medium inter esse reale, & rationis, ut Thomistae Scoticum idioma non intelligentes comminiscuntur, sed est purum esse rationis, qualis est esse visum in pariete, & esse intellectum in objecto intellectui repraesentato, non quidem esse rationis formale, & fabricatum, sed materiale, & derelictum, quemadmodum iam explicavimus disp. 3, logicae q. 2, art. 1, concl. I, in fine conclusionis. Here, *esse visum* in regard to the extramental wall is on the sensory level. *Esse intellectum* is on the intellectual level and has to do with the intramental object represented to the intellect.

49. *DM* d. 8.1.2, §17 (2:60a): esse cognitum creaturarum esse eiusdem rationis cum esse exemplato, & repraesentato Homeri, dum est in opinione, quod est opinatum satis se constat esse purum ens rationis; . . . tale esse [cognitum] inquit [Scotus] esse omnino eiusdem rationis cum esse Caesaris repraesentato in statua. See Duns Scotus, *Ordinatio* 1. d. 36.1, §15 (6:284); §45 (6:288). On extramental statues here in the context of ens rationis, see Suárez on those who claim that artifacts are beings of reason, *DM* 54.1.5 (26: 1016). For the background associated with *in opinione* and *est opinatum* here in the above text, see J. P. Doyle, "Supertranscendental Nothing: A Philosophical Finisterre," *Medioevo Revista Di Storia Della Filosofia Medievale* XXIV (1998): 4, nn. 18–20.

50. See n. 47 above.

51. *DM* d. 8.1.2, §21 (2:63a): quare dicendum est aliud esse loqui de creaturis ab aeterno cognitis, aliud de esse possibili, quod a divino intellectu noscitur eis non repugnare, & aliud tandem de simplici denominatione, quam suscipiunt ex eo, quod terminant divinam cognitionem, nam hoc esse simplicis denominationis est purum esse rationis, ut diximus (see n. 48 above). It is here that heed must again be given to the equivocal character of esse cognitum referred to in n. 12 above. For it surely comes to the fore in Mastrius, *DM* d. 8.1.2, §16 (2:59): siquidem per tale esse cognitum, ac diminutum, quod [Scotus] tribuit creaturis ab aeterno in mente divina, solum [Scotus] intelligit illud esse possibile creaturarum, secundum quod ab aeterno objiciatur intellectui divino virtute suae intellectionis ratione cuius dicuntur ab ipso divino intellectu secundum quid produci, hoc est, representari, ita Doctor explicat. See Scotus, *Ordinatio* 1. d. 36.1, §60 (6:296). Here *esse cognitum* in Mastrius clearly refers to the *res denominata,* the possible essence of creatures. See in the same place, §17, 59b, where Mastrius refers to *esse cognitum* as the extrinsic denomination *quoad denominationem* (to use Suárez's terminology) of the above *res denominata:* omnino distinguendum esse illud esse cognitum, quod creaturae possibiles accipiunt formaliter in intellecto divino cognoscente, ab illo esse, quod attingitur per divinam cognitionem eis non repugnare, penes quod dicuntur esse in potentia logica, ac etiam in potentia objectiva ipsius Dei, a quo realiter produci possunt. See the reference to *esse cognitum* in n. 48 above that concerns *illud esse cognitum prius* that is *purum esse rationis.*

52. See the end of the text cited in n. 48 above and nn. 56, 76, 88 below.

53. *DO* d. 3.1, §9 (296b): vel clarius potest rem dupliciter cognoscere, vel sicut est, vel aliter ac est, cum primo modo cognoscit, tunc utique praesupponit objectum esse, sed dum cognoscit secundo modo, tunc efficit objectum suum & nullo modo supponit quia tale objectum non habet aliud esse, nisi quod tunc ei tribuit intellectus, ita vero cognoscit dum efficit ens rationis, nam

illud efformat cognoscendo rem aliter, ac sit; *DO* d. 8.1, §112 (347b): quia objectum considerari possit in duplici statu, primo secundum quod est in se, et secundum attributa ei convenientia ex natura rei; secundo ut est in apprehensione, & secundum attributa ei convenientia ex intellectus operatione, qui status, ut liquet, posterior est illo; merito cognitio, quae exprimit objectum sub primo statu dicitur prima intentio, & quae illud exprimit sub posteriori, dicitur secunda, & consequenter quae talem conceptionem terminant, entia rationis erunt. See n. 55 below for additional considerations of formal and objective concepts.

54. See n. 47 above and *DM* d. 8.1.2, §18 (2: 60b–61a): Caeterum advertit Doctor ibidem hoc versari discrimen inter divinum intellectum, & creatum quoad productionem rerum in esse cognito, quod cum intellectus creatus res intelligit, non praestat eis per talem intellectionem primum omnino earum esse, quia in proprio esse supponuntur eius intellectioni, qua respectu intellectus creati res sunt prius intelligibiles, quam intellectae. See n. 58 below; *DM* 19 (61b): . . . esse cognitum a nostro intellectu rebus tributum, non sit primum earum esse, sed secundarium ut dicebamus.

55. *DO* d. 3.8, §111 (347a): advertendum est non sumi hic intentionem presse pro tendentia voluntatis in suum finem sed late pro tendentia intellectus in rem cognitam seu pro conceptu intellectus; sed quia conceptus intellectus est duplex, formalis, & objectivus, sic etiam duplex erit intentio formalis, & objectiva; formalis est actus ipse intellectus tendens in objectum, objectiva est ipsa res, in quam tendit intellectus, & utraque duplex est, prima et secunda; *DO* d. 3.8.1, §112 (347b–48a): si nulla daretur fictio intellectus, adhuc illa attributa ipsi objecto convenirent, talis cognitio dicitur prima intentio formalis, & objectum illud sic cognitum dicitur prima intentio objectiva, ut v. g. quando intellectus cognoscit naturam humanam participari a Petro, & Paulo, natura humana cognita cum hoc attributo dicitur prima intentio objectiva, & cognitio, qua intellectus tendit in naturam humanam sub ea ratione, dicitur prima intentio formalis. Cum vero hac occasione motus intellectus, quia scilicet videt naturam humanam communem Petro & Paulo, concipi illam universalem, & illam veluti speciem actu de illis praedicat haec universalitas concepta in ipsa est secunda intentio objectiva, & cognitio eam exprimens sub tali formalitate est secunda intentio formalis quae licet sit realis, id tamen, quod ei correspondet ex parte objecti reale non est, quia universalitas non datur a parte re, sed sit per opus intellectus, ut dicemus disp. seq.

56. *DA* d. 6.6.1, §169 (455): non solum intelligibilitas motiva, sed etiam terminativa sit entis realis propria. See also *DO* d. 3.1, §9 (296); §95 (338b): licet intelligibilitas motiva sit propria passio entis realis, terminativa tamen communis utrique, quia objectum adaequatum terminativum intellectus non est ens reale, sed communissime sumptum ad reale, & rationis. *DM* d. 5.6 ad ult., §135 (1:428b): distinguendum est ex dictis disp. de Anim., q. 6, a. 1, §146 de duplici intelligibilitate terminativa entis una primaria, altera secundaria, quae tribui solet entibus rationis, & creaturis in divina essentia terminantibus actum divini intellectus . . . color enim nedum est objectum hoc modo terminativum visus, sed etiam motivum, quia est productivus specierum in oculo, et visionis cum oculo mediantibus speciebus. Heed must be given to Mastrius's response to Franciscus Herrera, OFM, in *DM* d. 8.1.2, §22 (2:63b–64a); Resp. supposita distinctione data in logica de ente rationis materiali, & formale, seu fabricato, & derelicto, negando esse cognitum praecise acceptum pro denominaione cogniti a potentia cognoscente in objecto derivata esse quid commune ad ens reale, & ens rationis, ut comprehendit tam ens rationis formale, quam materiale, quia continetur sub ente rationis sic accepto.

57. See n. 49 above.

58. See nn. 53, 54 above as well as *DM* d. 8.1.2, §18 (2:61a): Doctor ipse docet 2 d. 1, q. 1 sequitur secundum instans naturae, ubi proinde comparat productionem hanc creaturarum in

esse cognito effectioni secundarium intentionum in intellecto nostro, in quo non dicuntur habere prius esse intelligibile, quam intellectum. Hinc deducitur quod esse cognitum ab intellectu nostro rebus tributum, non est primum omnino earum esse (nisi in entibus rationis, ac secundis intentionibus) sed secundarium. See Scotus, *Opus Oxon., In Sent.* 2. d. 1.1 in *Opera Omnia* (Paris: Vives, 1893), 11:26.

59. See n. 55 above. On behalf of the metaphysics of the possible, one must heed the following text: *DM* d. 8.1.4, §57 (2:83b): Ad ult. pariter scientiae dicuntur esse de entibus realibus, & non rationis, quia rerum quidditates considerant, non secundum esse objectivum, quem habent in intellectu, sed secundum se, vel quatenus aptae sunt ad existendum a parte rei cum talibus naturis, ac proprietatibus dicuntur etiam esse de rebus aeternis, quatenus abstrahunt ab existentia rerum hic, et nunc, quae sunt conditiones contingentiam inducentes. See Suárez, *DM* 31.2.10 (26:232ab).

60. See nn. 53–56 above. See also *DO* d. 3.1, §9 (296b): quare esse intelligibile in entibus rationis non est aliquod intrinsecum ut in entibus realibus, sed potius est mera denominatio extrinseca a potentia intellectiva procedens, quatenus quae non sunt, nec esse possunt, concipere ad modum entis potest; *DM* d. 2.9.1, §233 (1:235b) and *DM* d. 5.6.1, §134 (1:428ab): & sic in proposito verum est cognoscibilitatem extrinsecam in objecto desumi totaliter, & adaequate a cognitione ut possibili, sicut actu cognitum adaequate sumitur a cognitione actuali, & actu terminata ad objectum. See J. P. Doyle, "'Extrinsic Cognoscibility': A Seventeenth Century Supertranscendental Notion," *The Modern Schoolman* 68 (1990): 57–80.

61. See nn. 43, 44, 49 above.

62. See n. 56 above and nn. 90, 98, 101, 139, 143 below.

63. See nn. 42–44 above.

64. See n. 43 above.

65. See n. 56 above and *DO* d. 3.2, §22 (303b): illud esse cognitum, quod est denominatio extrinseca, potius formaliter, & subjective esse in intellectu, quam objective, quia ut ait Scotus realiter participat in intellectu illud idem esse, quod habet formaliter ipsa cognitio, realiter, enim non est nisi ipsa cognitio ad objectum terminata. See Scotus, *Ordinatio* 1. d. 36.1 §46 (6:289); Suárez, *DM* 54.2.13 (26:1021); Mastrius, *DM* d. 2.9.1, §238 (1:239ab). See also *DO* d. 2.6, §90 (283b): Sed quia Denominativa sunt duplicis generis, alia per intrinsecam denominationem, quae sumitur a forma intrinseca, seu inherente subjecto, quomodo paries dicitur albus ab albedine ei inherente; alia per extrinsecam, quae sumitur a forma in alio subjecto, quomodo paries visus a visione, non in ipso, sed in oculo existente. See J. P. Doyle, "Prolegomena to a Study of Extrinsic Denomination in the Work of Francis Suarez, S.J.," *Vivarium* 2 (1984): 121–60.

66. See n. 48 above.

67. See *DO* d. 3.7, §99 (340b et seq.). See J. P. Doyle, "Another God, Chimerae, Goat-Stags and Man-Lions: A Seventeenth-Century Debate About Impossible Objects," *Review of Metaphysics* 48 (1995): 771–808.

68. *DO* d. 3.7, §103 (343a).

69. *DO* d. 2.1, §4 (293a): quia multa saepe cogitamus, ac si essent, quae tamen nec sunt, nec esse possunt, ut patet de Chymera, Hircocervo, & similibus, ergo cum aliud esse non habeant, quam cogitari, et tamdiu sint, quamdiu cogitantur, vere sunt entia rationis. Tum quia cum intellectus concipit negationes, privationes, ac extrinsecas denominationes, eas utique concipit ad modum entium, cum enim eius objectum adaequatum sint ens reale, nihil concipere potest nisi ad modum veri entis, unde tenebram in aere, caecitatem in oculo concipit per modum quarundum formarum luci, ac potentiae visivae contrariarum hoc autem efformare ens rationis. See nn. 72, 89 below.

70. See n. 48 above and n. 88 below.

71. See n. 69 above and nn. 74, 75, 88 below. Also see *DM* d. 8.1.2, §22 (2:64a): cum esse cognitum in objecto concipitur per intelligentiam reflexam accipit maius esse intra latitudinem entis rationis, quia ubi prius erat ens rationis materiale duntaxat, & derelictum, acquirit per intelligentiam reflexam formale esse rationis.

72. *DO* d. 3.4.2, §60 (325a): cum enim actu simplici, & positivo privationes, negationes, et alia impossibilia, item & extrinsecas denominationes, quae omnia sunt entia rationis materialia concipimus, & efformamus entia rationis formalia, utique illa concipimus ad instar veri entis, nempe caecitatem, ut pravam organi dispositionem, tenebram ut quamdam aeris dispositionem, creationem activam in Deo, ut relationem quamdam ad creaturam, & visionem passivam in pariete ut aliam relationem activae in oculo correspondentem, & sic de aliis, ut discurrenti constabit.

73. See n. 75 below.

74. *DO* d. 3.7, §102 (342b–43a): in qualitate concipimus famam, & honorem ut dispositiones convenientes personae honoratae, & ipsas denominationes extrinsecas concipimus in rebus denominatis per modum correlationis, ut relationem cogniti ad cognitionem . . . & tandem alia quoque fingimus cum cogitamus Deum replere hunc mundum ad modum corporis, stare in Caelo, vel sedere, infinito temporis spatio durare & esse amictum tanquam vestimento. See *DO* d. 3.8.1, §118 (350b–51a); ita per relationem cogniti in objecto ad potentiam cognoscentem exprimimus, id, quod est a parte rei, scilicet habitudinem cognitionis ad objectum, & objectum a parte rei terminare actum mentis, ergo sicut hac ratione exclusimus a numero secundarum intentionum relationem creatoris in Deo, sic in proposito excludere debemus relationem concepta in objecto cognito ad potentiam cognoscentem.

75. John Poinsot, OP, *Tractatus De Signis: The Semiotic of John Poinsot*, Interpretive Arrangement by John Deely in consultation with Ralph Austin Powell (Berkeley: University of California Press, 1985), First Preamble, a. 1:49. See also *DO* d. 3.2.1, §15 (299b–304b), that is entitled: Ens rationis formaliter non consistere in extrinseca denominatione, neque in aliqua relatione ex ea resultante in rebus.

76. *DO* d. 3.2.1, §15 (299a–300b): est advertendum hic nos non loqui de denominatione formaliter, ut nimirum est ipsamet actualis appellatio, nominisque, sic enim cum non pertineat ad ordinem rerum, sed nominum (nam res, non ut res sunt, sed ut nominibus significantur, denominari, vel denominare dicuntur) est ens rationis, siquidem est ipsa significatio, est opus rationis, quia intellectus est qui imponit nomina rebus; sed loquimur de denominatione quasi materiale, & prout spectat ad ordinem rerum, nempe secundum quod forma tribuendo suum effectum formalem subjecto, & aliud respiciendo pro termino, dicitur hoc quidem extrinsece, illud sensu asserimus, quando forma denominans est realis denominationem tam intrinsecam quam extrinsecam, ab ipsa procedentem esse realem, id est vere dari a parte rei nullo cogitante intellectu, paries enim v. g. dicitur a parte rei albus ab albedine sibi inexistente, & visus a visione existente in animali. See also *DO* d. 3.2.1 ad 1m, §22 (303b). In *DO* d. 3.2.1, §15 (299b) Mastrius notes that extrinsic denominations forthcoming from real forms are characterized as real in the same fashion that privations and negations are real even though they are not real beings.

77. *DO* d. 3.2, §11 (297b): Prima satis famosa [opinio] constituit formalitatem entis rationis in denominatione extrinseca . . . ita sensisse videtur Fonseca 5 Met., c. 7, q. 6, sect. 3 & Vasq. I.p., disp. 115, n. 2 & p. 2, disp. 95, c. 10 ubi denominationem extrinsecam inquit esse aliquid rationis. For Suárez on this issue, See J. P. Doyle's translation of Suárez's 54th Disputation, *On Beings Of Reason* (Milwaukee: Marquette University Press, 1995), 26–27, 69–75.

78. See n. 69 above.

79. See n. 49 above.

80. *DM* d. 8.1.2, §19 (2:61b): unde sicut hac ratione esse quod noster intellectus secundis tribuit intentionibus, non est eis extrinsecum nec eis omnino convenit per extrinsecam denominationem, quae rem supponere solet, cui advenit in proprio esse, sed est eis intrinsecum & formale secundum quid, ac diminutum, est tamen extrinsecum primis intentionibus; ita esse cognitum in quo producuntur creaturae a Deo, est intrinsecum, proprium, & formale ipsis creaturis, licet diminutum, & secundum quid. This consideration will be revisited again in the context of *esse cognitum divinum*. For Mastrius is inspired by Scotus's comparison of the origin of the *esse cognitum* of possible creatures in the divine mind to the production of second intentions in the human mind. See n. 58 above. See also *DM* d. 8.1.2, §18 (2:61a): proinde comparat [Scotus] productionem hanc creaturarum in esse cognito effectioni secundarum intentionum in intellectu nostro, in quo non dicuntur habere prius esse intelligibile quam intellectum. See as well nn. 112, 113 below.

81. See nn. 53, 54, 55 above.

82. See nn. 56, 58 above.

83. See nn. 53, 58, 65, 80 above.

84. See n. 65 above. See Suárez's remark in n. 40 above on *esse objectivum*, a synonym for *esse cognitum*, to the effect that "it is not *esse*, but it is *cogitari* and *fingi*."

85. See n. 80 above.

86. See n. 88 below and nn. 43, 56, 72, 74 above.

87. See n. 12 above and nn. 101, 111, 114, 115 below.

88. *DO*, d. 3.4, §48 (318): Rursus cum ens rationis ex dictis q. 2, a. 1, [disp. III, q. 2, a. 1, n. 20: 302b] duplex sit, aliud materiale, derelictum, ac potentiale, quia nimirum formalitatem entis rationis actu non participat, utique participare potest per actum potentiae fingentis, quo sensu negationes, privationes, & omnes extrinsecae denominationes reales dicuntur entia rationis materiales, & fundamentaliter, quia possunt intellectui, vel alteri potentiae praestare fundamentum fictionis, ut concipiat id, quod non est, ac si esset; aliud vero formale, & actuale, quod nimirum actu participat formalitatem entis rationis, quia scilicet actu fingitur esse ab intellectu, aut alia potentia, & ita objective existit in ea, ut extra illam nec existat, nec existere possit. Heed must be given here to what Mastrius claims in *DO* d. 32, §20 (302b): Itaque Doctor in hoc sensu appellavit illud esse cognitum creaturarum ens rationis, quatenus scilicet fundare potest per opus intellectus aliquod esse, vel relationem rationis, ut ipse expressit in sol. ad 2 prin. Nec mirum esse debet, quod Scotus ibi denominationes extrinsecas appellet entia rationis; tum quia interdum solet ipse confundere ens rationis materiale & formale, ut patet in eodem I, d. 30, q. 2 L. For the reference to sol. ad 2 princ., see *Ordinatio* 1. d. 36.1. §44 (6:288).

89. See n. 40, 48, 51 above.

90. See *DA* d. 6.6.1, §169 (455a): potest etiam & alter dicendi modus sustineri, quod non solum intelligibilitas motiva, sed etiam terminativa sit entis realis propria, & tunc declaranda est intelligibilitas entium rationis virtute entis realis, sicut declarari solet intelligibilitas creaturarum virtute divinae essentiae, ut Doctor explicat 2 d. p. q. p quare sicut essentia divina respectu divini intellectus in ordine ad cognitionem creaturarum nedum ponitur objectum motivum, sed etiam primario terminativum, creaturae vero terminare dicuntur actum divini intellectus secundario tantum, nam ideo terminant, quia divina essentia prius natura terminat, sic pariter in proposito ens reale erit per se primo intelligibile, tam motive, quam terminative, ens vero rationis in virtute entis realis erit intelligibile terminative, non quidem per se primo. sed tantum per se secundo. See also *DT* d. 3.13, §42 (113a).

91. See n. 7 above.

92. *DM* d. 8.1.2, §16 (2:59a): fatendum est hoc esse [cognitum] convenire creaturis ab aeterno, qua convenit ipsi Deo scire creaturas, quare sicut prorsus irrationabile foret concedere oculum parietem videre, & deinde negare parietem esse visum, ita in proposito mera dementa foret concedere Deum ab aeterno scientia simplicis intelligentiae cognoscere creaturas possibiles, & negare istas habere esse cognitum ab aeterno in divina mente.

93. *DM* d. 8.1.2, §16 (2:59a): statuendum est omnes fateri, ut certum nedum in fide nostra, sed etiam in vera Philosophi, divinum intellectum omnes creaturas possibiles cognoscere ab aeterno quoad earum possibilitatem scientia, quam dicunt simplicis intelligentiae.

94. See *DM* d. 8.1.2, §18 (2:61a): at intellectus divinus cum res intelligit. producit eas in primo esse intelligibili, vel intellecto, res enim nequeunt habere esse intelligibile proprium & formale priusquam ab intellectu divino intelligantur, sed tantum virtuale in divino essentia.

95. *DM* d. 8.1.2, §18 (2:61a): essentia divina, ut prior intellectione praecise secundum rationem essentiae non est exemplar actuale, & formale creaturarum, nec in ea veluti in speculo res ipsae relucent, sed tantum virtuale, et eminentiale . . . unde ante actum divini intellectus creatura nullum esse formale proprium habet in Deo nec cognitum, nec possibile, nec intelligibile, licet haec quasi virtualiter in divina essentia.

96. See n. 94 above.

97. See n. 56 above.

98. See n. 94 above and *DM* d. 8.1.4 ad 1m, §57 (2:83b): Ad 1 itaque dicendum ex tractatu theologico de scientia Dei, Deum non cognoscere res possibiles ab aeterno ex seipsis, quasi in seipsis aliquod esse haberent, per quod moveant intellectum divinum, vel eius actu primario terminent, sed Deus illa attingit per modum objecti secundarii, & pure terminativi. See *Ordinatio* 1. d. 35.1 §15 (6:250): Hoc videtur vilificare intellectum divinum, quia tunc erit passivus respectu objectorum aliorum cognitorum per istas rationes, per quae actuabitur ad cognitionem istarum rationum.

99. *DM* d. 8.1.2, §17 (2:59b): major intelligentia istius esse cogniti.

100. See nn. 12, 51 above and *DM* d. 8.1.2, §17 (2:59b): omnino distinguendum esse illud esse cognitum quod creaturae possibiles accipiunt formaliter in intellectu divino cognoscente, ab illo esse, quod attingitur per divinam cognitionem eis non repugnare, penes quod dicuntur esse in potentia logica, ac etiam in potentia objectiva ipsius Dei, a quo realiter produci possunt. On potentia objectiva, see nn. 127–28 below.

101. *DM* d. 8.1.2, §17 (2:59b): quamvis enim hoc esse [possibile], quod eis cognoscitur non repugnare, & est terminus divinae cognitionis, velut objectum secundarium eius, sit esse reale potentiale, quod appellari solet ens reale nominaliter ut late explicabimus art. sequenti. This is what Mastrius had characterized to be *esse cognitum* as it designates the *res denominata* in n. 51 above. See also n. 12 above.

102. See nn. 15, 41, 48 above and n.123 below.

103. See nn. 48, 65, 88 above and nn. 105, 106 below.

104. See n. 49 above.

105. See n. 51 above. For the quo/quod distinction, see *DO* d. 3.2.1, §319 (302a): Tandem quol. 3, ar. 1 ab initio ait [Scotus] ens rationis esse illud, quod est praecise habens in intellectu considerante, & haud dubie loquitur de consideratione, qua cogitatur ipsum ens rationis, sed cum primo res cognoscitur, tunc denominatio cogniti non cognoscitur, neque consideratur, quia in illo omnino primo signo se habet ut quo, non ut quod; ergo secundum Scotum denominationes extrinsecae ut sic, non sunt entia rationis formaliter, sed novus actus intellectus requiritur, per

quem tale esse suscipiant; Scotus, Quodlib. 3. 1 in ed. Alluntis, 93–94. See also *DO* d. 3.2.1, §19 (301b): ergo non eo ipso, quod objectum causatur ab intellectu in esse cognito per actum rectum, causatur in eo ens rationis, sed potius objectum supponitur cognitum, tum virtute sui, tum intellectus, ex his enim duobus causa totalis cognitionis integratur, & deinceps intellectus se solo operans circa objectum, ut cognitum apprehendendo nimirum per actum veluti reflexum illud esse cognitum, ut quid intrinsecum objecto, causat in illo ut cognito ens rationis.

106. See nn. 48, 51 above and *DO* d. 3.2.1, §20 (302ab): Quando autem Doctor I, d. 36, q. un., 'Concedo, illud esse cognitum, quod habent creaturae ab aeterno per actum divini intellectus, vocat ens rationis, notat Fuentes loc cit. Scotum revera non vocare ens rationis illud esse diminutum creaturarum, sed relationem quandam in ipso fundatam ad Deum cognoscentem, & inquit Doctorem ita se explicuisse in 'Ad secundum, & ita loquitur in 4, d. 1, q. 5 in fine; sed quando etiam loqueretur de illo esse diminuto, & denominationis extrinsecae, dicendum cum P. Vulpes Doctorem non appellare illud ens rationis formaliter, sed materialiter tantum, quo sensu illud dicitur ens rationis, quod per actum intellectus potest formaliter esse rationis suscipere; hinc communiter distingui solet, & praesertm in schola subtilium, ens rationis in materiale, & formale, seu ipsi loquuntur, in ens rationis a ratione fabricatum, & a ratione derelictum. See Scotus, *Ordinatio* 1.d. 36.1., §26–29 (6:281–82).

107. See *DO* d. 3.2.1, §22 (303b): illud esse cognitum, quod est denominatio extrinseca.

108. *DM* d. 8.1.2, §19 (2:61ab).

109. *DM* d. 8.1.2, §19 (2:61ab).

110. DM d. 8.1.2, §19 (2:61ab).

111. See *DM* d. 8.1.2, §19 (2:61b). This can only be construed to mean that Mastrius is no longer using *esse cognitum* to indicate an extrinsic denomination (*quoad denominationem*), but to indicate the *res denominata* (*quoad rem denominatam*).

112. See n. 80 above.

113. *DM* d. 8.1.2, §19 (2:61b).

114. *DM* d. 8.1.2, §19 (2:61b). Again, the emphasis here on res in *esse cognito* clearly indicates a *res denominata*.

115. *DM* d. 8.1.2, §19 (2:62a). The use here of *cognitum*, referring back to the *res in esse cognito* in the previous note, sustains the emphasis on *esse cognitum quoad rem denominatam*.

116. See *DM* d. 8.1.2, §20 (2:62a): ly cognitum esto non sit determinatio distrahens, quia non tollit significationem creaturae, nec oppositum inducit scilicet privationem omnimodam possibilitatis; est nihilominus determinatio diminuens, quia minuit esse creaturarum, & constituit illud in esse secundum quid, & diminuto. Quare autem hoc esse rationis absolutum appellet Doctor, quod respectum rationis fundat ad divinam cognitionem.

117. *DM* d. 8.1.2, §20 (2:62a): ex dictis disp. 3. log. q. 7. ubi docuimus ens rationis dividi in absolutum, & respectivum ad instar entis realis, ad modum cuius & concipitur, & dividitur; absolutum nempe est, quod concipitur, vel concipi potest vero quod concipitur ad modum entis ad se, respectivum vero quod concipitur per modum entis ad aliud, sicut sunt omnes secundae intentiones. See n. 55 above on that example of a second intention wherein the human nature, initially conceived on the level of a first intention as shared by Peter and Paul, is conceived again as predicable of many.

118. *DM* d. 8.1.2, §20 (2:62ab): cum igitur esse cognitum creaturarum possit concipi per modum fundamenti respectum rationis fundantis ad divinam cognitionem, seu divinum intellectum, veluti ad causam producentem secundum quid, hac ratione optime appellatur ens rationis absolutum, nam proprius munus absoluti est fundare respectum. In regard to Mastrius's

allusion here to a *causa producens*, see n. 133 below where he insists that, since possibility involves no actual reality, the issue of a *ratio* is more pertinent than a *causa*.

119. *DM* d. 8.1.2, §20 (2:62ab). Heed must be given to the ease with which Mastrius moves from the *esse cognitum* in the preceding text to the *esse possibile* in this text. It is here that *esse cognitum* refers to the *res denominata*, the intramental *ens reale potentiale*. For Mastrius on creabilis here, see n. 143 below.

120. *DM* d. 8.1.2, §21 (2:62b): Ex hactenus dictis facile diluvi possunt quaecunque objecta solent conglomerare Thomistae contra hoc esse cognitum creaturarum.

121. *DM* d. 8.1.2, §21 (2:62b–63a).

122. *DM* d. 8.1.2, §21 (2:63a): esse vero possibile creaturarum, quod a divino cognitione attingitur est ens reale potentiale seu nominaliter ut dicemus art. seq. creatura tandem si praecise accipitur secundum illud esse possibile est ens reale potentiale, si vero reduplicative, ut substat denominatione cogniti est ens rations; & sic creaturae ipsae hac ratione partim entia realis, partim entia rationis dici possunt, entia quidem realia secundum illud esse quod a divino intellectu noscitur eis non repugnare; entia vero rationis, prout secundum illud esse substant denominationi cogniti, quia sic considerantur solum, ut habent esse objectivum in divina mente. It is important to note that these references to *ens rationis* have to do with an *ens rationis* taken materially See nn. 88 and 106 above. It would appear that Mastrius here is responding to a position of Francis de Meyronnes he alluded to earlier. See *DM* d. 8.1.1, §12 (2:57a): solum reperio Maironem, qui I. d. 42. q. 2. in fine dicit quidditates rerum ab aeterno non esse entia rationes, nec etiam realia, quod etiam in bono sensu potest intelligi, ut postea explicabimus.

123. *DM* d. 8.1.2, §21 (2:63a): Resp. Thomistas quoque teneri ad solutionem difficultatis propositae quia & ipsi fateri tenentur Deum cognoscere ab aeterno creaturas possibiles, quod idem est ac eas esse a Deo cognitas in sua possibilitate per scientiam simplicis intelligentiae, cumque cognoscantur a Deo, ut possibiles, ac producibiles, non erunt pura entia rationis, quia hac non sunt producibilia ad extra, at neque sunt entia simpliciter realia, ut ipsi ultro concedunt, erunt ergo quid medium inter esse reale, & rationis.

124. *DM* d. 8.1.2, §21 (2:63b).

125. *DM* d. 8.1.3, §26 (2:66a).

126. Mastrius is taking issue with Petrus Hurtado, SJ, in no. 27:66ab. On this position, see Jeffrey Coombs, "Modal Voluntarism in Descartes's Jesuit Predecessors," *Proceedings of American Catholic Philosophical Association* 70 (1996): 237–47. Also see n. 100 above.

127. *DM* d. 8.1.3, §26 (2:66a): quia circumscripta omnipotentia activa in rerum natura, adhuc multa dicerentur possibilia potentia logica, id est, multa non repugnarent in rerum natura. The *per impossibile* hypothesis is stated in no. §27, 66b, §29, 67b, and again in §30, 68a. See also §27, 66b: ergo talis possibilitas, vel impossibilitas logica non est mera denominatio extrinseca ex omnipotentia Dei desumenda, sed ex rationibus formalibus hominis, & chimerae; §30, 68a: At loquendo de possibilitate logica, quam Recentiores intrinsecam appellant, falsum est hanc denominationem sumi ab omnipotentia Dei, potius enim desumenda est ex rationibus formalibus ipsarum rerum possibilium; §29, 67b: Ex quo rursus sequitur potentiam objectivam supponere logicam, veluti fundamentum eius adeo quod res prius dicitur possibilis logice, quam objective; §28, 67a: ergo aliquam repugnantiam habet in se chimaera, quam non habet lapis, ratione cuius dicitur impossibilis, & aliquam non repugnantiam lapis, ob quam possibilis dicitur, quae non reperitur in chimaera, independenter ab omnipotentia divina.

128. *DM* d. 8.1.3, §31 (2:68b): Respondetur haec, & similia argumenta concludere tantum de potentia objectiva, extrinseca, & proxima, quia haec re vera constituitur per respectum ad

potentiam activam agentis non autem de logica, intrinseca, & remota, quae a tali respectu prae-scindit, & ideo dici solet possibilitas absoluta, quia consistit in sola non repugnantia rei prae-scindendo ab eo, quod illa res sit ab alio producibilis, vel a seipsa existat, qua de causa etiam ipse Deus dicitur possibilis logice, quod utique dici non posset, si haec possibilia imbiberet respectum ad potentiam activam agentis. See n. 119 above for a reference to *potentia absoluta*. For other texts on the inclusion of God and creatures under logical possibility, see §36, 71b; §42, 75b; §53, 81a.

129. *DM* d. 8.1.3, §32 (2:69ab).

130. Mastrius fails to mention that this is the position of Suárez, Bañez and Soncinas. See Suárez in *DM* 31.3.4 (26:234); 31.3.1 (26:233), where he refers to a real negative distinction between *ens in potentia* and *ens in actu* such that they are not *duae res,* but one. Rather, they are conceived and compared by the intellect as if they were two things. For all of his efforts here to deny any positive reality to the uncreated essences of his adversaries, Suárez, in explaining what he means by *identitas negativa,* acknowledges that "comparamus rem positivam objective exis-tentem in intellectu ad rem actu existentem." See *DM* 31.2.9, §26 (230). For the texts of Soncinas and Bañez, see N.J. Wells, "Javelli and Suárez on the Eternal Truths," *The Modern Schoolman* 72 (1994): 13–36 esp. n. 61. See the texts of Fonseca on negative diversity, in n. 79, that contains the correct reference to Fonseca since Mastrius has an incorrect one. J-L. Marion, *Sur la théologie blanche de Descartes* (Paris: Presses Universitaires de France, 1981), 53, fails to appreciate this tra-dition in Suárez when he accuses him of maintaining a doctrine of "positive possibility." For Suárez, "positive possibility" is extrinsic, not intrinsic. See *DM* 30.17.10 (26:209). Marion's claim should have been applied to Mastrius as the two following notes attest.

131. *DM* d. 8.1.2, §32 (2:69ab): Hic dicendi modus non placet, quia conceptus objectivi rerum in mente divina sunt positivi, & important esse essentiale rerum, quod est esse positivum.

132. *DM* d. 8.1.2, §32 (2:69ab): Tum quia negatio negationis est quid positivum, ut negatio tenebrae est lux, negatio caecitatis est visus, sed negatio repugnantiae est negatio negationis, quia est negatio impossibilitatis, ergo quid positivum importare debet.

133. *DM* d. 8.1.3, §35 (2:70b): sciendum est non hic esse sermonem de causa vere, & proprie dicta . . . sua possibilitas nullam prorsus importet actualem, frustra quaereretur aliqua talis eius causa, sumitur ergo causa pro ratione . . . unde attendenda sit prima ratio possibilitatis, & impossibilitatis rerum, num ex parte Dei, aut potius ipsarum rerum, adeout ex se, & a se dicatur possibiles vel impossibiles independenter a Deo. For all of this emphasis on *ratio,* Mastrius doesn't sustain it. See the references to a quasi-efficient cause in no. 43: 76a and b.

134. *DM* d. 8.1.3, §35 (2:71a). Punch, Vasquez, Suárez, Molina, Aversa, Soncinas and Cajetan are listed on behalf of the independence thesis. Gabriel Biel is cited for the voluntarist thesis. Pasqualigo is assigned the intellectualist position.

135. *DM* d. 8.1.3, §35 (2:71a): Mediam sententiam docet Scotus I d. 36. & d. 43. ubi ait rerum possibilitatem, ac etiam impossibilitatem extrinsece quidem, & principiative sumi ab intellectu divino, intrinsece vero, & formaliter ex suis rationibus formalibus. Mastrius had introduced this critical distinction—extrinsece & principiative; intrinsece & formale—early on in his disputa-tion vs. Punch. See no. 14:58a: hoc est directe contra mentem Doctoris, qui I d. 36. & 39. & d. 43 ex professe creaturas ab aeterno habere illud esse formaliter ex seipsis, & principiative ab intel-lectu divino. Cf. n. 142 below. See Wolter, "Scotus on the Divine Origin," 107, n. 27. Simo Knuut-tila, "Duns Scotus," 138–39, has misgivings on this issue. See Scotus, *Ordinatio* 1. d. 36.1. §39 (6:286–87); d. 43.1 (6:351–61).

136. *DM* d. 8.1.3, §36 (2:71ab) : contra Poncium; ut autem adhuc amplius in praesenti absur-ditas huius asserti eniteat advertendum est quod aliud est dicere quod res habeat possibilitatem

ex seipsis, & aliud, quod habeant a seipsis, primum est omnino verum.... at secundum est prorsus falsum.

137. See the following note for Punch and Vasquez. Also see §36, 71b: [a seipsis] significat quod illam intrinsecum possibilitatem habeant a seipsis, & non communicatam ab altero, sed independenter a quocumque extrinseco... ergo poni debet aliquo modo dependens a Deo etiam in illa sua realitate potentiali.

138. See *DM* d. 8.1.3, §39 (2:73b): In oppositum instat I. Poncius loc. cit. probans creaturas non habere esse possibile principiative ab intellectu divino, sed praecise a seipsis, quia objectum scientiae speculativae, non fit per illam, sed potius praesupponitur ipsi, sed scientia, qua novit Deus creaturas ab aeterno est speculativa, ergo non dat creaturis esse illud, secundum quod cognoscit illas. In Ad 1m; §40, 74a, this is identified as an *argumentum desumptum a Vasquez* that is paraphrased by Mastrius in §43, 75b. At the end of §40, 74ab, Mastrius noted that "instat Vasquez intellectum divinum apud Scotum esse mere speculativum, atque ideo non operativum rerum." It is striking how Descartes' reaction to the tradition represented by the likes of Vasquez and Punch manifests an affinity to that of Scotus. See *To Mersenne* 6 May 1630 (ed. Adam Tannery), 1:149.21–24: je dis derechef que sunt tantum verae aut possibles, quia Deus illas veras aut possibiles, cognoscit, non autem contra veras a Deo cognosci quasi independenter ab illo sunt verae.

139. *DM* d. 8.1.3 obj. 5, §39 (2:73b): Tum 5 quia nisi creaturae haberent esse aliquod possibile a seipsis independenter ab actu intellectus divini, non esset ratio quare homo esset possibilis, quam chimaera, nam intellectus divinus intelligit utrumque, tanquam objectum secundarium, nec esset ulla ratio, cur tribueret possibilitatem uni potius, quam alteri. In view of Mastrius's response in n. 140 below, this objection seems to be connected to an interpretation of Vasquez referred to by Mastrius. See §35, 71a: & adeo aperte loquitur [Scotus] illis in locis ut immerito prorsus illi imponat Vasquez cit. asseruisse possibilitatem rerum ab intellectu divino totaliter causari, non autem ex earum rationibus formalibus ullo pacto desumi. See n. 143 below.

140. *DM* d. 8.1.3, §38 (2:72b): ergo possibilitas in rebus consurgit ex rationibus formalibus, interveniente judicio intellectus & unum absque alio non sufficit. Conf. Quia si nullus daretur intellectus potens judicare aliqua extra esse inter se compossibilia, vel impossibilia, nulla daretur possibilitas, vel impossibilitas logica. ergo utrum in solidum concurrit ad constituendum possibilitatem, vel impossibilitatem logicam.

141. *DM* d. 8.1.3, §39 (2:73a): possibilitas enim procedit ab intellectu divino proxime, & immediate, impossibilitas vero remote, & mediate. Sicut Deus suo intellectu producit possibile in esse possibili, ita producit duo entia formaliter utrumque in esse possibili, & illa producta seipsis formaliter sunt incompossibilia, neque aliquid tertium ex eis.

142. *DM* d. 8.1.3, §39 (2:73a): hanc incompossibilitatem, quam habent formaliter, habent ex se, & principiative ab eo quodammodo qui produxit ea, idest quasi mediate, & remote.

143. *DM* d. 8.1.3, §39 (2:73ab): quare Doctor in ea questione dixerit ex esse cognitum creaturarum resultare in ipsis esse possibili, negant etiam chimeram, & quodcumque aliud impossibile objici divino intellectui, veluti unum per se objectum primarium, vel secundarium, & ab eo intelligi immediate, sed intantum dicitur cognosci, inquantum cognoscit illa plura possibilia, quae invicem repugnant, et ideo sicuti non habet unam naturam sibi propriam, ita nec dici debet habere esse proprium intelligibile, in quo producatur intentionaliter ab intellectu divino, quemadmodum produci dicuntur possibilia." See Scotus, *Ordinatio*, 1. d. 36.1. §60–62 (6:296–97). See also *DO* d. 3.5.2, §72 (331a): duplex est esse objectivum, alterum entis rationis proprium, & est illud, quod nullum prorsus aliud supponit esse in objecto, sive reale, sive rationis ex vi prioris cognitionis: alterum commune cum aliis rebus, quae objiciuntur intellectui, per

quod non constituitur ens rationis; dum autem Deus cognoscit entia rationis a nobis facta tribuit illis esse objectivum secundi generis; *DM* d. 8.1.3 §78 (2:335a): Ad 3 dat [intellectus divinus] illis [entibus rationis] esse objectivum extrinsecum, & denominativum, quale est illud, quod convenit etiam entibus realibus, non autem intrinsecum, & formale, quod solum constituit ens rationis ex dictis concl. I., & ideo licet illud esse objectivum primi generis a solo pendeat intellectu divino, non idcirco dicuntur ab eo entia rationis fieri, sed tamen facta, vel factibilia cognosci. Mastrius devotes a whole question to entia rationis in the divine mind in *DO* d. 3.5, §69–80 (329–36).

144. See nn. 131–32 above. See another consideration of the same point in §48, 78ab.

145. See n. 30 above.

146. *DM* d. 8.1.3, §46 (2:77b): Caiet. docuisse videtur cap. 4. De ente et essentia qu. 6 ubi monet ens reale dupliciter accipi, & prout distinguitur a nihilo, & de ente rationis, & prout contradistinguitur ab ente existente; & hoc tandem admittere tenetur quicumque admittunt famigeratum illam in scholis distinctionem de ente nominaliter & verbaliter sumpto, seu participaliter quam declaravimus disp. 2 de natura entis ab initio n. 1.

147. *DM* d. 8.1.3, §47 (2:78a): Denique ibidem respondendo ad 2 princ. concedit [Scotus] intellectionem lapidis ab aeterno fuisse Metaphysicam, & realem ex parte objecti, non autem logicam; ergo lapis possibilis, etiam ut ab existentia praescindit, potest & debet dici ens reale, alioquin cognitio divina lapidem attingens ab aeterno non posset dici realis objective quod negat Doctor ibidem. See Duns Scotus, *Ordinatio* 1. d. 36.1 ad 2, §53 (6:292). On this score, possible creatures are creatable. See *DM* d. 8.1.4 ad 3m, §55 (2:82b): Ad 3. constat ex nu. 46. creaturam possibilem ab aeterno esse ens reale nominaliter, licet non verbaliter; constat etiam ex dictis nu. 21. posse quoque dici ens rationis, quatenus substat divinae cognitioni, & habet esse objectivum in divina mente, licet non secundum hanc rationem dicatur creabilis, sed secundum priorem. It must be noted here that, as positively creatable, possible creatures, however intramental they may be in terms of their objective presence in the divine mind, are altogether other than that divine mind. For the divine mind is clearly not creatable.

148. *DM* d. 8.1.3, §48 (2:78b): Contra, quia oppositum ostendi nu. 32 tum quia ostendo modo, quod ibi [no. 32:69b] sum pollicitus, ens possibile significare formaliter, & in recto illud ens positivum, quod postea in tempore existeret, si produceretur.

149. *DM* d. 8.1.3, §48 (2:78b): ens in actu, & ens in potentia ex 9 Met. tex. com. 13 non sunt tantum eiusdem generis, & speciei, sed etiam eiusdem numeri, illud enim individuum, quod nunc est in actu, illud idem fuit in potentia.

150. *DM* d. 8.1.3, §48 (2:78b): Forte dices opus non esse, ut sint positive idem, ad hoc ut possint ad invicem praedicare, sed sufficere quod sint idem negative, idest, quod non sint duo positiva distincta

151. *DM* d. 8.1.3, §48 (2:78b): haec [realis identitas] autem inter extremum positivum, & negativum versari nequit. falsum enim est hominem, ac non ens non esse diversa, & e contra, verum est hominem nunc existentem non esse diversum ab eo, qui possibilis erat. It must be acknowledged here that by *non ens* Mastrius means that which is opposed to *ens reale.* Cf. no. 50: 79b.

152. See *DM* d. 8.1.3, §40 (2:74ab): Cum vero instat Vasquez intellectum divinum apud Scotum esse mere speculativum, atque adeo non operativum rerum; Hoc non obstat, quominus sit earum operativus, & productivus rerum in esse cognito, sed tantum quin nequeat dictare voluntati divinae res extra faciendas per modum regulae.

Recollections of Times Past

ARMAND MAURER

As a conclusion to this volume, the friendly editor has invited me to write a brief intellectual autobiography. I agreed to do so on the condition that its intent be not simply to recount events in my intellectual life, but rather to offer tribute to the teachers and institutions that have made that life possible. I have limited these reflections to the years of my general education and philosophical formation.

I suppose everyone who has led a philosophical life can recall the first awakenings of interest in philosophy that led him or her to devote their lives to its pursuit. In my own case, I felt these stirrings when I was a student at Aquinas Institute high school in Rochester, New York. At that time the school was not run by the Basilian Fathers, though there were several on the staff. This was my first, but not my last, encounter with these priests. The education Aquinas gave to its students was well-rounded and generally excellent. I recall with particular pleasure courses in English literature and French and Latin (languages that I would use all my life). A course in apologetics gave me a vivid awareness of the power of reason. I can still remember the teacher (Fr. Wurtzer) showing how conclusions can be drawn from principles, for example in proving the existence of God. For the first time I was experiencing deductive reason as a powerful instrument for increasing knowledge and arriving at truth. Mathematics reinforced my awareness of the power of deductive reason, used in this case with greater ease and clarity. The experiments in chemistry and physics classes were less appealing to me. It did not help that our teacher's experiments sometimes went awry, and the fiery mass had to be thrown through an open window! Later, I came to understand how some could be strongly drawn to the scientific method, and even regard it, mistakenly, as the only way to unravel the secrets of the universe and human life. Perhaps through some weakness of my own I simply was not attracted to it. But one has to fulfill his own destiny and follow his own star.

During my high school days my older brother, who was studying physics at the University of Rochester, brought home books in philosophy that began my interest in the subject. Among them were Plato's *Dialogues* and red-bound volumes of Aquinas' great *Summa theologiae* in the translation of the English Dominicans. I do not recall reading much of the *Summa,* but I was enthralled by Plato's dialogues and avidly read some of the short ones, like the *Symposium, Apology, Phaedo,* and *Meno.* Without knowing the meaning of the word, I was being introduced to dialectic as a method of grasping principles, through the pro and con discussion of a topic, leading to conclusions that, according to Plato, should be taken as true. Much later I encountered the dialectic of the medieval schoolmen, based on Aristotle's *Topics,* in which opinions are advanced for and against a position and concluding, not necessarily with the truth, but with a well-founded probable opinion. I also learned that Aristotelian dialectic features in the structure of the *quaestiones* of Aquinas's *Summa theologiae,* which offer arguments pro and con for a certain topic, reserving the determination of the truth to the master's own *respondeo.*

I came as an undergraduate to St. Michael's College in Toronto in 1933. It is a small Catholic college, one of several affiliated with the large secular University of Toronto. It is run by the priests of the Congregation of St. Basil, some of whom had been my teachers at Aquinas. I was drawn to the college by my friendship with them, but more importantly by the college's growing reputation as a center of Christian philosophy. In 1929 it had founded an Institute of Mediaeval Studies, in which philosophy played a leading role. The primary agent in this foundation was the world-renowned French philosopher, Etienne Gilson, and its staff included the outstanding philosophers Anton C. Pegis and Monsignor Gerald B. Phelan. Though the Institute was a graduate institution, its influence extended down to the undergraduate students of the college like myself, who were enrolled in the course of Honour Philosophy. We heard public lectures of the Institute philosophers and sometimes managed "to listen in" to Gilson's graduate lectures. I recall my excitement in hearing Gilson's lectures on Descartes (published as Part Two of his *The Unity of Philosophical Experience*) in the West Hall of University College. I returned to St. Michael's late for dinner, to be rebuked by Fr. Joseph O'Donnell. When I told him that I was attending Gilson's lecture he easily forgave me. Another time I sat on the steps of the Institute building (then House number 10, Elmsley Place, now demolished) to hear Gilson lecture on Duns Scotus.

Some of our teachers in the Honour Philosophy program were graduate students in the Institute, and through them the philosophical ferment of the Institute trickled down to us. They gave us seminars in Greek and medieval philosophy, Thomistic metaphysics, and Jacques Maritain's *Degrees of Knowledge.* The latter seminar was given by John Consitt, a graduate student in science; it was my first encounter with the philosophy of this remarkable thinker. Besides these seminars, we attended lectures on logic by Fr. Viator McIntyre (using Maritain's *An Introduction to Logic*), on the human person by Fr. Henry Bellisle, on Aristotle's *Ethics* by Fr. Basil Sullivan, on Thomistic metaphysics by William Walton, and in modern philosophy by Herbert Johnson. Social issues were vigorously addressed by Fr. Joseph McGahey. A course in metaphysics was given in the fourth year by Monsignor Gerald B. Phelan, by far the most accomplished philosopher and metaphysician in the undergraduate program. The course was a deep analysis of the first article of St. Thomas's *De veritate:* What is Truth? Even before hearing the lectures of Gilson on Thomas's existential notions of being and truth, Phelan showed us that they emerged from Thomas's *De veritate.*

A priest of the Halifax diocese, Fr. Phelan had studied at the Catholic University of America and Louvain, obtaining from Louvain the *Agrégé en Philosophie* under Auguste Mansion, Maurice DeWulf, and Léon Noël. He had already won a doctorate in experimental psychology under Albert Michotte. Louvain was a busy center of scholastic philosophy as early as 1893, when Cardinal Désiré Mercier set up its influential Institut Supérieur de Philosophie, also known at that time as the École Saint Thomas d'Aquin. Its aim was to implement the directives set forth by Leo XIII in *Aeterni Patris* (1879). It was to probe the philosophy of the Middle Ages, and especially that of Thomas Aquinas, in order to use its principles for contemporary needs, particularly in experimental psychology and sociology. Phelan was an outstanding product of the Louvain Institute, and when the Basilians at St. Michael's wanted, in their own way, to put the pope's encyclical into effect, they brought Phelan, along with DeWulf and Noël, to Toronto. Phelan stayed and became the first President of the Toronto Institute of Mediaeval Studies.

In the 1940s there was a growing interest on the Toronto campus in existentialism and phenomenology, but no courses in these subjects were available. In 1948 Lawrence Lynch taught the first course in Toronto in these areas of philosophy, introducing many of us to the thought of men like Edmund Husserl, Martin Heidegger, Karl Jaspers, Jean-Paul Sartre, and Gabriel Marcel. This opened up for us new vistas and possibilities in the way of doing philosophy. Analytic philosophy was less well received, though much later the college brought over an analyst from Oxford, and it moved into new fields, such as medical ethics.

Impressive courses in psychology were given by Paul O'Sullivan, a medical doctor and professor of medicine at the University of Toronto. At St. Michael's he offered courses in genetic psychology, the psychology of character, and physiological psychology. The latter was a study of the organs of perception, culminating in the dissection of a bull's eye and a human brain. A man of wide erudition, Dr. O'Sullivan was well-versed in languages and literature, and he brought them to bear on his subjects.

Some of the philosophy majors formed an Ethics Club to examine social, political, and philosophical topics. At its meetings a student would read a paper, followed by a discussion of the subject. One year we decided to read Marx's *Communist Manifesto*. Frankie Firth (later a Basilian) demurred because the work was on the Index. He removed this obstacle by going to the superior of the college and getting permission to read it.

In the 1930s we were living in the Depression and Toronto felt the pinch of poverty. The Baroness Catherine De Hueck, a Russian emigré and friend of Dorothy Day, established a Friendship House for the poor and unemployed. Feeling the urge to get into Catholic action, I visited the house a number of times with fellow students. We used to peddle the *Social Forum* and talk to the men who lived there or came for a handout. During a visit from Dorothy Day the Baroness said she needed more mattresses, whereupon Dorothy Day told all of us to get down on our knees and pray for mattresses. We did this, and in the afternoon a truck arrived loaded with mattresses. I do not know by what agency—natural or supernatural—she brought about this minor miracle. This must have been the year (about 1936) when Dorothy Day came to St. Michael's College and spoke to the students about her work with the poor and unemployed in New York. I do not recall much of what she said, but I remember her dress—a long, shapeless green gown, clearly not purchased in a fashion boutique. She lived poverty as well as teaching it.

The Institute was in full vigor in 1938, when I graduated from the University of Toronto and enrolled in graduate studies both in the Institute and the Graduate Department of Philosophy of the U. of T. As I have indicated, the Institute arose from the happy conjunction of the college's efforts to excel in philosophy, particularly in Thomism, and Gilson's desire to establish an institute of medieval studies. His program for the Institute made it clear that it was to cover a wide range of areas in medieval culture and thought. The first year in a three-year program leading to the license in medieval studies was once described by him as "the minimum background for reading Dante." An Institute professor whose field was not philosophy anxiously asked him if he intended to found a school of philosophy. Gilson assured him that he did not. Though his primary concern was the philosophy of St. Thomas, he realized that his works could not be read intelligently without understanding the whole culture in which they were produced.

To staff the Institute, a group of young Basilians was selected by Gilson and Fr. Henry Carr and sent to leading centers of study in Europe. They were Frs. George B. Flahiff (later Cardinal), Terence P. McLaughlin, J. Reginald O'Donnell, and Alex J. Denomy. T. Vernon Kennedy and Wilfrid J. Dwyer came later. By 1938, the year I entered the Institute, they had all returned and were on the staff, along with Gilson himself, Fr. Joseph T. Muckle, Fr. Hupert P. Coughlin, Jacques Maritain, and Fr. Gerald B. Phelan. Fr. Ephrem Longpré, a Franciscan, was considered but was unavailable. In 1939 the Franciscan Philotheus Boehner was a guest lecturer in paleography, and in the same year Gerhart Ladner, a Viennese, joined the staff, lecturing in medieval history and archeology. Unfortunately, Ladner stayed only a few years, leaving for Howard University and later achieving an enviable reputation at the University of California at Los Angeles. The courses of instruction comprised the histories of medieval theology, philosophy, canon law, and Christian worship; also medieval history, medieval Latin and vernacular literature, paleography, and archaeology. All first-year students took these courses, specializing in later years. Paleography (taught by Frs. Muckle and O'Donnell) was considered an especially important tool, for without it one could not do original research in the medieval manuscripts that kept their secrets in the European libraries. In 1939, ten years after its foundation, the Institute was given a papal charter; it became the "Pontifical" Institute of Mediaeval Studies, with the right to confer the license and doctorate in medieval studies.

Gilson usually lectured for a half-year in Toronto, teaching the other half-year at the Collège de France in Paris. He lectured on a great variety of medieval subjects, always with wisdom and wit, drawing his material directly from the works of the medieval authors. He taught us always to write with the works of our author in front of us, and not to rely on text books or manuals. From his own experience he knew how harmful they can be. In seminars we could choose from among subjects he had listed; we were then left to develop them as best we could. He was rigorous in his standards of scholarship, but always kind and helpful to his students. On several occasions he was very kind to me. Once when I was suffering from a bad cold and was low in spirit, he invited me to his home at 8 Elmsley Place and played records of medieval music composed by Perotinus, one of the creators of polyphony. He brought out a bottle of cognac, and before serving it told me to look at the label. It was a map of the cognac country with a small red dot in the center. "That," Gilson said, "is where this bottle came from." Many years later he invited me to collaborate with him in writing his multi-volume *History of Philosophy.*

Gilson was often asked to lecture in universities and other institutions and he almost always obliged. He acknowledged, however, that he was no good at answering questions after the lecture. He said, "I generally think of a good reply the day after the lecture." After a pause, he added: "No, once I was brilliant. Someone arose and asked: 'But sir, what are we to do with science?' To which I replied: 'Learn it!'" After giving a lecture in (I believe) Vancouver, in which he defended the existence of necessary or absolute truths, a questioner asked Gilson to give an example. He probably thought Gilson would bring out the old chestnut of the principle of non-contradiction: that something cannot both be and not be at the same time and in the same respect. For this he perhaps had a ready reply, but Gilson said: "Even the rich have need of friends." The questioner thought for a moment and then sat down.

Though Gilson could be a harsh critic of his contemporaries, he was always respectful to his predecessors. During a seminar a student criticized De Wulf. Gilson immediately stopped the seminar and told the student never to criticize De Wulf. The Louvain historian had done pioneering work in medieval philosophy and without it we would not be in this classroom.

Gilson was convinced that beyond all the other philosophical disciplines, metaphysics is concerned with the ultimate issue of being or existence, and no philosopher threw more light on this subject than St. Thomas Aquinas. In Gilson's interpretation, being is a dynamic act of existing, participating in a limited way in the pure Act of Existing that is God. Gilson loved to lecture and write on this theme, claiming for Thomism alone the title of a true existential philosophy. As God revealed his name to be "He who is" and "I am," this existential metaphysics is thoroughly in accord with scripture, and indeed it owes its inspiration (if not its rational justification) to the divine word.

In the school year 1939–40 Gilson gave a series of sixteen lectures entitled "Roman Classical Culture from Cicero to Erasmus." Here he was no longer speaking as a metaphysician but as a humanist, tracing classical humanism from the Ciceronian ideal of culture through the Middle Ages to the Renaissance. As he had shown that the Middle Ages preserved and revolutionized the philosophy of the ancients through the influence of Christianity, now he demonstrated that these so-called dark ages did the same for classical humanism. He did not want these lectures published, for he considered them too incomplete; but for us who heard and recorded them they opened up new vistas of medieval culture and the Renaissance.

Gilson brought Jacques Maritain to the Institute, adding to it a new world-acclaimed philosophical voice. Maritain was teaching at the Institut Catholique in Paris, but considered a permanent appointment to the Toronto Institute. Eventually he arranged with Phelan to "maintain a permanent tie with the Institute and come there when he wished." Maritain's first courses were given in the fall term of 1933, and after that he came to Toronto intermittently. His influence on the campus, through both his occasional lectures and his books, was extraordinary. When Gilson and Maritain were around, the philosophical temperature on the campus rose considerably. Maritain was gentle in manner and of soft complexion, reminding one of Aristotle's dictum that an intellectual person is *mollis carne.* I recall the emotion I felt when Maritain began lecturing on natural law. Here was a man who was philosophizing and not simply repeating formulae! I felt I was in the presence of a true philosopher. Observing him on the campus, I was also aware of his deep spirituality. In those days the convent of the contemplative order of the Sister Adorers of the Precious Blood was located on St. Joseph Street, where St. Michael's library now stands. Students used to visit it, particularly during exam time. We often saw Maritain there, with his customary scarf around his neck, deep in prayer. The last year Maritain was in Toronto he caught a bad cold during the winter, not knowing how to turn on the radiator. For fear of pneumonia he spent a few days in the hospital. He did not return to Toronto; it was rumored that his wife, Raïssa, forbade it.

Among other Institute philosophers who influenced me was Anton Pegis. Lecturing on Greek philosophy, he probed the Presocratics and Plato so thoroughly that he had little time left for Aristotle and Plotinus. His lectures on St. Thomas's doctrine of the human person left a deep impression. Many years later he gave considerable attention to the phenomenology of Husserl and Heidegger, which led me to study their philosophies.

I must not pass over the Dominican Ignatius T. Eschmann, who came to Toronto as a refugee from Nazism. Having edited Aquinas's *Summa theologiae* in Ottawa with precious notes and references, he was thoroughly acquainted with the work, and his lectures were drawn directly from it. He was an expert in the field of Thomistic ethics and politics, and he spoke on these subjects with a sonorous voice and great precision. At the end of a term Fr. Phelan, the president of the Institute, called him in and strongly suggested that next year he give a course in metaphysics. Taken aback, Eschy (as he was called) somewhat reluctantly bowed to authority and prepared lectures on William of Ockham's doctrine of universals. Ockham's name was heard around the Institute at that time, for the Franciscan Philotheus Boehner, another refugee from Germany, had been there, preparing an edition of Ockham's *Summa logicae.* As noted above, he taught paleography as a guest lecturer for one semester, then left and took up residence at the Franciscan Institute in St. Bonaventure College, where he continued his edition. Always a master of his subject, Fr. Eschmann opened up for us the influential school of medieval Franciscan philosophers and theologians, and when I came to choose a subject for my doctorate at the University I decided to write on Ockham's critique of Duns Scotus. I owe my lifelong interest in these Franciscans to Fr. Eschmann.

I did not choose to write my thesis on Ockham because I was sympathetic to his nominalism (or better, conceptualism), but because he was a major figure in medieval philosophy still in need of investigation. More specifically, I was intrigued by his complex relations with his predecessor, John Duns Scotus. When I compared any point of Ockham's doctrine with Thomism I found the latter more convincing. Indeed, of all the philosophers I was studying none excelled Thomas's rationality and cogency of argument.

It was usual for students at the Institute who were also proceeding to University graduate degrees to take some of their courses "across the campus." A popular seminar was given by Fulton Anderson, the chairman of the graduate school of philosophy. Anderson conducted his seminar acting the role of Socrates, questioning his students and eliciting replies that he often found unsatisfactory. He then guided the students to more acceptable solutions.

An expert in the English empiricists, Anderson's favorite philosophers, on the contrary, were Plato and the nineteenth-century idealists, F. H. Bradley and Bernard

Bosanquet. He was interviewed on the radio after publishing a book on Francis Bacon. At the end of the session, the interviewer, wishing to conclude on a positive note, said to Anderson: "Now you do consider Bacon a great philosopher, don't you?" After a moment of embarrassing silence, Anderson retorted, "I certainly do not!" Taken aback, the interviewer asked him why Bacon was not a great philosopher. Anderson replied: "He ruined metaphysics!" At this, my admiration of Anderson rose considerably. He started to write a book on John Locke, and knowing my interest in Ockham he told me one day that he had found the link between Ockham and Locke. With some excitement I asked him what this link was, but he replied that I would have to wait until his book was published. Alas, he died before it was completed, and the possible link remains unknown.

Having completed courses for the Master's degree at the University, I was in debt to both the Basilians and the University. I went to Fr. Phelan, then president of the Institute, and asked his advice about continuing graduate work. Perhaps I should drop out and work for a few years and then return. Fr. Phelan replied gently: "No, come back next year and everything will be all right." About the same time, the wise Fr. Basil Sullivan, knowing my predicament, said: "Armand, it would be much easier if you just became a Basilian." As I had been thinking about doing so for a long time, Fr. Sullivan's nudge helped me to decide to apply for entrance in the Congregation. When I told my decision to Fr. McCorkell, the superior of St. Michael's, he put his arm around me and welcomed me into the fold. Incidently, this episode is at the origin of a saying that circulated among my confreres, that I joined the Basilians in order to pay my debts! What we learn from this episode is rather the Basilian preferential option for the poor.

There followed four years of theology in preparation for ordination to the priesthood. I was concurrently studying at the Institute. At that time theology did not seem to me to be a very lively and interesting subject, though the course of Fr. Coughlin in dogmatic theology, based on Aquinas's *Summa,* and that of Fr. Daniel Dillon in moral theology were excellent. But I was not tempted to switch from philosophy to theology. After Vatican II the situation of theology changed and I became more interested in the subject.

Having received the Institute's Licentiate in Mediaeval Studies in 1945 and the Ph.D. from the University in 1947, I was sent to Paris in 1948 for a year's post-doctoral study at the École Pratique des Hautes Études, a graduate division of the University of Paris. Through Gilson I received a French government scholarship that gave me passage on French liners (the *DeGrasse* and *Ile de France*) and a small monthly stipend. Accompanied by Fr. Laurence Shook I resided in the rather bleak but friendly rectory of the church Notre Dame de Travail near the Gare Montparnasse, where Institute Basilians customarily lived when in Paris.

At first I thought of living at the more suitable Collège Canadien in the Cité Universitaire, and I went to visit it. On ringing the doorbell, I was greeted by a Franciscan dressed in his long brown habit. To my surprise it was Fr. Ephrem Longpré, the Canadian historian and editor of Franciscan medieval authors, who was known to me only by his works. Even before showing me the Collège, he told me with some agitation of his dismissal as editor-in-chief of the works of Duns Scotus in favor of his fellow Franciscan Fr. Carlo Balić. As a complete stranger to him and to his situation, I could only offer my sympathy.

The editing of Scotus's works was not the only bone of contention between the two Franciscans. Fr. Longpré was convinced by documents he discovered that Duns Scotus was born in Scotland at Littledean in the village of Maxton. One day Fr. Balić decided to make a pilgrimage to Littledean in order to venerate the birthplace of the famous Franciscan. He got as far as the village of Duns, just across the border of Scotland, where he encountered an historian who took him to the home in which, according to local tradition, Duns was born. After studying documents in Duns and being persuaded by the local legend, he decided that Duns had in fact been born in Duns. He stopped his pilgrimage there and never went to Littledean.[1]

At the École des Hautes Études I followed the lectures on late medieval philosophy by Paul Vignaux, a former student of Gilson, and those of the Dominican Marie-Dominique Chenu, entitled "Symbolisme au Moyen Âge." Chenu's lectures made me aware of a new dimension of medieval thought and culture. Knowing that he was a close friend of Gilson's and that he was among the first professors of the Institute, I visited him in his Dominican convent. He welcomed me warmly, sat me down in a chair facing him, took my two hands in his own, and spoke encouragingly to me about the studies I was about to begin.

At the Sorbonne, the undergraduate division of the university, I followed the course of the famous historian Henri Marrou on the Fathers of the Church. Among the Fathers he lectured on were the Cappadocians St. Gregory of Nazianzus and his friend St. Basil. I was struck by the lively interest the students showed in these lectures, which were given with great warmth and understanding.

Both Fr. Shook and I attended Gilson's lectures on Duns Scotus at the Collège de France. Gilson emphasized the central role of infinity in the Franciscan's thought, comparing it to the part played by *esse* in Thomism. In Scotism, he said, infinity identifies God as God and divides him from every other being, exactly as in Thomism God stands apart by his pure act of existing. This insight proved valuable when, years later, I wrote on Francis of Meyronnes, a follower of Duns Scotus.

I was told that Gabriel Marcel held a soirée for students every Friday afternoon. Remembering Larry Lynch's lectures on his philosophy, and having read with appreciation some of his essays on moral topics such as fidelity and disponibility, one Friday I walked over to his apartment building near the Sorbonne to join the group. On the stairway I ran into a small, rather unprepossessing man whom I thought might be a

workman. I spoke to him: "Pardon, monsieur, je cherche Monsieur Gabriel Marcel."
He answered with a smile: "C'est moi." He led me up to his apartment, which was
already crowded with students. One of them read a paper, followed by a lively discussion, after which Madame Marcel served refreshments. Years later Marcel gave a lecture at St. Michael's College entitled, characteristically, "Mon Théâtre."

At the Bibliothèque Nationale in Paris I made the acquaintance of Mlle Marie-
Thérèse D'Alverny, the *Chef des manuscrits.* She kindly assisted me in obtaining the
manuscripts I needed, as she did over the years for so many professors of the Institute.
Another permanent figure at the Bibliothèque who became a friend was Fr. Léon
Baudry, a secular priest who was preparing a philosophical lexicon of William of
Ockham. Baudry, who, like Fr. Boehner, was attached to Ockhamism, had a private
desk in the library where he patiently wrote out the entries of his lexicon on old envelopes
and other scraps of paper. Living in poverty, he eked out a livelihood by tutoring lycée
students. His lexicon is very helpful for the study of Ockhamism, but it needs to be
redone, now that the critical edition of Ockham's works has been published.[2]

When June came and Paris was in full bloom, I sailed for home, not without regret,
but eagerly looking forward to September and the beginning of teaching and directing
students in Toronto.

Looking back over these formative years, it is apparent that, after my family and
the Church, my primary indebtedness is to the Basilian Congregation and its institutions, particularly the Pontifical Institute and St. Michael's College. They welcomed
me long ago and provided an ambiance for cultivating both a spiritual and an intellectual life. We Basilians have often used a phrase referring to the esteemed men who had
gone before us: *Laudemus viros gloriosos* (Sirach 44). These memoirs pay homage to the
remarkable Christian educators and builders mentioned above, who labored for no
earthly wealth but for the love of God and humankind.

Armand Maurer

Professor Emeritus, Pontifical Institute of Mediaeval Studies and University of Toronto

Notes

1. Fr. Balić tells this adventure in "Note di un viaggio al 'Natio loco' del beato Giovanni Duns
Scoto," *Vita Minorum* 6 (November–December 1953): 1–7.

2. L. Baudry, *Lexique philosophique de Guillaume d'Ockham: Etude des notions fondamentales*
(Paris: Lethielleux, 1958).

Bibliography of the Writings of Armand A. Maurer, CSB

JAMES K. FARGE, CSB

Books

1. *Medieval Philosophy*, vol. 2 of *A History of Philosophy*, edited by Etienne Gilson. New York: Random House, 1962. Pp. xviii, 435. Rev. ed. Toronto: Pontifical Institute of Mediaeval Studies, 1982. Spanish trans. Buenos Aires: Emecé, 1967. Slovenian trans. *Srednjeveška Filozofija Zahoda.* Celje: Mohorjev Druzba, 2001.

2. *Recent Philosophy: Hegel to the Present*, vol. 4 of *A History of Philosophy*, in collaboration with Etienne Gilson and Thomas Langan. New York: Random House, 1966. Author of sections on English and American philosophy. Pp. 411–663, 813–876. Polish trans. Warsaw: Pax, 1977.

3. *St. Thomas and Historicity.* Milwaukee: Marquette University Press, 1979. Pp. 57.

4. *About Beauty: A Thomistic Interpretation.* Houston: Center for Thomistic Studies, University of St. Thomas, 1983. Pp. 135.

5. *Being and Knowing: Studies in Thomas Aquinas and Later Medieval Philosophers.* Toronto: Pontifical Institute of Mediaeval Studies, 1990. Pp. 496.

6. *The Philosophy of William of Ockham in the Light of its Principles.* Toronto: Pontifical Institute of Mediaeval Studies, 1999. Pp. 590.

Translations

7. *St. Thomas Aquinas: On Being and Essence*, with an introduction and notes. Toronto: Pontifical Institute of Mediaeval Studies, 1949. Pp. 63. 2nd rev. ed. 1968.

8. *St. Thomas Aquinas: The Division and Methods of the Sciences.* Questions 5 and 6 of his Commentary on the *De Trinitate* of Boethius, with introduction and notes. Toronto: Pontifical Institute of Mediaeval Studies, 1953. Pp. 232. Rev. eds. 1958, 1963, 1986.

9. *St. Thomas Aquinas: Faith, Reason and Theology.* Questions 1–4 of his Commentary on the *De Trinitate* of Boethius, with introduction and notes. Toronto: Pontifical Institute of Mediaeval Studies, 1987. Pp. xxxviii, 122.

10.   *Master Eckhart: Parisian Questions and Prologues*, with introduction and notes. Toronto: Pontifical Institute of Mediaeval Studies, 1974. Pp. 123.

11.   Etienne Gilson, *Christian Philosophy: An Introduction*, with introduction. Toronto: Pontifical Institute of Mediaeval Studies, 1993. Pp. xxv, 139.

12.   Etienne Gilson, *Thomism: The Philosophy of Thomas Aquinas.* A translation of *Le thomisme*, sixth and final edition. With Laurence K. Shook†. Toronto: Pontifical Institute of Mediaeval Studies, 2002. Pp. xv, 454.

EDITIONS

13.   Adam of Buckfield, *Sententia super Secundum Metaphysicae*, in *Nine Mediaeval Thinkers*, edited by J. Reginald O'Donnell. Toronto: Pontifical Institute of Mediaeval Studies, 1955. Pp. 99–144.

14.   *St. Thomas Aquinas 1274–1974: Commemorative Studies.* Editor-in-Chief. 2 vols. Toronto: Pontifical Institute of Mediaeval Studies, 1974. Pp. 488, 526.

15.   Siger of Brabant. *Quaestiones in Metaphysicam.* Louvain-la-Neuve: Éditions de l'Institut Supérieur de Philosophie, 1983. Pp. 479.

16.   Étienne Gilson, "Three Lectures 'In Quest of Species'" (in preparation).

ARTICLES

17.   "*Esse* and *essentia* in the Metaphysics of Siger of Brabant," *Mediaeval Studies* 8 (1946): 68–86.

18.   "Henry of Ghent and the Unity of Man," *Mediaeval Studies* 10 (1948): 1–20.

19.   "Ms Cambrai 486: Another Redaction of the *Metaphysics* of Siger of Brabant?" *Mediaeval Studies* 11 (1949): 224–32.

20.   "*Ens diminutum:* A Note on its Origin and Meaning," *Mediaeval Studies* 12 (1950): 216–22.

21.   "Siger of Brabant and an Averroistic Commentary on the *Metaphysics* in Cambridge, Peterhouse, Ms 152," *Mediaeval Studies* 12 (1950): 233–35.

22.   "Revived Aristotelianism and Thomistic Philosophy," in *A History of Philosophical Systems*, ed. V. Ferm. New York: The Philosophical Library, 1950: 197–210.

23.   "Scotism and Ockhamism," in *A History of Philosophical Systems:* 212–24.

24.   "Form and Essence in the Philosophy of St. Thomas," *Mediaeval Studies* 13 (1951): 165–76.

25.   "Siger of Brabant's *De Necessitate et Contingentia Causarum* and Ms Peterhouse 152," *Mediaeval Studies* 14 (1952): 48–60.

26.   "Henry of Harclay's Question on the Univocity of Being," *Mediaeval Studies* 16 (1954): 1–18.

27.   "John of Jandun and the Divine Causality," *Mediaeval Studies* 17 (1955): 185–207.

28.   "Boetius of Dacia and the Double Truth," *Mediaeval Studies* 17 (1955): 233–39.

29.   "St. Thomas and the Analogy of Genus," *The New Scholasticism* 29 (1955): 127–44.

30. "The *De Quiditatibus Entium* of Dietrich of Freiberg and its Criticism of Thomistic Metaphysics," *Mediaeval Studies* 18 (1956): 173–203.

31. "Between Reason and Faith: Siger of Brabant and Pomponazzi on the Magic Arts," *Mediaeval Studies* 18 (1956): 1–18.

32. "The State of Historical Research in Siger of Brabant," *Speculum* 31 (1956): 49–56.

33. "Henry of Harclay's Questions on Immortality," *Mediaeval Studies* 19 (1957): 79–107.

34. "Ockham's Conception of the Unity of Science," *Mediaeval Studies* 20 (1958): 98–112.

35. "A Neglected Thomistic Text on the Foundation of Mathematics," *Mediaeval Studies* 21 (1959): 185–92.

36. "Henry of Harclay's Questions on the Divine Ideas," *Mediaeval Studies* 23 (1961): 163–93.

37. "Henry of Harclay: Disciple or Critic of Duns Scotus?" in *Die Metaphysik in Mittelalter: Ihr Uhrsprung und ihre Bedentung*, ed. P. Wilpert, Miscellanea Mediaevalia, bd. 2 (Berlin: DeGruyter, l963), 563–571.

38. "St. Thomas and Henry of Harclay on Created Nature," *La Filosofia della Natura nel Medioevo: Atti del terzo congresso internazionale di filosofia medioevale* (Milan: Società editrice Vita e Pensiero, 1964, publ. 1966), 542–49.

39. "Cajetan's Notion of Being in His Commentary on the *Sentences*," *Mediaeval Studies* 28 (1966): 268–78.

40. with William Dunphy, "A Promising New Discovery for Sigerian Studies," *Mediaeval Studies* 26 (1967): 364–69.

41. Six articles in *The Encyclopedia of Philosophy*, ed. Paul Edwards (New York: Macmillan, 1967): Boetius of Dacia, Orestes Brownson, Jonathan Edwards, Henry of Harclay, Samuel Johnson, Nicholas of Cusa.

42. Nine articles in *The New Catholic Encyclopedia* (New York: McGraw-Hill, 1967): Latin Averroism, Boethius of Dacia, John Baconthorp, Marsilius of Inghen, Nicholas Oresme, Gerald B. Phelan, Robert Holcot, Siger of Brabant, Etienne Gilson.

43. "Francis of Mayron's Defense of Epistemological Realism," *Studia Mediaevalia et Mariologica P. Carolo Balić septuagesimum explenti annum dicata* (Rome: Antonianum, 1969), 203–25.

44. "St. Thomas on Eternal Truths," *Mediaeval Studies* 32 (1970): 91–107.

45. with Alfred P. Caird, "The Role of Infinity in the Thought of Francis of Meyronnes" *Mediaeval Studies* 33 (1971): 201–27.

46. "St. Thomas on the Sacred Name 'Tetragrammaton,'" *Mediaeval Studies* 34 (1972): 275–86.

47. "A Thomist Looks at William James's Notion of Truth," *The Monist* 57 (1973): 151–67.

48. "Analogy in Patristic and Medieval Thought," in *Dictionary of the History of Ideas: Studies of Selected Pivotal Ideas*, ed. Philip Wiener (New York: Scribners, 1973), 1:64–67. See http://extext.lib.virginia.edu/cgi-Pocal/DHI.

49. "Medieval Philosophy and its Historians," in *Essays on the Reconstruction of Medieval History*, ed. V. Mudroch and G.S. Couse (Montréal/London: McGill–Queens University Press, 1974), 69–84.

50. "The Unity of a Science: St. Thomas and the Nominalists," in *St. Thomas Aquinas 1274–1974: Commemorative Studies*, ed. A. Maurer (Toronto: Pontifical Institute of Mediaeval Studies, 1974), 2:269–91.

51. "Henry of Harclay's Disputed Question on the Plurality of Forms," in *Essays in Honour of Anton Charles Pegis*, ed. J.R. O'Donnell (Toronto: Pontifical Institute of Mediaeval Studies, 1974), 125–159.

52. "Medieval Philosophy," in *The New Encyclopaedia Britannica*, 15th ed. (1974), 14:256–61.

53. "Ockham on the Possibility of a Better World," *Mediaeval Studies* 38 (1976): 291–312.

54. "The Role of Divine Ideas in the Theology of William of Ockham," in *Studies Honoring Ignatius Charles Brady, Friar Minor* (St. Bonaventure, NY: Franciscan Institute, 1976), 359–77.

55. "Some Aspects of Fourteenth-Century Philosophy," *Medievalia et Humanistica*, n.s. 7 (1976): 175–88.

56. "Orestes Brownson: Philosopher of Freedom," *Proceedings of the American Catholic Philosophical Association* 50 (1976): 162–76.

57. "St. Thomas and Changing Truths," in *Tommaso d'Aquino nel suo settimo centenario: Atti del congresso internazionale di filosofia medioevale* 6 (Naples: Edizioni Domenicane Italiane, 1978), 267–75.

58. "Method in Ockham's Nominalism," *The Monist* 61, no. 3 (1978): 426–43.

59. "Anton Charles Pegis (1905–1978)," *Mediaeval Studies* 41 (1979): xvii–xix.

60. "The Sacred Tetragrammaton in Medieval Thought," *Actas del V Congreso Internacional de Filosofia Medieval*, ed. S.G. Nogales (Madrid: Editora Nacional, Torregalindo 10, 1979), 2:975–83.

61. "Time and the Person," Presidential Address, *Proceedings of the American Catholic Philosophical Association* 53 (1979): 182–93.

62. "The Legacy of Etienne Gilson," *One Hundred Years of Thomism: "Aeterni Patris" and Afterwards. A Symposium*, ed. V.B. Brezik (Houston: Center for Thomistic Studies, 1981), 28–44.

63. "Siger of Brabant on Fables and Falsehoods in Religion," *Mediaeval Studies* 48 (1981): 515–30.

64. "William of Ockham on Language and Reality," *Miscellanea Mediaevalia* 13/2. *Sprache und Erkenntnis im Mittelalter*, ed. A. Zimmermann (Berlin/New York: Walter de Gruyter, 1981), 795–802. Italian trans. in *Logica e Linguaggio nel Medioevo*, ed. R. Fedriga and S. Puggioni (Milan: Edizioni Universitarie di Lettere, 1993).

65. "Nicholas M. Häring, 1909–1982," *Proceedings of the Royal Society of Canada*, series 4, vol. 20 (1982): 93–94.

66. "C.S. Peirce and Duns Scotus," *Krisis* 1, no. 1, *International Circle for Research in Philosophy* (Summer, 1983): 6–9.

67. "Ockham's Razor and Chatton's Anti-Razor," *Mediaeval Studies* 46 (1984): 463–75.

68. "Gilson on Linguistics and the Philosophy of Language," *Doctor Communis* (1985): 335–44.

69. "James A. Weisheipl OP (1923–1984)," *Mediaeval Studies* 47 (1985): xii–xx.

70. "Maimonides and Aquinas on the Study of Metaphysics," in *A Straight Path: Studies in Medieval Philosophy and Culture. Essays in Honor of Arthur Hyman*, ed. R. Link-Salinger (Washington, DC: Catholic University of America Press, 1988), 206–15.

71. "Orestes A. Brownson (1803–1876)," in *Christliche Philosophie im katholischen Denken des 19. und 20. Jahrhunderts*, ed. M. Coreth et al (Graz/ Wien/ Köln: Styria, 1987), 1:729–36.

72. "Reflections on Metaphysics and Experience," *Proceedings of the American Catholic Philosophical Association* (Aquinas Medalist Address) 61 (1987): 26–34.

73. "Siger of Brabant and Theology," *Mediaeval Studies* 50 (1988): 257–78.

74. "Etienne Gilson," in *Christliche Philosophie im katholischen Denken des 19. und 20. Jahrhunderts*, ed. E. Coreth et al (Salzburg: Styria, 1989), 2:519–45.

75. "Gilson's Use of History in Philosophy," in *Thomistic Papers* V, ed. T. A. Russman (Houston: Center for Thomistic Studies, University of St. Thomas, 1990), 25–48.

76. "Reflections on Thomas Aquinas's Notion of Presence," in *Philosophy and the God of Abraham: Essays in Memory of James A. Weisheipl OP*, ed. R. J. Long (Toronto: Pontifical Institute of Mediaeval Studies, 1991), 113–27.

77. "James Ross on the Divine Ideas: A Reply," *American Catholic Philosophical Quarterly* 65 (1991): 213–20.

78. "Gilson, Etienne," *Handbook of Metaphysics and Ontology*, ed. H. Burkhardt and B. Smith (Munich: Philosophia, 1991), 1: 309–10.

79. "Orestes Brownson and St. Augustine," *The Modern Schoolman* (Vernon Bourke Festschrift) 69 (1992): 463–74.

80. "Orestes Brownson and Christian Philosophy," *The Monist* 75, no. 3 (1992): 341–53.

81. "On Divine Sendings," *The Canadian Catholic Review*, 11, no. 7 (July–August, 1993): 19–23.

82. "Thomists and Thomas Aquinas on the Foundation of Mathematics," *Review of Metaphysics* 47 (1993): 43–61.

83. "Descartes and Aquinas on the Unity of a Human Being: Revisited," *American Catholic Philosophical Quarterly*, special issue: *Descartes*, ed. S. Voss, 67 (1993): 497–511.

84. "Gilson and *Aeterni Patris*," in *Thomistic Papers* VI, ed. J. F. X. Knasas (Houston: Center for Thomistic Studies, University of St. Thomas, 1994), 91–105.

85. "William of Ockham," in *Individuation in Scholasticism: The Later Middle Ages and the Counter-Reformation 1150–1650*, ed. J. J. E. Gracia (Albany: State University of New York Press, 1994), 373–96.

86. "Ockham's Razor and Dialectical Reasoning," *Mediaeval Studies* 58 (1996): 49–65.

87. "Walter Henry Principe," in *Proceedings of the Royal Society of Canada*, series 6, vol. 7 (1996), 181–82.

88. "Dialectic in the *De Ente et Essentia* of St. Thomas Aquinas," *Roma, Magistra Mundi: Itineraria Culturae Medievalis. Mélanges offerts au Père L. E. Boyle à l'Occasion de son 75e anniversaire*, éd. J. Hamesse (Louvain-la-Neuve: Fédération des Instituts d'Études Médiévales, 1998), 573–83.

89. "Armand A. Maurer, CSB: The Eighty-Fourth Birthday. Interview with Donald J. Lococo and Sean McGrath," *The Canadian Catholic Review* 17, no. 1 (1999): 13–25.

90. "Introduction to Etienne Gilson: The Terrors of the Year Two Thousand," *Logos: A Journal of Catholic Thought and Culture* 3, no. 1 (Winter, 2000): 13–19.

91. "Darwin, Thomists, and Secondary Causality," *Review of Metaphysics* 57 (2004): 491–514.

92. "Étienne Gilson, Critic of Absolute Positivism" (in preparation).

Book Reviews

93. Robert Guelluy, *Philosophie et théologie chez Guillaume d'Ockham* (Louvain/Paris, 1947). In *Traditio* 5 (1947): 398–402.

94.	George P. Klubertanz, *The Philosophy of Human Nature* (St. Louis, 1951). In *The Modern Schoolman* 29 (1952): 315–18.

95.	Matthew C. Menges, *The Concept of Univocity Regarding the Predication of God and Creatures according to William Ockham* (St. Bonaventure, NY, 1948). In *The Modern Schoolman* 31 (1954): 143–45.

96.	Dom Mark Pontifex and Dom Illtyd Trethowan, *The Meaning of Existence: A Metaphysical Enquiry* (New York, 1953). In *The Modern Schoolman* 33 (1955): 54–56.

97.	*Averrois Cordvbensis, Commentarivm Magnvm in Aristotelis De Anima Libros*, ed. F. Stuart Crawford (Cambridge, MA, 1953). In *The Modern Schoolman* 33 (1955): 44–45.

98.	Gordon Leff, *Bradwardine and the Pelagians* (Cambridge, 1957). In *The Modern Schoolman* 36 (1959): 240–42.

90.	Gerard Smith and Lottie H. Kendzierski, *The Philosophy of Being: Metaphysics I* (New York, 1961). In *The Modern Schoolman* 40 (1962): 70–73.

100.	Fernand Van Steenberghen, *Dieu Caché* (Louvain/Paris, 1961). In *The New Scholasticism* 37 (1963): 120–24.

101.	Frederick J. Roensch, *Early Thomistic School* (Dubuque, Iowa, 1964). In *Manuscripta* 10 (1966): 170–72.

102.	Leslie Dewart, *The Future of Belief* (New York, 1966). In *The Ecumenist* 5 (1967): 22–25.

103.	Arthur Gibson, *The Faith of the Atheist* (New York, 1968). In *Commonweal*, April 25, 1969: 175–76.

104.	John F. Wippel and Allan B. Wolter (eds.), *Medieval Philosophy from St. Augustine to Nicholas of Cusa* (New York/London, 1969). In *The Thomist* 34 (1970): 167–68.

105.	Roland André Delattre, *Beauty and Sensibility in the Thought of Jonathan Edwards: An Essay in Aesthetics and Theological Ethics* (New Haven/London, 1968). In *The Philosophical Quarterly* 20 (1970): 399–400.

106.	John M. Quinn, *The Thomism of Etienne Gilson: A Critical Study* (Villanova, PA, 1971). In *The Thomist* 37 (1973): 389–91.

107.	Alessandro Ghisalberti, *Guglielmo di Ockham* (Milan, 1972). In *The Review of Metaphysics* 27 (1973): 126.

108.	Joseph Bobik and James A. Corbett, *The Commentary of Conrad of Prussia on the "De Ente et Essentia" of St. Thomas Aquinas* (The Hague, 1974). In *The Thomist* 40 (1976): 174–77.

109.	Thomas R. Ryan, *Orestes A. Brownson: A Definitive Biography* (Huntington, IN, 1976). In *The New Scholasticism* 52 (1978): 456–59.

110.	Gerard Verbeke, *The Presence of Stoicism in Medieval Thought* (Washington, DC, 1983). In *Journal of the History of Philosophy* 24 (1986): 264–66.

111.	John Marenbon, *Later Medieval Philosophy (1150–1350): An Introduction* (London, 1987). In *Journal of the History of Philosophy* 28 (1990): 128–29.

112.	Fran O'Rourke, ed., *At the Heart of the Real: Philosophical Essays in Honour of the Most Reverend Desmond Connell, Archbishop of Dublin* (Dublin, 1992). In *American Catholic Philosophical Quarterly* 67 (1993): 394–97.

Contributors

STEPHEN F. BROWN is Professor of Theology at Boston College, where he is Director of the Institute of Medieval Philosophy and Theology. He was educated at the Franciscan Institute of St. Bonaventure University and at the University of Louvain. After completing the edition of many volumes of the *Opera Philosophica et Theologica* of William of Ockham, his research interest turned to the history of medieval theology. His works include two translations, *Bonaventure: The Journey of the Mind to God* (Indianapolis: Hackett, 1993) and *Aquinas: On Faith and Reason* (Indianapolis: Hackett, 1999), and three volumes in the "World Religions Series" of Facts on File: *Catholicism and Orthodox Christianity, Protestantism,* and *Judaism.*

LAWRENCE DEWAN, OP is Professor of Philosophy at the Collége Dominicain, Ottawa, Canada. He was educated at the Pontifical Institute of Mediaeval Studies and the University of Toronto, where he studied under Fr. Maurer in the 1960s. The Dominican Order awarded him the signal honor of the degree of Master of Sacred Theology in 1998. He is the author of numerous articles on medieval philosophy, especially Aquinas.

LEO J. ELDERS, SVD was born in the Netherlands, where, among his many other appointments, he has been Professor of Philosophy at the Major Seminary Rolduc since 1976. Educated at the Universities of Utrecht, Harvard, and Montreal, he is the author of fifteen books and editor of thirteen more. He was recently honored with his own *Festschrift,* edited by Jörgen Vijgen: *Indubitanter ad veritatem: Studies offered to Leo J. Elders SVD, In Honor of the Golden Jubilee of his Ordination to the Priesthood* (Budel: Damon, 2003).

GIRARD J. ETZKORN is Professor Emeritus, The Franciscan Institute, St. Bonaventure University, New York. He was educated at Quincy College, Illinois, and the University of Louvain. His fourteen books include Latin editions of Roger Marston, William Ockham, and Walter Chatton, and *Iter Vaticanum Franciscanum: A Descriptive Catalog of some 100 Codices in the Vaticanus Latinus Collection* (Leiden: Brill, 1996).

JAMES K. FARGE, CSB is Senior Fellow and Librarian of the Pontifical Institute of Mediaeval Studies, Toronto. Educated at the University of St. Thomas, Houston, and the University of Toronto, his specialty is the history of universities. He has published five books on the University of Paris and its Faculty of Theology, and he is currently editing *The Correspondence of Erasmus*, in The Collected Works of Erasmus 13 (Toronto: University of Toronto Press).

R. E. HOUSER is Professor of Philosophy in the Center for Thomistic Studies at the University of St. Thomas, Houston. He studied under Fr. Maurer in the 1970s at the Pontifical Institute of Mediaeval Studies and the University of Toronto. His articles cover ancient and medieval philosophy, especially Aquinas, Avicenna, and Bonaventure. He is author and translator of *The Cardinal Virtues: Aquinas, Albert, and Philip the Chancellor* (Toronto: Pontifical Institute Press, 2004). He has also edited *Medieval Masters: Essays in Memory of Msgr. E.A. Synan* (South Bend, Ind.: University of Notre Dame Press, 1999). With Timothy Noone, he is currently translating philosophical selections from Bonaventure's *Commentary on the Sentences* for the Franciscan Institute Press.

R. JAMES LONG is Professor of Philosophy at Fairfield University and the President of the Society for Medieval and Renaissance Philosophy. He was educated at the Pontifical Institute of Mediaeval Studies and the University of Toronto, where he studied under Fr. Maurer in the 1960s. He has published numerous editions and studies, including his latest book (with Maura O'Carroll), *The Life and Works of Richard Fishacre OP: Prolegomena to the Edition of his Commentary on the "Sentences"*. He currently serves as general editor of Fishacre's *Sentences* commentary, which is being published under the auspices of the Bavarian Academy of Sciences.

TIMOTHY B. NOONE is Ordinary Professor in the School of Philosophy, The Catholic University of America. He was educated at the Pontifical Institute of Medieval Studies and the University of Toronto, where he studied under Fr. Maurer in the 1980s. He heads the Scotus Project located at Catholic University and has coedited Scotus's *Quaestiones in libros Metaphysicorum Aristotelis* (St. Bonaventure, NY: Franciscan Institute Press, 1997) and his *Quaestiones in librum Isagoge Porphyrii* and *Quaestiones super Praedicamenta Aristotelis* (St. Bonaventure, NY: Franciscan Institute Press, 1999). He is coeditor with Jorge Gracia of *A Companion to Philosophy in the Middle Ages* (Oxford: Blackwell, 2003). With R.E. Houser, he is currently translating philosophical selections from Bonaventure's *Commentary on the Sentences* for the Franciscan Institute Press.

CALVIN NORMORE is Professor of Philosophy at the University of California, Los Angeles. He was educated at the University of Toronto, where he studied under Fr.

Maurer in the 1970s. He specializes in the history of logic, especially Scotus and Ockham. Among recent works are: "Scotus, Modality, Instants of Nature and the Contingency of the Present," in *John Duns Scotus: Metaphysics and Ethics*, ed. L. Honnefelder, R. Wood and M. Dreyer (Leiden: Brill, 1996) and "Some Aspects of Ockham's Logic," in *The Cambridge Companion to Ockham*, ed. P. V. Spade (Cambridge: Cambridge University Press, 1999).

JAMES P. REILLY, JR. is Fellow Emeritus of the Pontifical Institute of Mediaeval Studies, Toronto. He was educated at the Pontifical Institute and the University of Toronto, where he has been a colleague of Fr. Maurer for many years. He is a member of the Leonine Commission for the editing of the works of Thomas Aquinas and has edited Aquinas's *Commentary* on the *Metaphysics* of Aristotle.

JOHN M. RIST is Professor Emeritus of Classics and Philosophy at the University of Toronto, where he was a colleague of Fr. Maurer. He was educated at Cambridge University and currently resides in Cambridge, England. His series of books on ancient philosophy is now complemented by *On Innoculating Moral Philosophy Against God: The Aquinas Lecture 2000* (Milwaukee, Wis: Marquette University Press, 2001) and *Real Ethics: Reconsidering the Foundations of Morality* (Cambridge: Cambridge University Press, 2002).

MARY C. SOMMERS, formerly Director of the Honors Program at the University of St. Thomas, Houston, is now Director of its Center for Thomistic Studies. She was educated at the Pontifical Institute of Mediaeval Studies and the University of Toronto, where she studied under Fr. Maurer in the 1970s. She has edited *Questions on the Posterior Analytics* by Walter Burley (Toronto: Pontifical Institute of Mediaeval Studies Press, 2000).

RICHARD C. TAYLOR is Associate Professor and Director of the Graduate Program in Philosophy, Marquette University. He was educated at the University of Toronto, where he studied under Fr. Maurer in the 1970s. Author of numerous articles on medieval Islamic philosophy, he is the translator, with Vincent Guagliardo, OP, and Charles Hess, OP, of *St. Thomas Aquinas: Commentary on the Book of Causes* (Washington: Catholic University of America Press, 1996). He has recently completed a translation of Averroes' *Long Commentary on the "De anima"* with Th.-A. Druart. He is also coeditor with Peter Adamson of the *Cambridge Companion to Arabic Philosophy* (Cambridge: Cambridge University Press, 2005).

DAVID B. TWETTEN is Associate Professor of Philosophy at Marquette University. He was educated at the Pontifical Institute of Mediaeval Studies and the University of

Toronto, where he studied under Fr. Maurer in the 1980s. He specializes in ancient and medieval metaphysics, natural philosophy, and philosophical theology. Among recent works are: "Averroes on the Prime Mover Proved in the *Physics*," *Viator: Medieval and Renaissance Studies* 26 (1995): 107–34; "Albert the Great's Early Conflations of Philosophy and Theology on the Issue of Universal Causality," in *Medieval Masters: Essays in Memory of Msgr. E. A. Synan* (Houston: Center for Thomistic Studies, 1999), 25–62; "Come distinguere in realtà tra *esse* ed essenza in Tommaso d'Aquino: Un contributo da Aristotele," in *Tommaso d'Aquino e l'oggetto della metafisica: approfondimenti e dibattiti* (Rome, 2004).

NORMAN J. WELLS is Professor Emeritus, Boston College. He was educated at the Pontifical Institute of Mediaeval Studies and the University of Toronto, where he studied under Fr. Maurer in the 1950s. His many works focus on late medieval and early modern philosophy, especially Suarez and Descartes.

MSGR. JOHN F. WIPPEL is the Theodore Basselin Professor of Philosophy at The Catholic University of America. He was educated at The Catholic University of America and Louvain University. The latest of his many books on medieval philosophy are *Mediaeval Reactions to the Encounter between Faith and Reason: The Aquinas Lecture, 1995* (Milwaukee, Wisc.: Marquette University Press, 1995) and *The Metaphysical Thought of Thomas Aquinas: From Finite Being to Uncreated Being* (Washington, DC: The Catholic University of America Press, 2000).

Index

a fortiori, 64, 188, 272, 273, 277
a posteriori, 306, 308
a priori, 119
a seipsis, 328, 329, 341, 347, 348, 360
ab aeterno, 299, 328, 329, 330, 335, 342, 347, 348, 349, 351, 356, 357, 358, 359, 360, 361
Abelard, Peter, 240, 241, 285
ability, 24, 39, 100, 161, 202, 243, 248, 249, 250, 255, 257, 291
abstraction, 8, 9, 83, 108
    of form, 8
    by separation, 9
    of the whole, 8
accident, 8, 30, 42, 63, 64, 76, 85, 87, 94, 95, 96, 98, 99, 100, 106, 133, 135, 136, 143, 147, 155, 156, 157, 160, 162, 175, 177, 180, 183, 217, 218, 235, 246
act, 6, 9, 10, 24, 26, 28, 29, 33, 36, 41, 42, 43, 44, 62, 64, 67, 78, 80, 90, 91, 92, 97, 101, 102, 113, 119, 121, 123, 124, 134, 138, 162, 193, 194, 199, 200, 202, 204, 210, 215, 221, 225, 227, 228, 234, 241, 247, 249, 257, 285, 287, 288, 292, 293, 295, 332, 342, 367, 370
action, 26, 47, 48, 49, 63, 77, 78, 123, 161, 162, 188, 199, 227, 233, 247, 248, 365
    intentional action, 48
active, 1, 10, 46, 61, 67, 78, 196, 197, 198, 200, 201, 202, 208, 214, 228, 250, 315, 333, 340
activity, 8, 14, 15, 17, 20, 21, 22, 46, 47, 48, 156, 161, 175, 185, 188, 189, 190, 191, 192, 195, 196, 197, 198, 199, 200, 201, 202, 204, 210, 250, 257, 333, 334, 336, 346
actuality, 9, 42, 44, 45, 46, 47, 56, 57, 58, 61, 77, 87, 156, 221, 225, 328
Adam, 28, 33, 34, 62, 222, 224, 360, 374
Adams, Marilyn M., 6, 292, 296
Aeterni Patris, 364, 376, 377

affection, 248
agent, 37, 47, 58, 124, 144, 214, 216, 225, 228, 285, 291, 363
    free agent, 255, 257, 329
    natural agent, 255, 257
agnosticism, 149
Albert the Great, 154, 382
Albertinus, Francis, 327, 328, 329, 330, 345, 346, 347, 348, 349
Albertism, 4
Alexander of Abonoteichos, 17
al-Farabi, 39
al-Ghazali, 91, 94, 95, 96, 97, 100, 101, 108, 176
Al-Juzjani, 79, 83, 102
Ambrose, St., 116, 129, 177
an sit, 155, 175, 176, 177, 182
analogy, 47, 78, 87, 119, 123, 132, 134, 135, 136, 137, 138, 139, 140, 141, 142, 144, 145, 188, 200, 258
analogy of names, 132, 137, 141, 144
analytic mode, 85
Anderson, Fulton, 368, 369
angel, 28, 29, 33, 36, 61, 62, 63, 64, 89, 90, 91, 92, 93, 96, 98, 99, 101, 102, 106, 111, 130, 157, 214, 215, 216, 217, 218, 222, 225, 228, 229, 232, 245, 246, 254, 289, 290
Anselm, St., 69, 285, 296, 322
anti-mendicants, 185, 186, 187, 188, 202
apocalypticism, 184
Apostles, 13, 17, 27, 195, 252, 254
appetite, 210, 211, 215, 221
    natural, 210, 211
    rational, 210, 211
    sensible, 210
Aquinas Institute high school, 362
argument
    affirmative, 83

argument (*cont.*)
 deductive, 82, 88, 91, 93, 94, 96, 97, 100, 258,
  259, 362
 dialectical, 43, 75, 76, 80, 81, 82, 84, 85, 86, 88,
  101, 102, 104, 251
 inductive, 96, 97, 324
 intellectus essentiae, 93
 predicables, 87, 91, 98
 probable-inductive, 148
 reductio, 78, 82, 137, 241, 329
 saving the appearance, 83, 88, 90
 sufficiency, 85, 86, 87, 91, 93, 94, 96, 99
 synthetic, 94, 98, 107, 250
Arias, David, 10
Aristotelian, 3, 5, 8, 18, 40, 41, 42, 43, 48, 50, 52,
  65, 66, 76, 94, 95, 115, 118, 119, 122, 124,
  125, 130, 147, 151, 153, 154, 156, 159, 160,
  165, 166, 167, 169, 172, 173, 174, 177, 234,
  238, 240, 242, 245, 246, 285, 288, 295, 363
 radical Aristotelian, 5
Aristotelian methodology, 154, 159, 160, 165
Aristotle, 3, 5, 8, 13, 14, 21, 28, 30, 31, 34, 35, 36,
  40, 41, 42, 43, 44, 45, 46, 47, 48, 49, 50, 51,
  52, 53, 54, 55, 57, 58, 62, 63, 64, 65, 74, 76,
  77, 79, 82, 83, 85, 87, 90, 91, 96, 97, 98, 104,
  105, 106, 114, 118, 119, 120, 121, 122, 123,
  124, 125, 126, 128, 130, 131, 133, 134, 142,
  143, 144, 145, 154, 155, 156, 157, 158, 159,
  163, 166, 170, 172, 173, 174, 175, 176, 187,
  218, 219, 240, 242, 243, 244, 245, 246, 247,
  249, 250, 251, 256, 257, 284, 288, 289, 344,
  363, 364, 367, 368, 381
Arius, 186
Ark of Noah, 245
atheism, 17, 114, 149
atheist, 146, 148, 150
atomism, 120
Augustine, St., 15, 21, 24, 25, 27, 28, 30, 31, 32, 33,
  34, 35, 36, 26-28, 37, 61, 64, 69, 74, 112, 116,
  117, 118, 122, 186, 187, 200, 221, 240, 242,
  243, 251, 255, 256, 258, 330, 377, 378
Augustinian, 66, 196, 197, 239
Augustinism, 4
Augustino Nifo, 119
Aureoli, Peter, 132, 255, 258, 259, 297
Averroes (Ibn Rochd), 5, 38, 39, 40, 41, 42, 43,
  44, 45, 46, 47, 48, 49, 50, 51, 52, 53, 54, 55,
  56, 57, 58, 59, 88, 90, 121, 166, 174, 246, 251,
  253, 282, 288, 381, 382
Avicenna (Ibn Sina), 5, 10, 39, 41, 52, 55, 75, 76,
  77, 78, 79, 80, 81, 82, 83, 84, 85, 86, 87, 88,

 89, 90, 91, 92, 93, 94, 95, 96, 97, 98, 99,
  100, 101, 102, 104, 105, 106, 107, 108, 166,
  380
axiom, 23, 76, 82, 83

Báñez, Domingo, 150, 171
Barker, Mark, 10
Basil, St., 1, 118, 363, 364, 369, 370
Basilian Fathers, 362
Baudry, Léon, 371
beatitude, 111, 118, 123, 127, 138, 256, 257
 formal, 257
 human, 242
being, 7, 8, 9, 10, 14, 15, 20, 21, 22, 23, 25, 26, 28,
  29, 30, 32, 33, 37, 38, 39, 43, 44, 45, 46, 47,
  48, 49, 54, 56, 57, 58, 60, 61, 63, 64, 65, 69,
  76, 77, 78, 79, 80, 84, 85, 86, 87, 88, 91, 97,
  98, 99, 100, 103, 104, 105, 106, 107, 108,
  110, 111, 112, 117, 119, 120, 123, 124, 125, 130,
  132, 133, 134, 135, 136, 137, 138, 139, 140, 141,
  142, 144, 145, 147, 148, 149, 150, 152, 153,
  157, 160, 161, 162, 163, 164, 165, 166, 167,
  168, 170, 171, 172, 176, 179, 180, 193, 197,
  198, 199, 200, 201, 202, 204, 209, 210, 211,
  213, 215, 216, 217, 218, 219, 222, 225, 229,
  230, 233, 242, 243, 244, 246, 248, 250, 284,
  288, 289, 290, 291, 292, 295, 296, 330, 331,
  332, 333, 334, 335, 336, 337, 338, 339, 340,
  341, 342, 343, 344, 363, 364, 367, 370, 380
 al-mawjûd, 77
 being qua being, 45, 46, 110, 119, 123
 mawjûd, 78, 79, 86
Bellisle, Henry, 364
Benedict, St., 184, 192, 200, 203, 207
Bernard, St., 192, 240, 245, 368
body, 3, 5, 26, 30, 31, 41, 42, 47, 48, 52, 58, 63, 112,
  122, 123, 126, 133, 134, 135, 136, 138, 139,
  140, 142, 145, 147, 156, 187, 195, 214, 215,
  216, 217, 218, 223, 225, 228, 229, 240, 245
Boehner, Philotheus, 365, 368, 371
Boethius, 8, 25, 35, 64, 74, 79, 88, 129, 135, 144,
  153, 154, 159, 163, 166, 172, 177, 180, 186,
  213, 286, 373, 375
Boethius of Dacia, 213, 375
Bonaventure, St., 3, 4, 6, 52, 65, 89, 90, 120, 130,
  171, 238, 241, 242, 243, 250, 251, 252, 259,
  322, 368, 376, 378, 379, 380
Bonaventurianism, 4
Boniface VIII, 240
Book of Revelation, 15, 16, 156
Bradwardine, Thomas, 233, 295, 378

Brinkley, Richard, 255, 256, 258, 259
Brown, Claudia Sommers, 11

Caesar, 60, 61, 332
Cajetan (Thomas de Vio), 130, 132, 137, 138, 139, 142, 145, 150, 171, 181, 345, 359, 375
canons regular, 194
Capreolus, Johannes O.P., 132, 142, 327, 328, 329, 330, 345, 346, 347, 348, 349
Carr, Henry, 365
categories, 21, 22, 77, 78, 79, 80, 119, 188, 192
causa esse alterius, 90
causality, 46, 48, 58, 141, 152, 153, 160, 166, 167, 168, 182, 183, 329, 347, 348
    angelic, 228
    creative causality, 46, 329
    efficient causality, 46, 47, 329, 330, 343, 348
cause, 9, 16, 17, 25, 31, 32, 33, 34, 36, 41, 45, 46, 47, 48, 54, 56, 57, 60, 62, 64, 82, 83, 84, 85, 86, 87, 88, 89, 90, 91, 92, 98, 99, 100, 101, 106, 108, 111, 112, 115, 117, 119, 122, 123, 135, 143, 144, 149, 151, 153, 154, 155, 157, 158, 159, 160, 166, 167, 168, 169, 170, 174, 176, 179, 183, 187, 188, 228, 234, 247, 248, 249, 257, 286, 291, 292, 330, 340, 343, 347
    efficient, 42, 46, 100, 165, 166, 228, 248, 256, 329, 330, 338, 343, 347, 359
    of existence, 84, 85, 86, 88, 90, 91, 92, 98, 99, 100, 106
    final, 42, 46, 47, 48, 161, 176
    formal, 46, 158
    genera of, 119
    material, 176
Celsus, 25, 26, 27
certitude, 79, 86, 104, 118, 120
change, 62, 64, 76, 82, 86, 89, 147, 167, 205, 229, 285, 287, 288, 289, 290, 291, 292, 293, 295
chastity, 194, 256
choice, 19, 28, 29, 109, 111, 120, 210, 214, 222, 248, 249, 250, 291
Christian philosophy, 4, 5, 7, 13, 16, 20, 34, 35, 122, 363
Cicero, 116, 240, 247, 282, 367
Clement I, Pope, 15, 21, 22, 32, 34, 35, 36, 37, 114
cleric, 192, 199
Cluny, 185, 203
cognition, 106, 120, 157, 163, 175, 177, 182, 210, 286, 297, 298, 332, 335, 337, 338
common nature, 6, 136
compatibilism, 38, 51, 292
Comte, Auguste, 8, 9

condemnation, 213, 214, 219, 220, 221, 222, 224, 227, 229, 230, 231, 233, 234, 251, 252
consequences, 49, 82, 83, 98, 156, 157, 238, 239, 245, 285, 288, 294, 295, 330
conservation, 293
consistency, 108, 124, 285
Consitt, John, 363
contemplation, 37, 196, 198, 199, 200, 201, 202, 207, 257
contingency, 166, 249, 283, 291, 292, 293
    diachronic contingency, 249
    synchronic contingency, 249
contingent, 115, 240, 286, 290, 291, 293, 294, 330
corruptible, 134, 136, 139, 144
Coughlin, Hubert, 365, 369
counsel of poverty, 186, 200
Cousin, Victor, 2, 3, 4
Craig, William Lane, 149, 170
creation, 22, 23, 39, 46, 58, 61, 63, 67, 85, 100, 115, 122, 238, 287, 293, 329, 343
    con-creation, 64
    de Deo, 21, 175, 233, 276, 301, 305, 310, 311
    de novo, 63, 286
    ex Deo, 24
    ex nihilo, 20, 21, 22, 23, 24, 25, 29, 30, 31, 32, 33, 46, 329, 343
creative, 21, 22, 24, 33, 46, 63, 64, 100, 150, 169, 239, 259, 287, 329, 330
creator, 30, 33, 47, 68, 88, 110, 128, 130, 147, 149, 150, 161, 168, 199
creature, 19, 25, 33, 45, 60, 64, 75, 81, 82, 83, 85, 86, 87, 88, 89, 90, 91, 92, 93, 97, 99, 100, 101, 103, 106, 111, 135, 136, 137, 142, 144, 160, 161, 172, 180, 209, 210, 211, 242, 258, 289, 327, 328, 329, 330, 331, 333, 335, 336, 337, 338, 339, 340, 341, 342, 343, 344, 346, 347, 348, 351, 355, 359, 361
Crescens, 18
Cynic, 18, 247

Day, Dorothy, 365
De Hueck, Baroness Catherine, 365
De Wulf, Maurice, 3
Decretum, 187, 281
Deely, John, 10, 354
definition, 76, 77, 78, 108, 118, 143, 149, 150, 151, 153, 155, 157, 159, 160, 166, 171, 176, 182
    nominal definition, 149, 156, 157, 158, 159, 160, 161, 163, 164, 165, 166, 167, 168, 169, 171, 174, 175, 176, 177, 182, 183
    real definition, 156, 157, 158, 159, 175, 176, 182

deity, 148, 149, 150, 160, 168, 177, 179, 181, 343
demerit, 255, 256
Demiurge, 30, 31
demonstration, 40, 41, 53, 54, 55, 75, 76, 91, 97, 100, 103, 107, 116, 118, 144, 151, 157, 160, 175, 241
denomination, 333, 334, 337, 339, 340, 344, 346, 349
    extrinsic denomination, 332, 333, 334, 335, 337, 339, 340, 344, 345, 346, 351, 354, 357
    intrinsic denomination, 333, 337
Denomy, Alex J., 365
Descartes, René, 1, 7, 8, 358, 359, 360, 363, 377, 382
desire, 49, 58, 112, 113, 119, 161, 168, 176, 188, 193, 203, 210, 215, 221, 232, 365
determinism, 51, 248, 292
determinist, 250
DeWulf, Maurice, 364
Dietrich of Freiberg, 5, 375
difference, 8, 23, 63, 87, 94, 95, 96, 98, 110, 118, 133, 137, 138, 141, 143, 153, 156, 167, 175, 179, 183, 218, 245, 256, 288, 291, 294, 342
dilectio, 210, 212
Dillon, Daniel, 35, 369
Dionysius, 153, 160, 171, 172, 177, 178, 187, 192, 206, 321
divine, 6, 9, 14, 19, 23, 27, 35, 36, 45, 46, 57, 60, 61, 62, 65, 98, 110, 111, 116, 117, 118, 121, 122, 127, 130, 133, 135, 144, 147, 148, 149, 152, 153, 154, 156, 160, 161, 162, 163, 164, 165, 166, 168, 170, 172, 175, 177, 178, 179, 180, 181, 183, 186, 198, 199, 200, 202, 209, 210, 211, 216, 229, 241, 242, 255, 256, 257, 258, 286, 287, 288, 294, 328, 329, 330, 331, 335, 336, 337, 338, 339, 340, 341, 342, 343, 344, 345, 346, 350, 355, 361, 367
    essence, 98, 133, 156, 160, 161, 162, 175, 178, 256, 257, 335, 336
    illumination, 242
    intellect, 328, 335, 336, 337, 338, 339, 341, 342, 343, 344, 345, 350
    intervention, 65
    revelation, 110, 127
    science, 116
Dominic, St., 55, 191, 197, 206
Dominicus Gundissalinus, 78
Dondaine, Hyacinth, 103, 143, 175, 185
double truth, 50, 53, 110
doubt, 5, 50, 173, 204, 230, 245, 248, 291

Dufeil, Michel-Marie, 185, 187, 190, 191, 203, 205, 206
Duhem, Pierre, 238, 251
Dumont, Stephen, 249, 253, 290
Düring, Ingemar, 124
Dwyer, Wilfrid J., 365

effect, 4, 20, 32, 37, 47, 48, 54, 62, 63, 66, 85, 86, 90, 100, 111, 135, 144, 151, 152, 153, 155, 157, 158, 159, 160, 162, 165, 166, 167, 168, 174, 175, 182, 183, 195, 201, 210, 214, 228, 238, 239, 245, 247, 248, 249, 287, 291, 293, 295, 342, 355, 364
    actual effects, 247
    potential effect, 247
eminent, 168, 179
end, 1, 5, 10, 16, 17, 43, 51, 58, 63, 76, 78, 79, 80, 83, 84, 91, 103, 110, 113, 123, 145, 148, 149, 161, 163, 167, 169, 176, 200, 202, 211, 215, 231, 243, 255, 257, 259, 292, 298, 351, 360, 368, 369
    goal, 33, 53, 92, 112, 187, 255, 257
enlightenment, 38, 51
ens, 9, 72, 74, 76, 77, 78, 79, 86, 88, 104, 130, 131, 143, 161, 166, 179, 180, 182, 270, 304, 310, 323, 326, 327, 329, 330, 331, 333, 334, 335, 336, 338, 339, 340, 342, 343, 346, 348, 349, 350, 351, 352, 353, 354, 355, 356, 357, 358, 359, 361
    ens commune, 9
    ens inquantum ens, 9
    ens participatum, 330, 348
    ens possible, 342, 343, 361
    ens rationis, 327, 331, 333, 334, 335, 336, 338, 339, 346, 349, 350, 351, 352, 353, 354, 355, 356, 357, 358, 361
    ens reale, 331, 333, 336, 338, 339, 340, 342, 350, 352, 353, 355, 356, 358, 361
    entia rationis fundata, 333
Epicurean, 17, 34, 247
epistemology, 35, 55, 119, 129
Eschmann, Ignatius, 368
esse, 6, 9, 63, 66, 70, 71, 73, 74, 78, 79, 86, 88, 89, 90, 92, 101, 102, 103, 104, 105, 106, 107, 108, 127, 128, 131, 135, 136, 137, 139, 141, 144, 158, 159, 162, 166, 180, 182, 211, 215, 219, 225, 232, 233, 235, 236, 248, 252, 253, 261, 266, 267, 268, 272, 273, 274, 275, 276, 277, 278, 279, 282, 299, 300, 301, 302, 303, 304, 305, 306, 308, 309, 310, 316, 319, 322, 323, 327,

328, 329, 330, 331, 332, 333, 334, 335, 336,
337, 338, 339, 341, 342, 343, 344, 345, 346,
347, 348, 349, 350, 351, 352, 353, 354, 355,
356, 357, 358, 359, 360, 361, 370, 382
esse cognitum, 327, 331, 332, 333, 334, 335,
336, 337, 338, 339, 341, 342, 344, 345, 346,
347, 349, 350, 351, 352, 353, 354, 355, 356,
357, 358, 360
esse cognitum divinum, 331, 333, 335, 337, 341,
350, 355
esse cognitum humanum, 331, 335, 337
esse exemplatum, 332, 334
esse existentiae, 330, 348, 349
esse opinatum, 332, 334, 336, 349
esse possible, 268, 336, 337, 338, 339, 342, 348,
349, 351, 358, 360
esse secundum quid, 332, 344, 349, 357
esse visum, 332, 333, 335, 336, 351, 356
essence, 9, 10, 44, 45, 46, 56, 64, 69, 75, 76, 78,
79, 81, 82, 85, 87, 88, 89, 90, 91, 92, 93, 94,
95, 96, 97, 98, 99, 100, 101, 102, 103, 105,
106, 107, 118, 123, 124, 133, 143, 152, 155,
156, 157, 158, 159, 160, 161, 162, 169, 173,
174, 175, 176, 177, 178, 180, 186, 214, 219,
225, 256, 257, 329, 330, 331, 336, 340, 341,
343, 347, 348, 349, 351
divine essence, 98, 133, 156, 160, 161, 162, 175,
178, 256, 257, 335, 336
essentia, 9, 44, 75, 76, 78, 95, 103, 104, 106,
107, 133, 142, 143, 174, 265, 266, 267, 272,
273, 274, 275, 276, 277, 299, 308, 309, 310,
312, 313, 318, 325, 348, 349, 350, 352, 355,
356, 361, 374
eternal life, 112, 257
eternity, 64, 65, 110, 112, 120, 122, 147, 179, 238,
286, 288, 293, 294, 335
ethic, 26, 115, 120, 121, 123, 124, 364, 368
Eudes of Chateauroux, 114
Eve, 28
Ex corde ecclesiae, 8
ex seipsis, 329, 341, 344, 347, 348, 356, 359, 360
excellence, 49, 50, 51, 56, 195, 224
excommunication, 219, 220, 221, 226, 229, 230
existence, 9, 23, 33, 37, 41, 42, 43, 45, 46, 52, 64,
75, 78, 79, 80, 81, 82, 83, 84, 85, 86, 87, 88,
89, 90, 91, 92, 93, 94, 95, 96, 97, 98, 99,
100, 101, 102, 103, 105, 106, 107, 108, 114,
117, 120, 121, 130, 133, 140, 146, 147, 148,
149, 150, 151, 153, 154, 155, 156, 157, 158, 159,
160, 163, 164, 165, 166, 167, 168, 169, 170,

171, 172, 173, 174, 176, 181, 182, 183, 194, 195,
210, 219, 285, 286, 287, 289, 328, 329, 330,
331, 338, 339, 342, 347, 348, 349, 362, 366,
367
in actuality, 87
necessary, 79, 80, 83, 84, 86, 87, 91, 98, 99,
107
non-existence, 33, 84, 86, 93, 94, 287
possible, 79, 80, 83, 86
wujûd, 78, 79, 86, 104, 105
existent, 23, 32, 45, 46, 58, 63, 85, 86, 87, 98, 170,
337
existential truth, 330
Existentialism, 7, 364
extramental, 332, 333, 334, 336, 337, 338, 351

Fabro, Cornelio, 119, 129
faith, 4, 5, 7, 8, 15, 16, 19, 22, 103, 109, 110, 111,
112, 113, 114, 115, 116, 117, 118, 120, 121, 122,
123, 126, 155, 169, 186, 187, 195, 196, 220,
224, 243, 245, 246, 250, 251, 255, 256, 257,
258, 335
mystery, 114, 116, 126
Farge, James K., 11, 373, 380
fear, 13, 17, 191, 209, 220, 367
felicity, 138
Fides et ratio, 109
first intention, 332, 334
first philosophy, 116, 119, 123, 143
First Principle, 45, 114, 123, 124
Firth, Frankie, 365
Fishacre, Richard, 60, 61, 62, 63, 64, 65, 66, 67,
68, 69, 71, 259, 380
Flahiff, George B., 365
foreknowledge, 218
form, 3, 4, 5, 7, 10, 17, 21, 22, 28, 30, 31, 33, 38, 39,
42, 43, 44, 46, 52, 53, 56, 57, 60, 61, 63, 64,
68, 79, 81, 82, 87, 88, 89, 90, 92, 96, 97, 99,
101, 106, 114, 123, 132, 133, 143, 144, 161,
162, 165, 177, 178, 179, 180, 192, 209, 217,
222, 223, 232, 239, 241, 245, 249, 283, 284,
286, 295, 333
Form, 79, 374
formula, 24, 150, 151, 152, 155, 156, 167, 171, 172,
174, 176, 182
nominal formula, 155
Fraassen, Bas van, 288
Francis of Meyronnes, 5, 370, 375
Franciscan, 5, 65, 68, 89, 92, 171, 191, 196, 235,
238, 239, 240, 242, 243, 244, 245, 248, 250,

Franciscan (*cont.*)
    252, 254, 255, 259, 297, 298, 322, 344, 365,
    368, 369, 370, 376, 379, 380
free, 14, 15, 20, 23, 27, 28, 29, 30, 31, 32, 34, 41,
    44, 60, 61, 80, 90, 91, 103, 107, 110, 116, 117,
    147, 184, 196, 197, 198, 199, 200, 204, 210,
    211, 221, 247, 248, 249, 250, 255, 257, 289,
    290, 291, 293, 329. *See also* freedom
free choice, 27, 28, 60, 210, 247, 248, 249, 250,
    289
free will, 20, 27, 28, 29, 30, 31, 32, 117, 247, 250
freedom, 27, 29, 51, 61, 115, 221, 234, 238, 247,
    249, 257, 291, 292, 293
Friendship House, 365
future, 18, 27, 28, 59, 60, 64, 69, 227, 285, 286,
    287, 288, 289, 290, 295, 296

Gallagher, Jack, 10
genera, 67, 70, 71, 77, 79, 80, 119, 139, 218, 262,
    308, 320
generality, 91, 283
generans, 63, 72, 315
genus, 44, 45, 67, 77, 80, 81, 87, 94, 95, 98, 99,
    133, 134, 138, 139, 140, 141, 143, 144, 145,
    153, 156, 157, 160, 162, 166, 201, 217, 219,
    324
Gerardus de Calcar, 255, 257, 258
Giles of Rome, 221, 234, 328, 346
Gilson, Étienne, 2, 3, 4, 5, 6, 7, 11, 65, 75, 103, 119,
    166, 178, 182, 363, 364, 365, 366, 367, 369,
    370, 373, 374, 375, 376, 377, 378
God, 152, 161, 164, 171, 174
    Deus, 24, 67, 70, 71, 72, 73, 152, 161, 162, 171,
        177, 179, 180, 181, 182, 211, 232, 236, 261,
        270, 272, 273, 274, 280, 281, 299, 301, 310,
        313, 314, 318, 319, 320, 322, 324, 330, 340,
        348, 349, 356, 359, 360, 361
    eminence of, 152, 153, 160, 166, 167, 168, 182,
        183
    First Cause, 44
    First Principle, 45, 114, 123, 124
    nature of, 20, 22, 24, 25, 39, 40, 41, 154, 169
    unmoved mover, 41, 42, 44, 153, 166
Godfrey of Fontaines, 213, 214, 215, 216, 217, 218,
    219, 220, 221, 222, 223, 224, 225, 226, 227,
    228, 229, 230, 231, 232, 233, 234, 235, 236,
    237, 239, 251, 347
good, 17, 25, 28, 29, 30, 31, 32, 33, 36, 37, 62, 68,
    77, 91, 101, 113, 115, 119, 120, 122, 133, 145,
    147, 156, 161, 165, 166, 172, 176, 178, 179,
    189, 190, 193, 196, 198, 199, 200, 201, 204,
    210, 211, 215, 220, 226, 227, 242, 243, 248,
    249, 256, 257, 283, 298, 366
    highest, 166
Gospel of John, 14
governance, 209, 210, 211
    divine, 209, 210, 211
    human, 209
    limited, 209
grace, 36, 96, 111, 112, 116, 117, 118, 127, 221
Gregory of Nyssa, 27, 118
Gregory of Rimini, 255, 258, 259
Gregory the Great, 129, 187, 199
Grosseteste, Robert, 63, 67, 114, 120, 154, 157,
    158, 159, 173, 175, 176, 177, 289

Hanrahan, Barbara, 10
happiness, 35, 39, 48, 49, 50, 119, 122, 123, 131,
    132, 176, 257, 365
Harclay, Henry, 5
Harnack, 13, 14
Hauréau, Barthélémy, 2, 4
Heidegger, Martin, 6, 364, 368
Heloise, 2
Henry of Ghent, 214, 215, 232, 233, 234, 235, 239,
    293, 327, 328, 329, 330, 343, 345, 374
Heraclitus, 240
Hermas, 22
Hilary, St., 258
Hintikka, Jaakko, 173, 284, 296
Hissette, Roland, 213, 230, 231
Holy Spirit, 238, 256
Holy Trinity, 27, 118, 178, 181, 205, 256
Horst, Ulrich, 185, 203
Hugh of St. Victor, 243, 258
Humbert of Romans, 66, 197, 207
Hume, David, 3, 241
Husserl, Edmund, 364, 368
hypothesis, 81, 85, 86, 87, 88, 90, 91, 93, 98, 99,
    100, 101, 105, 106, 108, 126, 358

Ibn Gabirol, 89
imagination, 83, 109
immaterial, 33, 42, 43, 44, 45, 46, 57, 90, 91, 101,
    114, 120, 121, 123, 157, 159, 170, 222, 234
    immaterial actuality, 42
    immaterial entity, 42, 43, 45
inclination, 111, 112, 113, 124, 210
incorruptible, 43, 134, 136, 139, 144, 174
indetermination, 248

individual, 6, 8, 15, 42, 43, 49, 52, 78, 80, 81, 89,
    106, 107, 115, 120, 124, 125, 133, 135, 143,
    144, 163, 164, 177, 180, 200, 220, 223, 245,
    246, 321, 342, 361
infinite, 25, 27, 42, 45, 67, 77, 86, 91, 99, 100, 101,
    110, 148, 150, 161, 162, 168, 286
iniquitas, 33
intellect, 44, 54, 56, 57, 76, 95, 111, 118, 123, 134,
    135, 145, 157, 161, 214, 215, 216, 220, 221,
    223, 224, 225, 228, 232, 234, 242, 248, 250,
    255, 257, 331, 332, 334, 336, 337, 338, 341,
    342, 344, 351, 359
  agent, 124
  immaterial, 42, 44, 45, 57
  passive, 223
  separate, 42, 43, 44
intellectual, 2, 15, 17, 19, 39, 42, 43, 44, 45, 46, 49,
    51, 81, 83, 90, 92, 120, 143, 214, 239, 243,
    245, 250, 251, 255, 258, 297, 298, 332, 342,
    351, 362, 367, 371
  intellectual activity, 46
  intellectual entities, 44, 45
  intellectual imagination, 258
intelligence, 44, 80, 82, 89, 91, 92, 96, 100, 105,
    214, 218, 223, 225, 228, 243, 330
intention, 45, 47, 48, 52, 108, 121, 134, 135, 141,
    142, 226, 256, 334, 357
intramental, 330, 331, 332, 333, 334, 335, 336,
    337, 338, 339, 340, 341, 344, 346, 351, 358,
    361
intuitive, 270, 275, 283, 297, 298, 299, 302, 304,
    310, 311, 312, 314, 318, 319, 320, 322
Irenaeus, St., 18, 20, 21

Jaffa, Harry V., 124, 131
James of Venice, 120
Jaspers, Karl, 364
Jerome, St., 115, 116, 117, 187, 199, 200
John of Damascus, 152, 161, 171, 172, 178, 180
John of Jandun, 5, 374
John of Ripa, 255
John Paul II, Pope, 8, 109, 126
Johnson, Herbert, 172, 364, 375
Jovinian, 186
joy, 112, 113
judgment, 9, 16, 76, 78, 97, 191, 219, 221, 222,
    243, 260, 342
justice, 25, 26, 28, 189, 190, 209, 256
Justin Martyr, St., 15, 16, 17, 18, 19, 20, 21, 22, 23,
    24, 25, 26, 28, 29, 32, 35, 114

Kant, Immanuel, 8, 9, 343
Kennedy, T. Vernon, 365
Kilwardby, Robert, 197
knowledge, 8, 13, 18, 19, 22, 29, 39, 41, 42, 43, 45,
    46, 47, 48, 50, 53, 54, 56, 57, 60, 77, 89, 96,
    97, 110, 111, 113, 115, 116, 117, 119, 120, 123,
    124, 126, 130, 133, 143, 148, 154, 155, 156,
    157, 158, 159, 174, 175, 176, 177, 178, 187, 195,
    199, 218, 219, 220, 221, 224, 225, 233, 250,
    257, 287, 327, 330, 332, 335, 336, 344, 347,
    362
  eternal, 257, 330
  nominal, 218
  particular, 45
  perfect, 257
  potential, 45
  universal knowledge, 89
Kretzmann, Norman, 147, 148, 149, 150, 170,
    292, 296
Kripke, Saul, 284
Kügelgen, Anke von, 38, 51

Ladner, Gerhart, 366
Lambertus de Marchia, 255, 257, 259
Langston, Douglas, 292
Latin Averroist, 5
Le thomisme, 4, 234, 374
Leo XIII, Pope, 3
Lewis, D. K., 287, 296
light, 26, 43, 44, 51, 60, 62, 63, 64, 68, 83, 110,
    117, 118, 121, 124, 151, 154, 156, 158, 159, 160,
    166, 168, 216, 217, 226, 244, 246, 255, 257,
    336, 340, 343, 367
Locke, John, 369
logic, 39, 79, 87, 94, 95, 119, 132, 133, 134, 135, 142,
    143, 150, 151, 153, 154, 161, 166, 335, 364, 381
  logical *intentions,* 132, 134
  logical notions, 132, 133, 135, 139, 144
  logical potency, 340, 343
Lombard, Peter, 60, 129, 142, 154, 160, 187, 254,
    255, 256, 258, 259, 298
Longpré, Ephrem, 365, 370
Louvain, University of, 2, 3, 11, 55, 68, 74, 103,
    104, 131, 170, 174, 230, 231, 234, 364, 367,
    374, 377, 378, 379, 382
love, 17, 111, 113, 118, 148, 169, 196, 200, 201, 202,
    209, 210, 211, 257, 290, 371
Lucinus, 200
Luther, Martin, 13
Lynch, Lawrence, 364, 370

magic, 62
Maimonides, 161, 163, 178, 376
Malivus of Saint-Omer, 255, 258
Manichaean, 35
Mansion, Auguste, 174, 364
manual labor, 184, 186, 188, 190, 198, 199, 200, 201, 204, 207
Maqâsid al-falâsafa, 94
Marcel, Gabriel, 364, 370, 371
Maritain, Jacques, 8, 363, 364, 365, 367
Marrou, Henry, 370
Martin, Christopher, 10, 173, 179, 181, 183, 295
Mastrius, Bartholemew O.F.M., 327, 328, 329, 330, 331, 332, 333, 334, 335, 336, 337, 338, 339, 340, 341, 342, 343, 344, 345, 346, 347, 348, 349, 350, 351, 352, 353, 354, 355, 356, 357, 358, 359, 360, 361
material, 8, 9, 16, 19, 21, 23, 26, 30, 31, 32, 33, 52, 82, 88, 89, 99, 112, 114, 121, 130, 133, 142, 155, 162, 166, 174, 176, 177, 222, 223, 232, 246, 332, 335, 336, 337, 366
matter, 2, 4, 8, 9, 18, 19, 21, 22, 23, 24, 27, 30, 31, 32, 33, 34, 36, 41, 42, 43, 44, 45, 47, 48, 52, 56, 57, 58, 60, 61, 62, 63, 64, 68, 81, 82, 87, 88, 89, 90, 91, 92, 99, 100, 101, 102, 106, 110, 114, 115, 120, 121, 130, 132, 133, 138, 139, 141, 144, 145, 170, 172, 192, 201, 217, 218, 221, 222, 223, 224, 225, 232, 240, 241, 244, 245, 246, 295, 329, 342, 344
  pure matter, 60, 67
Matthew of Aquasparta, 239, 240, 250, 251
Maurer, Armand A., 2, 3, 4, 5, 6, 7, 8, 9, 10, 11, 12, 13, 97, 103, 104, 105, 107, 145, 181, 295, 296, 298, 347, 362, 371, 373, 375, 377, 379, 380, 381, 382
Mayronis, Francis, 297, 298, 321, 322, 324
McGahey, Joseph, 364
McInerny, Daniel, 10
McInerny, Ralph, 132, 135, 137, 138, 139, 140, 141, 142, 144, 145, 171, 176, 178
McIntyre, Viator, 364
McLaughlin, Terence P., 365
mendicant, 185, 187, 194, 196, 200, 201, 202
Mercier, Desire, 3, 364
mercy, 194, 195, 196, 198, 202, 205, 248, 249
merit, 3, 116, 138, 150, 186, 256
metaphysics, 7, 8, 9, 10, 13, 20, 27, 42, 55, 57, 76, 77, 78, 79, 80, 81, 82, 83, 84, 87, 89, 101, 102, 103, 120, 121, 123, 124, 130, 132, 133, 134, 135, 142, 143, 147, 148, 158, 159, 218, 335, 353, 363, 364, 367, 368, 369, 382

Michotte, Albert, 364
Middle Platonism, 15, 16, 32
miracle, 61, 62, 66, 111, 112, 114, 365
mobile, 64, 218, 269
modal, 78, 283, 284, 285, 289, 291, 295, 296
monism, 120
monk, 184, 186, 191, 192, 193, 194, 197, 199, 203, 204, 205, 207
monotheist, 147, 149, 150, 163, 164
Montagne, H. A., 119
moral, 123, 187, 220, 224
motion, 9, 41, 42, 47, 63, 64, 102, 158, 160, 167, 168, 214, 215, 219, 228, 237, 288, 292
movement, 2, 9, 17, 38, 41, 52, 120, 122
mover, 47, 149, 153, 157, 160, 165, 166, 174, 215
Muckle, Joseph, 365, 366
Mutakallimun, 39

name, 2, 3, 4, 32, 63, 80, 94, 132, 133, 135, 136, 137, 138, 139, 140, 142, 143, 144, 148, 150, 152, 153, 154, 156, 160, 161, 162, 163, 164, 165, 166, 171, 172, 177, 178, 179, 180, 181, 192, 195, 241, 246, 260, 337, 350, 367, 368
  adjectival names, 161
natural law, 110, 111, 117, 210, 367
natural philosophy, 8, 9, 65, 76, 382
nature, 9, 13, 14, 20, 22, 23, 24, 25, 26, 27, 28, 29, 30, 32, 34, 39, 40, 41, 42, 43, 44, 45, 46, 47, 49, 52, 53, 54, 55, 57, 61, 62, 63, 64, 66, 77, 79, 81, 82, 83, 85, 86, 89, 90, 99, 101, 102, 104, 106, 108, 109, 110, 111, 112, 113, 114, 116, 117, 118, 119, 120, 121, 122, 123, 124, 125, 126, 133, 136, 141, 142, 147, 151, 152, 154, 157, 160, 161, 162, 163, 165, 166, 168, 169, 170, 172, 177, 178, 179, 180, 183, 184, 185, 189, 191, 198, 201, 211, 214, 217, 218, 221, 222, 223, 224, 229, 232, 234, 244, 248, 256, 259, 285, 290, 340, 357
necessary, 34, 37, 42, 45, 47, 48, 51, 78, 79, 80, 81, 82, 86, 87, 105, 147, 166, 210, 283, 284, 287, 288, 290, 292, 293, 294, 295
  al-darûrî, 77
  necesse, 77, 105, 107, 265, 275, 301
  suppositionally necessary, 294
Neo-Platonism, 114
Nestorius, 186
New Testament, 17, 24, 113
Noël, Léon, 364
Nominalism, 368
non-prescriptive, 150, 151, 168, 169, 171
Noone, Timothy B., 68, 183, 238, 290, 380

notion, 3, 4, 6, 7, 18, 20, 22, 26, 27, 29, 30, 32, 37, 40, 41, 47, 48, 52, 61, 77, 78, 79, 80, 85, 133, 134, 136, 139, 141, 143, 144, 145, 151, 152, 171, 173, 175, 194, 197, 202, 223, 249, 283, 285, 287, 289, 295, 296, 343

obedience, 188, 194, 220, 256
object, 8, 35, 45, 46, 57, 64, 116, 117, 119, 127, 130, 161, 163, 174, 204, 210, 211, 248, 250, 256, 257, 332, 333, 334, 335, 336, 339, 342, 344, 351
    formal object, 256
    intelligible, 43, 56
    sensible, 43
Ockhamism, 4, 371, 374
Olivi, Peter John, 239, 242, 243, 244, 245, 246, 247, 248, 249, 250, 251, 252, 253
omnipotence, 6, 15, 20, 24, 25, 26, 27, 28, 29, 30, 31, 32, 34, 35, 36, 60, 111, 147, 161, 285, 340, 341
omniscience, 147, 330
ontological, 8, 43, 45, 80, 82, 89, 90, 91, 179
ontology, 81, 176
operation, 161, 171, 201, 210, 214, 215, 216, 225, 227, 228, 229
opinion, 48, 102, 115, 116, 122, 125, 126, 145, 165, 222, 224, 225, 228, 240, 241, 242, 243, 245, 247, 250, 258, 259, 286, 297, 328, 329, 330, 363
Order of Preachers, 190, 191, 196, 197, 198, 202, 205
Origen, 25, 26, 27, 30, 32, 36, 37, 245
Osborne, Thomas, 10
Owens, Joseph, 103, 106, 119, 124, 130, 131, 173, 174

Paris, University of, 8, 36, 51, 52, 53, 59, 65, 69, 103, 104, 108, 110, 114, 120, 122, 128, 129, 130, 131, 170, 174, 178, 179, 181, 182, 184, 198, 203, 213, 219, 221, 223, 224, 226, 227, 228, 230, 231, 233, 234, 238, 239, 240, 242, 251, 252, 254, 255, 259, 345, 349, 353, 359, 366, 367, 369, 371, 377, 378, 380
Parmenides, 21
passion, 3, 77, 78, 104, 221, 225
passive, 60, 61, 78, 214, 223, 228, 250
past, 10, 36, 60, 61, 64, 65, 69, 198, 285, 286, 287, 288, 289, 290, 291, 292, 293, 294, 295
Paul, St., 29, 30, 115, 116, 117
peace, 199, 209, 227
Pecham, John, 197, 238, 240, 321

Pegis, Anton, 170, 172, 363, 368, 376
Pelagianism, 186, 378
perfection, 47, 48, 49, 58, 111, 114, 136, 147, 161, 162, 166, 178, 179, 181, 186, 189, 196, 202, 203, 210, 211, 214, 220, 222, 223, 224, 227, 228, 256, 257
perseverance, 257
Peter, Apostle, 254
Peter de Trabibus, 242
Peter of Candia, 254, 255, 256, 257, 258, 259, 260
Phelan, Monsignor Gerald, 363, 364, 365, 367, 368, 369, 375
Phenomenology, 249, 364, 368
Philo, 24, 28, 36, 37
physics, 14, 125, 133, 142, 218, 362, 363
Piché, David, 213, 223, 230, 231, 232, 233, 235, 236
pity, 249
place, 10, 14, 28, 29, 37, 42, 45, 58, 62, 75, 99, 109, 111, 119, 120, 126, 128, 135, 148, 151, 152, 153, 155, 157, 160, 164, 166, 170, 175, 182, 183, 187, 196, 198, 199, 201, 202, 215, 216, 220, 225, 226, 229, 231, 232, 248, 286, 331, 351
Plato, 15, 16, 19, 21, 22, 23, 24, 26, 27, 29, 30, 31, 34, 35, 36, 37, 50, 51, 55, 114, 119, 120, 121, 122, 124, 130, 131, 142, 170, 173, 264, 265, 363, 368
Plotinus, 27, 28, 29, 30, 32, 33, 34, 36, 162, 368
Plutarch, 30
Pontifical Institute of Mediaeval Studies, 1, 11, 12, 104, 108, 181, 206, 363, 364, 366, 371, 373, 374, 375, 376, 377, 379, 380, 381, 382
Porphyrian tree, 77
position, 2, 4, 21, 23, 25, 29, 42, 44, 50, 53, 63, 69, 110, 111, 115, 118, 120, 121, 132, 137, 143, 165, 178, 185, 186, 187, 191, 193, 197, 202, 206, 218, 219, 221, 223, 224, 225, 226, 227, 237, 241, 242, 245, 246, 248, 255, 256, 257, 258, 259, 327, 328, 329, 330, 331, 335, 336, 337, 339, 341, 343, 347, 348, 358, 359, 363
possibility, 14, 19, 21, 23, 26, 28, 29, 31, 32, 33, 40, 61, 64, 80, 81, 91, 105, 107, 129, 142, 169, 173, 216, 218, 219, 229, 232, 284, 285, 293, 294, 295, 328, 330, 335, 339, 340, 341, 342, 343, 344, 358, 359
potency, 9, 41, 44, 46, 61, 62, 65, 78, 80, 90, 91, 92, 99, 101, 102, 106, 107, 111, 112, 119, 121, 138, 228, 234, 247, 249, 285, 288, 295, 340, 342, 343, 359
    active potency, 61, 67
    passive potency, 61

potential, 29, 92, 211, 247, 343

poverty, 185, 186, 190, 194, 200, 201, 203, 256, 365, 371

power, 19, 24, 25, 26, 27, 29, 37, 42, 60, 61, 62, 65, 67, 89, 112, 161, 162, 178, 186, 188, 189, 191, 214, 215, 216, 223, 228, 229, 247, 249, 250, 285, 289, 290, 291, 294, 295, 362

præambula, 117, 129

praecognitio, 218

predicate, 46, 48, 85, 159, 173, 340, 341
  divine predicates, 161

predication, 134, 143, 174, 181, 294, 343

prescriptive, 150, 151, 167, 169, 183

presence, 17, 55, 86, 87, 111, 125, 165, 184, 191, 210, 216, 231, 232, 250, 334, 342, 343, 346, 361, 367

present, 6, 15, 20, 21, 22, 27, 28, 34, 39, 40, 44, 47, 57, 60, 64, 69, 78, 95, 101, 104, 109, 115, 118, 121, 123, 125, 134, 137, 142, 145, 154, 166, 167, 172, 179, 192, 210, 213, 214, 215, 216, 217, 221, 228, 229, 255, 259, 260, 286, 287, 288, 289, 290, 291, 292, 295, 297

pride, 32, 33, 202, 244, 248

primary, 7, 10, 30, 32, 54, 77, 78, 81, 102, 148, 163, 164, 165, 175, 181, 182, 191, 193, 332, 342, 346, 363, 365, 371

principle, 50, 51, 57, 62, 64, 65, 75, 76, 77, 81, 82, 83, 85, 86, 87, 88, 89, 98, 99, 101, 103, 105, 113, 118, 119, 121, 144, 151, 152, 153, 158, 161, 162, 163, 164, 165, 171, 172, 173, 175, 176, 179, 180, 214, 216, 217, 227, 234, 247, 290, 291, 366

Priscian, 163

privative, 340, 342

Proclus, 5, 36

proof, 4, 40, 41, 90, 93, 95, 96, 97, 115, 121, 122, 132, 146, 147, 148, 149, 150, 151, 154, 155, 157, 158, 159, 160, 163, 164, 165, 166, 167, 168, 169, 170, 171, 172, 174, 176, 182
  existential proof, 157, 158, 159, 165, 167, 176, 177
  five ways, 146, 147, 148, 149, 150, 151, 153, 154, 156, 165, 166, 167, 168, 170, 171, 172, 181, 182, 183

property, 37, 80, 87, 98, 99, 100, 150, 152, 164, 169, 175, 184, 194, 198

proposition, 15, 30, 49, 52, 53, 61, 77, 89, 147, 175, 215, 219, 221, 222, 232, 259, 293, 341

providence, 22, 28, 35, 47, 48, 49, 111, 116, 117, 121, 152, 171, 182
  particular, 45
  universal, 45

psychology, 38, 42, 43, 247, 249, 364

Punch, John O.F.M., 328, 341, 344, 345, 347, 348, 359, 360

purpose, 4, 121, 123, 132, 137, 190, 194, 195, 196, 204, 213, 224, 241, 297, 338

quaestio, 60, 63, 68, 218, 252, 260, 261, 262, 280, 308, 322, 324

quality, 10, 16, 111, 140, 141, 145, 193, 210, 235

quantity, 8, 9, 200, 216, 217, 218, 232, 235

quasi-species, 77

question, 15, 16, 21, 22, 24, 27, 28, 29, 30, 31, 32, 33, 36, 40, 60, 61, 62, 63, 65, 68, 85, 93, 116, 117, 118, 123, 124, 125, 134, 137, 140, 143, 144, 145, 147, 148, 150, 151, 154, 155, 156, 159, 161, 165, 167, 168, 172, 173, 174, 175, 177, 178, 179, 182, 191, 194, 196, 197, 202, 205, 214, 215, 216, 218, 219, 220, 221, 222, 223, 224, 226, 227, 228, 229, 233, 235, 237, 239, 240, 242, 245, 248, 250, 254, 255, 258, 259, 260, 285, 288, 289, 297, 328, 331, 333, 334, 340, 343, 361

quid sit, 155, 159, 175, 182, 212

quiddity, 44, 77, 78, 79, 80, 81, 82, 84, 85, 86, 87, 88, 91, 92, 93, 94, 95, 97, 98, 99, 101, 102, 105

quod quid erat esse, 79

Rahner, Karl, 126

Ratzinger, Joseph, 109

realism, 89, 119, 155

reality, 4, 8, 18, 20, 39, 41, 47, 50, 52, 53, 64, 91, 93, 96, 97, 110, 119, 120, 124, 125, 126, 127, 129, 130, 133, 139, 141, 145, 153, 158, 159, 163, 169, 173, 180, 217, 254, 255, 256, 340, 342, 343, 358, 359

realizability, 285

reason, 2, 4, 5, 7, 8, 28, 34, 39, 52, 53, 61, 62, 66, 67, 70, 72, 73, 75, 78, 81, 85, 88, 89, 91, 92, 93, 97, 98, 99, 100, 103, 107, 109, 110, 111, 112, 113, 114, 115, 116, 117, 118, 120, 123, 127, 129, 134, 137, 138, 141, 145, 146, 147, 152, 157, 161, 162, 167, 169, 170, 172, 176, 179, 182, 210, 212, 214, 219, 221, 222, 224, 225, 229, 232, 234, 236, 240, 242, 245, 246, 247, 248, 250, 258, 260, 262, 267, 268, 270, 272,

273, 275, 276, 277, 278, 279, 280, 286, 303, 309, 310, 311, 312, 313, 333, 334, 335, 337, 338, 339, 340, 341, 344, 351, 358, 359, 360, 362, 368

ratio causalis, 62

Reid, Thomas, 241

Relation, 45, 46, 47, 48, 49, 57, 58, 86, 96, 97, 102, 106, 109, 132, 135, 138, 143, 153, 161, 162, 163, 168, 172, 176, 178, 182, 186, 188, 256, 284, 285, 286, 287, 288, 289, 295, 333, 338

Religion, 2, 7, 8, 14, 17, 20, 38, 39, 40, 48, 49, 50, 51, 52, 53, 112, 147, 163, 169, 185, 196, 202, 244, 257

religious, 184

religious life, 184, 185, 187, 189, 190, 191, 192, 193, 194, 196, 197, 198, 200, 201, 202, 204

repugnance, 270, 285, 335, 338, 340, 341, 342, 359

non-repugnance, 331, 335, 338, 339, 340, 341, 343

responsibility, 19, 37, 133, 187, 249

responsible, 19, 20, 25, 28, 29, 31, 33, 47, 188

Richard of Mediavilla, 242

Rochester, University of, 363

Roland of Cremona, 120

Roman Catholic Church, 3, 13, 116, 117, 118, 185, 188, 189, 191, 192, 193, 194, 198, 201, 204, 220, 245, 258, 370, 371

Ross, Sir David, 36, 58, 124, 377

Rowe, William, 149, 169, 170

Rufinus, 25

Rufus, Richard, 60, 61, 62, 63, 64, 65, 68, 69, 71

Sabellius, 186

Sacred doctrine, 110

Saint, 4, 16, 61, 62, 128, 130, 131, 170, 172, 174, 188, 197, 199, 203, 243

Saint Jacques, convent of, 102

salvation, 110, 127, 190, 199, 220, 240

Sartre, Jean-Paul, 364

scholastic, 3, 4, 7, 14, 38, 156, 188, 193, 364

Scholastic Synthesis, 3, 4

scholastic teaching, 193

scholasticism, 2, 3, 4, 13

science, 7, 8, 9, 41, 42, 43, 44, 55, 65, 75, 76, 77, 97, 109, 110, 114, 115, 116, 117, 119, 123, 126, 127, 128, 129, 132, 133, 134, 135, 142, 143, 147, 149, 155, 159, 172, 238, 251, 363, 366

Scot, Michael, 120

Scotism, 4, 6, 327, 328, 337, 344, 347, 370, 374

Scotus, Duns, 132, 233, 249, 250, 251, 253, 255, 285, 286, 287, 288, 289, 290, 291, 292, 295, 296, 297, 320, 321, 322, 327, 328, 329, 330, 336, 338, 340, 341, 342, 345, 346, 347, 348, 349, 350, 351, 353, 355, 356, 357, 359, 360, 361, 363, 368, 370, 375, 376, 380, 381

scripture, 38, 39, 187, 198, 199, 367

secundum esse, 73, 136, 137, 138, 139, 140, 353

secundum intentionem, 121, 125, 136, 138

secundum intentiones logicales, 132

secundum rationem, 128, 136, 214, 356

secundum rem, 290

self-determination, 211

semantic relationship, 284

seminal nature, 60, 61, 62, 66, 67, 70, 72

semiotic, 251

shame, 248

Shook, Lawrence, 369, 370, 374

Siger of Brabant, 5, 11, 213, 221, 234, 374, 375, 376, 377

simultaneity, 64, 69, 219, 286, 288, 289

singular, 6, 22, 80, 163, 180, 290, 291

Smith, Ben, 10

Socrates, 16, 19, 35, 89, 200, 247, 290, 368

Sommers, Mary C., 10, 184, 207, 381

Sorbonne, 3, 109, 213, 370

soul, 8, 18, 30, 31, 32, 33, 37, 42, 43, 44, 52, 61, 63, 76, 77, 78, 89, 111, 112, 114, 120, 123, 124, 134, 145, 156, 163, 168, 175, 195, 199, 221, 222, 223, 224, 234, 235, 250

species, 43, 61, 72, 77, 79, 80, 87, 91, 98, 99, 104, 106, 108, 130, 133, 134, 143, 144, 155, 160, 163, 180, 196, 210, 217, 218, 222, 223, 224, 225, 232, 245, 246, 253, 255, 257, 258, 261, 273, 275, 276, 301, 302, 303, 304, 305, 308, 309, 310, 311, 314, 315, 316, 317

spiritual militia, 195

Stagirite, 54, 119, 120, 121, 122, 123, 124, 246. See also Aristotle

Stephen of Bourret, 227

Suárez, Francisco, 327, 328, 345, 346, 348, 349, 351, 353, 354, 355, 359

subject, 2, 9, 16, 42, 56, 76, 85, 86, 94, 95, 102, 110, 115, 123, 125, 130, 133, 134, 143, 157, 161, 163, 169, 170, 172, 174, 178, 179, 185, 190, 192, 209, 228, 243, 244, 290, 293, 294, 329, 333, 336, 337, 339, 340, 341, 363, 365, 367, 368, 369

substance, 8, 21, 35, 37, 42, 44, 56, 63, 64, 69, 76, 81, 82, 85, 87, 88, 89, 90, 91, 118, 120, 133,

substance (*cont.*)
134, 135, 136, 139, 145, 152, 161, 162, 164, 178, 180, 181, 214, 216, 217, 218, 219, 222, 223, 225, 227, 229, 232, 235, 245, 257
  composite substance, 88, 89
  material, 82, 88, 133, 222, 232
substitution, 284
substratum, 42
succession, 64
sufficient, 84, 107, 265, 267, 268, 279, 280, 306
Sullivan, Basil, 364, 369
Swinburne, Richard, 147, 148, 169, 170
syllogism, 41, 53, 54, 91, 93, 94, 96, 97, 108, 146, 153, 155, 165, 224

Tatian, 20, 23, 114
Telfer, W., 28, 36
temperance, 113
Tempier, Stephen (Bishop of Paris), 213, 214, 220, 221, 224, 232, 233, 234, 239
Ten Commandments, 110, 238
Tertullian, 31, 35, 114
theism, 146, 147, 148, 149, 150, 169
  classical theism, 147, 148
  non-theism, 146
Themistius, 55, 57, 154, 157, 158, 172, 173, 176
theology, 3, 4, 5, 7, 8, 16, 109, 110, 112, 113, 114, 115, 116, 117, 118, 119, 123, 126, 127, 129, 147, 153, 154, 169, 172, 174, 184, 219, 221, 226, 230, 239, 242, 243, 244, 245, 246, 247, 250, 251, 258, 259, 290, 366, 369, 379, 382
Theophilus of Antioch, 23, 32, 35
thing, 6, 33, 52, 56, 58, 77, 78, 80, 81, 84, 85, 86, 88, 89, 92, 94, 96, 98, 99, 100, 102, 104, 106, 108, 111, 113, 133, 134, 135, 138, 139, 140, 141, 145, 150, 151, 154, 155, 156, 157, 158, 159, 160, 161, 162, 163, 164, 165, 166, 167, 168, 172, 173, 175, 176, 177, 190, 193, 200, 201, 217, 218, 228, 234, 239, 242, 249, 285, 293, 331, 332, 334, 336, 337, 340, 342
  al-shay', 77
  res, 6, 17, 42, 46, 48, 54, 66, 70, 71, 77, 78, 89, 90, 98, 108, 134, 135, 155, 158, 159, 162, 178, 179, 182, 200, 212, 240, 266, 277, 281, 299, 302, 304, 312, 313, 314, 318, 319, 321, 333, 334, 336, 337, 338, 339, 344, 345, 346, 348, 349, 350, 351, 352, 354, 356, 357, 358, 359, 361
  singular, 6, 345
Thomas Aquinas, St., 2, 3, 4, 5, 6, 7, 8, 9, 10, 11, 12, 65, 75, 76, 77, 78, 79, 81, 82, 84, 86, 88, 89, 90, 91, 92, 93, 94, 95, 96, 97, 98, 99,

100, 101, 102, 103, 104, 105, 106, 107, 108, 109, 110, 111, 112, 113, 114, 115, 116, 117, 118, 119, 120, 121, 122, 123, 124, 125, 126, 127, 128, 129, 130, 131, 132, 133, 134, 135, 137, 138, 139, 140, 141, 142, 143, 144, 145, 146, 147, 148, 149, 150, 151, 152, 153, 154, 155, 156, 157, 158, 159, 160, 161, 162, 163, 164, 165, 166, 167, 168, 169, 170, 171, 172, 173, 174, 175, 176, 177, 178, 179, 180, 181, 182, 183, 184, 185, 186, 187, 188, 189, 190, 191, 192, 193, 194, 195, 196, 197, 198, 199, 200, 201, 202, 203, 205, 207, 208, 209, 210, 211, 213, 219, 221, 226, 227, 229, 230, 231, 233, 234, 238, 239, 241, 242, 245, 246, 250, 255, 285, 286, 287, 295, 349, 362, 363, 364, 365, 367, 368, 369, 373, 374, 375, 376, 377, 378, 379, 380, 381, 382
Thomism, 4, 6, 7, 119, 131, 365, 367, 368, 370, 374, 376, 378
Thomist, 3, 6, 7, 103, 119, 142, 149, 150, 155, 170, 173, 328, 375, 377, 378
time, 6, 10, 13, 16, 21, 24, 25, 32, 34, 53, 56, 60, 61, 62, 63, 64, 65, 69, 76, 80, 101, 113, 120, 126, 127, 141, 150, 154, 156, 164, 167, 178, 186, 188, 192, 195, 196, 197, 200, 201, 203, 205, 213, 215, 220, 221, 227, 230, 234, 239, 242, 245, 247, 248, 249, 259, 284, 285, 286, 287, 288, 289, 290, 291, 292, 293, 295, 327, 329, 331, 335, 341, 346, 362, 363, 364, 366, 367, 368, 369
Tolomeo of Lucca, 75, 103
Toronto, University of, 1, 35, 295, 363, 364, 365, 371, 379, 380, 381, 382
  St. Michael's College, 1, 363, 365, 371
Torrell, Jean-Pierre O.P., 103, 104, 172, 185, 197, 203, 207
truth, 1, 2, 4, 6, 9, 14, 15, 16, 18, 19, 23, 27, 28, 30, 39, 40, 41, 43, 45, 46, 47, 49, 50, 51, 52, 53, 54, 55, 57, 61, 62, 64, 70, 71, 75, 77, 83, 86, 90, 94, 96, 98, 99, 100, 103, 106, 110, 112, 113, 114, 115, 116, 117, 118, 120, 121, 124, 125, 126, 134, 135, 136, 137, 138, 139, 141, 142, 143, 145, 157, 179, 186, 199, 200, 214, 215, 217, 219, 220, 221, 222, 224, 225, 226, 227, 228, 234, 240, 241, 242, 245, 246, 248, 250, 257, 258, 260, 262, 263, 264, 265, 267, 268, 269, 276, 283, 284, 285, 287, 290, 291, 292, 293, 294, 297, 324, 330, 335, 343, 351, 356, 358, 362, 363, 364, 366, 367
haqiqa, 86
practical truth, 49

unicity of God, 149

unity, 1. 2, 3, 4, 5, 6, 10, 11, 14, 15, 16, 17, 21, 23, 25,
27, 28, 29, 30, 32, 33, 35, 39, 40, 41, 43, 45,
49, 50, 51, 52, 53, 54, 55, 56, 57, 58, 60, 61,
64, 76, 77, 78, 79, 80, 81, 82, 83, 84, 85, 86,
87, 88, 89, 90, 91, 93, 95, 96, 97, 98, 99,
100, 101, 102, 104, 108, 110, 112, 113, 115,
116, 117, 118, 119, 120, 121, 122, 123, 124, 125,
126, 127, 130, 132, 133, 135, 136, 137, 138,
139, 140, 141, 143, 144, 145, 146, 147, 148,
149, 150, 151, 152, 153, 154, 155, 156, 157, 158,
159, 160, 161, 162, 163, 164, 165, 166, 167,
168, 169, 172, 173, 175, 177, 178, 180, 181,
183, 184, 185, 186, 187, 188, 189, 191, 192,
194, 195, 196, 198, 199, 202, 204, 209, 210,
213, 214, 215, 216, 217, 218, 219, 220, 221,
222, 223, 224, 225, 226, 228, 229, 233, 239,
241, 242, 243, 244, 245, 247, 248, 249, 250,
251, 255, 256, 258, 284, 285, 288, 289, 290,
292, 293, 295, 327, 330, 331, 333, 334, 335,
336, 337, 342, 343, 346, 349, 353, 359, 362,
363, 366, 367, 368, 369, 370
   numerical unity, 217
   transcendental unity, 104, 216, 217
universal, 8, 9, 42, 43, 45, 47, 48, 49, 50, 68, 76,
77, 78, 89, 108, 109, 119, 122, 134, 144, 161,
170, 174, 179, 180, 187
universe, 16, 21, 22, 23, 24, 31, 32, 46, 48, 114, 119,
124, 149, 250, 293, 362

Van Steenberghen, Fernand, 149, 150, 153, 165,
170, 171, 172, 176, 181, 182, 378
Vasquez, Gabriel, 327, 328, 334, 341, 344, 345,
346, 347, 348, 359, 360, 361
Vaticanus Latinus, 297, 298, 379

Vicaire, M. -H., 197, 206
Vigilantius, 186, 187
Vignaux, Paul, 370
virtue, 33, 42, 44, 47, 49, 56, 86, 113, 118, 135, 138,
142, 176, 186, 189, 193, 194, 196, 200, 204,
209, 294, 332, 333, 334, 336, 337, 341, 344
   intellectual virtue, 49, 51
   moral virtue, 49, 51, 58

Walton, William, 364
Weisheipl, James, 103, 143, 197, 376, 377
Whately, Richard, 241
White, Kevin, 10, 349
Wielockx, R., 221, 231, 235
will, 9, 14, 16, 19, 20, 21, 22, 25, 26, 27, 28, 29, 32,
33, 34, 37, 41, 42, 45, 48, 50, 51, 54, 55, 56,
59, 61, 62, 65, 82, 83, 86, 94, 96, 111, 112,
113, 115, 122, 125, 131, 134, 135, 137, 140, 141,
142, 146, 148, 149, 150, 151, 153, 156, 157,
158, 161, 163, 168, 169, 185, 191, 192, 200,
201, 202, 209, 214, 215, 216, 217, 219, 221,
222, 223, 224, 225, 228, 231, 232, 234, 241,
245, 247, 248, 249, 250, 251, 252, 255, 257,
258, 260, 286, 287, 288, 289, 290, 291, 292,
293, 295, 297, 333, 335, 339, 341, 345, 355,
369
William of Ockham, 5, 6, 11, 287, 288, 289, 290,
291, 292, 293, 294, 295, 296, 297, 298, 368,
369, 371, 373, 375, 376, 377, 378, 379, 381
William of St. Amour, 187, 191, 192
Wippel, John F., 03, 176, 178, 213, 231, 235, 238,
251, 347, 349, 378, 382

zeal, 248, 249
Zents, Jeffrey, 11